Pétain

Charles Williams

LITTLE, BROWN

LITTLE, BROWN

First published in Great Britain in May 2005 by Little, Brown
This edition first published in November 2005

A CIP catalogue record for this book is available from the British
Library.

ISBN 0 316 73233 8

Typeset in Bembo by M Rules
Printed and bound in Great Britain
by Mackays of Chatham plc, Chatham, Kent

Little, Brown
An imprint of
Time Warner Book Group UK
Brettenham House
Lancaster Place
London WC2E 7EN
www.twbg.co.uk

For Justin and Caroline,
Tim, Katharine, Peter,
Eleanor and Hannah

CONTENTS

INTRODUCTION

'Quoiqu'on puisse penser de Vichy c'est tout de même quelqu'un.'

It is always a mistake to end up on the wrong side of history. History, as has often been remarked (not least by Adolf Hitler), is written by the winners. Winners, of course, tend to emphasise their own virtues and the wickedness of their opponents. Outright losers, on the other hand, are not allowed – or are in no position – to write history (nobody, for instance, has heard much from the Hittites defeated by Ramses the Great, from the Persians defeated by Alexander or the Gauls defeated by Julius Caesar). But if, having lost, the losers end up on the winning side, the history they write inevitably attempts to mitigate their embarrassment at their initial defeat by fierce attacks on those they pronounce to have been responsible. France is an illustration of the general rule. In the First World War, she was one of the winners, and history was written accordingly. Pétain, for instance, was a great figure in 1918 – a Marshal of France and the 'Victor of Verdun'. In the Second World War, however, she was a loser – but a loser who ended on the winning side. Pétain was deemed to have borne the main responsibility for the collapse of 1940 and was duly condemned for treason. Again, history was written in a suitable manner. His reputation has thus gone up and down, like a float, on the consecutive waves of French adulation in 1918 and French excoriation in 1945. Since the second wave came after the first, and since there was no third wave, his reputation has never recovered. He has ended up on the wrong side of history.

Pétain was born into a dysfunctional peasant family in the north of France in the early years of the second half of the nineteenth century. As a boy, he was lucky enough, after losing his mother, to be nurtured by a grandmother and two clerical uncles. For an intelligent peasant lad of the day there were only two careers which could lift him out of the drudgery of subsistence farming – the Church and the Army. The Church soon lost its attraction, and the Army was his choice. Coming as he did from a peasant background, he fitted uneasily into the officer class of the French Army which he aspired to join. Faced with the arrogance of his new colleagues he became shy in their company and caustic in his comments about them. In fact, throughout his life, although he was able to command obedience, respect and even devotion among his juniors in rank, he made no true, long-lasting, male friends. Nor was he good at forming permanent relationships with women. Blessed with inordinately good looks – piercing blue eyes, blond hair, smooth and slightly babyish skin – and an apparently insatiable sexual drive, he was able to knock over the ladies of provincial France pretty much at will. In short, during the long years climbing slowly up the army ranks, he was a serial fornicator – until he met his match in one of his many mistresses, who determined, after a long but casual relationship, that she would not settle for anything less than marriage. (Even after marriage, however, he did not lose the taste; he then became a serial adulterer.)

At the onset of the First World War Pétain, ambitious as he undoubtedly was, found himself at a dead end. He was due to retire in 1916 at the age of sixty and had set about finding a suitable place for his retirement. Circumstances intervened, and within four years he found himself, almost to his own surprise and certainly to the surprise of his more aristocratic colleagues, a Marshal of France and Commander-in-Chief of the French Army. In fact, there is little doubt that, had Pétain died in the 1920s, he would even now be celebrated as a great military French hero. France had borne the main brunt of the slaughter on the western front during the First World War and had come out as winners. Pétain, thanks to the defence of Verdun in 1916 and the reconstruction of the French Army after the mutinies of 1917, would quite rightly have been rewarded with all the honours France had to offer. Furthermore, had he been allowed to pursue his plan in November 1918 to drive into Germany to pursue and destroy a defeated German Army which had retreated in good order, he might even have occupied a place higher than the much lauded Marshal Foch.

In May 1940, however, France (and Britain, for that matter) suffered an overwhelming military defeat. Pétain, having witnessed the early stages of the defeat from his embassy in Spain, came to the conclusion that Britain would soon collapse and made his dispositions accordingly: an armistice would be followed by a peace treaty, and France would take its place in its own right in a Europe dominated by Germany. It was far from an isolated view. Indeed, there are few, even now, who do not recognise that in mid-1940 the odds were very firmly in favour of a German victory – sooner rather than later.

In the event, and in the end, Germany lost the war in Europe. Yet the story of winners and losers was far from over. De Gaulle, who had fought on the losing side in May, took off to London in June 1940 without any immediate prospect of success – and ended up on the winning side in 1945. Even so, he could hardly claim to have been victorious (although, of course, he did). In truth, the Second World War in Europe was won by the Soviets, the Americans and the British. Up until 1943 the contribution of Free France, or Fighting France as it was by then called, was negligible; and, after that, it was no more than peripheral. None the less, de Gaulle and his followers had the undying distinction of saving what remained of France's honour. But the shame of defeat still remained. To help wipe it out the official propaganda machine held the losers of May 1940 up to obloquy – needless to say, conveniently forgetting that almost all of those who were most vocal, including de Gaulle, had been themselves in one way or another among those who had lost.

The attempt to wipe the slate clean was fully illustrated in Pétain's trial. As a judicial event it was little more than ridiculous. But the point is that the main burden of complaint about Pétain at his trial, and the one on which de Gaulle laid his own particular emphasis, was not what had happened at Vichy but that Pétain in person was responsible for the ignominious 'capitulation' of 1940 – in other words responsible for France's shame. He was convicted of treason mainly on that count. The losers of 1940 had turned into winners – and had written an almost predictable script.

Vichy was never going to be easy to deal with in the post-war period.

Of course, many – perhaps most – people in France claimed by then to have been members of the Resistance (even though their participation might previously have escaped everybody else's notice). But de Gaulle was contemptuous of the Resistance. In fact, one of his first acts was to disband it – telling its leaders to go back home and do a proper job. Moreover, Pétain and de Gaulle – de Gaulle was, after all, Pétain's protégé in the 1920s – shared most of the opinions of the French military of the time. Both of them were suspicious of politicians, fervently nationalist and even more strongly anti-communist. Nobody can say what de Gaulle would have made of the National Revolution, but President Roosevelt, for one, certainly thought that de Gaulle was authoritarian almost to the point of fascism. Besides, de Gaulle thought that the whole development of Vichy was easily traced to Pétain's fundamental mistake, the signature of the Armistice in 1940. The fate of the Jews – the dreadful conditions of deportation, the horrors of the holding camps at Compiègne and Drancy, the dreadful round-ups in Unoccupied France which followed the Paris round-up that has gone down in infamous history as the 'Vel d'Hiv', let alone the final horror of the death camps – seemed at the time of Pétain's trial to be of little concern. Nor was there much mention of the persecution of Freemasons, the brutal sadism of the Milice and the feebleness of 'collaboration'. In all these matters Pétain might legitimately have been held to be either complicit, through the turning of a blind eye, or directly responsible, but they were, for a long time, hardly mentioned. In fact, it took many years after the end of the war, and much wringing of hands, before historians, let alone politicians, were prepared even to look beneath the stone under which the corpse of Vichy had been buried.

After his conviction in 1945 Pétain spent his last years in prison until his death in 1951. But things did not stop there. Campaigns to reverse his conviction continued, and were to continue, as he himself had instructed his lawyers, 'even after his death'. For more than thirty years his supporters demanded his reburial in Douaumont at Verdun. Committees were formed to defend his memory. In 1973 his remains were dug up from his grave in the Île d'Yeu off the west coast of France and shipped to the mainland for reburial, only to be discovered in a garage in a Paris suburb – and shipped back again. Moreover, surprising as it may seem, successive French presidents, starting with

Charles de Gaulle in 1968 and ending with Jacques Chirac in 1998 – among them, most notably, President François Mitterrand – arranged for flowers to be placed on Pétain's grave on each anniversary of the Armistice of November 1918.

'Pétainisme', such as it is or ever was, is by now dying. Young people in France hardly recognise the name itself. Vichy has become a regional centre for tourism in the Auvergne. The Île d'Yeu is now a favoured resort for intrepid surfboarders. The battlefield of Verdun is no more than a vast area of unsightly bumps in the ground. The past, as well as its lessons, is being put out of mind. None of that, of course, is necessarily a bad thing. The past can sometimes be too painful. But the past can never be truly forgotten; and Pétain was, and is, part of France's past, not least because he was, above all, a patriot. He was a fine general – not great, since he did not have the genius for surprise of a Napoleon, but fine enough to stand high among the mediocrities around him in the First World War. To be sure, like many ambitious generals before and since, he was bewildered by the world of politics. Blunders and misjudgements became daily characteristics. He was lax, to say the least, in standing out against the persecution of Jews and Freemasons and the brutal excesses of his subordinates. History has recorded all that in detail. But he loved his country and had a touching faith in what de Gaulle was to call the eternal France. Inadequate he may have been for the task for which he thought himself qualified, but he was not, and had never been, a traitor. In that particular at least, and perhaps – dare it be said? – generally, Clio, the maverick Muse of History, has not played it entirely fair.

1

'THE SON OF MY SORROW'

'Il en est ainsi de notre passé. C'est peine perdue que nous cherchions à l'évoquer, tous les efforts de notre intelligence sont inutiles.'

It was raining. It was also, for April, unseasonably cold. At the Swiss frontier station of Vallorbe, the checkpoint lights had been turned on earlier than usual, and a larger than usual contingent of Swiss frontier guards had moved in, as well as a few journalists. There was, it was said, to be an important event that evening. A special train had arrived in the late afternoon with some distinguished passengers, who even then were resting in the modest railway station waiting room. Word also had it that more than one hundred armed police and soldiers were mustered on the French side.

There was, indeed, to be an important event. On 26 April 1945, at 7.27 p.m. precisely, so the Swiss official report runs, Marshal Philippe Pétain crossed into France for the last time. As his car reached the checkpoint a platoon of Swiss soldiers presented arms – his due as a Marshal of France. Waiting for him on the French side was General Pierre Koenig, the former Free French general but by then Governor of Paris, whose task it was to escort the Marshal to Paris to stand trial. Once out of his car Pétain, again as a Marshal of France, saluted the French soldiers. Some moved to present arms in their turn, others just shuffled about uncomfortably. Koenig stood to attention. Pétain held out his hand; but Koenig remained fixed at attention, merely inclined his head, according to one newspaper report, 'in deference to an old man' – and refused the proffered hand.[1]

The warrant for Pétain's arrest was then read out. The charges were 'plotting against the internal security of the state' and 'collusion with the enemy'.[2] Pétain identified himself in the manner the law required, stated that he was in his ninetieth year, signed the form acknowledging his arrest and returned to his car. His Swiss chauffeur had by then been replaced by a French police driver. The car was escorted under heavy guard for the eight kilometres to the railway station at Les Hôpitaux-Neufs, where he boarded another special train, this time for Paris, in which a coach had been set aside for him and his wife. Apart from the reading of the warrant, nothing of consequence had been said.

When the train arrived at Pontarlier, just before ten o'clock, a crowd besieged Pétain's coach. There were shouts of 'Traitor' and 'Hang him', and some in the crowd spat at his window. It was a complete – and to Pétain unexpected – contrast to the scenes which had greeted him a year earlier, on that precise date, when he had visited Paris. Indeed, Pétain would have been less than human if he did not at that moment recall all the adulatory crowds of compatriots such as these whom he used to address as his 'children'. He would also have been less than human if he had not reflected that his return to France to face his accusers was at his own insistence. He had, after all, refused the offer of a secure and peaceful home in Switzerland. The conviction that he had saved France in the hour of her greatest danger had overcome his inherited peasant caution. What had not been obvious to him, although it was obvious to everyone else, was that the political tide had turned so decisively against him that he was, without any doubt, returning to a sentence of death.

It was, perhaps, naïve; but it was not dishonourable. There was also an element of self-importance, the belief that his rank would allow him special treatment, and even that he might successfully negotiate with his former protégé, Charles de Gaulle; but self-importance and pride in himself had long been a feature of his life. For instance, he had always prided himself on what he supposed to be an almost mystical relationship with the people of France. It came, he said, from his own peasant ancestry and upbringing. In speech after speech he had extolled the virtues of the peasant: thrift, honesty, hard work, loyalty to country and to God; and, needless to say, his picture of the peasant became progressively more idealised as he grew older. What he revealed only when the mask slipped was that his own peasant childhood had not been quite the idyll he was accustomed to describe. As a matter of fact, he had been only too content to leave his family and his birth-place as soon as he could, and, apart from fleeting visits, never to return.

Pétain's childhood was typical of the time and the place. He was born at Cauchy-à-la-Tour, a village of some four hundred inhabitants in the Department of Pas-de-Calais, at 10 p.m. in the evening of 24 April 1856. The birth was apparently without complications. His mother Clotilde Pétain, née Legrand, was attended by the local mid-wife, and the formal witnesses were the boy's two grandparents. But they were not the only people present. As was the custom, there were others from the extended family milling about – cousins, neighbours, other relations, even the baby's elder sisters. It was all quite normal. A new birth, particularly a healthy one, was a matter of general celebra-tion, and privacy was by no means a priority. Omer-Venant Pétain, the baby's father, was particularly glad that it was a boy. Until then he had only managed three daughters. For a family whose life depended on working the land a son was a gift of providence; daughters were no more than a burden.

The new baby was duly baptised as Henri Philippe Benoni Omer Pétain, within the official limit of two and a half days from birth pre-scribed by the Catholic Church, at the little church in Cauchy by its first priest – it had previously been deemed too small to be worthy of its own priest and services had been taken by the vicar of the neigh-bouring parish, Auchel. He was given the names of his maternal uncles, his grandfather and his father (Omer also being a saint of par-ticular local veneration as the founder of a Benedictine abbey in the town which bears his name). Perhaps the only oddity to modern ears is the name of his Pétain grandfather – Benoni. Biblical names were, of course, not uncommon, but this one, although not unknown in the district, was unusual elsewhere. The name had originally been taken from a passage in the Book of Genesis. Rachel, Jacob's second wife, gave birth to a son as she lay dying. Before she died she gave him his name, Benoni, 'the son of my sorrow'. Jacob, more prosaically, called him Benjamin. But it had gained some sort of mystic meaning by the time the new baby was baptised. Some said that in its meaning it reflected a nostalgia for the *ancien régime*, others that it signified no more than the normal pain of childbirth. Others, perhaps rightly, claimed that it was no more than right and proper that the boy should bear the name of his grandfather Benoni, regardless of any undertones of meaning.

There is no suggestion (however interesting it might be in the light of subsequent events) that the name indicated any Jewish blood in the Pétain family veins. Originally of Flemish stock – the name itself is a French version of *Piet-heim* (Peter's home) – the Pétains had settled in Cauchy at the end of the seventeenth century. They had married and intermarried, had bred copiously, had worked the land for their subsistence, and had, above all, lived by the maxims of the Catholic Church. As marriages took place, land was transferred by way of dowry; and as deaths took place the same land was divided up or transferred back again by way of inheritance. This constant movement of land ownership, and rented tenure, had generally taken place between the larger peasant freeholders in Cauchy, the Tahons, the Legrands, the Lefebvres, the Carons, the Pétains and the Cossarts, for the simple reason that they tended to intermarry.

It was a feature of these peasant families of high standing that they called themselves *cultivateurs* as opposed to *paysans*. They were literate, and, from time to time, adventurous. Omer-Venant Pétain, for instance, had decided in the late 1840s to escape from peasantry to participate in the excitements of the wave of industrial inventions which were a feature of the time. Indeed, he had even tried his luck in Paris. There he had for a time been apprenticed to Louis Daguerre on the then new invention of the daguerrotype, an early form of photography, and had written to his parents in 1846 of his enthusiasm for it ('The person who showed me was earning by himself more than 100 francs a day')[3] and about his ambitions to set up shop on his own account – while requesting fifty francs to tide him over until that time should come. The revolutionary days of 1848, however, had put an end to all such thoughts, and Omer-Venant had returned swiftly to the family farm.

His brother Cyrille also had ambitions. At first, he had been unlucky in drawing a '*mauvais numéro*'[4] in the ballot for conscription to military service, but he had been able to buy himself a replacement – as was

Abbe Lefebvre – great-uncle.

Benoni and Françoise Pétain –
grandparents.

Omer-Venant Pétain – father.

Abbe Legrand – uncle.

allowed under the law of the time. It was, of course, at some cost to his parents, who had to sell a hectare of land for the purpose; but it allowed him to continue to teach in a village not far from Cauchy. Strangely enough, Cyrille then decided that after all the Army was an attractive proposition, and signed up for fifteen years' service. It was not a sensible decision. After a posting to Algeria, Cyrille was assigned to the Crimea. That was altogether too much. He deserted and, to the surprise of his family, settled in the Caucasus. The Pétains thus gained a branch of cousins in Russia, but Cyrille Pétain's name, to the shame of his French relatives – and, presumably, to his nephew, the future Marshal - was posted in Cauchy as a deserter.

However embarrassing Cyrille's career, it illustrates a point. One of the traditional – and convenient – ways to escape from the drudgery of peasant life was to enrol in the Army. This was particularly true in the Pas-de-Calais, where memories of unremitting warfare were part of the folk inheritance. The history of the place is scarred by stories of battles. The Pas-de-Calais had been, give or take some boundary changes imposed by the Revolutionary government in 1790, the old province of Artois. Ever since the arrival of the Romans – the name Artois itself, like the name of its capital Arras, is no more than a cor-ruption of the name of the Gallic tribe the Atrebates – the territory had been fought over. Indeed, it had changed hands times almost without number. Romans, Franks, Normans and English had all, at one time or another, laid their claim. By the twelfth century it had fallen to the Count of Flanders, then over the years to pass, by con-quest or by marriage, to the King of France, to the Dukes of Burgundy, to the Habsburg dynasty of Austria, to the King of Spain, and from time to time to the English, before the Treaty of Utrecht in 1713 confirmed the sovereignty of France. All around are the sites of ancient battles: Crécy, Azincourt, Lens, Cassel, Ramillies, Mons-en-Pévèle, Bouvines, Fontenoy; and the area is dotted with towns fortified by Vauban himself.

It is not difficult to see why there was such constant military mayhem in Artois and the adjoining provinces of Flanders and Picardy. They were obvious targets for incursions from England: witness – over the centuries – the campaigns of Edward III, Henry V and the Duke of Marlborough; they lie at the western end of the extensive plain of northern France and are thus open to attacks from the east; and, not least, the northern border of the provinces lies exposed to attacks from the lowlands of the Rhine delta.

The geography has thus made for easy incursions, over the centuries, from west, east and north. Peasants living there had to be continuously on their guard. Anybody, at any time, could march into their land and inflict the brutalities of victors. The English were particularly feared – the Duke of Marlborough's soldiers had been more than usually unforgiving. Moreover, if life was dangerous, there was little compensation to be gained from either a fertile soil or a beautiful environment. The soil is chalky and the landscape can only be described as dull. To the traveller it seems almost without feature as Artois merges, almost without notice, into Flanders and undulating only gently from time to time towards its southern boundary with Picardy. Admittedly, there is a line of hills running from the northwest of the province to the south-east; but it can hardly be said to be very impressive. There is one peak of more than 200 metres near the town of St-Omer, but even that seems curiously out of place. Nor, apart from the constant coming and going of armies, has the area attracted much attention. For tourists, it seems always to be on the way to somewhere else. The traffic hurtles through on the Calais–Paris motorway on its way south; and even the old Roman road to and from the legionary camps at Arras and Thérouanne is left friendless and almost deserted.

In the middle of the nineteenth century, outside the major towns, Arras, Béthune and St-Omer, the countryside around was largely populated by peasants, each family with a smallholding which provided them with the basics of life. The coal mines of the prolific basin south of Lille were then only gradually extending eastwards. Certainly, when they arrived, a new and different population encroached on to what had until then been peasant territory. There was little love lost between the two. The miners were paid by the day, their wages some four times the average daily wage for an agricultural labourer; they spent their money in the local bistro; they were rough and their children undisciplined; worst of all, they showed no inclination to go to church. But they brought money, and with the mines and the money came roads and railways, and a new generation of subsidiary industries. By the end of the century the Pas-de-Calais had changed for good.

Nevertheless, for the Cauchy of the 1850s that process was only just beginning. Like many other villages up and down the length and breadth of France, Cauchy was still little more than an agglomeration of family farms in a largely subsistence economy. As Karl Marx put it in his study of French rural sociology, '. . . a smallholding, a peasant and his family; alongside them another smallholding, another peasant and another family. A certain number of these families form a village, and a certain number of villages, a department. Thus the great mass of the French nation is made up of a simple addition of units bearing the same name, just as a sack filled with potatoes forms a sack of potatoes.'[5]

The Pétain family farm was one such unit. By the time of Pétain's birth, the family smallholding consisted of some 10 hectares under ownership, some of which was Legrand land which Clotilde had brought as dowry, and a few more rented hectares dotted about within the boundaries of the hamlet. There were two horses, five or six cows, a few pigs and a scattering of chickens. The farmhouse itself was from an earlier date, but over the decades pieces had been added on, to the point where in the mid-nineteenth century it was a house of some substance. In fact, the house still stands, by the side of the main road from Arras to Thérouanne – a rectangular structure surrounding a central courtyard, partly in the traditional chalkstone and partly in brick. The wall facing the road was divided by an archway which led from the road to the courtyard behind. The barn to the right of the courtyard housed the animals – their stalls are still visible. Beyond it was a storehouse for the produce of the farm and a brick annexe for the primitive machinery – cart, harvester and tools – which was essential for the proper running of the farm. To the left of the arch-way were the living quarters, one large kitchen off which lay two little rooms and a small dairy.

To work the farm, there was Omer-Venant himself, his wife Clotilde, their children and, as circumstance required, one or two neighbours. There was also grandfather Benoni, who had built a little house for himself and his wife Françoise some fifty metres from the main farm, to which they moved after Omer-Venant's marriage in 1851. In other words, Pétains of all generations, together with their animals, lived in close – and presumably at times suffocating – proximity to one another.

True, the property was at the richer end of the peasant range, and by the peasant standards of southern France they were relatively prosperous.

But at the time of Pétain's birth, prosperity was only relative. The collapse during the period 1853 to 1855 in the price of the two main cash crops, wheat and potatoes, had brought misery to the lesser peasant farmers. There were even beggars on the roads, and the richer families were asked (with varying results) to contribute to their welfare. But relatively prosperous though it might be, the Pétain farm was nevertheless far from comfortable. There was no indoor sanitation; the one living room served as kitchen as well; and apart from the central fire in that room there was no heating.

Nor was there much light. The house had only a few narrow and primitive windows (since anything else would have allowed penetrating draughts to enter); daylight mainly came in through the door, and in the long winter evenings there was only the light provided by poor-quality tallow candles. Summer was bearable, since the animals could be put out of doors and the days were long. When the autumn rains came, however, life became very much less pleasant. The days became shorter; rainwater leaked into the house, and since there was no internal drainage there was no method of drying the floors. The stench must have been dreadful. There could be only one possible result. 'Life is hard; hygiene does not exist, and promiscuity gives rise to a high level of infant mortality or the rapid spread of disease.'[6] In Cauchy in 1859, for example, nine out of fourteen babies died in infancy. Life was, indeed, hard.

Nor was there any comfort to be had from clothing or good food. Working clothes were rough, and, apart from a rather smarter set for wearing on high days and holidays, worn continuously day and night – including underwear – and only changed once a week. Since water was too precious to allow for baths – or even for cleaning teeth – clothes became dirtier, and more pungent, as the week progressed. Food, too, was monotonous. The daily fare was soup, cooked in a large pot which hung on a tripod over the central fire. It was generally known as 'eternal soup', since it was topped up from time to time with water, grain and green vegetables in the summer and root vegetables in the winter.

Occasionally, the soup might be seasoned with lard or, even more occasionally, salt; more frequently, it was little more than coloured water. To accompany the soup the family baked bread. Barley and rye – the wheat crop was for the market, to be sent to Paris for the fashionable white bread – were laboriously milled and baked in the oven, either in the home or at the local bakery. But so laborious was the process that it only took place once every few weeks, and the product, a coarse dark brown loaf, rapidly became so stale and hard that it was almost impossible to cut with a knife; a hatchet was the only possible solution. The resulting pieces were then soaked in the soup to soften them to the point where at least they became edible.

This miserable diet was only varied at times of great celebration such as marriages or religious feast days by the eating of meat. There was no question of eating the horses or the cows, or even the chickens; they were far too valuable for working (the horses for working and transport) or for produce (the cows and chickens). The delicacy to mark the celebration was pork. A pig would be killed and eaten. But it was not just a question of a change of diet; the process of killing the pig was in itself an elaborate ritual. First, of course, the unfortunate pig had to be caught, since it would be grazing in the open on common land. This process involved the whole family, and presumably a good deal of shouting and waving of arms. Once caught, the pig was strung up – there were even harnesses made for the purpose – and its throat was cut. The blood (important for making sausages) was collected in a bowl as it gushed out. Once the pig had bled to death, it was minutely dissected. No part was wasted. '*Tout fait ventre, pourvu que ça y entre*' was an old peasant saying.[7] The main meat was eaten at the feast, in which the whole family and favoured neighbours – properly dressed for the occasion – participated; and what remained was cured and stored away for future consumption.

As for social life, there was not much of it. To quote only one account, 'there are no friends in the countryside; only relatives or neighbours'.[8] The women gathered round the communal washing place and the men in whatever establishment was available to provide a cheap glass of beer or cider. Certainly, there was a local market, or a more elaborate but more distant one at the town of Lillers, at which the valuable produce of the Pétain farm – wheat, potatoes, eggs, milk or home-made cheese – could be sold for cash to pay for essentials not available on the farm. The market, too, was part of social life. There was also the communal assembly, at which the great and the good of Cauchy would deliberate about local problems. They were elected by the male universal suffrage which had been revived (for males over twenty-five only) in 1848; but it always seemed that the same names were returned. The Mayor for the year of Pétain's birth, for instance, one Pierre Castelin, had also been Mayor in 1852. Above all, however, there was the church, and the Pétains, as good Catholics, attended without fail and, no doubt, took the opportunity of extended conversation with their neighbours.

On 1 October 1857, three weeks after the birth of her short-lived fourth daughter, Pétain's mother, Clotilde, died. For Omer-Venant it was a triple blow; he had lost a wife, a mother to his children and a fellow worker on the farm. The children were, for the time being, looked after by a neighbour, but, not unnaturally, he looked for another wife. At the age of forty-two, upright, good-looking and even tempered, and with what passed for a substantial property, he was certainly an attractive proposition; and soon he was engaged to Reine Vincent, from the nearby village of Aumettes. They were married on 7 April 1859.

It was not long before there was a problem. Reine produced three children in quick succession. Seven children were far too many for one person to look after, particularly when she had to work on the farm as well. It was only normal to ask relatives to help. It was equally normal – and at the time not at all unusual – for the children of the first marriage to be the ones to be parked with their nearest relatives. The young Pétain, by then aged five or six, was lodged, together with his sisters Marie-Françoise and Adélaïde, with the neighbouring grandparents. The younger daughter Sara, on the other hand, went to the much more salubrious surroundings of the presbytery at Bomy, a village about twice the size of Cauchy and some ten kilometres to the north-west, where Clotilde's brother, Abbé Jean-Baptiste Legrand, was the priestly incumbent.

In later life, Pétain complained that his stepmother had forced him out of his childhood home, and that the only motherly love he had known had come from his grandmother. The complaint was certainly an exaggeration. For a start, his stepmother referred to him as 'my son' rather than as 'my stepson'.[9] Equally, far from being the Wicked Stepmother of legend (legends with which the young Pétain was certainly familiar) she was by all accounts a kindly soul, and anxious to ensure a good upbringing for all her husband's children.

Nor, for that matter, was grandmother Françoise particularly demon-
strative in her affection. Her fierce blue eyes, a physical characteristic
which she had passed on to her grandson, betrayed an almost fanati-
cal sense of religiosity. No doubt she was devoted to her
grandchildren, but the devotion seems largely to have consisted of
warnings that earthly life was no more than a sinful vale of tears
through which we must pass before – on the assumption of good
behaviour and attention to Catholic precepts – attaining the blessed-
ness of the afterlife.

It is little wonder that for the boy Pétain the establishment at Bomy
held the greater attraction. The house was, by his standards, one of
luxury. It had two storeys, with four separate rooms on the ground
floor. Admittedly, the rooms were little larger than monastic cells, but
they were separate – and separately furnished. Although the journey
to Bomy took several hours, the boy took every opportunity to visit
his uncle and his elder sister, most frequently in the summer months
before work began on the harvest. He was, apparently, always welcome. Abbé Legrand had spent all his adult life as a priest, first as a
teacher in St Omer and then as a curate in the village of Samer before
taking over the parish of Bomy in 1852 – and staying there until
1879. By all accounts he was a popular priest – shy but without any
pomposity (he too came from a peasant family). He had also been
responsible for the building of the church of St Vaast de Bomy, a
matter of great pride to his village and, it needs hardly to be said, to
the Abbé himself.

Abbé Legrand also took the boy's education in hand. True, there
was primary education in Cauchy, in which a M. Demont had the
task of teaching the elements of reading and writing to the children of
the village, and there was a priest to teach them their catechism. But
at Bomy Abbé Legrand insisted on a much higher standard. Besides,
by the time Pétain reached his sixth birthday, M. Demont's small
establishment – a small peasant house which served both as his classroom and his lodging – was being overrun by the children of miners
newly arrived in the village. It was under Legrand's tuition, therefore,
that the boy's handwriting developed the characteristic sloping hand of
later life, his reading widened in scope and his devotion to the
Catholic Church was – needless to say – heavily reinforced.

There was, however, another, and quite different, source of information – this time from a wider world than that of a parish priest. Pétain's great-uncle, Clotilde's mother's brother, Abbé Philippe-Michel Lefebvre, had led a more varied, even at times exotic, career. After studying science and philosophy he had entered the seminary at Hinnin and was about to be ordained deacon when the seminary itself was suppressed under the Revolution. He was then called up into the Army, fought at Jemappes in 1792 under General Dumouriez and in Italy, under Napoleon, in 1794. Posted to a garrison in Italy, it was not until 1799 that he returned to France – just as Bonaparte himself was on the way back from Egypt. After the Napoleonic Concordat he was released from the Army, resumed his theological studies at Douai University, and was ordained. A subsequent – and quieter – career in the priesthood led finally to retirement at the presbytery at Bomy, where he was happy to regale anybody who would listen with anecdotes of his life as a soldier in both the Revolutionary and Napoleonic armies.

One such, of course, was the young Pétain. But the old Abbé's influence on his young great-nephew should not be exaggerated. The young boy, like any young boy, would certainly have listened to his great-uncle, but since Lefebvre died in 1866, just before Pétain's tenth birthday, and since visits to Bomy were by their very nature special occasions, it would be an exaggeration to maintain, as some have done, that it was in listening to stories of heroic military exploits that Pétain decided on a military career. As a matter of fact, his uncle was a much greater influence, and it was under that influence that Pétain resolved to follow the well-trodden path of the priesthood. His Confirmation and First Communion in Cauchy church in 1867 only served to reinforce his young resolve.

But to accomplish this he had to follow a more elaborate educational route than that provided by M. Demont at Cauchy. Again, his uncle Legrand came to his aid. Matters were so arranged between Abbé Legrand and his former pupil Abbé Graux that in October 1867 the ten-year-old Pétain embarked on the first stage of his formal education, at the school of which Graux was the director – the Collège Saint-Bertin at St-Omer. It was the first and welcome step away from the confines and hazards of peasant life – up until then the only one which he had known. Childhood and the peasant family were left behind; adolescence, with all its difficulties, lay ahead.

2

FROM THE CRUCIFIX TO THE SABRE

'Vous ne vous doutez pas de la sombre atmosphère où nous sommes grandis dans une France humiliée et meurtrie . . . élevés pour une revanche sanglante, fatale et peut-être inutile.'

The emotions of a ten-year-old boy leaving home for his first board-ing school can easily be imagined, and for some, perhaps, even remembered. They are a mix of shyness and sheer terror. Further-more, even though the young Pétain's relations with the rest of his family – apart from his uncle and great-uncle – were far from har-monious, the thought that he would be spending almost all his time with a wholly new set of hitherto unknown companions in a strange environment must have been particularly daunting. Add to that the probability that the boy had never been to St-Omer before or, if he had, only for fleeting visits, and the prospect becomes even more frightening. It must therefore have been with a wildly beating heart that the new pupil, Philippe Pétain, stood in front of the huge gates of the Collège Saint-Bertin on a day in the first week of October 1867.

In fact, although it must have seemed overwhelming to the new schoolboy, it can hardly be said that the town of St-Omer in the mid-nineteenth century was a place of great excitement. Indeed, one description of the town in the 1840s was quite simple: it was 'a very dull place'.[1] The description certainly held good for the 1860s, during Pétain's schooldays, and – at least arguably – holds good today. What it did have, however, was an aura of holiness. It was not simply that many of the priests of Artois, such as Abbé Lefebvre and Abbé Legrand, had been educated there. Nor was it simply that the town boasted two properly promoted saints. It was as though through the whole town there pervaded a lingering smell of incense. In total contrast, the city of Arras, the capital of Artois and the seat of the diocesan bishop, seemed strangely heathen by comparison. The tone there was one of a bustling provincial capital city, where the tone of St Omer was by comparison almost of a monastic quietness. It was in these surroundings that the young Pétain was to grow up – surroundings, to be sure, carefully selected by his uncle to encourage the boy's ecclesiastical ambitions.

Nevertheless, holy though it might be, the town was still dull. Even its eponymous saint, Omer, hardly excites the imagination. With all respect, he can only with difficulty lay claim to a higher status than that of a junior non-commissioned officer in the illustrious army of the blessed. A bishop of Thérouanne in the seventh century, Omer's only obvious qualification for sainthood – apart from his no doubt exceptional piety – was to found a settlement not far from the Benedictine abbey built by his monastic colleague Bertin – also in his turn elevated to middle-rank sainthood – on the Île de Sithieu, an inhospitable piece of marshy land watered by the River Aa.

Omer correctly decided that the hill overlooking the marsh was altogether more attractive, and built there a small chapel dedicated to the Virgin Mary. In doing this, Omer was presumably aware of the story that Bertin only built his abbey in the middle of the marsh because the boat in which he was sailing came to a halt there – an event which Bertin took to be a direct sign from heaven, but which, perhaps more plausibly, is now regarded as the result of an exceptionally low tide on the Aa. Omer, it appears, knew better. A small and flourishing settlement grew up around Omer's chapel, rivalling the settlement around Bertin's abbey. Needless to say, there was little love lost between the followers of the two saints.

In the course of time a larger church was built on the site of Omer's chapel, and after nearby Thérouanne had been razed to the ground in the religious wars of the sixteenth century, it became in 1559 the cathedral of the new diocese of St-Omer, a distinction which it held until 1801. It seemed that Omer had won a decisive victory over Bertin, and this was confirmed when, as was inevitable, the two religious centres were joined. The resulting ensemble reflected, and still reflects, the junction of the two holy places in its lay-out, the road pattern appearing like a series of parallel umbilical cords between the two holy places. But it was Omer who was accorded the privilege of giving his name to the new town.

Dull it may have been, but St-Omer had had its fair share of history. It was overrun by the English in 1337 and 1339, and after its annexation by France in 1677 was again besieged – this time by the Duke of Marlborough and Prince Eugen – in 1711. Fortunately, as local legend has it, on that occasion a heroine by the name of Jacqueline Robins came to the rescue by sailing down the River Aa with a boatload of arms and provisions for the defenders. Unlikely as it may appear today, the heroine, if such she was, or, indeed, if she ever existed, is revered in St-Omer as a local Joan of Arc.

But it was not only a matter of battles, however dramatic they were. St-Omer, given the distinction of its two religious foundations, was a major attraction for Roman Catholics who, for one reason or another, were excluded from England or the Netherlands. There had been, for instance, a Jesuit school for the Catholic youth of England and Scotland – Titus Oates was one of its pupils – which flourished until it was moved, first to Bruges, then to Liège and finally to Stonyhurst in the English county of Lancashire. Even after the Jesuits left, others – most particularly the Collège Saint-Bertin – followed in their steps, to the point where the town not only maintained but enhanced its distinct reputation as a haven for Catholics from the barbarous Protestant countries to the north and west.

Little now remains of the great abbey of Saint-Bertin. The Revolutionaries achieved the major part of the work of destruction; but it was completed by the municipal administration after 1830 – on the dubious grounds that the work of destruction was worthwhile since it gave employment to the local populace. Nevertheless, whatever the fate of the abbey itself, one of the main umbilical cords between the site and the former cathedral still carries its name: the rue St-Bertin. And it is in this street, together with the old military hospital and a former recruiting office, that there rises the gaunt red-brick building of the Collège Saint-Bertin.

It is not, by most standards, an attractive building. The architect, a M. Lejeune, had hitherto confined his attentions to the design of railway stations. Indeed, one look at the Collège is enough to convince the bystander not just that M. Lejeune had failed to move beyond the constraints of his earlier career but that he ought not to have left it. It is hardly surprising that the building is known – with more than a trace of mockery – as the 'gare du nord'. The design replicates, almost to a brick, the design of the London railway station of St Pancras. Nor was this vast construction easy to erect. Work started in 1850 and continued until 1868. Even then, there were still bits and pieces to be added. Thus, during the whole of Pétain's stay there, between 1867 and 1874, workmen were going in and out, hammering and sawing and sculpting away – and hardly helping serious study.

There was, in fact, good reason for the project of building a large school, as was appreciated by the then Superior of Saint-Bertin, Constant Poulet. Not only had his predecessor been able to buy the piece of land previously occupied by a community of Franciscan friars but, more important, the Collège itself had changed its fundamental role.

It had originally been founded in 1812, after a Napoleonic edict restricting the number of Catholic secondary schools to one for each new Napoleonic department. As an ecclesiastical secondary school, it had, however, been required to abstain from teaching subjects on the state curriculum and send its pupils out for the purpose to the local lycée. It was not a happy existence. Nevertheless, the Collège, such as it was, survived, and by 1835 it had become a boarding establishment, by then firmly under the direction of the Société de Saint-Bertin, a group of priests of the diocese of Arras – 'a company of priests devoted to education'.[2]

Everything changed for the Collège in 1849. With the proposed introduction of new legislation by a government elected in that year after the ructions of 1848, the Société de Saint-Bertin sprouted new wings. The Falloux Law, so called after the Minister for Public Instruction of the day, allowed the Church not only to take full control of its own schools but also to found others as and when it thought appropriate. Furthermore, the schools were allowed to teach their pupils the curriculum leading to the baccalauréat, the examination devised and controlled by the state, which was the only gateway to higher education. To be sure, the curriculum had to be correspondingly adjusted, but apart from that, the 'free schools', as they were known, and of which Saint-Bertin was one, were able to set their own agenda. So important was Saint-Bertin in the eyes of the authorities in Paris that, in anticipation of the passing of the Falloux Law in 1850, the Collège was given the full rights of a 'free school' some months before the legislative event.

As a result of this new freedom, by the end of the 1860s the priestly company counted ten schools in its portfolio – not just in the diocese of Arras but in the diocese of Cambrai to the north. Furthermore, flushed by success, the company requested in 1866 canonical recognition from Rome as a separate order. The request was even repeated in 1869 – during the time when Pétain was a pupil. All this was too much for the Bishop of Arras. It was intolerable that a mere educational body should try to separate itself from his jurisdiction and be responsible only to the Pope himself. The bishop, a Monseigneur Lequette, was no fool when it came to ecclesiastical politics, and managed to block the bid of the unruly priests to escape his jurisdiction. Nevertheless, the spirit, as it were, lived on. The schools were run on a Catholic curriculum with a strong ultramontane flavour. The atmosphere was as close to the Jesuit formula of 'the Militia of the Pope'[3] as it was possible to get while retaining diocesan allegiance.

It was to this gloomy establishment that the ten-year-old Pétain arrived in October 1867 – in a peasant cart drawn by his family's two horses. There is little doubt that, even after the manoeuvring of his uncle Legrand to get him accepted, he could only have gone with the encouragement of a legacy from his recently dead great-uncle, Abbé Lefebvre. Indeed, it is impossible to see how Pétain could have possibly afforded to go to Saint-Bertin without financial help. It was, after all, a boarding school; and the boys had to wear a special uniform – a frock coat with tails with a row of buttons in front and a peaked cap – all of which cost money.

Pétain's arrival at his new school marked his first – and decisive – separation from his peasant family. There were new faces, and new friends. To be sure, he retained the close friendship of one of the Occre boys – Cauchy neighbours – but the other boys were almost entirely from middle-class families. None of this is surprising. At the time only about one in fifty pupils at all secondary schools was the son of unskilled workers, and there is no reason to suppose that at Saint-

Bertin the proportion was any greater. Moreover, bourgeois families preferred to keep their sons away from the state-run colleges, which were regarded by the higher ranks of society as demeaning. As for peasant families, it was not everybody who could benefit from a great-uncle's legacy to pay the many extras (the boarding and tuition being provided free by the Church). They preferred to keep their children away and teach them the simple precepts of subsistence farming.

It was thus that, for the first time in his life, the young Pétain met boys from quite a different class; and, on all the evidence, he seems to have taken to them. None the less, Pétain's new life with the sons of the bourgeoisie was far from easy. The school itself was of an architecture which nowadays would be regarded as primitive. For instance, in the dormitories there was no heating; pupils shivered throughout the long nights of the winter. Even the water froze from time to time in the washbasins. Furthermore, it was reported that 'the only equality is won with the fist',[4] and there seems little doubt that the crowding of adolescents in dormitories led to obvious results. Bullying was commonplace, and Pétain was no doubt bullied in the way that a peasant boy could expect to be.

There was little escape. The pupils were at Saint-Bertin for by far the greatest part of every year – in all nearly eleven months out of twelve. The main holiday was in the summer. By early October they were back at school until the second week of August of the following year, with breaks only for Easter and Christmas – although at Saint-Bertin religious zeal required the boys to stay at school for Christmas Day and curtailed the Easter and New Year holidays to no more than three days each. During the year there were three free days: in mid-November, on Shrove Tuesday and at Pentecost.

The working day was equally rigorous. It started early, at 5 a.m. From 5.30 to 6.15 there was a period of prayer, followed by thirty-five minutes' study before the daily Mass at 6.50. Only after Mass were the pupils allowed their breakfast. There was a class from 8 to 10, to be followed by a short recreational break before a further period of study leading to lunch at noon. After lunch there was a forty-minute period of recreation, study at 1.20 p.m., a class from 2 p.m. to 4 p.m., half an hour recreation, and then study from 4.30 p.m. until 7 p.m.; after which there was a short lecture on a spiritual subject, prayers, supper at 7.30 and bed at 8.

It was certainly a tiring day. But the day was made worse by what might politely be called the teaching methods. Classes were conducted by the priest in charge from behind his desk, and were largely devoted to an exposition of the matter in hand, with minimal contribution from the pupils. Study consisted of written work, frequently of an essay or translation by the pupil, in or from Latin or Greek, on an improbable topic – such as an imagined conversation between two characters from Roman or Greek mythology or history. (Pétain's only known contribution to this literature is a translation of a text describing the heroics of one Critognatus in the defence of Alesia in 52 BC, in which the hero recommended that non-combatants should be eaten.) After such exercises it is little wonder that by the end of the day the pupils were exhausted.

Discipline, of course, was strict. For instance, reading was closely controlled. Given the severely ultramontane bias of the school, pupils were only allowed to read improving literature, such as the lives of the saints or, as a concession, the right-wing Catholic newspapers – *L'Univers*, *Le Monde* or *L'Union*. Any attempt to smuggle in subversive material, such as *Le Figaro*, was punished, as were all other infractions (such as moving restlessly on the seat during class), by extra work, known as the '*pensum*',[5] to be completed during the periods normally reserved for recreation. Corporal punishment, however, was forbidden, and for all the strictness there was no resemblance to English schools of the period – which seemed to give a licence to schoolmasters tantamount to official sadism.

Although Pétain arrived at Saint-Bertin in 1867, it was not until 1870 that he began the five-year course of studies in the French language which was designed to take 'with honour the examination for voluntary enlistment and other examinations unconnected with the teaching of ancient languages' (in other words, the baccalauréat).[6] Up until then it had been a question of learning Latin and Greek grammar, of getting by heart long texts from the classics and, of course, pursuing the unremitting study of the teachings of the Catholic faith.

Pétain's scholastic record was not altogether bad. Indeed, in later life he claimed to have been proud of it. On the other hand, it was far from good. In his first-year class, known as the *septième*, he won a (second) prize for 'good sense'. In the next year, the *sixième*, he could only manage third place in 'Greek themes', 'history and geography' and 'arithmetic'.

The pattern continued through the cinquième, the quatrième, and troisième. It was not until he reached the deuxième in the school year 1872–3 that he made any particular impact: first prize in English and geometry and second prize in Greek translation and music. But these efforts were not followed through to his last year, in the Rhétorique, in which he could only manage a commendation for his skill in gymnastics.

None of this should be a matter of particular surprise. It is nowadays received wisdom that children from middle-class families do much better on average at school than children from working-class families. Certainly, in spite of his stays with his uncle Legrand, it would be a mistake to believe that Pétain, when he arrived at Saint-Bertin, had the kind of questioning mind that makes for a successful schoolboy. That was to develop later. Moreover, the work of the Pétain farm was not, in any sense, intellectual; nor were his parents and siblings. Yet Abbé Legrand had not worked in vain; he had taught the boy diligence in his studies, and that served him well.

It need hardly be said that it was to his religious studies that Pétain at Saint-Bertin seems to have had the greatest commitment. The Church, of course, was quite clear on the purpose of education. It had been set out in the Syllabus of 1864 for elementary schools. 'Schools for the masses', it pronounced, 'are established principally with a view to giving people religious instruction, to bring them to piety and to a truly Christian moral discipline.'[7] One textbook put it more pithily: 'In order to teach letters properly, children must first be taught to make the sign of the cross.'[8]

The young Pétain was not backward in following the teachings of the Church. It was not just a question of particular diligence in attendance at the morning Mass or the evening Rosary. These were anyway compulsory. Nor was it simple obedience to the declaration of the Emperor Napoleon III that by spreading education he was winning 'to religion, morals and comfort' the large section of the population 'that barely knew the precepts of Christ'.[9] In fact, he went out of his way in his piety. In 1873, for instance, at the age of seventeen, he was an active member of the Society of St-Vincent-de-Paul, whose purpose was to alleviate the sufferings of the poor – presumably by offering them scraps of the already inadequate food of Saint-Bertin.

He went even further. In February 1874 he was received into the Congregation of the Virgin, an organisation, as its name implies, dedicated to the veneration of Our Lady. He participated, as was customary, in the processions through the town on appointed days – in particular the feasts, dear to the Collège Saint-Bertin, of Saint Catherine and Saint Nicolas – and was no doubt diligent in times set aside for special prayer. All in all, it was a particularly pious adolescence, and there is every reason to suppose that Pétain's respect for the Church hierarchy and the rhythms of its worship were ingrained – whatever his later religious beliefs – during his time at Saint-Bertin.

Yet Saint-Bertin was not only concerned with religion. Even before the events of 1870 there was something of a military flavour as well. It was not just the uniform, which made the boys look like young soldiers 'or municipal guards'.[10] There was a good deal of marching up and down in recreation periods, no doubt to encourage respect for military virtues. Nevertheless, the tone changed quickly in 1870. It was then, about halfway into Pétain's career at Saint-Bertin, that France blundered into what was, at best, an absurd and – in the outcome – a catastrophic war with Prussia.

The whole complicated story has been recited many times. But the simple truth is that, after the victories of the 1850s over Russia and Austria, there was a general belief in France that she was militarily invincible. It followed that any slight was taken by the French political right as a pretext for military action; and the attempt by Prussia to put a Hohenzollern on the throne of Spain, followed by some brusque treatment of the French Ambassador in Berlin, was certainly considered to be slight enough.

Few in France had taken the growing military power of Prussia at all seriously. Admittedly, the Prussian victory over the Austrians at Königgrätz in 1866 had sparked off a process of reform of the French Army. Numerical parity with Prussia was to be achieved. A French-made breech-loading rifle was to be introduced in response to the perceived success of the Prussian version against the Austrians. But the reforms were far from complete by 1870. Moreover the general opinion of Paris society was that the Prussians were 'dim-witted, beer-drinking, pipe-smoking peasants, led by inexperienced officers good only at military theory and usually portrayed in French cartoons as wearing spectacles'.[11]

Popular enthusiasm in Paris for the war – apart from the political left – was unbounded. It was widely assumed that the French Army would merely stroll across the north German plain until it reached Berlin. At that point Prussia would sue for peace, the price for which would be the cession of the Rhineland to France. The reality, when it came, was something of a shock. By the middle of August 1870 the bulk of the French regular army had been pushed back to the fortress of Metz, where it was trapped. In early September a second army, mostly reservists of one sort or another, under the direct command of a painfully ill Louis Napoleon, was surrounded at Sedan. 'Nous sommes dans un pot de chambre,' noted General Auguste Ducrot, 'et nous y serons emmerdés.'[12] His prediction was borne out. A hundred and thirty thousand men, including the Emperor, surrendered. The German advance on Paris was swift, and by mid-September the capital was surrounded. Finally, Metz itself capitulated on 29 October.

Events then took on a bewildering pace. A new Republic was declared; a Government of National Defence was formed; there was a resurgence of fighting spirit, symbolised by the escape from Paris of the Minister of the Interior, Léon Gambetta – in a balloon. But however successful Gambetta might be in rallying the remaining French army at the Loire, it was not long before the position in the north was desperate. The territory north of Rouen was soon virtually cut off from the south. The only communication with the south was by telegraph lines running through England and Le Havre. It seemed only a matter of time before the Germans marched into St Omer.

The effect at Saint-Bertin was electric. Students were encouraged by their tutors to train to become soldiers in the defence of their country. Particularly enthusiastic was a Father Jérôme Ducroos, who had obtained a copy of a military manual. It was not, perhaps, the best manual for the training of the future defenders of the new Republic – but it had to do. Under the supervision of Father Ducroos, the older students paraded up and down in the courtyard of the vast building, shouting orders and going through the motions of presenting, ordering and shouldering arms. Of course, there were no real arms. The 'rifles' for the purpose were made of wood – the Fathers were particularly dexterous in woodwork – and, furthermore, cost each student some three francs. Nevertheless, the students engaged happily in this charade, and none more so than Pétain. By early 1871, he had become a leader in these events, apparently by self-appointment.

'I made myself captain', he reported in later life, 'with the tacit agreement of my soldiers'.[13] Equally, in the sometimes robust theatrical
events which the students put on Pétain seems to have allocated to
himself any military role that was available.

This was all very well. But, in truth, it was little more than adolescent whistling in the wind. More seriously, there is some anecdotal
evidence that the students of Saint-Bertin were marshalled to help in
the field hospitals behind the front line. If that is true, the students
were perilously close to the real action. In fact, as they might have
found out, the rearguard action was being conducted with great skill.
The general in charge of the northern front was Louis Léon
Faidherbe. An old Africa hand – he had been Governor of Senegal –
Faidherbe knew the virtues of military discipline, and he enforced
them rigorously. He was also a master of tactics, and he knew, furthermore, that the German troops were on the point of exhaustion.
The result was that the confrontation between the French and
German armies in the north became a succession of skirmishes until
'the French and Germans withdrew north and south like exhausted
boxers to their corners at the end of an inconclusive round'.[14] St-
Omer was safe, and the efforts of the Fathers of Saint-Bertin and
their pupils could, at least temporarily, be suspended.

But there were soon to be further developments. The front in the
north might be static, but Paris was in uproar. Even by the end of
October 1870 the city had become uncomfortably detached from
the rest of France and, Paris being Paris, near the point of insurrection.
Since then, the privations of a siege in which the staple diet had been
horsemeat or – if any could be captured – rats, and the belief that the
government, by then in Tours, was preparing to accede to a peace
with Bismarck which would allow German troops to march down the
Champs-Elysées, had led, in March 1871, to a political eruption. On
the 18th, a detachment of troops tried to recover some guns which
had been paid for by public subscription and spirited away. They
were met by a crowd of men, women and children who blocked
their path. There was a mêlée. A general was shot and killed; troops
broke ranks; the authorities quickly moved out of Paris to the safety of
Versailles. So it was, in bloodshed and confusion, that the Paris
Commune was born.

The Commune was dominated by the same spirit as had flourished in the working-class districts in eastern Paris at the time of the Revolution. It was half idealistic – but half revengeful, too, against those who they thought had betrayed them. Among those were the priests of the Catholic Church. The Communards closed church schools, threw out the nuns who had been working in the hospitals, ransacked parish churches and arrested the Archbishop of Paris. In late March, some twenty-four priests were rounded up and shot.

None of this, to say the least, was welcome in the Collège Saint-Bertin. Each of the Fathers either knew, or knew the name of, a priest who had fallen foul of the Paris Communards. The newspapers told a grim story. Nevertheless, the conservative priests were to have their day. In April 1871 the French government, after agreeing a peace with the invading Germans, instructed the Army to lay siege to Paris. After five weeks of Parisian misery, the government troops broke through the defences of the Communards on 21 May. There followed the worst bloodshed seen in Europe since the French Revolution. Between 21 and 28 May, more than two thousand – possibly as many as ten thousand – men and women were summarily shot and another twenty thousand arrested (most of whom were sentenced to deportation after a cursory trial). In Saint-Bertin the news was no doubt received with relief. In the town of St-Omer – traditionally Bonapartist – perhaps less so.

The immediate psychological impact of the events of 1870–1 on the adolescent Pétain can only be guessed at. But two conclusions are sure. The first was that he, and the other boys at Saint-Bertin, became much more conscious of the movement for 'revenge' against Prussia – stimulated by Abbé Bled's library, which had the newest books by the historian Fustel de Coulanges on the subject. Moreover, the young man came to know and admire – and perhaps went out of his way to know and admire – the officers of the light infantry battalion which was stationed at St-Omer at the time. The second conclusion is that, under the influence of his ultramontane mentors, Pétain was conditioned to detest all that the Communards stood for. Hatred of the Communards became, in the course of time, hatred of communists (or 'bolshevists' as he was to call them), which lasted until his dying day.

In the event, there was an immediate upshot. Pétain decided against the priesthood as his future career and decided on the Army. Whether the decision was caused by admiration for the young officers of St-Omer or disillusion with the priests of Saint-Bertin – or even, perhaps, rebellion against his uncle Abbé Legrand – is not known. Nor can it be. Nor can the timing be known. But what is certain is that by the time he arrived at the penultimate year of his course at Saint-Bertin in 1873 he had determined that the Army rather than the priesthood was to be his future.

At this point Pétain had a piece of good luck. In 1873 a decree was promulgated by the government of the new Republic which abolished the advantage (apparently '100 points')[15] hitherto enjoyed in the competition for entry to the military academy of Saint-Cyr by those candidates who had passed their baccalauréat (the final examination in the secondary school system). The result was not only that anyone could compete with *bacheliers* on equal terms, but also that a student who was only a year or two away from his baccalauréat and who intended to apply for Saint-Cyr was able simply not to bother to take the examination.

Whatever the reason, Pétain decided to ride his luck; and it was this path which he chose. Thus, instead of attending Saint-Bertin for what would have been his last year, he simply left. What happened then is a mystery. He apparently left Saint-Bertin in the late summer of 1874, only to reappear in the autumn of 1875 at his new college in Arcueil on the outskirts of Paris. There is no sign of his whereabouts in the intervening months. There is certainly no sign, for instance, that he stayed either at Bomy or at Cauchy.

All that is certain is that he had firmly decided on a military career. The decision was approved by his uncle Legrand, who furthermore gave it as his opinion that if the young Pétain was to go into the Army he should go in as an officer. (His stepmother, on the other hand, considered that it would be cheaper for him to go in as an ordinary soldier.) At a family conclave in 1875 the Abbé's view carried the day. So it was that Pétain prepared for his next step, a move to the Collège Albert-le-Grand at Arcueil. Yet again his uncle had secured his entrance there; and yet again his uncle had made sure that he did not stray from the narrow path of piety. The college was run by Dominican monks. The long shadow of the Catholic Church was still to loom over the young man even as he prepared himself for war.

In fact, the Dominicans at Arcueil prove on a closer look to be

At Saint-Bertin: Pétain – and with fellow pupils (Pétain standing top left).

something of a surprise. This was no gloomy monastic establishment. The monks turn out to have been enthusiastic sportsmen. The college itself had been founded in 1863 by a Father Captier, and its motto demonstrated the good father's intentions: *Citius, altius, fortius.* It was no accident that this was also to become the motto of the revived Olympic Games of 1896. The fathers were determined that their charges should follow the principle of sporting excellence. This, they thought, combined with proper religious teaching, gave the best results in the chosen vocation, which was to prepare their pupils for the examination for entry to the great schools of the Navale, the École Spéciale Militaire de Saint-Cyr, the École Polytechnique and the Centrale.

Their task had not been an easy one. For two years after the foundation in 1863 the Fathers had been prohibited from wearing their monastic habit on the grounds that their order was not recognised in France. That obstacle was finally overcome, and the college became well known for its success securing entry for its pupils – who numbered well over two hundred – to the major schools. But the success was interrupted at the time of the Commune. There was, indeed, an incident of dreadful savagery which put an abrupt stop to all activity.

In May 1871, during the last days of the siege of Paris, the college provided space for a hospital for wounded soldiers. On the morning of 18 May – the hospital still in place – the Communards invaded the premises. They arrested a number of monks and lay helpers on the grounds that they had taken the side of the government in the massacre of fifty or so revolutionaries a fortnight earlier. They took them to the nearby fort of Bicêtre. Soon afterwards, on hearing of the approach of government troops, the Communards took most of their prisoners, including Father Captier, out on to the Avenue d'Italie – and gunned them down.

Such was the resulting trauma that it was only two years after this murderous event that the remaining Fathers were able to resume their full curriculum; and it was only two years later, in the autumn of 1875, that Pétain presented himself at Arcueil. Since he had no family prepared to accompany him, which was the custom, he had to go for his first interview by himself. Furthermore, he had to explain that the funds which had supported him at Saint-Bertin were no longer available and that he would have to support himself on the small legacy from his mother.

After the events of 1871, the management of the school had been taken over by the Vicar-General of the Dominican teaching order, Monsignor Laurent Lecuyer. In his opening address after the murder of his predecessor Monsignor Lecuyer was forthright. 'For the generation we are raising,' he proclaimed, 'the future is revenge: revenge against the foreigner . . . revenge also against the revolutionary spirit which surprised us . . .'[16] The message could hardly have been clearer. That, and the knowledge of the cold-blooded slaughter of the monks in 1871, only served to reinforce the signals Pétain had received at Saint-Bertin: revenge against the foreigner and revenge against those who pursued violent revolution at home.

Pétain was a diligent student at Arcueil, concentrating, as was natural, on the subjects which he was to take, when it finally came to it, in the entrance examination to Saint-Cyr: French, Latin translation, history, mathematics and drawing. He learned the sports specified by his Dominican teachers, becoming, in particular, a proficient horseman. He is also said to have been a robust leader of his colleagues in the parades they held. All in all, it was a confident young man who, in 1876, took the Saint-Cyr examination at the military college in Nancy. But in the event he only just scraped through. Of the 412 who were accepted by Saint-Cyr in that year Pétain came no higher than 403rd in merit.

It was not a particularly happy outcome. But at least he had not fallen at the first hurdle, and his uncle and the rest of his family could be proud of him. He was about to embark on a career as an officer in what he still considered, as did others, to be the greatest army in Europe. In his view, there was no greater honour than that. For a lad from Cauchy, it was almost beyond his dreams.

3

THE LONG APPRENTICESHIP (1)

'Froid. Gagne à être connu, n'est peut-être pas encore complètement fait, sera un bon officier.'

On the morning of Wednesday 25 October 1876 Officer Cadet Designate Pétain presented himself at the doors of the École Spéciale Militaire of Saint-Cyr. There is no doubt that it was an immensely proud moment. The young man had emerged from his peasant family background, had survived adolescence in Saint-Bertin and Arcueil, and had reached the gate through which lay a career – almost undreamed of in Cauchy – as an officer in the Army of the Republic.

True, the results of his entry examination had not been anything other than average, but that in itself had its advantages. He was not to be considered in any sense an intellectual, as were those who had headed the list of entrants for his year, and therefore was not expected to shine in the more cerebral elements of the school's curriculum. This would have suited him well. But there was another dimension. The intake of which he was part was largely composed either of sons of the aristocracy – up to about a third – or of sons of serving officers, policemen and minor civil servants or – another third – of non-commissioned officers; in other words of his social superiors. Pétain would as a matter of course have expected to be treated with social disdain; but social snobbery is perhaps easier to tolerate if intellectual snobbery is not piled on top.

As a matter of fact, both the social and intellectual composition of intakes to Saint-Cyr had changed markedly in the decade prior to Pétain's arrival. Indeed, even before then, the dominance of the sons of the aristocracy, which had been a marked feature of Saint-Cyr after the Restoration in 1815, had diminished. Sons of serving officers or of minor civil servants – most of them intellectually superior to their aristocratic contemporaries – had begun to appear on the list of entrants. But the major change had come with the Falloux Law of 1850. Schools run by the Catholic Church, such as Saint-Bertin and Albert-le-Grand, had been enabled to specialise, if they so wanted, in the preparation of their pupils for military careers, and, at the upper end, in preparation for Saint-Cyr and its civil equivalent – another Napoleonic creation – the École Polytechnique. True to form, the Jesuits had been particularly successful in this endeavour. The great Jesuit colleges of Sainte-Geneviève in Paris, Saint-Joseph in Rheims and the École de l'Immaculée Conception in Toulouse stood out, to the point where there were rumbling political complaints about the religious, and therefore supposedly anti-Republican, nature of the new officer class.

The list of the 1876 intake illustrates these points. Certainly, the aristocratic names still stand out – de Bacquencourt, Serpette de Bersaucourt, de Beaurepair-Derrion, de Cazes, de Châteauneuf-Randon, Pourroy Lambérivière de Quinsonas, d'Oncieu de la Batie and so on – but equally remarkable is the roll-call of names of a clear middle-class origin – for instance, and at random, Baron, Caplain, Carlain, Cochin, Ducrot, Deneuve – and even Froelicher, Frisenhauser, Dalinzy, Roederer and Schmit, many of them, without a doubt, educated in religious schools. All in all, Pétain's fellow cadets designate seem to have formed a reasonable cross-section of the upper and middle class of the France of their day. Yet peasants were few and far between. Pétain was clearly at the bottom end of the social ladder.

On the morning on which they were due formally to enter the school, the new cadets designate assembled in front of the imposing entrance to their new residence. They would have been aware – or if not they would soon be made aware – of the strange history of the institution they were about to enter. Thanks to the munificence of Mme de Maintenon, the then *maîtresse en titre* of Louis XIV, a building had been constructed in the late seventeenth century on the fringes of the park of the royal palace of Versailles. Its original purpose was as a school to educate the daughters of impoverished nobility. The school, for no known reason, was named after one of the youngest saints in the Christian calendar (Saint Cyr had been martyred at the age of three). Another oddity is that the hymn which was composed by Lully to be sung in greeting when Mme de Maintenon entered a classroom to view the results of her generosity was the precursor, later suitably arranged, of what is now the national anthem of the United Kingdom.

Be all that as it may, Mme de Maintenon's school was abolished at the time of the Revolution – and its head teacher guillotined for her pains. The building was then taken over during the First Empire and turned into a military academy to replace a much more modest officer-training unit at Fontainebleau. In subsequent years and decades it was added to extensively, to the point where, in the mid-1870s, the dormitories could accommodate over eight hundred cadets.

The new academy flourished, both academically and in prestige, in the first half of the nineteenth century; but by the time of the Franco-Prussian War signs of decadence were in clear evidence. A contemporary account notes that the smell of boot polish in the dormitories was often overwhelmed by that of perfume, that 'the fashionable cadets had cosmetic kits far more elaborate than many girls'[1] – and that the richer ones hired the music rooms simply in order to have somewhere to smoke and lounge about. Furthermore, the behaviour of cadets outside the school became a matter of public scandal. It was not just a question of cadets visiting the local bordellos – and contracting unpleasant diseases. There were riots, and behaviour that by any standards was outrageous. In 1872, for instance, the commandant of the school received a substantial bill from the railway company, detailing the damage caused by cadets on the Paris train, 'mostly by sabre thrusts applied to upholstered parts of the carriages'.[2]

By the time of Pétain's arrival at Saint-Cyr stricter discipline had been enforced. Non-commissioned officers were posted on the Paris trains, as well as in the dormitories. Civilian teachers who were unable to keep order were replaced by military officers. Punishments were reported to cadets' subsequent regimental postings. In 1876, just prior to his arrival, cadets were dispatched to learn discipline by participation in the annual autumn manoeuvres.

Some things, however, seemed to be immutable. Like all institutions of such a nature, Saint-Cyr had developed its own arcane rituals. 'Those who scored under half marks', reported a subsequent commandant, 'were called *"officiers galettes"* – and were called *"fines galettes"* when they were at the end of the roll of entry.'[3] Instead of being looked down on, they were generally regarded as being possessed of practical common sense – quite unlike the supposed intellectuals at the top end of the roll. Pétain, by virtue of his entry marks, was a *'fine galette'*. The oddity was compounded by the original meaning of the French word *'galette'*. It is a variety of flat cake; but what was on the epaulette of the cadet at Saint-Cyr looked so like a flat cake that it was taken up, first in mockery and then, more grandly, as the symbol of the school itself.

Fine galette or not, the Pétain who presented himself on that day in October 1876 was a most handsome young man. At Arcueil he had cultivated a rather plaintive adolescent wisp of a beard; but that had now disappeared in favour of a military moustache shaped, as was the custom in the Army, in the form of a sabre. His hair had, at Arcueil, been parted on the left, with a hint of adolescent vanity in its wave; at Saint-Cyr it was now parted in the middle, and brushed smartly down on either side. As his registration for military service at the *mairie* of Béthune reports, he had 'blond hair, blue-grey eyes, a wide forehead, and an oval face', and that his height was a modest '1.74 metres'.[4]

This attractive young man seems, in spite of his social origins, to have adapted without too much difficulty to the life of a *'fine galette'*. To be sure, the required dress was somewhat odd. The uniform at the time consisted of breeches, a frock coat with the flat *galette* on the shoulder and a képi. The distinctive mark of the lowly newcomer was that the peak of his képi 'had to abandon its horizontal position to take a vertical direction',[5] in other words to lie uncomfortably flat against his forehead. In compensation, the new intake were graciously allowed to share in the communal pleasures of their seniors. There was a large room with a piano and a billiard table available to all; and there were, of course, the same opportunities to show off in swaggering strolls in the streets of Versailles.

For Pétain there were some pleasures which had to be denied. He had, after all, to take good care of his money, since he had little of it – a small allowance from his uncle Legrand and perhaps an even smaller

The Young Officer.

supplement from the family farm at Cauchy. But the one pleasure that he denied himself without difficulty was participation in the expensive feasts or drinking bouts of the better-off cadets. The simplicity of living which had been his peasant heritage stayed with him – at least until his success in his career allowed at least a measure of relaxation.

For a cadet from Pétain's background, the curriculum was not unduly harsh. Five a.m. was the wake-up time – but he was used to that. At first, in the early days, cadets designate were taught how to make their beds, how to salute, and the detail of the hierarchy of the Army. Later on, the régime was somewhat relaxed, but cadets still did not see their first meal until 9.30 a.m., and then only for a quick fifteen-minute breakfast. Moreover, lunch at 12.30 was for only ten minutes. In between, following the curriculum of 1872 – designed, it was said, to 'prepare for the hour of *revanche*' – the cadets were required to study military tactics and capabilities, to practise riding, shooting, fencing, boxing, gymnastics, swimming and, last but by no means least, an important attribute of the peacetime officer – and one at which Pétain showed himself to be particularly adept (though how it aided the '*revanche*' is unclear) – dancing.

The curriculum may not have been unduly harsh, but it was tiring. Pétain took to it much better than some of his colleagues, and gradually moved up the ladder of promotion within his intake. Moreover, he had made a great friend of one of the cadets senior to him, Alphonse Guide. Guide's origins were in the south – in Antibes. His parents were Provençal bourgeois, with means enough to keep their son in a reasonable, but not unduly luxurious, style of life. He and Pétain forged the kind of friendship which was typical of young men of their age and background. They walked together in the streets of Versailles and even, on days off, took the train to Paris – like any other day-trippers – to see the sights. It was only on their holidays that the two friends separated, Guide to return to his home in the south and Pétain to the rectory at Bomy – with occasional visits to his family at Cauchy and occasional escapades, mostly shooting rabbits, with his old friends from the Collège Saint-Bertin.

By the time Pétain had completed his first year at Saint-Cyr, he seems to have adapted to its particular culture. The ceremony which transformed the officer cadets designate into officer cadets apparently held no terrors. To others it had been intimidating. Known as the 'baptism' of the intake, it resembled an elaborate and rather grotesque religious service. There was a great deal of shouting, and singing of idiotic songs dedicated to the '*noble galette*'. At the high point of the ceremony, the juniors knelt in front of the Tricolor and their seniors, and, in the solemnity of the moment, found their intake 'baptised'. Like most ceremonies of its kind, to an objective observer it was ridiculous, but it was held in much reverence by the participants, and there is certainly no evidence that Pétain was any more cynical about the whole thing than were his cadet colleagues.

The intake was duly baptised, the name chosen being 'Plewna'. It was a name which was very much in the news in the middle of 1877, for reasons which were evident then but which perhaps are less evident nowadays. Plewna, or, in the anglicised version, Plevna, is a small town on the banks of a barely significant tributary of the River Vid in what is now Bulgaria. The reason it was very much in the news at the time was that it was the scene of one of the greatest defensive military engagements of the nineteenth century. The choice of the name, and the fact that the engagement would have received special study by the intake which bore it, is of at least some interest in the light of Pétain's own subsequent views of the importance of defensive war strategies. Of course, not too much should be made of it. It would be absurd to imagine that Pétain's future views were solely determined by the study at Saint-Cyr of a far-off battle in a Russo-Turkish War, but the coincidence is worth noting.

The facts of the defence of Plevna by the Turkish commander Osman Pasha can be easily rehearsed. It lasted from mid-July 1877 until Osman's final capitulation in mid-December. Three Russian assaults, two in July and one in September, were repelled by the Turks with heavy casualties on both sides, but with the Russians at a clear disadvantage. Frustrated by the failure of all their efforts, the Russians called on General Todleben, the defender of Sevastopol in the Crimean War, who laid siege to the town. As supplies ran out Osman Pasha requested permission from Constantinople to withdraw, but this was refused. A Turkish sortie on the night of 9–10 December failed. Osman Pasha realised that his game was up, and surrendered soon afterwards.

Osman Pasha had conducted a brave and skilful effort. There was, however, a lesson to be learned, a lesson which was certainly not lost on the cadets of Saint-Cyr. It was simply that mere defence is not enough. On either of the three occasions when he had defeated the Russians, Osman could have broken out on to the offensive. His failure to do so led to his eventual defeat. Plevna thus became a symbol of defence to the – ultimately unsuccessful – end.

The Plewna *promotion*, to use the French word, came to its day of stardom on 13 September 1878. At their passing-out parade, the cadets, soon to be junior officers in the Army of the Republic, knelt on one knee in front of the Tricolor and solemnly swore to live and die for their country. It was a splendid occasion, attended by the parents and relatives of the cadets who were about to receive their commission. Some cadets, of course, had no surviving relatives; others had relatives who did not come. Such was the case with Cadet Pétain. None of his family attended the ceremony.

On the same day, the Ministry of War published the list of successful candidates in the *Journal Officiel*. Of the 386 considered worthy of their commission, Pétain was ranked – by merit – number 229. It was not perhaps a wholly successful result, but at least the peasant boy had performed better than his entry score might have led him to expect, and he could therefore hold his head up high as a newly commissioned officer.

All in all, in spite of Pétain's relative poverty, Saint-Cyr was for him a time of reasonable contentment. 'I would have been perfectly happy in this School', he wrote in later life, 'if they had not required us to master the finer points of theory.'[6] In other words, if it had not been for the more cerebral parts of the curriculum, he would have found himself at home there. But he had to move on. As it turned out, his result was not good enough for him to have his pick of regiments in which to serve. As a good horseman, he might at first have hoped to go into the cavalry, whose training at Saint-Cyr had been amalgamated with that of the infantry and whose subsequent recruitment was by then no longer confined to the sons of the nobility. But all available positions were occupied by those who came higher than him on the roll. The infantry was therefore his only option.

He could have chosen to join the infantry in the colonies. Some of his colleagues did so, and achieved an initial rate of promotion faster than those who had chosen to remain in metropolitan France. Moreover, by serving in fields where there was live action, colonial officers gained valuable experience in real warfare denied to their domestic brothers (and, as a result, learned to look down on them). But Pétain chose, presumably on the simple grounds that he did not want to leave France, to opt for the domestic infantry. This being so, his ranking at Saint-Cyr was good enough for him to have the pick of domestic infantry regiments. Apparently under the influence of his friend Guide, Pétain's choice lighted on the 24th Battalion of Chasseurs Alpins, stationed at the time on garrison duty not far from Guide's home at the little Mediterranean port of Villefranche-sur-Mer.

It was in many respects a happy choice. There was a short delay, since in preparation for this posting he went on a course in rifle shooting at the Rifle School at La Valbonne, near Lyon. This occupied the early weeks of 1879 – and also awarded him the distinction of 'marksman'. But it was a good introduction to his career as an infantryman; and it was with pride and a suitably light heart – and a somewhat romantic idea of soldiering – that he took up his post as 'sous-lieutenant' (second lieutenant) at his new home in his battalion.

His pride, and the light heart, were to some extent justified. The prestige of the Army, even after the catastrophe of the Franco-Prussian War, remained high. It was generally regarded as the guardian and symbol of the nation. Moreover, it was in the process of re-equipment with modern artillery and rifles, and a series of impressive fortifications on the eastern frontier. The idea of 'revenge' for the defeat of 1870 was to many, not just in the Army, an inspiration. War memorials, particularly the black-veiled statue of 'Strasbourg' in the Place de la Concorde in Paris, became the sites of emotional ceremonies. With these ideas in mind, the young sous-lieutenant could take up his post at Villefranche, guarding the French frontier with Italy, with enthusiasm.

The pride, the light heart and the enthusiasm did not survive long, even in the Provençal sunshine. In fact, it turned out that there was really not very much for a junior officer to do. There was no great call to arms. Furthermore, the longer-serving officers of the 24th Battalion regarded the newcomer from Saint-Cyr with suspicion and, since most were former non-commissioned officers, with ill-disguised jealousy. Besides, Pétain had by that time developed a caustic wit which was not at all appreciated by his seniors – or, as it happened, by the fiery southerners he accosted on his walks in neighbouring Marseille. Moreover, the pay was poor, the company indifferent, and the battalion was struggling with the reputation of garrison life as seen from the outside, as one of 'threadbare boredom, drink, debt, duels, pox and suicide'.[7]

Nevertheless, Pétain enjoyed his four years in Villefranche, and looked back at them with nostalgia. 'It is of our first garrison, of our first regiment,' Colonel Pétain declared in 1912 to the lieutenants of his then battalion, 'that we retain the most lasting impression.'[8] There were, of course, moments when he was doubtful about the whole business: the discipline was harsh, the tasks of a sous-lieutenant were in many respects menial, and the life for a young man was, compared with Saint-Cyr, monotonous.

But there were three things which made life for Pétain in the 24th Battalion not just bearable but enjoyable. The first was that his commanding officer, Colonel Cazé, understood the frustrations of the young man. It so happened that within the light infantry certain battalions had been chosen to specialise in mountain warfare and, because it was stationed on the coast below the Alpes Maritimes, the 24th was one of those selected for the task. Cazé in turn chose Pétain to lead the training. Here was, after all, an athletic young man who seemed to have no difficulty in getting on with his inferiors in rank. Pétain, in his turn, felt himself to be in his element. 'We climbed the mountains together,' he wrote later, 'helping each other without regard to rank. Living together for several months each year made it easy to discover men's inmost thoughts . . .'[9] Clearly, he was already discovering his own particular talent for military command.

Secondly, life was made more bearable by the rise, after 1870, in the social standing of junior officers. Admittedly, they were still badly paid, but they were no longer shunned in local society. 'It was not so long ago that many officers, the last hold-outs of the old school,' reported the *Avenir Militaire* of 16 May 1875, '. . . found the idea of presenting themselves into a family perfectly noxious. Consorting with women of doubtful morals, spending all day in the café, gambling, conversation peppered with oaths and vulgarities . . .These opinions, thank God, have had their day.'[10] By the time Pétain arrived in Villefranche junior officers were accepted in society. Doors were not closed to them. Indeed, if they were young, good-looking and intelligent they made a welcome change from the young men of the bourgeoisie who had previously been the staple fare of the social circuit.

Thirdly, Pétain had his friend Alphonse Guide as companion and, to put it crudely, they went on the hunt together. Guide provided the entry to the bourgeois society of the Côte d'Azur; Pétain provided the looks and the charm. They went swimming together – Pétain recalled swimming across the port of Villefranche and back. They went gambling together at Monte Carlo – strictly not allowed to officers but Pétain, at least, disguised himself in civilian clothes for the purpose. But, above all, they chased women.

It so happened that the terrain was favourable for their purpose. The starchy rectitude of the Second Empire had given way to the greater freedom of the Third Republic. Women, for instance, no longer shied away from open awareness of the facts of life or, for that matter, from reading the romantic – and, at times, near-pornographic – novels that were a feature of the day. The inevitable result was that dissatisfied wives felt able to engage in extra-marital affairs; and there were few more ready to oblige them than the handsome young garrison officers. Indeed, in some regiments officers were specifically permitted to form such attachments, in order to avoid their constant attendance at the local brothels, 'provided that the relationship remained discreet and the woman displayed a certain distinction'.[11] Once introduced to the world of the theatre, the balls, the soirées and the salons which formed the essence of social life on the Côte d'Azur, it seemed that a young man could take his pick; and Pétain was certainly not slow to join in the fun.

There is, for instance, a photograph of him dressed as a jockey at a fancy-dress ball in Menton in 1881. Oddly enough, it was on that occasion that Pétain met his future wife, Berthe-Alphonsine-Eugénie Hardon, known generally as 'Nini'. At the time she was four and a half years old and she appeared dressed as a flower girl to dance with the other children in the afternoon. The 'jockey' was due to dance in the evening with the grown-ups. Somehow the two met. The young Nini – obviously rather skittishly – explained to Pétain that her father was a successful civil engineer. She even might have gone so far as to mention that he was involved in the construction of the Panama Canal. What apparently she did not add was that her mother was exceptionally beautiful, her beauty enhanced by the pallor of tuberculosis.

Introductions to the family followed, and Pétain frequently thereafter visited their home in Menton. There is no particular reason to believe that the visits were anything other than innocent. But Pétain's reputation was well known to the family. 'In those far-off days', Nini was later to recall, '*sous-lieutenant* Pétain courted many pretty ladies . . . people often talked, with a smile, of his conquests.'[12] In the light of this, it is perhaps not too fanciful to assume that Pétain's real target was the mother rather than the daughter, and in dandling the daughter on his knee he was pursuing a well-known technique – the way to a mother's heart through a demonstration of affection for her child.

Be that as it may, there is no doubt that *sous-lieutenant* Pétain carved something of a furrow through the female society of the Côte d'Azur during his years at Villefranche; and, no doubt, one or two tears were shed when he announced in December 1883 that he was to be posted

The 'jockey' and little Nini.

to a rather more stern environment – the 3rd Battalion of Chasseurs in the garrison town of Besançon. But it was not only the ladies. His platoon also gave him a friendly send-off. After all, they had spent many days and weeks in the mountains together and, to celebrate the New Year of 1883, had all been drinking together (Pétain apparently producing a bottle of eau-de-vie of walnuts – with the unlikely claim that it had been distilled specially for him by his stepmother).

Besançon proved to be quite different from Villefranche. 'Not particularly jolly' was Pétain's own verdict.[13] It is easy to sympathise. Lying as it does at the end of the Jura mountain chain in the middle of eastern France, the city, although it still boasts an attractive centre within its original site of the meandering horseshoe of the River Doubs, carries even now an air of dissatisfied gloom. Historically, the territory had been fought over many times, but the worst moment in the city's life had come with the Franco-Prussian

War. It had been little less than a disaster. In January 1871, General
Bourbaki had retreated to Besançon in an attempt to stem the Prussian
advance and, if possible, to relieve their siege of Belfort to the north.
This attempt having failed, Bourbaki had then tried to commit suicide – without success. The result had been that a hundred thousand
men of the French 'Army of the East' were interned in Switzerland,
Belfort was lost, and in the negotiations leading to the treaty of
Frankfurt, which formally ended the war, France only just managed to
keep Besançon in her territory.

Those wounds, like all wartime wounds, took a long time to heal.
Not least among the scars was the unwelcome arrival in the Franche-
Comté, and its capital Besançon – their migration sanctioned by the
Frankfurt Treaty – of a number of Alsatian Jews, among them a family
by the name of Dreyfus. Moreover, perched on the eastern frontier of
France, the city suffered an industrial decline, only alleviated by the
founding of a watch industry by refugees from Switzerland. In the
last quarter of the nineteenth century it was overtaken by Dijon in
terms of both population and wealth. The railway passed it by: the
Paris–Geneva route, thanks to Besançon's refusal, was snapped up
by Pontarlier to the south. All in all, it was a city in decline at the gates
of which Pétain, now a full lieutenant by virtue of seniority, arrived in
January 1883.

Besançon was much more serious a garrison town than Villefranche,
facing, as it did, any future German threat. It offered little more than,
as Pétain recorded, 'one resource: work'.[14] This, as it happened, was
something less than the truth. Certainly, there is little doubt that
he found Besançon, as a place, worthy but boring. There was a society
of sorts – the theatre which you came out of, on his own account,
humming the tunes of the operetta you had heard, receptions, the
occasional ball or wedding celebration – where a young lieutenant
might meet an engaging lady or even an entertaining civilian male
friend who would turn out to be a good drinking companion. There
was always the possibility of a visit to a brothel or, more likely for an
officer, a quick excursion with a young secretary who wished to
supplement her income.

Nevertheless, all this was becoming somewhat repetitive – and
more dangerous, in that the Army was becoming more strident in its
disapproval of its lieutenants either contracting venereal disease or

fathering illegitimate children on the ladies of the garrison towns where they were stationed. Therefore, having spent six months testing the Besançon social climate, Pétain decided, in mid-1883, that it was time for him to get married. He was, after all, in his late twenties. He had sown, and perhaps more than sown, his wild oats. It was time, in the hallowed phrase, to 'settle down'.

This proved to be more difficult to achieve than he might have imagined. His first choice of bride was almost predictable. She was a girl from his home country of Artois and a distant cousin from the well-to-do peasant community around Cauchy, by the name of Célina Brassart. The business seemed at first sight easy enough; but it turned out that there were problems. Although Pétain was able to present himself as a full lieutenant with the prospect of an honourable if unadventurous career in the Army, the lady in question did not find the prospect enticing. For a start, she was nine years older than Pétain and dedicated to holy and good works. For instance, 'she looked after the young girls of the parish. She made them sing, and accompanied them on the harmonium. Very pious, she had sworn herself to celibacy in order better to serve the Lord . . .'[15]

The handsome lieutenant was thus unceremoniously turned down by his pious cousin. But he was not discouraged. His next step was to research the field of possible candidates in Besançon. His eye lighted on one of the girls he had met on the social circuit: Antoinette Berthelin. Her father was an engineer in the employ of the government, well respected in the community and, in principle, happy to welcome a young officer with suitable prospects into his family as a son-in-law. But when approached about a possible wedding, he quite properly pointed out that he would have to make enquiries before making a decision. Unfortunately, M. Bertholin's enquiries showed that there was little future for the lieutenant other than a long and frustrating slow march towards eventual obscure retirement. They would continue to remain friends, M. Bertholin assured Pétain, but he did not think that the lieutenant was the husband he would wish for his daughter.

Pétain had now drawn two blanks. Nevertheless, still undeterred, he was prepared for one more shot. A year later, he tried again. This time the target was Angéline Vuillaume, the daughter of the Besançon manager of the Société Générale, one of the most powerful banks in the region. Again, his initial approach to M. Vuillaume was well received; and, again, enquiries were made by the prospective father-in-law. Presumably, M. Vuillaume asked the opinion of the same people who had given their opinion to M. Berthelin, since the answer was the same: a polite refusal of the daughter's hand.

For the time and place – the last quarter of the nineteenth century in provincial France – such a series of marital rebuffs for an officer of at least reasonable standing was, to say the least, unusual. For Pétain it was more than a blow. He had, after all, had numerous amatory conquests. His manner with men was perhaps a little caustic, but he was at ease in provincial society. In fact, he had become rather pleased with himself, and obviously proud of his eyes and of his moustache. He could not understand why the bourgeoisie of Besançon would not take him to its heart. They, on their side, understood quite clearly that – whatever the view of their daughters – Pétain was by origin a peasant, and that, consequently, he could not possibly have the connections which would allow him anything other than a humdrum career in the Army. As such, although welcome in their society, he was not regarded as fit to become a member of their family.

This series of rebuffs was bad enough. But things got worse. What had obviously started out as a considered and rational campaign became very emotional. For a start, on 5 May 1888 Pétain learned that his father, Omer-Venant, had died. Although relations between father and son had not been particularly good since the father's second marriage, the death of the second parent is, however benign the circumstances, a matter of distress. It is the intimation of mortality of the child himself that is always so striking, and Pétain, having just reached the age of thirty-two, would, like anybody else of that age, have felt it deeply.

Whatever emotional turmoil there was became very much more intense a few weeks after his father's death. Invited, along with his fellow officers in Besançon, to a ball in the house of M. Léon Regad, the owner of the Forges de Quingey and one of the richest men in the province of Franche-Comté, Pétain met and danced with 'a girl of a rare beauty'.[16] It was immediate, and apparently reciprocal, love. By the end of the evening the couple had exchanged sighs and promises – and had even agreed, well beyond the social conventions of the time, to address each other by their Christian names, Marie-Louise and Philippe.

The following morning, Pétain asked his commanding officer, Captain Louis Ernest Maud'huy, to approach M and Mme Regad on his behalf to request the hand of their daughter Marie-Louise in marriage. This de Maud'huy did. But, much to the distress of 'Marie-Louise' and 'Philippe', there followed the usual investigation of the prospective bridegroom's fortune and prospects with which Pétain was wearily familiar. The result was the same as on previous occasions: there was to be no wedding. Nevertheless, thanks to the entreaties of the daughter, the parents offered Pétain a compromise. If, they said, he would abandon his military career, resign from the Army, and join the family firm in Besançon, then – under those circumstances, but only under those circumstances – they would give their consent to the marriage.

Pétain did not know which way to go. Should he give up the Army for love, or should he give up love for the Army? Faced with this dilemma, he concluded that there was only one thing to do. He sought advice from his uncle, Abbé Legrand – by then translated from Bomy to the nearby parish of Mazinghem. There the two of them apparently spent a number of days – and the odd night – in serious deliberation. In the end, the uncle's decision was clear: forget the lady and stick to your career. Pétain, after much hesitation, agreed. He would go back to Bésançon and tell Marie-Louise that he would not marry her. In fact, he did not dare to do so. Marie-Louise had asked her parents to prepare for another ball to celebrate her engagement. But nothing happened. The charming lieutenant did not send so much as a word. There was only a message from Captain Maud'huy. There was to be no engagement. The ball was cancelled.

Of course, it is easy to criticise, or to mock, Pétain's decision, and his cowardice in not himself telling Marie-Louise the result of the consultation at Mazinghem. He had, after all, committed himself to the beautiful girl (who never married subsequently) and had formally requested her parents for consent to their marriage. Nevertheless, there are some, albeit slender, mitigating factors. The law which required the man as well as the woman to secure parental consent to marriage was still in force. Since both Pétain's parents were dead, it was to the uncle he had to look for a parental view. It followed that, whatever his own feelings, he could not marry Marie-Louise without breaking the law. Whatever love there was between the two – and it seems to have been perfectly genuine – had to be stifled. His uncle, with the authority, moreover, of the Church, had spoken. Besides, since matters of marriage were properly a subject of communication between parents, a message from Maud'huy *in loco parentis* was probably the most elegant way out.

Whatever the truth, Pétain's last failure successfully to achieve the married state led him in a different direction. To be sure, he continued the flirtations and seductions which were a feature of garrison life. But there entered into his life at that point a more serious note, which was to echo down the years almost to his death more than sixty years later. Abbé Legrand had reminded him of the oath which he had taken at Saint-Cyr 'to serve France'. This had been interpreted during their discussions at Mazinghem as equivalent to a monastic vow. Like a monk, the officer was to give himself to his country – without let or hindrance. That oath taken and reaffirmed, the Army was to become for ever the officer's family, and the service of France and her people his destiny. It was a hard view, but Pétain seems to have accepted it. Of course, the oath did not prevent philandering. It did not even prevent marriage. What it prevented was a marriage whose condition was the abandonment of the fundamental belief that the graduate from Saint-Cyr had acquired a mystical relationship with his country. It therefore comes as no surprise to find Pétain himself describing his years at Besançon as 'decisive for my career'.[17]

With this emotional baggage now on his back, he devoted himself to his study for the entrance examination for the École de Guerre, the staff college for aspiring young officers. The examination duly passed, on 1 November 1888 he returned to Paris and, along with thirty-nine other officers from the infantry, entered the gaunt building in which was housed his new college. Lieutenant Pétain was now formally classified as a 'high-flier', with a career on the general staff lying before him.

It was at the École de Guerre that the professional Pétain started to flourish. After the personal difficulties of Besançon, he seems to have found a new equilibrium. To be sure, the military doctrines which were taught at the college still dated from the Napoleonic era – it was not until the Germans published their accounts of the Franco-Prussian War, in the early 1890s, that the curriculum was brought up to date – and there was little scope for discussion. But in some ways this suited Pétain's by now apparent ambition. His paper on the defence of northern France against a possible attack through Belgium, for instance, put forward ideas for defensive warfare which were certainly not Napoleonic. He also played his full part in other activities. In May 1889 he scored a mark of 16 out of 20 in a field exercise. In June there was a week's course with an artillery battery, firing live ammunition, at Nîmes. On his return to Paris in July, he was again marked 16 out of 20 for map-reading and 17 out of 20 for infantry training.

High marks continued into his second year at the École de Guerre. It was noted that he had 'a voice of command – clear and firm'.[18] So it went on: always good marks, reports of an officer who was 'serious', 'reflective', 'willing' and so on. There was also the frequent qualification: 'cold', 'cold character', 'cold aspect' and 'difficult to understand'. Pétain was quite clearly no longer the sparkling young officer of Villefranche-sur-Mer; he was an older, perhaps sadder and more bruised, middle-ranking infantry officer. To be sure, women were still on his agenda, but there is no mention of any serious liaison, let alone any suggestion of marriage.

This mood is clearly carried over into his next posting. On 7 July 1890 he was promoted to the rank of captain – yet again only on the basis of seniority – and was sent as a staff officer to XV Army Corps at their headquarters in Marseille. There 'I spent three years bound to the most monotonous office job, doing my best to carry out the duty of staff writer for which, I confess, I had no inclination.'[19] To cap it all, Pétain was a victim of a mild version of typhoid fever – a common occurrence in the Marseille of the day – which put him in hospital for two months. At the end of 1893 he moved again – Army Regulations required former pupils of the École de Guerre to alternate between staff appointments and field commands. This time it was to the command of a company of the 29th Battalion of Chasseurs, then stationed at Vincennes, a short distance to the east of Paris. There were, he subsequently reported, manoeuvres in the woods around the town, and some decent riding. Apart from that, there seems to have been little else to do.

Pétain was by then nearing forty. He was on the way to becoming a confirmed bachelor. Indeed, at this time he seems to have developed some characteristics which would normally be associated with disappointed bachelorhood. For instance, he was happy to claim that he had finally abandoned the religious faith of his childhood (attendance at Mass being confined to the requirements of social and military convention); he took, in a fit of personal vanity – as though to demonstrate his good looks to the world – to riding on a white horse and, at Vincennes, to reviewing his company on it; above all, he became much more querulous towards his army superiors. Nor had he any of the normal means of solace of bachelorhood. His reading was no more than army texts; his musical ear did not reach further than an army band or the tunes from an operetta; and the visual arts were a closed book.

Nevertheless, Besançon had been decisive in his career. The disappointments of his amorous manoeuvres served to concentrate his mind on his future in the Army, and, if the Army was to be his career, he was ambitious enough to wish to make a success of it. The study of the history, the doctrine and the governing regulations of the French Army became daily reading. The peasant mind developed into an acute analytical instrument. He had set himself to learn, not through formal education, but in the evenings of marital disappointment.

This, in short, was the – rather different – Pétain who was posted back to Paris in July 1895 to the staff of the Military Governor of Paris. Here, he was at the centre of events; and, as it happened, events were unusually exciting. It had only been six months earlier that Captain Alfred Dreyfus had been stripped of his badges of rank, and his sword broken in front of him, in a humiliating public ceremony. His alleged crime was treason. But the evidence against him, the nature of his conviction, and his sentence to a life on Devil's Island were even then being widely challenged. The whole affair was throwing the Army into turmoil and provoking civil disputes almost to the point of civil war. The ambitious Captain Pétain was to be at the centre of it all – in the eye, as it were, of the hurricane.

4

THE LONG APPRENTICESHIP (2)

'. . . et pourtant je refusai de me rendre pour ne rien devoir à l'un des agents les plus en vue de l'affaire Dreyfus.'

'Cold, even icy, this beautiful blond man, his head already almost totally bald, attracted both men and women by the power of his blue eyes.'[1] Thus only one description of the Pétain of the early 1900s. Others told the same story, of a man who was glacial in his relations with his fellow officers but who exercised an apparently irresistible attraction for women. Similarly, the photographs of Pétain at the time, few as they are, show the face and physique typical of a military man of the day – upright in posture, authoritative in the frown and direct look, heavy eyebrows, classically moulded moustache, and a well-formed chin. The only oddities in the head are the premature baldness – normally obscured in photographs by his képi – and the protuberant, but rather small, ears. There is also in the carriage more than a hint of personal vanity. He was quite conscious of all – and in this context all means all – of his physical attributes.

Many commented on the major's good looks. His baldness was explained away, somewhat improbably, as the result of his typhoid attack a few years earlier. The piercing blue eyes came, again it was said, from his peasant background in the Artois. His blond moustache, on the other hand, was remarked upon as being the purest signature of a successful staff officer. What was never in doubt was these characteristics made him fascinating to the opposite sex.

True, to the modern eye it is not a particularly attractive image. Compared with the image, to judge from a similarly contemporary photograph, of Pétain's friend Alphonse Guide, who seems to be all that a French officer should be, Pétain's face seems unrelaxed and his posture affected. But there is no reason to pursue the comparison between the two. Guide had, quite soon after their joint amatory endeavours in Villefranche-sur-Mer, succumbed to a bout of tuberculosis which made him unfit to pursue an active military career. Given that he was a man of independent means, he could afford to live a life of comparative leisure; and this he had proceeded to do.

Pétain, on the other hand, had, until his promotion to the general staff, moved from garrison town to garrison town, when not in barracks or in the field living in a hotel or in furnished rooms, taking with him, on each transfer, his personal effects and his limited collection of books. He had no doubt left behind him, on each occasion, a number of broken hearts. The names of Jacqueline Cyprien-Fabre, Amélie Racine, Jehane Saby, flit across the pages of his private life. Almost certainly, too, there had been a number of unwanted results of his liaisons: a girl assistant at a toy shop in Besançon, for instance, seems to have become an unintentional mother. There were, almost certainly, others; but Pétain was careful enough to escape the consequences, or at least callous enough not to bother about them.

Once Pétain joined the general staff his lifestyle – though not his habits – to some extent changed out of necessity. After all, the life of a staff officer was very different from that of a field officer, and Pétain, like most others, soon adapted to the change. Apart from the fact that he worked in an office and only visited manoeuvres in the comfort of a car or, at worst, on a horse, where the field officer was expected to muck in with his men, the staff officer was regarded, or at least regarded himself, as a member of the Army's élite. In fact, such was the self-regard of the general staff that it can reasonably be said that they were largely responsible for the refusal of the Army to admit to a mistake over the Dreyfus affair.

The main events of the Dreyfus affair are by now well known. Dreyfus himself was an artillery officer attached to the general staff when, in September 1894, a list of French military documents had been found by a cleaning lady doing daily duty sifting through the contents of a waste-paper basket in the German Embassy in Paris. The counter-espionage service of the Army, operating as it did under the strange title of the 'Statistical Section', mounted an inquiry and concluded that there was a German spy in the Ministry of War in the rue St-Dominique. Since Dreyfus was not only not a permanent member of the general staff but was an Alsatian Jew, it became immediately obvious to the 'Statistical Section' that he was the culprit.

Dreyfus was duly tried in a secret court martial, found guilty and, because he failed to do the honourable thing and commit suicide, received his dreadful sentence – to be publicly stripped of his rank and sent to Devil's Island to forced labour for life. At the time, in mid-1895, when Pétain took up his office in the Military Government of Paris, Dreyfus's case was only being pursued by his brother Matthieu. But by the time Pétain left, in the autumn of 1898, the row had escalated. Not only had a vigorous campaign proclaiming Dreyfus's innocence been mounted by Georges Clemenceau, then proprietor of the newspaper *Aurore*; not only had the Vice-President of the Senate, Auguste Scheurer-Kestner, taken on the job of lobbying influential politicians on Dreyfus's behalf; not only had the author Emile Zola launched a vitriolic attack on General Mercier, the Minister of War at the time of Dreyfus's arrest (in an open letter entitled *J'accuse*'), accusing him of a judicial crime; but, most important of all, the 'Statistical Section', by then headed by Colonel Georges Picquart, had become convinced that they had picked the wrong man. The true culprit, it appeared, was another staff officer, Major Ferdinand Esterhazy.

In early 1898, Esterhazy was tried but, to the disgust of many, he was acquitted. (It subsequently turned out that the evidence which led to his acquittal had been forged by yet another officer of the general staff, who, when exposed, committed suicide.) Zola was also tried and quickly condemned. At that point it seemed that the general staff had conclusively won that particular war; and it was at that moment in the drama – which was by no means finished – that Pétain, in September 1898, was posted to the 8th Battalion of Chasseurs stationed in Amiens. From then on he was no longer at the centre of events.

To this day there remains the delicate question of whether or not Pétain believed in Dreyfus's guilt. He must have had a view. He was far too intelligent not to have formed one; and he had been, after all, at the centre of things. But it is also reasonable to suppose that he must have been pulled in two opposite directions.

The first would have been towards suspicion of the Dreyfus verdict. The office of the Military Governor of Paris in the Place Vendôme was not large, and those who worked there were naturally loyal to their senior officer. A staff captain would certainly have known most of what was going on, and in this case would have picked up all the rumours that were running around at the time. There was, furthermore, an inbuilt rivalry between the Military Government of Paris and the Ministry of War. Each was suspicious of the other's machinations – understandably so. If the attack on Dreyfus had come from the ministry, as it had, this in itself would lead to suspicion in the Place Vendôme. But by far the most important pointer of all was that General Félix Saussier, Pétain's immediate superior as Military Governor – and Vice-Chairman of the Conseil Supérieur de la Guerre, a job which carried with it the command of the French Army in the event of war – had enough doubts about Dreyfus's guilt to sign the warrant for Esterhazy's trial. In the jargon of the day, Saussier was a 'Dreyfusard'.

On the other hand, the Catholic hierarchy, led by the Archbishop of Paris, formed a solid front against Dreyfus. The question, it was said from many pulpits, was not whether a wretched individual was guilty or innocent; it was whether the Jews and the Protestants were or were not the masters of the country. The 'anti-Dreyfusard' writer Maurice Barrès even managed to convey the impression that what was at stake was the integrity of the nation. Furthermore, only a fortnight after signing a warrant for Esterhazy's arrest and trial, Saussier retired – to be replaced by General Emile Zurlinden, who immediately back-pedalled on Saussier's position.

All that, in turn, would have led Pétain in the opposite direction. Although he had lost whatever remained of his childhood faith he was always very respectful of clerics and clerical opinion. He was also loyal to the Army and to the general staff of which he was a member. Moreover, although the French peasant was perhaps less vociferous in anti-semitism than the bourgeoisie there was no doubt that the Army and the Catholic Church were deeply anti-semitic, and there is no evidence that Pétain was any different from his military colleagues.

But there was the matter of Saussier. If his military superior – and a respected general – had doubts about the whole procedure, would that not be persuasive? In fact, there is no means of even guessing at the answer to the question, since there is no contemporary evidence of Pétain's opinions on the affair, and his later comments are, to say the least, delphic. All that can be said with certainty is that after Saussier's retirement he continued to work with, and, as aide-de-camp, was trusted by, General Zurlinden, who was certainly not prepared to fight Dreyfus's cause (and was even implicated in the general staff's efforts to smear Dreyfus further). But it might also be reasonable to speculate that Pétain was reluctant openly to take sides. In other words, whatever his feelings, it was a time for him to keep his head down.

Pétain's posting to Amiens in 1898 came at the time when the Dreyfus furore was at its height; it was clearly a good moment to be out of Paris. In that he was perhaps fortunate. But there was also something better than avoiding the storm. In 1900 he made a further step in his slow progress up the ladder of rank. His promotion to the rank of major came through in July of that year. At long last, after ten years as a captain, he could take command of a battalion instead of languishing as a quasi-permanent company commander, as was the fate of many of his colleagues. But it was not just the promotion which was cause for satisfaction. He had been noticed by no less a figure than General Guillaume Bonnal, who reported Pétain as 'a remarkable captain . . . top flight'.[2]

Bonnal's remarks were indicative. Although his progress up the ladder of rank had been slow, by the time he became a battalion commander Pétain was quite clearly a considerable figure in the military world. He had matured from the youthful and somewhat cavalier *sous-lieutenant* of Villefranche-sur-Mer into a responsible and thoughtful staff and field officer. He had read much military history and was giving a good deal of attention to developing his own views on strategy and tactics. His stay in Paris had allowed him to make influential contacts in the higher reaches of the general staff, contacts which were certainly to prove useful in the future.

Those, however, were not the only features of his stay in Paris from 1895 to 1898. There were, of course, the liaisons which, with his new status as a staff officer in the Military Government, Pétain was only too enthusiastic in pursuing. The disadvantages of a peasant background and the relative poverty of a junior officer by then put aside, he had been able to reach into a more socially elevated class of female society. Of course, there was no question of him storming the heights of the aristocracy. Nor was he interested in the substrata of Parisian life. But it was the upper middle class – the *haute bourgeoisie* – which he found attractive. There is, for instance, an account of the seduction of an eighteen-year-old daughter of the Mayor of Provins ('We both profaned the moonlight,' she wrote to him)[3] during the Christmas holidays of 1898. But, in particular, his eyes had become fixed on one of the daughters of the *haute bourgeoisie*, none other than the little girl he had dandled on his knee all those years ago in Menton – Nini Hardon.

Nini, like Pétain, had travelled a long distance since then. For a start, she had grown into a tall and comely young lady in her early twenties. Her mother had died in early 1898, her father had married again, and she was living with her grandmother, father and stepmother in a pleasant apartment in the reasonably – but not too – fashionable rue Cambon. How Pétain and Nini met again is not clear. But meet they did, and Pétain's mind wandered again towards marriage. After all, Nini was attractive, had no apparent suitor and, of some importance to the middle-ranking officer, would bring with her a substantial dowry.

Two things prevented Pétain from pursuing this new idea. The first was the illness of his uncle Legrand which was to lead to his death in 1899. If anybody had set the young peasant boy on his road to advancement it was Abbé Legrand. Apart from that, there was always a welcome for Pétain in the *curé*'s house, first in Bomy and then in Mazinghem. When it came, his death was correspondingly a solemn event for the now middle-aged protégé, and it was treated accordingly. Pétain was present at his uncle's deathbed, and at his funeral behaved with all the dignity and restrained emotion that the occasion demanded. His true father had been Omer; but his spiritual father had been Abbé Legrand.

The second problem was his posting to Amiens, which came only a few months after his meeting with the prospective bride. It was hard in those days to be a pressing suitor at more than a hundred kilometres' distance. Besides, Nini's stepmother would certainly wish to have her say in the matter, and Pétain had hardly met her, let alone paid her the courtesies and the attention which would be the necessary part of his wooing of her stepdaughter. In short, the stars were at that moment not favourable, and Pétain had to be content with the ladies of Amiens.

No sooner had he been promoted to the rank of major than he was given the command of the 133rd Regiment of Infantry, then stationed at Belley, another garrison town near Aix-les-Bains in south-eastern France. It was to be the shortest of all his postings, since he was almost immediately assigned to the Rifle School at Châlons at the instigation of his former teacher at the École de Guerre, General Millet, by then the most senior general in the infantry. The assignment, as it happened, was not a success. Current theory required that riflemen should simply saturate the battlefield with indiscriminate fire. Pétain, himself no mean marksman, thought differently. Quite apart from his contempt for his superiors (he later wrote that he found at Châlons 'a school of mutual admiration'),[4] he believed in accuracy of fire above all.

Although at the time this seemed radical, this view was already gaining ground in the Ministry of War. There is evidence to show that Pétain was not producing a novel theory but acting as an instrument for those in Paris who argued for change. Nevertheless, Pétain's lectures on the matter profoundly irritated the commander of the Rifle School, Colonel Vonderscherr. But, however irritated, there was nothing much he could do while Pétain was under Millet's protection. After six months of irritation, however, Vonderscherr had a stroke of luck. Millet was replaced, and his successor was much more sympathetic to the prevailing philosophy of the School. Pétain was accordingly invited to resign. It was an invitation which was not to be refused; all that Pétain managed to achieve was the assurance of a posting back to Paris. This was duly arranged, and in February 1901 Pétain took command of the 5th Regiment of Infantry, then stationed in the barracks of Latour-Maubourg.

Yet again, this was to be a short posting. In the autumn of 1901 Pétain was invited to become Assistant Professor of Infantry Tactics at the École de Guerre. The pendulum had swung again. He was back in favour, at least with some. The appointment was certainly prestigious, but it was entirely due to General Bonnal, who had by then become the School's Director. Pétain's immediate superior, too, was a figure from his past – the same Maud'huy who had acted so unsuccessfully as Pétain's intermediary in his attempts at marriage at Besançon.

Little is known about Pétain's teaching during his two-year period from 1901 to 1903 at the École de Guerre. But it appears that even then there was a clear division of opinion on infantry tactics among the teaching staff. There were those who still taught the Napoleonic guiding principle – throwing maximum force against the enemy – and there were those who held that not even a large force could withstand well-directed and accurate fire from a determined opponent. Pétain certainly took the latter view, and was presumably duly put out when a draft regulation in 1902 came down firmly in favour of the former.

But, by such accounts as there are, he was a good teacher – meticulous in the preparation of his subject and effective in engaging the attention of his audience. As an example, one of his techniques in the seminars he conducted was particularly clever: he invited his students to recount any experience which they, their family or friends had had of enemy fire. By asking them, in effect, to teach themselves he made the lesson more vivid. But he seems not to have tried to charm his students. One of them, René Pichot-Duclos, described the assistant professor as 'clear-eyed, cold, bald . . . he spoke in icy tones'.[5] He was also reported as having a particularly dry, even sarcastic, sense of humour.

The teaching of infantry tactics were not the only thing on

Pétain's mind. On his return to Paris in late 1901 he had decided to renew his pursuit of Nini. Accordingly, he made an approach to her stepmother and grandmother, but it comes as something of a surprise to learn that Pétain omitted to mention his project to Nini herself. Moreover, neither Nini's grandmother nor her stepmother thought it worth consulting her. As a result, Nini was in total ignorance of her suitor's request for her hand.

The grandmother and the stepmother put their authoritative heads together – and decided that the difference in their ages made a marriage between the two out of the question. Pétain was duly informed of their decision. But Nini was still not told. 'If he had told me', she said many years after, 'I would probably have married him on the spot in spite of my family.'[6] Pétain's reaction to this latest rebuff is not the least surprising feature of the whole affair. Instead of retreating in dudgeon, he took Nini aside and advised her to get married – to somebody else. This she promptly did. The upshot was that Pétain's curious tactics in romance lost him some twenty years of married life.

There were other matters which were profoundly to affect Pétain's future. In the middle of his period at the École de Guerre the political climate changed dramatically. The Dreyfus affair had all the time been rumbling on. In June 1899 a young royalist baron had approached President Loubet at the Auteuil spring race meeting and, with a sweep of his cane, had knocked off the President's top hat. This was, as all admitted, going too far. The ensuing uproar quickly took on a political dimension. The coalition of the moderate right which had run France for most of the decade collapsed, to be replaced by a left-leaning anti-clerical coalition. The new government brought such pressure on the Army's high command that Dreyfus had been brought back the following month from Devil's Island – an emaciated ruin of a man – and tried again in a secret court martial in Rennes. The court found him guilty again but cited 'extenuating circumstances' in giving him a shorter sentence. The general staff was still trying to shore up its now dubious position. Indeed, one officer was heard to remark, 'I am convinced of Dreyfus's innocence but . . . I would convict him again for the honour of the army.'[7]

Needless to say, the verdict and such a fatuous justification commanded the headlines in the press not just of France but of the world outside. The row was such that the government was obliged to offer Dreyfus a pardon, which, although still protesting innocence, he accepted. (In fact, it was not until 1906, at a hearing in the appeal court, that Dreyfus was acquitted and that there was a somewhat grudging official admission that the whole thing had been a most regrettable miscarriage of justice.)

The overall result of the affair, and, in particular, of the fierce anti-Dreyfus and anti-government offensive mounted by the hierarchy, was that in the national elections of May 1902 the Catholic Church became almost the sole issue. Other matters, in reality of equal but of mundane importance, faded into the background. In the event, the left-wing grouping, whose main constituent was the Radical Party, won a majority in the National Assembly of just over eighty seats. The sitting head of government, René Waldeck-Rousseau, who had led, in terms of the Third Republic, a long-lasting and remarkably successful administration (but whom his opponents considered to be a weak man of few great political principles – he was dubbed 'a pike in aspic'),[8] threw in his hand and gave way to a new government headed by the fiercely anti-clerical Emile Combes, a somewhat eccentric elderly country doctor who was at the time carrying on a fond correspondence with an aristocratic nun, Princess Bibesco. Moreover, it was noted that Combes's Council of Ministers was composed entirely of Freemasons.

Pétain's reaction to this new government needs little imagination. French Freemasonry had long been the enemy of the Church, and Pétain, for all his avowed loss of faith, maintained his respect for the priesthood which had so strongly influenced him and supported him in his early years. Distrust of Freemasons was ingrained, and distrust of politicians quickly followed. This distrust was exacerbated by the immediate actions of the new government. It was quick to run its colours up the anti-clerical mast. Soldiers were dispatched to close down convents, three in Brittany and one in Tarascon. To use the Army against the Church was, in the view of most officers – of whom Pétain certainly was one – wholly unacceptable. If that was the way the Masonic government were going to behave, then the sooner they were turned out the better.

At that point the Vatican intervened, with a volley of encyclicals directed at the newly elected French government. As might be expected, a protracted row ensued, which ended only with the repeal of the Napoleonic Concordat between Church and state in 1905. In the interim period, however, the government pressed forward with its programme, one feature of which was a proposal to 'republicanise' the Army.

The chief promoter of this campaign – whatever 'republicanisation' meant in practice – was the new Minister for War, General Louis André. At first sight, he had looked an unlikely choice. True, he was a Freemason like his cabinet colleagues; but he was regarded in the Army as little more than a competent technician, rather colourless in character, although not without courage (he had been decorated for bravery at the time of the Commune). Moreover, he and his private secretary at the Ministry of War, Colonel Alexandre Percin, had been active in securing the conviction of Dreyfus, which was not a cause that endeared them to the Radicals.

Nevertheless, when given the task, André embarked on his campaign with energy. It turned out that the real meaning of 'republicanisation' was a purge from the Army of all officers with Catholic sympathies. Key positions in the ministry, the general staff and the military schools were filled with André's trusties. The main target for removal was any officer who was known to be a practising Catholic. Three colonels in the general staff, for instance, were removed only for that reason.

It was around this time – the date is uncertain – that Pétain was sent for by Percin, who had been impressed by his grasp of infantry tactics, to be offered the command of the Rifle School at Châlons. It was an odd move by Percin, since the school, as Pétain pointed out, was usually under the command of a lieutenant-colonel, not of a major such as himself. The objection was brushed aside. He would be promoted immediately. 'This would place me', Pétain wrote later, 'in a very advantageous position for future promotions'.[9] In spite of this, Pétain turned the job down.

The reasons for Pétain's refusal are far from clear. It was certainly damaging to his own interests. In fact, he had to wait another four years for promotion to lieutenant-colonel, a delay which effectively barred him from further promotion before his retirement date, due in 1916 when he reached the age of sixty. He himself claimed that he did not wish to be indebted to one of the main protagonists in the Dreyfus affair; but that explanation should perhaps be treated with caution. A more plausible reason for Pétain's refusal is that he did not wish to get too close to the group of Freemasons who were by then running the Army. Indeed, there are some anecdotes which support this view. For instance, it is said that when André made his first visit to the École de Guerre Pétain refused to shake hands with him.

After a period of nine months of what might be called statutory exile in command of the 104th Regiment of Infantry at Argentan, Pétain returned to Paris in March 1904 – yet again as a teacher of infantry tactics at the École de Guerre. His lectures – whatever their controversial content – were clearly of too much value to be dispensed with. So far, as it were, so good. He had returned to the capital, to a job which he enjoyed and at which he was becoming more and more confident and competent. But, to the obvious dismay of senior officers – of whom Pétain was by now one – in November of that year there were revelations about André and Percin's conduct of affairs that threw relations between the Army and the Republic into turmoil.

The policy of the Ministry of War since the 1902 elections had been quite clear. It was not simply to 'republicanise' the Army. It was to assert the authority of the ministry to promote those officers who were considered reliable and 'in this way to block the road to the students of the Jesuits'.[10] This was perhaps bad enough, but worse still were the methods used to discover who was reliable and who was not. Percin had relied on a network of Freemasons of the Grand Orient Lodge to assemble a store of cards, or *fiches* – some twenty thousand in all – each one recording for a particular officer information about his religious beliefs, his wife's beliefs, where his children went to school, and so on.

On 4 November 1904 the deputy for Neuilly, a former army officer named Jean Guyot de Villeneuve, revealed to an astonished National Assembly the extent of Percin's machinations – and of André's ultimate responsibility. The ensuing debate was suitably rowdy, the *France Militaire* noting that 'as for material damage (breaking of desks etc.) [the deputies] surpassed the maximum achieved up to today'.[11] In the event, André, after putting up a feeble defence, was saved by the fact that a Nationalist deputy punched him on the nose. This was enough to gain the sympathy of the majority, and the government won the ensuing vote.

But it was only a temporary reprieve. André recognised that he had lost all authority and, one month later, he resigned. Nevertheless, that was far from the end of the affair. Duels between officers and Masons were widespread. Major Bader, for instance, of the 37th Regiment of Infantry at Nantes fought a duel with a local Mason who had reported on him; others fought at Bastia, Montélimar, Toulouse, Biarritz and Marseille. Officers who reported on their colleagues were often forced to change regiments. All in all, during 1905 the talk in the Army was of little else.

The affair, which became known as the 'Affaire des Fiches', gradually died down, but there were permanent scars. For instance, it now appeared certain to those seeking promotion that it was no longer a matter of how good you were; it was a matter of whom you knew in the rue St-Dominique. They were clearly right. The 1906 promotion lists, for example, were drawn up by a captain on the War Minister's staff, a young friend of his who happened to be a diplomat and the diplomat's girlfriend – who apparently went by the name of Blanche – over lunch at Maxim's. By any standards, the whole thing had become very odd.

There is little doubt that among the twenty thousand or so fiches there was one on Pétain, although it has not come to light. The mere existence of a fiche would have been unpleasant enough. But for Pétain the situation was even worse than that. He did not count many influential politicians among his acquaintance. His prospects for promotion, under the new dispensation, were correspondingly diminished. Furthermore, although he had grown out of the faith of his childhood, he retained his respect for the cloth, and was therefore instinctively on the side of Catholic officers against Freemasonry. The events of the Affaire des Fiches only served to reinforce that ingrained view.

Yet if his political acquaintance was limited, Pétain's military acquaintance was expanding fast. His lectures at the École de Guerre were attracting attention. He was by now an expert not only on infantry tactics but on military history as well. He was also an impressive lecturer. On the days when he was lecturing the large semicircular hall in the School filled rapidly. Indeed, so many senior officers from the general staff crowded in that little room was left for the students. But Pétain was listened to in silence, such was the interest in what he had to say. His delivery, too, was arresting: cold, impassive, without gestures or rhetorical flourishes.

The message was simple and direct. *Le feu tue*. Firepower kills. It was accurate firepower that made movement possible. Artillery and infantry had to work together. 'Offensive?' he said. 'Of course, on condition that gunfire which was powerful and destructive enough had opened the way.'[12] These precepts were delivered in the clipped voice which earned him the nickname of 'Précis-le-Sec'. But they were far from popular with many of his superiors on the general staff. The prevailing view was that artillery could operate on its own, and that the cavalry would provide the momentum for attack – as it had in the days of Napoleon.

Although Pétain's lectures on infantry tactics in this period never rose to the level of controversy of the disputes about the deployment of armies later in the decade, they were enough to earn him, as he himself put it, 'a bad press at the Ministry'.[13] The result was that in 1906 he was posted not, as he had hoped, to a battalion of the eastern army but to the 118th Regiment of Infantry at Quimper in Brittany. It was not at all to his liking. As a lieutenant-colonel, and for a few months as battalion commander, he found himself caught in a hierarchy which forced him to keep his distance from his fellow officers. Besides, the winters were cold – and there was nothing much to do. The only relief lay in his visits to his sister Sara at Mazinghem where he would see some of his old friends from the Artois.

It is hard to see in the Pétain of 1905 much sign of anything resembling the fulfilment of his ambition. The long apprenticeship seemed to be leading to nothing; his promotion up the ranks had been desperately slow. True, he had over the years broadened his intellectual horizons, but these were no compensation for the lack of a settled family life or a truly successful career. Moreover, he would soon have to start thinking about his retirement, which was only eleven years away. Life in a peacetime army was hardly a good preparation for what in all likelihood would be a lonely old age. The best he could do, as he wrote to a nephew in December 1907, was to 'find the means, by working a great deal, not to be bored'.[14] It is hardly a message of unalloyed joy.

5

THE ROAD TO RETIREMENT

'Vraiment le petit écolier de Saint-Bertin ne s'attendait pas à faire une si belle carrière.'

Pétain was rescued from his Quimper exile in April 1908. A newly appointed commandant of the École de Guerre, General Joseph Maunoury, had met Pétain some years earlier (personal endorsements were a prerequisite for appointments in those days) and invited him back – this time as a full professor. From 1908 to 1911, therefore, Pétain was able to expand on his views on infantry tactics without running the risk of his superior's disapproval. Furthermore, he had the active support of Percin – by then promoted to the rank of general. In fact, such was Percin's support that he invited Pétain on secondment as his divisional chief of staff for the period of the autumn manoeuvres of 1910. (It was, of course, the same Percin that had been heavily involved in fixing the case against Dreyfus.) Pétain's later expressed distrust of Percin, if indeed it ever existed, seems to have vanished like the morning mist after Dreyfus's final acquittal in 1908. Furthermore, the episode of Pétain's refusal of promotion as commandant of the École de Tir seems also to have been conveniently forgotten.

Back in Paris, Pétain found himself yet another two-room apartment, conveniently close to the large building on the Champs de Mars which housed the École de Guerre. Once there, he renewed acquaintances – and formed many more. He was in touch again, for instance, with Nini, whose marriage, in spite of the birth of a son, was not altogether happy. He moved up the social ladder – the Marquis Louis de Chasseloup-Laubat was one of those who introduced him to what passed for the proper society of the day. His old partner in the hunt for female company, Alphonse Guide, was a frequent companion for lunch or dinner. Pétain started to relish his food, and became something of a gourmet, although still not much of a connoisseur of wine.

It was not only the social ladder that commanded his attention. Intellectually, too, his horizons were expanding. He now read more widely. For instance, the philosopher Henri Bergson was the flavour of the intellectual day, and Pétain apparently read and mastered his views to the extent that he was able 'to conduct a detailed conversation on Bergson and his works'.[1] In itself, this was no mean feat. Bergson was far from an easy read, and his ideas were, on first acquaintance, difficult to grasp. Many – better educated than Pétain – professed themselves defeated. (In a series of lectures at the Collège de France, published in 1907 in his book *L'Évolution créatrice*, Bergson asserted the primacy of the freedom of the human spirit – *l'élan vital*, which inspired all life. The idea, whatever it signified in practical application, was little short of revolutionary for the time, and for those brought up in the careful discipline of the Catholic Church and of the French Army, not far short of blasphemous.) Nevertheless, Pétain added Bergson to his reading list as, in the past, he had added Clausewitz, Machiavelli and the range of military strategists from Alexander the Great through to the German generals of the Franco-Prussian War. In short, even at a late stage in his life, Pétain was starting to educate himself in matters of high philosophical moment – many of them, at this point, wholly unrelated to his military career.

Pétain's lectures at the École de Guerre, now that he was a full professor, took on an air of theatricality. They were directed at the full assembly of students – the small seminars which formed part of their course, and which he had been content to take as assistant professor, were no longer a duty. As in earlier days, the large semicircular auditorium was crowded with senior officers who had just come in to listen and, further back, row upon row of student junior officers, each sitting at a small table – only large enough for a few papers and a képi – with quill pens poised. They all knew that the notes which they were about to take would be crucial to their success in passing out with honour. They therefore wrote 'with rigour, discipline and seriousness'.[2]

At the appointed hour, when all were assembled, Pétain strode into the hall. There was silence while he took his place on the small dais framed by four cast-iron columns at each corner and placed his képi on the small table in front of him. When he started his lecture, there was hardly a murmur. '[He] knew how to seize his audience.'[3] The sentences were short. He stared at his students, only turning round to the blackboard behind him to illustrate his points with quick strokes of the chalk which he held in his hand throughout the lecture. There were no flourishes and no extravagant gestures.

In one sense, it was as it had been before. But there were some important differences. For instance, in his earlier lectures at the École de Guerre, Pétain had set out his stall with a certain degree of modesty. That had now disappeared. As a full professor, he was confident in his delivery. Furthermore, the argument had moved forward. By 1910 there was no longer much debate about infantry tactics. In one form or another all the theorists accepted that, tactically, infantry, properly supported by artillery, should look to the offensive, whether it be immediate attack or quick counter-attack. Moreover, the experience of the British in the Boer War and a clear appreciation of modern weaponry had led to the view that the infantry front would have to be dispersed to avoid the menace of the machine gun and the modern rifle. But if, the consensus went on, artillery could be brought to bear in sufficient quantity to destroy small arms emplacements in support of an infantry attack, whether initial or counter, all would be well. By the time of Pétain's lectures, there was almost no disagreement among the theorists of the day. The importance of firepower, artillery support for infantry and a dispersed infantry front were no longer in dispute.

In fact, Pétain's lectures had little to offer which was not part of the consensus of the time. They were, none the less, rigorous in their analysis and in their presentation. He concentrated on three basic themes. The first was an analysis of the role of the infantry in the Napoleonic Wars and the changes in weaponry which had ensued. He pointed out that the rifle in use in 1802, itself a development of the

1777 rifle, had difficulty, even when correctly aimed, in hitting at 400 metres 'a four-storey building'.[4] Moreover, the fierce recoil of the rifle inflicted its own injuries on the rifleman, and the smoke from the exploding cartridge frequently made the ground in front of him invisible. It was for this reason, he claimed, that Napoleon had decided that the best solution lay in marshalling his infantrymen into three separated ranks.

The second theme was the analysis of the Franco-Prussian War of 1870–1. The potential of the Chassepot rifle introduced in 1866 had, he argued, largely been misunderstood by the generals of the day. The development had been regarded as no more than a technical matter. The fact that the Chassepot was accurate to a metre at 400 metres, and the tactical implications of that single fact, had simply passed them by. Nevertheless, Pétain was also critical of the Instruction of 1867 which claimed that 'with the new weapons the advantage lies with the defensive'. 'Only the offensive', he went on, 'could lead to victory'.[5] Pétain was quite clear that there had to be an offensive if ground was to be won and the battle successfully brought to an end; but the enemy had to be severely damaged first.

The third theme was built around a study of the various infantry regulations which had appeared between 1875 and 1902. Pétain criticised the 1875 regulations on the grounds that they too relied too much on passive defence. His message was the same. The point was, he insisted again and again, that the modern rifle, properly handled, could inflict such damage that it was foolhardy to rush into an offensive without having prepared the ground with firepower. The Boer War provided a clear example of how the accurate use of the modern rifle in the hands of skilled marksmen could stop a traditional heavy-infantry advance in its tracks. The whole point of this was that, in order to mount a necessary offensive, infantry had to be careful not to rush in without adequate preparation.

As a support team, as it were, Pétain had Colonel Maud'huy – the unsuccessful Pandarus of Besançon – and Colonel Victor Debeney, a former colleague of Pétain's as a junior officer in the same battalion. Both supported in their different ways. Pétain lectured – yet again – on the importance of firepower, Maud'huy lectured on the psychology of the infantryman and his need to master his fear, while Debeney illustrated the relevance of – carefully selected – views of previous

generals in the context of modern war. All of them advocated the
'offensive'. None of them, least of all Pétain, disputed the general
position that the 'offensive', in whatever form, was a necessary condition for winning ground – provided that the enemy had been
suitably softened up.

If nothing else, Pétain's lectures of 1908–11 show how far the peasant boy of the Artois had come in the discipline – and expansion – of
his intellect and of his personality. The analysis is rigorous. The form
is precise and effective. Given confidence in the delivery, which by
then Pétain had, the impact on the assembled company must have
been not just theatrical but intellectually convincing. The rogue lecturer of earlier years had become the spokesman for the consensus on
infantry tactics – and was regarded by then as a repository of the
wisdom of the day.

Nevertheless, another debate was engaged in late 1910 – towards
the end of Pétain's tenure of office at the École de Guerre. It was a
debate not about infantry tactics but about the strategic deployment,
and the shape, of armies in the field – in other words what was known
in French as 'la grande tactique'.[6] A clear view – or, at least, a reasonably
clear view – was set out in a decree of 28 May 1895 containing regulations on the matter. In the initial phase of a battle, the regulations
stated, an advance guard of infantry and artillery would reconnoitre
enemy positions in force. It would penetrate the enemy's defence, stop
an enemy attack and start the inevitable process of wearing him down.
At a suitable moment the main body of the army would engage in
battle. The whole operation would be phased and maximum force
would only be applied gradually. This doctrine, based as it was on
Napoleonic principles but with a genuflection to Prussian military
theory, was proclaimed as the last word on the matter in a book, *De
la Conduite de la Guerre*, written by one Colonel Ferdinand Foch in
1896 on his appointment as the new Director of the École de Guerre.

An opposite view was put by a relative newcomer – Lieutenant-
Colonel Louis de Grandmaison. De Grandmaison gave two lectures at
the École de Guerre in late 1910 criticising the 1895 regulations on
the grounds that the system they advocated – the phased introduction
of maximum force – was too slow, allowed successively deployed
waves of support attack to be challenged successfully at any given
point and was still – for the historical reasons on which the regulations

were based – too fearful of defeat. 'There is no other means', de Grandmaison declared, 'than immediate and total attack'.[7] Using the battles of 1870 as an illustration, he went on to argue that the proper system was to pack the front line with as many divisions as possible and advance on a broad and extended front. Reconnaissance was no doubt important, but what was more important was to attack on such a wide front that the enemy would either be outflanked or, if he were to be dispersed to counter the threat to his flanks, would open up points of weakness which could be exploited.

De Grandmaison's language was, admittedly, intemperate. He did not, however, use the expression '*offensif à l'outrance*' ('offensive to the end') as has been claimed. Instead, he used the expression '*offensif sans arrière pensée*' ('offensive without second thoughts').[8] But his central message was clear. It was no good trying to mount an attack half-heartedly – while trying to anticipate enemy moves or, worse still, trying to make preparations for possible defeat.

Much has been made of the supposed clash of opinion between the followers of Pétain and the followers of de Grandmaison. In fact, there was no such clash. Apart from the timing, Pétain's supporters – notably Debeney and Maud'huy – supported de Grandmaison without reservation. The reason is simple – a matter of, in the colloquialism, 'apples and oranges'. De Grandmaison was dealing with the deployment of whole armies and Pétain was dealing with infantry tactics in localised battles. Both of them, and their followers, favoured the 'offensive'. Moreover, as a matter of fact, the de Grandmaison view was reflected in the new regulations on strategic deployment of 1913.

After the supposed, and misunderstood, controversy, Pétain, much as he may have disliked it, then had to move on. His professorship at the École de Guerre came to an end in June 1911. He was due for another posting in the field. By then he had moved up a rank to full colonel, with, as it happened, an enthusiastic recommendation from Foch. On his promotion, he was posted to command the battalion of the 33rd Regiment of Infantry, then stationed in Arras. Although he did not particularly like the posting, Pétain took it as a compliment that those who were posted to guard France's northern front were the élite of the French Army of the day. It was regarded as the most vulnerable front by the Ministry of War, and word had it –

whether rightly or not – that the most able commanders were posted there.

Whether he liked his posting or not, Pétain had taken a further step in his private life. Before he left Paris he renewed his friendship with Nini. It had turned out that her marriage had been going so badly that she had engaged in a series of extra-marital affairs. The temptation was too much for Pétain, who was never one to decline such an obvious opportunity. Friendship became rather more. Indeed, when he got there, he regularly deserted his command to travel to Paris for an assignation with Nini – having set up a small pied-à-terre for the purpose.

The new command brought its own difficulties. According to available reports, discipline in the 33rd had become very slack. The long years of peacetime boredom had taken their toll. The Schramm barracks in Arras, where they were quartered, were uncomfortable. Too much was drunk by both officers and other ranks in the local cafés. Worst of all, soldiers of all ranks simply did not bother to come back from leave on their due date.

It was obvious that the situation had to be remedied, and Pétain set about his task. He wrote to the families of defaulting soldiers demanding a greater degree of patriotism, and he was not slow to punish those who persisted in ill discipline. He was nothing if not persistent, and his efforts seem to have been successful; by the middle of 1912 the regiment was held up as an example to others. Pétain, moreover, was helped in his efforts by a shift in the political wind. The trauma of the Dreyfus era had worn off by the time he took command in Arras. The climate of opinion was no longer pacifist. Patriotism was back on the agenda. The Radical government, such as it was, had been a disappointment, and its leaders were trying to shore up their position in a traditional manner – by recognising hitherto unsuspected virtue in patriotic and even militaristic sentiments. It was even possible for a Radical deputy to say in 1911, 'When the guns begin to speak it is best that the politicians keep quiet.'[9]

No doubt encouraged by the new mood, Pétain became even more diligent in his efforts to discipline his previously errant troops. But there were interruptions. During 1912, apart from romantic excursions to Paris, there were two forced breaks. Early in the year he was sent, along with General Léon Durand, to reconnoitre the defences in the area around Namur in Belgium. The suspicion, perfectly justified in the event, was that if war came Germany would not hesitate to violate Belgian neutrality. As it happened, it did not take the two officers much time to realise that the Belgian defences were wholly inadequate. This was duly reported to the Ministry of War. Pétain's Belgian task was thus shorter than he had expected. But there was to be a second break – to run a course on infantry tactics at the cavalry school in Saumur on the River Loire. Although at first sight these breaks might have been a pleasant diversion, Pétain – leaving aside the temptaions of Paris – much preferred to continue the work of pulling his battalion into shape. Any diversion was an irritant. His priorities were clear: the 33rd had to be ready to fight in any future war.

It was to this by then well disciplined unit that a tall young officer, fresh out of Saint-Cyr, was posted in October 1912. It was not wholly by accident. The new *sous-lieutenant* Charles de Gaulle was pleased to be posted to Arras, and particularly to the 33rd. Apart from the attraction of his own background in the north of France he much admired his new commanding officer. Pétain's lectures at the École de Guerre were still remembered, and de Gaulle admired both his analyses and his authoritative delivery. Pétain, in turn, took to de Gaulle. 'Graduated from Saint-Cyr 13th out of 211,' runs his report for the first quarter of 1913, '[de Gaulle] has immediately established himself as an officer of real worth, who promises much for the future.'[10] There it was. Thus did the strange relationship between the two, which was to be such a feature of both their lives, start – with de Gaulle's posting to Arras – in the ambiguous light of a northern French autumn.

By all accounts, Pétain led his battalion well in the annual autumn manoeuvres. They were, in truth, a curious affair. They involved virtually the whole French Army, strung out in large formations across various plains in metropolitan France. In some years the manoeuvres were held in the flat country around Toulouse. In other years they were held in the northern French plain. But in all cases the procedure was the same. Umpires would blow whistles and wave flags to indicate that this or that battalion or company or platoon had been blown up or wiped out – or whatever fate the umpires decreed. This done, and the manoeuvres completed, everybody went home, satisfied that all was well in the world.

These manoeuvres were, as a matter of course, observed by other parties. Indeed, they were invited so to do. In the autumn manoeuvres of 1913, for instance, many representatives of foreign governments were invited to observe. It so happened that the French High Command thought it better for the manoeuvres to be held well away from the German frontier, since it was felt that the whole thing would then be less irritating to the German government. This was done, and the manoeuvres were deemed to have been a great success. There had been, unfortunately, one casualty. On investigation, it turned out that the casualty in question was the German Military Attaché, whose car had run off the road while he was on his way to observe events. Nevertheless, and despite this minor incident, the Kaiser felt able to write to the French President to say how pleased he was that the whole exercise had gone so well. (It was, as a matter of fact, only a few hours later that he told the King of the Belgians that he was tired of the French and determined to finish them off 'by a necessary and inevitable war'.)[11]

There was, as it happened, another curious incident. It was during the 1913 manoeuvres that Pétain, as a commander in the field, displayed what can only be described as flagrant insubordination. At one point the 33rd was ordered to storm a hill and capture the village on its summit. They set off with flags flying and a band leading them up the hill. It was quite obviously absurd, but it was the way the infantry conducted themselves at the time. The hill duly stormed, and the village duly captured, the umpires declared that the matter had been concluded satisfactorily and that there had been no casualties on the French side, while the enemy had been successfully eliminated to a man.

Pétain was unable to contain himself. When his divisional commander asked him to give his opinion on the exercise, Pétain turned to his men and pronounced in a loud voice that he was 'sure that the intention of General Le Gallet, in order to impress it on your minds, was a catalogue of all the mistakes that a modern army should not make'.[12] General Le Gallet's reaction has not been recorded.

It was by then quite clear that Pétain had become convinced that further promotion was out of the question. He knew that he had made too many enemies by his sarcasm and his disrespect for senior officers. In short, his career was finished. By way of confirmation, word had it in the Ministry of War that he would never be promoted to the substantive rank of *général de brigade* (brigadier-general). Nevertheless, as he was to remark himself, he had not done badly. The French Army, other than the colonial forces, had been at peace for forty years and promotion was inevitably slow. Furthermore, promotion to brigadier-general would have brought with it posting to divisional command, and at the time there were no vacancies.

Pétain was still a colonel, therefore, when on 24 April 1914 he left the 33rd in Arras to take command of the 4th Infantry Brigade. Such a posting was not unusual. Typically, a brigade was commanded by a colonel. Pétain's brigade, however, was not an obviously cohesive force. It was spread widely across northern France. The 110th Infantry Regiment was stationed just outside Dunkerque, and the 8th Infantry Regiment was spread between St-Omer, Calais and Boulogne-sur-Mer. Of all the choices he could make among those battalion headquarters, Pétain chose to make his own brigade headquarters in St-Omer – the city of the two saints which he had known in his childhood. In fact, by then he had come to the conclusion that this was to be his last posting. He would retire with the rank of colonel; any thought that he might be promoted to brigadier-general, a promotion which would have put off his retirement date by a further two years – let alone promotion to full general which would have put off his retirement date indefinitely – was out of the question. In short, his military career, which had followed a pattern typical of a peacetime officer of some (but not outstanding) distinction, was coming to a gentle end.

There was one consolation, if that is the right word. His relationship with Nini, after a bad break in April 1913, had been restored. Nini had become tired of their secret trysts. Making love in a small pied-à-terre with a gentleman who had quickly to leave her to return to his duties – and to the affection of other ladies – was apparently no longer to her taste. Perhaps she had even transferred her own affections elsewhere – she was not, to say the least, known for constancy. Moreover, by December 1913 Pétain was writing that he loved her more than she him and that, because he was so jealous, the only solution was total separation. It had seemed as though the relationship was at its end.

There were, however, second thoughts. A few months later, things were getting better. Pétain had a nasty fall from his horse, which needed a quick operation on his knee. He used the opportunity – a frequent male ploy – to write to Nini asking for sympathy, and perhaps more. 'I had given you all my love,' he wrote, 'all my devotion, all my life. I shall never recover from this . . .'[13] It was, of course, not wholly true. He had been philandering with the ladies of Arras all the time. But it seems that Nini fell for it. Once out of hospital, Pétain wrote again suggesting a meeting. Nini agreed. The result was predictable. 'With what intoxication', he wrote afterwards, 'my lips took your kisses in total forgetfulness of everything which separates us.'[14]

So far, as it were, so good. It was, however, not all sweetness and light. Nini accused Pétain of being obsessed with sex. She wanted something more spiritual – this time it was her turn to use a well-established female ploy. Pétain tried to wriggle his way out of this charge – uncomfortably near to the mark as it was. 'If I did not love you physically it would not be love,' he wrote, 'since love takes over the entire physical and intellectual being.'[15] It was a good try, but for those who were familiar with Pétain's philandering it rang false. In fact, it was, as might be imagined, a great deal of nonsense.

Nonsense or not, Nini seems to have been satisfied, and by the time Pétain left Arras for St-Omer in April 1914 the visits to the pied-à-terre in Paris had been resumed. Needless to say, once that particular objective had been achieved, Pétain showed his usual reluctance to abstain from casual acquaintance with the ladies of Artois. His performance at the parade in St-Omer on Bastille Day 1914, for instance, set many hearts beating faster. Mounted, in ceremonial dress, on a white horse, Pétain rode on to the parade ground at a brisk trot. He came to a halt in front of the stand on which the assembled local dignitaries were seated, saluted them with a flourish of his sword and moved away, followed by two aides-de-camp, to inspect his troops at the walk. That done, he turned his horse round, spurred it to an immediate gallop and came to an operatic halt in front of the dignitaries he had just left. He then dismounted, announced the names of those who were to be decorated 'in a clipped voice which carried [throughout the parade]',[16] pinned their medals to their chests, mounted his horse and left the parade ground – again at a full gallop.

It was meant to be Pétain's farewell to the Army. He thought it fitting that he should make his final display in the city of his childhood.

Not only that, but he had found, through a local *notaire*, a small house just outside St-Omer to which he planned to retire. He even bought a pair of secateurs in the expectation of a long career as a gardener.

There was, however, to be a hitch in his plans. On 28 June 1914, just over two weeks before Pétain's final parade, Archduke Franz Ferdinand, the heir to the empire of Austria-Hungary, was assassinated at Sarajevo. Europe suddenly found itself hurtling towards war. The world was about to change – and to change for good. Pétain's plans for retirement moved quickly off his agenda. There was a job to be done; and, in practice, there was no alternative for him but to stay in the Army and help to do it.

There is little doubt that, had the Pétain story ended there, it would rate no more than a short footnote in the history of the French Army. The long apprenticeship would have led nowhere. It would have been yet another military career spent without seeing a shot fired in anger. In short, he would have retired quietly to a small house – which was all he could afford. He would probably not have married Nini, for whom marriage to a colonel and retirement in the country would have had limited attraction; and therefore his old age, which, if he had lived as long as he did, would have lasted some thirty-five years, would certainly have been lonely and bitter. Nevertheless, that is not the way Pétain saw it. By the middle of 1914 he was rather pleased with himself. He thought that his career had been a great success, given his peasant background. What neither he nor anybody else could have expected was that his career was about to be much more spectacular and infinitely more successful. At the age of fifty-eight he was on the point of retiring as a colonel. At the age of sixty-two he was to be still in active service as a Marshal of France.

6

THE DOGS OF WAR

'Ce fut . . . vraiment la première journée "cruelle" de la guerre'

To the general public, the outbreak of war in early August 1914 came as something of a surprise. True, there had been intense diplomatic activity in the weeks following the assassination of Archduke Franz Ferdinand, but diplomacy in those days was conducted by a select group, speaking to each other in the most elegant French, whose deliberations were not usually disclosed to the outside world. The press, whether in London, Paris or Berlin, was hardly bothered. The assassination in Paris on 31 July of the French Socialist leader, Jean Jaurès, for instance, created a much more interesting storm.

Besides, the summer was exceptionally fine; the social season in London and Paris had been quite brilliant; and it was time, for those who understood the proper rhythm of events, to go on holiday. The Kaiser set off for his customary three-week cruise in the Norwegian fjords; the President of France, Raymond Poincaré, embarked on a state visit to Russia before, in his turn, taking his holiday; and the beaches all over Europe were filling up. In mid-July, it seemed that the summer storms of Sarajevo were no more than a passing moment. Certainly, Pétain, in his last flourish in St-Omer, gave no sign that he was aware that he would be at war within three weeks.

By the last week in July, however, the atmosphere had changed. Austria had sent an ultimatum to Serbia on 23 July, demanding the immediate arrest of Serbian officials believed to be implicated in the outrageous crime, and, moreover, demanding that Austro-Hungarian prosecutors should sit alongside the Serbian authorities both in the investigations and in any subsequent trials. In this, as in its language, the Austrian ultimatum was noticeably fierce; and at it was at that point that the diplomats went, as far as they were able, into overdrive. Notes sped all around Europe, counselling caution, advising the Serbs to accept the terms of the Austrian ultimatum, warning all concerned about the dangers, proposing meetings of all parties. It was to no avail. On 28 July Austria formally declared war on Serbia, sparking off in Russia, Serbia's traditional friends, at first partial and then total mobilisation. Germany, in its turn, issued a series of ultimata – to Russia, to France and, lastly, to Belgium, demanding free access through her territory for operations against France. Britain, too, issued an ultimatum. But by then, whatever its merits, the war of the ultimatum was over. Everybody mobilised; and, in practice, mobilisation meant real war.

Both Germany and France had their own plans for war, if and when it came. Both rightly assumed that mobilisation, once the orders were issued, would lead inexorably to armed conflict. The Germans, in their plan, even referred to the day of mobilisation as *M-Tag*, in other words, the day on which it all starts. But from one assumption followed another. In the development of their plan it had become clear to German strategists that it was no use massing troops on France's eastern frontier. The rail connections from the Rhine bridges were too difficult – and, furthermore, the French frontier was too well fortified. In particular, the rail connections from Cologne, which was a central point of assembly, were much easier if the movement of troops was directed towards the immediate west – in other words, towards Belgium.

The use, if it can be put in that way, of Belgian territory was therefore necessary for the execution of the German war plan. In its original version, the plan, which came to be named after its author Graf Alfred von Schlieffen, required a mass movement of German cavalry and infantry through Belgium and down into France. This concentration of military power would allow German armies to move southwards to the west of Paris and subsequently turn eastwards to envelop the French army which lay along France's eastern frontier;

which, after the inevitable French surrender, would conclude the war. The war, it was estimated, even after many revisions to the plan, would be over in forty days.

That was all very well in theory; but, like all plans, it remained to be seen how well it would work out in practice. In fact, even after all the years developing the Schlieffen plan, there were still those who had their doubts. Field Marshal Helmuth von Moltke, for instance, the Commander-in-Chief of the German armed forces which would have to execute it, certainly had his doubts, and amended it to show greater caution. The plan would not work, he thought, if the enemy massed enough troops and military hardware to defy the German assault through Belgium. The German frontier, and Alsace and Lorraine, could not just be ignored. By that time, even before any action, it was clear that the mice were nibbling at the plan itself.

The French, too, had a plan, known – without any personal attribution – as Plan XVII. This was also supposed to lead to a quick end to the war. By ensuring a speedy and efficient mobilisation – the lessons of the chaotic 1870 mobilisation had been carefully studied – a dashing French offensive would rush through Alsace and Lorraine and into Germany, cross the Rhine and not stop before it arrived at the gates of Berlin. In fact, Plan XVII, in its final form, was little more than a plan for the mobilisation of large units. It was certainly not an operational plan for the use of those units. Nevertheless, such was the optimism of the French military establishment – and their belief in the virtue of an immediate offensive to the east – that it was difficult to know what was to be done with successfully mobilised troops unless they were marched into the lost provinces of Alsace and Lorraine. Moreover, the plan was firmly based on the assumption, which had been argued to and fro for many years, that the Germans would not violate Belgian neutrality for fear of bringing Britain, one of its guarantors, into the war. This assumption was, of course, quite wrong. Finally, the textbook methods of attack had been rigorously followed: the artillery would destroy the enemy's firepower, allowing the cavalry to charge freely and the infantry to occupy the ground. Unfortunately, there was no reasonable method of communication between the three arms and the artillery barrage was unco-ordinated and ineffective.

In the event, neither plan was successful. The German thrust through Belgium was unexpectedly held up, first by the resistance of the forts at the entry point of Liège and then by some further stout defence by the small Belgian Army. In its turn, the French mobilisation was indeed efficient, but the subsequent attack eastwards was met by such resolute German artillery and machine-gun fire that it was halted after gruesomely heavy French casualties.

By then, the French Commander-in-Chief, General Joseph Joffre, had ordered Plan XVII to be quickly modified to allow troops to be moved up into Belgium to block the German attack. In doing so, they were to link up with the British Expeditionary Force (BEF), dispatched to Belgium under the command of Field-Marshal Sir John French. The BEF was, even at the moment Joffre changed the plan, disembarking at the Channel ports. The original Plan XVII was consigned to the waste-paper basket and Plan XVII(b) emerged. In brief, it was an order to send troops with immediate dispatch – not to attack in the east but to defend in the north. Needless to say, the order was to generate a good deal of confusion.

The area of Belgium to be defended, the order went, was the triangle of the southern Belgian plain bordered by the River Sambre to the north and the River Meuse to the east. This, apparently, would not only be enough to halt the German advance but also, once that had been done, to provide a springboard for a counter-attack eastwards. But, whatever the assumptions behind Plan XVII(b), it was clear that French strategy had fundamentally changed. Troops, and the public, who had thought that there would be an immediate breakthrough to the east, which would not stop until the gates of Berlin were stormed, suddenly found themselves confronted with the idea that French soil had to be defended. The north had to be made secure; and the force which was chosen for the role, the order went on, was the French 5th Army; and one of the 5th Army's units was the 4th Infantry Brigade, commanded by Colonel Pétain.

The French generals whose job was to implement Joffre's Plan XVII(b) were something of a motley crew. Joffre himself was a bull of a man, heavily overweight as a result of his fondness for a good – and extended – lunch followed by an afternoon sleep, but nevertheless of intelligence and clarity of vision. By training first as a railway engineer and then as a gunner in the artillery, he had a formidable ability to bring his subordinates into line, either by his refusal to panic or by the use of his temper which, when unleashed, was ferocious. 'His anger when roused', goes one contemporary account, 'was terrific in its concentrated quiet force, and was never withstood. There were then a few short gestures of the arms, the muffled voice rose half a tone, whilst the head was thrown slightly back; and the words that came forth from under the shaggy moustache were never either disregarded or forgotten.'[1] Yet his main characteristic was imperturbability. He was placidity and calmness personified. Indeed, his placidity was such that at times his subordinates were left baffled. For instance, there were occasions when Joffre would turn up at a headquarters, listen to what he was told by staff officers urging one course or another, and then leave again without saying a word. It was, by any standards, unnerving.

General Charles Lanrezac, the commander of the 5th Army which had formed the left flank of Joffre's initial order of battle and which was now to move into Belgium, was a quite different matter; and, needless to say, the two men did not get on. To be sure, they were both corpulent, but beyond that they had little in common. True, Lanrezac was something of an odd fish. It was said that he had some mulatto blood in him – his dark and flabby face was said to show it – but he had inherited the title of 'marquis' which, apparently, he never used. When he was teaching at the École de Guerre – inspirationally, according to accounts – his nickname was '*le voyou*' ('the hooligan') because of his habit of shouting at his pupils. 'He spoke as if delivering a lecture, with his eyeglasses hitched over his right ear.'[2] In short, although he was certainly able, he was rude and morose. But the main disadvantage of his present command was that he was irrevocably opposed to everything British. Since part of his job was to link up with, and work with, the BEF, this was hardly a suitable qualification; and, as events were to show, it proved disastrous. Nor was his contempt confined to the British; the Belgians were just as bad. Nor, it seems, did he have any great opinion of his own subordinates. He simply refused to talk to them.

General Louis Franchet d'Esperey, on the other hand, the commander of the 1st Army Corps under Lanrezac, was a character from a quite different mould. Nicknamed 'Desperate Frankie' by the British, he was short and squat, and in figure not unlike a rectangular brick. He cut his hair '*en brosse*'. 'Seen from the back,' it was said, 'his

head reminded one of a howitzer shell.' Even his face seemed to be
made up of right angles – 'straight jaw . . . straight top to his head,
straight eyebrows, straight toothbrush moustache, straight chin'.[3] His
preferred method of command was to shout instructions in a high-
pitched voice. There was no question of asking for advice or of
permitting any questions. As it happened, however, Franchet
d'Esperey had his courteous side, and, furthermore, was anglophile. In
sending telegrams to the British he signed them punctiliously
'Franchet d'Esperey KCVO', in recognition of the British knighthood
he had received in April 1914.

It was this mixed bunch that Pétain had to deal with as a subordinate commander in the field. He certainly liked and admired Joffre.
Equally, in the days to come, when communications between
Lanrezac and Sir John French virtually broke down, he would absorb
at least some of the former's intense dislike of the British. As for
Franchet d'Esperey, he was so far from Pétain's peasant background
that a meeting of minds was, to put it mildly, not, in August 1914, on
any foreseeable agenda. It was only to come later on in the war.

Thus it was that Pétain, having three weeks earlier thought he
was on the point of graceful retirement, found himself, on 5 August,
ordered to assemble his brigade in Arras and to move, with the utmost
dispatch, on a long trail from the Artois some 100 kilometres to the
east to the town of Hirson on the Belgian frontier, there to join
up with rest of the 1st Army Corps and to move northwards. It was
far from an easy task. To be sure, he was confident in the spirit of
his troops – the *'gars du nord'*,[4] the lads from the north, as he called
them, using the patois of his peasant childhood (which he did when
talking to his soldiers – to crucial effect later on in the war). But the
life of the infantry on garrison duty, spread out as his brigade was,
was no serious introduction to the real thing. Moreover, the brigade
had only a nucleus of regular soldiers, the remainder being con-
scripts or recalled reservists. It is little wonder that Pétain, when he
received the orders to move on what was to be a long and perilous
journey, complained that he had had no time to pull his brigade into
shape. Moreover, to himself he must have recognised that he himself
had no experience of the fearful nature of warfare – or, indeed, of
any war at all – and, certainly, little idea of what it was to become in
the future.

Nevertheless, orders were orders, and the 4th Brigade set out on a forced march eastwards to join the rest of the 1st Army Corps, and the rest of the 5th Army. It was a long, hard struggle, particularly for the reservists, who had been civilians only a week earlier. Not only were they in the middle of a blistering heatwave, but they were carrying, in addition to their rifle, a pack containing spare clothes, a jacket, one day's provisions and six hard-tack biscuits, on top of which sat a rolled blanket, a pair of shoes and cooking equipment, and to the side of which was attached an entrenching tool and an ammunition pouch. The whole thing weighed some 22 kilograms. Moreover, they were required to wear the traditional uniform of the infantry of the line – red trousers and a blue open jacket made of wool. The Grande Armée of Napoleon had worn it, and it would strengthen morale, so it was said, for modern soldiers to show themselves as the descendants of the Emperor's formidable military machine. The German infantry, of course, wore field grey; and the British, after the experience of the Boer War, wore khaki (making at least one of them appear, to French eyes, to be 'disguised as a dusty canary').[5]

Even by the time they reached Hirson, Pétain's troops were dead tired. But there was to be no rest. On 10 August 1st Army Corps was ordered to march north-east to take up positions between Mèzières and the frontier town of Givet, guarding the west bank of the River Meuse. This they did – shadowed, as it happened, all the way by a German spotter plane. Yet again, the march was exhausting. There were many stragglers and some men collapsed from the heat. It was even said that non-commissioned officers had to use sticks to get their men off the ground where they lay and beat them into resuming the march. Nevertheless, on the evening of 12 August they reached their positions. The 4th Brigade itself arrived at Revin, a village perched on a loop in the river. On arrival, Pétain's troops threw off their clothes and equipment and settled down to sleep. But even then they were not given any time to rest. That night 1st Army Corps was given further instructions – to move northward into Belgium to occupy the area east of Philippeville, and in particular to secure the bridge at Dinant; and – yet again – they rose to their blistered feet and marched.

It was at six o'clock in the morning of 13 August that the first detachments of the advance guard of 1st Army Corps arrived in front of Dinant bridge. Just as they sat down to rest, the German artillery and machine guns, strategically located on the citadel on the other side of the river, opened up. The point platoon tried to rush the bridge. Almost immediately the platoon commander, Lieutenant de Gaulle, was hit in the knee, and only escaped with difficulty. He left his platoon sergeant on the bridge – dead, along with several of his platoon. As he crawled away, de Gaulle noted 'the dull thud of bullets entering the bodies of the dead and the wounded which lay there'.[6] It was de Gaulle's introduction to real warfare. Pétain's introduction was not long in coming.

The 4th Infantry Brigade was not far away. Their march, apart from the fact that they were all tired, had been severely hampered by the flood of refugees trying to escape the German advance. The Belgian farmers had woken up to the German invasion – and had decided that it was time to migrate westwards. They had no idea of their destination; it was simply a time to move. For a day or two the weather had broken, leaving the roads a sea of mud. It then cleared again and left the roads a desert of dust. Indeed, at one point Pétain had found himself giving orders for road repairs so that the soldiers could make their way past the refugees going in the opposite direction. By way of entertainment, such as it was, he also kept a diary of the journey, in pencil on the leaves of a school notebook. He noted the warmth of the reception given to the French troops, and, incidentally, took evident pleasure in describing the characteristics of the women of the homes where he was billeted.

Yet, as he also noted, the going was exceptionally hard (not least, though this was not noted, because they had little idea where they were going – the brigade staff officers had lost the only two maps they had). But on the morning of 14 August the brigade managed to reach the village of Florennes, some twenty kilometres west of Dinant; and on 15 August they finally arrived in front of the Meuse bridges of Yvoir, Houx and Anhée which they had been ordered to protect. Here, in whatever state they were, they were to prepare for battle.

It was on that day that Pétain saw his first action – shots fired in anger, to kill rather than to hit imaginary targets in exercises. In fact, as so often in war, the whole thing was due to a mistake. There had been an unauthorised salvo from an over-enthusiastic French artillery battery at Dinant. The Germans had responded, and the commander of the 1st Infantry Division, General Deligny, had to move his troops in haste to deal with a possible follow-up German attack. This duly happened. The German retaliation was swift and effective. In the ensuing exchange, General Deligny himself was wounded when a shell burst in front of him. Furthermore, some hundred soldiers of various ranks were subsequently registered as killed, nearly six hundred were registered as wounded, but no fewer than five hundred simply 'disappeared' – presumably blown to pieces by German shells. It is little wonder that Pétain wished to withdraw his brigade, and to order them to construct all the defences they could in the way of trenches and barbed wire. To say the least, it was not a happy baptism of fire.

Pétain wrote as much to Nini, whose divorce had become final in March 1914 and who, according to the harassed colonel, had been pursuing him ever since. True, he had been something of a willing victim; but war had brought a different tone. 'We had a bloody engagement', he wrote, 'on the 15th. A great battle is coming; I go to it without regret and without fear, since I have made the sacrifice of my life; the physical sufferings which may be inflicted on me are little compared with the moral tortures undergone because of you.'[7] In other words, he was inviting her to let him get on with his war. Nini obviously understood the message, and ceased bombarding him with letters – at least until 1916.

By then, the German strategy had become clear to the French High Command. The German 1st Army, under General Alexander von Kluck, was to strike westwards to Brussels and then turn left to make for the French frontier. The 2nd Army, under General Karl von Bülow, was also to move westwards, past Namur, follow the line of the River Sambre to the south-west and, again turning left to guard von Kluck's right flank, join alongside him in the race to the frontier. The 3rd Army, under General Baron Max von Hausen, was to cross the Meuse at several points between Dinant and Namur, and then imme-diately to head southwards, in turn guarding, as they went, von Bülow's left flank. The race for the French frontier was thus for three German armies, marching side by side, each to protect the other.

But there was a weakness. As his army moved westward, von Bülow's left flank would be exposed. Joffre saw an opportunity. Accordingly, he ordered Lanrezac to attack von Bülow on the Sambre at Charleroi. The BEF would advance to protect his left flank. At the same time, Franchet d'Esperey's 1st Army Corps was to hold or destroy the Meuse bridges to prevent von Hausen from attacking Lanrezac's right flank. With any luck, von Bülow's army would by that time be crippled, leaving von Kluck isolated and vulnerable to attack from both Lanrezac and the BEF on his left. The plan was clear, decisive and, on paper, excellent. On 21 August 1914, therefore, the Battle of Charleroi began.

Needless to say, it did not go according to plan. Obviously in ignorance of the French dispositions, units of von Bülow's army succeeded in crossing the Sambre. In the face of this incursion on what should have been a secure front, Lanrezac ordered Franchet d'Esperey immediately to leave his position on the Meuse and engage them. But that left his own flank – and the Meuse crossings – unprotected, allowing von Hausen in his turn to cross the Meuse in their rear. On the 23rd Franchet d'Esperey changed direction yet again, ordering Pétain to cover his flank as he tried to push von Hausen back across the river. The battle was hard, and much blood was shed – but to no apparent effect. By the evening of the 23rd Lanrezac had realised that he risked being attacked on both flanks at once and possibly encircled. The Battle of Charleroi had undoubtedly been lost. This being so, there was only one possible conclusion. Lanrezac promptly ordered a general retreat. The instruction was firm: 'With the aim of evacuating as soon as possible an area where the deployment of the offensive capability of our troops and the co-ordination of efforts are difficult, the general commanding the Army has decided to resume the retreat [*reprendre la marche rétrograde*].'[8] The 1st Army Corps was to form the rearguard for the 5th Army; and 4th Brigade was to form the rearguard of 1st Army Corps. The British, apparently, could do what they wanted – which, in the end, was what became known as 'the retreat from Mons'.

It was full of danger. At any moment Pétain's brigade could have been surrounded; the rest of his war would have been spent in a prison camp. Bitterly, Pétain seized on the expression '*reprendre la rétrograde*'. What it really meant was defeat. Depressingly, the excursion of the 4th Brigade into Belgium had lasted only eleven days. The morale of his troops was low; they were tired and dishevelled. In short, it no longer looked like a serious army at all. Besides, the reserve forces had amply revealed how badly trained they were. All in all, their first action had shown that the French troops were no match for the Germans. Pétain, in his own mind, tried to shift the responsibilty on to the government. He was starting on the long road, familiar to military men and a recurrent theme in his future, of blaming civilian politicians. 'Maybe', he wrote in his diary, 'they are going to hold the army to blame yet again for something the government did. A nation has the army it deserves.'[9]

For Pétain, the news was not all bad. On his arrival at the town of Iviers, he learned that he was to be promoted to the rank of brigadier-general, and that he might soon be given the command of a division. Moreover, on 28 August there was a halt to the retreat. Joffre had planned another counter-attack, to block the German advance in order to allow the assembly of a newly constituted 6th Army under General Michel Maunoury, whose task it would be, if the retreat continued, to defend Paris. Joffre ordered Lanrezac to attack von Bülow's 2nd Army by crossing the River Oise and heading west for St-Quentin. At first light on 29 August, therefore, units of Lanrezac's army duly crossed the river, took the Germans by surprise, and managed to advance some four kilometres towards St-Quentin. The Germans soon regrouped, however, and by midday had retaken the lost ground and were even beginning to launch their own attack on Lanrezac's northern units.

Lanrezac quickly perceived the danger, and ordered Franchet d'Esperey to counter-attack to the north with vigour. Franchet d'Esperey, who had been waiting impatiently all day, needed no further encouragement. Divisional commanders were goaded into action. They and their troops were clearly more frightened of their general than they were of the Germans ahead. 'The little square man with the bullet head, whose gestures were like cracking whips, as violent as dynamite' was terrifying in his energy. But he was also respected 'and liked, too, for men love a real leader'.[10]

By 5.30 p.m. all was ready, and Franchet d'Esperey, on horseback and surrounded by mounted staff officers, gave the order for general attack in the direction of the town of Guise. The bands started playing, the colours were unfurled, bayonets were fixed and the 1st Army Corps went on a brisk offensive. Franchet d'Esperey placed himself at the head of one of the leading brigades. 'As he rode by, he spotted a sad, stern-faced officer with a drooping moustache the colour of pepper and salt standing with the small staff of [his] brigade . . . and called out to him as he rode by "What do you think of this manoeuvre, *Monsieur le Professeur à l'École de Guerre?*"[11] The officer was, indeed, Colonel Pétain.

Pétain's 4th Brigade, which up until then had been held in reserve, was ordered into the attack late in the evening. He moved his troops forward in open order, to take advantage of any features of the ground that could give shelter from enemy fire. But time was short. To be sure, a farm was captured; but by that time it was difficult to see much apart from the burning farmhouse. There were dead men lying on the open field; the wounded were screaming in the near-darkness. That apart, there was a danger that his troops, unused to night-time fighting, would lose their way. In fact, much of the night was spent in finding out where they all were, and regrouping them for a further assault in the morning. All in all, it had been a dreadful introduction to the horror of war.

Nevertheless, Franchet d'Esperey had led a successful action. French soldiers had shown the enemy what they were capable of. But, in truth, it did not lead to much. On the morning of 30 August, 4th Brigade found itself isolated. Lanrezac had sent orders that the general retreat should be resumed. As it happened, he was right; there was, once more, the danger of encirclement. Depressing as it was, in the moment of their first success the French were moving backwards again. Pétain took his brigade with them – at some speed. They were glad to be out of it. Yet, in spite of it all, Franchet d'Esperey had made a point. The Battle of St-Quentin might have been lost, but the Battle of Guise had been won. It was the French Army's first victory of the war. It showed that the 'Boches' could be defeated, and – at least temporarily – it stopped the German advance in its tracks.

Pétain's brigade had played only a limited part in the Battle of Guise, but Pétain himself had by then earned the reputation of being a competent, disciplined and strict, if somewhat undistinguished, officer. At least he had not failed, and, in the midst of so much failure, that in itself was merit. It was certainly this that allowed him to survive

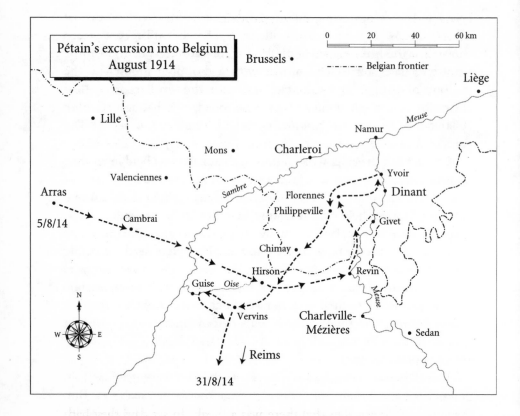

Pétain's excursion into Belgium
August 1914

the purge of senior officers undertaken by Joffre in the late summer
and autumn of 1914.

The purge was brutal, understandably so, since, apart from the prevailing incompetence, the average age of a general in July 1914 was
just over sixty-four years. Many generals had been appointed under
André's efforts at 'republicanising' the Army. Moreover, a number of
retired generals had been called back with the mobilisation of the
reservists. Certainly, there was much weeding to do. By 6 September
three army commanders (including Joffre's immediate target Lanrezac,
who was replaced by his erstwhile subordinate Franchet d'Esperey)
had been sacked, along with seven corps commanders, thirty-four
divisional commanders and fourteen brigadiers. In the remaining
weeks of September, a further thirty-eight divisional commanders
went, followed by another eleven in October and twelve in
November. By January 1915 all but seven of the forty-eight

commanders of peacetime infantry divisions had been dismissed or moved.

Pétain was a clear beneficiary of Joffre's purge. Others' bad fortune was his good luck. Thus it was that on 1 September he took leave of the 4th Brigade (after no more than four months in command) to take command, on 3 September, of the 6th Infantry Division, part of the 3rd Army Corps of the 5th Army. When he arrived, however, he found his new division in a sad state. The soldiers were 'like skeletons . . . They turned their exhausted eyes towards the as yet unknown commander and seemed to implore him to give them some respite from the long catalogue of their miseries.'[12] It was a struggle to refashion the division as a fighting unit, but it seems that Pétain made a good fist of it. He brought units into close order, so that their commanders were able to exercise more efficient oversight; he was severe in punishing laziness and negligence – not to mention sporadic looting; but he was equally ready with a word of encouragement to his troops.

Yet the orders were still to retreat. They had turned back and marched – and they marched on. By the time Pétain took command, at the village of Fismes, they were deep into French territory only thirty kilometres from the city of Reims. By the time they were called to a halt, they had crossed the Rivers Serre, Sambre, Aisne and Marne and both the Grand and Petit Morin. It was not until the evening of 5 September that there was a break. In six days they had marched – in retreat – over eighty kilometres, in difficult terrain and in constant fear of enemy ambush. But they had marched. It was now time to stand and fight.

Surprisingly, von Moltke had by then changed the purpose and direction of the German advance. On 2 September he issued orders to von Kluck to abandon the route west of Paris and to move southeast to protect von Bülow's right flank. In other words, the Schlieffen Plan had been consigned to the waste-paper basket. 'Without pause or preparation, [Moltke] was shifting the conceptual base of the German advance from envelopment to breakthrough.'[13] Von Kluck was, understandably, confused. Already ahead of von Bülow, convinced that he had a clear run to attack the French 5th Army, he decided to ignore the order to protect von Bülow's flank and simply march on. On 3 September units of his army crossed the Marne.

All this was carefully observed, through intercepted signals and by spotter aircraft, by Joffre and the Military Governor of Paris, General Joseph Galliéni. It seemed to both of them that von Kluck, on his new course, was dangerously exposing his right flank to an attack by Maunoury's 6th Army, whose job hitherto had been to sit tight and defend Paris. Furthermore, a gap was opening up between his advance and the slower von Bülow, which could be exploited by the BEF, by now south of the Marne and east of Paris, to aide Maunoury in an attack. This, in turn, would allow Franchet d'Esperey's 5th Army to mount a frontal assault on von Kluck's left wing. Moreover, the 9th Army, under General Foch, could then attack the by then unprotected von Bülow. Joffre and his staff drew up their plan carefully. The stage was thus set for the first Battle of the Marne.

On 5 September, Joffre made visits to the headquarters of Franchet d'Esperey, Foch and Sir John French. He explained in detail his plan for the coming engagement. He issued orders to his two subordinates, and appealed to Sir John French to accept his plan. Fortunately, the sour relations which had marked the BEF's manoeuvres in Belgium in August had improved since the dismissal of Lanrezac. Sir John agreed. The British would march alongside their French allies.

At half past six on that evening Franchet d'Esperey issued his orders to his corps and divisional commanders. The battle, he told his generals, would last several days, and corps commanders were instructed not to commit all their infantry at the outset. These orders were reflected in Pétain's orders to his division – but Pétain added the provision that the infantry should not leave their positions for the advance until the artillery had done its work to his satisfaction. That done, all was ready.

The following morning the French artillery laid down a heavy barrage on the German lines, and in the afternoon the infantry moved forward. Almost immediately they came under equally intense artillery attack – and started to waver. One of Pétain's brigades lost six hundred men in two hours attempting, in the end successfully, to capture one farm. It looked as though the attack would stall, at least in his sector, until Pétain himself, in an extraordinary display of bravado, rode up to his front line and, seemingly oblivious to the shells raining around him, took personal control of the forward troops in the assault.

It may have been brave, but it was also foolhardy. Divisional commanders were not meant to throw away their lives. Besides, the idea of

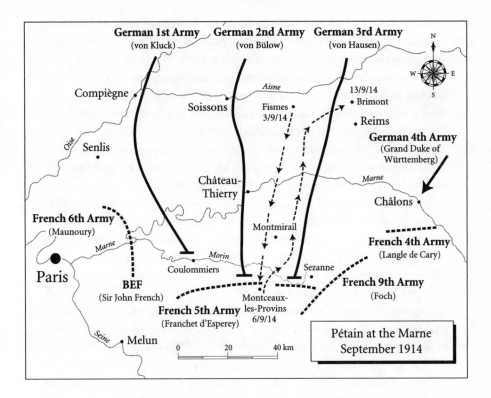

German 1st Army **German 2nd Army** **German 3rd Army**
(von Kluck) (von Bülow) (von Hausen)

Compiègne

Aisne

Soissons Fismes • Brimont
3/9/14 13/9/14

• Reims

German 4th Army
(Grand Duke of
Württemberg)

Senlis
Oise

Marne

Château-
Thierry Châlons •

French 6th Army
(Maunoury) Montmirail

Marne **French 4th Army**
(Langle de Cary)

Morin Sezanne
Paris Coulommiers

BEF **French 9th Army**
(Sir John French) Montceaux- (Foch)
French 5th Army les-Provins
(Franchet d'Esperey) 6/9/14

Seine • Melun

0   20   40 km

Pétain at the Marne
September 1914

directing an infantry attack on horseback, in the days of effective light
artillery and the machine gun, was little short of suicidal. As a matter of
fact, the practice was abandoned soon after the Marne. But it says a
great deal about the state of morale of his troops that Pétain had to
resort to such desperate measures.

As Pétain had calculated, the gesture was effective, and 6th Division
rallied to its commander. By nightfall, the German 6th Brandenburg
facing them had been driven back over two kilometres and had abandoned the strategically important village of Monceau-les-Provins. A
brigade from the neighbouring 18th Army Corps was able to move
through and secure the village. At that point, it was clear that there
would be little more action that day. 6th Division had attained the
objective set for it. It was time to reorganise – and bury the dead. As
the sun set, Pétain turned to his staff officers and said: 'The sun is
going to bed; we will do the same.'[14] With that, he turned his horse
around and trotted back to his headquarters.

The German line had been broken, and during the next few days Pétain's division's main task was to advance northwards, harrying the retreating enemy as it went. They crossed the Petit Morin near Montmirail, the Marne near Dormans, the Vesle just to the west of Reims and reached the Aisne Canal on 13 September. They had marched nearly 90 kilometres in six days. By any reasonable standards, the feat must go down as one of the most remarkable achievements in military warfare. An army which, three weeks before, had looked irretrievably beaten had roused itself, defeated its enemy and pursued him right up to the bounds of physical endurance.

It was along the line of the Aisne Canal that the German retreat was called to a halt. On the evening of 13 September Pétain ordered an attack across the canal in the direction of the village of Brimont. For the first time for many days the French met determined German resistance. The attack floundered with heavy casualties. As it turned out, this was to be the pattern over the next few weeks. The German defensive positions were so strong, and their artillery so powerful, that they could not be shifted. A series of French attacks failed dismally. Even a small farm on the other side of the canal was not taken, let alone Brimont. Nevertheless, it was essential to maintain the rhythm of these attacks to keep the German troops pinned down, in order to prevent the movement of units to defend the area north of Reims, which the rest of the 5th Army was trying to clear, or to attack the right flank of the BEF, which was advancing into the gap which had opened up between the German 1st and 2nd Armies.

The series of French attacks continued: assaults at divisional level on September the 22nd, 23rd and 25th. There were German counter-attacks, on the 26th and 27th. On 1 October, Joffre ordered aerial reconnaissance to see whether it was worth having another shot. The answer came back that it might be. A further major French offensive was announced for 12 October, but few thought that it had much chance of success. Certainly, Pétain was gloomy about its prospects, and only ordered one battalion of infantry, supported by artillery, to take part. He was not far off the mark. The offensive was a failure.

Pétain by then had become pessimistic about this form of warfare. On 16 October, he wrote to his corps commander, General Hache. The whole picture, he said, had changed. The campaign, such as it was, now resembled siege warfare. It was no good wasting human lives in futile assaults. The whole concept of war needed to be thought through again. In the future, it would be heavy artillery which would determine the course of a battle. The French 75mm light artillery was all very well when used in support of infantry movements, but it was no good in static trench warfare. In fact, in this opinion he found himself in surprising company. Others, for instance Generals Édouard de Castelnau and Auguste Dubail, commanders respectively of the 2nd and 1st Armies along the eastern frontier, were coming to the same conclusion. None the less, it was to be some time before the general staff would be brought round to their view.

But, for Pétain, it was, yet again, not all bad news. He and his division had performed well in the Battle of the Marne, and recognition was not long in coming. On 16 October 1914 he was appointed officer of the Légion d'honneur – the citation records that he was 'remarkable in his bravery, his calm when under fire, and in the example that he sets to his men . . .'[15] Moreover, on 20 October he was ordered to report to General Foch, by then commander of the armies of the north. He was to be given the command of 33rd Army Corps, whose headquarters were at Aubigny near Arras. His immediate superior, as commander of the 10th Army, was his old friend General Maud'huy. Thus in a matter of under three months of war Pétain had achieved a rate of promotion unthinkable in the previous forty years of peace.

The appointment, although again due to Joffre's purge, was perfectly sensible. Pétain knew the country well. It was, after all, his home, and before the war he had conducted manoeuvres with his battalion on the Lorette plateau and on Vimy Ridge. Be that as it may, he hardly had time to settle in before he was called on to repel a ferocious German attack aimed at Arras itself. By the time he took up his command German advanced units were within three kilometres of the outskirts of the city. The situation was desperate. Pétain had to respond immediately, which he did. In the event the German attack was halted, but French casualties were noted as being very severe. Pétain was not slow to draw the lesson.

The German attack had not been an isolated occurrence. In fact, it was to set the pattern of the next few weeks, in what became known as the Battle of Artois. The Germans would attack, and initially gain ground. The French would resist, and then counter-attack to regain the lost ground. From time to time, the position would be reversed.

The French would attack and gain ground, which the Germans would recover in their counter-attack. Both sides suffered horrendous casualties.

It was obvious to Pétain, if not to others, that new tactical thinking was required. Seeing the number of French casualties in these attacks and counter-attacks, Pétain adopted a much more subtle approach. In defence, camouflage became all important, as were centres of resistance in built-up areas. Trenches were dug deeper and machine guns more carefully hidden. Above all, a second line of defence was constituted, on which a German attack would break if it managed to pierce the first line. Counter-attacks were only permissible when the enemy had been weakened by his own attacks. Random and meaningless offensive movements were no longer on the Pétain agenda.

As it turned out, the tactic was successful. By the end of October it had become clear that the Battle of Artois had ground to a stalemate. To be sure, Arras had been saved, but the French troops were far too exhausted, and morale was far too low, to allow any major offensive in the foreseeable future. The German troops, too, were exhausted, and started to wonder what they were doing so far away from home. The conclusion was unavoidable. It was time to dig in.

7

KILL OR BE KILLED

'Adieu 1914 et vive 1915 qui sera l'année de la victoire.'

'I got to know Pétain well when he commanded the 33rd Corps on the deadly Lorette Ridge, today covered by a forest of wooden crosses. In those early days of the War it buttressed the Vimy Ridge near the junction with the British Army, where my duties as a liaison officer with the French often led me. From almost daily visits to this sector, careful examination of the tactical methods employed by Pétain, his use of fire power, the combination of artillery and infantry power, his disciplinary practices which were both firm and stern, the ingenuity with which he set up small factories and workshops to provide him with some of the weapons and objects his men needed but could not obtain from army sources, I soon realised that there was much to be learned from him which could be of benefit to our own army.' Thus Lieutenant (acting Captain) Edward Louis Spears, the official liaison between the British and the French army headquarters in the autumn of 1914. 'I presently found out,' Spears went on, 'and wondered at my discovery, that General Pétain had a marked sense of humour deeply concealed under his frozen exterior, like *edelweiss* beneath a snowdrift, as unexpected as a spring of fresh water in the desert.'[1]

Spears had accompanied the BEF after the Battle of the Marne to their new station at the northernmost end of the Allied front line at the same time as Pétain had taken command of the 33rd Army Corps.

For the BEF it had been a long and exhausting railway journey, but the move, requested earnestly by Joffre, had proved to be right. After the Marne, both armies had tried to manoeuvre round their opponents on their northern flank. Sometimes called the 'Race to the Sea', the operation consisted of attacks by both sides where generals perceived that the enemy line ended. It was not finished until both sides had completed their front. It was the BEF's task, by then supported by reinforcements shipped in numbers into Belgium, to seal off the northern section, which, after the bloody engagement of the First Battle of Ypres, they finally succeeded in doing. The line of trenches, although not yet as fully developed as they were to become later in the war, by the end of 1914 stretched without a break from the Belgian coast to the Vosges and the Swiss frontier.

Spears was, on the face of it, almost the perfect liaison officer between the two Allied armies. He was bilingual in French and English. On the other hand, he was neither one thing nor the other. He fitted into no identifiable social or national category. The son of a raffish commission agent, probably of German origin but with at least a drop of Jewish blood, known as 'Charlie' Spiers, and Melicent Hack, whose own mother had been of Irish Aylmer stock, he had had a signally unhappy childhood. Delicate in health, he had been dragged around the various health resorts of Europe in the summer and had spent winters in Menton with his grandmother. 'The sense of isolation', wrote his biographer, 'lasted all his life'.[2] He had then grown into an unruly and frequently violent adolescent. But he was ambitious; and his chief ambition was to rise so far socially as to be accepted as a true member of the English aristocracy. As it happened, in that ambition he very nearly succeeded. As part of that ambition, he anglicised his parental name, becoming 'Spears' instead of 'Spiers', in September 1918.

Thanks to his Aylmer connection, Spears joined the British Army through the Irish militia at the age of sixteen in 1903 and was gazetted into the Royal Irish Hussars in 1906. At the end of the war, still intent on establishing his English credentials, he moved in 1922 seemingly effortlessly into the House of Commons as an MP. (He was elected unopposed as a National Liberal in November 1922 for Loughborough. He stood again as a Liberal in 1923 and squeaked through with a majority of 873. In 1924 he stood as a Liberal and came third behind the Conservative winner and the Labour runner-up. He joined the

Conservative Party in 1925, fought Bosworth in May 1927, Carlisle in May 1929 and was elected for Carlisle as a National Conservative in October 1931 and represented the town until he was defeated in July 1945.) Yet he could never quite slough off his origins. His English was grammatically perfect, but there was always just the trace of an accent which was vaguely Central European, and he was never able to pronounce the English *r*. In short, for all his life Spears was to be an outsider.

As such, he took to Pétain, and, in fact, their paths crossed repeatedly during the war, the inter-war period, and, most notably, in June 1940. Pétain was, of course, something of an outsider himself. His efforts to marry into the bourgeoisie had come to nothing, and he had failed to establish any sort of equal relationship with the cavalry officers who formed the social élite of the French Army. It was these failures which converted shyness into coldness and brittle sarcasm, and made him at times impertinent to his superiors. In sum, both Pétain and Spears, in different ways, had chips on their shoulders – and therefore took to one another immediately.

Spears's undoubted charm was spread widely. Maud'huy, too, enjoyed his company – Maud'huy, according to Spears, said that he gave 'them all gaiety here' – and both he and Pétain invited Spears to eat in their mess whenever he paid a visit. Indeed, on one occasion Maud'huy persuaded him to accompany himself and three of his corps commanders (of whom one was Pétain) on a visit to the ruined city of Arras. (Spears thought the idea 'really stupidly dangerous'.)[3]

If Pétain's adoption of this strange half French, half Irish Hussar showed the 'outsider' aspect of his character, his friendship for two officers in his command, Bernard Serrigny and Emile Fayolle, showed the other – the Army as a surrogate extended family. Serrigny, doting but self-important, had been known to Pétain as a junior officer in the 8th Infantry Battalion when he had joined in the celebrations of Pétain's promotion in July 1900. Fayolle, on the other hand, was an older acquaintance. A fellow member of the 'Plewna' year at Saint-Cyr, he had been on Pétain's staff at the École de Guerre (they were frequently seen lunching together at Chez Gangloff, a restaurant just off the Champ de Mars), and was now one of Pétain's divisional generals. As an aside, Spears thought Fayolle 'one of the very sweetest and wisest old men I have ever met'.[4] Yet although these two can reasonably be called Pétain's friends, there was a divide. There was, after all, a difference in rank – of which Pétain was always punctiliously aware. Both Serrigny and Fayolle were admirers rather than friends of equality, although Serrigny's admiration, which comes out very clearly in his diaries, is much more devoted than that of Fayolle, who from time to time in his own diaries had some harsh opinions of his friendly superior officer.

When Pétain was given command of 33rd Army Corps it was understood, whatever his own feelings on the matter, that he would follow the instructions of his army commander, Maud'huy, to take the offensive wherever possible. This was accepted. But Pétain knew perfectly well that to follow Maud'huy's instructions successfully he had to restore the battered morale of his newly inherited troops.

Pétain found various ways of doing this. For instance, during the days of inaction after the hectic defence of Arras, his soldiers had become bored. The phenomenon was not uncommon. Throughout the war, between the bloody engagements there were long periods of calm; and in that calm the men's fighting spirit tended to sag. They even started to ask themselves awkward questions about why they were there. In short, they had to be found something to do. Pétain's solution in the dreary autumn of 1914 was to allow them to go on leave to Amiens, and even to make contact with what Serrigny chastely described as 'female elements'.[5] There were, too, weekly entertainments behind the lines. The men's food was much improved (along, in fact, with Pétain's own mess – minions were sent to Arras or even to Boulogne to stock up on oysters or Bordeaux wine).

But, above all, Pétain went out to meet his troops on the ground. He visited each of his three divisions, talked to the brigade and battalion commanders, went down into the trenches, and at one point even told the machine-gunners in a trench where their line of fire should be. He noted the poor state of their equipment and clothing and hectored the Army's quartermasters for more supplies. He – and Serrigny, whose experience was in army administration – noted carefully the shortage of ammunition and complained bitterly about it to Maud'huy.

All this served to alleviate what Serrigny described as the 'depressing monotony' of the front.[6] There were, of course, other unofficial diversions for the troops – all, to be sure, unthinkable later in the war. On 12 November 1914, for instance, a hare, obviously startled, ran into the hundred metres of no man's land which separated the trenches of 10th Army Corps from the enemy. Immediately, fire from both sides was concentrated not on the enemy but on the hare. To general surprise, the hare was hit and killed. But at that point there arose a difficult problem: to whom did the unfortunate hare belong? The problem was solved by German soldiers shouting that they would rather have tobacco than the hare. A delicate negotiation followed. In the end, the exchange rate was fixed: four packets of tobacco for the hare. The deal done, a French soldier went out, deposited the tobacco and collected the hare; whereupon a German soldier came out and collected the tobacco. After that, the two sides started shooting at one another again.

The story of the cow is similar. Again, this time on Pétain's front, the two lines of trenches were particularly close. There was a spring between the two in no man's land. Each morning a cow emerged from the German trenches to drink at the spring and to graze. The cow made a convenient conduit for messages between the two lines – messages which were tied to the cow's tail. On the same day as the hare met its fate further down the line, the cow was bringing a message from the Germans to the French: the French were to get their water from the spring at 10 a.m. and the Germans at 11 a.m. The French sent back a message – via the cow – that they accepted the arrangement. It was rigorously adhered to.

To be sure, there were times when the rules of this macabre game broke down. On Christmas Day 1914 the Germans suggested a truce, which the French accepted. Soldiers of the French 269th Infantry Battalion – not part of Pétain's army corps – were invited by German soldiers from Baden to come over for a guided tour of their trenches. The offer was accepted. The French soldiers were duly impressed by the German trenches, and also grateful when the Baden soldiers told them that they were soon to be relieved by a Prussian regiment – unpleasant Protestants, they implied – but they would let the French know when that happened (which they later did, by hanging out the agreed signal: a white flag). The French, however, were not playing the game. On their guided tour they made careful note of where the Germans had sited their machine guns. The following day they blew them to pieces. Fraternisation one day; killing the next.

It took some time for these shenanigans to be reported upwards to divisional and corps commanders. Officers on the ground in many cases still regarded war as an extension of chivalry, and had a gentlemanly respect for their opponents – to be regarded as human beings rather than mere targets; in other cases they were only too keen to see their men occupy themselves harmlessly. Moreover, they knew, and their men knew, that senior officers lived a life which was far removed from the rigours of the front. Pétain, for instance, had his corps headquarters in a requisitioned inn at Aubigny, a village a few kilometres to the west of Arras. It was well out of the range of even the heaviest German artillery; nor were there any bombers – aviation at that time being confined to reconnaissance in support of the guns. In fact, life in Aubigny was not far short of normal. There was no black-out. There were plenty of servants to man the Mess. Staff officers had comfortable rooms – only Pétain insisted on his usual Spartan surroundings – and were only too keen to bask in the patriotic admiration of the villagers. Needless to say, word of this seeming luxury was quickly passed around the troops at the front.

When he finally heard what the troops were up to, Pétain took immediate action. By mid-December, as far is his soldiers were concerned, he put a stop to it. 'The German', ran his order of 14 December 1914, 'is the enemy under whatever pretext he presents himself, and the first duty of every soldier is to shoot at him as soon as he shows himself.'[7] Improving morale was one thing; slackness in discipline was another. Indeed, Pétain was enough of a martinet to have no compunction about enforcing military discipline. Fayolle noted that Pétain's dealing with self-inflicted wounds was particularly fierce. On one occasion he was prepared to have twenty-five men who had shot themselves in the hand or the foot taken out and executed by firing squad; on reflexion, he commuted the sentence. He ordered that the offenders should be tied up and left in no man's land near the German trenches for a night.

The morale of the senior officers of the 33rd Army Corps was supposed to be further raised by a visit, on 3 November, by the President of France, Raymond Poincaré. It was, apparently, a reward for their successful defence of Arras the previous month. Poincaré, 'small, square and precise' with 'the persistence of a leech rather than that of a bulldog',[8] was accustomed to descend on those who had fought a successful engagement, review a detachment of troops and hand out

medals. On this occasion the detachment to be reviewed was a mixture of light infantry and cavalry, with a section of Zouaves from
Algeria thrown in for good measure. After the review, there was the
medal ceremony. One of Pétain's divisional generals was decorated (as
it turned out, he was killed a few days later) and – perhaps surprisingly
but on Maud'huy's recommendation – Spears was made a Chevalier of
the Légion d'honneur (he reported mournfully that he was decorated
beside a rifleman who had lost an arm and who had to be carried to
the ceremony).

All in all, the day passed peacefully, apart from the impression given
by both Poincaré himself and his aide-de-camp. 'Tireless and auto-
matic,' Spears reported,

> [Poincaré] went from place to place pecking at the cheeks of the
> bearded warriors whom he was rewarding in the name of France. A
> certain reserve, shyness perhaps, prevented him from appearing gra-
> cious on these occasions, but he certainly handicapped himself
> unnecessarily in the eyes of the troops by the kit he had devised for
> himself. A chauffeur's cap with a dark blue band on which could be
> discerned the oak leaves that appear in gold on a French general's
> headdress, a kind of Norfolk jacket and black leggings, made up an
> outfit which would have made Napoleon look ridiculous.[9]

Not to be outdone, Poincaré's aide-de-camp turned up heavily
scented and in a pair of highly polished yellow boots.

Even before – and through – Christmas 1914 serious hostilities, however bizarre the interruptions, were unremitting. The Christmas escapade
of the 269th had, in fact, come in the middle of the second phase of
the Battle of Artois. Once the Allied front had been completed, Joffre
and his staff had assessed the strategic situation. It was intolerable, they
concluded, that French territory should be occupied by an enemy.
Moreover, the territory which was occupied contained the heart of
the French coal and steel industry and much of its manufacturing base.
War could not be fought without the tools with which to fight. The
French Army must therefore continue to take the offensive.

That conclusion reached, it only remained to decide where on the
front the breakthrough should come. The wetlands of Flanders were
no good. An offensive there would soon get bogged down. The hilly

country around the Meuse and in the Vosges was equally no good. The Germans had positioned themselves cleverly on reverse slopes and would simply mow down any attackers. The conclusion was again clear. The most promising areas for attack were the Artois – and, in particular, the German salient in the chalklands of the Somme around Arras – and the Champagne. It was therefore in Artois that the 10th Army was ordered to attack.

The plan was carefully prepared by Pétain on Maud'huy's instructions. The phasing of the battle was worked out in detail, and Pétain made sure that there was proper co-ordination between artillery and infantry. On 17 December, the first wave went over the top. On the 18th the 33rd corps went into action. A German trench was taken; then a line of German trenches. A point platoon was held up by heavy machine-gun fire from its flank. The attack was redirected towards the village of Carency. But it was to no avail. Progress was minimal and casualties heavy. The only relief was that on the following day the battlefield was enveloped in thick fog. At that point, all attacks were called off.

The weather did not clear up until the 27th. Yet again the men were ordered forward, on the same line of attack. Yet again losses were heavy – the 226th Infantry Battalion lost nineteen officers and eight hundred men in the first assault – and the ground was atrocious. Advancing troops found themselves at times up to the waist in water in the shell holes, and mud jammed their rifles. The attack was brave but fruitless. It seemed fortunate that in the night of the 28th–29th there was a storm so intense that trenches and galleries started to fill up with water. Further action was pointless. The French generals, even the optimistic Maud'huy, admitted as much. The 10th Army withdrew to lick its wounds.

1914 thus came to a bitter end. The French Army had sustained losses on a dreadful scale: more than 160,000 killed, wounded, missing or taken prisoner in August; more than 200,000 in September; over 80,000 in October, 70,000 in November and more in December. Yet there was little public weeping, except among the families of those concerned, at this haemorrhage of French youth. Nor, apparently, was there much weeping in the trenches for those who were lost. It seemed that the bulk of the Army, of peasant stock, had developed a peasant stoicism, even fatalism, about death or mutilation.

Pétain seems to have shared this mood. He is recorded as worrying about the extent of the loss of manpower, but much more as a damaging effect on the war effort than as a pitiful waste of young human life. Peasants, after all, had been brought up to hardship and random fatality. One more or less, a hundred more or less, a thousand more or less; it seemed to make little difference.

Nor, it seemed, was Joffre much concerned. On 15 January 1915 he wrote to his army commanders that 'there was not enough vigour in attack and not enough stubbornness in defence'. Moreover, he went on, 'the present war has by no means weakened the principles which are the basis of our offensive doctrine . . .'[10] There was, he ordered, to be another offensive in Artois as soon as possible. But given the dreadful weather – and the subsequent thaw which had filled the trenches with water and the roads with pot-holes – an immediate offensive was out of the question. All the planning was directed towards the spring.

The overall plan for the 1915 spring offensive was worked out in meetings at Northern Army Group headquarters at Chantilly in March, and approved by Joffre on the 24th. General Victor d'Urbal – another contemporary of Pétain's at Saint-Cyr – who had replaced Maud'huy as commander of the 10th Army (to Pétain's evident disgust, since he was hoping for the job), fleshed it out on 6 April. The attack was to be launched by the 10th Army on a front of 6.5 kilometres. The target was the row of low hills which blocked any French breakthrough into the northern plain and whose main feature was the ridge of Vimy. In this attack, the five army corps were to move forward together in line, 33rd Army Corps taking the central role.

Once this was decided, Pétain settled down with his staff to map out not just a battle plan but a programme of training exercises at division and brigade level. He again toured the trenches, visiting every front-line battalion, talking to officers – commissioned and non-commissioned alike – engineers and, above all, the artillery. Each battery was required to fire one shot in Pétain's presence to satisfy him that they were properly aimed. His corps was further reinforced by the arrival, on 19 and 20 April, of three more artillery batteries and on 25 April by a Moroccan division. It was not by any means what Pétain had wanted, but it was all he could get.

On 6 May Pétain was able to write to d'Urbal that 'the preparatory works for the attack are complete'.[11] But there was an unpleasant prelude. On 22 April the Germans had launched the first gas attack against the Algerian divisions defending the Ypres salient. It was deadly. Troops fled from the gas, clutching their throats, coughing, screaming as they turned blue in the face. Furthermore, as they fled, the neighbouring Canadians were instructed to shoot them down for fleeing in the face of the enemy. Fortunately, since the gas was chlorine – and therefore soluble – wet cloths tied round the mouth gave protection. But the damage was done. An extra dimension of fear touched the men who were about to embark on the spring offensive. Moreover, on that day perished once for all the idea that war was a gentlemanly pursuit.

Throughout 6, 7 and 8 May it rained, only clearing late on in the evening of the 8th. Last orders were given to the aircraft which were to patrol the front observing enemy troop movement and locating his artillery positions. Troops waited nervously in their trenches. All was ready for what would be the biggest engagement of the French Army since the Battle of the Marne, and the last phase of the Battle of Artois.

At first light on 9 May 1915 the French guns opened up. The barrage was massive, and well directed. Between 9 and 10 a.m. the infantry moved forward in wave after wave, running as fast as they could across the muddy fields, leaving the comparative safety of the trenches to face a hail of small-arms fire on open ground. As it happened, the preliminary artillery barrage had done its work, and the German resistance was less robust than expected. With the Moroccan Division in the van, the French troops surged forward. Within an hour the German line had been broken and the Vimy Ridge occupied.

The orders for 33rd Corps had been clear. They were to attack along a ten-kilometre line stretching from the village of Camblin-l'Abbé, some twelve kilometres north-west of Arras, south-eastwards through the little hamlet of La Targette and on to Roclincourt, almost on the outskirts of Arras. To the north of them the 20th Army Corps were due to attack at Lorette; to the south, the remaining units of the 10th Army were to advance along the line of the River Scarpe.

The Moroccans, supported by 77th Infantry Division, achieved a startling success. Not only had they achieved their objective of Vimy

Ridge ahead of schedule, but their forward units had penetrated as far as the villages of Petit-Vimy, Givenchy and Souchez. By midday they were on the eastern slopes of the ridge. They could see the town of Lens lying undefended in front of them. Moreover, in achieving all this they had captured two German artillery batteries, dozens of machine guns and between 1,200 and 1,500 prisoners. By mid-afternoon there was no doubt about it. Reconnaissance aircraft reported German troops fleeing in all directions. Not only was the German line broken but discipline seemed to have been cast to the winds.

None the less, there was a problem. Spotter aircraft had discovered German reserve regiments moving up to close the breach in the line. At the same time the Moroccans came under heavy fire from Souchez to their north and Mont Neuville-St-Vaast to their south. It was plain that the French attacks on the rest of the front were going badly. By nightfall on 9 May both forward divisions of 33rd Corps had reported heavy losses – and the supporting artillery had almost run out of ammunition.

But it had been a good day's work – the best for the French since the Marne. On the following day, Joffre sent a message to Pétain, raising him to the rank of Commander of the Légion d'honneur and urging him to continue the attack. At last, it seemed to Joffre, the long-awaited breakthrough had been achieved. Foch, too, was enthusiastic – and d'Urbal could hardly be contained. 'Push on at all costs' was the message.

Pétain, however, knew perfectly well that the enthusiasm was misplaced. Neither on his left nor his right had the French made any progress. German reserves, unlike the French reserves, had been moved up quickly. His troops were exhausted, and their formations badly depleted by casualties. They were in a pocket, in danger of attack from three sides simultaneously. Around 7 p.m. they had faced a German counter-attack – repulsed only with greater loss of life. That done, they had dug in for the night, posted sentries and slept where they were.

On the morning of 10 May d'Urbal sent another message to Pétain. 'This is the decisive day . . .' he wrote. 'The 33rd Army Corps will have the honour of landing the great blow . . .'[12] Admittedly, Pétain then did his best. He ordered a further attack, following d'Urbal's instruction to take the village of Souchez on his northern flank. But the German machine guns did their work. Both the Moroccan Division and the 77th suffered dreadful casualties without making any progress.

May 11 was little different. There was a further attack to the north – without success. In the evening, Pétain sent a long report to d'Urbal drawing the lessons to be learned from the attacks of the previous three days. He pointed out that the 'breakthrough' was only possible when an assault was meticulously planned, launched on a broad front and in open country. Improvised attacks on fortified positions were doomed to failure.

Pétain's complaints remained unheard. He was ordered to continue his attacks, which he did on 13, 14 and 16 May, again without success. By then, d'Urbal was obviously becoming impatient. When Pétain protested about the lack of ammunition d'Urbal told him sharply to make sure that there were, for instance, enough home-made grenades to deter the enemy. So it went on: daily attacks, daily loss of life, daily failure. D'Urbal, too, went on regardless. 'I demand a fresh attack on 29 May,' he wrote, '33rd Corps must be ready like the others to meet this date.'[13] The familiar '*tu*' of 9 May had given way to the more distant '*vous*'. In short, tempers had become frayed to breaking point.

It was not until late June that Joffre finally threw in the towel. By then, the 10th Army had lost well over a hundred thousand men. All the ground which had been gained had been lost to enemy counter-attack. The series of attacks which had been launched throughout June had been met by stout German resistance and, the weather having turned again to rain, had become bogged down in the mud. Whatever the initial tactical success, the whole thing had been an expensive strategic failure. It is little wonder that Joffre's placidity deserted him; he was profoundly and obviously depressed – anecdote has it that he was reduced to tears – that yet again the 'breakthrough' had eluded him.

By that time, Pétain was well out of it. On 22 June 1915 he had been appointed commander of the 2nd Army, which held an extended line north of Châlons-sur-Marne in the Champagne. His promotion had been quick – and remarkable. In less than a year, Pétain had risen from field commander of a brigade to strategic commander of a full army – by any standards, as Joffre remarked, an

exceptionally rapid rise. Yet Pétain by then had come to differ fundamentally with the super-optimists – particularly Foch and d'Urbal –
over the conduct of the war. He wrote as much in another long note
dated 29 June. 'The present war', he wrote, 'has taken on the character of a war of attrition. There is no longer a decisive battle as there
used to be. Success will in the end belong to the side which will have
the last man.'[14] He was, however, rather more circumspect in a letter
to Foch written a month earlier. Indeed, it was Pétain's boasting about
his achievement of 9 May which seems to have persuaded Joffre that
he was the right person to be promoted to the command of a full
army.

On 22 June 1915 Pétain arrived at his new headquarters in the little
town of Souilly. A shock awaited him. Such was Joffre's concern for
the element of surprise that he had ordered de Castelnau, commander
of the Centre Army Group, to announce the disbandment of the 2nd
Army and the transfer of their positions to the British. Furthermore,
he should give out that elements of the disbanded army were being
posted to Italy and the Dardanelles. This was essential, he considered,
since Pétain's reputation had gone before him and once the Germans
got wind of the fact that Pétain was in the area they would know precisely when and where the next attack would be. Pétain therefore
arrived to find his supposedly new headquarters redesignated as the
headquarters of the 9th Army. He was not to be General Commander
of the 2nd Army but Deputy Commander – to de Castelnau – of the
Centre Army Group. The 2nd Army in turn was redesignated as 'the
Pétain Group' and did not recover its proper title until 17 September.
It was all very confusing.

Nevertheless, Pétain proceeded to review the disposition of the
troops under his – at least notional – command. They were, he discovered, well dug in. In fact, apart from a small skirmish in late May
against an inconvenient German salient, the front had been quiet for
six months. Their trenches were laid out carefully, as was noted by a
visiting British staff officer. 'The system', he reported, 'consists of i. a
strong first line, and with support trenches about 80 yards in rear, not
continuous but opposite points where support is likely to be wanted;
ii. Points of appui, generally villages or other tactical points, to hold up
the enemy in case the first line is broken through; iii. A second line,
which should be as strong and perfect as the first and at such a distance

from it that the enemy will have to move his heavy artillery before being able to bombard it.'[15] True, there was still work to be done. Communications between units and between units and headquarters were inadequate. Reinforcements already earmarked for a future campaign had to be fitted in. Water supplies were insufficient. But on the whole things were not too bad, and at least his troops were reasonably cheerful.

Nevertheless, Pétain knew that the Germans had learned the lessons of 9 May. Their second line of trenches was now just as strong as the first. The tactics which had been successful then might not work again. Pétain said as much to President Poincaré during his visit on 9 July. Nevertheless, by the time Pétain arrived at Souilly Joffre had almost reached his decision: to launch an offensive across the whole front of the Centre Army Group. The objective: to break the German front by the power and surprise of the assault. The final decision was made in mid-July. In announcing this to de Castelnau on 25 July Joffre gave instructions that the methods employed on 9 May in the Artois should be used in the planning of the offensive: careful preparation, meticulous orders to both the artillery and the infantry and, above all, surprise.

Indeed, so impressed was Joffre by this element of surprise that he devised an elaborate camouflage for Pétain himself. On 13 September Joffre instructed Pétain to spend some days in Nancy, putting himself about and openly declaring that there would be an offensive in the east. To top it all, a dummy army headquarters was constructed at Bayon, facing the frontier with Alsace. He was only to return, almost incognito, on the 20th.

Whether these manoeuvres confused the German High Command or not is, to say the least, uncertain. At all events, another great offensive, the second major action of the French Army in 1915, was set to begin on 25 September. The main attack was to be in the Champagne, but planned to coincide with a lesser French offensive in the Artois and a British attack to the north at the village of Loos. The stage was set; the planning was finished; precise targets had been set for each unit; command of the air had been assured by five attack aircraft brought in for the purpose; pilots of reconnaissance aircraft were instructed carefully on which targets to look for and how to report back; the guns had tested their range; all was ready.

Pétain's train carriage office, autumn 1915. (*Ken Welsh/Bridgeman Art Library*)

The 2nd Army, commanded by Pétain, and the 4th Army, commanded by General Fernand de Langle de Cary, attacked along a front of some thirty-five kilometres with seventeen divisions, a further fifteen being held in reserve. The pattern was by now familiar. At first light a thousand guns launched their barrage on the German first line. Gas attack followed – then the waves of infantry. It had rained the previous night, which made the gas attack ineffective, but the sun shone in the morning – carefully picking out the French infantry as they emerged from the cloud of gunsmoke and dust. Some regiments even went so far as to advance in the old style, with flags flying and bugles sounding. Others, which had learned the lessons of previous engagements, were more cautious.

Although the German High Command suspected that an attack was imminent, the actual date was unknown, and the French, as Joffre had wanted, achieved at least a measure of surprise. The 14th Army Corps, at the centre of Pétain's line, in two hours overran the first German trenches opposite them and moved forward a further kilometre and a half. The 11th Army Corps, to their right, pushed even further to reach almost to the village of Tahure. By nightfall on 25 September it seemed that the French were heading for a great victory. Pétain gave orders for the offensive to continue. Perhaps, de Castelnau thought, the 'breakthrough' might be achieved at last.

They were all to be disappointed. The following day there was no progress. The French infantry had run up against the German second line, which the artillery had been unable to reach and where, consequently, the wire was intact. Continued attacks only resulted in men stumbling into barbed wire, presenting easy targets to the German machine guns. The story was the same on the 27th. Yet there was still a glimmer of hope. De Langle de Cary had succeeded in advancing some two kilometres on his front. De Castelnau ordered Pétain to support him by further attacks at Tahure. This he did, and further ground – the hill above the village – was captured. Perhaps, again de Castelnau thought, this was the moment when the German line would break, as it had at the Marne.

Yet again there was to be disappointment. De Langle de Cary reported that he had failed to overrun the German second line and was held up. Pétain considered that in that case continued attacks by the 2nd Army would inevitably fail. It was time, he suggested to de Castelnau, to consolidate his positions and to prepare carefully an attack at a later date. De Castelnau agreed. But time was running short. The Germans were bringing up reserves. On 6 October the French tried again; but yet again they made no progress. Both armies were held up – and then subjected to fierce counter-attack. For the rest of October there was only sporadic fighting, as each side tried to consolidate their positions and remove the salients which the offensive earlier in the month had left behind. The 2nd Army was in action again on 21 and 24 October, with a degree of success, but on 30 and 31 October German gas attacks practically wiped out twelve companies and the subsequent infantry assault dislodged the French from the hill above Tahure which they had taken at such cost only a month before.

At that point all attacks were called off. The overall result, the French generals concluded, was minimal. The German positions remained intact. The cost in human life had been horrific: the total casualties of the 2nd and 4th Armies from 25 September to 31 October were officially estimated at '191,797 men'[16] – in itself probably a gross underestimate. It could hardly have been more depressing.

Each general made his own post-mortem (or, more to the point, *post mortes*) analysis. Pétain, for his part, concluded that the battle showed the difficulty of taking the enemy second line – usually placed on a reverse slope and so invisible to ground attackers until they breasted the summit of the hill – without preparation at least as thorough as that for the original attack. Yet shortage of artillery ammunition would at present make that impossible. The answer, he considered, was a tactic of limited strikes at the enemy front line. Once that had been overrun, the attackers should retreat. But if there was to be a more general attack it should be on the basis that 'the breakthrough is not an end in itself, but the means of arriving at an engagement in open country . . .'.[17] De Castelnau, while not accepting all Pétain's conclusions, agreed that it was no good attacking the enemy second line without proper preparation. Foch and d'Urbal, in their turn, came to the same conclusions about the failed attacks both in Artois and in Champagne.

In all, 1915 was the bloodiest year of the war for the French Army. The total number of casualties for the year came to nearly 1.5 million men. Even Joffre realised that casualties at that rate were not sustainable. There were simply not enough men of military age in France. Not that Joffre himself was particularly popular in Paris. His promotion in early December to the new post of Commander-in-Chief of the French Armies was more an attempt to enhance the status of France in the campaign for a joint Franco-British command than a sign of confidence in his leadership.

But Joffre was still there – and in command. Although he did not agree with Pétain's conclusions about the offensive in the Champagne, he valued Pétain as a source of new ideas – of which Joffre himself seemed notably short. Perhaps the idea of the 'breakthrough' had perished in the mud of the battlefields and in the cemeteries of the French dead; but Joffre would not give up. 1916 was another year, and another spring offensive. The lessons of 1915 had to be learned. More artillery, more troops and more training were needed.

Joffre set about this programme with his usual energy. Once the exhausted troops had been stood down for the winter, he asked Pétain to direct the training of four army corps of reservists who were to be employed in the spring offensive he was planning for 1916. Pétain agreed. The posting was duly announced just after Christmas. Pétain's headquarters for this exercise were to be at Noailles, just outside Paris. His new posting took effect on 31 December 1915.

Pétain, of course, knew Noailles well. He had been stationed there before the war. Indeed, the place had memories. The surroundings were peaceful; he could ride in the forest as before; and he could even make trips into Paris. There were other memories too. Waiting for him on his trips to Paris was the ever devoted Nini. That particular wheel, it seemed, was about to come round full circle.

8

THE VICTOR OF VERDUN?

'The fall of each one of your soldiers was a stab in the heart of his general, and the impassive expression under which you hid your feelings masked constant and unremitting grief.'

The best part of a century has gone by since the Battle of Verdun of 1916. With the passage of time, the living experience of those dreadful ten months has to a large extent been drowned in the quicksand of historical analysis. Of course, there is nothing wrong in that. History will always have its say. But it is worth pausing for a moment to reflect. Those months left indelible, haunting, nightmare memories for the survivors of the battle and left families up and down the length and breadth of France in grief for her sons who were lost. Indeed, it is not too much to say that if there is one single battle which defined the Great War for France, it is, without a shadow of any reasonable doubt, Verdun.

The memories and the grief, each in their own rhythm, needed time for healing. Those same dreadful months, however, also saw the birth of a legend. To have 'done Verdun' became an accolade in the France of the inter-war years which no patriot could do other than respect. France herself, it was said as the legend developed, had 'done Verdun'. Individual memories of the hideous slaughter faded as the collective heroism was honoured. In time, too, legend developed into myth. Verdun was, the myth-makers asserted, a war within a war.

Whatever happened elsewhere, it stood for all that was French, noble and courageous, the true revelation of the Gallic spirit. As it happened, no one was a greater beneficiary of that particular myth than Philippe Pétain.

The city of Verdun stands astride the River Meuse as it gently wends its way northwards through the surrounding hills. The countryside around is still scarred with the remains of battle, but for the casual visitor the landscape beyond the site of the battle could easily be taken as one of gentle and almost nostalgic tranquillity. History, however, tells us otherwise. Like so much of eastern France, the quiet fields are, inch-deep below the surface, soaked in the blood of war.

As the Roman Verodunum, the city itself held the line against incursions from the east – most notably in the third century AD, when its defence was organised by that most redoubtable of Christian saints and the city's subsequent patron, Saint Vanne. It fell to Attila's Huns after the collapse of the Roman Empire, was reclaimed by the Frankish king Clovis in AD 502, only to be signed away again by Louis the Pious in AD 843. For seven hundred years thereafter it remained the fiefdom of German bishops, until reclaimed again for France by Henry II in 1552. In 1792 the city was unwise enough to open its gates to the Prussians – a weakness rewarded by the mass execution of its inhabitants by the Revolutionary Army a few months later. Thereafter, for a large part of the nineteenth century the place remained unusually tranquil, concentrating with worthy attention on the production of sweets and rope – and on the distillation of liqueurs.

The tranquillity could not last. Nor did it. In September 1870 the Prussians invaded again, laying siege to the city and bombarding it on three fearsome occasions. After courageous but hopeless defence, it surrendered once more in November. Returned to France under the Treaty of Frankfurt in 1871, the city then found itself once more at the centre of French military attention. What had been a small fortress built by Louis XIV's architect Vauban became the hinge of a great line of powerful forts designed to rule out for ever a future German invasion.

The new line was built by the sapper general Séré de Rivière, on plans laid down by the Ministry of War in Paris – temptingly leaving a gap through which German armies could march only, so went the plan, to be encircled and destroyed by French counter-attack. It was at

Verdun that the line of forts was at its strongest. Verdun thus became the lynch-pin of the whole massive line. Around the city there were sixteen major and some twenty smaller constructions in a protective ring fifty kilometres in perimeter. The names of those forts, to those who remember, echo down the years – Douaumont, Vaux, Souville, Moulainville, Tavannes, Belrupt, Rozellier, Houdainville – like some melancholy roll-call. Even today, the sight of their ruins is a gloomy reminder of the tragedy they witnessed.

The stabilisation of the western front in the autumn of 1914 left Verdun tactically vulnerable. The forts on the eastern, or right, bank of the Meuse had been enough to deter a further German advance there, while the movement of the French 1st Army to defend the western, or left, bank had secured a front some twenty kilometres to the west of the city. A salient was formed, digging in to the German front. Throughout 1915 the salient had held, not least because there was no sustained German attack. The front in that sector was known to the French as 'quiet'. In fact, it was only towards the end of the year that German planners, fearing a Franco-British assault to the north-west along the line of the River Somme, thought about attacking Verdun.

All salients are weak points in a front. The accepted way to attack a salient is to move against both flanks simultaneously with the intention of cutting off the defending army and forcing its capitulation. The salients at Ypres and Arras had been attacked in this way – unsuccessfully, as it happened. But the Verdun salient was flatter in shape. Sealing off its neck would have been difficult. The German planners took the view that the best chance of success lay in an assault at the top of the salient, along the front due north of the city. The assault would be in force, and would be concentrated on the most direct route to the city along the right bank.

There was much detailed planning to be done. But the planners needed to know the strategic aim. In fact, in spite of all that has been written about Verdun – and is still being written – the German intentions remain obscure. At the end of the war, Graf Erich von Falkenhayn, who had replaced Moltke as German Commander-in-Chief after the Marne, published in his memoirs the text of a draft memorandum written, he claimed, in December 1915. The memorandum purports to set out in detail the strategy of a static battle around a place which, for reasons of prestige, the French would be bound to defend to the last man. 'If they do so,' the memorandum goes on, 'the forces of France will bleed to death.'[1]

Whether the memorandum ever existed at all in December 1915 is now a matter of doubt. What is not in doubt, however, is that it was the Kaiser himself who approved the assault on Verdun in mid-December 1915 and who, after the success of the first assault, went himself to the front line in order to view – through a heavily protected periscope – the fall of the city. Furthermore, one of Falkenhayn's most trusted generals, Schmidt von Knobelsdorf, who had been appointed to keep an eye on the Crown Prince Wilhelm – the heir to the Kaiser's throne and the commander of the German 5th Army which was to lead the assault – not only gave the news to the Crown Prince himself but, as the Crown Prince's Chief of Staff, drafted the orders to the Army 'to capture the fortress of Verdun'. In the normal run of things, those orders must have been approved by Falkenhayn, in spite of his previous directive to the 5th Army, which only mentioned 'an offensive in the direction of Verdun'.[2]

There was thus strategic confusion at the start. Indeed, when all this was relayed to the Crown Prince Rupprecht of Bavaria – in his own right a general of distinction – he could only write in his diary the comment that Falkenhayn 'was not clear what he really wanted . . . and was waiting for a stroke of luck that would lead to a favourable solution. He wanted a decision in the spring, while declaring a breakthrough impossible, but how else should the change from the war of position to the war of movement be achieved?'[3] That was probably the truth of it. In other words, it was a question of 'either' or perhaps 'or'.[4] Knowing the fickle nature of his master, Falkenhayn was hedging all his bets.

From this uncertain strategic start the German tactical build-up during January 1916 was efficient and massive. Engineers built ten new railway lines across the marshy Plain of Woevre to the east of the city. Some 1,200 guns were brought up, ranging from the huge 380mm Krupp naval guns down to the 77mm field pieces, which were to continue their battle for supremacy with the French 75s. Two and a half million shells, it is said, were delivered in more than a thousand trainloads. The Crown Prince's army was reinforced to the point where it boasted seventy-two battalions – some four hundred thousand men, the best trained and most experienced in the German Army. To ensure surprise, the German sappers burrowed into the earth to build large concrete *Stollen* (dug-outs) in which the infantry could be concealed up until the moment of assault. Finally, no fewer than 168 aircraft were assembled, not just for reconnaissance but, for the first time ever, in support of a ground attack. The build-up was indeed impressive, and the operational planning was faultless. The problem, and perhaps the Achilles heel of the whole enterprise, was that smaller ventures on the battlefield of individual initiative and audacity fitted uneasily into the overall scheme of things. The planned juggernaut rolled on regardless.

Opposite them the French defences were notably weak. On Joffre's orders in 1914–15, the forts had been largely denuded of guns, which were transferred to other parts of the front. At the time there had been sense in this. Joffre was a gunner. He knew all about the inferiority of the French artillery, particularly in heavy pieces of over 75mm calibre. (In fact, the heavy guns were not just taken from Verdun. Forts at Toul and Epinal were stripped as well.) Moreover, enthusiasm for a defensive line of forts had gone out of fashion. Since the front had been quiet for a number of months the French trenches had been badly maintained, and the third line was almost non-existent. As it happened, this was pointed out by one of the many deputies in the National Assembly who had signed up for service and who, much to Joffre's displeasure, reported what he saw directly to his fellow politicians in Paris. True, as the leaks of the German movements became more frequent and more threatening, a battalion of engineers was sent to shore up some of the trenchwork, but beyond that little was done. Joffre's mind, and that of his staff, remained concentrated on preparations for the spring offensive on the Somme.

Pétain's mind, on the other hand, was elsewhere. Nini had by that time returned to the charge. She had read of his promotion to three-star general in the newspapers and had written to congratulate him. At first, all went well, and in January there were assignations at the Buffet-Hôtel at the Gare du Nord where Pétain arrived on his train from Beauvais, the nearest main-line station to his quarters at Noailles. There was, however, an unpleasant fly in this otherwise clear ointment. In short, Pétain was jealous. It appears that after her divorce Nini had been rather freer with her favours than was appropriate –

there had been talk of various liaisons, not only with army officers but, it was reported, even one with a salesman of heating appliances. This would obviously not do. Pétain insisted that he was too proud to accept anything other than monopoly rights. In order to make his feelings perfectly clear, he added a postscript to his letter to her of 11 February 1916 in tone much more like the one he used with fellow officers, or politicians, than the one customary with ladies of high standing. 'Your writing paper', the brutal postscript went, 'has the same smell as the suffocating gas used by the Germans. It reeks of chlorine.'[5]

Nini's reaction to this onslaught does her credit. She was not in the least deterred, and apparently gave her difficult general without delay the assurances he required. The path after that ran more smoothly. Nini was summoned to further assignations, usually to meet the Beauvais train at 4.45 p.m. by standing at the bottom of the staircase of the Buffet-Hôtel and waiting for him there. Pétain's letters became more enthusiastic. A letter dated 22 February, for instance, summoning Nini for the following Thursday, concludes: 'It seems a century since I saw you . . .'[6]

On the day before that letter, the first shots were fired in what was to become the Battle of Verdun. On the morning of 21 February, as overnight snow turned to early frost, the German heavy guns opened up. Their noise could be heard two hundred kilometres away in the hills of the Vosges. After three hours, their bombardment was supplemented by the medium and light artillery, attacking directly the French positions on the Meuse right bank. Every metre seemed to be the object of specific attack. Within minutes the air had been turned grey with smoke, snow, earth and splinters of trees thrown into the air. If men were caught in the open they were torn apart. 'A great pile of earth,' ran one account, 'round, shaped like a pyramid with a hole gouged out all round. Sticking out of it, symmetrically, to a distance of about 40 centimetres, were legs, arms, hands and heads like the bloody cogs of some monstrous capstan.'[7]

It was a gruesome day. But worse was to come. Just as dusk was falling, patrols of German stormtroopers broke from their trenches, not in the customary waves but in small groups, zigzagging, crouching, running and then pausing, all to avoid the defensive fire. As though that were not difficult enough for the French defenders, dazed after a day of ferocious artillery assault, the attackers brought with them a terrible new weapon – the flamethrower. In the first attack, French defenders were burned to death as they stood. Others simply ran away in desperate fear.

There was, to be sure, much courageous resistance. At the Bois des Caures, manned by the same deputy who had complained about the French defences, Colonel Emile Driant, the German attack was held up for a crucial twenty-four hours. But whatever the courage shown by the French troops, the advantage always lay with the enemy. By the evening of 24 February the Germans had made their breakthrough. The way to Verdun was open.

The reaction to these events at the French headquarters, the Grand Quartier Général (GQG), at Chantilly was mixed. Joffre still seemed unconcerned; but that was his customary reaction to any crisis. De Castelnau, his deputy, was much more worried. With Joffre's agreement, and, as always, together with his nephew, who doubled as his personal father-confessor, he rushed to Verdun on the evening of 24 February. At breakfast time the following day they reached the city. From there, after suitable prayers, de Castelnau quickly went on a visit to the troops, such as they were, on the front line. He then returned to the regional headquarters, only to find chaos and panic. To stiffen everybody's backs, de Castelnau immediately issued an order that the defence of the Meuse had to be made on the right bank, 'cost what it may'.[8]

In one move, de Castelnau had made the defence of the right bank an imperative. Any idea, then or in the future, of a tactical retreat from the right bank to narrow the salient and preserve the integrity of the Meuse left bank – whatever a future commander might think – was thus ruled out. At the same time, however, de Castelnau urged Joffre to appoint Pétain, a general known to be prepared to countenance tactical retreats, to the overall command of French forces at Verdun. Even on the French side, there was strategic confusion.

Joffre, as always, wanted time to consider all this. He was not to be deprived of his usual prolonged nightly sleep. Nevertheless, before he finally went to bed, Joffre agreed that Pétain should be summoned to Chantilly. But there was a snag. Only half an hour after de Castelnau's call to Joffre, Pétain had told Serrigny that he was going off – again – from Noailles to Paris, and would not return before lunch the following day. Since there was nothing particularly pressing, Pétain did not tell Serrigny where he would be that night. In fact, it was his latest assignation with Nini for the evening – and night – of Thursday 24 February. The pair duly met at the bottom of the staircase of the Buffet-Hôtel, presumably had something to eat in a discreet establishment, and retired for the night to the Hôtel Terminus near the Gare du Nord.

In the event, it was hardly to be a night of languid and amorous calm. At around 10 o'clock that evening at Noailles, while Serrigny was playing a quiet hand of bridge in the officers' quarters, a telegram from Joffre was brought in. 'General Pétain', it read, 'should present himself at GQG Friday at 8 a.m. to be received by the Commander-in-Chief . . .'[9] At that point, there was in the officers' quarters a degree of panic. It was clear that this was a matter of urgency. It was not just a matter of summoning General Pétain. Staff officers had to be rounded up, told to get ready for a new assignment, cancel all social engagements, say goodbye to the horses and so on. The Quarter-master had to be told that the whole staff establishment would be on the move the following morning; the Transport Officer had to be told to provide transport for the General and his effects; the Mess Officer had to be told to ensure that the General's favourite wines were prop-erly packed up. In short, there was much to be done; and, as it was being done, word had it that they were destined for Verdun.

All that took some time. But the problem was: where was the General himself? Serrigny set off for Paris to find him, guessed – from previous experience – where he would be, and duly arrived at the Hôtel Terminus in the small hours of the morning of 25 February. At first, the owner of the hotel denied hotly that Pétain was in her hotel, but soon retracted when Serrigny told her that it was a matter of 'the safety of the country'. Serrigny then ran up to the room which she had pointed to, recognised a general's yellow boots sitting alongside two 'charming little, wholly feminine, "molière" shoes',[10] and knocked loudly on the door. Sure enough, Pétain emerged – in his nightshirt. A quick conference ensued. Pétain, once appraised of the situation, told Serrigny to find a bed somewhere in the hotel. They would leave together at seven o'clock that morning. This done, Pétain returned to Nini, told her that he was going to Verdun – whereupon she burst into tears – spent an apparently passionate remainder of the night with her, and left her, by all accounts somewhat drained, in the early morning.

Without any noticeable signs of exhaustion themselves, Pétain and

Serrigny arrived at Chantilly on time at 8 a.m. on 25 February. They found panic everywhere. It was said that the Germans had taken twenty to twenty-five thousand prisoners, that they had captured eight hundred guns, that Verdun was about to fall. A few minutes later Pétain was ushered in to Joffre's office. 'Well, Pétain,' Joffre said at once, 'you know things are not going badly at all.'[11] (They were, of course, going disastrously.) He went on to say that de Castelnau was on the spot with full powers to change the Verdun regional command. Pétain's 2nd Army, at present in reserve, should be made ready to shore up the defence of the city. Pétain himself should go forthwith to Bar-le-Duc, prepared to assume immediate command.

At ten o'clock, as instructed, Pétain set off. As it happened, the journey was far from easy. There was deep snow on the road and, although Pétain's car managed to get through, the staff cars behind him became bogged down. Pétain, in a letter to Nini several days later acknowledging the three letters he had received from her since 'we

With Joffre at Verdun. (*Keystone*)

left each other', wrote that the journey had been very unpleasant with 'five degrees of frost' but that 'I think of you a great deal and with infinite tenderness'.[12] Nevertheless, however much he thought of Nini during the journey, Pétain was still able to give his mind to the task ahead. In fact, Joffre's summons had not been unexpected, however inconvenient its timing. Pétain knew that he was the only senior general without a current active command, and that his army had been resting for three months since the abortive Champagne offensive. It made sense for Joffre to give him this command. There was, in truth, no one else.

Eventually, at least the important section of the party arrived at Châlons in the early afternoon – to find General Gouraud (apparently another of Nini's former lovers) with a message from de Castelnau telling them to make as quickly as possible for the château of Dugny, the headquarters of General Herr, the commander of the Fortified Region of Verdun. Gouraud, however, persuaded Pétain and his party to stay to lunch at Châlons. 'Since we had been without food since the early morning,' Serrigny sighed, 'and since love and other emotions generally serve to sharpen the appetite, the invitation of the Commander of the 4th Army was accepted with gratitude.'[13] Although the lunch was reasonably jovial – there was apparently much shared reminiscence of Nini, which Pétain gave no sign of resenting – Serrigny noticed that Pétain had developed a tic in his right eye. It was, he noted, a sure sign of worry.

Pétain was right to be worried. At four o'clock in the afternoon the party left Châlons. But they were soon held up. There were large and haphazard convoys on the road. Not only that, but the surface was frozen. Lorries were skidding, horses were sliding about and falling; passing became impossible. It took four frustrating hours to reach Dugny. Once there, they found 'a madhouse'.[14] Everybody seemed to be talking at once – de Castelnau, de Langle de Cary (the commander of the Centre Army Group), General Herr, as well as a gaggle of junior staff officers. Indeed, the news could hardly have been worse. The great fort at Douaumont had fallen without a shot being fired. Although they had been held up by initial fierce French resistance, the Germans had advanced eight kilometres – into open ground and only four kilometres from the last line of defence in front of the city itself.

De Castelnau insisted that Pétain take command at midnight.

Pétain wanted to wait. Most of his staff, he pointed out, would not arrive until the following day. De Castelnau would not budge. Finally, Pétain agreed, but as a parting shot he said to Serrigny, in a voice loud enough to be heard by others, 'in that case we will set ourselves up at Souilly where I hope we shall find a little bit more calm'.[15] This they did. But it was 11 p.m. before they reached Souilly, only to find that the house of the local notary, where Pétain was to stay, was freezing cold.

On the following morning, 26th February, Pétain woke with a high temperature and a bad cough. A doctor was summoned – and diagnosed double pneumonia. There was immediate and understandable consternation. News of Pétain's arrival had leaked out to the troops. His reputation as a careful commander had run before him. If he were now to die or be incapacitated the blow to the Army's morale would be disastrous. At all costs, the whole business must be kept under the strictest wraps. Pétain therefore spent the next five days confined to the notary's bedroom, issuing orders none the less to his staff officers, who in turn conveyed them to the soldiers in the field.

As Pétain subsequently wrote to Nini in his letter of 3 March – without reference to his illness – it was 'a hard task'.[16] Nevertheless, however hard the task, the tactical appraisal of the situation shows Pétain at his analytical best. He very quickly saw that there had to be a line of defence which must be held at all costs. He even got up from his bed to draw a line with a piece of charcoal on a map to instruct his generals precisely where their respective positions were to be. There were, he also ordered, to be three lines: a forward line, designed to blunt an enemy offensive but not to be held at all costs; a principal 'line of resistance', to be held come what may; and a third line, which would serve as a base from which counter-attacks would be launched. Secondly, he realised that since the Crown Prince Wilhelm had only attacked on the Meuse right bank, the field of battle was narrow. It was therefore all the more important that the French heavy artillery should be concentrated under central command, to be deployed and targeted at a moment's notice. Thirdly, he recognised that the army at Verdun would be slowly strangled if there were no quick solution to the problem of reinforcements and supplies of food and ammunition.

It was here that Pétain had a piece of luck. There was only one road – of inferior quality – leading from Bar-le-Duc into the Verdun

salient. The narrow-gauge railway, known as the 'Meusien', was of
limited use. It so happened that a member of Pétain's staff, a Major
Richard, had been in civil life an engineer in the maintenance of
bridges and roads. He turned out to be something of a genius. Pétain
faced him with the problem of how to convert this inferior road into
a road capable of carrying traffic the like of which it had never seen.
It was not, Pétain explained, just for reinforcements and provisions.
Soldiers could only stand so much at the front. Whole battalions,
even brigades, had been decimated. It was no good just putting new
troops into the line. The units themselves lost the collective will to
fight. There was, he said, to be a system of constant replacement – he
called it the 'millwheel' after the primitive mechanism for irrigation,
a chain of buckets attached to a wheel, dipped into a river, brought up,
emptied and sent down again. Whole units would be taken out of the
line and replaced by new units. They, in their turn, would in the
course of time be replaced by the old units, suitably, it was hoped,
refreshed.

Major Richard was up to the task. He discovered that the road
could be reinforced and widened to take two lanes of traffic by constantly digging out the limestone shale which lay on both sides of the
road, shovelling the pebbles on to the surface of the road, and relying
on the lorry traffic to act as steamroller to bed it down. Richard's idea
worked. Eight thousand territorials were put to work with shovels,
working in shifts day and night. More than a million tons of pebbles
were shovelled on to the road. Some three and a half thousand lorries
acted as daily steamrollers – one passing by every twenty-five seconds.
To be sure, many broke down, but they were simply pushed off the
road – spare parts, if required, were produced at factories which sprang
up almost overnight at each end of the road – soon to be baptised by
Maurice Barrès as the 'Sacred Route' (which soon became the more
euphonious 'Sacred Way').

By the first week of March it seemed that the 'line of resistance' had
held. The Kaiser had gone home, disappointed once more by the failure of his son and heir to take Verdun. In a mood of optimism,
Poincaré and Joffre visited the headquarters at Souilly to urge Pétain
to take the offensive. Pétain was unreceptive; official visits, even by the
President of the Republic, were a regrettable diversion from the
matter in hand. Yet again he was at his most abrupt. When Poincaré

told him that he assumed that Pétain would not be evacuating the right bank – which had always been at the back of his mind as a tactical retreat – Pétain replied brusquely: 'I do not know whether I will be obliged to abandon [the city of] Verdun, but if such a measure seemed to me necessary I would not hesitate to consider it.' Poincaré was quick in repartee. 'Don't even think of it,' he replied. 'It would be a Parliamentary catastrophe.'[17] It was hardly the most cordial of conversations.

Poincaré and Joffre might be optimistic, but Pétain knew that the position was far from stable. Certainly, Crown Prince Wilhelm had other thoughts in mind. On 6 March he attacked on the left bank, this time on a broad front. The French first line was quickly overrun but the 'line of resistance', along the ridges of Mort Homme and Hill 304 down to the hamlet of Avocourt, was not breached. Moreover, for the first time the German losses were this time as heavy as the French.

Yet throughout March the German attacks continued – at enormous cost to both sides. The assaults on Mort Homme and its neighbour Hill 304 were particularly expensive. In fact, day after day the pattern of battle was the same. At the beginning of an attack there was a crushing German bombardment. This was followed by patrols of stormtroopers running out from their trenches to find gaps in the French lines. They were in turn followed by a full infantry charge across the broken ground. There was then a confused mêlée, with soldiers hiding randomly in shell holes and fighting in groups at close contact with grenades. Once the German advance was seen to falter the French in turn launched a heavy artillery barrage and then counter-attacked with infantry. For the most part, the ground which had been captured by the Germans in the morning was recaptured by the French in the afternoon. In fact, in this grisly warfare there was only one consolation: the German flamethrowers, which had proved such a horrifyingly effective weapon at the start of the battle, had been neutralised. The French had discovered that the canisters of fuel which were carried on the back 'turned their bearers into writhing torches'[18] when hit by a rifle bullet or shrapnel from a shell.

It is hardly surprising that morale on both sides was by the end of March beginning to crack. There were, for instance, reports of

German soldiers refusing to charge, and of French soldiers surrendering too easily. In fact, it seems to have been one such incident which lost the French the strategic point of Avocourt Wood together with a whole brigade of nearly three thousand men. Nevertheless, by the end of March the German pressure was starting to tell. Gradually their front moved closer to the city. The little hamlets, or what was left of them, fell one by one: Malancourt, Haucourt, Bethincourt.

It was getting close. On 9 April the Germans launched yet another offensive, this time on both the left and right banks. Mort Homme was taken after desperately heavy fighting. The 'line of resistance' was broken. Pétain felt it necessary to issue an order to his troops to bolster their morale: '*Courage! On les aura!*' ('Courage! We'll have them!')[19] Fortunately, the French guns on Hill 304 had exacted such a heavy price that successive French counter-attacks during the following ten days finally won Mort Homme back. All the initial German gains made in the early-April offensive were lost again in a fortnight. Mercifully, on 22 April it started to pour with rain. Carnage was, for the moment, suspended, and on 26 April Pétain, in the moment of calm, was able to celebrate – if that is the right word – his birthday.

By then, there was no doubt that the 'millwheel' was working as planned. A constant supply of reinforcements and munitions had been assured. Although the rations for the troops were meagre, at least they got through – thanks to the notably courageous ration-carriers dashing through the lines to avoid instant death. Water, too, was no longer a problem, thanks to the ingenuity of the French engineers in laying pipes. True, living conditions were still miserable, but by the end of April it seemed at last as though the German assault had finally been blunted and held.

For Pétain, this was a mixed blessing. While the position was critical he had Joffre's confidence. But he was starting to get on Joffre's nerves with his unceasing demands for troop reinforcements. By the end of April some forty French divisions – nearly half the entire French Army – had been on the 'millwheel' through the fire of Verdun. Yet Joffre was still concentrating on what he thought would be the decisive battle of the western front on the Somme. Moreover, Pétain was still in no mood to launch a sustained counter-offensive. In his view, the French successes, such as they were, did not constitute a platform from which a counter-attack could be launched. In other words, he was not ready. Joffre thought he was just being over-cautious.

As though all this was not irritating enough, Pétain was starting to get some unpleasantly favourable press limelight. When he was first posted to Verdun, the press searched in vain for a suitable photograph. None existed. It was not that Pétain had been particularly reluctant. Unlike Joffre, de Castelnau, de Langle de Cary or Foch, he was simply not a public figure. By the end of March, however, the press had taken an intense interest in this hitherto unknown general who was apparently performing such heroic feats at Verdun. Reverential articles – complete with illustrations – started to appear in the Paris press. This only served to annoy not just Joffre but the politicians in Paris, who tended to feel that the function of generals was to get on with the job and not to hog the limelight which was properly theirs.

Added to the general irritation was Poincaré's own personal annoyance. In fact, he had good reason. During March and April he paid several visits in his special train to Verdun. He thought that it would be good for morale – and certainly not bad for his own public image. On those occasions Pétain would be invited to dinner. The invitations were unwelcome, but he could not refuse. He therefore made it his business to be as rude as possible. During one such dinner, for instance, he told Poincaré crisply that proper co-ordination of the machinery of government could only be assured by a head of state acting as a dictator. When Poincaré raised the small matter of the Constitution Pétain replied, in the rudest possible manner, 'La Constitution, oh! Moi, je m'en fous' (perhaps translated in modern vernacular as 'Stuff the Constitution').[20] On another occasion, Poincaré asked whether he could sit in on one of Pétain's daily briefings of his senior commanders. Pétain grudgingly agreed. At the end of the session Pétain asked Poincaré whether he would like to say anything to his officers. Poincaré, unusually modest, declined the invitation, whereupon Pétain turned to his officers and said drily, 'The President of the Republic has nothing to say to you.'[21]

Pétain had thus succeeded in annoying both Poincaré and Joffre. But he was nevertheless fighting a successful defensive engagement at Verdun. Although he had started as a stop-gap, he had done all that had been asked of him. Admittedly, even in early March there were rumours that he would soon take over the command of the Centre Army Group 'when de Langle de Cary retired at the end of April'.[22] But for the moment that idea had been put aside. It was resurrected by no less a figure than the Prime Minister, Aristide Briand. His suggestion was that de Langle de Cary's command should be put in abeyance, for Pétain to take it up once he had finished the job at Verdun. That was not enough for Joffre. He wanted Pétain out of Verdun. In fact, he had in mind to promote General Robert Nivelle, one of Pétain's army corps commanders, to Pétain's job.

Nivelle was almost all that Pétain was not. For a start, he was adept at dealing with politicians. He was good-looking, cultured, sure of himself, silver-tongued and charming. He was also fluent in English, thanks to his mother, which endeared him to the British. Moreover, as an officer, although he subsequently chose the artillery for a career, he retained all the spirit of his alma mater, the cavalry school at Saumur. Again unlike Pétain, although he could smile winningly at politicians and was jollity itself in the officers' mess, he was stiff and overbearing to the infantry soldiers he commanded – and refused to look at the casualty lists. Like Foch, he believed that battles could be won by the sheer force of morale and will-power. Poincaré found him irresistible.

Nivelle at the time was commander of the 3rd Army Corps, and thus one of Pétain's subordinates. His closest ally was one of his own divisional generals, Charles Mangin. Mangin – not to put too fine a point on it – was a thug. He had spent most of his career in Africa, and his square, sunburned face showed it. As long ago as 1898 he had been on the expedition to Fashoda, and had worked his way up through the colonial army. He was competent, brave and exceptionally aggressive. 'Reckless of all lives and of none more than his own,' Winston Churchill was to write of him, 'charging at the head of his troops . . . Mangin beaten or triumphant, Mangin the Hero or Mangin the Butcher as he was alternately regarded, became on the anvil of Verdun the fiercest warrior figure of France.'[23] On the day he arrived at Verdun, 2 April, he had immediately flung himself into battle – with startling success. From then on he was always looking for opportunities to attack wherever he could find an enemy. He seemed, it was said, always to be charging at something.

On 19 April 1916 de Castelnau telephoned Pétain from GQG at Chantilly. De Langle de Cary was definitely going to retire at the end of the month, and Pétain was to replace him. The conversation was confirmed officially on 28 April. Pétain's 2nd Army was to be commanded by Nivelle but under the overall command of Pétain as commander of the Centre Army Group. Nivelle was to take over Pétain's headquarters at Souilly. Pétain was to move to Bar-le-Duc. Underlying the promotion, of course, was Joffre's intention that the day-to-day conduct of the Battle of Verdun would be left to Nivelle. Pétain left Souilly feeling, in the jargon of the day, that he had been 'sent to Limoges' – in other words sacked.

For Pétain it was an uncomfortable situation. Formally, he was still responsible for the 2nd Army at Verdun along with the three other armies in his group. But Nivelle, as the general commanding the 2nd Army, pulled all the immediate strings. To add to the discomfort, Pétain himself reported to Joffre. He was thus caught in the middle of a sandwich. Both Joffre and Nivelle were in favour of an immediate and decisive counter-attack at Verdun, while Pétain thought that the time was not yet ripe. Moreover, Joffre's eyes were still fixed on the Somme, where he expected the final breakthrough to be made. Pétain's eyes were still fixed on Verdun.

The result of these changes was that the 'millwheel' was halted on Joffre's own instruction. The 2nd Army were told to get on with the battle by themselves. But this was much easier said than done, as Nivelle soon found out. On 3 May the Germans took Hill 304 – the first breach of Pétain's 'line of resistance'. On 8 May a huge explosion inside the fort at Douaumont convinced Mangin that the fort itself was there for the taking, and on 13 May he launched his attack. But after ten days of slaughter the Germans fended it off. Moreover, by the end of May the German attack on the left bank had been successful to the point where the whole of Mort Homme had fallen.

From that platform, on 1 June the Crown Prince launched his own offensive. It was the largest in scale since the initial assault of late February. On 7 June Fort Vaux, the second most important strategic point after Douaumont, surrendered. The way was then open to Fort Souville and to the city of Verdun itself. Nivelle, in desperation, immediately called for reinforcements. Pétain supported him – and made daily visits to Souilly to keep in touch with a situation which was obviously becoming ever more dangerous. He telephoned Joffre to tell him bluntly that 'the situation at Verdun is very serious; unless there are immediate reinforcements I shall be obliged to evacuate the right bank'.[24] It was, of course, bluff; but it worked. Joffre immediately ordered a further four divisions to Verdun. Even if the Somme was to be deprived, Joffre knew that it would be a military and political catastrophe if Verdun fell.

In retrospect, it is clear that by 23 June 1916 the Battle of Verdun had reached its climax. The Germans had failed to break through to Verdun itself. Fort Souville had held. A gas attack with the new, more deadly, phosgene gas had created panic, but the French had a new gas mask and their field artillery – the 75s – was destroying the German assault troops as though they were rabbits running out of a corn field. And then, the following day, 24 June, there was distinctly heard a rumble, like distant thunder, to the north-west. Both the Germans and the French knew very well what it was. The British guns had started their massive barrage on the Somme. At that point both sides knew that Verdun was saved.

The battle itself, of course, dragged on – through the autumn of 1916 and into the winter. But the French grew in confidence as German morale collapsed. Falkenhayn was sacked. Crack German regiments were withdrawn for redeployment on the Somme. Pétain himself even found time to spend a weekend with Nini in Châlons. The new German Commander-in-Chief, Field Marshal Paul von Hindenburg, ordered all German attacks to cease. By mid-September Nini was permanently settled in Châlons, and Pétain was fighting off her allegations that he had been too heavily involved with a nurse in one of the Verdun hospitals – which, of course, he had been. In other words, life – at least to some extent – was returning to normal.

The French counter-offensive started on 19 October. It had been carefully planned by Nivelle and Mangin, and was decisive. By mid-December the battle was to all intents and purposes won. Nivelle rightly claimed the victory, and on the strength of it was appointed Commander-in-Chief in December 1916 – in succession to Joffre, who had lost his job after the failure of the Somme offensive. As for Pétain, he was understandably aggrieved at Nivelle's promotion over his head, but more important, in the story of his life, was the effect of those dreadful months.

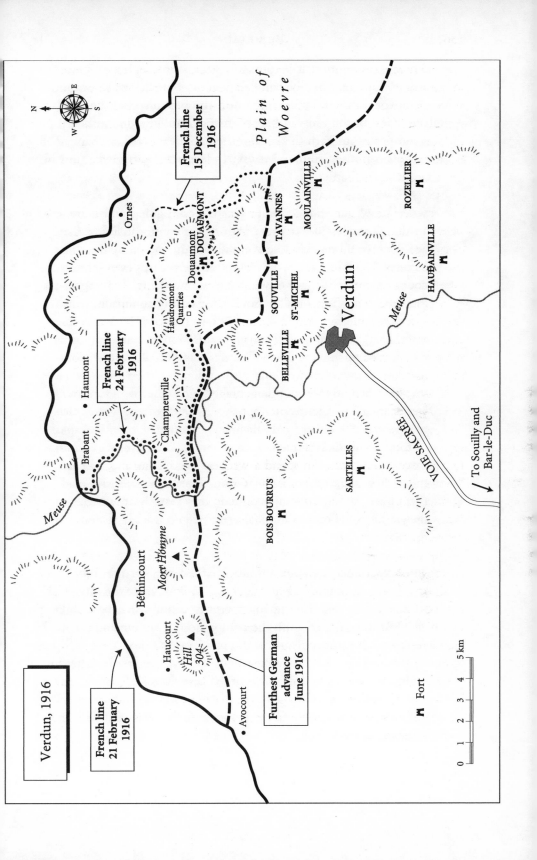

Verdun, 1916

French line
21 February
1916

French line
24 February
1916

French line
15 December
1916

Furthest German
advance June 1916

Plain of Woevre

N
E
W
S

Ornes

Haumont

Brabant

Champneuville

Haudromont
Quarries

Douaumont

DOUAUMONT

TAVANNES

SOUVILLE

ST-MICHEL

BELLEVILLE

MOULAINVILLE

ROZELLIER

HAUBAINVILLE

Verdun

Meuse

Meuse

Béthincourt

Mort Homme

Haucourt

Hill
304

Avocourt

BOIS BOURRUS

SARTELLES

VOIE SACRÉE

To Souilly and
Bar-le-Duc

Fort

0 1 2 3 4 5 km

There is no doubt that Verdun was decisive in changing his view of casualties. Up until then he had been – almost intellectually – cautious in the expenditure of human lives on the grounds that the military effectiveness of the units in his command would be diminished if he was too profligate with the lives of their soldiers. Verdun changed all that. Pétain himself summed it up. 'Indeed my heart bled', runs his account of the battle,

> when I saw our young twenty-year-old men going under fire at Verdun, knowing as I did that with the impressionability of their age they would quickly lose the enthusiasm aroused by their first battle and sink into the apathy of suffering, perhaps even into discouragement, in the face of such a task as was theirs. As I stood on the steps of the Town Hall of Souilly, my post of command, which was excellently situated at the crossing of the roads leading to the front, I singled them out for my most affectionate consideration as they moved up into the line with their units. Huddled into uncomfortable trucks, or bowed under the weight of their packs when they marched on foot, they encouraged each other with songs and banter to appear indifferent. But the discouragement with which they returned! – either singly, maimed or wounded, or in the ranks of their companies thinned by their losses. Their eyes stared into space as if transfixed by a vision of terror. In their gait and their attitudes they betrayed utter exhaustion. Horrible memories made them quail. When I questioned them, they scarcely answered, and the jeering tones of the old *poilus* awakened no spark of response in them.[25]

The experience without a doubt marked him for life. None the less, he was too much a product of Saint-Cyr to be mawkish. 'Fortunately,' he told a writer on a visit to Souilly, 'I have a chilling mask.'[26] As it happened, both the compassion of Verdun and the mask were to be in evidence in the year which was to follow.

In truth, there was no 'Victor of Verdun'. The whole gruesome episode did not allow for a 'victor'. There were, of course, many heroes on both sides, and, if any group can be singled out, it should be the *poilus*, the rank and file of the French infantry. But even with them Verdun had taken its toll. As it happened, in the extremity of the hell

Stretcher bearers at Verdun. (*Photos12.com/Hachedê*)

Pétain saluting fresh troops. (*Harlingue/Rex Features*)

of battle there were those who started to wonder whether the whole game, in crude terms, was worth the candle. Indeed, many of them were soon to make their views felt. 'Victory' at Verdun was little compensation for the suffering of those ten months. None the less, Pétain emerged at the end of it – even though he had spent no more than two months out of ten in direct command of the battle – as the figure who would in the future be seen, in almost mythological terms, as the emblem of the French spirit which had kept the ordinary soldiers – the *poilus* – fighting with heroism to defend their homeland. The mythology, powerful as it was, carried Pétain through even to the end of his life. If there was in reality no 'Victor of Verdun', this did not prevent Pétain from being awarded the title. It need hardly be said that he showed no reluctance in accepting the palm. In fact, it was to stay with him – even in 1940 and after – both as a prop for his own ambition but, more important, as a mythic symbol of France's will to victory.

9

'THEY REFUSE TO ADVANCE TO BE BUTCHERED'

'On ne m'appelle que dans les catastrophes.'

'Pétain believes he is a great man; he says seriously that the Republic is afraid of him.'[1] Thus Pétain's fellow general, Fayolle, in January 1917. There was, in fact, some justification for Fayolle's otherwise rather caustic opinion. Pétain's reputation at Verdun had placed him firmly on the domestic – and, indeed, international – political map. Even the British press had taken notice, thanks to a series of laudatory articles written by the energetic military correspondent of the London *Times* and to the award in June 1916 of the Grand Cross of the Order of Saint Michael and Saint George. Moreover, there was a good deal of coming and going between Paris and Pétain's headquarters at Châlons – some of it more welcome than others. Clemenceau, for instance, was, unlike Poincaré, always welcome. In fact, when he arrived on 7 January to tell Pétain that the Briand government was losing support and had limited life expectancy Fayolle thought that the two were plotting something.

There were visits, too, from foreigners – American journalists, Italian generals, Spanish war correspondents, Belgian and Dutch liaison officers, and so on – who were interested in making contact with this new military phenomenon. Pétain, reasonably enough, was much pleased by the foreign attention, although he grumbled to Nini that they 'take my house for a hotel'.[2] The Paris press was another matter. He had certainly enjoyed the attention, but, as 1917 went on, what looked like a honeymoon at Verdun changed into divorce over the coverage of the mutinies of the summer.

Nini herself, much to Pétain's only too clearly expressed regret, had left her nursing post in Châlons (whatever in truth it might have been). She had not been well and disliked the cold winter. She was certainly not used to the temperatures of minus 10 degrees Celsius which Pétain regularly recorded during January, and preferred to remove herself to the south of France with her son Pierre. Pétain clearly missed her. At one point he even proposed to take a week off to spend with her in the warm south, but, in the event, his – admittedly improbable – project came to nothing. He also took care to behave himself, writing to her that he had been 'very good'[3] since she had left. He was, of course, tempted. Serrigny's daughter Chantal, by all accounts an attractive young lady, paid a visit of several days to Châlons with a friend. Pétain immediately whisked them both off on a tour of Reims. (Serrigny was much relieved when they returned, apparently without incident.) Then there were Mesdames Pierrat and Dussane of the Comédie Française who made frequent visits to entertain the troops. Pétain expressed a preference for Madame Dussane; he liked the way she sang patriotic songs, although he was much impressed by the splendour of Madame Pierrat's *Phèdre*. Whatever the preference, Pétain was attracted to both. Whether they, one or the other of them, resisted his attentions is conveniently not recorded.

Although life at Châlons during the winter of 1916–17, apart from these diversions, was relatively quiet – leaving aside the regular visits of German bombers – much was going on elsewhere. In November 1916 Joffre had planned an offensive for the spring of 1917, but it was a modest affair compared with the new plan of his successor Nivelle. Nivelle's strategy was forthright: it was to hit violently at the bulge in the German front line which had resulted from the Allied advances on the Somme. The British, the strategy went, were to attack the northern flank of the German salient at Arras and the French were to attack the southern flank at Soissons. After the German armies on both flanks had been broken a joint Allied reserve force would smash through the middle – and thereby end the whole war in a few days.

As such, and as an intellectual exercise, Nivelle's strategy was perfectly sensible. The German salient was exposed, and therefore vulnerable to attack. The British Army, in spite of the heavy losses on the Somme, was growing in numbers. True, the French losses were taking their toll – the President of the Senate Army Commission, André Maginot, admitted that the 'problem is serious',[4] but Nivelle thought that he could make up for that by raising the morale of his troops. It was all a matter of inspiration, and Nivelle considered that he was admirably equipped to provide it.

Pétain did not share Nivelle's heroic optimism. The main French attack, he noted, would almost immediately run into the heavy defences and difficult terrain of the Chemin des Dames, a rugged and wooded ridge which runs from east to west to the north of, and parallel to, the River Aisne. In his view the French artillery would be unable to get close enough to hit the German second line. Pétain said as much to Nivelle when they reconnoitred the front of the planned attack on Christmas Day 1916. His alternative suggestion was to direct an attack towards the north-east with more limited ambitions. Nivelle's response was to tell General Fayolle openly that Pétain 'was not offensive enough',[5] to remove the 5th Army from Pétain's command, and to put the main French attack under the command of General Alfred Micheler – leaving Pétain with only a minor role in the whole affair.

In early January 1917 the Allied leaders, the British Prime Minister David Lloyd George, Briand and the Italian Premier Giovanni Borelli, met in Rome to discuss plans for the year. They agreed that there should be a joint Franco-British offensive on the western front, but they could not see how to avoid another Somme – which would be, for obvious political reasons, wholly unacceptable. But on his way back to England Lloyd George stopped in Paris, where he had a hurried conversation at the Gare du Nord with Nivelle. Nivelle, just before the train drew out, explained his plan, and it was plausible enough to convince Lloyd George that he should be invited to London to explain it in detail.

Nivelle's visit to London on 15 January was a great success. He explained to the British in perfect English that his plan was in essence simple: to mass enough artillery to break all the German lines at once – rather than concentrating only on one line at a time. That would be followed by a creeping barrage, behind which the infantry would advance, carefully avoiding any strong enemy positions that might slow them down. The whole thing, he went on, would be over with minimal casualties in a matter of hours. True, the British generals, when they heard the plan, were doubtful. What had worked on a small scale at Verdun, they thought, would not necessarily work on a larger stage. Lloyd George, however, not only overruled them but insisted that the British forces under Field Marshal Sir Douglas Haig be placed under Nivelle's command. Haig himself took this badly, to the point where he complained to King George V over the Prime Minister's head.

Whatever the intrinsic merits of Nivelle's strategy, the one crucial component for its success was the element of surprise. In the event, this was signally lacking. In his efforts to raise the fighting spirit of his troops, Nivelle allowed details of his plan to be circulated widely, and to lower ranks. Needless to say, at an early stage they fell into the hands of the German High Command. The German response was, in tactical terms, quite (there is no other word) brilliant. On 9 February Operation 'Alberich' was launched, named after the devious and wicked dwarf in Wagner's *Ring of the Nibelung*. The plan was to retreat to a line which would smooth out the bulge, in other words to eliminate the salient. Not only was this line to be well fortified but the territory which was to be vacated was to be rendered virtually uninhabitable. Bridges and roads were mined; booby traps were laid; all trees were cut down and the wood burned; houses were systematically blown up; dead animals lay everywhere, gorged on by rats – which grew to a truly terrifying size. By the time the actual withdrawal started, on 15 March, the gruesome work had been completed. There was almost nothing left for the French to occupy other than a burnt-out and barren desert.

When they heard of the German withdrawal, most French officers in GQG – now in Beauvais where Nivelle had moved it from Chantilly – were elated. 'How far would they go? To the Meuse?'[6] To their surprise, however, the Operations Department, the 3rd Bureau as it was known, at first refused to believe the news of a German retreat. When, by mid-March, it was plain for all to see, Nivelle refused to accept the obvious logic of the event: if there was no salient there was no salient to attack. The whole basis of his strategy had been removed from under him. But instead of announcing that the attack was off, Nivelle defiantly insisted that the attack was on. It would be directed at the southern end of the German line – the Hindenburg Line as it was called, after the German Commander-in-Chief – and the connecting Chemin des Dames.

By that time, politicians in Paris had started to worry. The Briand government, as Clemenceau predicted to Pétain, had on 19 March given way to a government headed by the eighty-year-old, somewhat ramshackle and heavily bearded Alexandre Ribot. He was hardly a figure to inspire wartime confidence, but, more to the point, his Council of Ministers included the Radical Socialist Louis Malvy, generally regarded as the creature of the most prominent pacifist of the day, and a former premier, Joseph Caillaux. But from Pétain's point of view there was one significant appointment: the new Minister of War was to be Paul Painlevé.

Painlevé was far from being a professional or even a skilled politician. At an early stage in his life he had attained some considerable distinction as a mathematician. It was perhaps something of a surprise to him that he found himself, at the age of fifty-three, projected into the position of Minister of War. Moreover, his physical characteristics did not, on the face of it, suit him for the job. He was short in stature, with a 'square head and face built around a nose rather like a turned up thumb',[7] and a voice that sounded, as was remarked at the time, like a strangulated contralto. He was not an obvious person to confront the great generals of the French Army.

Nevertheless, he was there. Not only was he there, but he was a Pétain supporter. He had had occasion to meet Pétain in the spring of 1916 when he filled the post of Minister of Inventions. As such, he had become interested in the development of the tank as an instrument to break the deadlock of the trenches. He had visited Pétain at Souilly and found a ready interlocutor. In fact, Painlevé seems to have been the one politician to whom Pétain was not insufferably rude. It therefore comes as little surprise that Painlevé, as the new Minister of War, wished to consult Pétain about Nivelle's plans. It equally comes as no surprise that Pétain, when consulted, told Painlevé that in his view they were nonsensical.

On 1 April 1917 Painlevé went to Châlons to spend an afternoon with Pétain. Pétain told Painlevé firmly that all idea of a 'breakthrough' was no more than wishful thinking. He recognised Nivelle's point that the war must be won in 1917 because the French Army could not hold out for another year, but he argued that a series of limited offensive operations would sustain morale without risking the whole Army on what was, after all, one throw of a rather doubtful dice. On the following evening Pétain and Franchet d'Esperey, by then a general and commander of the Group of Armies of the North, dined with Painlevé in Paris and gave him the same message. Painlevé reported all this to the new Premier, Alexandre Ribot, who passed it on to President Poincaré.

By then the row was escalating. On 3 April Nivelle was summoned to Paris to explain to ministers how he responded to the objections of Pétain and Franchet d'Esperey (and Micheler). He was, understandably, furious. His subordinates had, in his view, used their connections with politicians to undermine their superior general. In a speech brimming with confidence he assured Painlevé and his ministerial colleagues that this was not to be another Somme, that he had a perfectly clear and workable plan which would lead to a 'breakthrough' in forty-eight hours. Not content with that, he strode to a map which was hanging in the minister's office and, with a sweep of the hand, pointed to the large swathe of territory which his lightning offensive would recapture. As a rhetorical performance it was most impressive. Even Painlevé himself was almost convinced.

Nevertheless, in spite of Nivelle's rhetorical success, Painlevé still persisted. At a meeting of French ministers on 5 April he explained his objections. Moreover, in his explanation he introduced another factor into an already difficult equation. It had become clear, he pointed out, that the United States, having resolutely maintained its status as a non-belligerent until then, was so offended by the loss of its innocent citizens to torpedo attacks by German submarines that it was about to declare war on Germany. The whole balance of forces would thereby be changed, not only because of American industrial strength but, much more important, because of the reserve of manpower which America could mobilise to reinforce the severely depleted French Army. There seemed to be no reason, he argued, why French manpower should be wasted on a doubtful offensive when American reinforcements were not far away.

Painlevé's argument was enough to persuade Poincaré to call a conference for 6 April of all the main figures in the drama, soldiers as well as politicians, British as well as French, to be held in the presidential train at Compiègne, which was now, after Operation Alberich, out of the range of the heavy German guns and to which Nivelle had moved GQG. It was an impressive array of the most senior French politicians and generals, although it was noted that the British only fielded generals, and that politicians seemed to be excluded. The atmosphere at the meeting was apparently 'very strained and gloomy'.[8] Poincaré reproached Painlevé for asking the opinions of subordinate generals behind the back of the Commander-in-Chief. Painlevé countered by complaining that Nivelle had been talking to foreign governments without reference to him. Pétain 'was quite impassive, presenting an exterior of ice as he always did on formal occasions', while Ribot looked detached, 'looking like a great, beaked, stooping bird, scanning with mild interest the tops of his colleagues' heads'.[9]

There was then, it appears, a good deal of shouting. The generals present were asked to give their opinion on the proposed offensive. When it came to Pétain's turn, he gave it emphatically but in his customary low voice. Nivelle interrupted him constantly, shouting at him so much that he was unable to finish his speech. As soon as he paused, waiting for the chance to continue, Nivelle proclaimed loudly that since he was in agreement neither with the government nor with his subordinates the only course open to him was to resign. With that, he stood up and made to leave the train.

At that point there was general clamour. Everybody stood up. Poincaré, Ribot and Painlevé tried to calm Nivelle down. It was unthinkable, they all said, that a commander-in-chief should resign on the eve of an offensive. There was then a long pause in the meeting while the clamour subsided and Nivelle returned to his seat. When they had all sat down again, Poincaré did his best to sum up. What he said is even now not entirely clear. He seems to have wobbled between stating that the offensive should be limited in scope and saying that it really was a matter for the military to decide what to do. At all events, his summing up was ambiguous enough to allow Nivelle to interpret it as sanctioning his original plan. In fact, it was all irrelevant anyway. The Nivelle plan could not be changed. The French artillery had already received its orders for the opening barrage.

As it turned out, the whole thing was a fiasco. To start with, the weather was appalling. On the eve of the assault there was rain and sleet, which persisted through the night. The troops of General Mangin's 6th Army, due to lead the assault, already numb with cold struggled to their positions through the mud. The noise of the barrage made sleep impossible, with the result that when the whistles blew for attack at six on the morning of 16 April, the original enthusiasm for the battle had collapsed. It was then discovered that the creeping artillery barrage had moved forward too fast. The infantry were cru-elly exposed to the German machine-gunners who had time to come out of their dug-outs. Furthermore, the French guns had not suc-ceeded in destroying all the German barbed wire.

By then the artillery commanders had no idea where the infantry were. Some believed that the infantry had not yet left their trenches, and ordered their barrage to be brought back to the starting point. The soldiers in front were treated to the horrific spectacle of their own barrage gradually coming back to rain shells on them. But that was not the end of it. French aircraft had lost control of the air to the Germans. One German pilot even managed to fly low and machine-gun a field hospital.

All was then confusion. Early in the afternoon, Nivelle sent his tanks forward. Instead of being the key to victory, they proved cum-bersome and ineffective. They could only move at walking pace, were frequently bogged down in the mud or tipped into shell holes, and their armour was no protection against the armour-piercing bullets the Germans had invented, let alone the accurate German field artillery. Almost all the tanks were destroyed, and the infantry which followed them killed almost to a man.

Very soon thereafter the German counter-attack was launched. The forward French troops were halted – but the reserves kept on moving up behind them. The chaos from the subsequent telescoping of a large section of the French Army was unimaginable. Moreover, the French Army Medical Service, which had expected to receive no more than fifteen thousand wounded, found themselves quite unable to cope with the nearly ninety thousand needing drastic attention by the time night fell.

At the end of the dreadful day of 16 April 1917, the French had failed in all their objectives. Instead of breaking through to open ground beyond the Chemin des Dames, where the tanks would be able to operate effectively, the whole front had hardly moved.

Mangin's 6th Army was stalled. Micheler's 10th Army was piling up against them from behind. For the first time in the war, the morale of the *poilu* had collapsed. '[The wounded men] were not the men the nurses expected, were used to; mangled, but gallant and very courteous. These men were broken in spirit as well as in body; not a laugh among them, not a smile of greeting. They were discouraged as French wounded had never been discouraged before. "It's all up," they said, "we can't do it, we shall never do it."'[10]

For a few days, Nivelle tried to continue the offensive against the German positions on the Chemin des Dames. The battle meandered wearily on. Back at GQG Nivelle tried to blame Mangin for the failure – and then Micheler. But it was no good. They both knew, as did everybody else, that Nivelle's gamble had failed; and nobody knew that better than the *poilu* in the field.

On 16 April, the day of the attack, five soldiers and a corporal of the 151st Infantry Regiment had refused to go into battle. On 17 April, seventeen men of the 108th Infantry Regiment deserted their post. The *'crise d'indiscipline'*[11] had begun. But there was to be more – much more – to come. On the night of 21 April, troops of the 1st Colonial Division, one of Mangin's crack units, while being brought back from the front, started shouting 'Long live peace' and 'We have had enough of killing.'[12] On 18 April the survivors of the 2nd Battalion of the 18th Regiment of Infantry, which had been first into the attack on 16 April but had been broken apart by the German counter-attack, staggered into miserable billets just outside Soissons. They were told that they were going to another area of the front, the border with Alsace. But by 29 April the battalion had been reconstituted with other straggling survivors. They were then told that they were going back to their original position for a further assault on the German positions on the Chemin des Dames. This was the last straw.

The men of the 2nd Battalion went on the rampage. Their wine ration quickly drunk – as well as many other bottles which had been hoarded – they roamed around their quarters in drunken rage, shouting that they were fed up with the war and wanted no longer to have anything to do with it. By the time they had sobered up and were back to normal discipline the damage had been done. As they marched off yet again to the front, a few of their number were hauled out of the ranks – as suspected ringleaders – and arrested. After a trial with no more than what turned out to be uncertain evidence five men were summarily shot.

Word, of course, quickly spread around the other units on Nivelle's front line. Moreover, Nivelle himself was being called to account. Someone had to take responsibility for the fiasco, and although Nivelle tried again to put the blame on Mangin and Micheler they were not standing for it – and openly said as much. As it happened, on 27 April Nivelle had arrived in Châlons to see Pétain, whose instructions to his 4th Army on an attack to the north-east – avoiding the Chemin des Dames – had been only for a very limited offensive. Nivelle started by reproaching Pétain for his caution, but ended up by offering him a job as his Chief of Staff. Pétain, not unnaturally, refused.

Two days later, on the day the men of the 2nd Battalion went on the rampage, Pétain was summoned to Paris to see Premier Ribot. Nini was told, in a letter of 28 April, that it was possible that he would be in Paris the following day, but was 'unlikely to be able to have dinner with you'.[13] Nevertheless, she was summoned to an after-dinner rendezvous at the Buffet-Hôtel. The following day the message became more urgent. He would now be staying at the Continental Hotel (Room 222), and would she please turn up in his room some time after 10 p.m.

Pétain duly met Ribot on 29 April. Ribot told him that the government had decided to revive an old office – Chief of the Army General Staff, in other words immediate adviser to the Minister of War – which had been dormant for many years. It was a way, Ribot pointed out, of dislodging Nivelle without admitting that the offensive had been a disastrous failure. Furthermore, it was widely believed that any Pétain appointment to the highest levels of military command, unless carefully orchestrated, would meet with the greatest resistance. Even the suggested appointment, Ribot further pointed out, would be widely resented.

So it was. The British, particularly Lieutenant-General Sir Henry Wilson, head of the British Mission to GQG, objected on the grounds that a Pétain appointment would mark a diminished French interest in any offensive. The politicians in Paris objected that Pétain was now so widely known for his dislike of politicians in general, and of President Poincaré in particular, that he would be a threat to the Constitution.

Maginot, a former infantry sergeant who had lost his leg earlier in the war at Verdun, apparently threw his crutch on the table in disgust at the prospect when it was mentioned at a meeting of the Senate Army Commission.

But in the end Painlevé had his way. He threatened to resign if Pétain was not appointed to the post he wished. On 30 April, therefore, the *Journal Officiel* published an exchange of correspondence between Painlevé and Poincaré in which the latter, presumably with gritted teeth, gave his assent. The British noted the reaction of the Parisian press, which came out on Pétain's side – although the British Ambassador commented, perhaps rather oddly, that 'the fact of his being a practising Catholic causes him to be "persona grata" in conservative circles'.[14] The Military Attaché in the British Embassy added, in a telegram to General Sir William Robertson, the Chief of the Imperial General Staff in London, that 'this arrangement is only provisional and after a short time a mission abroad will be invented for General Nivelle'.[15]

There is in fact no evidence, apart from the British Ambassador's comment, that Pétain had resumed his devotion to the Catholic faith. He was much more interested in Nini – although custom at the time had it that devotion to the one did not at all exclude devotion to the other. Nevertheless, the fact that Nivelle was a Protestant and that his fellow generals, de Castelnau, Franchet d'Esperey, Micheler and others, were devout Catholics may well have led Pétain to resume regular observance. It would have been, after all, the sensible thing to do.

Be that as it may, Pétain moved into his new office, a magnificent affair decorated in the full pomp of the Second Empire, on 1 May 1917. Since the office of Chief of the Army General Staff had been in abeyance for such a long time, nobody was quite sure what the holder of the office was meant to do other than give general advice to the Minister of War. But on 3 May Painlevé received a document from Pétain setting out his views on his new duties. The Chief of the Army General Staff, the document proclaimed, would be the delegate of the War Committee (of the Council of Ministers). He would take command of the Allied armies on the Franco-British (western) front and in the Balkans. He would 'ensure the co-ordination of those operations with that of allied armies in other theatres'.[16] In other words, Pétain was saying that he would run the war.

Painlevé lost no time in cutting Pétain down to size. The Chief of the Army General Staff was to be subordinate to the Minister of War and no more than a technical adviser to the government. He was not to be in direct command of anything. Serrigny put Painlevé's reaction down to indecision, but the truth is that it was a notable example of decisiveness. Whatever Pétain thought of his own ability, which by then, of course, was a great deal, he certainly was not going to be allowed to run the war – even if the British would let him. He was to be technical adviser, and that was that.

Even so, there was much to be done. On 4 May Lloyd George, accompanied by Robertson, Haig and Admiral Jellicoe, arrived in Paris with their respective staffs for a conference about the future conduct of the war. On the French side were Ribot, Painlevé, Nivelle, Pétain and Vice Admiral Le Bon. The Italian and Russian governments were represented by their ambassadors in Paris, the Marchese Salvago Raggi and Mr Iswolski. The discussions, after the failure of the Nivelle offensive, were never going to be easy, nor were they. Nevertheless, Pétain, at a meeting of the military on the morning of 4 May, managed to persuade the others that it was no longer realistic to mount an offensive designed to secure a 'breakthrough'. The French Army simply no longer had the men to do it. Even Haig, forever wishing to go on the offensive, agreed that the French would only attack 'vigorously to wear out and retain the enemy on their front'.[17]

This conclusion was relayed, as the unanimous conclusion of the Chiefs-of-Staff, in a memorandum submitted to the political leaders the same afternoon. The memorandum was read out loud by Robertson – and its conclusions agreed. The only worry which was expressed was by Lloyd George, who wished to continue offensive action towards the Belgian ports to stop their use by the Germans as bases for their submarine war in the Atlantic. This was agreed, but it was pointed out that the United States, now an active belligerent, had come to the aid of the anti-submarine campaign by putting its Atlantic fleet at the disposal of the Allies. It was also noted that America was even then sending over a detachment – admittedly small but nevertheless symbolic of its commitment – of the United States Army, which was due to land in Liverpool in a few weeks' time. 'Waiting for the Americans' was creeping on to the agenda of both Allies.

If the New World was coming to redress the balance of the Old, the very old world, in the shape of Russia, was in disarray. Such was the disaffection with the war that the Tsar had been compelled to abdicate and give way to a more populist government. In his first pronouncement to the Russian Duma the new leader, Alexander Kerenski, struck a reassuring note. He proclaimed to the Allies that Russia would continue to fight. But it was not to be as easy as that. True, one of the spokesmen of the new delegation of 'workers and soldiers of the front' dismissed fraternisation with the enemy, stating that 'the entire proletariat rejecting with indignation a separate peace, every soldier who concludes, so to speak, a separate peace with the Germans harms the whole cause of Russian democracy'.[18] Nevertheless, it was already clear that the tensions inside Russia made her future contribution to the war a matter of serious doubt.

The arrival of two Russian brigades on the western front brought with it first-hand accounts of the agitation in Russia. Equally, news of the impending arrival of the American saviours spread quickly to the French soldiers in the trenches. The conclusion, on the face of it, was simple. There was no cause for them to be hurled into battle to no purpose, when the Russians were giving up and the Americans would soon be coming to take over the burden.

On 15 May 1917 Pétain replaced Nivelle as Commander-in-Chief of the Armies of the North and North East. The appointment came as no surprise, even to those who were 'unaware of the great antagonism existing between the two generals [Nivelle and Pétain] or of the struggle which has for some time been going on between the President of the Republic and the Minister for War on the subject of the High Command, M. Poincaré having done his utmost to retain General Nivelle and M. Painlevé insisting on his substitution by General Pétain'.[19] Pétain's appointment was supported both by Foch, who took over Pétain's position as Chief of Army General Staff – thus completing his rehabilitation after his failures on the Somme in the offensive of July 1916 – and by other generals, including – most important – de Castelnau. The Parisian press were all on Pétain's side, at least for the moment.

So it was that the peasant boy rose to become Commander-in-Chief of a French Army of more than a million men. In that sense, it was a personal triumph. But there was no time for gloating, or, for that matter, even telling Nini. Pétain was much too busy. On 17 May he moved into GQG at Compiègne. As it happened, Nivelle was there out of courtesy, but at dinner that evening neither of them spoke and the party, such as it was, broke up early. Nivelle left in silence. Pétain then proceeded immediately to occupy Nivelle's room in the Compiègne palace – the room which apparently had previously been occupied by Marie Antoinette. He felt able to write to Nini on 21 May that he found his accommodation 'charming' but that in the previous four days he had seen 'so many different things'.[20] Of course, he went on to write that he saw her image at the end of every path in the garden, but this may be little more than lover's rhetoric. True, he tried to stop Serrigny commandeering a bust of the Empress Eugénie, but Serrigny fended him off with the jocular remark that there were too many women around him already. This was probably true, since there survive other letters which demonstrate that Pétain was far from faithful to Nini in the distribution of his favours, and that his favours were enthusiastically accepted by those on whom they were conferred.

Youth, as many will tell, is not everything in what are politely described as matters of the heart. There is no doubt that, even at the age of sixty-one, Pétain was still absorbingly attractive to women, particularly, of course, to those whose menfolk were away at the front. With the position of authority which he now had, Pétain looked – and sounded – the part of a successful and confident military commander. 'None approached nearer than he', wrote one of his staff officers in GQG, 'to what the Latins termed "Great Men".'[21] He was of above average height, had put on enough – but not too much – weight and was, the same officer continued, 'a majestic sight in his blue uniform'.

Leaving aside the distribution of his favours to his various female admirers, Pétain, as the new Commander-in-Chief on the western front, had two immediate tasks. The first was to get to know the British; the second was to deal with the indiscipline in the Army which by then was reaching alarming proportions. The British were certainly a problem. In Paris their Ambassador, Lord Bertie of Thame (known, because of his aggressive manner, as 'The Bull'), verged on eccentricity. He sported not just a white moustache but long and flowing white hair. Apart from his habit of riding around Paris in his state coach, he was remarkable in his capacity for telling a seemingly endless number of obscene jokes. He also disliked intensely his Military Attaché, Colonel Herman LeRoy-Lewis. It is not difficult to see why. LeRoy-Lewis was not only bad-tempered but also regarded Bertie as an old fool; he much preferred to report to Lord Esher, who lived in Paris but had no position at all – except that he had the ear of the King. Besides, LeRoy-Lewis lived in the Ritz Hotel with a French lady who was already married to a German. Lord Bertie thought that she was a spy.

For Pétain, this whole situation was made easier by the return to France in May of the by then Major Spears. Pétain had taken to him in 1914 and was certainly glad to see him back again. Spears was appointed in May as Liaison Officer reporting directly to the British War Office. As such, he had an office close to Pétain's in the Boulevard des Invalides. Just before he left for Compiègne on 17 May Pétain sent for Spears and told him that when he arrived there he did not expect to see General Wilson. Wilson was, explained Pétain, an intriguer, a supporter of Nivelle and too much involved with Foch. Spears, albeit with some reluctance, since Wilson, whatever his faults, was an officer much senior to him, duly complied with Pétain's request. Wilson, understandably, left the premises in a fury – and became a Pétain enemy.

Pétain's first contact as Commander-in-Chief with his opposite number in the British Army, by then acclaimed as Field Marshal Sir Douglas Haig, was in a visit paid to Haig at Amiens on 18 May. Their meeting was held in a salon in the rue Gloriette, where, Serrigny noted, 'I had danced . . . many times as a lieutenant at Amiens'.[22] It was cordial, although Pétain could not help noting that General Wilson had appeared again – at Haig's right hand. None the less, Pétain made what he thought would be a friendly gesture by offering to put six French divisions at Haig's disposal for his proposed offensive in Flanders.

Haig was, as always towards the French, patronising. He found, as he recorded, Pétain 'businesslike, knowledgeable and brief of speech . . . a rare quality in Frenchmen',[23] but he received Pétain's offer well. Haig, although he admitted that he read French much better than he spoke it – or indeed English, since he was notoriously inarticulate in speech – expressed gratitude. Yet Serrigny noted that the British were deeply suspicious. Pétain's reputation as a cautious military commander had gone before him. Haig put the question: 'Will you take the offensive?'[24] The question was repeated. The minute of the meeting puts it more politely. On receipt of Pétain's proposals for four separate but limited attacks, Haig 'saw no objection to the proposals, which were workable provided that there was determination and goodwill on the part of all concerned'.[25] But Wilson, much the sharper of the two, pointed out that Pétain's commitment to the offensive was 'suspiciously vague'.[26]

Pétain was indeed evasive, for two good reasons: first, he did not believe that hurling live bodies at barbed wire and machine guns was a sensible way to proceed; and, second, he knew perfectly well that the troops in his command would not obey orders to do so. What he was unwilling to do, of course, was to explain to his patronising British allies that a substantial part of the French Army was in a state of disarray.

During the second week of May there had been further sporadic outbreaks of protest, amounting to mutiny, among the infantry divisions lined up along the front of the Chemin des Dames and the reserve divisions who were soon to go up – yet again – to the trenches. The protests, as Pétain fully understood, were nothing to do with hopes about America or despair about Russia. The real problem lay in the way the men of the line infantry were treated. Their trenches were little more than rivers of mud, urine and excrement. Their food was cold and maggot-ridden; their 'rest areas' behind the front were squalid and rat-infested; the army medical service could not cope with the diseases, let alone the wounded; they were expected to go into battle at short notice with no clear idea what they were fighting about – only that they would be lucky if they survived. Above all, they were infuriated at being denied their proper entitlement to home leave.

Superimposed on discontent with his dreadful life in the trenches and high-handed treatment by the French High Command, the hitherto unprotesting, and suffering, *poilu* was encouraged to protest by the knowledge that there was growing disenchantment with the war throughout France. Even the severe censorship of press and post was unable to disguise the fact that the failure of the Nivelle offensive had demoralised not just the Army but the civilian population as well. In fact, the two went together. If the civil population was supportive the

Army would do its job; if morale in the Army collapsed, the collapse quickly spread to the civil population. And this is what had happened. There were strikes in major industries and defeatist talk in Paris. The British were scathing in their comments about the 'jelly fish who just now sit in the French Ministries'.[27] The soldiers at the front wanted to know what was going on at home – but the arrangements for leave were at best uncertain and at worst random, and in any event cancellable at short notice. This was the grievance around which all other grievances coalesced. The men simply wanted to go home. Furthermore, those at home wanted to have them back.

By 20 May 1917 it was clear that there was something near what can only be described as a general mutiny in the French armies along the line of the Chemin des Dames. General Maistre, the new commander of the 6th Army, postponed an attack because 'we risk having the men refuse to leave the trenches'. When he asked for fresh troops, Franchet d'Esperey promised five divisions but added, 'they are in a state of wretched morale'.[28] On 20 May as well a group of soldiers from the 128th Infantry Regiment, when told that they were yet again destined for the front, marched in the streets. On 26 May four battalions of the 158th Infantry Division refused to accept orders to go to the front. Troops stormed railway stations demanding trains to take them home. Even when they arrived in Paris soldiers on leave proceeded to wreck the railway stations and insult those Parisians who had been unwise enough to greet them on their return from the front.

Nothing can be worse, as Serrigny remarked, than to take command of an army only to find that it is disappearing under your feet. Pétain was precisely in this situation. Although the common view of the rebels was that they would defend their trenches against an enemy attack – but would not go on the attack themselves – and although the Germans seemed to have no perception of the state of French morale, it was immediately clear that Pétain had to assert the authority of command or disappear in inglorious defeat. There was, in truth, a challenge which could not be ducked.

His first act was to issue a formal Directive. It was addressed to the generals commanding the three army groups and nine armies, and one army corps. The language was terse and to the point. The balance of forces on the front of the north and north-east did not allow, for the moment, for a breakthrough. Efforts should therefore be directed to wearing down the enemy with the minimum of losses. 'To secure such attrition', the Directive went on, 'it is wholly unnecessary to mount huge attacks with distant objectives.'[29] In the future, attacks would have limited objectives, be conducted with maximum artillery support, make use of surprise, cover different sectors of the front and follow each other rapidly so as to deny to the enemy his freedom of action.

It was all quite revolutionary – and also extremely sensible. It recognised the extent of the losses that the French Army had suffered since the beginning of the war and the need to economise on future losses to allow time for the build-up of American troop numbers. It also recognised one of the grievances of the rebel soldiers. All along the Chemin des Dames front the fruitless attacks came to a halt.

Nevertheless, the Directive was only a preliminary statement of principle. As the situation became more volatile, direct action was necessary. First, Pétain set out to reform GQG. The Nivelle supporters were sent packing. Alcohol in the Mess was strictly limited. Officers only spoke when they were spoken to – meals often passing in silence unless Pétain himself thought he would tell an anecdote from his military past. He himself stayed up late in the evening, reading military history or the plays of Corneille – or writing to Nini. High living in GHQ was no longer on the agenda.

Then there were the men. On 23 May Pétain wrote to Nini that he was 'going away for several days. Don't worry if you hear nothing from me . . .'[30] He was concentrating on the problem at hand. There was no time for frivolities, however attractive they might be. First of all, leave arrangements had to be improved. GQG issued an instruction that seven days' leave must be granted every four months without exception. The number of trains for those going on leave was increased. Reception facilities at the Paris terminals were overhauled, and the French Red Cross were asked to set up canteens for arriving soldiers.

But all this took time to set up, and in the meantime the virus was spreading. From 25 May to 10 June there were eruptions in almost every unit along the line of the Chemin des Dames. Furthermore, the eruptions of indiscipline were taking on a much more sinister form. In short, what could hitherto possibly be described as 'military strikes', in the sense of simple refusal to obey orders, had become what can reasonably be described as 'mutinies', in the sense of taking over direct leadership of military units. The protests of May, which were largely about the conditions under which soldiers were required to live, assumed in early June clear overtones of social revolution. 'Down with the War!' 'Throw down your arms!' were slogans heard more and more frequently as the mutineers gained confidence in their numbers. Whole companies were disappearing into the forests. By the time of the emergency Cabinet meeting on Sunday 3 June it was glumly noted in the Ministry of War that between Paris and the front of Chemin des Dames there were only two divisions which could be 'absolutely and wholly relied on'.[31]

Pétain noted all this in a memorandum he sent to Painlevé on 29 May. He was clear in his view that there were factors within his control, such as the living conditions of the troops and the problem of postponed leave. But there were also factors outside his control. He was particularly severe on the Parisian press, even suggesting that they might have deliberately set out to destroy the morale of the Army, and on politicians from the National Assembly who sowed discontent and reported back in the most pessimistic terms. In other words, it was up to the government to deal with the factors outside his control.

Yet Pétain was still not prepared to come clean with the British. On 27 May he repeated his promise to Haig to provide six divisions for a British-led Flanders offensive, but by then the British were becoming aware that someting was badly wrong. Spears, in particular, was reporting to London that the situation in the French Army was much more serious than they let on, and by the end of May Haig was convinced – vaingloriously, as it turned out – that the British would have to win the war on their own. His view was reinforced when General Debeney, Pétain's Chief of Staff, was sent by Pétain on 2 June to explain in a rather roundabout way that a French offensive – one of four that had been promised only a fortnight earlier – was to be postponed. Spears, in his further reports over the next few days, emphasised that now the situation 'in Paris and France is serious'.[32] This was duly reported to the British War Cabinet. Pétain himself went to see Haig on 7 June, admitted that some recalcitrants had been shot, but left the impression that the troubles were confined to two divisions only. He clearly was not prepared to tell Haig the whole truth. Indeed, he admitted as much to Haig after the end of the war.

Apart from what he did or did not tell the British, Pétain had a domestic political problem. In order to suppress the mutinies a proper and efficient system of justice was essential. After the Dreyfus affair the old system of courts martial had been replaced by a system of *conseils de guerre*. This allowed any soldier convicted of a crime to appeal to a civil court and, in the case of the imposition of the death penalty, to appeal directly to the President of the Republic. That was all very well, but the system obviously would not work when it was necessary to deal quickly with major collective events such as mutinies. Pétain saw this clearly and, stretching his legal powers to the limit, on 1 June gave the armies in his command the authority to summon *conseils de guerre* without reference to a higher command. Painlevé – who throughout the whole affair was to be much more lenient than Pétain – noted the action, but urged caution.

That done, on 5 June Pétain issued another Directive – to all offi-cers. Inertia, it said, is equivalent to complicity. But it was only on 9 June that he got what he really wanted: an order from Painlevé abol-ishing the right of review of sentences in cases of 'collective disobedience'. At that point, on 11 June, he felt able to send out a ferocious message to the commanders of army groups and armies that 'all officers, from the commander of a platoon to the commander of an army corps, must have the same sense of duty. It is necessary that all realise that they must exercise their responsibilities or else they will themselves be brought before *conseils de guerre*.'[33]

On 15 June Pétain felt able to move even more directly. 'For some days now,' he wrote to Nini that evening, 'I have been less anguished by the national morale. If I manage to bring things back to a proper state and if I apply myself as best I can, I will have rendered a consid-erable service to the public cause. I have much to do . . .'[34] Indeed he had. By the time calm was restored approximately forty thousand troops had been involved in episodes ranging from indiscipline to outright mutiny. Some fifty divisions were affected in one way or another, almost half the French Army. In all, 554 men were con-demned to death by *conseils de guerre*, of whom 49 were actually shot. Nearly 1,400 were sentenced to deportation and forced labour. Fierce as it was, it was part of the price Pétain was prepared to pay – not just to whip his army into shape but for the 'public cause', the restoration of civil morale.

By then, visible help was at hand. An American advance force had arrived at Liverpool on the morning of 8 June. It, and its general, John J. Pershing, was greeted with what can only be called hysterical enthusiasm. The Americans were, to a war-weary crowd, to be the saviours of all that was decent in the world – particularly the lives of British men still engaged in the seemingly endless battle. On their arrival in London, Pershing and his men were greeted by the great dignitaries of the realm led by no less a figure than King George V. 'It has always been my wish', the King intoned to the assembled company, 'that the great English speaking peoples unite in the pursuit of a great cause.' 'The Anglo-Saxon race', he went on, 'must save civilisation.'[35] (Nobody apparently remarked that King George V was of largely German blood and was born with the surname of Saxe-Coburg-Gotha.)

The Americans, still in their distinctive Boy Scout hats, were welcomed with equal enthusiasm when they arrived in Paris on 13 June. They marched up the Champs-Elysées singing their marching song,

Pétain and King George V, July 1917. (*IWM*)

'Over there! The boys are coming!', to a welcome which bordered on delirium. Flowers were flung at their feet by normally reserved Parisian ladies. The crowds were ecstatic. Again and again it was said that these new, healthy boys would win the war for us.

In practice, it was not to be quite like that. General Pershing, on the instructions of President Woodrow Wilson, was at pains to point out that his was only an advance party of an army that still had to be assembled. Such an assembly needed time. Although conscription had been well received – those who were chosen by the ballot considered themselves fortunate – the process of mobilising and training the manpower which the United States, in its new enthusiasm for the war, wanted to put on the ground in Europe would take time. Pershing, as a veteran of the 1898 hostilities with Spain over Cuba and the Philippines, knew what he was talking about. The United States had not fought a real war – as opposed to a colonial war – since their own Civil War. They had to learn how to do it. In the mean time, there was no question of United States troops serving under anything other than United States command.

On 16 June Pershing arrived at Compiègne to meet Pétain over lunch and to explain the American position. 'He has a kindly expression', Pershing noted, '[and] is most agreeable, but not especially talkative. His keen sense of humour became apparent from the jokes he told at the expense of some of his staff.'[36] What his staff thought of the jokes is, of course, not reported. Nor did Pershing reveal what Pétain had said to him about the condition of the French Army – or even if, as is more likely, he said nothing at all.

The following day Pétain set out on his travels. His programme was to visit, one by one, the units of his disaffected army. Almost every day thereafter he set out from Compiègne in his car to drive to one or another divisional headquarters. His day was always the same: discussion with senior commanders, an address to the troops – standing on a mound or on a tree stump – in which he reiterated, time after time, his strategy of holding ground with limited and well-prepared offensives until the French industrial base had been fully converted to build the machinery of modern warfare – guns, tanks and planes – and until the Americans arrived to give the Allies superiority in manpower. There was, he said, to be a reorganisation of the medical service, and a new decoration for troops in units which had been mentioned in

Pétain visiting soldiers, June 1917.

Orders of the Day more than four times. The troops' resting quarters would be cleaned up. As a speech it was perhaps not very eloquent. The Pétain of the time – or ever, in fact – was not a good public speaker. His delivery was too crisp and peremptory. Nevertheless, whatever its shortcomings in delivery, there is no doubt that his speech, repeated over and over again, hit the mark with the *poilus*. At least, they thought, they had one general on their side.

Pétain then turned to the junior officers. He was much less accommodating. In fact, he was inclined to harangue them. 'Look at these men,' he was apt to shout, 'all they need is an example. Advance and they will follow you.'[37] Needless to say, many officers resented this treatment. After one such lecture, a junior officer wrote in his diary: 'Is that the way to raise morale and to ask people to go out and fight? . . . Pétain has not shown himself a great leader, at the very least not human. There were so many ways to make us feel what he wanted – without saying it!'[38]

Nevertheless, the round of visits – perhaps to as many as ninety units – bore fruit. By mid-July outbreaks of indiscipline were on the wane. A violent German assault on the Chemin des Dames front was contained. The Army seemed to be convalescent. The 77th Infantry Division, for instance, had been mutinous throughout May and June, but the troublemakers had been weeded out, the division had been to one of the newly improved rest camps and was back in the trenches. On 19 July it not only survived a heavy German bombardment but was able to counter-attack and repel a fierce infantry offensive.

It was now time to demonstrate that the French Army was still a fighting force – that, with proper direction, it was as good as, if not better than, the German or British Armies. The six divisions which Pétain had promised Haig were collected under the command of one of Pétain's most trusted officers, General Anthoine, and were dispatched to Flanders to fill the gap to the south of the Belgian Army and to the north of the British. Haig was curmudgeonly: 'I am afraid that Anthoine and his Frenchmen will be a terrible drag until the enemy begin to fall back.'[39] In fact, Anthoine's operation was a spectacular success. His troops prepared thoroughly. They built some thirty kilometres of roads, laid eighty kilometres of rail track, set up three field hospitals, assembled large quantities of ammunition to service the nine hundred guns which were moved up to the front. The French barrage started on 15 July with heavy artillery followed by howitzers and trench mortars. By the time the infantry attacked, on 31 July, the German lines were a tangled mess. By the end of the day, the French had captured the German third line. On hearing that the Germans were moving in reinforcements Anthoine ordered his troops to dig in and hold what they had. In the assault, he had lost only 180 men. Haig was (reluctantly) impressed.

Three weeks later, on 20 August, the French went on the attack again, this time with eight divisions striking north of Verdun on both banks of the Meuse. The objectives were the forts which had been lost the year before and the heights of Mort Homme and Hill 304. Again the limited operation was a success. Once the objectives had been achieved and the infantry appeared to wish to advance beyond the range of the artillery, Pétain called a halt. French casualties were again low.

The third major action, the largest since the mutinies, was in October. General Maistre's 6th Army attacked on a twenty-kilometre front north of Soissons at Malmaison – precisely the area where Nivelle had failed so disastrously in April. There was a preparatory barrage lasting a full ten days before the infantry assault on 26 October. Again, the attack had limited objectives: to drive the Germans out of their positions along the Chemin des Dames. Again, the operation was a success, and Pétain ordered a halt to the attack on 1 November, once the Germans had been forced to retreat behind the River Ailette. General Pershing, who had been invited by Pétain to observe the event, was suitably impressed, and stopped off at Compiègne on his way back to congratulate Pétain in person.

It was by then time to start planning for 1918. But two events intervened. The first was the battle of Caporetto at which the Italian Army was broken, leaving a dangerous southern French flank. The second was the Bolshevik revolution in Russia which, on the assumption that the new Soviet government would conclude a separate peace with Germany, would allow the Germans to move troops from the eastern to the western front. It was in the light of these two events that Pétain put forward a draft plan to Haig.

It was what would now be called a working hypothesis. If Russia made a separate peace, the Germans might increase their forces on the western front by as much as fifty divisions – in which case the defensive security of the front would need reinforcing. On the other hand, if Russia stayed in the war, there could, and should, be a general offensive in the spring of 1918 by all the Allied forces, including the Americans. It followed that, if Russia pulled out, there should be only limited offensives with local objectives, until the time came, probably in the late summer, when there would be a more general offensive on a broader front.

It was quickly noted by Haig that Pétain's anxiety related only to the defensive security of the French line. Haig took the view that even if Russia pulled out 'the vigorous prosecution of our [British] offensive would still be not only possible but the wisest military policy'.[40] At that point, it was clear that a difference between Pétain and Haig was starting to open up. Pétain, in short, had been much affected by the 1916 experience of Verdun. Haig, on the other hand, seemed hardly to have been affected at all by the 1917 experience of Passchendaele.

Up to that point, the difference was only reflected in the tactical approach. Although Haig continued to mutter into his diary that the French were a broken reed – and that General Pershing had perceived as much, which, of course, was untrue – he felt able to write, on 17 December 1917, that he was 'much struck with the different bearing and attitude of the present Officers at GQG. The present ones seem much more simple, more natural than their predecessors, and are more frank in their dealings with the British. In fact, the relations between GQG and GHQ are better than I have ever known them.'[41] 1918, of course, would tell a different story.

10

WILL IT EVER END?

'L'armée française est ce qu'elle doit être, ce que je voulais qu'elle fût.'

The war dragged wearily on into its fourth year. But the war at the end of 1917 was very different from the war of 1914. For a start, the *dramatis personae* had changed. Russia had collapsed, to be replaced by the United States as an open belligerent. Austria-Hungary was suing for peace. Italy was only just holding a line on the River Piave and could no longer be considered a serious force. In short, Germany had won in the east and could now turn her attention to the west. All now turned on America. America, in the Allied view, was to provide the resources that would win the war for them. As it happened, the German High Command had arrived at the same view. One way or another, 1918 would be the decisive year. Either the Germans would destroy the British and French Armies in 1918 before the American forces could be fully deployed or the weight of American manpower would turn the tide against Germany and force her into surrender in 1919.

Nevertheless, whatever the change in the cast of belligerents, and whatever their forecast on the likely outcome of the war, nobody on either side of the western front had yet found the solution to the main military problem. The truth was that the stabilisation of the front in late 1914 had led to a new and unexpected form of warfare. It was discovered that the combination of the machine gun and barbed wire ruled the field. Offensives and counter-offensives came and went, but turned out to be little more than bursts of murderous fighting over narrow strips of territory. Even by the end of 1917 the problem had not changed. True, tanks were intermittently successful, and the deployment of artillery was becoming more efficient. But the lines on the western front, give or take a few kilometres, were more or less where they had been at the beginning of 1915. In truth, as 1917 drew to its close, it was difficult to see any solution other than a continued and wearisome battle of the trenches.

Just as the war had changed, so had Pétain. He had started the war as an unknown infantry officer, commanding no more than a brigade in the north of France. By mid-1917 he was Commander-in-Chief of the French Armies of the North and North East – in other words, of the whole western front. In 1914, he rode, and occasionally marched on foot, with his men while they were trudging south on the long retreat. He made a lonely figure, with almost no friends, usually dismissive of his superiors and caustic or morose – depending on the circumstances – with his equals and subordinates. In 1917, by contrast, he was living in the royal Palace of Compiègne, out of range of even the heaviest German artillery and with only the occasional inconvenience of visits from German bombers, with a comfortable Mess, an attendant staff, an official car – and regular visits to Paris (by train, of course) for assignations with his mistress. Furthermore, on the evidence he appears to have been actually liked, as well as admired, by his subordinates, and have developed at least a form of wit.

He had also changed his view of war. In 1914, like all his officer colleagues, he was a commander on the offensive. But the battles around Arras in 1915 had been enough to show him the futility of uncontrolled and ill-timed infantry attacks. The machine gun and the barbed wire would defeat them. He, unlike others, had then applied his accumulated military skill and experience to the problem. True, the solutions he developed were cautious, and were considered by most of his fellow generals to be 'pessimistic' – an epithet that was more and more used against him – but there were few who would stand up to deny their logic.

The successive years had brought with them another by-product of war. In 1915 and early 1916, the French civilian population still man- aged to live relatively normal lives, largely – it must be admitted – in

ignorance of what was being carried out in their name. But 1916 –
and Verdun – had brought with it a much greater civilian involvement. Almost every family in France by then had lost a son, a husband
or a brother. Many had seen their menfolk return from battle either
with grotesque physical wounds or, perhaps even worse, mentally
deranged. War could no longer be quietly ignored.

Furthermore, the balance between man and woman had changed.
For so long regarded as the guardians of house and home, and as
mothers of children, women were now on active service, as nurses at
the point of danger or, more prosaically, in munitions factories.
Whatever their task, women, in one way or another, became part of
the war. For the daughters of the respectable middle class the preferred
way of showing their allegiance was to volunteer for nursing duty, for
which, of course, there was always an unsatisfied demand.

One such was Eugénie Hardon. But after her experience as a nurse
in Châlons in 1916, Nini seems, like many others, to have been put
off front-line nursing by the injuries she witnessed there. Certainly,
there was no pressure from Pétain to persuade her to continue her
profession, such as it was, at or even near the front. There were, of
course, many other places behind the line where help with convales-
cents was required. Nini may well have helped there from time to
time. But, whatever her nursing career after 1916, she seemed to be
able to drift about France – apparently waiting, as always, for a summons from her lover general. The letters which Pétain wrote to her
during the winter of 1917–18, for instance, carry various addresses,
many in the south while she was spending her time with her son
Pierre. Others could labour, or expose themselves to the same danger
as their men. Nini's main patriotic task, it seems, was to give physical
succour, when required, to the Commander-in-Chief.

The war was also coming ever closer to home. By the second half
of 1917, German Zeppelins and Gotha bombers could reach Paris or
London to unload their own form of destruction. British and French
planes could in turn reach the Ruhr. Whistles announcing an air raid
became a common event in London and Paris. Shelters were manu-
factured on the spur of the moment to cope with the resulting panic.
In London, bugles announced the end of an air raid. In Paris it was
another blast of whistles. Such was the danger that Pétain was constantly advising Nini that she should not return from the south to

Paris, whatever they both might wish. It was too dangerous. She should stay away.

Civilians were also subjected to intensive propaganda in a way unimaginable in the war of 1914. By the beginning of 1918 all sides had learned the techniques of psychological warfare, of the use of grotesque images of enemy sins to stiffen the resolve of their people and to undermine the enemy's morale. The relatively courteous war of 1914 had become a ferocious and uncompromising struggle to the death. The press itself, indeed, became a weapon of war. Also, as might be expected in what was perceived to be a great cause, God was invoked by all sides – German soldiers had GOTT MIT UNS carved into the buckle of their belts while English bishops pronounced, from pulpit after pulpit, that theirs was a just war. In short, the whole of Europe was beginning to learn the meaning of 'Total War'.

Pétain fully understood the necessity for all this, and, indeed, played his part. As far as the press went, he was certainly alive to its importance. In fact, one of his first acts after his arrival at Compiègne was to give an interview to Henri Simond of the *Echo de Paris*, on the grounds that 'the Press must prepare the country for the truth as to the duration of the war and the efforts still to be made'.[1] (As it happened, the interview was not a great success – Simond did not feel that Pétain was enthusiastic enough about the prospect of victory.)

Be all that as it may, as far as God was concerned, Pétain was at a distinct disadvantage compared with his fellow, heavily Catholic, generals such as Foch, de Castelnau, Franchet d'Esperey or Fayolle, or even his devout British Protestant counterpart Field Marshal Haig. They all seemed to believe that men killed in battle would go immediately to a heavenly Valhalla as martyrs in a just cause. Pétain's agnosticism did not allow him to see them as such. To him they were just festering corpses hanging on the barbed wire.

Such was the dispiriting nature of the conflict that it comes as little surprise to learn that by then all the participants, in one way or another, were becoming tired of it. Soviet Russia signed a humiliating armistice in December 1917. There were tentative suggestions in the west – and in Germany – that it might be time to call it a day. In London, the Marquess of Lansdowne, a senior Conservative, advocated a negotiated peace. In Paris, the National Assembly held secret debates on the failure of the Nivelle offensive and the need for peace. Even ministers were involved in furtive conspiracies against their own governments.

Heads of government, on the other hand, continued to talk war. Clemenceau, at the age of seventy-six, became Premier and Minister of War in November 1917 with a promise of 'war – nothing but war'.[2] On 5 January 1918 Lloyd George set out the British war aims to trade unionists who might have been seduced into following Soviet Russia into peace. He was soon followed by President Wilson's Fourteen Points, set out in an address to the United States Congress (Clemenceau commented acidly that God had required only ten). But in spite of all this bravado many senior figures in all countries continued to whisper peace in private and discussions in the drawing rooms of London, Paris and Berlin were all about a possible armistice.

The problem was that nobody seemed to have a clear idea how to achieve it. In truth, the difficulty of devising a peace strategy was that it was no longer a matter of rational judgement. By then it had become a matter of the prestige of all belligerent governments. The war in Germany had always been a political event – the Kaiser in control. That had not always been true in France or Britain. But as a result of the bloodshed on the Somme in 1916 and the Nivelle fiasco of 1917, governments in both France and Britain had demanded greater control over military operations. The United States, on its entry into the war, also insisted on the same political control. Gone were the days when the French Commander-in-Chief could act, as Joffre had acted, almost independently of government. Indeed, not only did both Lloyd George and Clemenceau – and to some extent President Woodrow Wilson – follow events daily but the three governments went further. At a conference in Rapallo on 5 November 1917 they decided to create a co-ordinating unit for the western front, to be known as the Supreme War Council, to which the military were little more than advisers. (The ubiquitous Spears was to be its master of ceremonies.)

None of this, it need hardly be said, was to Pétain's taste. The creation of the Council in itself brought with it increased political interference in what Pétain regarded as purely military matters. It was already enough that he had had to defend himself against attacks from politicians who thought that he was being too cautious, even to the point where, at a meeting on 18 December in Paris with an aggressive group of senators, he lost patience – and offered to resign. Fortunately for him, both Poincaré and Clemenceau hurried to his support, and his offer was not accepted.

But Pétain saw a further menace in the Council. Foch, rather than he, was invited to become its French military representative. Foch declined, since he wanted to stay as Chief of the General Staff, but he managed to put his deputy, General Maxime Weygand, in his place. Pétain suspected, rightly as it happened, that Foch was using the post as a stepping stone towards a higher appointment as Allied Commander-in-Chief. Furthermore, he had no time for – and took a personal dislike to – Weygand, who had never commanded troops in battle and who had risen to his present rank by simply climbing up the general staff ladder. Although Pétain did not object in principle to there being an Allied commander-in-chief (in fact, he had himself earlier suggested it) he clearly thought that he rather than Foch should get the job.

Pétain took this view not just out of distrust of Foch or dislike of Weygand. It was because he had complete confidence in his military policy, and had retained it in spite of the buffetings it had received. It was, indeed, clear, simple and straightforward. There was to be no major spring offensive in 1918. Soviet Russia's acceptance of peace would allow the transfer of troops from the east to the west. A German spring offensive was therefore confidently expected. This was to be resisted by a strategy of defence combined with limited tactical offensives where appropriate. The overall objective was to contain the Germans until the American Expeditionary Force was strong enough to participate fully in a final strategic offensive. To contain the Germans, of course, the French Army had to be up to the task, in a high state of morale and with enough tanks, aircraft and artillery to be able to face the German onslaught with confidence. This was the task Pétain set himself in the winter of 1917–18. It was a task that he accomplished with diligence, method and, in the end, success.

Pétain's success in re-establishing the fighting spirit of the French Army and in re-equipping it was an achievement which ranks with his settling of the 1917 mutinies as a high point of his war. It has been little understood by British historians, who have tended to accept Haig's dismissive view that 'it is doubtful whether the French Army can now withstand for long, a resolute and continued offensive on the part of the enemy'.[3] (In fact, of course, it was the British Army which broke in March 1918.) The newly restored state of morale is demonstrated by the regular studies which Pétain commissioned. These noted that in October 1917 it was 'good' in 71% of units, a figure which rose to 85% in November, 84% in December and 83% in January 1918. These figures are not necessarily wholly accurate – the techniques for monitoring letters of other ranks (but not officers) from the front were hardly very sophisticated – but they do clearly indicate that the Army was again in reasonable spirits. The intake of 1918, further-more, were 'driven by the wish to do well' and the young soldiers had even 'cheerfulness and zest'.[4] In fact, morale in the Army was very much better than civilian morale, a point which Pétain was quick to note.

There was then the matter of equipment. First of all, Pétain gave attention to the artillery. By the end of 1917 French factories were turning out guns and munitions at a high rate, although, of course, slower than he hoped and had demanded. Heavy artillery was organ-ised half into a formidable general reserve which could be moved wherever most needed and half into divisional batteries. The same principle was used in the organisation of field pieces; speedy manoeu-vre was of the essence. Then there were the tanks. The Battle of Malmaison in October 1917 had shown that the lighter Schneider tanks were the most effective. Pétain asked for 3,500 of them (in practice, a quite unrealistic figure). After that came the aircraft. By January 1918 Bréguet and Hispano were producing more than four hundred fighters and nearly three hundred bombers a month. Pétain organised them, for the first time, into squadrons and gave them specific instructions on their tasks. Once more speedy transfer to the part of the front where they were most needed was to be the guiding principle.

Pétain's next concern was to make sure that all these forces were correctly deployed. On 22 December 1917 he issued Directive no. 4, setting out the principle of successful defence. The first line of defence, the Directive stated, should not be manned in force. There should only be enough troops to slow the enemy's advance. The second line, however, should be fully manned. It would be out of range of the enemy field artillery and therefore able to halt decisively the enemy advance. Reserves should then be used to attack the enemy in his flank as he went forward.

For no particular reason, since it was a sensible enough document, the Directive caused something near to uproar. The idea that a retreat from the front line, even if only for tactical reasons, was officially sanctioned by the Commander-in-Chief was, to generals trained in the doctrine of the offensive, wholly unacceptable. General Micheler even appealed to Poincaré on the matter. The upshot was that Pétain was obliged to visit all his army headquarters to explain and clarify what he was up to. But it was not by any means an easy ride. In fact, it was only eight days later that Foch made his views known to the military representatives at the Supreme War Council in Versailles. Without directly contradicting Pétain's directive Foch advocated 'powerful counter-offensives . . . prepared beforehand'.[5] Pétain, when he heard about it, was understandably irritated.

In the end Pétain got his way, thanks to Clemenceau's – perhaps unexpected – support. Strong defence was now official policy. The line of trenches on the French section of the front, particularly the stretch from Soissons to the Somme, was reinforced. Instead of relatively shallow trenches from which attacks could be launched, the 'second line' was constructed with deep trenches on the model of the trenches in the Hindenburg Line. To do this Pétain asked for, and obtained, no fewer than sixty thousand workers from Italy whose sole purpose was to dig. (Haig was very envious of this success. He asked Pétain if he could let him have up to twenty-six thousand of them – which Pétain agreed to – and requested another sixty thousand from Italy, a request which was politely refused by the Italian government.)

Pétain's efforts, however, were under constant attack throughout the winter as, indeed, was Pétain himself. Mangin, who been sacked after the failure of the Nivelle offensive but who was reinstated as an army commander by Clemenceau, nursed a deep dislike of Pétain – and so informed anybody who cared to listen. Joffre, now in semi-retirement in his small house at Auteuil, lost no opportunity of explaining that Pétain's tactics were far too cautious. Micheler was not afraid to talk to ministers behind Pétain's back. Pétain, in turn, gave as good as he got, denigrating the efforts of his subordinate generals when they were slow to follow his instructions – General Duchêne, commander of the 6th Army, being a particular target.

If Pétain was under attack, so, at the time, was Haig. There were seemingly endless British ministerial visits to Haig's headquarters, each minister assuring Haig of undying support while taking pains to report back to London his criticism of the Commander-in-Chief. But there was at least some comfort. His relations with his generals were cordial as well as respectful. Indeed, the same is true of Haig's relations with Pétain, at least up until late March 1918. Their dialogue was always frank, but neither felt that the other was deceitful – unlike their view of their respective political masters. Moreover, the agreement on 17 December whereby the British took over another section of the French line was only achieved, admittedly after long negotiations, thanks to the good will existing between the two commanders-in-chief.

Apart from his travails with fellow generals, and the odd spat with politicians, Pétain's winter was relatively calm. He visited London in late December – where he flirted with the Duchess of Sutherland – and Belgium in early January – where he flirted with the Queen. But most important of all was his relationship with Nini. By then, it had taken on the air of permanence. His letters are still full of passion, but instead of requiring her to meet him in various seedy hotels he had rented an apartment in Paris in the Square de Latour-Maubourg. Assignations with Nini were therefore much more leisurely matters.

Yet the war went on. By the end of January 1918 preparations for the spring were well under way. The British had met their undertaking to take over more of the French line by moving Sir Hubert Gough's 5th Army into an area south-east of Péronne and extending as far as Soissons. Haig's assumption, mistaken as it turned out to be, was that this was to be a relatively quiet part of the front, since the 5th Army needed time for rest and training its reserves.

That done, on 31 January the Supreme War Council met at Versailles. It was not an easy meeting. Haig complained to Lloyd George that the shortage of men was hampering his operations. 'The problem seems to me', he confided to his diary, 'how to bring home to our Prime Minister's mind the seriousness of our present position and to cause him to call up more men while there is yet time to train them.'[6] Foch, too, reproached the British for not providing more troops, claiming, rightly, that France had called up many more classes than Britain and had trained more men in each class. Lloyd George attempted to demonstrate that resources were adequate and suggested a diversionary attack on Turkey, whereupon Clemenceau gave him 'a real good dressing-down'[7] – most of which Lloyd George, who did not understand French, was able to ignore.

There was, however, one conclusion of the meeting which was ominous for Pétain. It was proposed to constitute an Inter-Allied General Reserve, to be kept ready for deployment as and when needed at any part of the western front. At Lloyd George's suggestion, Foch was to be in charge of it. Haig was very much against the proposal, claiming that his relationship with Pétain was such that no co-ordinating body was necessary. In the event Haig and Pétain were allowed to run the whole project into the ground, which they proceeded to do. After a few weeks of bad-tempered discussion, Haig wrote firmly to the Supreme War Council that all his troops were fully occupied and that he was 'unable to comply with the suggestion'.[8] But Pétain had carefully noted that it was the British Prime Minister who had nominated Foch for the job.

The meeting at Versailles had come to another conclusion much more palatable to Pétain. Foch argued, just as he had at a meeting of the military commands at Compiègne a week earlier, that the way to halt a German offensive was to launch a powerful counter-offensive. He claimed that the pressure on Verdun in 1916 had been to a large extent relieved by the offensive on the Somme. Both Haig and Pétain disagreed, Haig on the grounds that his troops were exhausted and that he had no reserves, Pétain on the grounds that the situation in 1918 was quite different from 1916. In the end, they persuaded both Foch and the Council. It was decided to 'adopt a defensive attitude for the present'[9] – much to Pétain's satisfaction.

The carefully constructed alliance between Pétain and Haig did not end there. They had even made a pact to come to each other's assistance. Haig made the deal clear in his note to the Supreme War Council rejecting the whole notion of an Interallied General Reserve. 'In the event', runs the text, of the enemy making a sustained attack in great force on any of the Allied Armies on the Western front it might be necessary to despatch a considerable force to the assistance of the Army attacked . . . For such a purpose . . . I have arranged . . . with the Commander-in-Chief of the French Armies for all preparations to be made for the rapid despatch of a force from six to eight British divisions with a proportional amount of artillery and subsidiary services to his assistance. General Pétain has made similar arrangements for relief or intervention of French troops on the British front.[10]

The conclusion of the alliance with Haig was the last piece in Pétain's jigsaw to restore the French Army to fighting fitness. By the middle of March 1918 everything had been put in place. Army morale was high; there was a clear statement of purpose; both the political and military leadership were resolute; the French had no fewer than four thousand aircraft; the Schneider light tanks were performing well in exercises; and the Franco-British alliance was cemented. To be sure, there were still some shortages of equipment, and some of the divisions were still under strength, not least because General Pershing refused to allow American troops to fill the gaps in either the French or the British armies. There was, he maintained, on instructions from Washington, to be a self-standing American Expeditionary Force under United States command. Nevertheless, the general state of French military preparedness was of a standard that could not possibly have been predicted at the height of the mutinies nine months earlier. Moreover, Pétain could reasonably claim the credit for himself. The French Army, in short, was by then Pétain's Army. Furthermore, it was as ready as it could be to resist the impending German offensive – far readier, as it turned out, than the British.

On 19 March, in fact, Haig himself was prepared to throw in the towel. He told his visitors of the day, Winston Churchill, the Duke of Westminster and General Birch, that he was ready for peace. Churchill asked his views. 'I stated', he replied, 'that from the point of view of British interests alone, if the enemy will give the terms Lloyd George recently laid down, we ought to accept them at once; even some modification of our demands for Alsace Lorraine might be given way on.'[11] In an aside, he went on, in his customary vein of contempt for the French Army and its officers ('fat tavern keepers'),[12] to tell Churchill that Foch 'was in his dotage'.[13]

Haig certainly had a point about his own army, albeit much less of a point about Pétain's. He knew that a German offensive was coming. He knew that his whole army was tired. He knew that Gough's 5th Army was weak and badly organised. He knew that they could not hold out against the imminent German offensive without massive American reinforcements – which were not yet there. There was only one way out. Haig, whatever the subsequent bluster, had by March 1918 joined the peace party. He was also remarkably insouciant. Although a German offensive was expected at any time, on 20 March he wrote to his wife that he thought it better to postpone his visit to England from that week until the following week. Furthermore, although disappointed, he took the trouble to continue that 'the cook is making some soup for you, and I am arranging to send it by King's Messenger on Friday'.[14]

It was at first light on the following day, Thursday 21 March 1918, that General Erich Ludendorff, the commander of the German armies in the field, launched the long-awaited offensive. Just at the point where the British and French Armies met, along a line stretching from Péronne on the Somme to the north and Noyon on the Oise to the south – some seventy kilometres – seventy-six German divisions followed a barrage, lasting no more than five hours – from 4.40 a.m. to 9.40 a.m. – of high explosive, chlorine, phosgene and tear-gas shells. The surprise was complete – the Allies were used to a much longer artillery barrage to start an attack – and there was dense fog on that morning. Stormtroopers, assembled the night before in the greatest secrecy, burst through Gough's first line. By the end of the day, the German infantry in their wake had occupied Gough's second line. His 5th Army had lost over seven thousand killed and, much worse in terms of morale, twenty-one thousand surrendered to be taken prisoner. As a fighting force, the British 5th Army no longer existed.

Haig's reaction to the day is, even to this day, astonishing. In spite of authorising Gough to withdraw, he sent a message of congratulation to the 5th Army, just as it was disintegrating, on a 'highly creditable' result.[15] As it happened, however, Pétain knew better. Before Haig had even asked for help, he put three infantry divisions, a battalion of *chasseurs* and a regiment of heavy artillery on alert to move into the gap which was left by the virtual disintegration of the

British front. On the following day Haig made his request, and the French troops went immediately into battle. But it was too little, too late. The Germans had advanced further and had broken through the third and last British line. The British 3rd Army, under General Byng, was holding firm to the north, but a breach was opening up between the two armies.

On 23 March Pétain went to see Haig at his headquarters. Haig told him that, much to his surprise, he had learned that Gough and the remnants of the 5th Army had withdrawn behind the Somme. He asked Pétain to concentrate a French force of twenty divisions to protect Amiens. Pétain replied that he would do what he could to help, and in particular to keep the two armies in touch, but he expected the Germans to attack to the south along the line of the Chemin des Dames. He could not leave that front too weak, since a German breakthrough there would open the route to Paris. Haig spoke openly of a crisis.

At this point it was clear that both Haig and Pétain, in their different ways, had woken up fully, each to his own problem. Haig's problem was that he had never fought a defensive battle. The BEF of 1914 which had fought at Mons and the Marne no longer existed. Haig had been used to ordering his troops to attack. Neither he nor they were accustomed to defend. The absence of a clear plan to manage retreat led to the breakdown of communications. Whole units wandered about in confusion and men, not knowing what to do, simply dropped their rifles or left their guns and ran away or surrendered. That was what had happened to Gough's 5th Army.

Pétain, on the other hand, was the master of defence. But it is precisely because of this that he understood the true gravity of the situation in a way which Haig did not. If the line was broken, if his carefully constructed defensive strategy was overturned and the Germans had succeeded in rediscovering the war of movement, Pétain had no solution. There was nothing – no plan at all – to stop the Germans chasing the French and British armies, the one to Paris and the other all the way to the sea. Once a breakthrough had occurred, after all those years of static defence, nobody knew how to deal with it. In fact, it was precisely the danger of such a situation that had confronted Joffre and Sir John French in 1914. Then Joffre had accepted that in the event of a German breakthrough the British

were bound to protect the Channel ports and the French were bound
to protect Paris. Pétain saw this happening in front of him precisely
as Joffre had imagined. He had no answer. Nor, for that matter, did
Haig.

Later that day, Pétain explained the full gravity of the situation to
Clemenceau, who was dining at Compiègne with his chief adviser,
General Henri Mordacq. The danger, Pétain told him, was that the
way to Paris was open and that Paris itself could not be defended.
They were joined by Fayolle, who made the same point. On the way
back to Paris Clemenceau remarked to Mordacq that after an interview like that one needed an iron-bound spirit to maintain
confidence.

On the 24th Haig and Pétain met again. Haig noted that Pétain
looked badly shaken, and so he was. The Germans had crossed the
Somme south of Péronne. Pétain told Haig that all available French
reserves were in battle, that further reserves were coming by rail, lorry
or on foot from around Reims and Belfort – distances of 150 to 250
kilometres – to be assembled under the overall command of General
Fayolle. He said that he was doing all he could. He had issued an order
to Fayolle that his reserve force should not be detached from the rest
of the Army, and that, if possible, the liaison with the British should
be maintained. But he was still worried about weakening his front
along the Chemin des Dames, where he expected a German attack at
any time.

That simply fanned the flames. Pétain was acknowledging that
the two armies might be separated. At that point, and in something
of a panic, Haig signalled London for help. The two armies must
not be separated. French morale, he thought, needed stiffening. Furthermore, he had finally come round to the view that there should be
a supreme Allied commander. He asked Wilson and Lord Milner, the
British War Minister, to come immediately to France 'to arrange that
General Foch, or some other determined General who would fight,
should be given supreme control of the operations in France'.[16] The
'some other general' was obviously not to be Pétain. Apart from the
by now clear breakdown in the relationship between the two men,
to have allowed Pétain to become supreme commander over his head
would have been an admission by Haig that he had been defeated in
battle and was in consequence being demoted.

That evening Clemenceau and Mordacq arrived again for dinner at Compiègne. Pétain was at his most gloomy – he was suffering from a recurrence of the influenza which had made him so ill in February and about which he had moaned to Nini. Moreover, it was far from a quiet evening. The German attack had made it necessary to move GQG to the little, and hitherto sleepy, town of Provins, and lorries full of files were churning up the mud around the palace. German bombs were falling at regular intervals on the railway station and the nearby crossroads. In the middle of this noise Pétain told Clemenceau that, although he now had command of the vital part of the front, including the remnants of the British 5th Army, the British 3rd Army were retreating northward. Since he could not give orders to Haig, the situation was not one which he could control. Moreover, his greatest concern was that the Germans were planning a second attack in Champagne.

As soon as Clemenceau and Mordacq had left, however, Pétain's mood improved. He immediately ordered an air strike by all available aircraft on the German divisions preparing to move into the gap left by the disintegration of the British 5th Army. On the following morning, 25 March, Fayolle found Pétain 'calm. There is a gap generally between Nesle and Péronne. But it is not finished. Although the road to Paris is open, the enemy will have to pass between the English and us . . .'[17] But by the time Clemenceau returned to Compiègne at about midday, this time with Poincaré, Foch and Lord Milner, Pétain had descended again into gloom. He claimed that he had no more reserves, that the British 5th Army no longer existed and that Haig was fighting a losing battle. In fact, gloomy or not, there was much truth in what he said. Indeed, by the end of the day the German advance had reached a point thirty-three kilometres from the initial line of attack. Clemenceau and Milner, after a long private talk, agreed on another conference, this time to include Haig and Wilson, to be held at Doullens.

At 11 a.m. on 26 March a convoy of official black cars rumbled into the narrow streets of the small town of Doullens. Clemenceau, Mordacq, Foch and Weygand had arrived. Poincaré was missing – his driver had lost his way in Amiens. Haig and his generals, Plumer, Horne and Byng, had already arrived and were discussing the military situation in a room on the first floor of the little *hôtel de ville*, where

Wilson soon joined them. Poincaré finally arrived, but while they were waiting for him Pétain explained to the others as they walked in the garden that Haig would soon have to capitulate and he would be very lucky not to be forced to do the same. Foch retorted furiously that Pétain had already given up the fight but that he, Foch, would fight to the bitter end.

The conference itself was under way by a quarter to one. It was immediately agreed that the key railway centre of Amiens must be held at all costs. If the Germans took Amiens the British would have to run for the Channel ports and the French would have to fall back towards Paris. The war would then in practice have been lost. Clemenceau asked Haig what he intended to do. Haig replied that he would hold the territory north of the River Somme, but that the area south of the Somme should be a matter for the French – he had already put his 5th Army under Pétain's command. Pétain intervened to reiterate that the 5th Army no longer existed, and went on to compare the whole British Army with the Italian Army at Caporetto. Foch could hardly contain his anger; Wilson kept on interrupting with snide remarks. Pétain said that he had already sent twenty-four divisions into the Amiens area, and turned the question back to Haig: what would he do? Haig replied that he had no more men fit to go into the line. The meeting fell into ominous silence.

There were then several whispered conversations in the corner of the room: Clemenceau and Milner; Milner, Wilson and Haig; Clemenceau and Foch, then Pétain. The meeting reconvened. Clemenceau then played his hand with the greatest skill. He announced that it was agreed to make a stand in front of Amiens with a joint Franco-British force. He went on to allow Milner to propose that Foch should be appointed to co-ordinate the operation. As Clemenceau hoped, Haig immediately saw the flaw in this proposal. Foch would be responsible to Pétain and himself. Haig considered it vital that Foch should control Pétain. He therefore recommended at once that 'Foch should co-ordinate the action of all the Allied Armies on the Western front'.[18] The meeting agreed to this with a sense of relief, and promptly broke up for lunch. Haig had sandwiches out of his lunchbox. Clemenceau and his French colleagues crossed the street to lunch at the Hôtel des Quatre Fils Aymon. As they sat down,

Clemenceau turned to Foch and said: 'Well, you've got the job you so much wanted.'[19] Foch was not amused.

By nightfall on 26 March the German advance had reached forty-three kilometres from its starting point. Noyon was lost, as was Roye. The French 1st Army, which was being assembled hurriedly as Fayolle's main strike force, was not yet in place. Byng's 3rd Army was retreating north-westwards. The gap between the two armies was opening wider. Yet even at that point Fayolle started to believe that the Germans could, after all, be held. The critical days would be the 28th and the 29th. So it turned out. Foch showed in full his characteristic energy. He bullied his generals into moving their exhausted troops to new positions around Beauvais. It was very high-risk, since it left Amiens exposed to the north. None the less, the tactic was successful. On Good Friday, 29 March, the first French counter-attacks went in. The German advance was halted. On Easter Sunday Fayolle went to Mass at the Convent of the Ladies of Pity. 'It is the day of the Resurrection,' he wrote, 'France and England were in agony. Today they are recovering. Glory to God in the highest!'[20]

The next day Pétain received a visit from the British Minister for Munitions, Winston Churchill. Churchill had been sent by Lloyd George (although Lloyd George – too late – thought better of his instruction and tried to reverse it) to report on the situation at the front. Churchill and Clemenceau went first to Amiens and then drove back to Beauvais, where Pétain was waiting for them in the French headquarters train, and conducted them, as Churchill recorded, into the 'sumptuous saloons of this travelling military palace, and a simple but excellent dinner was served in faultless style'.[21] Pétain had quite clearly recovered his composure.

All was calm and orderly . . . said Pétain at one moment, 'A battle like this runs through regular phases. The first phase through which we are now passing is forming a front of any kind. It is the phase of men. The second phase is that of guns. We are entering upon that. In forty-eight hours we shall have strong artillery organisations. The next is ammunition supplies. This will be fully provided in four days. The next phase is roads. All the roads will be breaking up under the traffic in a week's time. But we are opening our quarries this evening. We ought just to be in time with the roads, if the front holds where it is. If it recedes, we shall have to begin over again.'[22]

Churchill was mightily impressed. Pétain was showing the determination that seemed to be missing in the British generals. Nor was his confidence misplaced. The German advance on that front was held. But it was not to be long before the German Army delivered its next hammer blow – precisely where Pétain had expected it, along the Chemin des Dames.

11

The Strife Is Oe'r, the Battle Done . . .

'Est-il possible qu'on me refuse cela?'

On 27 May Ludendorff launched what turned out to be the last – and most dangerous – German offensive of the war. After a short artillery barrage, eighteen divisions swarmed on to the Allied lines on the Chemin des Dames. Of the six Allied divisions left to face the German attack, three were British – the remnants of Gough's 5th Army – which had been retired to what was considered to be a 'quiet' part of the front, and three French. They were the only defenders of a line of fifty-five kilometres. It is little wonder that by the evening of the 27th the German infantry had crossed the river Aisne and had almost reached the town of Fismes, some eighteen kilometres from their starting point.

Oddly enough, Ludendorff's attack on the Chemin des Dames had at first been no more than a diversion. His main thrust was to have been against the British between Arras and the Somme. He thought, not without reason, that he had the British on the run, and that, with one more push – as the jargon had it at the time – he could roll them back to the Channel and into the sea. Foch's analysis was the same. After his powers of command had been reinforced at a meeting of the Supreme War Council in Beauvais on 3 April (Pershing voluntarily put American troops under Foch's command on 28 April), he had taken stock of the whole situation on the front for which he was nominally responsible. He had decided that the main sector that needed reinforcing was the British sector in front of Amiens. Hence the continued movement of French troops to the north – and the virtual denuding of the Chemin des Dames sector to the south.

In fact, Ludendorff had already tried an assault on the British and Belgian positions in Flanders on 9 April. Haig had then appealed to Foch to send even more French divisions to shore up his position. 'Owing to very severe losses', Haig wrote in his diary, 'the British Divisions are fast disappearing.'[1] Foch responded that he would maintain a reserve of fifteen French divisions to support the British, but to do so he would have to put 'tired British Divisions'[2] on the Chemin des Dames front in place of the French divisions required to support Haig. Haig, supported by Lord Milner, replied that he accepted Foch's offer, but there could be no question of mixing French and British units on other than a temporary basis. Pétain, Fayolle and Franchet d'Esperey, the generals on the other Allied fronts, were furious and amazed at the same time. Not only were their troops being removed from under them, but they considered – rightly – that Haig was far from showing what had hitherto been normal courtesy between allies.

This whole episode, in fact, had shown the limitations of Foch's position. Although he had been nominated as Supreme Commander, the Beauvais meeting had specified that if any individual commander-in-chief objected to his instructions he had a right of appeal to his own government. In practice, this did not apply to Pétain (Clemenceau took the right away when he tried to exercise it) since Foch was a French general and as such Pétain's superior. He could therefore give orders to Pétain but only make requests to Haig and Pershing. Whether they accepted his requests was then a matter of negotiation. Haig realised early on that there was a double game to play – accept Foch's 'requests' when it pleased him and appeal to his government, and possibly the King, when it did not.

Nevertheless, as far as it went, the Foch arrangement was an improvement on what had gone before. But there had been then a further shift in positions at a conference of the Supreme War Council held at Abbeville on 2 May. To be sure, Lloyd George and Clemenceau complained, as they had on many occasions before, that the Americans were being too slow in building up their force, and that

Pershing's idea of a 'great self-contained American Army' was no more than wishful thinking. But on the major question of the day, whether the British and French Armies should be treated as one strategic unit or as two separate fighting forces, the meeting was unanimous in insisting that the main strategic priority was not to allow a breach between the two armies.

There was, however, a sting to the conclusion. If necessary to keep the two armies together, the meeting went on in its conclusion, the Channel ports would have to be abandoned and a retreat would be made southwards towards the Somme. In other words, Haig and the British government were accepting something which had been unacceptable to them only a few weeks before – Pétain and the French government's view that the defence of Paris was the strategic priority of last resort. But the question then raised, which Foch was unable to answer, was why French divisions were protecting the British when they might have been guarding the route to Paris – which lay precisely through the line of the Chemin des Dames.

There had also been a further discussion of Foch's position, this time on the sidelines of the Abbeville conference. The British claimed that they were not entirely happy with Foch's conduct of the war. Clemenceau, Lloyd George and Milner agreed to meet to discuss the matter, and, in particular, who might be his successor if, by design or mischance, he was unable to continue in the job. Milner, before going into the meeting, asked for Haig's view. Haig's response was that the 'best arrangement would be to decide that the C-in-C of the French Army should be *ipso facto* "Generalissimo" . . . Then the French Government should be asked to nominate (privately) either Anthoine or Pétain to be Foch's successor in case of necessity.'[3] In other words, Haig was prepared to continue what was in essence a double game – accepting any French supreme commander, even Pétain, secure in the knowledge that he had the right of appeal to his own government about any decision the Supreme Commander might see fit to make.

In the event, Clemenceau refused to engage in any lengthy discussion, claiming that Foch was his choice and that nothing was going to happen that required consideration about a possible successor. Armed with this confirmation of his position, Foch on 5 May had issued a general instruction virtually countermanding Pétain's Directive no. 4. All ground, he insisted, should be held. The front line should be fully

manned and the second line only lightly manned. 'Defence of territory, foot by foot, must be the priority.'[4] General Duchêne,
commanding the 6th Army along the Chemin des Dames, was quick
to follow Foch's instructions. Pétain, faced with the dilemma of either
insisting on his own directive, even to the point of dismissing
Duchêne, or accepting the instruction of the Supreme Commander,
chose the latter course – much against his better judgement. Franchet
d'Esperey, Duchêne's immediate superior as general commanding the
Army Group, did the same.

The result of all this political manoeuvring within the Allied camp
was that Ludendorff's diversionary attack on the Chemin des Dames
on 27 May achieved a surprising but immediately decisive breakthrough. Seeing this, Ludendorff cancelled plans for an attack in the
British sector and moved further divisions south to support what had
become his main thrust. Since there were virtually no Allied divisions
in reserve, it was impossible to contain the German advance. Fismes
fell, then Soissons and Fère-en-Tardenois. The River Ourcq was
crossed on 29 May. It was not until 31 May that the advance came to
a halt along the line of the River Marne. To the east, Reims itself was
only held thanks to the heroic defensive action of Gouraud's 4th
Army and the American 2nd and 3rd Divisions. As Fayolle wrote in
his diary, 'If we manage to surmount this crisis as well, it is only
because God wishes to save us.'[5] Pétain expressed himself doubtful
about defending Paris. Even Foch said that he thought that the war
might be lost.

The reaction in Paris to these events was one of panic. The government made plans to move to the Loire. Clemenceau told Mordacq
that he thought that Paris might be lost. Matters were made worse by
the presence of three Krupp long-range cannon (known as 'Fat
Bertha' after Krupp's daughter) on the edge of the Forêt de Villers-
Cotterets, able to lob shells into the centre of Paris itself. There were
angry scenes in the Assembly, many voices calling for the heads of both
Foch and Pétain. As the British Ambassador, the Earl of Derby (Lord
Bertie's successor in the post), reported, 'the good record [of reasoned
debate] was not kept up during yesterday's proceedings in the Chamber,
when a comparatively small but noisy group of Deputies on the Left
of the House created considerable disturbance'.[6] In short, they wanted
the government impeached. Clemenceau, when he finally managed to

speak, was only able to resist the attacks by a virtuoso show of angry rhetoric (although he privately admitted to Poincaré that he thought both Foch and Pétain had made mistakes).

The panic in Paris spread to Versailles, where the Supreme War Council met on 1 June. The meeting was both bad-tempered and fruitless. Everybody agreed that the Americans should be asked to make more of an effort – President Wilson was to be asked to aim for a hundred divisions. There was, however, a wrangle about where the American units should go. Haig wanted them to reinforce the British front, maintaining that it was a waste of time to relieve French divisions with Americans. Haig showed his by then customary contempt for his French allies, not even bothering to recognise that they had come to the rescue of his army after the defeat of 21 March. Foch just managed not to lose his temper, but countered with the justifiable complaint that reinforcements from Britain had been too slow in arriving.

As it happened, it was just at that point that Ludendorff's attack had been halted on the Marne. In fact, although the Allies could not know it, he had already decided that he would call a halt to the attack on 3 June, since he calculated that by that time his infantry would be at the limit of their supply chain. Nevertheless, it took a resolute combination of French and American troops to prevent a further breakthrough. The Americans, for the first time, played a full part. Pétain, in particular, admired the new verve and spirit they brought with them. 'We all had the impression', one of Pétain's staff officers wrote, 'that we were about to see a wonderful operation of transfusion of blood. Life was coming in floods to reanimate the dying body of France, almost bled to death since for four years that blood had flowed from countless wounds.'[7] Pétain himself was so impressed that he predicted that 'if we can hold on till the end of June, our situation will be excellent. In July we can resume the offensive: after that, victory will be ours'.[8]

The line of the Marne may have been held, but Ludendorff's offensive was far from ended. On 9 June, his supply columns having caught up with his infantry, he switched the direction of attack, driving westwards along the line of the small River Matz and then the larger Oise towards Compiègne. This time, however, the manoeuvre was less successful. To be sure, it started well. The French 3rd Army, under

General Humbert, followed Foch's defensive formula – to hold the first line at whatever cost. Again it was easily broken. Pétain lost his temper, and – unusually, given his normally quiet manner – gave Humbert a loud dressing-down in front of his subordinate commanders. Humbert could only reply that he had been following Foch's directive. Needless to say, an undignified row ensued, Pétain claiming that he and he alone was Commander-in-Chief and that his generals should obey him in all operational matters. Fortunately for everybody, at that point Foch ordered a counter-attack. It was organised – with his customary ferocity – by Mangin, by then commander of the 9th Army Corps and Humbert's superior commander. 'God protect us!', Fayolle wrote as Mangin's counter-attack went in on 11 June.[9] Protect them He did. By 13 June, Mangin had successfully used his tank squadrons to reclaim ground and throw the Germans on to the defensive. Foch was full of praise for Mangin; Pétain, still furious with Humbert and unwilling to concede anything to Mangin, said nothing.

By that time, all French reserve divisions had been brought into front-line battle. At Fayolle's insistence, Pétain asked Foch for British divisions to be placed as reserve to support the French front line. On receiving Foch's request Haig replied that he wished to consult his government. In his now customary fashion, he insisted that he was receiving 'a dismal picture of the French troops. But this I knew in August 1914. The Somme battle confirmed my view that much of the French good name as efficient fighters was the result of newspaper puffs.'[10] His tactic was to ask the British government to modify what he regarded as 'my responsibility for the safety of the British Army'.[11] If the government refused, as he assumed they would, he could reply to Foch that his overriding responsibility would not allow him to accede to his request. In short, he was using every tactic to resist having to move British troops to support the ally who was being attacked. Pétain could only note – with some bitterness – that Haig's response to him on 13 June was in marked contrast to his own response to Haig on 21 March.

In part, of course, Haig's reluctance to help may have been because he was aware that Pétain's own position was now threatened. Rumours were rife. It was freely said that Fayolle was to succeed him. He himself wrote to Nini on 28 June that 'it might happen that my services will no longer be required, since I am not supple enough to endure humiliation . . . But I view such an eventuality', he went on, 'with imperturbable calm.'[12] But, instead of Pétain, it was Anthoine, Pétain's Chief of Staff, who was sent on 'rest leave' for advancing 'defeatist notions'.[13]

It was in this mist of uncertainty about his own position that Pétain was left to face the fifth – and, as it happened, the last – German attack. In spite of his heavy losses and a near epidemic of 'Spanish influenza', on 15 July Ludendorff launched his remaining fifty-four divisions against the French 5th and 4th Armies around Reims. It was to be the final assault leading to victory – the *Friedensturm*, the Germans named it. But yet again he was to be disappointed. To the east of the city of Reims Gouraud held firm. His army had adopted the formula of Pétain's 4th Directive – a weak first line and a strong second line. The result was that the German opening barrage fell, as predicted, largely on open territory. The infantry attack was then slowed by the first line, and by the time that was overrun the infantry had lost touch with the creeping barrage – which had moved on ahead but had not the range to reach Gouraud's second line. The infantry advance was then halted and thrown back by a well-judged counter-attack. It was, as the official history points out, 'proof of the value of Pétain's defensive method'.[14]

General Berthelot's 5th Army, to the west of Reims, fared much less well. Berthelot himself, a creature of Joffre – but even larger (he weighed in at over 105 kilograms and his moustache was a wonder to behold) and an even greater believer in the 'offensive' – had been put by Foch in command of the 5th Army as part of his effort to introduce a more aggressive look to the whole French Army. But Berthelot was now required to fight an essentially defensive battle for which he was poorly equipped. True to form, he followed Foch's instruction to keep a strong first line and not on any account to surrender territory. Equally true to form, his army was quickly overrun. Nevertheless, Gouraud's resistance to the east of Reims, and the fact that the city itself remained in French hands, meant that a headlong German advance to the south and west ran the risk of a French counter-attack. That slowed the German impetus, and, in fact, the last attack was halted, yet again by determined French and American resistance, on 17 July – yet again along the line of the Marne.

Ludendorff was slow, or perhaps he even failed, to realise the danger

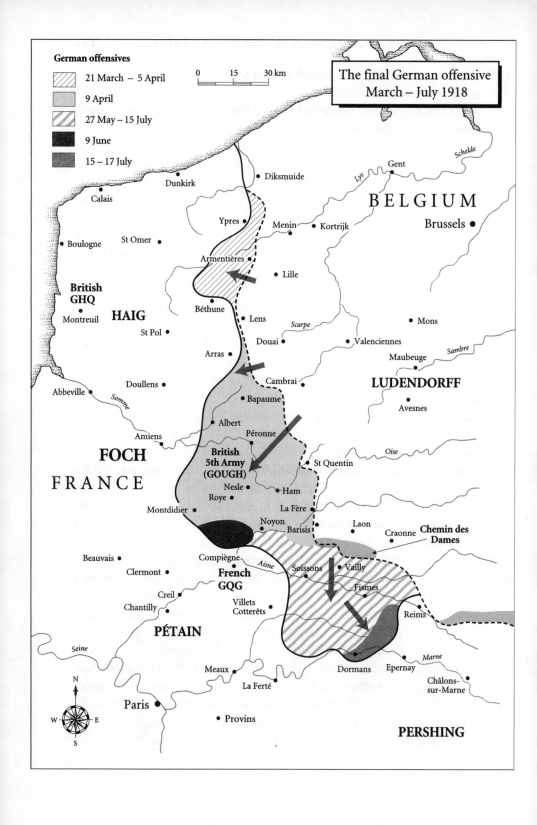

he was now in. He had established a large salient, along the line of the Marne from Château-Thierry in the west to Epernay in the east, but with a large and exposed western flank from Château Thierry in the south, across the Rivers Ourcq and Aisne as far as the Oise to the north, and with an eastern flank running from Epernay in the south, across the Rivers Ardre and Vesle to the north until it reached Reims.

The most vulnerable flank was the western, and it was against that flank that Foch ordered his counter-attack. On the morning of 18 July, while Ludendorff was in Mons discussing a transfer of German troops to the north for a further attack on the Flanders front, the French 10th and 6th Armies, under Generals Mangin and Degoutte respectively, supported by five American divisions – each twenty-eight thousand strong – attacked along the line of the Ourcq. At the same time Pétain ordered the 9th, 5th and 4th Armies, ranged along the southern and eastern boundaries of the German salient, to prepare for a general offensive.

The Second Battle of the Marne, as it became known, lasted some three weeks. It was fierce – Mangin saw to that – and ultimately successful. But the going was slow. The territory which Ludendorff had gained since 27 May was won back again, but only after three weeks of tenacious defence. Yet it was not only the disciplined German retreat which held up the French and American advance. The truth is that the Allied command and control was far from perfect. Foch's uncertain role – he was Supreme Commander but without the power to give direct orders other than to the French Army, and even then Pétain had a good deal of latitude in their interpretation – turned out to be a recipe for confusion. It was difficult for generals in the field to know the difference between an 'instruction' from the Supreme Commander (to the French) and a 'request' from the Supreme Commander (to the Americans). Furthermore, Foch had a limited staff at his disposal and was therefore obliged to pester his fighting generals for information on which to make his decisions.

Similarly, it was far from clear at what level – Foch or Pétain – general directives on policy should be made. On 12 July, for instance, only six days before the major counter-attack, Pétain issued his Directive no. 5. It had, in fact, been in preparation for some time. Pétain, as he had said at the end of May, had expected the German offensive finally to break its back on the rocks of French and American resistance. That being so, it was reasonable to expect – as was confirmed by prisoners taken at the front – that Ludendorff had run out of options. The losses sustained in the five major attacks since 21 March had, to recapture the expression allegedly used by Falkenhayn at Verdun, bled his army white. For Pétain, it was necessary in logic to spell out at that point his view of the new nature of offensive tactics. It seems that he discussed it with Foch before issuing it, but since Foch had himself issued directives which cut across those issued by Pétain, French generals could be excused for their doubts about its status. None the less, there it was.

Directive no. 5, of course, has some familiar material. Attacks should be 'audacious' and 'rapid', the follow-up 'immediate and far-reaching'. None of that was new. It could easily have been drafted in 1914. What was new, however, was the method of attack. There should be a bombardment of the enemy lines 'either by artillery or from the air' as short and as violent as possible. This should then lead quickly to an assault by heavy tanks 'opening the way to the infantry and artillery'. Lighter tanks should accompany the infantry to help it break down residual resistance and 'repel counter attacks'.[15] The Directive was followed to the letter in the counter-attack of 18 July: some thousand aircraft were deployed and some 750 tanks. (In fact, it is harder to think of a clearer description of what became known as the German *Blitzkrieg* of May 1940.)

Although Pétain's armies were prepared for offensive action along the whole of his front, Foch was surprisingly slow to allow them free rein. It was not until 24 July that he summoned Pétain, Haig and Pershing to his headquarters at Château Bombon to explain the conclusions he had drawn from the Second Battle of the Marne and the subsequent counter-attack of 18 July. Somewhat surprisingly, they were modest. It was time, he thought, generally to adopt a more offensive attitude. He hoped to achieve some 'useful' results, with the possibility of launching a more general offensive in late summer or autumn. In the mean time he requested Haig to prepare for an attack in front of Amiens and into the old battlefields of the Somme. The day set for the start of the attack was 8 August.

As it happened, Foch was made a Marshal on the day of the British attack. (Pétain was awarded France's highest military honour, the Médaille Militaire. This was added to the recognition by the British in the form of the Grand Cross of the Order of the Bath.) On the morning of the 8th, 530 British and 70 French tanks, ten divisions of the Canadian and Anzac Corps and eight French divisions from Fayolle's army group attacked on a front of thirty kilometres. It was a stunning, almost a decisive, blow. Within four days most of the old Somme battlefield had been retaken and the Germans were in full retreat towards the Hindenburg Line. On the evening of 12 August Foch, Pétain and Fayolle were invited to meet King George V to receive his congratulations. Haig, apparently, was 'very friendly'.[16] Since he had been in command of the eight French divisions it is perhaps not hard to see why.

That might have been a moment of bonhomie, but it did not last long. The now deep mutual distrust between Pétain and Haig continued to bedevil Allied operations right up until the November Armistice. Nor, for that matter, were Pétain's relations with Foch particularly good at the time – although this was due to differences of opinion over tactics rather than personal animosity. The first point of disagreement was about what Pétain perceived to be Foch's tendency to favour the British over the French. It was not just that the Chemin des Dames front had been denuded. Foch's playing down the results of the Mangin/Degoutte counter-attack of 18 July and his preference for relying on the British for the next step instead of encouraging his own army was little short of a betrayal. Joffre, Pétain claimed (rightly), had always been much more sensitive to the needs of France. In this, Pétain was on firm political ground. His view was shared by Clemenceau, whose own relations with Foch were by then, and for that reason, taking a turn for the worse.

The second point of disagreement concerned the Americans and the use to which American forces might be put. Pétain took the view that they were not sufficiently trained to embark on a sustained offensive operation. He believed that they should be kept in defensive positions or in reserve until properly trained for attack. Foch took the opposite view – that the enthusiasm of the American soldier made up for his lack of experience, and that he should be put on the offensive straight away. Both generals recognised the American potential – after all, they had by then some 1.2 million soldiers on French soil. The difference was over how to take advantage of it. General Pershing, it need hardly be said, agreed with Foch.

At their meeting of 24 July in Bombon, Foch had instructed

Clemenceau and Pétain, 1918. (*Photos12.com*)

Pershing to assemble his troops for the reduction of the small salient of St-Mihiel on the Verdun front. This Pershing had done. He had been proud on that day to announce the formation of the American First Army, with fourteen full divisions, of which he would be the first commanding general. In fact, he had been quietly planning the St-Mihiel operation with Pétain – who had to suppress his doubts – and his staff for some weeks. True, he had no tanks, but that problem was solved by Pétain allocating six divisions from de Castelnau's Army Group of the East to reinforce the American left. By 17 August Pétain was able to tell de Castelnau that he was satisfied that the operation had been properly and efficiently planned, and that Pershing would be in overall command of the whole force, including de Castelnau's six divisions.

On 30 August Foch changed his instruction. The major thrust of the attack was to be northwards. St-Mihiel was to be a secondary operation. As it turned out, Foch was right in his change of mind. The success of the Canadian and Anzac offensive had opened up new possibilities. There was now the chance of a major encircling movement, with a Franco-American push northwards from Verdun and a British push eastwards towards the Ardennes. If the two pincer movements could unite, the German Army would be trapped and surrounded on the Hindenburg Line.

It was an ambitious plan, and required much shuffling around of units. Moreover, it led to a major row between Pershing and Foch. The new commander of the American First Army was simply not going to accept Foch's instruction if it meant dividing up the American Army among various French units. Pershing even stood up in front of Foch to say: 'Marshal Foch, you have no authority as Allied Commander-in-Chief to call upon me to yield up my command of the American Army and have it scattered among the Allied forces where it will not be an American army at all.' On Foch's insistence, Pershing went on: 'Marshal Foch, you may insist all you please, but I decline absolutely to agree to your plan. While our army will fight where you decide, it will not fight except as an independent American army.'[17] Never were the limitations of Foch's command more brutally exposed.

It need hardly be said that Pétain was sympathetic to Pershing's case. Nevertheless, 'requests' from the Supreme Commander had to be listened to, and a limited St-Mihiel offensive started only two days behind the original schedule on 12 September, and St-Mihiel was taken within two days. Congratulations poured in. 'The boys have done what we expected of them', wrote President Wilson, 'and done it in a way we most admire.'[18] Clemenceau, Foch and Haig followed suit. Pétain was accordingly almost forced to reverse his previously held view. The St-Mihiel action had persuaded everybody else that the Americans were fully able to take offensive action. He could only bow to that judgement. Accordingly, after agreement with a rather bruised Foch, he requested Pershing to transfer his army from the right to the left bank of the Meuse, ready to participate in the major push northwards which Foch now planned for 26 September.

At that point there was another difference of opinion between Foch and Pétain. Foch was determined that the northwards push should be without pause. Pétain, true to his form, was more cautious. He was thinking in terms of successive phases. As it happened, when the day came, events conspired against Foch. The American First Army was badly held up. They had been instructed to attack northwards, and that they did. What Foch had perhaps not appreciated was that the route north towards Mézières and Sedan leading up the west bank of the Meuse and into the Argonne forest was by far the most difficult territory to attack and by far the easiest to defend outside the Vosges.

The failure of the American troops to meet their targets on the Meuse-Argonne front had knock-on effects. Gouraud's 4th Army, to their left, was also held up, fearful of exposing its right flank. This in turn threatened disequilibrium along the whole front – the attack of 26 September had, after all, been mounted simultaneously by British, French, Belgian and American armies, with a total of 180 divisions. It was not the time for one sector to flag while another moved on, and the British were making excellent progress in Flanders and on the Somme to the north. They had even succeeded in piercing the Hindenburg Line.

Clemenceau, as Chairman of the Supreme War Council, heaped all the blame for Pershing's failures on to Foch. He wrote two furious letters, telling Foch to pull himself together and act like a leader. Foch, stung – reasonably enough – by this attack, sent his Chief of Staff, General Maxime Weygand, to see Pershing with a proposal 'to interject the French 2nd Army between us and the French 4th Army', a proposal, Pershing's diary reports, 'which I disapproved'.[19] Pershing realised that the plan involved detaching the American divisions in and around the Argonne forest and placing them under French command. He was having none of it. In this he had an ally in Pétain, who recognised that the front was interdependent, and could not simply be shuffled around like pieces on a chess board. As Pershing reported, '[Pétain] fully appreciates difficulty of our task.'[20] In other words, Pétain was quietly undermining the proposals of the Supreme Allied Commander. In doing so, he must have allowed himself a wry smile at the thought that his suggestion of attacks by phases was now, due to the new circumstances, official policy.

What none of them, Clemenceau, Foch, Pétain or Pershing, knew at the time was that German morale was starting to crack badly. On 28 September Ludendorff had had something of a breakdown. He had flown into a 'paranoid rage'.[21] His staff had had to shut the door of his office lest his fury should be heard by all his subordinates. When he had composed himself, he went to Hindenburg's room and told him that there was now no alternative but to seek an armistice. The following day, when it became known that Bulgaria was opening negotiations for peace, the Kaiser was told firmly by a delegation from the Reichstag that Germany should prepare for her own negotiation by moving to greater democracy. On 3 October he accordingly appointed Prince Max von Baden, a known moderate and an advocate of peace, as Chancellor.

On 6 October, somewhat to his surprise, Foch read in the Paris newspapers the text of a note from Austria-Hungary, Germany and Turkey. It requested an immediate armistice and discussions of peace conditions on the basis of President Wilson's Fourteen Points. The note, it appeared, had been sent to the US government by the intermediation of the Swiss. Foch had previously known nothing about it. The German tactic was clear: they thought they could get a better deal from Wilson than the French and the British, who had borne the brunt of the struggle. But it is little wonder that not only Foch but both Clemenceau and Lloyd George were badly put out. Moreover, it was just at the point where Foch 'was very disappointed with the American attack west of the Meuse. Many of their divisions had been several days without food. Some had run off to get something to eat . . .'[22] Americans generally seemed to be under something of a cloud.

On 9 October there was a meeting of the Supreme War Council to respond to the German request for an armistice. Clemenceau and Lloyd George insisted on harsh conditions, tantamount to unconditional surrender. Pershing was in favour of precisely that. None the less, no decisions were taken, but it was agreed that there would be further consultation with other belligerents, and in particular that Foch would sound out the views of the Allied Commanders-in-Chief. In the mean time, the war went on. As it happened, it was not until 25 October that Foch was able to call a conference of the three, Haig, Pétain and Pershing. One by one, Foch asked for their views.

Haig spoke first. He reiterated what he claimed to have said to the War Cabinet in London the previous Saturday. To be sure, he seems to have left out the more insulting remarks about his allies. The French Army, he had apparently then said, was 'worn out and has not been really fighting latterly'. The American Army was 'ill-equipped and half-trained'. The British Army, on the other hand, 'was never more efficient than it is today'. On the basis of these absurdities – perhaps the high point of Haig's inbred xenophobia – he concluded that 'the French and American Armies are not capable of making a serious offensive now. The British alone might bring the enemy to his knees. But why expend more British lives – and for what?'[23]

Following that line of argument – but without the disparaging remarks about their troops (apart from a sideswipe at Pershing) – Haig proposed to the other Allied commanders that the terms of the armistice should be minimal: (a) immediate evacuation of Belgium and occupied French territory; (b) Metz and Strasbourg to be at once occupied by the Allied armies and Alsace-Lorraine to be 'vacated by the enemy'; and (c) Belgian and French rolling stock 'to be returned and inhabitants restored'.[24]

It could hardly have been more insulting to the French or, for that matter, to the Americans. France had, after all, been the main victim of the war. The battle had been fought largely on her territory, much of which was no more than a mangled desert. The French Army had fought battles, particularly at Verdun, in defence of its own land, which the British Army had never had to fight. Finally, although itself mourning the loss of more than a million of its sons, the French Army had come to the rescue of the defeated British Army in March 1918. The idea that France would agree lamely to lay down her arms on Haig's terms was one which every French officer, including Foch, found deeply offensive.

Pétain spoke next. He spread out on a table a map of the western front, on which he had marked out in red lines a progressive withdrawal of German troops from their present positions to the Rhine. He recommended immediate and prompt German withdrawal on the timetable he had prepared. If this happened, he argued, the Germans would be unable to remove their heavy guns and ammunition. Further, he recommended that the Germans should surrender to the Allies five thousand locomotives and a hundred thousand freight cars. When all that was completed, their armies should withdraw to the east of the Rhine and the Allies should establish bridgeheads at Mainz, Koblenz and Cologne. For good measure, he threw in the suggestion that Germany should pay a large indemnity to the Allies whose territory had been laid waste.

Pershing, when he came to speak, showed his irritation at Haig's performance. The thought that the flower of American youth had crossed the Atlantic to rescue Europe, and had died on the battlefields of France for the cause, only to be lectured by a supercilious British general for their pains, was more than he could bear. Although he had, only two days before, 'acquiesced' in Haig's views[25] his line was now quite different. He endorsed all that Pétain had said, and added for good measure that U-boats and U-boat bases should be put under the control of a neutral power 'until their disposition is otherwise determined'. At that point Haig bridled. 'That is none of our affair,' he said, 'It is a matter for the Admiralty to decide.'[26] Pershing, however, insisted that the American armies relied on a safe passage across the Atlantic. It was a matter of vital importance.

It had by then become clear that Haig was in a minority of one. The other three (supported, incidentally, by the Northcliffe press in London) clearly wished to impose harsh terms on Germany. Haig, on the other hand (supported apparently by Lord Milner) wanted only minimal terms. Above all, he thought that the British 'should set their faces against the French entering Germany to pay off old scores'.[27] Since he was firm in his view that, as he told Foch, 'the British Army has defeated the Germans this year',[28] he considered that the British view should be the one to go forward to heads of government. Militarily, Haig was on firmer ground. From July onwards Haig's armies had recovered impetus and, with the Canadian and Anzac Corps in the van, taken the initiative in the north with resounding success. Fighting bravely and with great tactical skill, they had driven the German armies back in what nearly became a rout. But however justified Haig's claim that his armies had at least played a major part in the German defeat – if not the whole of it – Haig's diplomacy was not up to the task he had set himself. In short, he was crass. 'The demands . . . for a humiliating peace for Germany were', he pronounced, 'against the best interests of the British Empire.'[29] Foch and the others took the wholly reasonable view that they were not there to defend the interests of the British Empire, and Haig was outvoted. Foch, Pétain and Pershing were firm. They were there to have their pound of German flesh.

By then, however, Pétain had hatched another plan. By the third week in October he and his staff were preparing a major offensive in Lorraine, starting from the area north-east of Nancy, moving northwards towards Metz, passing to the east of the heavy fortifications on the Metz–Thionville axis, striking – for the first time in the war – into German territory beyond the Saar, thus destroying communications between the homeland and the remaining German Army on the western front. German capitulation would then have been inevitable – and unconditional.

In Pétain's eyes, this was to be the last offensive of the war – the *coup de grâce*. Not only that, but it would be the French Army which would be seen to have delivered the mortal blow. Instead of having to share the glory of victory with the British and Americans, France could claim to have resisted the German onslaught in the first place, to have fought through the miserable middle years of the war and, finally, to have landed the knock-out punch.

It was not a sudden brainwave. As far back as 24 September Pétain had asked de Castelnau, in command of the Army Group of the East, to submit operational plans for the great venture. De Castelnau agreed with Pétain that the operation was both feasible and desirable. Intelligence reports showed the area around Metz to be feebly guarded by inexperienced German units. If the Metz–Thionville forts could be avoided there was no reason why a rapid advance should not be made along the lines that Pétain had suggested.

In a version dated 10 October the plan had become even more elaborate. There would now be a three-pronged attack – one along the western bank of the River Moselle to the west of Metz, one towards Metz directly to the north, running up the eastern bank of the Moselle towards Trier, and the third passing to the east of Metz in the direction of the German frontier and Saarbrücken. The initial attack would be on a front bounded by the River Seille to the west and the River Senon to the east, and would be mounted by the 2nd American Army (operational as of 16 October), forming the first prong, and the French 8th and 10th Armies forming the second and third prongs, with the French 7th Army in reserve. It would be the French 10th Army – Mangin's army – which would have the honour of crossing the German frontier.

By 20 October Foch was coming round to the idea, so much so that he asked Pétain to explain the plan in detail the following day. This he did, in the detail required, with supporting memoranda from his staff. On 27 October Pétain was able to give de Castelnau instructions for the French 7th, 8th and 10th Armies and to invite Pershing to do the same for the 2nd American Army. The 10th Army, his order went on, was to lead the assault as near as possible to 15 November.

But time was running out. On 3 November the German sailors in Kiel mutinied. Germany itself was descending into chaos, with crowds of armed soldiers roaming the streets of the major cities and near-revolution in Berlin. Prince Max von Baden gave way to Friedrich Ebert as Chancellor, who immediately said that the Kaiser, by then in the army headquarters at Spa, must abdicate. On 9 November the Kaiser accepted what had by then become inevitable. At that point, the German armistice delegation, which had already crossed into France, arrived at Rethondes in the Forest of Compiègne.

The terms of the Armistice were all that Foch, Pétain and Pershing had wished. In fact, they were precisely those which had been agreed at Senlis on 25 October. Pétain should have been pleased. Yet the evidence suggests otherwise. True, he wrote to Nini on the day to say

Signing the Armistice, November 1918. (*Bettman/Corbis*)

that 'my first thought this morning, learning of the signature of the Armistice, was for you. I would have wished you to be with me so that I could embrace you and show you my joy . . . I love you passionately . . .'[30] Nevertheless, this show of affection to his mistress may have concealed – it would not be the first or last time – his true feelings. He may have exaggerated when he claimed later in life to have pleaded in tears with Foch to postpone the Armistice, but it is impossible to dismiss the evidence of an extreme reluctance to give up his Lorraine offensive – due to start on 14 November. As Charles de Gaulle later pointed out, 'the hasty end to the combats . . . on 11 November 1918 came just at the moment when we were about to harvest the fruits of victory'.[31] Above all, in Pétain's eyes, it allowed Haig and the British to claim to be the true victors of the Great War.

Thus ended Pétain's war. From an obscure beginning he had risen to be one of France's greatest military heroes. He was also, without a doubt, the most accomplished defensive tactician of any army, French, British, Russian, Austrian, Italian or Turkish. (The only possible rival would be Ataturk for his defence of the Gallipoli peninsula in 1915.) But Pétain's methods were not one-off. Apart from the initial Ludendorff offensive of 21 March, which revealed a weakness in the application – though not in the theory – of Pétain's defensive system, it held firm from the time it was devised in 1917 to the end of the war. For that, and for organising the defence of Verdun at a critical moment, he was undoubtedly worthy of his marshal's baton, formally presented to him by President Poincaré in front of his fellow commanders-in-chief in Metz on 8 December 1918.

None the less, it would be wrong to suggest that Pétain was a perfect all-round military commander. There were moments, particularly in March 1918, when his courage deserted him, and his natural caution took on an air of gloom and despondency. Moreover, he found it difficult to summon up the enthusiasm for battle which leads men to put their lives at risk for a cause. Fayolle summed it up well. 'If Pétain had been alone [in command]', he wrote in his diary, 'we would not have attacked. We owe everything to Foch. It is not that he organised this series of victories, but he gave the order to fight. It is always the same thing: Foch said "Attack!"; Pétain provided the means . . .'[32] If the war ended in disappointment for him – 'is it

Receiving the Marshal's baton, Metz, December 1918. (*Keystone*)

possible that they will refuse me that?'[33] – it is perhaps because he did not quite have the ruthlessness to pursue his own ambition to the end at the expense of others and perhaps because his in-built caution did not allow for the dash needed to inspire men to attack. Furthermore, he was forever the outsider – a peasant in the company of swordsmen, a bachelor in the company of husbands, an agnostic in the company of Catholics. Yet, as a general, he was certainly superior in intelligent analysis, in tactical awareness and, above all, in humanity to both his colleagues and his opponents. He was not a Napoleon or a Wellington, but he comes very high in the ranks just below them.

12

NINI

'. . . je constate que je t'aime profondément . . .'

There is no denying that Eugénie Hardon was, in her prime, a particularly beautiful woman. True, in her mid-forties, when her relationship with Pétain blossomed, she was what kindly observers would describe as 'statuesque' and the less kindly as 'large and plump' (she was all of 5′ 10″ tall – the same height as Pétain – and was possessed of an imposing bosom), but her face was still her undoubted glory. A photograph taken at the time tells the story. Her face is shaped as an almost perfect oval. In the style of the day, her hair – a deep brunette – is done in ringlets kept in place by a discreet silver band. One of the ringlets drops down her forehead, to a point just above where her dark eyebrows – the right arched quizzically, the left slightly lower but slanting upwards as though in challenge – frame a narrow indentation at the top of her nose. Her nose is short and retroussé, and leads symmetrically downwards to her lips, full, sensual with just the faintest hint of a smile, and from there to a dimple on her chin. Above all, however, her face frames, and guides the onlooker towards, her brown, passionate and inviting eyes.

Men found her irresistible. So, by all accounts, did she find men. Even during her marriage to the painter François Dehérain she apparently had great difficulty in refusing alternative arrangements – one story is that she allowed herself to be spirited away to the United

Nini in her prime.

States by an American admirer shortly before her marriage broke up. After her divorce in 1914, and her resumption of her maiden name, she was frequently to be found in what were politely known as military circles, in other words in officers' beds. Nor was it clear at that time how she supported herself and her son Pierre financially. Her former husband had no money, and her family did not think much of her. In short, she seems to have acted out the traditional role of mistress – for which she was, without any shadow of doubt, admirably qualified in every way.

Her main lover during the latter part of the war was General Pétain. There were certainly others, in the same way, indeed, as Pétain had other women. But in the first flush of their renewed relationship, at the time of Verdun, Pétain's craving for her company – or rather, not to put too fine a point on it, for her body – was passionate. His letters to her are quite explicit in their assertion of his desire. By the end of the war, however, his letters seem to have become rather more mechanical in their expressions of devotion. The relationship was certainly settling down; Nini's outbursts of affronted dignity at her lover's peccadilloes were less convincing; and above all, hanging over the whole affair, there was talk of marriage.

The idea was not altogether welcome to Pétain. It was one thing to have a successful relationship with an attractive, but divorced, mistress. It was perhaps something to boast about, as Pétain did from time to time. It was quite another thing to marry her. For a start, there was the matter of his almost certain excommunication for living in sin with an adulteress, since they could not, of course, be married in church. Although Pétain acknowledged the loss of his childhood faith, there were residual emotional hang-ups which still demanded attention. Then there was the social problem. Nini could not possibly be introduced into society as his wife. She, and consequently he, would be shunned. Lastly, there was the problem of what to do with Nini's son Pierre. Pétain certainly did not want a stepson. It would be an intolerable encumbrance. Besides, Pierre was not an easy child, and his mother seemed over-protective of him.

Pétain himself had come out of the war as one of the two Marshals of France who were generally regarded as the architects of victory. In the public eye, in fact, Pétain even outshone Foch. The 'Victor of Verdun' was fêted wherever he went. It helped, of course, that he was extremely good-looking. He kept himself fit – a daily hour on horseback, walking long distances, fencing skilfully with foil, épée and sabre – so much so that his doctors could not believe that he had recently come through four years of war. But it was not only his good looks. His reading was by then widely drawn, by preference Corneille but extending to more modern authors as well. He made friends of Paris intellectuals, of Paul Valéry, Maurice Donnay, Pol Neveux, of the diplomat Maurice Paléologue and of the satirist Forain. Two literary clubs were happy to invite him to membership: the Déjeuner Paul Hervieu and the Dîner Bixio.

Nor was his company confined to intellectuals. At a time when *le tout Paris* was trying to forget the war and determined to forget the lost years in a self-indulgent spasm of enjoyment, Pétain was quite prepared to join in. He frequented the salons, joined the Jockey Club, lunched almost every day with one or other of the society lionesses who decorated the *vie mondaine*. He was invited to stay at the castle of his friends the Marquis de Chasseloup-Loubat and his wife, and at the luxurious home of the Citroën family. He was regularly invited by the de Rothschilds. Of course, Mme de Chasseloup-Loubat, the Citroëns and the de Rothschilds were all Jewish, but that did not seem to matter. In fact, at one point it was alleged that he was the natural father of a son to the Jewish wife of a prominent industrialist.

As a matter of fact, Pétain was doing no more than following the pattern he had set at his headquarters at Compiègne and Provins once he had become Commander-in-Chief. There he had entertained many of the ladies who were to be his hostesses once the war had ended. It almost goes without saying that for Pétain the line between hospitality and amorous adventure was thinly drawn. As the faithful Serrigny nervously observed, 'these women seized every pretext: charity, propaganda, politics, the needs of the sick etc. Today it was Baronesse Henri de Rothschild, tomorrow Mme Harjès, the wife of an American banker, Mme Morgan, actresses, women of letters, women in love . . .'[1]

Naturally enough, as Serrigny pointed out, 'many of these women received, I think, unequivocal evidence of the Chief's admiration'. So it was after the war in Paris. Germaine Lubin, a striking operatic soprano celebrated for her Isolde in Wagner's *Tristan*, was certainly a target – although she probably managed to escape Pétain's ultimate intentions by pleading an unfashionable fidelity to her husband. Jacqueline de Castex, the widow of one of Pétain's officers who had been killed at La Malmaison, was another. Marie-Louise Regad, by then grey-haired and stout, reappeared from Besançon and almost threw herself at him. And so it went on. Indeed, it is said that after Pétain's death Nini found a military trunk full of adoring letters written to him – some still carrying the scent of their author.

Under those circumstances, there was no particular reason that Pétain could identify why he should hurry to get married. Once the war had ended, of course, his excuse that he could not possibly get married while it was still on was no longer valid. Nini therefore redoubled her efforts. She started to follow him around the country when he was on official business. She wanted to go to Nancy with him, for instance, in early January 1919. He could hardly prevent her, but he certainly did not want her showing up in public. 'If you don't find me at the station', she was told, 'you will go to have tea at the Hôtel d'Angleterre, near the station. M will find you there. It is important that your name does not appear in the official list of those accompanying me . . .'[2] (M was a frequently employed intermediary. Among his other jobs he was on one occasion sent to rescue Pétain's briefcase, inadvertently left behind after yet another night of passion.)

Nini was also fully capable of making scenes when she chose. These were generally followed by soothing letters from her lover. 'Your letter moved me profoundly,' he wrote in February 1919, 'I fully understand your distress and the cause of it . . . on my return from my next trip we will explain ourselves as frankly as you wish . . .'[3] The explanation obviously did not satisfy Nini, who clearly threw a tantrum. A further mollifying letter followed, but this time it had a sterner message. Pétain argued that the tenderness with which she received him was due to the 'relative independence towards one another' which they enjoyed. 'Suppose', he went on, 'this independence, which allows a bad mood to be breathed away apart from one another, did not exist, and one of us let slip a word . . .'[4]

It was a nice try, but Nini was up to it. She then accused him of 'lacking drive and enthusiasm'. This provoked a 'long dissertation'. 'It is because I have made precise calculations,' it went, 'because I have undertaken nothing which was too much for the means at my disposal, because I have had an exact notion of the realities and possibilities, because I have clearly appreciated the strength of the forces against me after having analysed them with cold calculation, that I have obtained some successes these last few years.'[5] So it went on for several pages. He admitted that he was a man of few words, but words were useless unless accompanied by acts, and he was capable of 'generous gestures which have allowed me to inspire devotion'.[6]

Nini kept up the pressure. By March 1919 Pétain was consulting his old friend Guide about 'our projects'[7] – namely the purchase of a property in Provence. At first, Guide was pessimistic about finding anything suitable, but he started a search and soon produced one or two possibilities. Their preferred area was the hills above Antibes and Nice. Pétain had walked about those hills many years ago when he was a young officer at Villefranche and Nini's family had spent a good deal of time in Monaco. Since the Pas-de-Calais, which Pétain had chosen before the war for his retirement, had become a large coal-mining area and as a result had lost whatever agricultural charm it might have had, Provence was an obvious choice. Pétain, indeed, imagined himself retiring there to keep chickens.

But he was still a Marshal of France, and still on the active list. In fact, until peace was signed in June 1919 he was still Commander-in-Chief of the French armies in the west. There was much to be done to convert a wartime establishment into an arm of peace. The French Army at the end of 1918 was a formidable fighting force. More than a million men were under arms; the Hotchkiss machine gun was superior to all its rivals; there were some six thousand 75mm field pieces and seven thousand heavy guns, 2,500 light Renault and a hundred heavy Schneider tanks. Moreover, the French air arm was more numerous and better than any Allied rival in all four disciplines – fighter, bomber, reconnaissance and observation. The skill of French officers was in wide demand – Mittelhauser in Czechoslovakia, Berthelot in Romania and Gamelin in Brazil. The teaching staff at the École de Guerre was 'an élite which no other army in the world . . . would be able to assemble'.[8]

The problem facing Foch and Pétain at this point was not one they had faced before. Clemenceau considered that the Armistice had finished the war and that there should be substantial demobilisation. At the same time, Foch was required to produce a military plan which could be put into action in the event of Germany refusing to accept the Allied peace terms. On top of all this was the need for some hard thought about the configuration of a future peacetime army. There was still a threat from Germany but worse even than that was the danger from the great new enemy – 'bolshevism'. Indeed, it was not just what was happening in Russia or Germany. It was very close to home. In June 1919, only two weeks before the signature of the peace, the metalworkers went on strike. They followed the miners of Lorraine, bank employees and shop workers in demanding Soviet-style political change. Clemenceau promptly ordered tanks on to the streets of Paris and a force of seventeen thousand men behind them. The strikers were dispersed, but not before the fear of 'bolshevism' had become a reality in the minds of senior officers.

Addressing the question of what sort of army should emerge, Pétain at the beginning of 1919, even while his present army was being demobilised, had made his views clear. He asked for the next mobilisation to be of '6,785 tanks . . . under separate command . . . it is much to ask for, but the future belongs to those who have the greatest number of armoured warriors'.[9] Furthermore, along with Joffre, Pétain urged the importance of air power. The aeroplane, he had argued to Pershing as long ago as December 1917, could be the weapon of decision.

As it happened, demobilisation was little short of chaotic. Units were stripped of men seemingly at random, without much thought of merging them to give a rational structure to the army which was to emerge. On Clemenceau's direct and explicit instruction, Pétain reluctantly dissolved twenty-two divisions between 10 January and 10 February, and a further twenty-four between 22 February and 31 March. By the end of September there were only forty-one divisions left in France – little more than one-third of the army of a year earlier.

The Peace Treaty was signed in the Hall of Mirrors at Versailles on 28 June. Pétain was there, summoned, as he told Nini, back from Metz for the occasion, but Foch was conspicuously absent. It was no accident. Foch, and Mangin, had argued throughout the negotiations for a separate Rhineland state to be a buffer between Germany and France in the future. Foch had gone so far as to write about his plan in the press and to speak out at a meeting of the Peace Conference on 6 May. Lloyd George thought that he had gone off his head; Clemenceau was furious; Wilson was simply baffled. Weygand went on to incur general displeasure by attacking Clemenceau in his turn. President Wilson concluded that, as he put it, the worst thing in the world would be to leave Europe in the hands of General Weygand. In short, the period leading up to the signature of the treaty was marked by bad-tempered bickering among the Allies.

After the signature of the treaty France returned to its pre-war form of political supervision of the armed forces. Pétain's job was to be wound up as soon as demobilisation had been satisfactorily achieved. The Conseil Supérieur de la Guerre was revived, along with the Conseil Supérieur de la Defense Nationale. After Foch's antics at the Peace Conference there was no question of his getting the top military job, the vice-chairmanship of the Conseil Supérieur de la Guerre. That naturally fell to Pétain. On 23 January 1920 his appointment was announced.

For the whole of 1919 Pétain had managed to fend off Nini. True, he was away from Paris a great deal, leaving her with her son Pierre in a small house which she had bought in the rue Desaix – an unfashionable part of Paris. (In fact, from his letters it seems that they had resorted again to the Buffet-Hôtel for their assignations. Perhaps Pétain's apartment was too public.) She had spent September with Pierre in England – in Bournemouth, to be precise, where she was thoroughly bored. In her absence Pétain seems to have renewed contacts with his sister Sara – they had met again at the funeral of their elder sister Adélaïde, 'whom I never used to see'[10] – who clearly warned him against unsuitable relationships.

But by early 1920 Pétain's resistance to marriage was breaking. Nini sold her house in the rue Desaix, advised on the sale by her lover. The previous September Guide had found what seemed to be the perfect retirement home. Named, somewhat banally, L'Ermitage, it consisted of a modest two-storey house, a stable for the owner's horses, a barn, a small house for a caretaker and a pigsty. Just outside the hamlet of Villeneuve-Loubet, high up on the road to Vence above Antibes in the Alpes Maritimes, it commanded a panoramic view of the Mediterranean below. In short, it could hardly have been better. Pétain duly opened negotiations.

The vendors were asking a price of 140,000 francs (roughly some 60,000 of today's euros). Guide thought it was worth 125,000 francs. On the assumption, as Pétain wrote to Nini, that the vendors would accept that, his total outlay, including expenses, would be around 140,000 francs, which he considered 'severe'.[11] His annual salary as a Marshal was 150,000 francs – but that would rise over the years to 300,000 – which meant that he would have to borrow to do the deal. In the event the haggling went on for several months, the vendors finally accepting an offer of 130,000. On 12 April 1920 Pétain authorised the purchase. At the same time, however, he was asking Nini if he could see her portfolio – apparently to give her proper investment advice, but perhaps also to see whether she might be able to make a contribution towards the price of L'Ermitage. Pétain, the peasant, was always frugal with his money.

Pétain was by then virtually committed to marrying Nini. He had given up his pursuit of Mme Lubin – she had been suitably flattered by the Marshal's attentions, particularly when he rode his white horse over to her window to salute her while leading the 14 July parade in 1919, but had continued to plead fidelity as an excuse for inaction.

L'Ermitage at Vileneuve-Loubet (date unknown). (*L'Ilustration*)

Mme de Castex was still on his list – he had apparently asked her to marry him when Nini was not looking, but she replied that she was not yet ready for a second marriage. Finally, there was Marie-Louise Regad, who was still not prepared to take 'no' for an answer.

What followed has taken on the status of legend. A letter from a friend of Marie-Louise, Henriette Laurent, tells the story. Thinking that she had won Pétain over, Marie-Louise was one day dismayed to receive a message from him saying that 'Everything is broken. All is finished.' The message went on to express the thought that she might be owed some sort of explanation. He had, he said, wished to convey – as gently as possible – to Nini that the situation had changed. When he had tried to do so, his message went on, Nini had taken a revolver out of a drawer and, waving it at him, had simply said, 'It's going to be me or it will be a bullet for you.'[12]

Whether the story is true or not, Nini certainly won the day. On 14 September 1920 the pair were married at the *mairie* of the 7th Arrondissement in Paris. It was all very discreet. Fayolle, by then a

Victory parade, Paris, 1919. (*AKG*)

marshal himself, was Pétain's witness. After the brief ceremony the motley party went off to lunch at the Café de Paris.

The marriage was not well received. Pétain's sister Sara said she had no intention of knowing her new sister-in-law. A number of Pétain's acquaintances cut him from their address books. Nevertheless, the thing was done, and the new *maréchale* had to be recognised. A larger number therefore wrote to Pétain with congratulations, promising to recognise Nini as the Marshal's rightful spouse. But it was not to be as easy as that. Pétain considered it unwise to take Nini to official functions. Her position as a divorced woman might lead to difficulty with the heavily Catholic officers' wives. Even entertaining friends to dinner at Pétain's apartment in the Square de Latour-Maubourg was fraught with problems. Many among Pétain's large acquaintance would have professed themselves shocked to be found sitting at the same table as the disgraced female.

Pétain's solution to the problem was nothing if not ingenious. He acquired the apartment next door in the Square de Latour-Maubourg, no. 6, on the same level as his no. 8. A connecting door was installed, to be opened only from Pétain's side. When dinners were held, the door was kept firmly shut, and Nini was left to entertain herself as best she could. Next door, however, the hostess for the evening was selected by Pétain from among the ladies in attendance on that particular evening. Thus it was that Mme de Gaulle, the young – and very Catholic – wife of Captain de Gaulle, who had returned from his adventures in Poland to a job as Assistant Professor of History at Saint-Cyr and had become one of Pétain's staunchest admirers, frequently found herself hosting the Marshal's dinners at his own table.

It can hardly have been to Nini's liking. But then Pétain himself paid what he knew would be the inevitable penalties of marrying a divorcée. Although he had lapsed in his religious observance, he was certainly upset at being deprived of the Holy Sacrament for living in what the law thought perfectly proper but in the eyes of the Church were – at least formally – sinful circumstances. In fact, it seems that in 1920 or 1921 he took to mingling unnoticed with crowds going in and out of Mass on Sundays. Official functions were also a difficulty. Pétain was frequently invited – and attended – without his wife. Even his closest friends found the whole situation embarrassing. Louis Ménétrel, for instance, who had been his doctor before the war and took up the same position afterwards, was apt, on the long walks they took together, to be particularly hard on both Nini and her son Pierre. Moreover, Pétain's grander friends, the Chasseloup-Loubats, the Citroëns and the de Rothschilds, certainly would not have Nini, given her rackety past, in their grand houses – so Pétain went alone.

It was a strange existence. Pétain, one of the most powerful men in France, was required – and perhaps secretly wanted – to ignore his wife for a large part of his own life. True, on some of his many trips to visit army units he took her along, but she was always kept strictly under wraps when it came to official functions. In fact, neither Pétain nor Nini seems to have been particularly dismayed by this. The flow of letters when he was away from her, which turned out to be much of the time, continued unabated and in the same vein as before – although admittedly without the pulsating physical passion of the earlier years. But perhaps that was inevitable. Perhaps it was also inevitable that Pétain's eyes soon started to stray to other targets.

Indeed, only a few months after his marriage Mme de Castex makes a further appearance.

What Nini did with her days remains something of a mystery. She was a bad housekeeper – her house in the rue Desaix had always been untidy and she brought the same habits to her apartment in the Square de Latour-Maubourg. At one point Pétain had to call on the services of a friendly nurse from the Red Cross, Marie Provost (one of the few women with whom his relations seem wholly innocent), to 'bring some order' into her home.[13] The same Marie was employed to spend a large part of each winter at L'Ermitage for the same purpose.

There is little mention of the great affairs of the day in Pétain's letters. They are mostly about trivia. Nor was Nini particularly interested in those affairs. Yet much was happening in the wider world. By the time the two were married Clemenceau had retired. After the elections of November 1919 had produced a right-wing government, he had tried and failed to get himself elected President. The National Assembly elected Paul Deschanel instead, leaving Clemenceau to walk out in disgust. Alexandre Millerand became Prime Minister. But without Clemenceau's personal authority government became more diffuse and uncertain. Furthermore the problems were seemingly insoluble. The war had drained French resources to the point where the public finances were only propped up by massive short-term borrowing. Speedy demobilisation had thrown large numbers on to the labour market. Finally, by the autumn of 1920 the French economy had moved decisively into recession.

It was this deterioration in the public finances which put an end to Pétain's proposals for a large tank and air force. At a meeting of the Conseil Supérieur de la Défense Nationale of 12 March 1920 the Finance Minister, François Marsal, announced that although Pétain's proposals were undoubtedly excellent they could not be afforded. Various alternatives were canvassed. The Minister for War, André Lefèvre, claimed that he had recently seen Churchill, who had told him that the British could quickly equip thirty divisions. Foch pointed out that in 1914 it had taken the British six months to build up their strength on the western front. If the Germans attacked again, he said, France would be overrun before the British could conceivably come to the rescue.

Deschanel announced the conclusion. Savings were to be made in the air force. Some fifty-five infantry divisions were necessary as the main weapon for national defence. There was hardly a mention of tanks. These conclusions were reaffirmed at meetings on 27 October and 13 December, except that, under pressure from the Marsal, it was agreed to reduce the fifty-five divisions to thirty. After that, it was left to the Marshals, Pétain, Joffre and Foch, to pick up the pieces and to devise an alternative strategy.

The task was not easy. The occupation of the Rhineland, which served as a buffer against a future German attack, had a finite life. When the occupying forces withdrew, as they were bound to do under the Versailles Treaty, Germany would again be in a position to strike quickly at the industrial basin of Lorraine and from there progress to the northern French plain. If the French Army was to be drastically reduced in numbers and if French superiority in tanks and aviation was to be thrown away, a method had to devised that would make best use of the resources which would be left.

Throughout 1920 and 1921 a stream of notes and memoranda was produced by the general staff of the Army, now under General Edmond Buat, to address the problem. But there was a continuing dispute about the length of national service. Until there was at least a degree of certainty on that matter it was difficult to plan sensibly. Nevertheless, the general staff had begun to think seriously about a line of forts along the frontier with Germany. A report was first considered at a meeting of the Conseil Supérieur de la Guerre on 22 May 1922. It rejected the idea that in a future war ground might be ceded to the enemy and later recovered at the moment of victory in favour of the doctrine of 'inviolability of the [national] territory'.[14] The way to achieve this was to construct a line similar to the line of Séré de Rivières in the previous century. The idea was supported in the end by Joffre (surprisingly in view of his hostility to forts when he was Commander-in-Chief) as long as they were sited in a manner which was consistent with an overall operational plan. The meeting was unanimous in resolving to adopt the principle of a line of forts along the frontier with Germany which would serve to protect both French territory and French armies in the event of war.

At first sight, it seems astonishing that all three Marshals present, even Joffre and Foch, agreed a strategy which was precisely that of a defeated France in 1871. After all, all of them, in one way or another and with varying degrees of enthusiasm, had been proponents of the doctrine of the offensive in 1914 and all of them had seen the results of 1918. Indeed, both Joffre and Foch – Foch with greater conviction than Joffre – had argued at the meeting in favour of a more offensive strategy. Nevertheless, they were all forced in the end to grapple with the problem of resources. Reductions in defence spending dictated their conclusions. If there were to be a shortage of tanks and planes, the main strike weapons of the future, it was obviously no good devising an offensive strategy at the outset of a war. By the force of circumstance, France was in 1922 already locked into a defensive strategy. In fact, this logic would become even more obvious in the 1930s.

Pétain's ascendancy over his fellow marshals was confirmed by his appointment as Inspector-General of the Army in February 1922. He was now not only the commander designate of the French Army in time of war but also the supervisor of all military establishments, domestic or foreign. His position was further strengthened in 1923 by the appointment of General Marie-Eugène Debeney as Chief of the General Staff in place of Buat. Debeney had been a fellow cadet of Pétain at Saint-Cyr and a fellow junior officer at Besançon. Moreover, they were friends (both of them enjoying the same style of risqué joke).

The result of this new co-operation was the emergence of a new army manual, portentously entitled *Provisional Instruction on the Tactical Employment of Large Units*, which soon became known as 'the Bible'. It was certainly weighty enough – much larger than the 1913 manual which it replaced. The strategy for a new war which it set out was clear enough. Given the financial constraints imposed by the government, which in turn had given rise to the decision of principle of the meeting of 20 May 1922, the emphasis was very much on defence. But this was not the only point which it stressed. The shortage of tanks meant that an autonomous tank force was out of the question and that therefore tanks would have to be dispersed and become a support arm for the infantry. Similarly, if there were to be a reduced air force the planes that were available should be used for observation, reconnaissance and spotting for the artillery. Powerful firepower in defence was 'the preponderant factor of combat'.[15] As a matter of record, the document was approved by both the Conseil Supérieur de la Guerre and the Conseil de la Défense Nationale (which included all the surviving marshals).

More problematic was the effect of demobilisation and financial stringency on the infantry itself. This was first shown up in 1923 when French and Belgian troops were sent to occupy the Ruhr in an ill-judged protest about German failure to meet its obligations to pay reparations for the damage inflicted in the war. At one point 70% of the French infantry were on German soil in the Ruhr or the Rhineland, and when the question of reserves was brought up in a meeting at the time Pétain remarked sourly that he only had 'three regiments of blacks'.[16] That was bad enough, but it was not until 1925 and the campaign on the Rif in Morocco that the weaknesses became clear for all to see. It was this unsatisfactory army that Pétain was to command in what was to be his last venture on the field of battle. But, oddly enough, if 1925 was to mark the end of his active military career it was also coincidentally to mark his venture into serious politics. Needless to say, when this shift in Pétain's ambitions occurred, Nini was to be little more than a bystander.

13

THE SPANISH CONNECTION (1)

'Le Maréchal est un grand homme qui . . . est mort en 1925.'

It is difficult to convey to the modern reader the esteem in which the victorious French marshals were held in the years following the end of the First World War. In the French public eye, these were no ordinary run-of-the-mill generals. Whatever the bickering among them during the conflict, they were perceived after the war as a united body of heroes of Homeric valour. To be sure, the three who had received their marshal's baton before the end of 1918, Joffre, Foch and Pétain, were held in particular respect. The others, Fayolle, Franchet d'Esperey and Lyautey, who were awarded their batons in 1921, to some extent trailed along behind. Of the three greater Homeric heroes, if there were to be carping, perhaps Joffre, the 'Victor of the Marne', was thought to be a bit past it, and perhaps Foch had been too hysterical in his attacks on Clemenceau in the run up to the Armistice and during the Versailles Peace Conference. But there was no denying Pétain, the 'Victor of Verdun' as he was universally known – not least by himself.

In many ways, 1925 was the apogee of Pétain's whole life. (As de Gaulle was later to imply, it might have been better if it had ended there.) Wherever he went he was fêted. The weekly magazines were full of his exploits, of the speeches he made to veterans' associations, of the prize-givings, of the parades, and of the openings of official buildings and even of the dedications of the streets which carried his name – at least one in every town that considered itself of any importance. In short, he received the treatment which nowadays is reserved for the most elevated of sporting heroes, even to the extent of courtesy titles and beyond that to other, more specific, rewards. In 1925, for instance, Pétain was made a Curator of the Château of Chantilly – an honorary post which carried with it a comfortable and well-appointed apartment.

Pétain certainly enjoyed these attentions. But in 1925 he was to encounter attentions which put even the Homeric worship of a Marshal of France into the shade. Moreover, as a hitherto political *naïf*, he was to encounter a régime which appealed to all the instincts of a respectful peasant educated into the grand tradition of the French Army. In short, he was to meet Spain.

Don Miguel Primo de Rivera y Orbaneja, the 2nd Marqués de Estella, was a big man. Though not above average height, he was thick-set and heavily built. His life had been lived on an equally large scale. Born in 1870, he led a boisterous career in the Spanish Army in Morocco, Cuba and the Philippines. Eventually he found his way back, first to his native Andalucía as Military Governor of Cádiz and then to Cataluña as Captain General of Barcelona. While there, he gained a reputation for unnecessary brutality in putting down any sign of civil disturbance – proclaiming, nevertheless, his affection for his fellow citizens. He also gained an equally deserved reputation for sexual prowess and his ability to drink his fellow officers under the table. Moreover, it was said that when he went to a bullfight he would have the testicles of the bulls killed early in the afternoon cooked and served to him in his box while he continued to enjoy the entertainment. He had a vast repertoire of bawdy jokes, which he used to tell during endless hours in street cafés – usually in his native Andaluz. In short, he was everything a Spanish grandee was meant to be. To the Spaniards of the day, male and female, he was irresistible.

In September 1923 Primo de Rivera decided that the domestic political situation in Spain demanded resolute action. Accordingly, together with a group of senior officers, he announced a coup on a manifesto of 'Country, Religion, Monarchy'. King Alfonso XIII, who was conveniently on holiday in San Sebastián at the time, returned to Madrid and 'invited' Primo de Rivera to establish what was tantamount to a dictatorship under no more than the nominal authority of the monarch.

This he did. The Directorate which he set up was composed entirely of military figures, but there was no doubt who ran it. Once in place, it quickly set about suspending all constitutional guarantees, outlawing the Communist Party, forcing trade unions to arbitration at the risk of being disbanded and – needless to say – adding further to the existing privileges of the army officers who had supported the coup. In his endeavours he was enthusiastically supported by those who held the reins of Spanish finance – and by the Catholic hierarchy. But it so happened that, in the course of this constitutional hijack, he also declared himself High Commissioner for Morocco.

Up until that point, the history of the Spanish Protectorate of Morocco, set up by the Treaty of Fez in 1912, had been little short of disastrous. Many areas had remained out of Spanish control. In fact, over the years the Spanish Army had only been able to advance by slow steps into the Moroccan hinterland. In 1921, however, the policy had changed. The Berber tribe of Beni Urriaguel had succeeded in forming a series of alliances with neighbouring tribes along the extended ridge of mountainous country in northern Morocco known as the Rif. They were threatening to declare independence from the Sultan, who was under the protection of Spain. There was no doubt about it. Spanish pride was at stake.

As it happened, the Beni Urriaguel had acquired two charismatic leaders, the brothers Mohamed and Mhamed Abd el Krim. The elder brother, Mohamed, was the more politically assertive of the two, while the younger had the job of commanding the tribal army. Contrary to the Spanish propaganda of the time, both Abd el Krim brothers were men of intelligence and education. Mohamed, for instance, had attended a Spanish school in Melilla, and from there he went on to Fez to study in the Koranic theological school – where, perhaps surprisingly, he learned how to shoot and how to ride a horse. Moreover, his first career had been in journalism, as editor of the Arabic section of the Melilla paper *El Telegrama del Rif*.

The confrontation between the brothers Abd el Krim's Berbers and their Spanish Protectors came to its first climax in 1921. The Spaniards launched an army of some twenty thousand men under General Manuel Fernàndez Silvestre. Its task was to move into eastern Morocco,

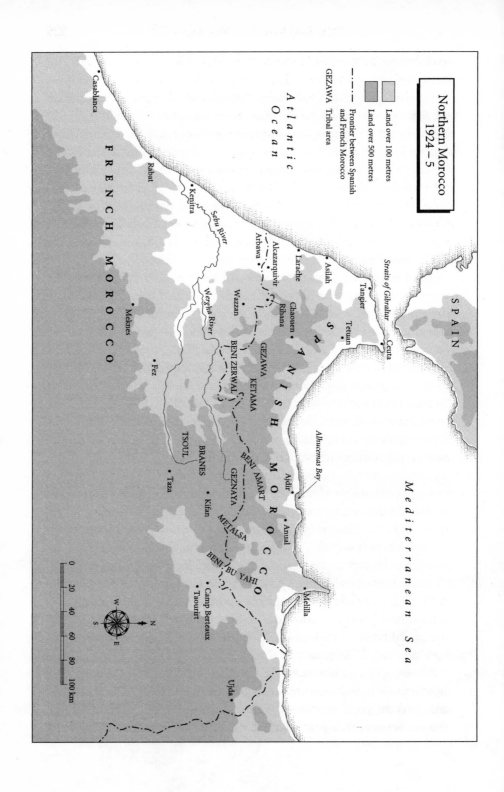

Northern Morocco
1924–5

Land over 100 metres
Land over 500 metres
— · — · Frontier between Spanish and French Morocco
GEZAWA   Tribal area

SPAIN

Atlantic Ocean

Strait of Gibraltar

Mediterranean Sea

FRENCH MOROCCO

SPANISH MOROCCO

Casablanca
Rabat
Kenitra
Sebu River
Asilah
Larache
Arbawa
Alcazarquivir
Wergha River
Wazzan
Chaouen
Rihana
Tanger
Tetuan
Ceuta
GEZAWA
BENI ZERWAL
KETAMA
Meknes
Fez
TSOUL
BRANES
GEZNAYA
Taza
Kifan
BENI AMART
METALSA
Ajdir
Anual
Alhucemas Bay
BENI BU YAHI
Camp Berteaux
Taourirt
Ujda
Melilla

0 20 40 60 80 100 km

N
W — E
S

to defeat the Berbers and to force their submission to Spanish rule. But things did not work out at all as planned. On 17 July 1921, at first light, the Berbers attacked, ferociously and in waves, all along a Spanish line defending a small settlement by the name of Anual.

It was a rout. The Spanish simply ran away from the fierce Berber onslaught. Those Spaniards who failed to surrender – and some even if they did – were either hacked to pieces or, in extreme cases, disembowelled and strangled with their own intestines. Headless and limbless bodies were left scattered at random on the field. General Silvestre's body was never found – it was assumed that it had been dismembered like the others. Only a handful of Spaniards escaped to tell of the full horror of the day.

For the Spanish Army, let alone Spanish pride, Anual was a catastrophe. Not only was it a human tragedy – 1,100 men had surrendered – but, worse still, the Berbers captured some 19,000 rifles, about 400 machine guns and 129 cannon. The Spanish prisoners were ransomed for a large sum of money, which allowed the Abd el Krim brothers to buy even more weapons and ammunition. Finally, in the enthusiasm of victory Mohamed proclaimed the independent Republic of the Rif, with himself as President.

By the time Primo de Rivera took power in Spain in 1923 the Rif Republic had established itself. Liberal opinion throughout Europe – and in particular the French Communist Party – pronounced the Berbers to be honourable natives who had thrown off the colonial yoke. As Abd el Krim himself said, 'We Riffians are no more Moroccans than the English are Dutch. Probably it is this racial mixture that makes us very like the English in our absolute will of independence and in our desire to be in touch with all the nations of the world.'[1]

Not unnaturally, Primo de Rivera took a different view. It was simple enough. Anual had to be avenged and the Rif Republic suppressed. But before that could happen the Spanish Army had to be reorganised into an at least reasonably efficient fighting force. It was not going to be easy, but the first step was to bring what remained back to safety. It so happened that there were still some forty thousand men sitting in relative tranquillity in the garrison of Chaouen, in the southern part of the Protectorate. Primo de Rivera gave orders that they had to be brought back sixty-five kilometres northwards to the capital Tetuan. But there was a problem. A protective line of four hundred blockhouses standing a quarter of a mile apart – to be known as the 'Primo Line' – still had to be built. The infantry at Chaouen could not possibly be brought back until the Primo Line had been built.

All in all, it was not until September 1924 that the final order could be given to evacuate Chaouen. But when it did get under way, the Riffians were lying in wait. The retreat from Chaouen turned out to be another Spanish disaster. The scale of losses has never been established, but by all accounts only half of the Chaouen garrison made it back to Tetuan. Furthermore, in all probability, casualties would have been much greater had it not been for the robust rear-guard action of the Spanish Foreign Legion – known as the Tercio – under the command of the young Colonel Francisco Franco. Nevertheless, in spite of Franco's rearguard action, it was not until 13 December that the stragglers from Chaouen finally found their way into Tetuan.

The Spanish withdrawal behind the Primo Line, leaving the centre and south of their Protectorate in the hands of the Riffians, had international repercussions. The Treaty of Fez had awarded France the protectorate of the southern – and by far the larger and richer – part of Morocco. The natural frontier to the north was the River Wergha, which rises in the mountains of the Rif and flows westwards to join the River Sebu and thence into the Atlantic Ocean. The legal frontier between the two protectorates, however, ran north of, and parallel to, the river. The French quickly realised that the Spanish withdrawal left the way open for the Riffians to make allies of the tribes which lived within their protectorate between the legal frontier and the natural frontier of the Wergha and to assert their authority over land that the French regarded as their own.

There was hurried consultation in Fez. Staff officers there wanted a quick pre-emptive strike against the Riffians. But the Resident-General, Marshal Hubert Lyautey, disagreed. His policy was, and remained, one of peace. It was he, after all, who had built the Moroccan Protectorate into a prosperous and peaceful country. In fact, he was the architect of a paternalist French colonial policy. Even as a lieutenant-colonel he had successfully settled and then administered the southern half of the island of Madagascar. He had been in Morocco since 1912, had overseen the building of railways, roads and, above all, schools. His attitude to the native inhabitants was paternal: they had to be educated, and it was up to the French Army to educate them.

Lyautey's answer to the Riffian threat was to construct and man a number of small forts in the territory between the Wergha and the frontier with the Spanish Protectorate. His strategy was to prevent the Riffians from launching a frontal attack in the way they had against the Spaniards. In the event, the strategy was a complete failure. On 13 April 1925 the Riffians, led by the younger Abd el Krim, overran the French forts in the west, hacked the defenders to pieces and put the villages of tribes which were friendly to France to the torch. The way to the town of Taza and from there to Fez itself was open.

The French establishment, both in Morocco and in Paris, was deeply shocked. After all, Pétain, in his capacity as Inspector General, had the previous January reviewed the military arrangements (and had 'lunch with Marshal and Madame Lyautey', as he wrote to Nini),[2] and had apparently found them adequate. He had even been relaxed enough to invite Nini to visit Morocco in February – a move which the Lyauteys, surprisingly given their strict Catholicism, warmly welcomed. All, at that point, had been well. But by the middle of June the atmosphere had changed. In Paris, Lyautey was personally blamed for the April failure.

It was the start of a whispering campaign against Lyautey. He was not well, it was said. He was too old, out of touch, too much the aristocrat, too Catholic and, to cap it all, a homosexual. Like all whispering campaigns, it contained an element of truth. Lyautey had indeed been ill and he had himself wished to be relieved of his direct military duties. But the mood in Paris was fiercer than mere gentle criticism. The centre-left ministers, newly elected in 1924, did not take to this fervently Catholic aristocrat. Moreover, he was thought to be too prone to run Morocco as though it was his own personal fiefdom. Almost worse than the political disapproval was the resentment of Parisian businessmen, whose hopes of exploiting the riches of the Protectorate had run up against Lyautey's paternalistic view that a large part of his job was to allow the Moroccans to build their own prosperity.

It was Painlevé, a figure from Pétain's past, and now once more Minister for War (as well as Prime Minister), who started the campaign to undermine Lyautey. He and his colleagues decided that the only way forward in Morocco was in joint military operations with the

Spanish. Lyautey had never thought that the Spaniards were anything other than boorish and brutal. Co-operation with them was simply not on his agenda. Worse still from Lyautey's point of view was that not only was Painlevé preparing to negotiate with the Spanish but at the same time he actually was negotiating – admittedly at arm's length – with Abd el Krim. Indeed, peace terms were handed to Abd el Krim's agents in Tangier at the same time as Lyautey was replaced as commander of the French army in Morocco by a hitherto obscure general, Alphonse Naulin. (Some thought that there had been a bureaucratic mistake: it should have been, they said, not Naulin but the much more distinguished Nollet). Not content with all that, Painlevé sent Pétain himself to make a detailed inspection of French forces there and report back to him.

At the time, Pétain was in Germany supervising the withdrawal of French troops from the Ruhr. He was, of course, already aware of the situation in Morocco – he had written to Nini in June that 'the direction of operations down there leaves much to be desired'.[3] On receiving Painlevé's instruction he hurriedly left the Rhineland and on 16 July he flew to Morocco, arriving in Rabat the following day. At first he was welcomed by Lyautey. But it became clear, as his journey of inspection proceeded, that he was less than impressed with the conduct of affairs. 'I am trying to arrive at a reasoned opinion',[4] he wrote to Nini on 22 July, the day he sent off his report to Paris.

The report was the first full account that the French government had of the gravity of the situation. Painlevé himself had visited Morocco in June but does not seem to have understood the urgency of the problem. He showed no enthusiasm in responding to Lyautey's admittedly rather plaintive requests for reinforcements. In any event, the centre-left government which Painlevé headed – the *cartel des gauches* – had no appetite for colonial military adventures. Furthermore, Lyautey had been less than open in his reports to Paris on the extent of the Berber incursions.

Pétain's report, however, came as a wake-up call. He described Abd el Krim as 'the most powerful and best armed enemy that we have met in the course of our colonial operations',[5] praised Lyautey's efforts – and then demanded massive reinforcements. Painlevé certainly woke up. During August and September troopships, on instructions from Paris, criss-crossed the Mediterranean loaded with men, animals and machinery – the *Oued Zem*, the *Doukkala*, the *Haiti*, the *Martinique* and the *Circassie* – sailing out of Marseille and heading for Rabat or Casablanca.

But the question was what to do with the troops when they were fully acclimatised and ready for action. Lyautey's original plan, which was adopted by Naulin, was to mount a series of limited attacks on dissident tribes together with attempts to maintain good relations with the tribes which had not given their allegiance to Abd el Krim. This was not good enough for Pétain. 'I considered the programme . . . insufficient', he later wrote.[6] Pétain's plan was to mount, together with the Spanish, a massive attack on Abd el Krim and remove him and his followers from the map. Once his report to Painlevé had been safely dispatched he therefore set off on 27 July from Casablanca to meet Primo de Rivera and to launch the process of planning a joint operation.

The following day at eight o'clock in the morning the French cruiser *Strasbourg*, with Pétain on board, duly arrived at Ceuta. Fifteen-gun

With Primo de Rivera, Tetuan, 1925.

salutes from the Spanish warships *Reina Victoria* and *Bonifaz* welcomed her in. As soon as she docked, Primo de Rivera and two of his generals went on board to meet Pétain and quickly accompanied him down the shaded ramp to a quay which was heavily decorated with flowers. Three bands, two Spanish and one French, played the '*Marseillaise*' and the '*Marcha Real*'. More Spanish generals joined in the review of the guard of honour. The whole company of Marshal, generals and officers then went to the railway station – to be greeted with a long speech by the Mayor of Ceuta. It was apparently some little time before they managed to get on to the special train which was to take them to Tetuan.

'The people of Tetuan', reported a journalist, 'gave Marshal Pétain a great reception.'[7] There were, of course, the formalities – welcome by the Grand Vizier, more generals, two more bands, another fifteen-gun salute and so on. Pétain and Primo de Rivera then drove in an open car through the crowded streets to enthusiastic applause. There was Moorish dancing in the Plaza de España and much singing of Andalusian songs. Pétain was obviously mightily impressed – and, it was reported, visibly moved.

It was not until they reached the official residence that the noise died down. In fact, the formal meeting lasted no more than an hour; but the celebrations were generous. There was a long lunch (to which the Grand Vizier was invited) and many toasts. Primo de Rivera's toast to France coupled with the name of Marshal Pétain was lavish in its praise of the 'Victor of Verdun'. Pétain, in turn, was full of praise for his host. The two men, with accompanying generals, then made their slow way back to the station to take the train back to Ceuta. After their farewells, Pétain and the *Strasbourg* sailed away. Primo de Rivera, for his part, took the trouble to congratulate the civil and military leaders on their performance, with a particular mention of the Tercio and its commander, Colonel Francisco Franco.

Pétain had been genuinely impressed with what on his departure he described as 'the fine Spanish Army'.[8] Primo de Rivera had sacked several generals and instituted a discipline which had brought the Army to a peak of competence quite unknown to the ragged mob which was destroyed at Anual three years earlier. In Paris, of course, the Spanish Army was still seen as something of a bad joke. Pétain was anxious to correct that impression. Captain de Courson, his liaison officer with Primo de Rivera's staff, was clearly expressing Pétain's view when he wrote that 'thanks to the long months of semi-armistice which followed the troop withdrawal and the organisation of the present lines of resistance, the army has been taken rigorously in hand, largely due to the authority of General Primo de Rivera'.[9]

Pétain was confident that he could safely recommend to Painlevé a joint military operation with the Spaniards. On 4 August, therefore, on his return to Paris, he explained to Painlevé and other ministers that he wished to mount not just the minor type of skirmishing favoured by Lyautey but a much more substantial attack designed to defeat Abd el Krim once for all. Painlevé agreed, but insisted that Pétain himself should take charge of it. Pétain accepted the job, but replied that he only wanted to run the military operation, not to replace Lyautey. He had, after all, been particularly complimentary about Lyautey in his report and, indeed, on his way back to France had called in at Barcelona and, in a press interview, had referred to him as 'my great friend'.[10]

On 18 August Pétain left Paris again for Morocco. The terms of Painlevé's proposals had been published a few days earlier, together with Abd el Krim's rejection of them. The stage was set for a major military confrontation. The nature of this was agreed between Pétain and Primo de Rivera at Algeciras on 21 August. The Spaniards would attack from the north and the French from the south. The attacks would be massive and carefully co-ordinated.

The following day Pétain arrived at Rabat after an uncomfortable flight. He was not in the best of moods. He was met by Lyautey. In their discussions Lyautey, according to Pétain, 'entered into my views and asked to let him know my definitive programme once I had fixed it'.[11] Pétain then left for Fez, where he made a detailed study of the front. By the 26th he was able to let Lyautey have the major points in his plan. The first two followed the limited plan sketched out by Lyautey himself and Naulin. The third point, however, specifically set out a plan for an offensive which 'aims for the foothills of Haut-Mbouz which give access to the heart of the Rif and open the possibility of establishing, along the general line of [the River] Kert, a Franco-Spanish base from which further progress may be made'. Lyautey told Pétain that he 'formally supported the plan'.[12]

The next day, Lyautey went to Paris for 'consultations'. They were, of course, nothing of the sort. It was an opportunity for the government to announce, on 3 September, that Pétain had been appointed sole commander of French forces in Morocco – without any responsibilities towards Lyautey as Resident-General. Lyautey's position was steadily being undermined. Three weeks later, worried and depressed, he returned to Morocco. He had finally recognised that the campaign to get rid of him was unstoppable. Only a week after that he wrote a dignified letter of resignation.

By that time, the military operation was under way. On 8 September the Spaniards landed at the beaches of Cebadilla and Ixdain in Alhucemas Bay, a point on the north coast halfway between Ceuta and Melilla. True, there was some confusion at the outset, when the slower landing craft were unable to manage the strong currents as well as the faster escorting warships. Primo de Rivera – initially in the background to allow General José Sanjurjo his proper place of command – took personal control and insisted that the landing go ahead. 'I have promised Marshal Pétain, he said, to land; I will land by force if necessary,' runs the French report of the operation.[13] Primo de Rivera left the cruiser he was sailing in, jumped into a pilot boat, changed to a torpedo boat and harangued the convoy – telling the faster ships without delay to take the slower in tow.

The landing turned out to be wholly successful. The Spanish Legionnaires, under Colonel Franco, were able to establish a bridgehead, which in turn allowed the disembarkation of regular and native units. The Riffians had expected a landing further to the west of Cebadilla beach and were taken by surprise. By nightfall the Spaniards were off the beaches and encamped in the hills behind. That was enough for Primo de Rivera to leave Sanjurjo in charge and to head back to Tetuan. Progress from there, however, was slow, and it was not until his return on 20 September that the Spaniards again took the initiative. On 2 October they were able to take Ajdir, Abd el Krim's capital. On 8 October they met the French columns which had been advancing in the territory north of the Wergha. On 15 October Pétain and Sanjurjo met – with much expression of mutual congratulation.

Five days earlier, Lyautey had left Morocco for the last time. He had had a last meeting with Pétain on the 3rd. When they were discussing the whispering campaign against Lyautey Pétain is said to have remarked, 'but certainly you don't suppose, my dear friend, that I have played a role in this affair?', to which Lyautey is said to have replied, 'No, my dear friend, I know you are too straight and loyal for that, but . . . are you sure that the role was not forced upon you?'[14] Privately, Lyautey thought that Pétain was implicated in a plot to dislodge him. He certainly bore resentment towards Pétain for some years afterwards. He also wrote a furious attack on Pétain's plan of attack (which he had earlier approved).

On 14 October the rains came – and snow in the mountains of the Rif. Further military action was impossible, and all sides dug in for the winter. The Rif was surrounded. Everybody, except perhaps the Riffians, knew that in the following spring the war would be concluded. Pétain said as much to Théodore Steeg, the civilian who had replaced Lyautey as Resident-General, when they met in Casablanca on 28 October. His mission apparently completed, on 2 November Pétain left for home. When he arrived at Marseille he announced, 'Morocco is henceforth quiet. Abd el Krim is no longer to be feared. My military task is now finished. I hand over the affair to political action.'[15] Two weeks later he was again travelling – this time to inspect French troops in the Rhineland.

Nevertheless, in early 1926 Pétain was once again back in Spain. On the night of 3 February his train crossed the frontier and stopped briefly at San Sebastián. Pétain told the small crowd which had assembled out of curiosity that he was very happy to be making the trip, 'since I have had a burning desire to come to Spain'.[16] On the 4th he arrived in Madrid in the morning, was met at the railway station by the Duke of Santa Elena, representing the King, by the usual posse of Spanish generals, by the French Ambassador, Count Peretti de la Rocca – and a band. Pétain and his aides, General Alphonse Georges and Colonel Émile Laure, then moved to the French Embassy where they were to stay. Hardly was the unpacking done than they were whisked off for an audience with the King in person. Then it was back to the Embassy for lunch with, among others, Primo de Rivera. By all accounts it was an extremely cordial occasion, culminating in the Ambassador presenting to the Mayor, to mark the friendship between France and Spain, a painting of Pétain and Primo de Rivera standing side by side. After lunch, the two leaders met by themselves in the Ambassador's office to discuss the war in the Rif. In truth, there was not much to say. Abd el Krim and his brother were surrounded; it was therefore only a question of tightening the noose once the weather improved. That was agreed between them in a meeting of less than an hour.

In the evening there was a truly splendid occasion – a state dinner in the Royal Palace hosted by the King and Queen María Cristina. The whole Royal Family was present, the Infanta Isabel looking particularly striking in a long beige dress, diamond necklace and the ribbon of the Order of María Luisa across her bosom. Some three hundred guests, the cream of Spanish society, all in full evening dress, made up the company. The place of honour on the Queen's right was, naturally enough, given to Pétain. On his other side sat one of Madrid's great beauties of the day, the Duchess of Talavera. Even the most cynical would have been impressed, and the peasant from the Pas-de-Calais was far from cynical about aristocracy.

It needs hardly to be said that the meal through which they all had to munch was enormous: consommé, soup, fillet of sole, braised *noix de veau*, gammon from Andalucía, pineapple sorbet, roast veal, salad, asparagus, ice cream, and, to fill any remaining space, Breton cake. All this was washed down with oloroso sherry, white Rioja 1919, a light red Rioja 1901, a darker red Rioja 1914, Champagne and sweet Muscat wine. To help them on their way the band of the Halberdiers played a selection of melodies, including, perhaps rather oddly, 'Reminiscences of England'.[17]

It was the first time that Pétain had been guest of honour at a royal state dinner. He had, of course, been entertained by royalty before – most notably by the King of the Belgians at a dinner throughout which he had flirted shamelessly with the Queen. But this was the first royal state occasion and, moreover, it was organised with traditional Spanish elegance and flair. Pétain even had to forsake his customary simple uniform of *horizon bleu* and don full marshal's regalia. Furthermore, the King and the royal princes went out of their way to engage Pétain in what was officially reported to be animated conversation. He was suitably flattered – and said so. At eleven o'clock, when the Royal Family retired, the guests left the Palace and were taken by Primo de Rivera to the Apollo Theatre where they were able to catch the second half of *Aida*. The audience stood up to a man (and woman) and applauded as they took their seats in the royal box.

Decorated by King Alfonso XIII. (*Keystone*)

There was to be no let-up in the social programme. The next morning there was a *vin d'honneur* at the Circolo Francés given by the Madrid branch of Anciens Combattants. Then, at 11.45 a.m. Pétain and the King – with the usual number of followers – left Madrid in a special train for Toledo. There was lunch on the train, finished in time for its arrival in Toledo at half past one. From there the party went immediately to the cathedral where they were greeted at the west door by the Cardinal Archbishop and Primate of all Spain. A tour of the cathedral followed, the King explaining to Pétain – in excellent French – the history of the cathedral's many treasures (including the only surviving copy of the Bible of Saint Louis). Pétain was duly 'astonished' at such richness.[18]

Later in the afternoon the King took Pétain to the Alcázar, which housed the officer cadet college. There, after a speech of some length, he presented Pétain with the Medalla Militar. Pétain made a somewhat shorter speech of thanks, in which he described the Spanish army which had fought in Morocco as 'the most courageous and admirable in all Europe'.[19] Further medals were exchanged between the lower-ranking officers, and the whole party moved off to see the Infantry Museum, various churches and the synagogue, before taking the salute at a march-past of a company of soldiers. Finally, the King presented his guests with swords of Toledo steel. All then took the train back to Madrid, arriving safely at Atocha station at 7.30 p.m. There followed a private dinner (and a film show) at the French Embassy.

The social programme still had some way to go. On the morning of the 6th there was a visit to the Museo del Prado, where Pétain, tact-fully wearing the Medalla Militar, expressed himself particularly interested in painting since 'in addition to his being a Curator of Museum at Chantilly his wife possesses widely recognised talents in painting'.[20] (This revelation of Nini's previously unannounced artistic genius comes as something of a surprise.) Then it was on to another formal meal, this time given by Primo de Rivera, in which Pétain announced that he had authority from the President of France to award to Primo the Médaille Militaire. The lunch ended at half past three 'in an atmosphere of extraordinary cordiality'.[21]

Pétain arrived back in Paris on 7 February. Once there, he was appalled to learn that the French government, under the pressure of public opinion, was ready to strike a deal with Abd el Krim. He and Primo de Rivera had agreed that the Riffians had to be crushed once for all, not least to give the Spanish Army its full revenge for Anual. Nevertheless, a peace conference was held at the end of April – at the town of Ujda, near the Moroccan–Algerian frontier. Both Pétain and Primo de Rivera urged their governments to be tough. Preconditions for a conference were therefore laid down: release of all prisoners and Riffian retreat from many of their most important strongholds. Although these preconditions were subsequently withdrawn, it proved impossible to establish any trust between the two sides, and the con-ference soon broke down. Further bloodshed had become inevitable.

It was then only a matter of time. On 7 May a joint Franco-Spanish attack was launched. Although the Riffians fought bravely, by the end of May Abd el Krim had had enough. On 27 May he, his mother, his brother, his two wives and four children with a mule train carry-ing all their possessions and, it was later alleged, a quarter of a million dollars, stole away from the main Riffian army and surrendered to the French. The Rif War was over.

There was a tidying-up conference in Paris on 14 June 1926, but the main celebratory event was the Bastille Day parade of that year. 'The Place de l'Étoile', the Spanish press reported breathlessly, 'presented an unforgettable sight.'[22] Assembled at the Arc de Triomphe were the whole Paris diplomatic corps, led by the Papal Nuncio in full fig, French ministers, Spanish generals (led by Primo de Rivera), French generals (led by Pétain), the Presidents of the Senate and of the Assembly, and a whole army of officials. At 9 a.m. precisely, to the accompaniment of deafening salvos, the '*Marseillaise*' and general applause, the President of the Republic and the Sultan of Morocco stepped out of their car in front of the assembled company. Decorations were exchanged, and the whole party moved off into a grand parade down the Champs-Elysées. At the end of it Primo de Rivera and Pétain lunched with the President and Sultan. In the afternoon, Pétain took Primo de Rivera off on a private visit to Chantilly.

There is no doubt that by then Pétain and Primo de Rivera had developed a strong personal friendship. Primo de Rivera obviously admired Pétain's war record. Pétain, on the other hand, was impressed with what he perceived to be his friend's political skill. In fact, his dictatorship followed the same ideological line as the other military interventions in politics in both Spanish and Latin American history. The military in these events sees itself as the ultimate guarantor of national cohesion; parliamentary democracy is believed to lead to confusion and corruption; the nation state has to be defended as the most efficient and reliable political entity – and source of pride; the Catholic religion is to be revered since it ensures continuity of conservative purpose, with the additional advantage of promising to its adherents eternal life. Primo de Rivera's seizure of power had all these characteristics. In this case, however, there was one further feature superimposed, as it were, on the traditional face. King Alfonso XIII was to remain head of state (although the wags nicknamed him 'Segundo de Rivera').

All this was familiar ideological territory for Pétain. Like all French officers of the day he was familiar with the most effective voice of the Catholic, anti-semitic, xenophobic and monarchist right, Action Française. Primo de Rivera did not follow the extremes of Action Française, but there was similarity between them on the need for firm social discipline supported by a Catholic monarchy. But although the ideology may have been familiar, Action Française had never been a political party, let alone taken power. In Primo de Rivera's Spain, Pétain saw for the first time a political system which answered to his instinctive – if as yet incoherent – political views actually in operation. Moreover, it seemed to be working.

Not only that, but Primo de Rivera had created for himself a public image that even a Marshal of France could only envy. To be sure, this had been carefully orchestrated by his movement the Patriotic Union, but Primo de Rivera himself had an extraordinary appeal to the Spaniard in the street or in the field. As a result, he was known as 'the saviour of the fatherland' or 'Titan fighting Jupiter' or an 'Atlas who with his stout unshakeable shoulders avoided the collapse of the lofty roof of our beloved Fatherland'. He was also a 'Christ, who carries the cross on his shoulders', 'the Messiah who carries the sun of justice in his right hand in order to illuminate the beloved Spanish soil'.[23] No Marshal of France, however great his reputation as a Homeric hero, could have dreamed of such accolades.

It is little wonder that the seventy-year-old Pétain was impressed, even to the point where, as de Gaulle later pointed out, he started to think that it might be he, in the future, who might follow Primo de Rivera's example. Indeed, he seems to have let slip as much himself, at a dinner given for him after their meeting in Algeciras on 21 August 1925. Under the headline ALLEGED TOAST BY PÉTAIN the Madrid agent of the *New York Times* reported carefully. 'Details received here of the banquet given by General Primo de Rivera to Marshal Pétain', he wrote, 'reveal a curious toast which the French Commander-in-Chief is alleged to have tendered to the head of the Spanish Directorate. He is quoted as saying: "I toast Primo de Rivera who through his intelligence and patriotism was able to re-establish discipline and order in Spain. Perhaps circumstances may make it necessary to do in France as was done in Spain."'[24] As a manifesto for the future, Pétain's toast could hardly be bettered.

14

'THE MEMORY IS WEAKENING'

Je n'avais jamais subi une telle avalanche de questions en trois jours . . .'

The Ossuaire at Douaumont is a truly dreadful monument. For a start, the architecture can conveniently be described as proto-Stalinist. But if the outside is bad enough, the inside is even worse. Row upon row of unidentified skulls and random bones lie in mute but furious testimony to the battle in which their owners had fought and died. And yet it is strangely moving. Nobody of any sensitivity can visit the place without at least a degree of humility. Pétain, as was fitting for the 'Victor of Verdun', was Président d'Honneur du Comité de l'Ossuaire. In 1920 he had laid the first stone of the sinister edifice. On 17 September 1927 it was his further duty to preside over the transfer of the fifty-two coffins – each representing one of the fifty-two sectors of the battle – from the temporary building where they had lain to the new building. This he did, with a speech in the memory, and honour, of those who had fallen. Pétain did not normally display emotions, least of all on public occasions, but his speech in this case is redolent of the memory of human suffering to which he himself had borne witness. He could not, nor would he ever, forget it; nor, indeed, would France.

It is no more than a banal truism to state that adjustment after a major war to what might be seen as peacetime normality has never been, nor will it ever be, an easy process. In the modern world, that has been shown many times over. Nevertheless, France in the 1920s found the post-war adjustment particularly difficult. It is not hard to see why. The loss in terms of killed, wounded, blinded or mentally damaged in the four years of conflict had been fearful. In total, according to official statistics, the war had cost France 1,382,400 male dead or missing in action. A further 3,594,889 men were wounded. Moreover, all classes had suffered equally. The officer class had, in fact, been somewhat worse hit – 20% of the 1894–1918 promotions of the École de Guerre, for instance, had lost their lives. But the peasantry was not far behind – nearly seven hundred thousand were killed and some five hundred thousand wounded. Admittedly, the statistics are far from reliable, but it is certainly true that almost every family had scars to bear. The lines of cemeteries in almost every village and town, with flowers withering on the graves, still remain as silent witnesses to the tragedy which was played out during those years on the plains of eastern France.

By the mid-1920s there was a general feeling that the apparently glorious victory of 1918 was not producing the rewards which the survivors felt they deserved. True, there was an outbreak of somewhat forced gaiety in the early years after the war. It was a long time since anybody had had anything which resembled a good time, and a good time people – at least in Paris – seemed determined to have. But the memories were still haunting. Painting, for instance, had changed to darker, surrealist colours and shapes. Music, apart from the frenetic dance music of the day, became more fractured and dissonant. Literature was questioning – in the last volume of Proust's novel, set after the end of the war, the narrator notes all these changes, and wonders at the almost unrecognisably altered faces of those he had known in pre-war days. In short, it had become quite clear that *La belle époque* could not be recreated in the way that many had previously wished.

It is not surprising that in this atmosphere of frenetic unease there were those who wished to huddle together for some kind of comfort. All sorts of groups were formed – most notably, of course, the veterans' associations, but also communist and anti-communist factions, trade unions, and groups of apparently well-meaning men who wished to set the world to rights. Redressement Français was one such group. Its founder was the industrialist Ernest Mercier, whose main achievement was to organise the distribution of electricity in France along lines that were considered to be the last word in modern technology. Mercier took the view that government could and should be modelled along the same lines. He recruited, as well as a number of like-minded captains of industry, senior officers in the armed forces and distinguished academics. Prominent members were François de la Rocque, Lucien Romier, Jérôme Carcopino, René Gillouin, Bernard Faÿ and Raphaël Alibert. To lend suitable dignity, Foch was the group's honorary president.

In its early days – it was founded in 1925 – the task was to develop a coherent programme for applying the concept of 'scientific management' to the economy as a whole and to the political system. Over two hundred 'experts' from all professions and none sat down to produce, over a period of four months, more than 120 reports. The role of the state was to be reduced, education reformed, agriculture made more efficient, the banking system overhauled, and a host of other worthy objectives spelled out in great detail. The Management Committee, headed by Mercier himself and including Lucien Ramier, the editor of *Figaro*, had the job of bringing coherence to it all.

At the outset, Mercier announced that the group was to be apolitical. Gradually, however, the group moved, albeit hesitatingly and with some wide differences of opinion, towards a political stance. Marxism was a particular enemy. To fight it off, strong government was needed, perhaps by successful senior military figures who had shown themselves to be capable of running large units during the war. If this meant a suspension of democracy and civil rights, it was a price worth paying. In support of this general view, the group lent its support to the Croix de Feu, de la Rocque's rumbustious collection of war veterans.

It is not entirely clear precisely when Pétain decided to form part of this group. He had known Mercier during the war as a technical adviser to the Minister for Munitions, his friend Louis Loucheur. But Mercier does not appear immediately as one of his closest post-war associates. Nevertheless, his experience of Primo de Rivera's Spain confirmed Pétain in the views which were the basis of Mercier's political attitudes, and when he was presiding over a meeting in 1934 he remarked that 'you know how much I am interested in Redressement

Français, as I have proved to you'.[1] He went on to say that whenever he was able to come to their meetings he did so with pleasure. It is not too much to say that this was Pétain's first introduction to what might be called political theory. Moreover, it chimed very neatly with what he had seen in Primo de Rivera's Spain.

For the moment, however, this was a minor preoccupation. What was worrying him much more was the state of the French Army. Morocco and the Riffians had shown him how badly it had deteriorated since the end of the war. The length of national service had been reduced from the two years fixed in December 1921 to eighteen months. It was impossible to retain an army of thirty-two divisions on that basis. Not only that, but a larger and larger part of the Army was taken by native colonial regiments – there were twenty-two of them in action in Morocco at the end of the Rif War. Finally, and most drastically from the point of view of Pétain and his fellow generals, a majority of the National Assembly had been elected in 1924 on a platform of reducing the length of service to one year.

The campaign for the reduction in army numbers was given impetus by the signature, in October 1925 at the Swiss town of Locarno, of a treaty. Under its terms, France, Belgium and Germany made a solemn commitment to the frontiers settled by the Treaty of Versailles, to the permanent demilitarisation of the Rhineland – and to Germany's admission to the League of Nations. It need hardly be said that the Locarno Treaty was hugely popular in all the capitals of Europe. This was, it was widely proclaimed, the final peace between the nations of Europe. The three main architects, Austen Chamberlain, the British Foreign Secretary, Aristide Briand, his French opposite number, and Gustav Stresemann, the German Chancellor, were fêted as heroes. In fact, in spite of the euphoria in Paris and London, the real winner was Stresemann. He had given no guarantee about Germany's eastern frontier with Poland and Czechoslovakia. Moreover, he had managed to secure a further reduction in the Allied forces occupying the Rhineland. All the French had achieved was a rather reluctant reaffirmation by Britain of her guarantee, already promised at Versailles, of Rhineland demilitarisation – which, in the event, was to prove worthless.

The Locarno Treaty, with its promise of permanent peace and good will between the nations of Europe, was precisely what French campaigners for a reduction in the length of national service required. By the end of 1925 their case was, at least in the press and public opinion, substantially won. Consequently, in January 1926 the Conseil Supérieur de la Guerre met to discuss the whole matter of army organisation, on the assumption that the reduction would indeed take place. The proposal put forward by the Chief of Staff, General Debeney, was certainly radical. After the event, he argued, there would be a totally new kind of army. Only twenty infantry divisions could be maintained on a standing basis. On mobilisation the three most recently discharged groups would have to be recalled. Officers from the standing army would then be posted to command and run the twenty further divisions thus formed. Thereafter, a further group of twenty divisions would be raised by recalling older reservists to the colours (known as 'Series B' reservists). It was all very complicated, but it had to do.

Debeney's proposals were agreed. In fact, in the circumstances there was nothing else to do. But the conclusions, even then, were clear. France would have to prepare for a wholly new kind of army. She would be reverting to the notion of a 'nation in arms' – the notion which had sustained the Revolution and the Napoleonic campaigns.

Pétain (centre) and de Gaulle (behind Pétain) in 1926.
(*Giraudon/Bridgeman Art Library*)

The standing army would be little more than an educational institution designed to train enough adult males to form on mobilisation an army of sixty divisions. The major part of that would consist of reservists. Pétain, of course, disapproved of the whole thing, pointing out, rather plaintively, that after all North Africa still had to be defended, and that in itself required a substantial standing army. But his cause was by then lost in the post-Locarno euphoria.

The legislative climax came in 1927 and 1928. The Army Organisation Law of 1927 – passed as a matter of confidence by the Poincaré administration of the day – was complemented by the One Year Law, finally passed in January 1928. At each stage in the debates, Pétain's name was cited and his reputation invoked – as it happened, by both proponents and opponents of each particular clause. Pétain himself kept his own counsel, at least in public, but recognised in private that the tide was flowing strongly against him and his fellow generals. Later, when all was done, he wrote that, after all, the French Army still occupied the city of Mainz on the Rhine and that the German Reichswehr was still 'in appearance, at least' within the limits of the Versailles Treaty limits.[2] Nevertheless, it was a difficult pill to swallow. But it was noted, and carefully stored in the ageing memory, that the Radical leader, Édouard Daladier, voted against the whole package, on the grounds that the Army was still too large.

While all this was happening, there was another event which caused something of a military stir. Captain Charles de Gaulle had joined Pétain's staff in July 1925. He had, of course, been one of Pétain's subalterns in the 33rd in Arras in 1910. But he had had an indifferent war – wounded twice in the early phases and then wounded again at Verdun, captured and then spending the remaining years of the war in a prison camp. Nevertheless, he had struck Pétain as an officer both of courage and of original views. It was de Gaulle's poor mark in his subsequent passage through the École de Guerre which prompted Pétain not only to take de Gaulle on to his staff but to invite him to give a series of three lectures at the École itself. It was unprecedented, but such was Pétain's prestige that nobody dared to say him nay.

De Gaulle's first lecture came on 7 April 1927. The great hall at the École de Guerre was packed. The crowd separated to let Pétain through, but Pétain pushed de Gaulle in front of him to give him pride of place – and to show that the lecturer was authorised by the Marshal himself to say whatever he wished. De Gaulle, in full dress uniform, his captain's braid on his arm and his war medals on his chest, strode up to the podium, removed the white gloves he affected at the time and, after Pétain's brief introduction, began his lecture – on military leadership.

'Powerful personalities', he proclaimed, looking directly at Pétain,

> organised for conflict, crises, great events, do not always possess the easy manners and superficially attractive qualities which go down well in ordinary life. They are usually blunt and uncompromising, without social graces. Although deep down the masses may obscurely do them justice, recognising their superiority, they are rarely loved and in consequence rarely find an easy way to the top. Selection boards are inclined to go more on personal charm than on merit.[3]

Warming to his theme, de Gaulle went on to quote by heart passages from Plato, Lucretius, Julius Caesar, Frederick the Great, Scharnhorst, Goethe and Bergson.

There was a good deal of muttering in the audience at the audacity of this young man who had never even commanded a company and yet presumed to lecture them on leadership. Nevertheless, he was under the protection of the Marshal and was not to be openly criticised. In fact, there was more to come in de Gaulle's second lecture, delivered a week later. Again staring hard at Pétain, he spoke at length about the real and lasting foundations of a true man of character. He went so far as to quote Admiral Fisher's judgement on Admiral Jellicoe after his failure to rout the German Grand Fleet at Jutland in 1916: 'He has all Nelson's qualities except one: he does not know how to disobey.'[4] By then, his audience had become used to the young and inflammatory lecturer. His third lecture, on the nature of prestige, was received in sullen silence. Senior officers in the audience simply referred to him as 'Pétain's foal'.

Later, in 1932, de Gaulle assembled the three lectures, with some additional material, in the form of a book. It was dedicated to Pétain. 'This work', de Gaulle wrote in the dedicatory note, 'could only be dedicated to you, *Monsieur le Maréchal*, since nothing demonstrates better than your glory what virtue can be brought to action through the illumination of pure thought.'[5] There can hardly ever have been a dedicatory note of greater adulation. Nor had the adulation been at a distance. During the years up to 1927 the social and family relationship had been very close. The de Gaulles were frequently to be seen at dinner at Square de Latour-Maubourg – Nini, of course, being excluded from the party so as not to offend Mme de Gaulle's religious sensitivities. Moreover, de Gaulle's son, although not Pétain's godson, as some have suggested, was given a signed photograph of the Marshal to hang over his bed.

But by the end of 1927 the adulation was starting to wane. In December de Gaulle left Pétain's staff to command a battalion of Chasseurs Alpins stationed at Trier in Germany. By the time he completed his two years there not only had his adulation of Pétain started to wane – he was not reappointed to Pétain's staff but to a staff post in Beirut – but there were the beginnings of what turned out to be a serious dispute between the 'foal' and his previously idolised mare.

The immediate cause of the coolness between the two during 1928 has an element of the absurd. During his time on Pétain's staff de Gaulle had drafted a section of what Pétain intended to be a compendium of his considered thoughts on 'the Soldier'. Pétain had even been prepared to invite de Gaulle down to L'Ermitage in order, as he wrote to Nini, 'to get stuck in to the work in which he is collaborating with me'.[6] In the event, Pétain was not at all happy with de Gaulle's work. It was obviously not written in Pétain's own style – simple and soldierly (adjectives, for instance, were considered 'ridiculous, like the silk sashes worn by officers in operas')[7] – but in de Gaulle's more literary style. Pétain therefore gave the manuscript to another member of his staff to be rewritten – and then locked away. Needless to say, de Gaulle was deeply offended, and muttered darkly that although it might not be published in the immediate future it would be one day – as indeed it was, but under de Gaulle's own signature.

Oddly enough, none of de Gaulle's lectures mentioned the burning military issue of the moment – the reduction of national service to one year. Even as he was speaking the Army Organisation Law was completing its parliamentary passage and the One Year Law had been published in draft. Nor did they refer to the reaction of military leaders, including his hero Pétain, to the consequential reduction in army numbers.

The reaction, of course, was to counter the proposed decline in manpower by stepping up preparatory work on a line of fortifications along the eastern frontier. Already the Conseil Supérieur de la Guerre, meeting on 5 December 1925 after the Locarno Treaty, had demanded immediate action. This was followed, such is the nature of 'immediate action', by six meetings of a new 'Commission de Défense aux Frontières', chaired initially by Joffre, which, in turn, led to two reports for Painlevé submitted in November 1926. The first proposed a plan of fortified regions for the north-east, the second a series of forts strung in a line reaching towards the Swiss frontier. The reports took time to digest, and it was not until early 1927 that the matter was moved to its next stage – a further discussion at the Conseil Supérieur de la Guerre.

In July 1927 Pétain himself went to reconnoitre the whole area, combining his visit with a ceremony to inaugurate the Ossuaire de Douaumont. Having spent a good deal of time at Belfort and Metz, marching up and down hills waving his walking stick in the air, he returned to Paris with a revised plan. It was this which was finally adopted by the Conseil Supérieur de la Guerre in October. It accepted the Commission's proposal for two fortified regions (Région fortifiée de Metz and Région fortifiée de la Lauter) with a supporting system of prepared inundations to make the area between them impassable in time of war. The Commission's second report was modified to provide for a further extension of light fortifications along the western bank of the Rhine to the south-east. The project, such as it was, and subject to the government providing the funds, was finally under way.

The Maginot Line, as it came to be called, occupied a good deal of Pétain's attention during 1928. Indeed, 1928 was a year in which he travelled extensively, visiting military installations up and down the country, although not all his stopovers, if rumour is to be believed, were on official business. Even at the age of seventy-two he had an eye for a pretty woman. In March there was a visit to Rome for the obsequies of his wartime colleague the Italian Marshal Diaz – followed by lunch with Benito Mussolini and a tour of St Peter's, the Janiculum and the Villa Medici. At the beginning of August, he wrote to Nini (letters now began 'My dear Annie' and ended 'very affectionately')[8] that he would be away for the whole month – which indeed was the truth, although his precise whereabouts were uncertain. In November he made a visit to Madrid to see his old friend Primo de Rivera, and in December he travelled to London to see his other old friend Spears, by then a member of the House of Commons.

By December 1928, however, it seems that Pétain started to think that he had had enough, both of travelling and being asked too many questions about every aspect of army policy. He let it be known that he wished to retire from the posts of Vice-President of the Conseil Supérieur de la Guerre and Inspector-General of the Army. He was tired; he was approaching seventy-five; and he wanted to spend his remaining years in tranquillity at L'Ermitage. In fact, de Gaulle even remarked that those who knew him well had started to notice 'small periods of emptiness'[9] and 'senile disinterest in everything'. Tired and senile he might look to some – though others, particularly his female acquaintances, claimed that he was in full possession of all his faculties. But the burning question was who would succeed him.

Needless to say, it was a matter of great debate, both among the military and among politicians. Furthermore, the debate became muddled with another matter of current debate – whether there should or should not be a command structure which brought the three services under clear and coherent control. True, the war, at least on the western front, had shown the preponderance of the Army, but after the retirement of Joffre, and even more after Nivelle's 1917 offensive, government had shown a much greater inclination – and ability – to grasp the reins of the somewhat recalcitrant horse. Moreover, aviation had developed to the point where it could lay reasonable claim to its own command structure. Finally, the navy, which had played only a modest part in the war, was by the end of the 1920s becoming an important strategic arm both in the Mediterranean and in the protection of France's enhanced empire. The balance between the three services had changed. Greater co-ordination was needed. The question was whether there should be a super-ministry overseeing three junior ministries – the solution which Pétain advocated – or whether that authority should be devolved to an operational commander.

Whatever the rights or wrongs of any theoretical solution, the nettle of vested interests, as is usual in such matters, proved too difficult to grasp. Instead, it was decided, yet again, to delegate the whole matter to a committee. In early 1929, therefore, the Conseil Supérieur de la Défense Nationale, a body which hitherto – particularly during the war – had played a role which can only be described as nebulous, was enlarged to include, as voting members, all members of the Council of Ministers, with, as advisers only, all members of the Conseil Supérieur de la Guerre. In itself, it can hardly be said to have been the most streamlined organisation for running a future war, but its role was the more complicated in that its function was only to provide technical advice to the government – not to take decisions. The problem, as General Weygand pointed out, was that since all members of the Council of Ministers were members of the enlarged Council of National Defence the process amounted to the government giving advice to itself, which was, Weygand went on with his customary sarcasm, like a donkey giving advice to his own tail.

Weygand, as it happened, was the leading candidate for Pétain's job when, or if, the old man finally retired. There was no doubt about his credentials. He had, after all, been Foch's Chief of Staff. Not only that, but he had almost been in love with Foch. 'When I knew him', Weygand is reported as saying, 'I loved him, and it is natural to do all one can for someone one loves.'[10] The difficulty was that he was small in stature, ugly, with the face of a fox – he reminded one Englishman of an 'aged jockey'[11] – was bad-tempered and a bigoted Catholic ('Up to his neck in priests').[12] Pétain, it need hardly be said, loathed him.

The other possible candidate was General Louis Maurin, a much more emollient character who had been Inspector-General of the Artillery since 1921. In some ways he was an ideal candidate, not least because of his ability to get on with politicians. Indeed, he was in the future to become a minister. It therefore comes as something of a surprise to learn that Pétain, in spite of his personal dislike, always had Weygand in mind as his successor. Yet, in truth, Pétain's endorsement of Weygand had always been conditional. Weygand was, to his mind, the best man for the job – such as it was at the time. Nevertheless, Pétain, in spite of his age and Nini's requests, never felt that he was out of the game. True, from time to time he wrote to Nini that there was nothing he wished for more than retiring to L'Ermitage and looking after his chickens. Indeed, he made elaborate plans for his retirement there – until he discovered that he had been defrauded by the guardian of the premises in his absence. But those were only plans. In spite of all, the real interest was still in Paris.

It was Maginot, the one-legged war hero, by then Minister of War, who took the matter in hand. But not only did he support Weygand; he wanted to give him complete authority over the Army. He proposed to return to the system enjoyed by Joffre between 1914 and 1916, in which the posts of Chief of the General Staff and Vice-President of the Conseil Supérieur de la Guerre (and therefore Commander-in-Chief of the Army in wartime) were united in one person.

Pétain objected to Maginot's proposals on the grounds that the two jobs were fundamentally different. The staff function was planning; the command function was directing troops on the battlefield. Pétain won the argument. The upshot was that Weygand was nominated as Vice-President of the Conseil Supérieur de la Guerre and General Maurice Gamelin – one of Joffre's protégés – was nominated Assistant Chief of the General Staff. Furthermore, Pétain, to general surprise, insisted on himself being nominated Inspector-General of Air Defence. Retirement, apparently, even at the age of seventy-five, was no longer remotely on his agenda.

On the face of it, Pétain's choice of air defence seems an odd one. In spite of his retirement as Vice-President of the Conseil Supérieur de la Guerre he was still a member – and a formidable member at that. By virtue of his rank he could command access to ministers at any time, and was by far the most influential voice on the Committee. Although he had shown himself fully aware of the importance of air power in the future, and had in 1928 supported the creation of an independent air force removed from the control of the Army, he had never shown a particular enthusiasm for the technicalities of air warfare. The most likely explanation for his acceptance of what was, after all, an inferior post is the simplest: like many old men, he just could not let go. It is also possible that he was reluctant to see Weygand with too much authority.

In September 1928 the first of the great French marshals of the First World War died. It was Pétain's old friend and witness at his wedding, Emile Fayolle. Not long afterwards, on 20 March 1929, Foch himself

With Lyautey at a reunion lunch for old St-Cyriens. (*Keystone*)

died. (Joffre survived until January 1931.) Their funerals were, of course, matters of great ceremony. But in Foch's death there was a particular consequence for Pétain. Foch had been a member of that most distinguished of bodies, the Académie Française. His death created a vacancy among the membership – strictly limited to forty – and Pétain was duly elected in his place. This, needless to say, gave him great pleasure. What gave him less pleasure, however, was the requirement that the new member deliver an encomium of his predecessor.

This was not easy. In fact, Pétain would have been wise to summon de Gaulle back from Trier, as was generally expected. De Gaulle certainly shared Pétain's view that Foch was responsible for the premature Armistice which allowed the German armies, as he later wrote, to march back home with their heads held high. But the summons never came. Pétain assigned the task to two of his staff officers, Majors Montjean and Audet.

The final version was an exercise in damning Foch with faint praise, long in the preparation, and cold in the delivery, when the event took place on 22 January 1931. But it did draw praise from an unlikely source. Léon Blum, writing in *Le Populaire*, complimented Pétain on his 'modesty, gravity and reflective and intelligent scruples'.[13] Nevertheless, it was in marked contrast to the speech of welcome, elegantly written and warm in its praise of Pétain, from Paul Valéry. The event itself, too, caused something of a sensation. Those who had exaggerated the row between Pétain and Lyautey over Morocco assumed that Lyautey would boycott the ceremony. He arrived, however, just before it all started, leaping over a table to get inside before the door closed.

Before all that happened, however, there was one event which caused Pétain great sadness. His old friend Primo de Rivera had been forced out of office on 26 January 1930. His dictatorship had come to an unhappy end. In the first week of March, suffering from heart trouble and advanced diabetes, Primo de Rivera arrived in Paris for treatment. Eight days later he died in the hotel where he was staying, his gaze apparently 'fixed on the church of St Thomas Aquinas' opposite his hotel.[14] There was, again, much ceremony to be performed. His body lay in the hotel chapel while mourners filed past. The Spanish Ambassador, Quiñones de León, accompanied Pétain on his sad journey. It was even sadder to say a last farewell as a special train, with the coffin covered in flowers, slowly pulled out of the Gare d'Austerlitz later in the day on its way to Madrid. As it left, Pétain stood stiffly to attention, in marshal's uniform, his hand smartly at the salute.

Official notice of Pétain's and Weygand's appointments came on 9 February 1931 in a decree signed by President Gaston Doumergue. Pétain surrendered his office at 4 *bis* Boulevard des Invalides and moved the short distance to Foch's old office at no. 8. It was very much less grand than his previous office, although almost as big. He took his armchair with him – genuine Louis XV, it was reported – and also recruited a new member of staff, Lieutenant Colonel Paul Vauthier, whose recently published book *Le danger aérien et l'avenir du pays* had been well received. At least there would be someone on Pétain's staff who was aware of the potential of air warfare.

In September, Pétain went for the first time to the United States to represent France at the celebration of the 150th anniversary of the American War of Independence. Pershing was, of course, on hand to meet him, and to escort him to the round of meetings, receptions and dinners which the occasion demanded. There was, too, the usual round of tourist visits – the Niagara Falls, Williamsburg, Richmond and, of course, New York. Pétain seemed to be almost skittish at his first sight of America, even to the point that he was reported as wandering incognito around New York, going to a baseball game and even a fashionable nightclub. As he left, with Pershing still at his side at the foot of the gangplank of the liner *Lafayette*, Pétain turned to him and said: 'We are real brothers.'[15]

As 1931 drifted into 1932, Pétain found himself able to spend more time with Nini at L'Ermitage. The house was by then simply but comfortably equipped, both for winter indoors and for sitting out in summer on the terrace. There was plenty of book space, many photographs of the pair together – and even more of Pétain by himself. Costs, of course, were always a worry, and there was the feeling that he was endlessly being defrauded by local tradesmen. But harvest time was their favourite. The grapes had to picked for the wine which was made locally (and usually distilled into a raw brandy) and olives were crushed for their oil. Pétain prided himself on his knowledge of farming – his correspondence about the type of chicken he wished to keep (and the disappointment at the final choice) is particularly detailed.

Yet times were hard, not just on the land but everywhere. Economic gloom was settling on all Europe. Pétain, too, was gloomy. He knew that he was growing old. As Emile Laure confided to a colleague, 'the memory is weakening. For events of the past, the Marshal's memory is perfect. As for new events, he does not take them in or, if he does, he takes them in badly.'[16] De Gaulle, too, thought Pétain 'gnawed' by old age.[17] One of his staff officers, Commandant Georges Loustanau-Lacau, was even more forthright. 'He has seen so many things and men,' he wrote, 'so many good and bad times, ups and downs, great matters and small, that the arrival of the car he is waiting for interests him as much or as little as the fall of a ministry or the death of a friend.'[18] That was no doubt true, but there were many more ups and downs to come, since Pétain, old and perhaps tired as he might be, was to show that he had certainly not lost what de Gaulle was to call his senile ambition. Interestingly enough, and in the context of future events, his first report on air defence, written, no doubt by Vauthier and advocating, of course, increased expenditure, was submitted in July 1931 to the Premier of the day, one Pierre Laval.

Although the manoeuvring in France for high military office seems today to be a matter of almost parochial unimportance, it would be wrong to accept that view as it stands. France in 1931 was a country at a summit of power and influence. As one distinguished historian has put it, writing – in 1932 – about 1931, '. . . France was the dominant military power in Europe in the air as well as on land; she was executing a naval programme . . . which was causing unease to the [British] Admiralty in Whitehall. Above all, she had extended her potency into the field of international finance. In 1931, the Bank of England was shocked to find itself dependent on the Banque de France, and the Federal Reserve Bank [of New York] to find itself not altogether independent of French good will . . .'[19] The squabbles at the time about position and tactics should not disguise the fact that these were matters which were seen – and rightly – outside France as affecting the whole security of Europe. It was only during the decade of the 1930s that France slipped towards weakness. But then it is not for nothing that these years were to become known as 'the hollow years'; and Pétain was to be part of them.

15

THE HOLLOW YEARS

'. . . je n'ai jamais fait de la politique et je ne veux pas en faire.'

Pétain's domestic arrangements in the 1930s verge on the bizarre. Until May 1939 Nini was kept in seemingly permanent isolation from her husband in her own apartment at no. 6 Square de Latour-Maubourg. She was rarely allowed to accompany Pétain when he went out with his friends, nor on his occasional visits to the theatre, and never to official functions. For instance, she was not allowed to attend his investiture at the Académie Française. Nor, perhaps more understandably, was she ever to be seen with him on his visits to military bases. Nor, indeed, were Pétain's friends allowed to meet her. Henry Lémery, a friend and colleague of Pétain's when he became a minister, was only one of many when he recalled that 'I never knew the Maréchale before Vichy'.[1] Moreover, even when they might have been alone together, Pétain very rarely invited her to have her meals with him, preferring to go out by himself to a restaurant. In short, Pétain was clearly distancing himself from what had become an uncomfortable marriage.

One reason for this distance was that Nini was infuriatingly unpunctual, which upset the militarily punctual Pétain. But Nini – understandably – felt neglected. She became careless both about the state of her apartment (not that she was ever a tidy housekeeper) and about her appearance. She was more than casual about her dress, in spite of the efforts of her maid, and gained the reputation of being somewhat 'bohemian'. To keep herself entertained, she gave tea parties to her friends, who, as Pétain readily acknowledged, were not at all to his taste. Of course, since she was divorced, the more prim members of Paris society – for instance, Mme de Gaulle – refused to go near her. In fact, the only time she was to be seen in Pétain's company on an official occasion was at the dinner he gave every year to his staff officers and their wives (who were unable to boycott the event) in a private room at the Café de Paris.

By way of compensation, Nini spent a good deal of time away from Paris with her son Pierre – whom Pétain gave every appearance of disliking. But as if the separation of their two lives was not bad enough, Pétain would from time to time graphically demonstrate it by – quite suddenly and without notice – simply disappearing. Sometimes it was with a mistress, as, for instance, to Rouen in 1932, but more frequently it was to see his family – sisters, nephews and nieces and, in turn, their children – to whom, as he grew older, he turned to more closely. Nini was never allowed to meet them nor they her – not that either they or she wished to do so. These family gatherings would usually take place outside Paris, at Arras or Amiens, on at least one occasion to mark his birthday. Nini was not invited to that event – even though it was her own husband's birthday party.

Nevertheless, the flow of correspondence between the two Pétains continued unabated. True, his letters no longer even bother to hint at the passion of 1916 and 1917. By 1932 they mostly consisted of recitals of his journey, details of an abscess in his mouth or, most important, instructions on domestic matters, usually at L'Ermitage (and most particularly about the making of wine – in 1934 all his grapes might have to be 'abandoned'), and warnings about spending too much money.[2]

It was not that Pétain's money was particularly short, but by 1932 the economic skies had perceptibly darkened. Moreover, in that year a government of the centre-left was elected. Politically, it was not at all to his liking, but it brought with it one domestic benefit. It served to reinforce his view that this certainly was not a time for reckless domestic expenditure, as he impressed on Nini. In the event, the new government took the same view. Led initially by Édouard Herriot, it seemed to believe itself to be the nation's household and, as such, felt the need to impose measures of severe financial stringency.

Herriot was certainly no financial genius. Nor were any of his ministers or their officials. A crisis was a crisis, and in those days there was only one way to deal with it: by drastic reduction in public expenditure. There were cuts in the salaries of all state employees, cuts in public investment and demands for retrenchment in the private sector. Above all, much to Weygand's disgust, there were severe cuts in the defence budget. For the military, in fact, it could hardly have been worse. Pay was reduced, conditions worsened, and orders for new weapons systems all but dried up. Furthermore, in 1932 and 1933 the summer manoeuvres were cancelled for lack of funds. Recruitment to the armed forces consequently fell off, to the point where Weygand, supported by Gamelin, warned vociferously and publicly of impending disaster.

But it was not just the customary bleating. The generals had a serious underlying point. France was about to enter what became known as the 'hollow years' for army recruitment. The birth rate between 1915 and 1919, for obvious reasons, had been only half the normal rate of a peacetime adult population. The unavoidable result was that eighteen to twenty-one years later there would be a shortage of men of military age. In 1928 the French High Command, fully aware of the impending problem, had hoped to mitigate the effect by raising the age of recruitment to twenty-one in the 'fat years' to then bring it sharply down again in the 'hollow years' to provide the extra manpower required. This hope proved illusory. By 1932 the programme had failed. By 1933, Weygand could reasonably claim, as he did, that the French Army was no longer a serious fighting force.

Weygand's claim was met by the government, by then led by Daladier, with something near to contempt. Almost by way of retaliation, they introduced measures to reduce the number of officers in the Army and to cut military pensions and pay. The measures were justified, in the government's eyes, not just by financial stringency but by the new spirit of international co-operation shown in the Disarmament Conference, finally taking place, after long delays, in Geneva.

The result of all this was a running battle between the High Military Committee, which had been formed in 1932 to attempt some form of co-ordination between the commands of the three services, and the civilians in the government. In this running dispute Pétain supported Weygand, but since he himself was not a member of the Committee he was forced to use Weygand as his mouthpiece. The authority of the 'Marshal's' views was thereby diminished. It was not at all satisfactory, not least since by 1933 Weygand's relations with ministers were, to say the least, fragile. But the row duly rumbled on, and, indeed, reached a pitch of ferocity when, to general consternation, Germany, under the chancellorship of Adolf Hitler, walked out both of the Disarmament Conference and of the League of Nations.

At that point, it was clear that both in Germany and in France the cast on the political stage was changing. Hitler had come to power in Germany. The old French warriors of the Great War had disappeared. Clemenceau had died in 1929; Poincaré was ill and was to die in 1934; Briand had died in 1931. André Tardieu, who had been the politician nearest to them in ability and stature in the period when, as Premier, he inherited Poincaré's majority in 1928, had seemingly sunk into general hostility to the whole parliamentary system of the Third Republic. Maginot died in 1932. Painlevé was to die in 1933. Paul Doumer, elected President in 1931 in succession to Doumergue, only served a year in office before being assassinated by a White Russian émigré.

The new actors were from a different mould. Doumer was succeeded by the even less charismatic Albert Lebrun. Herriot, the son of an impoverished army officer, had during the war been a reasonably effective mayor of Lyon and a minister in one of Briand's governments, but had deeply – and clumsily – offended the French financial establishment in 1925 and 1926, first by apparently refusing to admit the extent of the current financial difficulties and then by refusing to do much about them. Daladier, the son of a baker – known as the 'Bull of Vaucluse' – had fought the entire war at the front, but by the end of it had only achieved the rank of lieutenant. Subsequently, he had become leader of the left wing of the Radical Party, but, as a staunch supporter of the union of the left, was continually irritated by – and irritating about – his failure to induce the Socialists to join a Radical government. Laval, the streetwise trade union lawyer from the Auvergne, who had spoken up for peace in 1917 but had gradually moved to the right as he accumulated a large fortune through his investments in radio and the press, was personally charming enough – and clever – but fickle in his political allegiances. Léon Blum had

undoubted ability, but he presided over a fissiparous socialist movement which had not only refused to join the 1924 and 1932 centre-left
governments but was also uncertain – to say the least – about its
political ideology.

All in all, the French political leaders of the first half of the decade
were pretty much of a job lot. Faced with the gravest of economic
crises and international confusion, not least the problem of how to
contain a resurgent Germany, none of their governments pursued poli-
cies of any detectable strength or determination. Politics descended to
the level of personal bickering. If the Third Republic had been the
longest surviving republic up to that point, it needs little imagination,
even with the benefit of hindsight, to see in the personalities who
inhabited the political world at the time the start of its disintegration.

The first true political crisis came in 1934. On 8 January, a small-
time crook by the name of Serge Stavisky was found dead in a villa
near Chamonix. It was given out that Stavisky, or 'Monsieur
Alexandre' as he liked to call himself, had committed suicide when he
saw that the villa was surrounded by police. The police, the story went
on, were there to arrest him for fraud. Already rich through shady
dealing in securities, Stavisky had overreached himself by arranging for
the issue of a sizeable volume of bonds on the Paris market, the pro-
ceeds of which were apparently to be used to finance a small
municipal pawn shop in Bayonne. Thanks to his network of contacts,
the issue was fully subscribed. But the destination of the funds was not
as advertised. In short, the destination was Stavisky's own pocket.
When this came to light, Stavisky tried to escape to Switzerland.

It turned out that Stavisky had been under police surveillance for
the previous six years, but his contacts in high places had ensured that
on at least nine occasions he had avoided prosecution. These contacts
were mainly drawn from the pool of senators and deputies of the
Radical Party. The right-wing press immediately pronounced that
the Premier of the day, the Radical Camille Chautemps, had had
Stavisky murdered to shut him up. Action Française was particularly
harsh in the matter. There followed a few – but as yet unconvincing –
riots in the streets of Paris. Chautemps thereupon threw in his hand,
and Daladier was called back to form a government to sort out the
mess. In order to win the support of the Socialists for his goverment,
he decided to sack the – admittedly over-enthusiastic – Prefect of

Police, Jean Chiappe. This sparked the fury of the right wing, and on 6 February 1934 a group of demonstrators from a new group, financed by the perfume manufacturer François Coty and entitled Solidarité Française, gathered outside the Chamber of Deputies, chanting anti-republican slogans and proclaiming their intention of throwing all the Radical deputies into the River Seine. This time the riot was certainly convincing, the rioters being encouraged by the appearance in their midst of the venerable Marshal Lyautey, who proclaimed that the government had been subverted by a Masonic plot. This was all too much for the police, who proceeded to fire without warning into the crowd of demonstrators, killing fourteen and wounding a further two hundred and thirty-six.

Paris fell into almost catatonic shock. Still in the political subconscious was the folk memory of the anarchy of 1789, of the 'glorious days' of 1830 and 1848 and of the Paris Commune of 1871. Politicians believed that the riot had been carefully organised by right-wing groups intent on establishing a dictatorship along the lines of Mussolini's Italy – to be led by Lyautey. It need hardly be said that there were no conceivable grounds for this belief, but in times of crisis it is easy to believe in conspiracies where none exist. In short, it was time to panic. And panic there was. Daladier, instead of standing up to fight, resigned the following day.

The upshot was that the seventy-one-year-old Doumergue was dragged out of retirement by President Lebrun and invited to form a 'government of national unity'. So it was that, on the afternoon of 8 February, one of Doumergue's advisers summoned Laure to ask him whether Pétain would accept a position in the new government. Laure replied that 'the best thing would be to appoint the Marshal as Minister of State with the task of co-ordinating the three ministries of national defence'.[3] The suggestion fell on stony ground. Doumergue wished to form a government of national unity – without any experiments. Later that evening Laure was sent for again and asked to put formally to Pétain the invitation to accept the Ministry of War.

Pétain was at home preparing to go to bed when Laure arrived to bring Doumergue's message. At first, he grumbled at being disturbed. Then, after no more than a moment's reflection, he refused the offer. The administration of a department would be too much for him. Besides, he foresaw uncomfortable rows with the Chamber of Deputies.

Laure was therefore dispatched to break the news of his refusal. The following morning, however, Doumergue sent another message: France had need of Pétain. Almost immediately after that, Weygand turned up at Pétain's home and begged him to accept the job. The Army, he said, had need of strong ministerial leadership. Pétain relented, and at 11 a.m. on 9 February went to see Doumergue to accept the post. As he came out of the meeting, he was met by a group of journalists. 'The Prime Minister', he told them, 'said that the country had need of me. I did not hide, but I have never practised politics and I do not wish to do so.'[4]

The remark sounds pompous, and it was. But it is no more than an indication of Pétain's growing sense of self-importance. At the time he received his marshal's baton in December 1918 he was remarkable for the relative modesty of his demeanour. Now that the more flamboyant marshals of the Great War had disappeared (apart from Lyautey and Franchet d'Esperey – who was very much on the wild side) Pétain was regarding himself as 'The Marshal' and was tending to let everybody

Laval and Pétain leaving the Council of Ministers,
May 1934. (*Photos12.com/Hachedé*)

know it. He therefore felt it proper to explain to journalists that he was only taking the job because Doumergue had gone down on his knees.

On one point, however, he was genuine. He intensely disliked the rough-and-tumble of parliamentary debate – in fact, he only appeared once in front of the Chamber of Deputies during his ten months in office – and he certainly had not the debating skills of other members of the government such as Herriot, Louis Barthou, Pierre-Etienne Flandin, Tardieu and Laval. True, he was listened to in the Council of Ministers, not least because, given his marshalship, his colleagues felt obliged to do so. In fact, his main ally was the Foreign Minister Barthou. Extremely able and cultured, but with a roughness of tone which made many enemies, Barthou at least attempted to create a circle of allies to surround Germany. His difficulty was that the most obvious player in that game was the Soviet Union, and he pursued negotiations with the Soviets with enthusiasm. His chosen vehicle was a proposed Franco-Soviet mutual defence pact. At that point he completely lost Pétain's sympathy. Communists, after all, always had pride of place in Pétain's demonology.

All in all, Pétain was not an effective minister. On the major issue, that the Army's manpower needed reinforcement, he made no headway. As a member of government, he was forced to accept that he could not lengthen the period of national service as he wanted, and lost most of his battles with the Ministry of Finance. On the other hand, he managed to reverse Daladier's decision of February 1933 reducing the number of officers; he improved the recruitment programme for specialists; and he lengthened the training period by reducing holiday and leave entitlements. But this was not enough for Weygand. After Pétain had reported to the Senate Army Commission that 'we cannot now increase the length of service . . . the people will not allow it',[5] Weygand commissioned a formal report to the Conseil Supérieur de la Guerre claiming that the French Army was not in a fit state to resist a German attack. The report was signed by Lyautey and Franchet d'Esperey. When it came out, it turned out to be a clear and direct criticism of Pétain's ministerial performance.

The one matter on which Pétain could claim to have made progress was the Maginot Line. Although his initial argument, that the line should consist of a series of 'lighter but unbroken "prepared" battle-fields'[6] had been lost in favour of Foch's 'discontinuous fortified zones', he was prepared to adopt the generally agreed formula. In fact, owing to the shortfall in predicted army recruitment, it was undoubtedly the best option. Not only was the construction of the Line under way but its finances were the best preserved item in the military budget. They were sacrosanct. Very few deputies would dare to vote against them. So sacrosanct was it, in fact, that Pétain even secured an increase in the budget for the Line.

Nevertheless, there were two – interlinked – problems. The first was the matter of how far the Line should extend; the second was what, if anything, should be done to protect France's northern frontiers. Some suggested that the Line should be extended to run along France's northern frontier with Belgium, on the grounds that Belgium was an unreliable ally and could easily fall into German hands as it had in 1914. Others argued that the terrain along the northern frontier was too soft, that the industrial complex around the Lille coal basin was too close to the frontier for comfort, that Belgium would consider itself abandoned and, finally, that a defensive line would negate the main strategy of moving a sizeable force into Belgium at the outbreak of war with Germany.

Pétain was convinced by the second set of arguments. On the other hand, he recognised that it might be unwise to rely on Belgium being forever willing to invite a French army to march into and across its territory. He therefore favoured a scheme originally put forward by Tardieu when he was Premier from February to May 1932. The idea was to persuade the Belgians to erect a line of fortifications similar to those of the Maginot Line along their eastern frontier with Germany. The cost was to be met by a loan to Belgium of one thousand million French francs. Pétain revived the scheme in a series of conversations with his colleague Lucien Lamoureux, the Minister of Commerce. It was bold, and could easily have been effective. But the financial climate was even less promising in 1934 than in 1932 and the conversations came to nothing.

The strategy which emerged was therefore neither one thing nor the other. The Maginot Line would not be extended but would be defended in strength; Belgium would be assumed ready to invite France to send in an army to man the Liège forts and line up along the Albert Canal and the Belgian section of the River Meuse – the underlying threat being that the French Army would go in whatever the Belgians said; and the 'hinge' around which the two operations would revolve would be the Ardennes. The possibility that the Ardennes might provide the platform for a massive tank attack was never seriously entertained by any high-ranking French officer, from Weygand downwards (and certainly not by de Gaulle). Pétain himself ruled out the possibility. In answer to a question put by the Senate Army Commission he stated that the Ardennes were 'impenetrable as long as we make special provisions in them. We therefore consider this a zone for demolitions . . . We should erect blockhouses there.' Any enemy attacking there would anyway be 'pincered as he leaves the forests. This is not, therefore, a dangerous sector.'[7] Nobody, then or later, disagreed with him.

Yet the basic problem of manpower shortage remained. The Secretary-General of the Ministry of War, Alphonse Guinand, was a poor negotiator with the Ministry of Finance, a task which he accepted 'with as much courage as resignation'.[8] Besides, Pétain suspected him of being a Freemason. In fact, the old volcano of suspicions of Freemasonry, simmering in Pétain's mind ever since the days of the *Affaire des Fiches* in 1904, had started to erupt. At least one candidate for a job in his department was taken aside by Laure and told 'to reply frankly whether or not' he was a Freemason.[9] Pétain, of course, knew perfectly well that there were Freemasons in Doumergue's Council of Ministers – including Doumergue himself – as was President Lebrun. But they were civilians, and had no say in the running of the Army. He was certainly not going to let Freemasons into the Ministry of War.

Apart from his objections to Freemasons, Pétain was as meticulous in picking the senior members of his department in peacetime as he had been in picking the officers of his staff in wartime. Only the most able would do. They also had to be up early – he insisted that the day's work should have been mapped out for him by the time he arrived at the office sharp on nine o'clock. They also had to work late, since Pétain did not leave until half past seven in the evening. On the other hand, they had a two-hour lunch break – during which Pétain and one or other of his colleagues would eat together at a nearby restaurant.

Lunch was Pétain's preferred way of meeting friends and colleagues – not least because it avoided complicated questions about Nini, which those who did not know him were apt to ask if invited to dinner. De Gaulle was a frequent lunch companion, at least until the middle of 1934. It was at that point that de Gaulle sent Pétain a letter announcing the publication of his book *Le Fil de l'épée*, with the suggested dedication. Pétain was irritated on two counts: first, that de Gaulle was publishing the book at all, and, second, that de Gaulle, as a serving officer, was putting forward views – and making a nuisance of himself by trying to persuade politicians of their merit – which were contrary to official army policy. Not only did Pétain refuse to reply to de Gaulle's letter but he cancelled all luncheon arrangements forthwith. De Gaulle, needless to say, retaliated by publishing his book regardless, but with the dedication he had originally drafted.

If Pétain's relations with de Gaulle had become strained, his relations with Lyautey had become markedly cordial. Lyautey was particularly pleased that Pétain had taken the ministerial job. He thought that it would do credit to the Croix de Feu. It therefore came as something of a shock when, on 26 July 1934, Lyautey suddenly died. Pétain insisted on delivering the address at the funeral. 'It is for me', he told Barthou, 'to deliver the address, and I will do it.'[10] This he did. As might be expected, his address was flattering almost to the point of embarrassment. He spoke of Lyautey's 'method and imagination, warmth and prudence, will and flexibility, toughness and charm, intelligence and intuition'.[11] And so it went on. Lyautey's family were so impressed that all of them wrote letters to Pétain expressing their gratitude.

The autumn manoeuvres of 1934, reinstated by Pétain after the cancellations in 1932 and 1933, came and went. The official report made it clear that officers were poorly instructed, had little basic knowledge and no confidence. Non-commissioned officers had no sense of leadership and the soldiers had 'forgotten everything'.[12] It was a bleak assessment. But it was confirmed by Gamelin when Pétain asked him whether France had the military strength to intervene in the Saarland if the plebiscite to be held early in the following year resulted in the territory returning to Germany. Gamelin was clear. Any intervention would be a serious military error.

At that point Pétain did make an effort to secure further funds for the Army, but the Doumergue government was starting to look very shaky. On 6 October King Alexander I of Yugoslavia was assassinated in Marseille by a Croatian nationalist. In the hail of bullets Barthou was badly wounded and died soon after. General Georges was also wounded, but not fatally. Immediately the Chief of Police resigned, as did the Minister of the Interior, Albert Sarraut. There were various effects. There was a reshuffle of ministers, the most notable change being the appointment of Laval as Foreign Minister, eager to make alliance with Mussolini's Italy. Negotiations with the Soviets continued but, without Barthou, with diminished enthusiasm. But that was not all. When the new Council assembled, Pétain asked to see Doumergue privately. Aware of what was going to be said, Doumergue asked Pétain to speak out openly. 'With unaccustomed roughness', the account runs, Pétain said that in his view there was still a 'weak point in the government'. Henri Chéron, the Minister of Justice, asked, 'Who are you speaking about, Marshal?' Pétain looked him straight in the eye and replied, 'But of you, my dear Minister'.[13] Chéron wilted under the attack and resigned the following day.

The blood-letting was over, but the loss of blood had weakened the body itself. The press were certain that it was only a matter of time before the government fell. Pétain was relieved to be away from Paris, at least for a few days. He accompanied President Lebrun to Belgrade for the funeral of King Alexander. While there he made a new acquaintance: Hermann Göring. Göring had been a heroic aviator – perhaps the bravest after Baron von Richthofen – in the First World War. As old soldiers from opposite sides frequently do, the two got on famously, reminiscing about their experiences. Indeed, when he returned to Germany Göring spoke admiringly of Pétain, going out of his way to describe him as a 'man of honour'.[14]

The Doumergue ministry finally tottered to its end in early November. Doumergue had made a series of proposals for constitutional reform, one of which was to ban strikes by government employees. This was too much for Herriot and his fellow Radicals, who promptly walked out. According to his friend Henry Lémery, Pétain suggested, somewhat naïvely, that Doumergue could simply do without the Radicals if each minister took on a second portfolio. He himself would 'willingly take on National Education as well as War'.[15] But Doumergue would have none of it, and tendered his immediate resignation to Lebrun. Pétain was furious with Herriot for bringing down the government, but pleased to be no longer a minister. In fact when Flandin formed a government and asked him to stay as Minister of War he refused – in spite of a direct appeal from Lebrun himself.

He left the offices in the rue St-Dominique and returned to his old office in the Boulevard des Invalides. As he entered the familiar surroundings he was reported to be smiling.

Pétain might no longer be a minister, but his marshal's influence on military policy was undiminished. In fact, no longer shackled by collective governmental responsibility, and made a member by name of the High Military Committee on its reorganisation on 11 December 1934, he could be much more forthright in his views. Weygand retired on 21 January 1935, having delivered his 'last testament' to the Conseil Supérieur de la Guerre the previous week. At the first meeting of the High Military Committee on 23 January, with Gamelin now Commander-in-Chief designate, Pétain took up Weygand's reports on the state of the British Army. Weygand – and others – had been particularly impressed by the professionalism and imagination of the British exercises on Salisbury Plain between 1927 and 1931. In particular, the performance of the 1st Brigade Royal Tank Regiment in 1931 had been spectacular. One hundred and eighty tanks had manoeuvred successfully through dense fog and had turned up on time to parade past the visiting dignitaries.

But the manoeuvres which Weygand had watched at Tidworth in June 1934 were altogether a different matter. French military attachés in London had already been reporting a deterioration, but Weygand was shocked at the extent of it. He 'shook his head and walked away', went one British report, 'hoping that we really had something better.'[16] The difficulty was that there was not, in truth, anything better than what had been on show.

Pétain took up this theme at the meeting of the High Military Committee of the 23rd. He claimed that Britain was militarily so weak that it would be fruitless to look for assistance there in the event of a German attack. Even the Royal Air Force was not much good. He was supported in his view by Maurin, the new Minister of War. The inevitable conclusion was that France would have to go it alone. True, Laval had on 7 January signed in Rome an agreement with Mussolini which purported to resolve all outstanding differences with Italy, but even then it was far from clear that Mussolini would prove a reliable ally. (In fact, Mussolini interpreted the Rome Agreements as freedom to invade Abyssinia in October.)

Pétain pursued his campaign with an article in the *Revue des Deux*

Mondes of 1 March 1935. He (or perhaps, more truthfully, the officer who ghosted it for him) reviewed the history of the Army since it had effectively been reconstituted in 1927–8. At that time, he argued, the arrangement was adequate given the restraints on German rearmament in the Treaty of Versailles. But those conditions no longer obtained. Germany was rearming. The militia system could not possibly cope with a sudden attack by an enemy using armour and air power. This type of warfare could only be met by a standing army of trained soldiers. He had hoped that even with the one-year service there might be enough career soldiers to make the Army viable. But this had turned out not to be the case. In short, the only solution was to reinstate a compulsory two-year national service.

Pétain's article appeared only five days before Hitler, in the first of what became known as his 'Saturday Surprises', announced that Germany had a newly constructed air force. One week later, he announced that he would no longer abide by the military clauses of the Treaty of Versailles and was expanding the German Army from its Treaty strength of 100,000 to a force of thirty-six divisions comprising some 550,000 men.

The news could only add irresistible force to Pétain's campaign. But it also, at least in the mind of the press, endowed the Marshal with the quality of uncanny and almost superhuman prescience. If he could read the future so clearly where others were blind, then surely he was the man who should be leading France at this dangerous time. The idea, of course, was not new. There had been a move, for instance, immediately after the fall of the Doumergue government, by *Le Petit Journal*, a popular newspaper of generally right-wing circulation, to promote Pétain as a candidate for dictatorship. The paper even went so far as to conduct a poll – admittedly primitive in terms of modern polling techniques – to which nearly two hundred thousand readers responded. There was no clear outright winner, but Pétain came first in the result, announced in January 1935, with nearly forty thousand votes, well clear of Laval with thirty-one thousand votes.

Pétain did not respond. He was, of course, flattered, but he insisted on saying that he 'would not make use of this result'.[17] But the matter did not rest there. The theme was taken up by Gustav Hervé in *La Victoire*. On 14 February the paper produced an article with the headline *C'EST PÉTAIN QU'IL NOUS FAUT!*[18] The theme was taken up by *Le Jour* and, in April – after Hitler's two Saturday Surprises – by *L'Action Française* (particularly by the fiercely anti-semitic Léon Daudet). Whatever Pétain did, wherever he went, provided material for eulogistic commentary. He went to London in April for the inauguration of the Franco-British Association – to be greeted by Field Marshal the Earl of Cavan. He was therefore, in the eyes of the supporting press, the only Frenchman who was held in respect by the British aristocracy. In early May, he went, with Laval, to Warsaw for the funeral of the Polish Marshal Pilsudski (and another cordial meeting with Göring). *Le Jour* exclaimed that 'a country is on the slopes to disaster . . . when it governs itself in such a way that . . . it has no leader'.[19] The fact that Pétain found the ceremonies so exhausting that, as he wrote to Nini, 'after nine hours' sleep'[20] he went on a leisurely three-week tour of Kraków, Vienna and the Lake of Geneva was, of course, not mentioned.

Pétain's campaign to increase the length of military service to two years had been a success – thanks to Hitler, the Parisian press and some deft parliamentary footwork by Maurin, and in spite of a ferocious attack by Léon Blum. When the Flandin government fell at the end of May, therefore, Pétain felt able to respond to the call of Fernand Buisson to take ministerial office again. This decision was greeted with almost hysterical delight by his right-wing sycophants. But the delight was short-lived. Buisson's government fell after only three days in office. Hervé took this as a sign that democracy had failed – and that the answer, without any further doubt, was a Pétain dictatorship.

Apart from *L'Action Française*, none of the press campaigns need be taken too seriously. They were very much part of the Parisian hothouse. Certainly, Pétain did not take them too seriously. Laval formed a government without Pétain – and without much clamour for Pétain to be included – and in August Pétain went off to review works on the Maginot Line, which, as he wrote to Nini, 'was of the greatest interest'.[21] But he did note in passing that the third 'fortified region', around Belfort, was not built. (In fact, the Metz and Lauter 'fortified regions' proved adequate for the task and Belfort was never built.) Nevertheless, whatever else he was doing, he certainly was not angling for a political job. As a matter of fact, he stayed away from ministerial office until the crisis of May 1940.

Yet the press agitation in favour of a Pétain dictatorship did not die down. Indeed it even gained in momentum – fuelled by the prospect of general elections in May 1936. The conclusion by Britain of a naval pact with Germany which allowed the Germans to construct a surface fleet a third the size of Britain's but with parity in submarine strength, concluded in June by the British without even bothering to consult the French, added petrol to the flames. The news that Hitler, on a visit in October to the Oder-Warthe region east of Berlin, had suddenly taken a decision to accept the recommendations of his generals von Fritsch, Beck and Förster to build the *Westwall*, a line of heavy fortifications along the German western border to counter the Maginot Line, was equally disturbing. Moreover, it became clear that the general elections might well throw up a government that included Communists. Finally, the growth in strength and influence of the paramilitary *ligues* added to the fear of civil unrest – already present but which would become clearly very much fiercer if a Popular Front government came to power.

By the second half of 1935 there were several of these paramilitary or near paramilitary organisations. The Croix de Feu was the strongest in terms of numbers, but it was at times run close by Action Française, with the Jeunesses Patriotes and the Union Nationale des Combattants as also-rans. Francisme and Solidarité Française (apart from the latter's leading role in the riots of 6 February 1934) were of less consequence. Action Française was intellectually the most powerful – Catholic, anti-semitic, authoritarian and monarchist – but Croix de Feu, with its veteran base, could summon up more bodies if strenuous action was on the agenda. There was no doubt that if they combined forces they could pose a very grave threat to civil order.

Pétain, in common with other veterans of the Great War, was sympathetic to the Croix de Feu. When a Minister, he went to church services and other celebrations organised by the movement – as did others in the Doumergue government – but he was careful not to endorse either their political programme or their roughhouse tactics. Although he read – intermittently – the newspaper *L'Action Française*, he was careful to keep his distance from the organisation itself.

It was this distance from the activities of the *ligues* which inspired the most surprising endorsement of Pétain as the prime candidate to take charge of France and bring it to its senses. It appeared in a special edition in November of the left-wing journal *Vu*, and was written by the former Minister for Air in Daladier's Radical government of 1933, Pierre Cot. As such, he had known Pétain well as Inspector-General for Air Defence. Although he was a politician of the left (some claimed that he was a Soviet agent) and hence not to Pétain's political liking, Cot had impressed Pétain, and others, with his grasp of detail and his ability to assemble around him experts from any political affiliation or none.

In his article Cot claimed that the Army would never seek to overturn the Republic, but that if a crisis occurred, the President of the Republic had the right to appoint to the highest office someone of proven record and loyalty to the Republic who would take the reins firmly in hand for the duration of the crisis. 'Does such a man exist?' Cot went on. '. . . Such a man does exist. It is Marshal Pétain.'[22] So it was that, at a stroke of a left-wing pen, Pétain came to be seen as the 'Republican Marshal', not rampaging with the *ligues* in the way that Lyautey had done and Franchet d'Esperey was still doing, but acting against the *ligues* for the preservation of democracy in time of trouble. It was, indeed, a remarkable vision.

By the end of 1935, Radicals, Socialists and Communists had agreed a platform on which to fight the general election of the spring of 1936 under Léon Blum. As the campaign got under way, hysteria took over. The Franco-Soviet Pact, by then initialled but not yet signed, was waiting ratification by the Chamber of Deputies – the debates becoming ever more acrimonious and violent. The British were pressing for the imposition of economic sanctions (except for oil) against Italy as punishment for the assault on Abyssinia. The French right-wing press lashed out all round, raising the volume by several decibels. Blum himself was savagely beaten up on 13 February by an Action Française mob. To add to the political mayhem, Hitler seized his chance to spring another 'Saturday Surprise'. On 7 March, German troops marched into the Rhineland. As justification, the German government cited the Franco-Soviet Pact – which made Locarno no more than a dead letter.

Needless to say, there was consternation. But, in fact, nothing happened. The British Cabinet had been warned of the impending event, as had the French government, and had decided to back France – provided no military action were envisaged. So much for Locarno.

Gamelin pointed out that it was the job of the politicians to tell him what to do – but there had not even been a debate on the matter. German soldiers therefore walked into 'the garrisons and barracks that are already waiting and counting on the fact that we, prisoners of our internal discords and dominated by our love of peace, will not budge'.[23] And so it proved.

The first round of elections, on 26 April 1936, showed 5.5 million votes for the left against 4.5 million for the right on an 84% turnout. Pétain immediately decided to break cover. He gave an interview before the second round, due on 3 May, to the journalist Jean Martet of *Le Journal*. He made an unconvincing effort to pretend that he was not party political, but after a short and rather tedious introduction about military organisation he launched into an attack on the Franco-Soviet Pact, on communism in general, and on those who allowed communists intellectual respectability. He praised the Croix de Feu, not least because they 'occupy themselves with the moral and spiritual improvement of youth'. He claimed that both Germany and Italy were happier and had greater confidence than France. 'We have lost faith in our destiny, that is all. We are like sailors without a steersman, without a rudder.' When asked by Martet whether he could pass on his warning to the French people, Pétain replied – astonishingly – 'No. That would be politics.'[24]

Whatever else he was, Pétain was not stupid. He knew perfectly well that his words would be reported and he knew what slant the public would put on them. They were indeed reported and the slant put on them. But they had no effect. The result of the second count was equally crushing, and the Popular Front government was born. As though by some astrological coincidence, two days before the first round of voting Pétain had entered his eightieth year. He had also entered an arena which he had hitherto shunned and, indeed, which he had previously said he wished to avoid. In the Martet interview he had crossed the threshold into party politics. Far from being a soldier who would serve whatever government was legitimately elected, he had almost overnight openly associated himself with the political right. It was a move, however misjudged, of which his old friend Primo de Rivera would certainly have approved.

16

THE UNPOPULAR FRONT

'Si le baromètre annonce la pluie, est-ce le baromètre qui a tort?'

'We have a rotten government and I want to tell you that the French people won't fight.'[1] Thus ran Pétain's early verdict on the Popular Front government. He was not alone. The arrival of the Blum administration was greeted with a cacophony of poisonous abuse, not just from the right-wing press, which might have been regarded as a trivial if irritating normality, but also from the aristocrats of industry and banking, many of whom were among Pétain's acquaintance.

Admittedly, Blum got off to a bad start. Forever legalistic, he waited for more than a month for the previous Chamber to reach its constitutional term instead of seizing the initiative immediately after his election victory. However noble Blum's motives, the result was that the intervening month saw the worst demonstration of working-class discontent that France had ever witnessed. Factories were occupied by some two million impatient strikers – in what was claimed to be a celebration of their electoral victory and a demand for its immediate fruits. To further complicate matters, there was at the same time a prolonged capital flight. The mere idea that communists would be supporting a French government, if only from the sidelines, was more than any of the bankers of the day could stomach. In the end, Blum was obliged to settle the strikes by approving pay rises of up to 15% by recognising the rights of trade unions, by instituting a system of compulsory collective bargaining and – the last straw for Pétain and his friends – introducing a forty-hour week and paid holidays. Moreover, by September, in an attempt to satisfy the bankers and to stem the capital flight, Blum was forced to devalue the franc.

Pétain's objections to the new government led him into what was, for him, strange territory. For the first time, he felt it necessary to explain – if only to himself – what his political views, until then hardly defined, really were. This required many hours of unusual introspection. Finally, and after much thought, he chose to explain himself at the place with which in the public eye he was most associated – Verdun. The occasion was to be the twentieth anniversary of the battle, to be celebrated on 21 June 1936. He could be sure that his words from there would be heard, but, to make quite certain, he made a request that his speech should be broadcast live on radio to the nation.

Pétain prepared himself carefully, in dialogue with his godson (and, after the father's death in 1936, his doctor) Bernard Ménétrel. After extensive thought and dialogue with Ménétrel, Pétain finally made up his mind what he wanted to say and, having made up his mind, he was determined to say it in the clearest possible manner. But the subsequent preparation for the event turned out to be far from easy. He felt it only right to submit a draft of his speech to Blum. His most dramatic pronouncement – in draft – that 'having won the war [France] is on the point of losing the peace', was promptly struck out. Blum also vetoed the radio broadcast. Pétain's reaction was one of uncharacteristic fury. 'Here is a government', he raged to one his aides, 'which is stopping me from saying and broadcasting what needs to be said.'[2]

As finally delivered, Pétain's speech no doubt lacked the determined force of his draft, but it was none the less powerful. He started conventionally enough, by stressing the importance of remaining strong. 'Whatever policy is dictated by external circumstances, we have the duty to develop to the maximum our armed forces – land, sea and air. Force ensures independence, attracts alliances and maintains friendship.' So far, of course, it was all fairly routine stuff. But he then went on to more dangerous ground – domestic politics.

The physical and mental health of the French people require important reforms . . . The family is the essential cell which must be not only preserved but sustained and magnified . . . If the laws had defended it with care, the social disequilibrium which rages at the moment would not have assumed worrying proportions . . . There is a whole programme to be revived: family, school and army . . . the three guiding steps which make the child into a man . . . Teachers have in front of them an enormous task which requires a profound reform of national education . . .[3]

It was certainly powerful, but none of it can, in truth, be said to be particularly original. Indeed, most of it had been said before in Spain by his friend Primo de Rivera. Nevertheless, coming as it did from a Marshal of France – and a particularly respected one at that – it was both powerful and, given the circumstances, provocative. Even more provocative, however, were his private thoughts, relayed to Ménétrel on the evening before he was to deliver the speech. He explained that he was in favour of finding honest men (in other words, not politicians) who could run France successfully. Moreover, he did not rule himself out as their standard-bearer. But, unlike Primo de Rivera, he was firmly opposed to a *coup d'état*. He was far too deeply grounded in the old military tradition of service to the legitimate government, however distasteful that government might be. If he was destined to serve his country in public life, he had to be called to do so. He would, he implied, simply sit and wait to be called.

There was, at the time, one man who was fully prepared to do the calling. Pierre Laval had been Pétain's colleague in the Doumergue government of 1934, but the two had not had much contact since then. They were not, to be sure, immediate soulmates – Pétain, the rather distant, aloof Marshal of France, and Laval the slippery, chain-smoking, populist politician of the street. Nor did they move in the same social circles. But Pétain, almost in spite of himself, recognised Laval's ability, while Laval saw great use in Pétain's prestige as a marshal. After the Popular Front government's measure to outlaw the *ligues* (although de la Rocque was astute enough to convert the Croix de Feu into a fully fledged political party) Laval became convinced that there had to be an alternative to the system which had thrown up an administration of such disgraceful revolutionary socialism. In an interview with two American journalists, Laval claimed that he 'was convinced that the era of popular governments by parliaments was doomed . . .'.[4]

This conclusion struck a chord with Pétain, and in the middle of 1936 – he 'could not be precise about the exact date'[5] – Laval renewed contact. In the event, it was not difficult. Apart from the simple expedient of picking up the telephone, Laval could always claim a personal connection. His daughter was married to Pétain's other godson, Count René de Chambrun. Moreover, de Chambrun's father was not only a friend of Pétain but also a colleague, having persuaded Pétain in 1935 to become President of the French Information Centre in the United States. Laval, whatever else was subsequently said, was quite open about his intentions, although in the end they came to nothing. The meetings between the two were apparently 'not very frequent'. But they were frequent enough to allow Laval to conclude that Pétain 'had seemed disposed, if the occasion were to present itself to him, to accept the responsibility of power'.[6]

Whatever the nature and extent of Laval's contacts with Pétain, there was never any question of planning a *coup d'état*. Laval knew perfectly well that Pétain would not hear of any such suggestion. There were, of course, some who were thinking along those lines – including the other surviving marshal, Franchet d'Esperey – but Pétain had quite clearly distanced himself from all of them. Nevertheless, what Pétain seems not to have realised at the time was that even within his own office there was similar political ferment. Loustaunau-Lacau had come to the (doubtful) conclusion that communists were infiltrating the Army. Together with others, including Pétain's ever faithful ADC Captain Léon Bonhomme, he organised a counter-effort. They set up a network of officers, both active and reserve, who would gather information about their colleagues and report any sinister left-wing sentiments. The network was known, somewhat obscurely, as Corvignolles.

Corvignolles, as it happened, and however dubious its origins, enjoyed almost immediate success. It was not long before there was at least one member in every army battalion, every air base and every armaments factory. It was equally not very long, of course, before Pétain got to hear of it. When he did so, he insisted on seeing the reports sent in to Loustaunau-Lacau. He did not help to finance the network – he was much too careful with his money for that – nor was he formally a member, but he did from time to time provide helpful information. For instance, early in 1937 he gave Loustaunau-Lacau a paper on the situation in Spain which purported to describe the methods that would be employed by the communists if they wished to stage a 'putsch' in France. Embarrassingly, the paper was circulated to the commanders of all military regions by official military intelligence – whose commanding general, when the whole thing came out, was promptly forced to resign.

Much more sinister, however, was the Mouvement Social d'Action Révolutionnaire, commonly known as La Cagoule (the Hood). For a start, the committee which ran it, the CSAR, headed by a former naval engineer by the name of Eugène Deloncle, was quite prepared to use violence. Groups of carefully organised thugs were regularly sent to break up communist meetings. By the autumn of 1936 the movement had attracted the attention – and the cash – of Franchet d'Esperey, and by the end of the year Pétain himself was showing curiosity. He sent Loustaunau-Lacau to see General Duseigneur, who had recently retired but who was making a new career with Deloncle and La Cagoule. Duseigneur was nothing if not frank. He told Loustaunau-Lacau that indeed the group had arms, was well financed, and was in the process of organising attacks on communists. 'Marshal, there are arms!', Loustaunau-Lacau reported to Pétain. 'It is regrettable', Pétain replied. 'He who has arms is tempted to use them.'[7]

There is no suggestion, nor has there ever been any serious suggestion (apart from by the prosecutor at his trial), that Pétain was a member of either Corvignolles or La Cagoule. There were, of course, rumours, particularly when La Cagoule made a botched attempt at a *coup d'état* on 15 November 1937, that both Pétain and Franchet d'Esperey, the two surviving marshals, were up to their necks in both movements. But, at least in Pétain's case, these were no more than an attempt by his detractors to find guilt where there was none. On all the evidence, he was no more than an interested bystander. (The opposite is true of Franchet d'Esperey, but because he was a Marshal of France he was never even asked, when an official inquiry took place, what his role in either movement had been.)

Pétain's hostility to the Blum government was by then open. Apart from his general objections to the whole nature of the government, he also believed (unfairly) that Blum disliked him personally. His hostility was given further impetus by the government's reaction to the outbreak of civil war in Spain on 15 July 1936. Pétain's view was quite simple: his royal Spanish patron, Alfonso XIII, had been forced to abdicate in 1931 in favour of a parliamentary republic; the new republic had failed to deal with the problems with which it was confronted, and had allowed the elections of February 1936 to produce a Frente Popular which had won a parliamentary majority on a minority of votes cast; following the assassinations of José del Castillo and José Calvo Sotelo on 12 and 13 July, there had been a military uprising; the leading figure in this was the hard-faced young general whom Pétain had known in the Rif, Francisco Franco. It followed, as the night the day, that France should either support Franco or, at the very least, keep out of the affair.

That was not Blum's view. Personally, Blum was in favour of supporting the Frente Popular. But under pressure from the British government, which disapproved of the new Spanish government and all its works, and from his own ministers, he agreed that they should not be supported openly – with the proviso that they should be sent clandestine military aid. The decision, taken as it was in haste, managed to incur the odium of both sides of the argument. When it was leaked to the press on 23 July, the right screamed that Blum was a traitor and the left shouted that he was a coward. The Communists even refused to support the government when it came to a vote in the Chamber of Deputies in December. In the event, the policy itself fizzled out, after the export to Spain of 150 obsolete aircraft – masterminded by the Minister for Air, Pierre Cot, and a member of his staff, Jean Moulin.

In the course of all this, Blum and his colleagues recognised that the frontier with Spain needed, if everything went wrong, to be defended. They were also sensitive to the continued bleat from Gamelin and his fellow generals – and Pétain – that France's field forces needed substantial reinforcing and re-equipping. German rearmament and the remilitarisation of the Rhineland had strengthened the generals' case. Daladier, the Minister for War, finally accepted the argument, and on 7 September 1936 managed to persuade his colleagues – and a surprisingly sympathetic Blum – to adopt a four-year plan at the total expense of four thousand million francs. It was indeed an ambitious project – perhaps too ambitious, as the future would show. By 1938 national defence claimed a third of the whole French budget and absorbed 50% of tax receipts, an almost unsupportable burden for a government committed to social reform. But to Pétain, at least, it was a welcome recognition that the defence of France had been put in peril by successive governments and needed to be addressed.

It was only a month after the rearmament programme was announced that the whole French strategy for a future war with Germany was thrown into disarray. On 14 October King Leopold III of the Belgians declared that Belgium in the future would follow an independent foreign policy. Everybody knew what this meant in practice – Belgium would remain neutral in any future war. For the French strategists, it was a bad blow. In all their plans, they had relied on active and complete Belgian co-operation for a quick French move into the Low Countries in the event of war. The possibility of Belgian neutrality had not hitherto been on any considered French agenda.

French reactions to the Belgian declaration were, to say the least, confused. Gamelin tried to make a secret deal with his Belgian opposite number, and enthusiastic francophile, General Édouard Van den Bergen. The two quickly agreed that the Belgian Army, in the event of war, would immediately appeal to the French for help. As far as it went, that was all very well. But the problem with the deal was that Belgian generals, unlike their French counterparts, had no political clout. Gamelin was forced to concede this when he admitted that France would 'only enter Belgium if circumstances lent themselves to this'.[8] In other words, it would be a decision firmly in the political domain.

Daladier's mind was running along different lines. For him, the solution was to extend the Maginot Line along the Franco-Belgian border as far as the English Channel. France would then be protected along her whole frontier from Switzerland to the Atlantic. But as soon as serious study got under way, the familiar problems emerged, and Pétain again stressed them. The water table was too high; the mineworkings and heavy industry were too close; and the Belgians would simply be left hanging in the air. Moreover, work on the main part of the Maginot Line was badly behind schedule. It was delayed by strikes and supplies of faulty equipment. Besides, it had already cost some five billion francs and was due to reach between six and seven billion by 1939. The extra stretch which Daladier wanted would, in Gamelin's estimate, require another ten billion francs.

A third view was held by the French Ministry of Foreign Affairs. They hatched a plan to dangle in front of the British the prospect that French strategy would change as a result of the Belgian declaration. The outcome, it was hinted, would be very damaging to their British allies. The Channel ports would be exposed to a German attack and would be conveniently used as bases for U-boat operations in the Channel and the Atlantic. It was a clever try, and the British were suitably aghast. But General Sir John Dill, the Director of Military Operations at the War Office, pointed out acidly that the British Army would only be able to cobble together two poorly equipped infantry divisions for a cross-Channel operation. Besides, Dill, whatever the merits of the case, was not one to go out of his way to help the French.

Each of these proposals thus had its difficulties. Certainly Pétain, for his part, was very much against any arrangement with the British. But, having quite correctly appreciated the difficulty of extending the Maginot Line, he was left, as was Gamelin, with a half-hearted compromise, finally accepted by Daladier. There would, it was agreed, be some limited fortifications along the Franco-Belgian frontier, but not such as to inhibit a French sortie into Belgium at the beginning of any war. It was not just half-hearted; it was a messy compromise. But, in the circumstances, it was at least better than continued and acrimonious argument.

By then, Pétain's own thinking had moved on. Already, in a speech to the École de Guerre in April 1935, he had proclaimed that 'the military art is the swiftest-moving of all the arts. It would be ridiculous to be stuck in a study of the past without looking at the future . . . While remaining attentive to progress in chemistry and electricity or any other science, it is necessary to take full account of the perspectives opened by the tank and the aeroplane.'[9] This was followed by a preface written to General Sikorski's book *The Modern War*. 'The possibilities of tanks', Pétain wrote, 'are so vast that we can say that the tank will perhaps become tomorrow the principal arm [of warfare].'[10] He considered that the tank was best used in counter-attack, but he went further in a speech at St-Quentin on 4 October 1936. 'The concept of the defensive army has had its day . . . modern means of offence are the only ones capable of ensuring proper collaboration for an associate in danger.'[11] (By which, of course, he meant Belgium.) Moreover, he was very much in favour of a strong attacking bomber force to carry the attack to the enemy in the opening phases of a war. He was very much in support of Pierre Cot's Plan II, launched in September 1936, which gave priority to the production of bombers over fighters by nearly two to one. Indeed, he was even prepared to argue, along with Cot, for an arrangement with the Soviet Union for the joint manufacture of aeroplanes.

Where Pétain differed from Pierre Cot – and Daladier – was on the question of a unified overall command. When forming his government, Blum had revived the post of Minister for National Defence, originally created, if only for a brief life, by Tardieu in 1932. He had, however, weakened the position by appointing the new incumbent, Daladier, Minister for War as well. All this did, in Pétain's view, was to extend the remit of the Minister of War to allow some co-ordination with the Ministries of the Navy and Air – but nothing more. He argued repeatedly, from October 1936 onwards, that the Blum arrangement would not deliver a solution to the problem. A proper ministry was needed, to sit over, and dictate to, the three service ministries. Cot argued against this, on the grounds that it would allow the subordinate ministries to evade accountability to the National Assembly. Daladier agreed with Cot – as did the Chamber of Deputies when the matter was debated in January 1937. Although Pétain kept raising the matter again and again, it was clear that it was fast becoming a lost cause.

It was also in January 1937 that an article appeared in the magazine *Revue militaire générale* under the name of General Debeney. It soon appeared that, even if the signature was Debeney's, the thoughts were those of Pétain. Entitled 'The Mystique of Our Officer Corps', the article set out to demonstrate the role of the Army in healing the social and political divisions of the nation. As a theme, of course, it was not particularly new. But it was given particular relevance by the disputes of the day, which threatened, in 'Debeney's' view, to 'become mortal'.[12] In such a situation the Army was to be seen as an active force, even 'the true France', protecting the nation against the excesses of a political régime. Without a doubt, these were sentiments, as Pétain well knew, which would have found echo in Primo de Rivera's Spain.

The 'political régime' in question, was, of course, the Popular Front government, and Debeney's article, although he may not have intended it, served to set what he – and Pétain – thought of as 'the Army' against the Blum government. Fortunately, perhaps, at the time it never came to more than an article in a little-read military magazine, since by then Blum's problems were beyond solution. There was another wave of strikes in February and a good deal of marching in the streets. It was widely forecast that it was only a matter of days before the government would collapse. Indeed, so serious had the situation become that Pétain took several days off at L'Ermitage, complaining to Nini that 'at the moment I left the office the atmosphere of government had become impossible to breathe'.[13]

No sooner had Pétain escaped to the south of France than there was mayhem in Paris. In another attempt to pacify the bankers, Blum gave up his plans to introduce old-age pensions for workers and to create a National Unemployment Fund. The Communists, predictably, denounced the move as craven capitulation to a bankers' ramp; and there were more strikes. On 16 March, when the government refused to ban a meeting of de la Rocque's new political party, the Parti Social Français, protesters tried to storm the cinema in Clichy where it was being held. In the ensuing clash with police, seven people were killed and several hundred injured. The largest trade union, the Confédération Générale du Travail, called a general strike. By then, it seemed clear that the Blum government was mortally wounded. Although it limped on for another three months, it was effectively powerless, and on 22 June 1937 Blum threw in his hand. The 'popular front' experiment had, without any regret from Pétain, died its death.

By then, Pétain had missed the March Clichy riot and the subsequent general strike. It was not until mid-April that he returned to Paris. Even then, it was only because he had caught a cold at L'Ermitage and felt in need of treatment from Bernard Ménétrel that he came back. On his return, he duly underwent Ménétrel's treatment. Whether he knew with precision what he was letting himself in for is not at all clear. Ménétrel had inherited from his father some strange medical practices. One of his specialities was to treat gout and arthritis by attaching a copper cylinder to the patient's skin and heating the air inside to as much as 200 degrees centigrade. Another was to inject oxygen into the patient and a third, apparently favoured in Pétain's case, was bleeding. On this particular occasion, Pétain's cold was treated by Ménétrel, as he reported to Nini, with 'blue rays'. What these were is something of a mystery, but certainly he thought they did him some good, since on the following day he was coughing 'noticeably less'.[14]

Whatever their effect, Pétain managed to survive Ménétrel's practices (or malpractices). He recovered from his cold and got on with what, by then, was a fairly leisurely life. He had plenty of time, for instance, to answer the huge volume of mail he received for his eighty-first birthday. He also had time to consider making a will. While he had been at L'Ermitage he had been visited by his great-niece Yvonne, who was apparently surprised to see how modest the property was. In view of Pétain's stated intention to make a will – he had invited Yvonne to have a look at what might be coming her way – she might have hoped for something more splendid. But, quite apart from her obvious disappointment, she had to wait a long time for her great-uncle to declare his intentions. These were not revealed to his family until they met (without Nini) the following Christmas. One of the secrets that Pétain revealed was that he had made a codicil to his will requesting that he be buried at Douaumont.

The new government of June 1937, under the Radical – but intellectually bereft – Camille Chautemps, seemed to have little for Pétain to do. He therefore left Paris again in May for an extended tour of the Maginot Line, a tour which lasted, with one or two interruptions for cures at Bains-les-Bains in the Vosges (where he was again joined by Bernard Ménétrel and his wife), most of the summer. But while he was inspecting the Line, there were, whether he knew it or not, developments in Germany. On 9 March 1937 the Reichstag passed a law 'concerning the security of the frontiers and concerning reprisals'.[15] This was the formal authority for the building of the *Westwall*. The 'reprisals' in question referred to possible French retaliatory action after the remilitarisation of the Rhineland – and, looking ahead, after future German territorial expansion to the east. The *Westwall* was designed to mirror the Maginot Line – but, it was said, with superior German construction – along the whole length of the Franco–German frontier.

It is not clear whether Pétain either heard, or, if he heard, took any serious note of, the news from Germany. Certainly neither he nor any of his French colleagues are on record as drawing any conclusions from the news, let alone the right ones. So concentrated were they on a French response to a future German attack that they failed to understand that the Germans were equally worried about their own response to a possible future French attack. The German High Command had assumed that France would intervene in the Rhineland. That not having happened, they assumed that at some point a superior French Army would march into Germany on any suitable pretext. By the middle of 1937 it should have been clear to Pétain and the French General Staff that both they and their German counterparts were engaged in a very similar defensive strategy. Maginot and 'Siegfried' (as the *Westwall* came to be known) were, in truth, two of a kind.

In fact, German intelligence had been quick to understand the consequences of the Belgian declaration of October 1936. They were also fully aware of the compromise reached between Daladier and Gamelin. Their conclusion was that a French drive into a neutral Belgium could only be the prelude to an attack across the plain of east Belgium and southern Holland to strike directly at the Ruhr. The German High Command therefore started to badger Hitler to extend the *Westwall* northwards along the frontiers with Holland, Belgium and Luxembourg. There were, however, the customary delays, and Hitler did not give the necessary order until 9 March 1938. But the reason for the acceleration in the decision soon became clear.

Three days after that order was given, German troops moved to seal the annexation of Austria into the Reich. The reaction in France was, to say the least, surprisingly muted. But by then the Chautemps administration was on its knees. The Socialists had abandoned it in January in protest against the erratic – and pro-German – behaviour of Georges Bonnet, who had been brought back from the Washington embassy by Chautemps to be his Foreign Minister. In March 1938, the Socialists struck again, voting against the Chautemps government and bringing it down. If there was one consolation for Chautemps, it saved him from having to respond to events in Austria. As far as France was concerned, that was the end of the matter. In the confusion of the moment, a further Blum administration was formed – and lasted no more than a month.

The way was then open for a further attempt at something approaching a government of national unity that could face up to what was now perceived to be the threat from Germany. President Lebrun gave the task to an old parliamentary veteran. He called on Daladier to see what he could do. As it turned out, it was a good choice. Daladier had already served in no fewer than fifteen governments and had been Premier three times. He was also extremely popular, with a view of democracy which was widely shared (not least by Pétain), patriotic and, once a mandate had been given, authoritarian. In short, he was the only French politician who could possibly pretend to assume the mantle of the political heroes of the First World War, Poincaré and Clemenceau.

Once entrusted with the task, Daladier shifted the political centre of gravity sharply to the right. He brought in Paul Reynaud as his Finance Minister to torpedo the forty-hour week and Bonnet to pursue his policy of avoiding war until France was ready. The re-armament programme, which had badly lost momentum, was given new vigour, with the result that in the eighteen months after Daladier's arrival in office average monthly aeroplane production rose from just over forty to just under three hundred, and average monthly tank production from just over thirty to just under a hundred.

But the Daladier government, successful as it would turn out to be, in April 1938 had a long way to go. Although it was supported by a large majority in the Chamber and in the Senate, the fissiparous nature of the French politics of the time ensured that there was no guarantee that it would last. As Pétain in March wrote to his recently acquired friend – and prolific correspondent – Marie-Antoine Pardee, 'a new political crisis is beginning, and it worries me because it might become serious'.[16] As it happened, Pétain himself was one of the candidates offered to Lebrun as an alternative to Daladier, not least by Laval. But Pétain refused to play the game, and even went so far as to tell Lémery, who was peddling the same line in his newspaper *L'Indépendant*, to stop writing such 'stupidities'. Whatever Daladier turned out to be, Pétain, at least for the time being, was going to support him.

As in 1937, in the summer of 1938 Pétain preferred to be out of
Paris. In fact, as he wrote to Nini in September 1938, 'the last time I
went [to my office] . . . [was] in April last'.[17] But his 1938 summer
was far from idle. On 19 July King George VI and Queen Elizabeth
embarked on a four-day state visit to France. They arrived at
Boulogne in the royal yacht (bizarrely named *Enchantress*) and, as they
were steaming into the port, a vast monument in bronze was unveiled.
It was called 'Britannia'. Its object was to commemorate the first
landing of forward units of the British Expeditionary Force in August
1914.

There was an obvious point both to the huge statue and to the state
visit. Daladier and Bonnet needed allies in the west of Europe. After
Mussolini had declared the 'Axis' of Rome–Berlin and Franco had
virtually won the Spanish Civil War, the only place to look was
towards their old – and unreliable – ally, Great Britain. In consequence, a great fuss was made of the King and Queen. In Paris, the
Union flag was to be seen everywhere; an actress from the Comédie

Pétain and Queen Elizabeth in 1938. (*AP*)

Française intoned an artistically banal 'Ode to England'; and a special commemorative stamp was produced.

It was in Boulogne that Pétain, as befitted an old Marshal of France, gave the most fulsome speech in praise of the 'Entente'. At the unveiling of 'Britannia', he reminded Lord Cavan, as he welcomed him to 'this corner of French territory from where on clear days one can see the English coast', of the occasion in 1935 when they had met at the Franco-British Association in London. He went on to recall the flow of British troops through the port. 'During those unforgettable days', he continued, 'the general emotion which these new troops were also experiencing was such that this delightful detail was noted by an English observer: the shy Tommies offered to the young French women who were welcoming them the still-fresh flowers given by their fiancées just before their departure.'[18] (This was presumably said with a straight face – what the English 'fiancées' thought about it all is not mentioned.)

As a celebration of the Entente it was certainly impressive. But Pétain was only delivering what was appropriate for the moment. In other words, and in truth, he was being wholly insincere. His views about Britain, ever since his dispute with Haig in 1918 and his conviction that the British had stopped him from occupying the Rhineland and destroying the German Army, had, in private, been quite clear. What he said in public was, of course, a different matter.

Pétain had given his private view of the British on many occasions. But it had been expressed most explicitly in an informal conversation with the Italian Ambassador to Paris two years earlier. 'England', he stated – and there is no reason to doubt that these were his considered views – 'has always been France's most implacable enemy.' She only waged war at France's side because this served her own interests and then she backed Germany. (This was a clear reference to his belief that Britain had rushed the Armistice to prevent France annexing the Rhineland.) 'For all these reasons,' he went on, 'I believe that France has two hereditary enemies, the English and the Germans, but the former are older and more perfidious; that is why I would favour an alliance with the Germans which would guarantee absolute peace in Europe.'[19] 'Britannia', whatever else it did, did not change Pétain's mind.

The 'Britannia' event had an odd footnote. The huge and ugly statue was dynamited by the Germans in July 1940. Pétain's speech, however, remains as it was. But the significance, intended or not, was twofold. It reminded his audience, as was intended, of the 'Entente' with Britain. But it also reminded them of the slaughter of the First World War. In fact, Pétain's mere presence reminded them, and every other Frenchman, of precisely that. And if that was not enough, every 11 November, at the thirty-six thousand monuments to the French war dead, ceremonies around them made for an annual reminder of how appalling it had all been. In 1938, after all, those who had fought in the war and had survived would usually be no more than forty years old. Every speech Pétain made, whether he wished it or not, served to remind them of the dreadful sacrifice they and their fathers had made.

If Pétain was insincere in his 'Britannia' speech, Daladier was no less so. He, too, made a fulsome speech in praise of the Entente in Paris during the British royal state visit. But it was only six months later that he was telling the United States Ambassador to Paris, William Bullitt, that 'he fully expected to be betrayed by the British and added that this was the customary fate of allies of the British'. He went on to describe the British Prime Minister, Neville Chamberlain, as 'a dessicated stick', the King as 'a moron' and the Queen as 'an excessively ambitious woman who would be ready to sacrifice every other country in the world in order that she might remain Queen of England'.[20] The 'Entente', if indeed there was one at all, was at that point in frail hands.

It was not all doom and gloom. Daladier's Minister of Finance, Paul Reynaud, had come to a different view. He still believed that Nazi Germany was the main threat to the peace of Europe and had to be resisted by all means available. De Gaulle, Reynaud's political protégé, was of the same view. But de Gaulle was about to embark on the final stage of the simmering dispute which had stood between him and his erstwhile patron Pétain. On 2 August 1938, de Gaulle wrote to Pétain about the book he was due to publish. He asked Pétain to sign the preface. Pétain was in no mood to be generous – and curtly refused.

Pétain then left for his annual cure, this time at Eaux Bonnes – where again he was joined by Bernard Ménétrel. On his return to Paris on 29 August he found another letter awaiting him. After a further exchange of letters de Gaulle and Pétain finally met. De Gaulle set out to persuade Pétain to lend his name to the book, and in the end Pétain agreed to do so. On 5 September, therefore, Pétain produced a carefully written dedication. De Gaulle took this as a draft, rewrote it in a manner which subtly suggested that the publication was at Pétain's initiative – and sent it direct to his publishers. Pétain, as he often reminded others on future occasions, regarded this as a breach of trust. He wrote to de Gaulle's publishers to tell them so. De Gaulle brushed aside Pétain's objections as an irritating nuisance, and demanded that his publishers proceed as planned. By then it was clear that the breach between the two had become what can only be described as a chasm.

What might be called a chasm in the relationship of two men, however prominent they were or would in the future become, was as nothing compared with the crisis which was about to occupy the politicians of all Europe. On 9 September, Pétain wrote to Nini that he was hoping to leave Paris for L'Ermitage the following Monday, with the particular intent of supervising the picking of grapes for the vintage. But he ended his letter, after giving her precise instructions in the event of his being unable to leave Paris 'since it is necessary to envisage all possibilities', that his hope was 'in spite of the present difficulties'.[21] Nini was alarmed by this. The next day Pétain wrote another letter to calm her down. 'I do not believe', the letter ran, 'in serious events either today or tomorrow. Discussions will resume and finally the Czechs will accept. But I thought it would be stupid to leave Paris on the day on which Hitler is going to deliver his big speech.'[22]

The speech in question was delivered in Nuremberg on 12 September. It was a violent and vituperative attack on the Czech government. 'I have no intention', Hitler screamed, 'of allowing a second Palestine to be formed here in the heart of Germany by the labours of other statesmen ... The Germans in Czechoslovakia are neither defenceless nor abandoned ...'[23] Apparently undeterred by Hitler's histrionics, on 14 September Pétain wrote to Nini that 'I do not think that we can be caught up in the Czech row; our leaders would really have had to lose their compass bearing' (in other words, their mind).[24] There followed more instructions on how to organise the vintage. These were set out in even greater detail in letters on 20 and 24 September. In the early hours of 30 September Daladier, Chamberlain, Mussolini and Hitler met at Munich and signed an agreement which would deprive Czechoslovakia of a large slice of its population, its most important industrial sites – and its means of frontier defence against a German attack.

The Munich agreement was immensely popular in France, as it was in Britain. Daladier, who had expected to be booed in the streets, suddenly found himself a hero. From every town he received telegrams of congratulation. Tens of thousands signed books recording their enthusiasm, and there were subscription lists which collected substantial sums in appreciation of the government's action. In the Chamber of Deputies, the agreement was approved by 535 votes to 75 (73 of whom were Communists). Pétain echoed the public mood when, a few days later, he spoke to Bonnet. 'You have rendered a great service to France,' he said. 'I know how you have struggled to avoid war; you were right; we would have been beaten.'[25]

Nor was that the end of it. The anti-semitic tide in France was flowing again, swept on by Action Française and the even more outspoken *Ère Nouvelle* newspaper. When, on 9 November, there was an officially sanctioned pogrom in Germany, in which synagogues were

Pétain and Giraud inspect the army, October 1938.

torched, Jewish shops smashed into and Jewish homes raided (from the amount of glass broken the Berlin wits named it '*Kristallnacht*'), there was hardly a murmur in France. Furthermore, Bonnet let it be known that the German government was officially to be regarded as friendly – so friendly, in fact, that when the German Foreign Minister Joachim von Ribbentrop visited Paris in December Jewish ministers were excluded from the reception.

But it was not so much the anti-semitic tide that worried Pétain as what he perceived to be the general disintegration of French society. In November, he went to Metz for the twentieth anniversary of its liberation in 1918. In a speech to the Veterans' Association of Lorraine he again returned to great themes he had enunciated at Verdun two years earlier. France was gripped by material pleasures and desires; the benefits of the peace had been lost; spiritual life had been abandoned in the education and behaviour of the nation. As a result, France would no longer be able to defend herself. From then on those themes were constantly repeated. If anybody objected, he would say what he had said when Blum tried to water down his Verdun speech: 'If the barometer announces rain, is it the barometer which is wrong?'[26]

THE SPANISH CONNECTION (2)

'I do not believe that Pétain had, at that time, any sympathy for Germany beyond the reluctant admiration which all of us have felt, at one time or another, for her method and powers of organisation.'

'Yesterday evening I saw Monsieur Daladier and I agreed to go to Burgos for three or four months in order to redress French affairs in Spain or, at least, to help to do so. It was agreed that I should take two of my officers as well as civilian personnel. No women. Departure in 15 days.'[1] Thus Pétain's crisp announcement to his wife Nini on 1 March 1939. Almost as an afterthought, he added that in the evening he was to dine with Senator Léon Bérard.

Bérard had been a central figure in the complicated political dance which led to Pétain's appointment as French Ambassador to Spain. Sensing that the Spanish Civil War was gradually, if painfully, coming to an end, he went on his own initiative to Burgos, the then capital of the new Nationalist government, to see an old friend and francophile, Lieutenant General Francisco Gomez Jordana. The two talked – and struck an informal deal. Bérard reported this to Prime Minister Daladier and Foreign Minister Bonnet and was promptly given official status to conclude the arrangement in proper form. Thus the Bérard–Jordana agreements, as they came to be known, marked an important first step in the French effort to claw back the political ground lost by the Blum government's unofficial support in the Civil War of what turned out to be the losing side.

The agreements had seven main points. The most important, in Spanish eyes, were those requiring the release of gold deposited by the Republican government and contracted to the Banque de France as security for a loan; the repatriation of all military matériel, in particular the naval vessels and the fishing fleet which were held in French ports, and all lorries and other vehicles which had found their way to France during the conflict. The French, for their part, wanted to be rid of the five hundred thousand or so refugees who had fled Spain and who were housed, if that is the right word, in refugee camps at the French taxpayers' expense. They also wanted landing rights for Air France.

Until he took the ambassadorial job, Pétain knew nothing of the Bérard–Jordana agreements, which were only announced on the very day he saw Daladier. In fact, there was no reason why he should have known about them beforehand. He was not privy, after all, to political secrets; nor had he shown any particular interest in Spain since the outbreak of the Civil War. He had met Jordana, with Franco, in Morocco in 1925, and he knew that Jordana was now Foreign Minister in Franco's government, but that was about the sum of it. Moreover, Daladier's offer had been unexpected. Indeed, Pétain was not even the first choice for the job. After the announcement on 27 February of French *de jure* recognition of the Franco government, the press speculated on a number of names but there was no mention of Pétain. Daladier tried hard to persuade Bérard to take the job himself, but he turned it down. Only then was Pétain summoned from his winter break at L'Ermitage.

From Daladier's point of view the move was sensible. Pétain had fought alongside Franco in the Rif (although he had only met him once), and his name was well known and honoured in Spain. If anybody could build bridges the old Marshal was the best candidate. Besides, with another war with Germany in prospect, the French frontier along the Pyrenees had to be secured. In simple terms, this meant that in the event of a conflict Spain should be persuaded to remain neutral. Furthermore, by sending Pétain to Spain Daladier could push aside a figure who still had influence but was, in his view, given to moaning too much about France's lack of preparedness for battle.

For Pétain there were no such advantages. He was old, he claimed to be going deaf, he tired easily and openly admitted that he could not maintain a consistent work rate. But the truth is that he was also getting bored. Even at the age of eighty-three he was, in his sharper moments, perfectly capable of serious thought and, if necessary, action. Furthermore, by accepting even a relatively lowly position he would be officially in touch with political affairs rather than watching from the sidelines. Finally, to judge from the tone of his letters, he was quite happy to have a bit of time off from Nini.

The announcement of his ambassadorship was greeted with enthusiasm both in Paris and in Burgos. Even Weygand issued a long statement of congratulation. The only discordant voice was that of Blum who, while praising Pétain himself as 'the most noble, the most humane of our military leaders' thought it an 'error of taste' to send him to Spain.[2] The French press were, naturally, interested in Pétain's view of Franco. Pétain, however, was never one to air his opinions to the press, and they had to make do with the snippets they got. 'I met him once at Ceuta in 1925, during a review in which I accompanied General Primo de Rivera,' he told *Candide*. 'I have to say', he went on, 'that I was much taken with his character . . .'[3] There was more of the same, until Pétain launched into another lecture on the deficiencies of the French educational system – which the journalist faithfully reported.

On 16 March Pétain arrived in Spain. He crossed the frontier at Hendaye on foot (French cars were not allowed into Spain at the time), surrounded not just by his staff but by representatives of the departmental administration, a delegation of war veterans and a crowd of locals waving their handkerchiefs and cheering him on his way. On the Spanish side, he was met by the commander of the frontier station of Bidassoa, the Director-General of Police, the Governor of San Sebastián and one of Jordana's senior aides. There were speeches of welcome. It was the sort of occasion that Pétain revelled in. A Marshal of France, after all, was in his view entitled to nothing less than continued expressions of popular approval.

Pétain's staff was quite small, given the importance of the embassy. His own officers were Vauthier and Bonhomme, and his financial adviser was a young official from the Ministry of Finance, Henri du Moulin de Labarthète. The professional diplomatic staff was led by

Armand Gazel, holding the rank of counsellor. Their wives were duly left behind at the Hôtel Imatz in Hendaye, following Pétain's 'no women' rule. The Imatz was not a bad place – but no more than a small French provincial hotel. It was obviously not good enough for Nini, who much preferred the overblown surroundings of the Hôtel du Palais in Biarritz. The women, including Nini when she felt able to leave Paris, were invited to the embassy in San Sebastián at week ends – for lunch.

Settling in was to prove difficult. Pétain had forgotten his Spanish medals and his marshal's baton and wrote urgently to Nini in Paris to have them sent on. That apart, the house he was allocated, the Villa Zinza, in what before the Civil War had been an elegant suburb of San Sebastián, was in disrepair. It had not been lived in for three years and the interior badly needed patching up – doors, windows, heating, lighting and so on. Moving in was made many times more compli-cated by the weather – it rained without let-up. Added to the domestic difficulties was the reluctance of the Spanish government to invite him to Burgos to present his letters of accreditation. 'I haven't set foot in Burgos,' he complained to Nini on 17 March. 'Besides, they aren't in a hurry to see me . . . they are very severe about France and in some quarters show sentiments near to hatred. We are paying for the faults of our governments of the last few years.'[4]

There was, however, one good reason to be away from Paris: the election for the presidency. Lémery was canvassing Pétain's name in the Senate; others were doing the same in the Chamber. The object of this attention was adamant. He wrote to Lémery telling him not to pursue the matter, and to a deputy who was proposing to come to San Sebastián to sell him the idea that he should not bother. By 2 April, he was able to write to Nini that he had read in the newspapers 'some efforts at combinations in which I have refused to partici-pate . . . besides, it is quite amusing to look from afar at the game of parties and individuals'.[5] In the event, Lebrun was re-elected unani-mously.

Such was the Spanish displeasure, not at him personally but at France in general, that Pétain was not received in Burgos until 24 March. He was conveyed there by a special train. The ceremony was splendid in its choreography, but was spoiled by Franco's evident coldness. 'Franco didn't say a word, or hardly,' reported Gazel later.[6]

When – after the ceremony – he did, he pointed out to Pétain the failings of France in not supporting him in the Civil War. But he was at least grudgingly complimentary to Pétain himself, who, he said, 'having accumulated treasures of military virtue, is in the best position to understand the lofty sentiments of the new Spain, and cannot be indifferent to the proof of heroism and sacrifice which our people has given in this grandiose epic for the defence of its ideals and of Western civilisation'.[7] But it seemed that the defence of its ideals and of western civilisation depended very much on a far from lofty sentiment: the French obligation under the Bérard–Jordana agreements to release what was considered to be Spanish gold.

At that point, Pétain made a friend. On 6 April he met the new British Ambassador, Maurice Peterson. 'The Marshal', Peterson recorded, 'made a great impression on me. Of medium height, holding himself erect whether seated or on foot, the healthy colour in his face and the firm regard of blue eyes, made him appear, even in mufti, the very type of the great French soldier.' Peterson noted, however,

After presenting his credentials to Franco, Madrid 1939. (*L'Illustration*)

that 'vigorous and alert as I invariably found him in the morning, it was a different story if I had occasion to see him later in the day. For by then his age was almost painfully apparent and he looked more – though never wholly – like the figure which caricaturists have since made of him.'[8] Peterson obviously liked Pétain; and Pétain obviously liked Peterson. Moreover, Peterson never found Pétain 'defeatist'.

But Franco had set the immediate agenda. The Spanish gold must be released back to Spain. Pétain duly set about his task. On 10 April he left San Sebastián for Paris – leaving Nini stranded in Biarritz ('Man proposes, God disposes', he wrote to her).[9] He spent three days there, trying hard to explain to Daladier, Bonnet and their officials how much depended on the return of the gold. He explained that it was not just a matter of Franco's disapproval or of the carefully orchestrated press campaign. It was a question of French honour. But the argument – and the whole visit – was not a success. Officials at the Ministry of Finance pointed out politely but firmly that the loan from the Banque de France to the Banco de España had to be repaid before the gold could be released, and that was the end of the matter. Pétain returned to Spain empty-handed.

The Spaniards then dug in their sharp heels. Until the gold was returned, no progress could possibly be made on the refugee question or landing rights for Air France – or on any other matter. Pétain himself was coming in for criticism. The newspaper *Madrid*, for instance, produced a leader entitled WHAT WILL PÉTAIN THINK?[10] – the implication being that the old man had failed to persuade his political masters of the lapse in France's sense of honour. Pétain's ambassadorship had come to what seemed like a full stop. In truth, there was nothing much left to do.

What there was to do, however, was to attend a victory parade in Madrid. The ambassadors, as was the custom, were lined up in a stand on the route. Pétain found himself next to Peterson. They were neither of them in a particularly good mood. It was hot, and the German and Italian Ambassadors had been given pride of place – respectively wearing their Nazi and Fascist uniforms. When Pétain saw this, he turned to Peterson and said: 'Had I known that my German and Italian colleagues would wear uniform, I, for my part, would have put on civilian clothes.' Later in the same week, while the two ambassadors were waiting in the Escorial for a reception which

Franco had declared to be in their honour, Pétain's eye fell on a NO SMOKING notice on the wall. 'I see', he remarked drily, 'that it is forbidden here, not merely to smoke, but to spit.'[11]

But apart from expressing his distaste of the trappings of Nazism and Fascism, Pétain still had to occupy his time. His solution to this problem was to plan, and in May to execute, a long trip to the some of the major cities of Spain. He had always enjoyed travelling. In France he was accustomed to absent himself on trips to inspect this or that military installation. In Spain he considered it necessary to visit the French consular offices throughout the country. At least it saved him from the rain – and boredom – of San Sebastián. But the Spanish press, which followed his movements closely, were happy to call his trips 'recreation'.[12]

Pétain's May journey took him first to Salamanca, then by the evening train to Cáceres in Extremadura and on the following day by car to Seville. There he was met by the French Consul and the President and leading members of the French colony. He visited the cathedral and the Alcázar (and its gardens, which he is said to have much admired), halted for a moment in front of the 'Cross of the Fallen', and, in the evening, watched a procession in honour of Nuestro Padre de Gran Poder. Naturally enough he stayed at the finest hotel, where he was visited by the mayor of the city and the governor of the province. The next day he called on the Cardinal Archbishop before leaving by car for Jerez (where he had lunch with the Domecq family), Cádiz and then Algeciras. From there he crossed over to Gibraltar for lunch with Lady Ironside (the Governor, Sir Edmund Ironside, being absent on a visit to Rabat), and went on to Málaga, where he stayed another night before returning to San Sebastián.

No sooner had he returned to San Sebastián than he was planning another long trip, this time down the eastern side of Spain: Albacete, Cartagena, Murcia, Alicante, Valencia, Teruel, Tarragona, Barcelona, Lerida, Zaragoza, Pamplona and back again to San Sebastián. Again, he informed Nini, 'this journey is essential, to visit the consuls and consular agents'.[13] In fact, as with the previous trip, it was not necessary at all, but it was a convenient and pleasant way of killing time. Not that Pétain was indifferent to his surroundings or to the views of the people he met. He noted carefully the ravages left by the Civil

War – coming soon to the conclusion that Spain simply was not in a condition to join in a European war even if she were willing. He also told his driver (who doubled as his interpreter) to go out in the evening, to sit in cafés and listen to what people were saying – and report what, if anything, they were saying about France.

It was while he was on this journey that his preliminary report was delivered to Bonnet. It described the legacy of the Civil War, speculated about the country's future and expressed doubts whether it would ever be possible to determine what Franco really thought. The Falange, a semi-fascist movement founded by Primo de Rivera's son in 1934, preached a message of nationalism and regeneration in close alliance with the Catholic Church. Franco was believed to be sympathetic, but was unwilling to commit himself too deeply. He was also showing some sympathy towards the monarchists. As for foreign policy, Pétain noted that Franco was very appreciative of those who had come to his aid in the Civil War – and correspondingly hostile to those who had turned away from him. Nevertheless, the report's conclusion was clear. Franco, in spite of powerful pressure from Germany and Italy, would wish to keep Spain out of any future conflict.

The conclusion was thrown into doubt by the news that Franco had authorised the building of fortifications along the frontier of the Pyrenees. It was a bad blow to Pétain's efforts, which, at least in the matter of the gold, were beginning to show fruit. By the middle of June du Moulin de Labarthète had won officials in the Ministry of Finance over to the idea that there was political importance in the release of the Spanish gold, and agreement in principle had been reached on 24 June to return gold to the value of 1.7 billion francs to the new Spanish government, and to write off the corresponding loan in the books of the Banque de France. Pétain had hoped that this would open the door – hitherto no more than ajar – to a fruitful relationship between the two neighbouring countries which the Bérard–Jordana agreements had proclaimed as the ultimate objective. But the fortifications on the line of the Pyrenees were ominous.

On hearing the news, Pétain wrote directly to Franco. Writing as 'soldier to soldier', he assured him that France had no intentions that could remotely be called aggressive. 'Have confidence in a proven friend of Spain', he went on, 'who would not have agreed to come to your country were it not to tell the truth.'[14] Pétain's plea seems to have convinced Franco, since little more was heard of the Spanish fortifications. Moreover, in a spirit of unaccustomed generosity, Franco invited Pétain to another interview. 'The operations relative to the deposit of gold in Mont de Marsan happily concluded,' announced the falangist newspaper *Arriba*, 'in which Marshal Pétain, the French Ambassador, has so nobly and energetically intervened, His Excellency the Head of State received him this morning.'[15] It was Pétain's second interview with Franco. As in the first, there was little cordiality – it was not one of Franco's traits – but at least the date was convenient, since Pétain had just come back from another long trip to Barcelona and Gerona, diverting up the French coast and returning through Perpignan.

While Pétain was whiling away the time in Spain, there was much activity in the Square de Latour-Maubourg. The apartment in no. 8 which was to be Nini's had been secured. It was then a matter of making the necessary arrangements to their joint satisfaction. The delicate matter of communication between the two apartments resolved, Pétain decided in May 1939 that the necessary construction and decoration work should go ahead. Perhaps wisely, he allowed Nini to take charge of the whole business. It was, as he explained, a suitable time, since he was able to add his ambassadorial salary of 141,000 francs to his Marshal's salary of 150,000 francs. The work, he pointed out, came at a good moment.

Nini worked throughout a hot June and July to get the two apartments in reasonable order. Pétain sent her what he assumed was encouragement by writing that she should postpone any plans for further visits to Spain until she had finished her work. But he went further. 'If', he wrote on 7 July, 'when I come back to the apartment I find it completely finished, I will have the pleasure of giving you a good reward – much more substantial than the kiss which I send you today.'[16] Coming, as it did, from a man aged eighty-three, it was a heroic – and perhaps rash – promise.

Yet it seems to have done the trick. Nini did indeed spend her hours supervising the work in the Square de Latour-Maubourg. She was not present, for instance, at the party in San Sebastián for the 14 July national day. Pétain was not particularly generous with embassy funds – the French colony was only invited to an 'aperitif', and he was rather shocked when the assembled company, as he wrote to her, 'threw themselves on the food, which they devoured in one bite'. But at least they paid due respect to the old man. 'They didn't know how to thank me; the old ladies wept with joy and would not let go of my hand. They had never seen a reception like it.'[17] Admittedly, after that the day was spoiled for him by an attendance at a bullfight. He was so upset by the spectacle that he left after the second bull had been successfully slaughtered.

In the same letter to Nini he wrote that he wished to set a date for the end of his ambassadorship to Spain. He wanted to get back to L'Ermitage to supervise the vintage in September. He also felt that he had done as much as he could. The Spanish gold had been released. Franco had invited him for a third meeting (to take place after another long visit to refugee camps north of the Pyrenees), this time on much more cordial terms. Negotiations for a commercial treaty between the two countries were under way. Gazel, his right-hand man, had been recalled to Paris for a new posting. Finally, it would not be long before the government moved to Madrid, and the thought of the move – and setting up a whole new office – was daunting. In short, he felt that the time had come for him to end his mission and come home.

Nevertheless, he was still in San Sebastián when war broke out on 3 September. The event itself, of course, was momentous, but in France there was none of the enthusiasm which had greeted the outbreak of war in 1914. It was more a resigned belief that a job, however unpleasant, had to be done. But Pétain was even less enthusiastic than his compatriots. He did 'not approve the act of beginning the war and he had serious concerns about how it would be waged, given the still defective organisation of relations between the High Command and the government'.[18] In truth, he had a point. The previously strong relationship between Daladier and Gamelin had become very tense – and there were even doubts about Daladier himself. Interestingly enough, Pétain seems to have recognised that the rearmament programme was starting to bear fruit. In a few months France might have at least most of the equipment for war, if not the leadership. But the extra few months were badly needed.

The onset of war had an immediate effect on the kaleidoscope of French domestic politics. Straight away, Daladier made an effort to recreate the *union sacrée* of 1914. He decided to invite representation from all parties (except the Communists) and independents into a new administration. It almost went without saying that one of the first to be invited was the old and dignified hero of Verdun, Marshal Pétain. Pétain (just returned from another trip, this time to Bilbao, Santander, Oviedo and Santiago de Compostela) was duly summoned to Paris on 8 September. Daladier forthwith offered him the post of Minister of War.

After what he called 'long reflection' Pétain turned the job down. The reasons he gave in his letter to Daladier were that the government of national unity which Daladier proposed was merely a round-up of failed politicians. What was needed was something much broader. 'This decision firmly arrived at', he went on, 'allows me to be freer to tell you my thought about the cabinet you have in mind. The presence of certain politicians will be an obstacle to proper relations with Spain and Italy, and will have a deplorable effect on the morale of the country and the army.'[19] He was, of course, referring primarily to Herriot, who he considered had sabotaged the Doumergue government of 1934. But he was also having doubts about Daladier himself, let alone Gamelin. Moreover, as the Italian Ambassador to Paris pointed out in his dispatch at the time, Pétain confessed himself a very reluctant warrior.

Having delivered his broadside to Daladier, Pétain took the train back to Spain. This was not, however, a signal that he was about to abandon his customary close observation of the Parisian political scene. Quite the contrary. Loustanau-Lacau was buzzing to and fro between Paris and San Sebastián, as was Bernard Ménétrel. Pétain retained a 'liaison officer' in Paris, Colonel Henri Pellissier de Féligonde, whose task was to observe and report. True to their task, in early October all three reported a good deal of chatter about a possible change of government. Then, on 8 October, Lémery arrived in San Sebastián and spent two days with Pétain trying to convince him that a new government was an absolute necessity, and that only he, Pétain, could form an administration which would be able to continue the war. Moreover, he claimed that there was a substantial bloc, in the Chamber as well as the Senate, in favour of such a scheme. Equally, there would be no difficulty in forming a cabinet: Laval, Alibert and Adrien Marquet, the Mayor of Bordeaux, were willing and prepared (apart, he might have modestly added, from himself), and Hervé would stir up the press. But Pétain was not persuaded. He would be quite happy, he replied, to take the War portfolio in an administration which was not party political, but he would not head it. A premier, he pointed out, had to be able to answer questions on a multitude of topics, from agriculture to the merchant marine. He would only look foolish trying to do so. At that point the negotiation, such as it was, came to an end.

Lémery, however, did not give up. Pétain's reply had been firm enough in what he said but he was not wholly convincing in the way he said it. Besides, he had entertained himself by composing a list of possible members of a future cabinet, which he had shown to Gazel (it was absurdly injudicious to show it to a civil servant if it was meant to be taken seriously – and most unlike the cautious and usually secretive Pétain). Gazel's successor, Albert Lemarle, told later how Pétain had by mistake given him a note from Loustanau-Lacau with a message from Laval that proposed forming a Pétain government. Reynaud, too, later wrote that in his view Pétain was conspiring against the government during his ambassadorship in Spain. All that can be said is that if Pétain was conspiring he was a conspicuously bad conspirator. Much more probable is that he was doing what he had always done – waiting on uncertain outcomes while observing most closely, and with the greatest interest, the confused march of events. Indeed, it is no more than reasonable to take the view, along with André François-Poncet in his 1953 speech to the Académie Française after Pétain's death, that in the period of his ambassadorship he 'psychologically became accustomed to the idea that in a great crisis he would some day save the nation'.[20]

Be that as it may, Daladier was certainly full of suspicion about Pétain's intentions. Furthermore, he believed that Pétain listened too much to Laval, and that Laval had persuaded him not to accept Daladier's offer. When Pétain in mid-October asked whether he could be relieved in his post in order to take up his position in the Comité de Guerre, Daladier told him to stay put. As it happened, Daladier's refusal, however understandable politically, had for Pétain a number of unpleasant practical consequences. It was not just a matter of missing the vintage at L'Ermitage – for the first time since he had bought the property. Even worse than that, the Franco government had set up shop in Madrid. All embassies had to transfer there forthwith. This meant an annoying two weeks packing everything up and starting again in new embassy premises and a new home. It is little wonder that Pétain's letters to his wife at this time show distinct signs of tetchiness.

On 13 November he was due to leave for Madrid, but his trunks were not yet packed and, since he was busy saying his farewells in San Sebastián, he summoned Nini from Biarritz to help him. This she duly did, efficiently as it turned out, as he was able to write to her on 16 November to announce his arrival in the capital. His new home there was only five minutes from the Retiro park and its interior was 'not too bad, if one doesn't look into the corners'. Somebody had cleaned the place – though not entirely to Pétain's satisfaction – but none of the locks worked, the carpets in the corridors were crumpled and the hot water system was 'precarious'.[21] But he thought that it would all be sorted out in time. True, he missed his San Sebastián garden but liked the Retiro, which in future would be where he took his daily walk.

Once established in his home, Pétain had to undertake the task of visiting ministers, city authorities and ambassadorial colleagues, a task which he much disliked, particularly when there was another mountain of mail which needed answering. Three days later he was complaining that he still had twenty-five visits to make, and that the embassy building, which was meant to have been finished in time for his arrival, was still besieged by workmen – needing constant supervision. In fact, Pétain noted similar problems throughout Madrid – a city badly damaged by the Civil War, shortages of food, low morale and, when repairs were undertaken, generally shoddy workmanship. Yet, by way of compensation, the weather was quite beautiful, and his walks in the Retiro were suitably restful. There was also another bonus. Since all food was in short supply Pétain organised a weekly lorry service to Madrid from Bayonne. He shared out the load with his friend Peterson at the British Embassy. 'By that means alone', Peterson noted with evident satisfaction, 'was it possible to secure the supplies required for a dinner party of any size.'[22]

Pétain wrote all this to Nini, but his letters become increasingly critical of his hosts as the winter wore on – and as the weather worsened and his walks became shorter. The commercial negotiations were endless, even descending into 'comedy'. Du Moulin de Labarthète was doing an extremely competent job but his opposite numbers were without any sense of time. But he warns Nini: 'Don't give too many details about the situation in Spain and on the difficulties I have had with the Spaniards and on my manner of judging them, since everything will be reported and put down to my account.'[23] He was making sure, even with his wife, that there was nothing that could be held against him in the future.

The New Year came and went. There were rounds of visits to be made and responses to 'a cubic metre' of New Year letters to write.[24] There was a splendid dinner at the Palacio Real, but the high point of the season was the transfer of the remains of José Antonio Primo de Rivera, the founder of the Falange, to the Escorial. Primo de Rivera, the eldest son of Pétain's old friend, had been executed by the Republican authorities in November 1936 and, as such, had become something of a martyr for Franco and his followers. The ceremony at the Escorial was as elaborate as only the Spanish Catholic Church could make it. Pétain, of course, felt obliged – indeed, for his old friend, wanted – to be there. But there were those who noted that as he entered the basilica of the Escorial the whole diplomatic corps, led by the German Ambassador, rose to its feet. Furthermore, when he left, the German Youth of Spain saluted him by lowering their swastika flags in homage.

In fact, Pétain had become rather friendly with the German Ambassador, Dr Eberhard von Stohrer. He had advised von Stohrer on his French holiday plans before war broke out, and even when the two countries were at war the two ambassadors remained on reasonably cordial terms. At the ceremony at which Franco's ministers took their oath of allegiance, on 19 October 1939, Pétain seemed to go out of his way to shake hands with von Stohrer, a gesture which brought much critical comment in the French press, but which he regarded as no more than a simple act of courtesy to an ambassadorial colleague. (This courtesy, however, did not prevent von Stohrer from making some unfriendly comments about Pétain in his dispatches to Berlin.) Moreover, Peterson overheard Pétain's remark to an ambassadorial colleague: 'I always shake hands with those whom I intend to strike.'[25]

As the winter of 1939–40 moved slowly towards spring, it became clear in Paris that the Daladier government was in trouble. At the beginning of February Daladier, without consulting his British allies, suddenly announced that he would send a hundred planes and fifty

thousand troops by the end of the month to help the Finns in their
resistance to a Soviet invasion. Nobody knew where these forces were
to be found. It was widely said that Daladier was drinking too much.
That this was so became clear in a debate on 13 March in the
Chamber. During his speech he made remarks which were so crude
and offensive that they were struck from the official record. In the
Senate, in a parallel debate, Laval made a most effective speech opposing the war and demanding an immediate peace. On 20 March,
Daladier called for a motion of confidence. By then, as it happened,
the Finns had signed an armistice with the Soviets, and there was no
longer an obvious and urgent danger. But still, in the event, no fewer
than 300 out of 540 deputies abstained on the substantive motion. For
Daladier, there was no alternative to resignation.

Daladier's obvious successor was his Finance Minister, Paul
Reynaud. Reynaud, in fact, had been doing his best in the previous
weeks to undermine his government's own position. He had been
hostile to the Munich agreement and he loathed Daladier personally.
The sentiment was reciprocated handsomely. Indeed, during the
month of February the two men were unable even to speak to one
another, communicating only by way of notes. Their mutual hatred
was shared, and exacerbated, by their respective mistresses. Comtesse
Hélène de Portes, the object of Reynaud's affections – sallow in complexion, with a mouth too big for her untidy face, and blindly
pro-German – could not abide the Marquise de Crussol – a good-
looking if somewhat blowsy lady whose family had made their fortune
in sardine-canning. The two women quarrelled on every possible
occasion.

None of this made for happy relationships in government. Yet
such was the parliamentary arithmetic that Reynaud was obliged to
have Daladier in the cabinet which Lebrun asked him to form – as
Minister of Defence. He was also obliged to accommodate others,
such as Chautemps and the banker Paul Baudouin, who were known
opponents of the war. Even so, when it came to parliamentary endorsement of his administration, Reynaud's overall majority was down to
one.

In the first weeks of his administration Reynaud was all fireworks.
He thought himself the Clemenceau of his day, with a mission to
hector the generals and the country into a much more energetic pur-

suit of the war. There was much shouting – but to little effect. However intelligent he was, and however enthusiastic about the war, Reynaud had not the precious gift of being able to inspire men. Some attributed this to his height. 'Had Reynaud been three inches taller,' it was later said, 'the history of the world might have been changed.'[26] Others thought it was the malign influence of Hélène de Portes. 'You don't know', Reynaud sighed to a friend, 'what a man who has been hard at work all day will put up with to make sure of an evening's peace.'[27] But whatever the failings of Reynaud's own character there is no doubt that he was continually being wounded by Daladier's unceasing and sulky sniping at his flank.

Although the dispute between the two was primarily personal, there was an element of disagreement over war policy. French strategic planning in the 1930s was based on the experience of the First World War. An initial German attack was to be soaked up by vigorous defence (as at the Marne in 1914). This would be followed by stalemate. After a period the superior industrial might of France and Britain would wear down the enemy and lead to eventual victory. This was known as the strategy of the 'long war'. The original Plan XVII of August 1914, the all-out all-conquering offensive, was clearly quite the opposite – in other words, a 'short war'. The 'short war' was no longer an option for France in 1940, but there were those in Paris, particularly around Reynaud (but not around Daladier), who were worried that time, rather than working for the French, would in fact work against them. Such was the pace of German arms manufacture, they argued – all of it directed at the western front now that Poland had been overcome and the eastern front sealed off by the treaty with the Soviets of August 1939 – that the longer the war lasted the worse it would be for France. The Germans, of course, for their part were planning a very short war indeed.

By the end of March Reynaud was becoming convinced that Daladier was a serious liability. So too, he thought, was Gamelin. He then set about consulting his closest colleagues on possible courses of action. It so happened, whether by coincidence or not, that on 27 March Pétain wrote to Nini that he hoped to be in Paris the following week, but he instructed Nini 'firmly' not to talk to friends about his visit. 'I wish to keep incognito,' he went on mysteriously, 'at least until my first visit to ministers.'[28] Only four days later, however, he changed his mind. 'The news which I get from Paris', he told her, 'does not encourage me to make the trip I had in mind, which could be wrongly interpreted.'[29] If he had been one of those whom Reynaud was to consult, Reynaud would have to do it at long range – or do without him.

The fiasco of Norway – the south of the country was overrun by the Germans in April in a matter of days – allowed Reynaud to start dislodging Gamelin. When Daladier leaped to his defence Reynaud decided that he would have, one way or another, to be rid of him too. Nevertheless, he knew that the only possible way he could secure a parliamentary majority for a new administration, in which Daladier would no longer be involved in the conduct of the war, would be if he could assemble a cabinet which the Chamber and the Senate could not possibly reject; and the key to this was the 'Victor of Verdun', Marshal Philippe Pétain.

On 29 April Reynaud summoned Pétain back from Madrid. Pétain was mildly irritated. Ménétrel and his wife were staying with him, and, as he wrote happily to Nini, he had just finished arranging the let of a house for the summer overlooking the sea at San Sebastián. Moreover, he was engaged in planning the pilgrimage of a group of French Catholics to the shrine at Zaragoza for the end of May. Nevertheless, he took the train, leaving Nini in the Hôtel Imatz at Hendaye, and arrived in Paris on the morning of 1 May. He saw Reynaud in the afternoon. Reynaud immediately offered him the post of Minister of State in his cabinet. Pétain asked for a little time, but after consulting a few of his friends he telephoned his acceptance to Reynaud – provided he could return to Spain to settle his affairs, which he did on 9 May. On 10 May, at first light, the Germans launched their attack into Holland and Belgium. On 13 May they followed up with an assault through the Luxembourg Ardennes. The real war had started.

The pace of events quickened. On 16 May Pétain was summoned back from Madrid with immediate effect. He arrived in Paris at eight o'clock on the morning of 18 May at the Gare d'Austerlitz, to be told by Colonel Pellissier de Féligonde that the German Army had broken through the Meuse front and was heading for the sea. He went straight from the station to see Reynaud, who told him that he was personally taking over the direction of the war and offered him the post of Vice-

President of his cabinet – in other words, Deputy Premier. Pétain hesitated, but Reynaud wanted an immediate answer, as he was to announce the new members of the government that evening. He then went on to tell Pétain that Gamelin was to go, and be replaced by Weygand. When Pétain said that he did not much care for Weygand, Reynaud brushed his objection aside. He said that Pétain would soon come round to the idea that 'Reynaud and Weygand' would sound well with the Army. Pétain was left perplexed at such frivolity.

Later, after the war, Reynaud claimed that previously he knew very little about Pétain. He was not telling the truth. He knew perfectly well, since it had never been a secret, that Pétain had been opposed to the war in the first place, that he believed the politicians, above all those of the Popular Front, to be responsible for the mess that France was in, that he thought that France had not been ready for war, and that he was of the clear view that the present group of politicians were not up to fighting it. If there is any doubt about what Reynaud knew or did not know, on 26 May, when he went to see the new British Prime Minister, Winston Churchill, he told Churchill that if France were 'entirely invaded' they 'must reckon on the possibility of a move by Marshal Pétain in favour of an armistice'.[30] The truth is that Reynaud made Pétain Vice-Premier simply to trump Daladier. He only had himself to blame if the consequences of his petty manoeuvre turned out not to his taste.

18

DEFEAT

'. . . je fais à la France le don de ma personne pour atténuer son malheur . . .'

It is no more than commonplace to assert, as did Shakespeare's King Henry IV, that the wish is father to the thought. But it is much less easy to discern how, and at what point, a thought may become the father to a wish. When Pétain arrived in Paris on 18 May 1940 in response to Reynaud's summons, there is little doubt about the thought. He had persuaded himself that, if suitably called, he could be a leader of France in her current travail. If he had any doubts, his supporters had been, and still were, enthusiastic on his behalf. Precedents were mentioned: Joan of Arc, Napoleon, various saints and so on, who, in the mythology as it had developed, had come to the aid of their country in her deepest distress. It is not too much to say that it was in the shadow of that mythology that Pétain was welcomed back to Paris. If the precedents were, to put it mildly, not entirely appropriate to the matters of the day, there was no doubt that his reception by the Parisian press and, even more to the point, the standing ovation given to him by the Senate three days later, confirmed the general impression that he was destined to be the latest member of that illustrious band who had saved France by their mere presence on the scene.

For the Pétain of 18 May, however, although the thought was in his

mind, there is little sign of the wish. For a start, life had its own mundane imperatives. There were simple domestic matters to be attended
to, not least, as he reminded Nini – conveniently still confined to her
hotel – to ensure that the things he had left behind in Madrid,
his stock of wine, for instance, could be put in store for him in a
room, which he was sure would be available, at the Hôtel Imatz at
Hendaye. But, even leaving aside domestic matters, he was not in a
mood to provoke any political disturbance. True, he had been upset
at learning from Reynaud that Weygand had been appointed
Commander-in-Chief, but it was no good moaning about it, and
he reported to Nini that he was 'trying to adapt myself to my new
functions although the beginnings have been rather difficult. But I
want to remain in my role of adviser, so as to avoid conflicts with the
command',[1] adding, though not quite in those terms, that there were
too many cooks in an already overcrowded kitchen.

The Pétain of 16 June, on the other hand, when he was invited by
President Lebrun to form a government, was a quite different man. In
response to Lebrun's invitation, with well prepared confidence, he
produced, like a magician producing a rabbit out of a hat, a list of
ministers, proclaiming firmly, 'Here is my government.'[2] The contrast
between the Pétain of 18 May and the Pétain of 16 June could hardly
be more marked. There seems to be little doubt that the thought had,
by that time, fathered a wish.

It had been a hectic four and a half weeks. Pétain's moods had
swung with the flow of the events. Moreover, at the age of eighty-
four, his attention span was far from reliable. The faithful Bonhomme,
for instance, thought that he was 'very, very old. His thought no
longer puts action into gear'.[3] Georges Mandel, Clemenceau's right-
hand man all those years ago, and now Reynaud's Minister of the
Interior, dismissed him as simply senile, claiming that he fell asleep at
meetings of the Council of Ministers and, when he woke, started
reading papers which had nothing to do with the discussion of the
moment. Even Spears, his old friend, appearing yet again on the
scene on 25 May as Churchill's special emissary, found at their first
meeting that very day that 'the long fair moustache, although whiter,
was the same, but he seemed dead, in the sense that a figure that gives
no impression of being alive can be said to be dead'.[4] 'I knew
[Pétain's] reputation as a defeatist', Spears reflected the day after their

At his desk in 1940. (*Photos12.com/Hachedê*)

first meeting, 'but had never really believed it, for it chanced that I had always seen him either as a resolute, cold, calculating fighter, or as a man who by his moral ascendancy had quelled the great mutinies of the French Army in 1917. He had not the toughness of Foch, that was all I could have said. Was his cold objectivity, in so far as his mind possessed its erstwhile clarity, driving him to the conclusion that everything was lost? If so, what line would he take?'[5]

Spears, not for the first or the last time, read his man correctly. Pétain was not saying much to Spears about what he really thought. In fact, he was not saying much to anyone – other than to his doctor, Bernard Ménétrel. This was no accident. By then Ménétrel had become much more than his doctor. He had become what would, in modern jargon, be called Pétain's 'minder'. His job was now to make the old man's life – in all its respects – easier. For instance, it was Ménétrel who had been deputed to head Nini off from what would have been an unwelcome visit to Spain. Then, on Pétain's arrival in Paris on 18 May, it was Ménétrel who had booked him rooms at the

Pavillon d'Orsay, and it was Ménétrel who, after a couple of nights there, invited Pétain to stay at his own apartment – since the apartment in the Square de Latour-Maubourg had been shut and the servants laid off.

There was even more to it than that. Ménétrel can best be described, in the customary hackneyed manner, as the son that Pétain never had. Some went even further, asserting firmly that Pétain's relations with Ménétrel's mother had been such that Bernard was without a shadow of doubt the Marshal's natural son. Certainly, the dates and the history might seem to lend support to the assertion. Bernard was born in 1906, when Pétain was no more than fifty years old and eminently capable of fathering a son. Moreover, his relationship with Ménétrel's mother was well known. Furthermore, ever since his childhood Bernard had been the object of the Marshal's particular affection, in marked contrast to his unfortunate stepson Pierre. 'Bernard works well and is forthcoming,' Pétain had written to his mother, Renée Ménétrel, in 1924.[6] That was followed by a letter to her husband. 'We both regard [Pierre] as a cancer; he does not work, [and] he abuses the good faith of his mother, who gives him too much money . . .'[7] 'I am as much attached to your children', he concluded, 'as I am little attached to Pierre.'

Over the years, Bernard Ménétrel had studied medicine in some of the best hospitals in Paris, and had inherited a flourishing practice – with some dubious techniques as well as conventional medical proficiency – in 1936. After Louis Ménétrel's death he had married the young, and by all reports beautiful, Aline Montcocol, an heiress of some considerable substance whose father had made a fortune in tunnelling for the Paris Métro. The two young Ménétrels made a good-looking pair, Bernard with his dark hair carefully waved, dark prominent eyebrows above brown eyes and a firmly sculpted nose and jaw, Aline ('Line' to the obviously adoring Pétain) in her mid-twenties, small in stature but provocatively elegant in the fashions of the day. Pétain himself made a speech at the dinner following the wedding ceremony – much of it quite inappropriately devoted to a eulogy of the elder Ménétrel, who, in fact, had terrified the son. But that, however inappropriate for the occasion, was considered to be no more than a marshal's permitted foible.

Marriage (not to mention a generous dowry) brought with it a change in Ménétrel's social status. He started to take an amateur's interest in the right-wing movements of the time – without ever fully committing himself to any one faction. In 1937, he moved from the Left to the Right Bank to a larger apartment at no. 5 Avenue Montaigne, then, as now, one of the richest streets in the whole of Paris. Not only was the apartment in a rich street in a fashionable *arrondissement*, but it was also very spacious. Bernard's consulting rooms were kept separate from the living quarters and, such was the extent of the property, there was also a comfortable suite for guests.

It was this suite that Pétain occupied during late May and early June 1940. He had persuaded Ménétrel, who had joined up on mobilisation and had been posted to a cardiological centre at Chauvry-en-Oise, to transfer to his own staff as his personal doctor. That done, Ménétrel was able to devote all his attention to Pétain's health and well-being. Moreover, he became Pétain's favoured companion. In fact, they were almost inseparable. 'We dine together at the restaurant,' Nini was told. 'He does his business during the day and I do mine and we meet again in the evening. What will happen in the future? It is the attitude of the enemy which will tell us whether we are able or not to leave Paris. I have good hopes that we will hold on.'[8] Of all the people he could talk to without restraint, Ménétrel was without a doubt top of the (admittedly very short) list.

If Ménétrel helped with Pétain's domestic arrangements it was Raphaël Alibert – much disliked, as it happened by Ménétrel – who took charge of Pétain's office. It was set up in Pétain's old premises at no. 8 Boulevard des Invalides. Staff were recruited, both military and civil, to assist him in fending off persistent visitors – and seemingly hourly messages from Laval, possibly encouraged by Alibert, claiming that the war was lost and that Pétain should get up and say as much. There was also a great mass of letters and telegrams from well-wishers, which he resolutely refused to answer. 'If only', he wrote to Nini, 'people could understand that in such squalls one wants some peace!'[9] But the main 'business' seemed to be little more than continual dialogue with his colleagues about the conduct of the war and daily meetings with Reynaud held, as often as possible, with Weygand in attendance.

Nevertheless, the 'squalls', as Pétain called them, could not be ignored. The German panzers had broken through at Sedan on 15 May and by the time he arrived in Paris they had made their way as far as the English Channel. Their 'corridor', as it was called, stretched from Sedan in the east to Abbeville, at the mouth of the River Somme, in the west. The French 1st and 8th Armies, and almost the whole of the British Expeditionary Force, under General Lord (known as 'Boy') Gort, seemed to be in an inescapable trap.

Such events could hardly be dismissed as 'squalls'. They were more like a hurricane. But Weygand, as Pétain soon found out, had a plan: to attack the German corridor in a pincer movement from both north and south. Churchill, on a visit to Paris on 22 May, approved. Yet Weygand's plan was based on little more than optimism. It had been inherited from Gamelin, and relied on what can only be described as phantom armies. The British were not, any more than a newly constituted French Army on the Somme, in a fit state to execute any plan, let alone Weygand's. Furthermore, communications, and trust, between the two armies had long since vanished. As a result, the whole plan collapsed in general acrimony on 24 May. Reynaud, promptly and much to Pétain's annoyance, sacked sixteen French generals and then fired off two telegrams to Churchill complaining that the British were retreating much too far and much too fast. Weygand, too, felt betrayed by the British. Gort said stoutly that the French were plainly not up to fighting a war. The ghosts of 1918 seemed at that point to be stalking the stage.

Weygand's plan having collapsed in confusion, Reynaud's War Committee met in the evening of 25 May to decide what to do next. Lebrun started by asking what their reaction should be if the Germans offered some sort of settlement that would lead to a way out of the war. He thought that they ought at least to look at it, even though there was an agreement with Britain not to conclude a separate peace. Weygand and Reynaud, unusually, were in tandem. Both said that any offer should be discussed with Britain. Reynaud then agreed to go to London the following day. Weygand told him firmly to ask for more assistance. Pétain reinforced Weygand's demand by pointing out that the British had only put ten divisions in the field against France's eighty. Finally, they approved Weygand's next plan, to set a defensive line from the mouth of the Somme, along the Rivers Ailette and Aisne to Montmédy in the east, to be held 'without thought of retreat'. It seemed firm enough as an idea, and was generally welcomed.

But Weygand seemed not to have much faith in it, and certainly spoiled his presentation by remarking that if the Army fought to the end it would in all probability lead to the total destruction of all French armed forces. On that note of gloom the meeting broke up.

It was on the night of 25 May that Pétain gave up hope. In the morning, he confessed to Baudouin that he had spent a sleepless night. It would be wrong, he said, for France to fight to the death. At least part of the Army had to be saved to maintain order. The roads were clogged with refugees from the north. Weygand was worried about a possible communist uprising in Paris. The British were of no help: they refused to send aircraft to France, desperately needed to support Weygand's attempt to secure the Somme–Aisne line, and were busy getting their troops back home. It was all getting too much, and much too much for someone in his eighty-fifth year, and – here Pétain was near to tears – it was time to put a stop to it.

There was worse, much worse, to come. On the morning of 28 May, Weygand and Pétain met – at Weygand's request. Much as they disliked one another personally – Weygand was, after all, Foch's creature, and the old rivalry died hard – they were of one mind. By then, they had heard the news that the Belgians had asked for a ceasefire and that the British had started to embark troops at Dunkirk. For the first time, they raised between themselves the possibility of an armistice. Weygand was willing to write a fierce memorandum to Reynaud. He wanted to be sure that Pétain shared his views. They were simple. Should the Somme–Aisne line be broken, the battle for France was lost – and the British should be told as much. Pétain heard Weygand out, and then gave his opinion. He agreed.

Weygand's memorandum was presented to Reynaud that evening. Reynaud raised no objection, on Pétain's insistence, to inviting the British without delay to another meeting. Once more, on 31 May, Churchill, with a full entourage, arrived in Paris for what was minuted as the thirteenth meeting of the Supreme War Council. There was a great deal to talk about – much more than Weygand's memorandum – and the meeting, held in Reynaud's own room in the rue St-Dominique, had a full agenda. Apart from the Dunkirk evacuation, there was the matter of the repatriation of French troops who had been sent to Norway and who were trapped in an enclave around the port of Narvik; and there was, above all, the French request for British air reinforcements – necessary, Weygand said yet again, if the Somme–Aisne line was to be held. There was also the matter of Italy and what should happen if Mussolini declared war. The agenda was, at length, disposed of, and Churchill wound up the meeting with a fine rhetorical flourish. Reynaud replied in the same vein but, as the British Ambassador reported, 'one felt that it came rather from his head than from his heart'.[10]

Whatever the formal business, there is no doubt about the under-currents. Churchill wanted to stiffen Reynaud's spine – while limiting the number of aircraft sent to France, in case they were needed for the defence of Britain itself following a French collapse. There was no need to remind the French government of the solemn undertaking given to the British on 28 March 1940 that neither country would make peace without the consent of the other. That reminder would come in due course. The French, on the other hand, wanted to be assured of British readiness to commit themselves fully to the battle for France. Without that full commitment, Weygand repeated ever more aggressively, the Somme–Aisne line could not be held.

Throughout the whole meeting Pétain was silent. But, after the meeting, he found himself standing in the bay window of Reynaud's office overlooking the rue St-Dominique with Churchill, Spears and the young French diplomat Roland de Margerie, who was talking volubly about fighting on in North Africa if France fell. Pétain's atti-tude was, as Churchill later wrote, 'detached and sombre, giving me the feeling that he would face a separate peace . . . his reputation, his serene acceptance of the march of adverse events, apart from any words he used, was almost overpowering to those under his spell'.[11]

By then, Pétain's conclusion was evident to everybody present: a French defeat could not now be avoided. Nor was he the only one to arrive at that conclusion. Churchill, too, later on that decisive evening of 31 May, had given up on the French will to fight. When Spears went to bed that night, as he wrote, '. . . I knew, more from his tone than from a few words he had said before taking leave, that he realised in his heart that the French were beaten, that they knew it, and were resigned to defeat. He has not said so, it was as if he would not permit the thought to dwell consciously in his mind. But he knew.'[12] So, for that matter, did Spears himself. Thus, for different reasons and from different directions, Pétain, Churchill and Spears had all arrived at the same conclusion.

Pétain was more forthright to Spears on the evening of Sunday 2 June. He was tired and irritable. He had been with Reynaud the whole day, visiting anti-tank defences north of Compiègne. Obviously dissatisfied with what he had seen, he grumpily told Spears that Weygand had made an outspoken attack on the British at the morning's meeting of the Council of Ministers, in particular accusing Churchill of only producing fine speeches and of making promises which he did not keep. Although Pétain thought that Weygand was only covering up his own weaknesses, he nevertheless admitted that he thought Weygand had a point. Spears then lost his temper. He claimed that the difficulties in the north were largely due to inadequate French command. Pétain was too tired to argue and said that he ought not to have said anything about the matter. '"At the same time", he finished, "you should know what Weygand feels and how things appear to us."'[13]

On 4 June Pétain reported to Nini that 'we are living a quite anxious and active life'.[14] It was a majestic understatement. His days at the time were more than fully occupied – and, indeed, exceptionally anxious. Nevertheless, there was time for at least some creature comforts: his morning massage and heat treatment – although there were some days when, regrettably, the two had to be rolled into one. Moreover, he and Ménétrel had discovered a new restaurant in their neighbourhood, where the food was to his taste – although prices had doubled. Taking that as his cue, he complained about his money problems yet again, in order to impress Nini with his poverty to prevent her from spending too much on her own affairs. He was also much concerned about the bits and pieces he had left behind in Madrid, but 'the moment has not yet come for them to be sent to Paris'.[15]

This was indeed the problem, not just for Pétain's bits and pieces, but for them all. On 3 June Paris was bombed for the first time. On 5 June Dunkirk fell. Reynaud reshuffled his government – finally, much to Pétain's satisfaction, getting rid of Daladier and, much to Pétain's disgust, bringing de Gaulle into the Council of Ministers. But there was little time for Pétain's continued grievance about de Gaulle and his book, much as he was still complaining about it. That very day the Germans launched their attack on the Somme–Aisne line. Churchill refused to send further aircraft to help out the French. On hearing this, Pétain told Reynaud, 'well, there is nothing left but to make peace. If you do not want to do it you can hand over to me'.[16]

On 6 June the Somme line was breached, and the Aisne line was to give way soon afterwards. On 9 June the German Army was in Rouen. At that point, everything seemed to be in the Germans' favour, even the weather – perfect for tank attacks in seemingly endless days of clear sunshine. Pétain's mood, in contrast to the weather, was far from sunny. On 6 June he told Ambassador Bullitt, but without any conviction, that the only hope for France was immediate and decisive intervention by the United States. When Spears came to see him later in the morning, Pétain led him to a map on the wall. 'He adjusted his pince-nez, and his strong forefinger with its straight cut nail began to follow the line along which the battle was raging.' Pétain told him that there were no reserves. 'No doubt the men are fighting well, they have got over their surprise as they did in 1914, but they are fighting one against two . . .'[17]

All that said, the conversation then drifted. Spears said there was need of a Joan of Arc. As with all old men, memories of the past were much more vivid than the memory of the day before yesterday. Pétain immediately recalled a speech he had made about Joan of Arc, summoned help to find it in his files and, when it came, read the whole thing out loud. 'I cannot recall a single sentence, or even its gist. What I do remember was the terrible sadness I felt as I watched him, a sadness based on pity for a very old man for whom I had, till so recently, felt the deepest affection and regard. He was infinitely pathetic in his childish satisfaction as he read . . . As the interminable recitation went on, I felt that I could not bear it. I thought of France and the people of France . . .' Pétain, like all old men, was reminiscing. He went on to show Spears a speech he had made about peasants and a statuette of him on horseback, 'bending forward towards two very typical *poilus* of the last war who beamed up at him in fond and trusting respect . . . "I wish that group to commemorate me to the French people one day," he said.'[18]

On the morning of 9 June Pétain saw Reynaud at their customary daily meeting. Clearly doubtful about his ability to recall all his thoughts, he had prepared a written memorandum, which he proceeded to read out. It stressed the necessity of the government remaining in Paris. Whether he had written the memorandum himself or not, and whether it was intended seriously, is unclear, since the document has not survived. But what is certain is that by the time it was read to Reynaud it was badly out of date. Even his own staff were already making preparations for the move. When the Council of Ministers met the same evening and decided to decamp to a series of châteaux dispersed along the River Loire, Pétain seemed to Lebrun to be asleep during the meeting. Whatever the truth of that, he was certainly awake by eleven o'clock to tell Ménétrel to pack all essentials and be ready to leave. This done, and very soon after, a cavalcade – two outriders, Pétain and Bonhomme in the official car and Ménétrel bringing up the rear in his own – finally left Paris.

At 3 a.m. on 10 June the cavalcade arrived at the River Loire and the little town of Gien, after ploughing its way through the crowds of refugees determined to make the same journey. There was no room at any hotel and they were obliged to bed down in a small room at the Gien railway station. But there was not time for more than three hours' sleep. In the early morning they set off again, this time for Nevers, where they were housed for the night in the prefecture. It was only at midday on the following day, 11 June, that they were able to unpack and to start to get settled at their new perch, the Château de Saint-Amand-en-Puisaye, near Briare on the middle reaches of the Loire.

It is little wonder that Ménétrel was getting worried about his sleepless patient. But there was little he could do. No sooner had they arrived at the new perch than Pétain was summoned to a meeting of the War Committee at the Château de Vaugereau, some twenty kilometres away. On his arrival, he was told that they were all waiting for Churchill. Even then, there was to be no pause, not even for a discussion about what they were to say to Churchill when he finally arrived. Furthermore, as though to interrupt matters even further, when the numbers from the two sides were totted up it became clear that Vaugereau was too small. The meeting was then moved in haste to the nearby, but more spacious, Château de Muguet, 'a hideous house', as Spears described it, 'the sort of building the *nouveau riche* French *bourgoisie* delight in, a villa expanded by successful business in groceries or indifferent champagne into a large monstrosity of red lobster-coloured brick, and stone the hue of unripe Camembert'.[19]

Churchill, with Anthony Eden, his Minister for War, and a full complement of other ministers, officials and generals – and, of course, Spears – in his wake, arrived late in the afternoon of the 11th at Briare Airport. They drove immediately to the 'hideous house', and, at 7 p.m., the meeting began. Churchill did his best to rally the French – he returned to an idea, which had been going the rounds, of a retreat to the Brittany peninsula. Churchill cited the example of the British defence of the lines of Torres Vedras in the Napoleonic Wars as an example of what he meant. Weygand, rightly, dismissed the idea as impractical. He reminded Pétain of their meeting in Beauvais in March 1918 and Pétain's determination then to resist the German advance. It was to no avail. Seeing that both Weygand and Pétain were unreceptive to any and every scheme he could put forward, Churchill made one last, impassioned effort. If France were defeated, he said, Britain would fight on – in the air, with her unbeaten navy and with the blockade weapon. If Reynaud was encouraged by Churchill's speech, Weygand was unmoved, and Pétain was 'mockingly incredulous. Although he said nothing his attitude was obviously "*C'est de la blague.*"'('It's a joke.')[20]

The next morning Churchill made yet another effort, but it was to no avail. Pétain did not even go to the meeting. He knew what would be said. As far as he was concerned it was all too late. Sure enough, by mid-morning it was obvious that there was to be no progress. Churchill left again for Briare Airport – and England. When Spears saw Pétain later that day he found the Marshal in a mood of quiet resignation. '. . . He repeated that it was just a cruel self-deception to think that we could stand up to the Germans alone for more than a month.' Spears suddenly realised that 'if the French could but be made to believe we could fight on successfully, then many of them would stand by us'.[21] It was with that sudden, depressing for him – but vital – insight that Spears left for Tours. (It was also, as it happened, the last time that Spears spoke to Pétain in private.)

By then, Weygand had become impatient. At the Château de Cangé, where Lebrun was staying, on the evening of 12 June, he came out openly with a request for an armistice. He told the assembled Council of Ministers that if fighting continued French forces would be cut to pieces. There would be confusion and disorder – not merely military disorder, but general disorder. The response was one of shock. For most ministers, it was the first time they had been confronted with the stark military reality. After all, they said among themselves, the government had abandoned Paris in 1914. That had been followed by the heroic battle of the Marne. They were astonished – and shaken – when Weygand told them that there was no longer any question of a second Marne. He also implied that Britain could not possibly hold out and that consequently any retreat to Brittany or North Africa – or anywhere else for that matter – would be pointless. Pétain supported Weygand, but there was little agreement among the rest, and little sympathy for an immediate request for an armistice. Nevertheless, since the matter had been formally raised by the Commander-in-Chief, it could not just be ignored. On Chautemps' proposal, it was agreed to invite Churchill to France again for yet another discussion. That done, Pétain left Cangé for his new perch, the Château de Nitray, near Azay-sur-Cher, where Ménétrel had dutifully prepared a bed for him.

At midnight on 12 June Reynaud telephoned Churchill. He asked Churchill to come immediately to France. 'This looks', noted Churchill's private secretary, John Colville, 'as if the French mean to give in.'[22] As it happened, this was not yet the case. At Tours, where the two men met, Reynaud reported the discussion of the night before, adding that there had been no majority in favour of an armistice – but that many ministers were now veering that way. Churchill replied that he fully understood the problem and that he was much affected by French suffering. Nevertheless, he went on, Britain was not ready to release France from her formal undertaking of 28 March. The upshot was that it was agreed between the two of them that Reynaud would send a telegram to President Franklin Roosevelt requesting United States intervention, and that no decision would be made before Roosevelt's reply. That agreed, Churchill flew back to London.

Later that afternoon the Council of Ministers met again at Cangé. Everybody present expected to see Churchill, and there was much irritation, directed at Reynaud, when it was announced that he had gone back to London. They were hardly pacified when Reynaud told them that no decision had been taken at his meeting in Tours other than to appeal to Roosevelt. Pétain then delivered a statement, which he had had in his pocket for two or three days and which he had polished – in his own hand – that afternoon. As it was getting dark, and in order better to read his own writing, he moved his chair nearer to the bay window so that he could see properly, put on his pince-nez and delivered what amounted to a body blow to the Reynaud government.

If the government did not ask for an armistice, his statement made clear, the Army would probably stop obeying orders and give way to panic. It went on to assert the absolute necessity of the government remaining in France. As far as he was concerned, he preferred to stay and 'accept the suffering' which would ensue. The 'renewal of France' would be 'the fruit of that suffering'. There were only two options open: to seek an armistice or to leave. 'I declare', Pétain read solemnly, 'that, as for myself, I will refuse to leave metropolitan France – [I will stay], if necessary out of the government. I will stay among the people of France to share their trials and misfortunes. The armistice is in my view the necessary condition for the continued existence of eternal France.'[23]

In fact, this continued to be Pétain's theme in the days that followed. He would stay in France, come what may. He would make, in a rhetorical flourish, the gift of his person to France. In itself the assertion was dramatic, but it is far from clear whether Pétain really meant what he said or whether he was simply aiming for drama in asserting his own patriotism at the expense of others who would leave. But in making the assertion he manoeuvred himself into a political corner. He could not subsequently leave France without an embarrassing – and politically damaging – change of tack. In fact, he did admit, in his very old age and in prison, that the assertion was no more than a rhetorical flourish. But the flourish gained a life of its own.

There was then, as might be imagined, a bad-tempered argument. Reynaud claimed that what Pétain was suggesting was against the honour of France. Others were more sympathetic, but it was clear that there was no prospect of unanimity. The only thing on which they could all agree was to send a plaintive telegram to Roosevelt. Towards the end of the meeting Weygand lost his temper (yet again) and marched out of the room, slamming the door behind him. But before leaving he had told them all that the German Army was about to enter

Paris and would soon be on its way to the Loire. It was thus that, without any decision of substance, a divided and straggling government concluded that they had better retreat further. Their destination was, according to an old and prearranged plan, to be the haven in the south-west – Bordeaux.

Pétain's cavalcade was assembled again: two outriders to clear a path through the stream of refugees, Pétain and Bonhomme in the official car and Ménétrel in his own. This time, however, they were joined by Alibert and General Henri Bineau, who had taken refuge from Paris and were to set up Pétain's office when they arrived. The whole – now enlarged – group left Nitray at 2 p.m. and arrived in Bordeaux some four hours later. Unlike the departure from Paris for the Loire, the move to Bordeaux had been well planned in advance. Pétain was to stay in an apartment on the (aptly named) Boulevard du Président Wilson and his office was to be alongside that of the military commander of the region. Nevertheless, whatever the arrangements, Pétain's mind was made up. There had to be a decision. It was no longer possible to delay.

While ministers had been scattered around in different châteaux on the Rivers Loire and Cher, with uncertain communications and almost no contact between them other than the formal meetings of the Council, it was impossible for them to swap views in anything resembling informality. In consequence, it was equally impossible to hatch a conspiracy. Once in Bordeaux, however, all that changed. There could be meetings in cafés, bars, parks or hotels, or discussions on those telephones which worked. Moreover, sources of information were at a premium. Laval and Marquet held briefing sessions, at first in a small office in the Town Hall which Marquet, as Mayor of Bordeaux, had put at Laval's disposal and then, as the number of interested senators and deputies grew, in larger and larger rooms in the main hotels. Bordeaux at the time became no less than a political hot-house.

Laval, such was his nature, continued to bombard Pétain with messages. Pétain – in irritation – refused to read them. But although he agreed with Laval on the need for a quick decision about an armistice, there had been an unfortunate delay. On the morning of 15 June he tried to arrange for an early meeting of the Council, but it proved to be impossible, not least because Weygand did not arrive in Bordeaux

until after lunch. It was not until 4 p.m. that the meeting was con-
vened. By then Pétain's supporters had done the rounds. They had the
support of at least a third of the Council for an immediate armistice.
Reynaud and Lebrun, on their side, had the support of another third
in insisting that they should all wait for Roosevelt's reply. The others,
uncertain to the last, wavered to and fro. The result, needless to say,
was deadlock.

Reynaud then made another proposal: that they should follow the
Dutch example – negotiate a ceasefire and carry on the war as a gov-
ernment-in-exile in London. Strangely, he asked Pétain to go and
convince Weygand, who was waiting outside. He came back after no
more than a quarter of an hour to report that Weygand rejected the
idea out of hand. It would, Weygand had said, be no more than a
capitulation. There was, once more, deadlock.

It was Chautemps who came up with what seemed, at the time,
like a clever scheme. He suggested that a neutral party, perhaps the
Pope or the President of the United States, should sound out the
Germans on what their terms might be for an armistice. If the terms
were reasonable they should be discussed with the British, who would
no doubt then agree to the French looking at them seriously. If, on
the other hand, the terms were dishonourable, then France should
fight on. Pétain immediately accepted the proposal, saying that in
any event he had always envisaged an honourable armistice. Reynaud,
of course, immediately saw the flaw in Chautemps' proposal. As soon
as it became known, as it surely would, that the approach from the
'neutral' had come at the request of the French government the game
would be up. But the waverers were impressed by Chautemps, and
when Reynaud took a vote thirteen voted in favour of the proposal
and only six against. Reynaud immediately offered his resignation.
Lebrun, at this point shouting, refused to accept it. Reynaud, in his
turn, then had second thoughts. If he threw in the towel now, he
quickly realised that there would be a Pétain or a Chautemps government, which would immediately request an armistice.

In this angry debate, there was one voice which was decisive –
François Darlan. 'There is plenty of evidence', one account goes, 'to
show that, right up until 15 June, Darlan was prepared to sail away
with the fleet if any attempt was made to seek an armistice. Had he
done so, he would in Churchill's own words have become the master

of all French interests beyond German control . . . [and] the chief of the French Resistance with a mighty weapon in his hand . . . The whole French empire would have rallied to him. Nothing could have prevented him from being the Liberator of France.'[24]

Darlan had no love for the British; and he too believed in the inevitability of a British defeat. He could rightly claim that he had been responsible for the French fleet's undoubted reputation as France's most efficient armed force and as one which ranked in stature with the German, British and United States navies. Besides, it was undefeated. The question for him, at that moment, was which way he should go. Whatever his motives, in the event Darlan decided to go with Pétain – provided that 'his' fleet would not be surrendered to the Germans. Pétain agreed. So, up to a point, did Reynaud, who then informed the British government of the decision of 'the majority of the Council', asking their advice – but promising that under no circumstances would the French fleet be part of any deal.

During the evening of Saturday 15 June 1940 there was any amount of muttering in Bordeaux. Senators, deputies, ministers and hangers-on met in secret – and not so secret – conversations. Generally, the mood was gloomy, but there were two threads which, even then, ran along their conversations. The first was a distrust of England – always referred to as 'England' rather than 'Britain'. Old rivalries had not died. The second was a crude anti-semitism. Jews were somehow believed to be responsible both for the war and, at the same time, for the failure to resist the invader. There was no logic either in anglophobia or anti-semitism; but logic, in those tense days, was, to say the least, in short supply.

During the evening Pétain discussed with Darlan, and no doubt with his other allies, the composition of the government should Reynaud resign. He also drafted, or, more likely, asked Alibert or even Ménétrel to draft, a letter submitting his resignation from the Reynaud government. At the meeting of the Council of Ministers on the morning of 16 June, he proceeded to read it out. Lebrun took him aside and managed to talk him out of immediate resignation ('Ah, but you cannot do that to us at such a moment').[25] But Pétain, in agreeing, replied that he would only wait until the British reply to the Chautemps proposal was received. Reynaud then read out Roosevelt's response to his telegram. It was full of sympathy, and Roosevelt promised to continue to send equipment as long as France remained in the fight; but there was no possibility of any military commitment. Nor could there be; only Congress could make such a commitment.

The meeting then adjourned to await the British reply on the Chautemps proposal. It arrived early on that Sunday afternoon. Carefully considered, it said that, on all the balance, Britain would agree to the French request provided that the French fleet was sent immediately to British ports. In fact, this condition was at best unrealistic and at worst absurd. As Darlan was quick to point out, the manouevre would leave French North Africa at the mercy of an Italian attack.

At half past four, however, Reynaud was summoned to the telephone to hear an even more ridiculous proposal. At the other end of the line was de Gaulle, who had been sent to London to ask the British for assistance in moving the French government to Algiers. He was in a state of high excitement. The British Cabinet, he explained – first to de Margerie and then, after the call had been interrupted by Churchill, who had seized the handset himself, to Reynaud – had decided to offer a full 'and indissoluble'[26] union of the two countries and peoples. Moreover, Reynaud, if he wished, could become Prime Minister of the new union. It was all very exciting. In fact, such was the excitement that it was hardly noticed that King George VI had not been informed of the proposed disposal of his empire.

The whole thing, of course, would in normal times have been brushed away as quite absurd. But these were far from normal times. Reynaud thought the idea magnificent. The Council of Ministers met again at five o'clock to consider the British proposal. Needless to say, it found no support. Most of them thought the proposal ill thought out (as it was) and (rightly) not in the long-term interest of France. Pétain summed up their mood when he said that it was not in France's interest 'to fuse with a corpse'.[27] In yet another stormy meeting, Mandel accused his ministerial colleagues of outright cowardice. Pétain, after his first intervention, kept his silence. He knew perfectly well that Reynaud had lost the battle. The only option left was the Chautemps proposal. Reynaud, by now exhausted – and continually harried by Mme de Portes – said that he would submit his resignation to Lebrun. On that note, the Council adjourned. They were to meet again at 11 p.m.

The meeting never took place. Lebrun, as was his constitutional duty, sought the advice of Herriot and Jeanneney, the presidents of the two houses of parliament, on who should be the new head of government. Both answered 'Reynaud'. That said – and rejected – they replied that it was Lebrun's problem. There was, in truth, only one candidate. As ministers were waiting uneasily for the meeting Reynaud walked passed them saying abruptly that Marshal Pétain was even then forming a government. It was true. Lebrun had had no choice.

Pétain had been preparing carefully for the moment. Like others before him and others since, the thought, which had been in his mind in Spain, had become a wish. At the age of eighty-four, he believed he was the right person to rescue his country in her distress. He was not, perhaps, a new Joan of Arc, but he thought himself to be the next best thing. Oddly enough, his former protégé and now his antagonist, General de Gaulle, at the same time, but in a different place, felt precisely the same about himself.

19

THE ROAD TO VICHY

'Il arrive qu'un paysan de chez nous voie son champ dévasté par la grêle. Il ne désespère de la moisson prochaine.'

It was all to be so very simple. Pétain would form what was to be no more than an interim administration. Once Britain had surrendered there would be a peace treaty. France would be herself again, governed from her historic capital Paris. The spirit of 1871 would be revived, and France would, as she had before, regain her status as a major power in Europe and the world. Once that was all on course, Pétain himself would retire to L'Ermitage, secure of his place in history as another saviour of his country in her need. It may, even at the time, have sounded all too easy; but there were no more than a handful of those involved who had doubts. Pétain himself was certainly not one of them.

There were, to be sure, some inconveniences. The Germans turned out to be unexpectedly unpleasant; but, as Laval continued to assure those who listened to him, Nazism would in the course of time wither away. France herself, too, had to be cured of the mistakes of the 1930s; but this could be done by the programme Pétain had announced at Verdun in 1936 – with a nod to Primo de Rivera's Spain. Of course, those who were to blame for France's defeat had to be brought to book, a matter which, in the event, became muddled up with the fashionable attack on Jews and Freemasons; but that could be done by some – admittedly dimly perceived – procedure of justice. Finally, there was the matter of the timing of the peace treaty. There would without a doubt be a peace treaty before long, but there was no certainty when that would be; none the less, as one of the German negotiators of the Armistice, General Karl-Heinrich von Stülpnagel, pointed out, no more than confirming the general opinion, the British collapse could be expected 'in mid-August [1940]'.[1] A peace treaty would soon thereafter follow as the day follows the night.

Such was Pétain's acknowledged prestige as a Marshal of France that few in the political inner circle, least of all himself, believed that these minor inconveniences could not be overcome. Pétain, gratified as he was by the constant expression of devotion from both politicians and public, certainly believed that he was up to the job. But what he (and others) failed to take into account was the frailty of what de Gaulle was later to describe as the 'shipwreck of old age'. Whatever the prestige of a Marshal of France, the age of eighty-four was hardly the time to assume the leadership of a country even in the most healthy state, let alone one which had just suffered the worst defeat in its history. It was also hardly an age to resist the flattery, amounting almost to adoration, to which he had become accustomed in his role as a great saviour of France.

On the surface, of course, Pétain seemed reasonably fit. He still carried himself well and had not put on more than the normal amount of weight for a man of his years. True, on closer inspection it was clear that his face had taken on the distinguishing marks of an old man: the skin on his bald head had tightened and dried out, making his ears and the veins on the side of his head stand out; his nose seemed to have become an unsightly protuberance; his lower jaw had started to sag, and was etched with lines; his eyes were more hooded; the tic in his left eye when he was worried was more pronounced; and his moustache had become only a thin shadow of the former luxuriant bush which had attracted so many female admirers. It was no doubt sad, but no more than could be expected of old age.

Yet old age takes its toll on the mind as well as the body. Mentally, he could be either extremely alert – or almost vacant. Only Ménétrel seemed to be able to read the signs. He was also going deaf, as he himself admitted, and was tiring more easily – not so much with physical effort as with mental effort when concentration was required for anything other than short spells. Nevertheless, in spite of all, Pétain still stubbornly believed that it was his destiny to lead a defeated France into future, and calmer, waters.

But the one attribute necessary to accomplish the task, political judgement, was missing. As a result, even in the process of forming what he thought would be an interim administration Pétain managed to make a series of blunders. Moreover, through a combination of old age, susceptibility to flattery and political naïvety, he managed to surround himself with a dubious group of failed politicians of the Third Republic, to encourage the petty jealousies endemic in what was, after all, little more than a provincial government, and to upset both his potential allies and his declared enemies.

Pétain's first blunder came when he produced his list of government ministers to Lebrun on the evening of 16 June. The major surprise was that Laval was not given the job of Foreign Affairs but was offered Justice. When Laval got wind of this, he marched into Pétain's office – and after ten minutes came out announcing that he was after all to be given Foreign Affairs. Immediately thereafter, Weygand, with François Charles-Roux, the civil servant head of the department, in tow, marched in his turn into Pétain's office and, banging on the table, told Pétain that Laval's appointment would be disastrous for future relations with Britain and the United States and that he, for one, was not going to have it. Charles-Roux weighed in behind him, threatening to resign. Pétain then changed tack again and gave Baudouin the job. Laval remonstrated again, but Pétain, old and obviously confused, told him that he could not change his mind yet again. Laval stormed out, slamming the door behind him. That, at least for the moment, was that.

Another – perhaps subsidiary – blunder, of course, was not to put de Gaulle on his ministerial list. In fact, it was later claimed that in an earlier Pétain version de Gaulle's name had indeed been on the list – and that it was only out of pique at its subsequent removal that de Gaulle decided to stay in London. The claim, although made even now by Pétain's supporters, has yet to be substantiated by any documentary evidence.

Pétain had thus at the outset managed to upset almost everyone. But there was almost immediately another blunder. In the morning of 17 June somebody – it is still unclear who – told Pétain that Mandel was at the centre of an armed plot against the government. Pétain, without any delay, ordered his immediate arrest. Mandel was picked up while having lunch at a restaurant. The news spread quickly. When they heard about it, Herriot and Jeanneney went to see Lebrun. As guardians of parliamentary immunity they told him, correctly, that Mandel's arrest was illegal. At the same time, two of Pétain's new ministers, Charles Pomaret and Ludovic-Oscar Frossard, formed up to Pétain and told him he was making a grave mistake. Pétain, faced with an attack from both sides, climbed down yet again, changed tack, summoned Mandel and wrote him a grovellingly apologetic letter.

By that time, Baudouin had requested the Spanish Ambassador, José Felix Lequerica, to ask the Spanish government 'to transmit to Germany with all speed the request to cease hostilities at once and at the same time to make known the peace terms proposed by Germany'.[2] Without delay, the request was relayed to Berlin. Pétain then made another – and, in its result, even more serious – blunder. At midday on the 17th, at about the time Mandel was being arrested, he made a radio broadcast. He announced that, at the request of the President of the Republic, he had that day taken on the leadership of the government of France. He went on to say that 'it is with a heavy heart that I tell you today that it is necessary to cease fighting'.[3]

The effect on those listening to him – throughout the whole of France – was of stunned silence, and then of almost unimaginable confusion. Although the text was amended the following day in the official press release to read 'try to cease fighting',[4] the damage had been done. There was complete confusion. Platoons, companies, and sometimes battalions, of brave men, who were even then mounting an effective – and locally successful – resistance against a German Army which was tiring and at the end of a long supply chain, surrendered on the spot. Others fought on – pending further news. Those who fought on found that a unit on their defensive flank had laid down its arms. Just when French commanders and the troops on the ground had started to inflict serious damage on the hitherto all-conquering German Army, their efforts were undermined.

Even the Germans were perplexed. Their armies in the field sent urgent requests for further orders. In the event, the official German response to the French request for an armistice was not received until 6.30 a.m. on 19 June. A whole day and a half had gone by between

Pétain's radio announcement of a ceasefire and the German agreement to negotiate an armistice. Pétain's blunder had thus cost, at best, a chance to negotiate an armistice on better terms than that finally achieved, and, at worst, many unnecessary – and courageous – French lives.

If Pétain had been less reckless in his announcement, he could have made out a perfectly good case for an armistice. After the disaster of the panzer breakthrough at Sedan on 15 May the French had fought with courage and, in many areas, with determination. Indeed, Pétain could have claimed that the heavy fighting on the Somme–Aisne line had almost brought the same reward that Joffre had reaped at the Marne in 1914. Moreover, had he known the figures, he could have pointed out that no fewer than some 112,000 French soldiers had died in six weeks – more than in any six-week period at Verdun in 1916 – and a further 200,000 to 250,000 had been wounded. True, the Army had been defeated, but it had been an honourable defeat and not a rout. Under the circumstances, an armistice was a perfectly honourable way – in fact, the only honourable way – of stopping unnecessary slaughter.

There was to be yet another blunder. On the afternoon of 18 June Herriot and Jeanneney went to see Lebrun to try to persuade him and the rest of the government to go to North Africa. Lebrun called in Pétain – who reiterated his firm view that he would not leave France. It was then suggested that Lebrun and other ministers should go, along with one of Pétain's ministers specifically designated by him with plenipotentiary powers. Pétain agreed with the suggestion and accordingly nominated Chautemps to play the part. The matter seemed to have been settled. The decision was, according to Herriot, 'complete, absolute, and without reservation'.[5] That, to put it mildly, turned out not to be the case. Faced the following day with his undertaking, Pétain had forgotten about it.

Events moved on. On the morning of 19 June Lequerica reported to Baudouin that the Germans were prepared to talk. The Council of Ministers met again to appoint plenipotentiaries – and to do no more, without any commitment to Chautemps, let alone Herriot and Jeanneney, than study a possible move to North Africa. Herriot and Jeanneney, however, pursued their plans for evacuating deputies and senators. They were encouraged to receive, at seven-thirty in the evening, a note from Darlan telling them that a suitable passenger ship, the *Massilia*, would anchor off Bordeaux the following day at midday. When midday came, however, the ship was unable to enter Bordeaux harbour since it had been mined, and had anchored several kilometres downstream.

By that time ministers and their staffs had been badly rattled by an overnight air attack on Bordeaux itself. There was an immediate decision to move the government further south to Perpignan. The decision was suddenly reversed when Baudouin heard in mid-morning that the Germans were prepared to meet the French plenipotentiaries later that day at Tours. But nobody bothered to tell the deputies and senators who were scrambling on to whatever transport was available and making their way to the port at Verdon where the *Massilia* was anchored. Nor did anybody tell Lebrun, who was about to go with them when he was stopped – first by an urgent request from Weygand for a Council meeting in the early afternoon and subsequently by a letter from Alibert, written on Pétain's personal writing paper, to all members of the government instructing them to stay in Bordeaux until 8 a.m. the next morning. The signature was forged, as Alibert later admitted, but nobody seemed to notice. Anyway, by the time the letter was sent Pétain had gone to sleep and – as was the custom – could not be disturbed. Herriot, who had set out for Perpignan, rapidly retraced his steps when he was eventually told that the government was not moving after all.

The armistice negotiations were led, on the French side, by General Charles Huntziger. In fact, there was little room for negotiation. The Germans had already made up their mind about the terms. These were certainly harsh, but not unduly so. Two-thirds of metropolitan France was to be occupied by the victors, including Paris and the whole of the western coast; the remaining third would be self-governing; France was to pay the costs of the German occupying force; all French forces, except for those required for the maintenance of law and order, were to be disarmed and demobilised; the French fleet was to remain in its home ports and be disarmed under German and Italian supervision; finally, there was to be a simultaneous armistice with Italy.

The terms were considered by the Council of Ministers in Bordeaux during the night of 21 June and into the following morning. Various amendments were proposed, but, apart from two of little consequence, General Wilhelm Keitel, the chief German nego-tiator, brushed them aside. While all that was going on, the *Massilia* was on the high seas, Weygand was asking the Commander-in-Chief in North Africa, General Auguste Noguès, about the possibilities of continuing the fight there (and getting a surprisingly positive answer) and Pétain had finally decided to bring both Laval and Marquet into his government.

On the face of it, Pétain's decision was rather odd. After all, he did not like Laval. It was not just Laval's louche appearance – a badly groomed moustache, a crumpled suit and, usually, a smudged white necktie. It was worse than that. As Laval became more confident, he became more insolent to the old man, at times treating him almost with scorn. In particular, he had developed a habit of blowing ciga-rette smoke into Pétain's nose when talking to him which was particularly objectionable. Nevertheless, once the governmental circus had arrived in Bordeaux, Laval had started to play, as it were, on his home ground. He and Marquet often seemed better informed about events than government ministers. Certainly, they had the ear of sen-ators and deputies stranded in the unhappy streets of Marquet's city; and Laval's tongue was silvery and persuasive.

Pétain, in spite of the personal dislike, was impressed by Laval's abil-ity to persuade reluctant deputies. Moreover, he recognised that Laval's voice was one which he needed to be with him rather than against him. Apparently without consulting any of his ministerial colleagues, he therefore decided that Laval and Marquet were essential to his government and sent a message to Lebrun asking him to sign the nec-essary decree. The message did not go down well. Lebrun protested, on the reasonable grounds that the President of the Council should make the case in person. On the morning of 23 June, therefore, Pétain duly presented himself to Lebrun and the decree was signed without further ado.

Later that morning, Laval and Marquet turned up to their first ses-sion of the Council of Ministers – much to the surprise of those, including Baudouin, who only knew of their appointment a few minutes before the start of the meeting. In fact, the matter under dis-cussion was close to Laval's heart – an armistice with Italy; but Laval, wisely, did not intervene. In the event, the discussion, which spilled over into the next day, resulted in an accommodation which allowed the Italian Armistice to be signed at 7.15 on the evening of 24 June and for the armistice with Germany to come into effect at 12.35 on the morning of 25 June.

There was then the question of what to do next. Under the terms of the Armistice agreement, Bordeaux was to be part of the Occupied Zone. It could not possibly be the seat of the government of France. On the morning of 27 June, therefore, a long procession assembled to leave Bordeaux, much to the irritation of the Bordelais, who found their traffic inextricably snarled up. The destination of the procession was to be Clermont-Ferrand, much favoured by Laval, who owned the local newspaper and a radio station. Once there, however, the procession found that the place was impossible. There was no proper accommodation for ministers – let alone parliamentarians – and no office facilities in which a government could be properly conducted. Lyon was suggested, but Pétain refused to go there on the grounds that its mayor was none other than Édouard Herriot. There was only one solution: an old, somewhat decrepit, spa resort some sixty kilometres north of Clermont-Ferrand, by the name of Vichy.

In fact, Vichy turned out to be almost perfect for the purpose of an interim administration. The resident population was no more than 25,000, but, in the summer, when stressed gentlemen – and ladies – from Paris wished to take the waters, the population grew to some 150,000. The result was that there were spacious hotels, a casino, an attractive park along the River Allier surrounded by cafés and tea salons, and, for those who felt the need, baths in the reviving waters. Nothing could have been more agreeable or, for the rag-taggle of a government, more suitable.

Before they all arrived in Vichy much work had been done. During their stop at Clermont-Ferrand Laval had gone on the offensive. He had seized on Pétain's own ideas on the way the country should be run, by a small group of honest (that is, not political) men. On 30 June Laval suggested to Pétain, Baudouin and Alibert that the Senate and the Chamber of Deputies should be called together in joint session and, to put it shortly, invited to vote themselves out of office. Baudouin was against the proposal, on the grounds that 'you do not change the constitution of a country whose capital is in enemy hands'.[6] Pétain sided with Baudouin and raised the problem of

Signing the Armistice, June 1940.
(*Photos12.com/Photosvintages*)

Lebrun. Laval claimed that he was able to fix Lebrun, and went off to see him. An hour later he came back claiming that Lebrun agreed. Astonished at Laval's negotiating skills, Pétain gave him his personal authority to go ahead.

In fact, none of the ministers closest to Pétain was opposed to Laval's project. Baudouin, Yves Bouthillier (the Finance Minister), Weygand and Darlan all supported it, although with varying degrees of enthusiasm. But they all equally agreed that if the project failed Laval would be discredited – which was no bad thing. If the project succeeded, of course, Pétain would claim the credit. Pétain himself seemed almost uninterested. On the following day he went with Laval to see Lebrun about it all and hardly said a word. At a small meeting of ministers on 2 July he endorsed the project, but apparently without enthusiasm.

On 3 July Laval had a stroke of luck. Article 8 of the Armistice agreement had explicitly stated that the German government had no intention of using 'for its own purposes in the war the French fleet which is in ports under German supervision with the exception of those units needed for coastal patrol or minesweeping . . .'[7] But Churchill, for his part, had no faith either in German assurances or in French consistency of purpose. He therefore ordered that as many units of the French fleet as possible should be secured or rendered harmless. The most dramatic result of this order was at Mers el-Kébir near Oran in Algeria, where a large French battle fleet was berthed. A British naval task force stood off Mers el-Kébir and, on the morning of 3 July, issued an ultimatum to the French Admiral requiring him to sail his whole fleet immediately to a British port or to ports in the Caribbean or, alternatively, to scuttle his ships. A signal was sent to the Admiralty in Vichy asking for instructions, but it only mentioned the last alternative. The response was that the French should stand firm and that three cruisers were setting sail from Toulon to help. At that, on direct orders from London, the British opened fire on the station-ary French ships. In the ensuing orgy of destruction 1,297 French officers and men were killed and 351 wounded.

The effect of Mers el-Kébir at Vichy was politically decisive. There was general and vociferous outrage at this act of blatant treachery. Darlan, for instance, switched overnight from being moderately anti-German to being ferociously anti-British. He, and others, wanted immediate reprisals. Gibraltar should be bombed. A French task force should sail from Toulon to engage the British in the Mediterranean. Pétain, on the other hand, was more cautious. The upshot was that a whining note was sent to Roosevelt about the affair, Baudouin made a bitter broadcast, and diplomatic relations with Britain were broken off. It was not by any means a powerful response, but, for the moment, it had to do. As it turned out, what was much more powerful was the popular response in Unoccupied France. Mers el-Kébir was (and, for that matter, more than sixty years later still is) burned into people's hearts as a prime example of British perfidy. The thought of France working together with Germany in the future became that much more palatable.

Laval rode his luck. When the Council of Ministers met in Vichy on 4 July, although most of the discussion was about the possible responses to Mers el-Kébir, there was time enough for them to approve the proposed constitutional change, and Laval made sure they did. He then set about convincing the parliamentarians. But he did not have it all his way. When they heard of it, a group of ex-service senators decided to go directly to Pétain to express their anxiety. To do so, however, they had to get past Alibert – who was on Laval's side of the argument and was worried that Pétain would give in to them. It was not until 6.15 p.m. on 6 July that they finally found a way in. An obviously tired Pétain listened to them and responded that 'he did not intend to transform the nation without consulting [parliamentarians] in the process'.[8] He then asked them to prepare a text of a resolution, and all of them went away suitably reassured.

The resistance to Laval's project did not stop there. On 7 July Flandin arrived in Vichy. Addressing an evening meeting of deputies in the Petit Casino, he argued that there was no need for radical constitutional change. All that was needed was for Lebrun to resign and for Pétain to be elected President in his place. Pétain would thus combine in himself the jobs of President of the Republic and President of the Council of Ministers. The idea met with general approval, and Flandin went to see Laval about it. Laval rubbished the whole idea, stating firmly that Pétain would never approve. Flandin then went directly to Pétain who, unsurprisingly, thought the idea excellent. All he wanted, he said, 'was to be granted full powers until the conclusion of peace without being accountable to the Assembly in the meantime'.[9] Armed with this expression of approval, Flandin went off to see Lebrun. There, unfortunately for Flandin, the proposal ran into the ground. Lebrun refused to take any decision until he had seen Herriot and Jeanneney. They advised him to sit tight – which he did.

By then, Laval had made up his mind – rightly – that Pétain was not to be relied on. He was obviously agreeing, not for the first or the last time, with the last person who had spoken to him. On 8 July, therefore, Laval, after another unsatisfactory meeting with the ex-service senators, told Pétain that he could not manage the business unless he had clear and unequivocal authority. Yet again Pétain changed tack. He wrote a letter in his own hand, saying that as it was difficult for him to take part in the debates, Laval was to represent him. Furthermore, the passing of the measure which the government was putting before the National Assembly appeared to him to be essential to ensure the salvation of the country. Armed with this letter, Laval went off to a meeting in the Petit Casino to explain to assembled senators and deputies what the government had in mind. In doing so, he said that, now that France had been defeated, they must work together loyally with Germany and Italy and become integrated, sincerely and in good faith, in a reorganised continental Europe. The memorandum which accompanied the constitutional reform bill even mentioned a 'national revolution' to reinvigorate the country as a viable partner in the new Europe.

The formal debates in the National Assembly took place in the Grand Casino in Vichy on Tuesday and Wednesday, 9 and 10 July 1940. Laval's opening speech was generally agreed to have been one of exceptional parliamentary skill. If the Assembly was not immediately dissolved and a new constitution introduced, he told the Chamber of Deputies, the Germans would occupy the rest of France. If that did not happen, Weygand's soldiers at Clermont-Ferrand would simply take them all over. Accompanying the threats was a liberal spreading of Laval charm. In an hour and a half he displayed all the rhetorical tricks at his command, and there is nothing that parliamentarians like so much as a virtuoso display of rhetorical tricks. Laval by the end of the debate could be sure that he had mastered the Chamber.

The result of Laval's performance was that on that Tuesday afternoon the Chamber of Deputies carried, by 395 to 3, a motion to endorse the principle of constitutional reform. The same motion was later carried in the Senate by 229 to 1. That decided, on the next morning there was an informal debate of both Chamber and Senate in joint session, to debate where to go from there. Various proposals were made – Laval's proposal, the ex-service senators' proposal, by then produced in text, and yet another proposal, put forward by the Radical deputy, Vincent Badie, accepting the need to give Pétain full powers but rejecting the notion that the Third Republic should be wound up.

When the full National Assembly, the Chamber of Deputies and Senate in joint session, met in the afternoon of 10 July it turned out, thanks to Laval's tactical agility, that it was faced with two procedural motions which, under the rules, had to be taken first. One was to the effect that the government's bill should be voted on before any amendments were called and that if the bill was accepted all amendments would automatically fall; the second was to the effect that it should only require a simple majority of those present instead of – as was in the Assembly's Standing Orders in the case of a constitutional bill – a majority of those entitled to vote (in other words, out of those elected in 1936 the Communists and those on board the *Massilia* were excluded). Almost without demur, the Assembly accepted both these motions.

Accordingly, Jeanneney, who was presiding over the session, put the government bill immediately to a vote. Badie tried to protest but was dragged off the platform. The bill was carried by 569 to 80. All amendments, including that of the ex-service senators, then fell. The 'collective suicide', as it became known, had been accomplished with a minimum of fuss. At the end of the session Laval gave a speech of thanks. 'In the name of Marshal Pétain,' he said, 'I thank you on behalf of France.'[10] It was perhaps the shortest funeral oration for a parliamentary assembly that has ever been pronounced. The Third Republic in theory still existed – but it no longer had any parliamentary base.

Throughout all these parliamentary antics, Pétain remained detached. He had been glad to see his former – and much valued – subordinate Serrigny, who had turned up in Vichy on 6 July. Serrigny, in fact, did his best to argue against Pétain 'throwing himself into the arms of Germany where Darlan and some others were pushing him . . . If he relies on the German word, he will be eaten and we too'.[11] Pétain showed little interest. Two days later Serrigny saw Pétain again. They discussed how the Vichy government could administer Occupied France. 'It was not acceptable', Serrigny claimed, 'that the Führer should administer [Occupied France], contrary to the armistice treaty.' But Pétain had hardly given the point much thought. He suggested that he would send a 'high commissioner' to Paris. That was to be all. A clearly deflated Serrigny could only note: 'I have the impression that he is too feeble for the task in hand; it is a question of character, not intelligence.'[12]

Detached or not, on the evening of 10 July, after a long and tiring day, Pétain signed three 'Constitutional Acts', drafted by Alibert. The first announced that he himself was taking over the functions of the 'French state', in other words that he was becoming 'Head of State'. The second gave the 'Head of State' complete and overall power, both executive and legislative. The third adjourned the Chamber and the Senate *sine die*; they could only be reconvened by order of the 'Head of State'. There it was. Pétain, as Laval was to remark, had been granted more powers than Louis XIV.

On 11 July Pétain made another radio broadcast, in which he explained his new powers and how he proposed to exercise them. He had appointed a group of twelve ministers as his Council of Ministers. Laval was to be Vice-Premier, Baudouin was to continue at Foreign Affairs, Marquet was to be at Interior, Bouthillier at Finance and Weygand at Defence. France would thus be properly organised, with discipline and justice. Above all, the status of the family would be protected. Almost as an afterthought, he added that the Germans had been asked to move out of Versailles so that French ministers could be seen to run not just Unoccupied France but the whole country.

What Pétain did not mention was that there was still one constitutional matter which remained to be settled – the succession. He was, yet again, wavering. On 12 July he told Baudouin that he thought that the successor should be chosen by the Council of Ministers. He even suggested that Baudouin himself was the candidate that he favoured. Later that evening, however, Baudouin was astonished to learn that Pétain had changed his mind and had decided to make Laval his successor. Laval had persuaded him that there needed to be a civilian deputy to the military president. He had also pointed out how much

Pétain owed him. It was true. 'I could have done nothing without him', Pétain was later to say, '. . . [he] was extraordinary.'[13]

Constitutional Act no. 4, appointing Laval as Pétain's successor if he was ever 'hindered' from doing the job properly, was duly signed on the evening of 12 July. Weygand was furious, not at the emasculation of the Third Republic – far from it – but at Pétain's choice of his successor, the most flagrant example, in Weygand's view, of a shifty Third Republic politician. In truth, Weygand had a point. One of the many ironies of a supremely ironic period in modern French history was that the main instrument of the emasculation of the Republic had been nurtured by the Republic itself. Another, and little-noticed, irony was that the day on which Frenchmen woke up to the news that the emasculated corpse of the Republic had been put, as it were, in deep freeze turned out to be the day on which they all celebrated, with the usual joy, the storming of the Bastille in 1789 – 14 July.

20

NOUS, PHILIPPE PÉTAIN . . .

'Cette politique est la mienne . . . C'est moi seul que l'histoire jugera.'

The modern town of Vichy has, to be frank – and in spite of what the guidebooks say – really very little to recommend it. Like many provincial French towns, it has acquired both an accretion of ugly housing on its outskirts and a modern sector for fashionable shopping (Feng Shui is, for instance, in evidence) but has at the same time allowed the old town to decline into faded gentility. Lying as it does on the northern slope of the Auvergne volcanic massif, the town's only features of serious note are the Opera House and the Parc des Sources. Those who wish may enjoy by day the thermal – rather bitter perhaps but revivifying – waters emerging from the earth's broken crust and in the evenings wander in the cavernous halls of what is now called the Palais des Congrès. Indeed, surprising as it may seem, even nowadays there are those who go to take the waters, shunning the fierce sun and the no doubt younger spirits of the southern beaches of Provence. But they seem, like the peeling wrought-iron pillars of the covered walkways which border the Parc des Sources and the shabby painting on the outside of the Grand Casino, to be no more than relics from Vichy's great days in the time of the Second Empire.

Another feature, if it can be called that, is the Allier, by now a broad river meandering its way through the town on its way to debouch into the even more impressive – and historically royal –

River Loire. The Allier is bordered by parks on both banks, the one a golf course and the other (named after Napoleon III) a pleasant park boasting a wide variety of trees from all parts of the world, which provides, for those who are so minded, an agreeable walk in the spring or autumn sunshine. The summer climate, however, is less secure. Thunderstorms roll quickly off the Auvergne mountains to catch out those who walk out of doors without suitable precautions. But even those who are content to remain indoors or to make the limited excursions available along the streets of the old town are not much more favoured. The cuisine in the restaurants is no more than indifferent. There is, of course, the odd cinema, and a monument to the dead of the First World War and the Algerian War, but beyond that there is not much else to do or to see.

What is certainly not to be seen is much evidence of Marshal Pétain and his government. There is a Place Charles de Gaulle, a Place Victor Hugo, a rue du Maréchal Joffre, a rue du Maréchal Lyautey and an Avenue du Président Doumer. Varying the history, there is a Boulevard Gambetta, a Place du 8 Mai 1945, a Boulevard des Etats-Unis and a Boulevard du Président John Kennedy. There is even a Place de la Victoire, presumably commemorating the victory of 1918 rather than the defeat of 1940. Pétain himself gets little more than a footnote in the tourist literature of the town. Even the hotel where he stayed for all those years, the Hôtel du Parc, has been turned into apartments (Pétain's own, on the third floor, is preserved in its wartime state by those who still honour his memory). The Hôtel Thermal, which housed the Ministry of War, has been renamed and is now managed from America as a 'Best Western'.

None of this should be a matter for surprise. History moves on, even in Vichy. But there is a particular ability in France – shared, of course, by other states but in lesser measure – to rub out the names of those once prominent and even glorious who have ended up on the wrong side of history. Nevertheless, there was a period, between 1940 and 1942, when Vichy was at or near the centre of the attention of Europe and, at times, even of the wider world. The little spa town, hitherto ignored, suddenly became exciting – full of senators, deputies, ambassadors, officials, ministers, the mistresses of all of them, hangers-on and, it almost goes without saying, spies. A whole government apparatus, with all its accompanying baggage, settled in the town during the summer of 1940. There was plotting, gossiping, spiteful and, such is the nature of things, no doubt lustful intrigue. None of that hectic chaos, and indeed the enthusiasm, of those days is recognisable in the Vichy of today. History has, if only in that, taught her own lesson.

Pétain, in the early days, was the hub around which all revolved. In the first Constitutional Act he had adopted the royal 'we'. On the face of it, it was an odd thing to do. He certainly believed that responsibility for the defeat of the spring of 1940 should be laid firmly at the door of Republican politicians, but he never wished to assume the mantle of a Caesar. He himself claimed that he only wanted to serve until a peace treaty with Germany had been signed and he could retire to L'Ermitage.

The reason why he did so can be traced to the drafter of the Acts, Raphaël Alibert. At the outset, Pétain had impressed on his ministers that they must give the new administration a guiding theme, and Alibert, one of the most intense followers of Charles Maurras and Action Française, took up the challenge. Action Française, among other things, required a monarch; a monarch there should therefore be. Failing a credible descendant of the Bourbon or Orléans lines, a Marshal of France was the next best thing. In turn, Pétain was quite prepared to assume the role of surrogate monarch, however temporary it might be, if that was what was required. For a peasant boy to become even temporarily the surrogate monarch of France was, after all, more than he could ever have hoped for. Moreover, such was by then his opinion of himself, he considered himself a worthy monarch to look after his own people – whom, as though by way of asserting his monarchical role, he had started to refer to as his 'children'.

This was not the only matter on which Action Française had a decisive influence in the early Vichy. In fact, it had been Weygand who had set out the fundamental message, almost aping Maurras, in a letter to Pétain of 28 June. Weygand's message was then taken up by Alibert in drafting the document which Laval had read out to the deputies on 8 July. It followed – leaving aside the 'monarchist' element – the mantras recited over the years by Action Française: France must be reborn; the Catholic religion was to be restored to its proper place; the family was the fundamental unit of society; education was to have the highest priority; there should be a return to the land, to the values of the peasant; co-operation was to replace capitalism. The whole message was to be described as 'the National Revolution' (a phrase which Pétain did not care for – he preferred 'National Renovation') and could be summed up in the words *Travail, Famille, Patrie* (Work, Family, Fatherland). In passing, it is worth noting that it was a message which Primo de Rivera would have easily understood. In fact, it was little more than an updated version of the message he had put out himself.

Pétain set up his office and his living quarters – Nini joined him in late July – on the main floor of the best hotel in the town, the Hôtel du Parc. Ménétrel was given an office next door to Pétain, to protect his patient from unwanted visitors and to be ready with immediate medical attention if required. Bonhomme, Pétain's faithful orderly officer, was also nearby. In the early days of Vichy, Pétain's staff was headed by General Charles Brécard, under whom there were a military cabinet led by General Krantz and a civil cabinet led by du Moulin de Labarthète. Ménétrel was also given the job of sifting through Pétain's personal postbag; and his speeches were drafted by the former journalist Emmanuel Berl (as it happened, of half-Jewish parentage). On the floor below Pétain was Laval with his own staff. The two would usually meet each morning after Pétain's walk along the banks of the Allier, with Weygand, Baudouin, Bouthillier, Darlan and Alibert in attendance, in Pétain's office. There was not enough room there for the full Council meetings, which were held in the nearby Pavillon Sévigné.

The Council, as it happened, was to be fully occupied. There was much to be done, and, in those early days, Pétain's government showed surprising energy in doing it – surprising, that is, after the grim days and demoralisation of May and June. Pétain himself seemed a new man. He was no longer the grey-faced pessimist of a few weeks earlier. He even had a spring in his step as he walked. His old friend Serrigny noticed the difference. 'He is in excellent form . . . A curious thing: this silent man has become talkative. Before, you had all the trouble in the world to drag three words out of him. He really was the silent marshal. Here he is transformed.'[1] Others reported the same. Decisions came with unaccustomed speed.

There were, indeed, many decisions to make. Ministries had to be staffed and premises found. The civil service had been badly depleted during the move to Bordeaux – many officials decided to stay in Paris and, anyway, senior officials who had served the Third Republic loyally were not welcome in what was to be the new order. (Some, in fact, particularly in the Foreign Office, were given two or even three months' salary and told to stay away.) Judges, too, were not easy to find to staff the Supreme Court which was set up by Constitutional Act no. 5 of 30 July – to sit in Riom, a smaller town some twenty kilometres to the south of Vichy. Military officers, on the other hand, there were in plenty. There was no difficulty in staffing the military tribunal set up in Clermont-Ferrand to try deserters (including de Gaulle). Indeed, the military could enjoy the most sympathetic régime for fifty years. Not only was the Head of State a Marshal but, as was observed at the time, there were more military men in his government than had been in any government since that of Marshal Soult in 1832.

Action Française seemed to have set the agenda for the 'National Revolution'. It also played its part in the virulent anti-semitism of the day. Pétain himself was not, nor had he ever been, a follower of Maurras, but, in truth, he had never been one for ideology in any form. He was certainly anti-semitic in the sense that most army officers – and many others – in France then were anti-semitic. But he was not anti-semitic in the Nazi sense, regarding all Jews as a biologically inferior race. If he ever thought about it in recognisably intellectual terms, he would have told himself, as had many others, that there were two sorts of Jews – in short, those you knew and those you did not. The 'good Jews', that is those who were his pre-war friends or others, such as Berl, whom he knew personally or others who had fought bravely in the First World War, were to be protected. The general, unknown and unidentified mass of what the Catholics called 'deicide' Jewry, particularly those of foreign origin, were not to be given any special protection. The distinction is, of course, wholly bogus; but it appealed to many contemporaries – not least to Ménétrel, who wrote some notably unpleasant notes in the margins of a letter about '*juifs*' while going out of his way to help those Jews that he knew personally.

On the other hand, Pétain was certainly 'not anti-anti-semitic'.[2] In blaming the Third Republic for the degeneration of France, he accepted the view of many in the Gentile middle class that Jews had not only come to dominate the heights of industry and finance but were conspiring to reap the benefits for themselves rather than the community at large. Others even believed that there was a general conspiracy between Jews and Freemasons – although how that was organised was never made entirely clear. In fact, for Pétain, communists were a much more immediate – and permanent – target.

It was later said by du Moulin de Labarthète that Pétain signed the decrees which Alibert had drafted only with reluctance. That may be so; but he took a close interest in the drafting, and Baudouin reported that Pétain showed himself to be among the hawks. Legislation then came in, as it were, on the tide. On 12 and 17 July anybody other than of proven non-Jewish parenthood was disbarred from employment in the civil service. On 22 July a law appointed a commission to review concessions made under the Naturalisation Law of 1927. On 13 August all secret societies were outlawed, with a special reference to Masonic lodges. On 27 August the law which had been passed in April 1939 banning religious and racial defamation in the press was repealed.

This first wave of legislative action reached its climax in October with the Statut des juifs, which disbarred Jews from employment in the public sector and a large swathe of the private sector. They were not allowed to edit newspapers or even write in them (other than in scientific journals). They were prohibited from holding any post of responsibility in the military, the cinema, theatre or radio. Jews were defined as those who had three Jewish grandparents, or only two if they were also married to a Jew. At the same time, a special police section was set up to deal with foreign Jews, Algerian Jews were deprived of their citizenship and there was a further order authorising the internment of Jews born abroad in the camps created to house refugees from the Spanish Civil War.

During the debates about the legislation Pétain threw in a wild card. He instructed Alibert to exempt Jewish veterans of the First World War. He also, to put it bluntly, told Alibert to exempt his own friends who happened to be Jews. He also told him to introduce a blanket exemption, by simple decree, for anyone who had rendered exceptional services to the French state – in other words, anyone whom Pétain himself liked. As the result of Pétain's interventions, the legislation, however grotesque in principle, became impossible to apply with any degree of rationality, as almost immediately became apparent.

If there was a combination of Pétain's old age, political inexperience and dubious ideology in internal affairs in those early and energetic days of summer and autumn 1940, there was confusion in the new government's international dealings. Not that, initially, there was a great deal of activity. Various embassies took time moving into Vichy, and in the first few weeks ambassadors from countries who had hitherto had their homes in Paris had been busy finding their accommodation and setting up lines of communication in Vichy. True, Mers el-Kébir had thrown something of a stone into a hitherto quiet pond, but, apart from relatively minor ripples and a feeble response, the matter passed off without undue incident. The relative tranquillity, however, was not to last. The greater, and more extensive, ripples came with the British and Free French attack on Dakar, on the western coast of French Africa, in the last week of September 1940.

As a military operation, the Dakar attack turned out, for Pétain's supposed British allies, to be little more than an expensive and humiliating farce. For a start, the basic British intelligence was faulty. It was assumed that a 'majority of junior officers, garrison troops and population [at Dakar were] in sympathy with General de Gaulle'.[3] This assumption turned out to be wholly unfounded. Next, security was worse than inept. Spears, who was to accompany de Gaulle on the expedition, later wrote, 'I have never seen so many people from VIPs, civil and military, to wives and girl friends gathered together to see off the heads of an ultra-secret expedition.'[4] The Spanish Embassy in London was able to report almost daily to Madrid, and thence to Vichy, on its progress. Finally, the plans changed so often – at one point the British War Cabinet cancelled the expedition while the flotilla was on the high seas, only to reinstate it immediately – that nobody really knew what they were meant to be doing. It was almost a mercy when an unexpected fog descended to put an end to a miserable two days of unsuccessful action. The upshot of this ill-fated enterprise was that for the first time in the war Frenchmen fired at Frenchmen in anger, a British battleship was badly damaged and Britain's reputation for efficient organisation of a war effort took an almost terminal blow. As the *Daily Mirror* complained, 'we can't stand much more of this'.[5]

Worse than that, however, was the effect at Vichy. Up until then, Laval's efforts to move Vichy closer to Germany had stalled. The action at Dakar gave him his chance. Pétain was persuaded to agree that there should be further and more detailed negotiations with the Germans, with the objective – in return for suitable co-operation between the two countries – that France's fleet and the North and West African colonies would not be handed over to Italy (or Germany, for that matter) in any peace treaty. That decided, the negotiations were duly put in train through two separate channels: the military commission set up to monitor the Armistice, headed respectively by Field Marshal Walther von Brauchitsch and General Huntziger, and the diplomatic contacts between Laval and the German Ambassador to Paris, Otto Abetz.

The name of Otto Abetz runs through the whole history of Vichy almost like a Wagnerian *Leitmotiv*. It comes in at moments, at times friendly and at times sinister; is then silent; but then comes back again and then is silent again. On the surface, the Abetz *Leitmotiv* was francophile. Born near Mannheim in 1903, he started a career as a secondary-school art teacher. Actively engaged in youth work, he discovered a vocation for encouraging Franco-German friendship, and set about arranging meetings between French and German youth organisations in his native land of Baden through a loose organisation known as the Sohlberg circle. His French counterpart was the radical young journalist Jean Luchaire – Abetz married his secretary in 1932. In 1934, after a brief spell in the Hitler Youth, he was recruited by the future German Foreign Minister, Joachim von Ribbentrop, to become the head of the French section of his personal research staff, although it was not until 1937 that he summoned enough enthusiasm to join the Nazi Party. During a stay in Paris in the summer of 1939 he was accused (wrongly) of being a German agent and was expelled, only to return a few months later as Ribbentrop's personal representative. In July 1940 he was rewarded by being raised to the rank of ambassador.

Although the *Leitmotiv* was francophile on the surface – he was bilingual, charming, and a connoisseur of French wines and a lover of the French cuisine – Abetz nevertheless believed that, as he put it in a memorandum to Hitler before he became Ambassador, France should be reduced to 'a satellite state'.[6] But this policy, he went on to argue, should not be openly espoused since it would provoke a too hostile French resistance. The correct attitude, he concluded, was to encourage French aspirations for an *entente cordiale* with Germany – and then play on the divisions thereby caused. Hitler thought that Abetz's view was eminently sensible. The ground for Abetz's negotiation with Laval was clear – and was officially endorsed by the Führer himself. But, whatever the endorsement, their negotiations during July and August had gone very slowly. The only, rather unimpressive, result was that postal traffic between Occupied and Unoccupied France was made rather easier.

Nevertheless, the contacts, and the growing friendship between Laval and Abetz, helped to keep Laval in Pétain's government when he reconstructed it in early September. The reshuffle, if it can be called such, was in fact no more than the consequence of the demise of the Third Republic. Pétain, in the days of Bordeaux, had inherited ministers from Reynaud's Council, but he had always had in mind to dispense with the parliamentarians who 'annoy me . . . they make me waste valuable time and, what's more, they are unpopular'.[7] This, on 6 September 1940, he proceeded to do.

In the event, the only parliamentarian to survive in the government was Laval. Weygand, too, although in no sense a parliamentarian, was also a casualty – on the grounds that he was distrusted by Abetz as being pro-British. He was packed off to North Africa as Governor with what amounted to proconsular powers. But, even while confirming Laval's status in his government, Pétain was starting to have doubts about Laval himself. Although he had survived – Pétain realised, however reluctantly, that the relationship with Abetz was an asset to his government – Laval was far from popular with his colleagues and was consistently impertinent to Pétain himself. Pétain, an old man used to unquestioning obedience, did not like it. In fact, he had even started to doubt the wisdom of having made Laval heir to his throne.

Pétain's personal dislike of Laval led him in strange directions. In what appears to be a calculated attempt to undermine Laval, Pétain tried to open up his own line of communication with the Germans. On 15 September he sent a coded message to an old friend – and, as it happened, a dashing aviator of the First World War – Colonel René

Fonck, who was in Paris at the time. Pétain asked Fonck to get in touch with Göring, with whom he had swapped stories of derring-do in the years immediately after the war, to see whether a meeting between him and Hitler could be arranged. Fonck passed the message on to Abetz. Abetz thought Fonck's project ridiculous, but said, reluctantly, that since the request had come from Pétain he would nevertheless pass the request on to Berlin. In the end, Fonck's mission came to nothing – much to the relief of Serrigny, who thought that 'the Führer will play with [Pétain] as a cat plays with a mouse'.[8]

Such was the result of the Fonck mission, and the air of secrecy that had seemed to surround it, that Pétain felt it necessary to spell out his views in a radio broadcast on 11 October. 'France', he said, 'is prepared to work together with all her neighbours. She knows as well that whatever the political map of Europe and the world the problem of Franco-German relations, so criminally dealt with in the past, will continue to determine her future.'[9] Germany had a choice between imposing a peace or constructing a peace based on co-operation. 'The choice is first of all one for the victor; it depends too on the vanquished.' All that may have been true as Pétain saw it at the time. But at the time, too, he was also going behind Laval's back in contacting the British. Whatever the secrecy of the botched Fonck mission to the Germans, there was more secrecy to come in a new approach to the British.

It all started improbably. On 17 October 1940, there arrived in the office of Paul Baudouin a fifty-year-old French Canadian professor of philosophy from the University of Besançon by the name of Louis Rougier. Rougier claimed that he had a way of getting to London, and asked Baudouin to arrange a meeting for him with Pétain. Baudouin agreed, but the arrangements turned out not to be easy. Three days later Rougier was still waiting. He only got his chance when he was in the Pavillon Sévigné explaining his case to one of Pétain's aides, René Gillouin. Pétain himself suddenly came out of a Council meeting to smoke a – somewhat unusual – cigarette. Gillouin immediately seized the occasion to present Rougier and tell Pétain what was happening. Without checking any of Rougier's credentials or discussing the matter with any of his colleagues, Pétain, equally suddenly, told Rougier to go and negotiate with the British on his behalf.

On 22 October Rougier arrived in London. He first saw William Strang, then the official in charge of French Affairs in the British Foreign Office. The interview went well enough for a further meeting to be arranged the next day with Lord Halifax. Finally, on 25 October, he saw Halifax and Churchill together. Rougier suggested that there should be agreement whereby Vichy would agree not to try to recapture any of its colonies which had declared for de Gaulle and de Gaulle would agree not to invade colonies which had stayed loyal to Vichy. Furthermore, Pétain would undertake not to hand French ships and French naval bases over to the Germans or the Italians provided Britain relaxed the blockade – and provided that Churchill and his ministers would stop being rude about Pétain himself in the House of Commons and in BBC broadcasts. (In fact, the British had already come to the conclusion that personal attacks on Pétain were counterproductive.)

The day after Rougier's arrival in London, however, Franco-German relations took a new turn. On one of his visits to Paris Laval had been told by Abetz that he was to meet Ribbentrop, only to find out, on the appointed day, that he was in fact going to meet Hitler himself. The meeting duly took place at the railway halt of Montoire-sur-le-Loir, where Hitler's train had stopped as he was on his way to see Franco to try to persuade him to bring Spain into the war. Hitler raised a number of points with Laval about Vichy's attitude towards the war with Britain and Laval spoke of Franco–German co-operation and an honourable peace. Nothing was settled – except that Hitler said he would like to meet Pétain at Montoire on his way back.

The Council of Ministers met in Vichy on the evening of 23 October to discuss the proposal. Pétain initially showed some reluctance, not because he did not want to meet Hitler – he had, after all, himself been making efforts to arrange a meeting – but because he was concerned that he might be walking into some sort of trap. In the end they agreed that Pétain should go. Baudouin warned that Hitler would probably ask Pétain to declare war on Britain and said that he should be resisted. Pétain agreed and asked Baudouin to go with him. At this Laval objected, claiming that Abetz had specified that only he should accompany Pétain. Pétain then gave in to Laval – whereupon Baudouin wrote his note of resignation. 'I can only remain', he wrote in his diary, 'if I am in complete agreement with my two superiors, the Marshal and the Deputy Premier, and if I am able to exercise my functions with the necessary freedom and authority. Since this evening, this is no longer the case.'[10] Laval, as he had always wished, was duly appointed in his place.

At about seven o'clock on the morning of 24 October two cars set off from Vichy. The first was for Pétain, Laval and Ménétrel – dressed unusually in the uniform of captain, Pétain wearing the by then rather shabby marshal's regalia. The second was for Fernand de Brinon, an old friend both of Laval and Abetz (and a conspicuous Nazi sympathiser), and du Moulin de Labarthète. (François Charles-Roux had refused to go; he objected to the policy of co-operation with the Germans and resigned on the spot.) Lunch was at the prefecture of Tours, where there was much discussion about the fate of French prisoners and, in particular, Pétain's old friend General Laure. There was then a long interval while they waited for Laval to give news of the plane which was due to deliver von Ribbentrop and the train which was to deliver Hitler. While they were all waiting, Pétain entertained the company, as old men tend to do, with extensive reminiscences of the Rif campaign of 1925 and of his great friendship with the man he regarded as the greatest Spanish patriot of all, Primo de Rivera.

The leisurely afternoon finally came to its end. At a quarter to five the party left Tours under escort from German motor-cycle outriders. By six o'clock they were at Montoire. Hitler's train had arrived. There was, of course, careful security. Only Pétain and Laval were allowed to go near Hitler's own carriage; the others were banished to the restaurant car, where Ménétrel spent the time chatting to Hitler's personal doctor. When all were settled down, Pétain and Laval were ushered in to see the Führer himself.

There was the customary exchange of civilities. But by that time Pétain was tired. He immediately started to explain that he wished to co-operate with Germany, but he could not go into details on how that desirable objective might be achieved. Hitler replied with an extensive analysis of the military situation, and pronounced that Britain would soon surrender. The conversation then stalled. Laval intervened to try to give some flesh to the bones of Pétain's generalities about co-operation, but to little effect. Hitler then summed up the whole affair as follows: 'Marshal Pétain says that he is prepared in principle to consider co-operation' – the German word is

Zusammenarbeit, literally 'working together' – 'with Germany as outlined by the Führer. The conditions of this co-operation would be
established and settled in detail from case to case. Marshal Pétain
expects from this a more advantageous outcome of the war for France.
The Führer declares that he is in agreement.'[11]

That was the sum of it. Pétain and his party left Montoire at a quarter to eight to spend the night at Tours. But before leaving Pétain had
made another political blunder. He had shaken Hitler's hand. The
Germans were no fools. They understood perfectly well the propaganda value of what seemed to the old marshal to be no more than
courtesy. As a result, the photograph of the handshake was sent around
the world – and it arrived in London precisely on the evening before
Churchill was due to have his second meeting with Rougier.

The effect was volcanic. Churchill started shouting at Rougier as
soon as he arrived in the morning. Pétain, he claimed, had signed a
peace treaty with Hitler at Montoire. He would send the Royal Air

The handshake at Montoire (with Ribbentrop
in the background). (*Hulton Archive*)

Force to bomb Vichy and he would broadcast to the people of France to tell them that their government of traitors would be pursued wherever they went. Rougier managed to calm him down, but it was some little time before their negotiations were able to proceed.

Rougier was able to assure Churchill that nothing very much had happened at Montoire. This was no more than the truth. Pétain had achieved the release from prison camp of the ever faithful General Laure, but that was hardly a major victory. 'There was no conclusion at Montoire,' Laval said later. 'Nothing of any precision was asked at Montoire. Nothing of any precision was proposed by the Marshal at Montoire. Nothing was decided at Montoire.'[12] But what was also true was that Pétain was seen, and displayed by the world's press in one of the most famous photographs of the whole war, to have shaken the hand of the Nazi dictator and conqueror of France.

In the end, the Rougier mission did not amount to very much. Rougier, with the help of Strang, drafted notes on his meeting with Churchill. They were amended, with Churchill's approval. The notes still exist; but what is clear is that they were originally intended as a message to Weygand, whom Rougier was shortly to see. Somehow – it is not entirely clear how – the notes lost the name of Weygand in their heading. It was heavily crossed out. But Churchill did write, in his own hand, across the top of Rougier's notes, 'If General Weygand will raise the standard in North Africa, he can count on the renewal of the whole-hearted collaboration of the governments and peoples of the British Empire, and on a share of the assistance afforded by the US'.[13] Armed with this, Rougier went off to see Weygand, who would have none of it. Whatever his sympathies, Weygand was not prepared to allow himself to become a traitor to France. Rougier then reported back to Pétain, having at some point gratuitously added a second page to his note – and fraudulently attributed it to Churchill – which was much more explicit about an agreement between the two sides.

After the war the whole 'Rougier affair' became a matter of controversy, not least because Pétain claimed that he had in truth made a deal with Churchill. Flandin, who was appointed by Pétain to the government in December, also claimed that he would not have joined the Vichy government had he not thought that there was a 'secret agreement' between Churchill and Pétain.[14] Churchill was forced to make a statement to the House of Commons in 1945, and there was a British

White Paper on the whole matter, categorically denying any agreement of any sort. Nevertheless, when the circumstances were reviewed in 1964 by the British Foreign Office, a considered memorandum was cautious enough to state, while asserting that Rougier's second page was 'entirely spurious', that '. . . [the White Paper's] complete repudiation of any sort of agreement was couched in unduly strong terms'.[15] There were some further discussions, between ambassadors in Madrid, about a modus vivendi between the two sides, and some contacts in Geneva, but none of them came to very much. There the matter rests, at least for the moment. Nevertheless, it is safe to say that the British were in fact prepared to do a deal with their former ally – and that Pétain was more than prepared, behind Laval's back, to do some sort of deal with them – and had Weygand come over, or had Pétain been more experienced in diplomacy, a deal might have been done.

None of this should be called, as some historians have called it, a 'double game'. All that Pétain was trying to do was to keep open lines of communication with the British. They were, after all, and however much he distrusted them, his former ally and, as Peterson had noted in Madrid, generally preferable to the Nazis. All that the British were trying to do was to keep the French fleet out of German hands and, if at all possible, to detach Weygand in North Africa. But the Rougier affair was only on the periphery of the main events. What lasted from all the toing and froing between the various sides was the aftershock of Pétain's handshake with Hitler.

On his way back from Montoire Pétain was in fine form. There was an unscheduled stop in Amboise and then lunch with friends at Azay-le-Ferron. 'He is magnificent in his calm and self-possession,' one report goes. 'He is natural, as one imagines a sovereign to be; one sees straight away that everything in him is real . . .'[16] At Châteauroux crowds of children turned out to wave him on his way with flags and bunches of flowers. In short, it was a thoroughly satisfied Marshal who arrived back in Vichy on the evening of 25 October for dinner with Nini at the Hôtel du Parc.

The next morning Pétain woke up to the agonised cries of his colleagues (other than Laval) and the international press. Nobody could make out why he had put himself in such a position. There followed an almost desperate programme of damage limitation. On 30 October a chastened Pétain made yet another broadcast. He sounded nervous, not least because he had an irritating cough which Ménétrel had been unable to cure. 'Last Thursday', he started, 'I met the Chancellor of the Reich. This meeting has raised hopes and has caused anxieties; I owe you, on this matter, some explanation.'[17] This he went on to give. He claimed that sincere working together with Germany was the only possible policy for France. The Armistice was not peace. France remained sovereign. 'This policy is mine. Ministers are responsible only to me. It is me alone that history will judge.'[18]

The Rougier and Montoire episodes, although both were eccentric – to put it mildly – in their diplomatic method, showed that Pétain had gone to some trouble to think through his government's uncomfortable position, caught, as it was, between the former ally Britain and the victorious Germany. The course was difficult to steer. Nevertheless, Göring himself was later to say that the Armistice was Hitler's greatest mistake. Like Abetz and many others, he believed that France should have been reduced to no more than a satellite. Similarly Cecil von Renthe-Fink, who was to play his own role in Vichy's later stages, said after the war that for him Montoire constituted the greatest defeat of the entire German policy towards France; that Germany obtained nothing and almost lost what she had; that France was not won over to the German cause nor was the whole of French territory occupied; and that if there had been no Montoire, there would probably have been no Allied landing in North Africa and no German defeat thereafter.

On the other side, the British at the time were taking a relatively benign view of Vichy. 'The French', Colville wrote in his diary, 'have two great levers against Germany: their fleet and their Colonies.'[19] Churchill himself put his finger on it in January 1941. He conceived 'Marshal Pétain's main object', as he commented to the War Cabinet, 'to be to keep the Germans out of Unoccupied France by threatening that if they came in the fleet and North Africa would join this country.' But he then added, presciently, that it remained to be seen 'how long he could keep the Germans in play'.[20]

Rougier, the self-appointed ambassador, had opened up a dialogue. Certainly, the method was more eccentric even than Montoire – both Vichy and Britain had perfectly good ambassadors in Madrid, who did, in fact, continue desultory discussions about the British blockade for some months to come. But when Rougier left the scene, the baton was taken up by others. King George VI had already sent a carefully drafted message to Pétain on 25 October, during Rougier's visit to London. It soon became the turn of Pierre Dupuy, the Canadian Chargé d'Affaires in Vichy, to act as Britain's – and Vichy's – unofficial ambassador.

So far it was, for Pétain, so good. But by the end of November, the premise on which his whole international policy was based was starting to change. Britain had – unexpectedly – survived. The Luftwaffe had been defeated in the air and the German invasion of England had not taken place. At the same time, although German armies were victorious on all fronts, the Italians were not performing well. In short, it was even – just – possible to imagine a British victory and a German defeat. 'I have no love for the British', Pétain told the American Chargé d'Affaires on 16 November, 'and I shall defend French territory against them. But their victory is much better for France than that of Germany.'[21]

In the light of all that, it made perfect sense for Pétain to pursue contacts with Britain (behind Laval's back) and to play down Laval's efforts at single-minded collaboration with Germany. It so happened that Laval was pursuing these efforts even more energetically than before. In late October, he had instructed the French directors of the Bor copper mines in Yugoslavia to sell out to the Germans. In late November, gold which had been deposited with the Banque de France for safekeeping and had been subsequently ferried to French West Africa was brought back and handed over to the Germans on Laval's sole signature. Laval was at the same time, together with Huntziger and Darlan, having conversations in Paris with the German general Walter Warlimont about a possible military attempt to recover Chad for Vichy.

On the evening of 3 December 1940 Pétain told du Moulin de Labarthète and Laure that he was tired of Laval's initiatives – frequently made without proper consultation and always without the meticulous reports to which Pétain, as a soldier, was accustomed. Laure suggested Flandin as Laval's replacement at Foreign Affairs (an odd suggestion, perhaps, since Flandin had sent a telegram to Hitler after Munich congratulating him on preserving peace). Flandin was duly sent for and a letter was drafted explaining to Hitler the reason for Laval's dismissal. But then Pétain held his fire. He had learned that negotiations in the Armistice Commission had reached the point where he, together with a first tranche of his government, would be allowed to install themselves at Versailles. Nothing could be allowed to get in the way of that.

On 12 December Laval telephoned Vichy from Paris. Hitler was sending an invitation to Pétain to come to Paris on 15 December, the anniversary of the return of Napoleon's remains from St Helena. This time it was the turn of the ashes of Napoleon's son, the Duke of Reichstadt, to be repatriated. Pétain was invited to attend the cere-mony, to be held at night with the full panoply of searchlights sweeping the sky and swastika flags waving in the breeze. In Vichy, however, the invitation was seen as a trap – to get Pétain to Versailles by himself and force him there to sign over the entire government to Laval. There would then be a new government, which would include Marcel Déat, editor of the openly fascist newspaper L'Oeuvre and the author of a number of hostile articles. Pétain therefore refused to go. The next day Laval arrived in Vichy, determined to fetch him. At first Pétain resisted, but he then buckled under Laval's pressure and agreed to go, provided he was able to carry out some sort of ceremonial tour of towns in the Occupied Zone.

When they heard this news, Bouthillier, Darlan and Huntziger – quickly joined by Marcel Peyrouton, the Interior Minister, and Alibert – met in du Moulin de Labarthète's office at 4 p.m. to decide their tactics. Their aim was simple. Pétain had to be protected. It fol-lowed that Laval had to be sacked – immediately. They then marched into Pétain's office and told him so. Peyrouton was armed with infor-mation that the Germans wanted a 'more docile' French government.[22] The meeting was brief. Pétain was persuaded to immediate action. He summoned a Council meeting for 8 p.m. and asked all his ministers for their resignations (as was the custom in government reshuffles of the Third Republic). Pétain then left the room for a short while, came back and announced that the resignations of Laval and Georges Ripert, the Minister for Education, were the only ones to be accepted. In short, it was a clear political coup.

Laval was – understandably – furious. He demanded to know the reason. Pétain replied that it was because he did not make proper reports, because he was opposed to the transfer of the government to Versailles and because he was behind the Déat articles. None of that was particularly convincing. Finally, Pétain said simply that he had lost confidence in him. But that was not the end of it. As he was preparing to go back to Paris with his wife and daughter, Laval was told by an American journalist that his chauffeur had been arrested and his car removed. He tried again to get in touch with Pétain. In order to avoid having to talk to him Pétain instructed Ménétrel to tell Laval that he was asleep. By that time the building had been surrounded by police – and by some members of Pétain's personal bodyguard, many of whom were ex-Cagoulards. Laval feared the worst when he saw them with 'revolvers; they were showing them; they were threatening',[23] and was relieved when the chief of the official police came into his office to tell him that he had orders from Pétain to escort him to his home at Chateldon, some ten kilometres from Vichy.

Pétain announced Laval's sacking in a radio broadcast on the evening of 14 December. The following day Abetz, at the ceremony to mark the transfer of the Duke of Reichstadt's ashes to Paris, told Darlan and Laure, whom Pétain had sent to represent him, that the action of the French government was unacceptable. He reinforced this by travelling to Vichy on the next day, with ten heavily armed SS guards as his escort. He told Pétain that Laval's dismissal had been taken by Hitler as a personal affront. He demanded a wholesale reconstruction of the French government – to include Laval – and said that if that was refused Germany would not continue the policy of co-operation.

Pétain replied that since he had already announced Laval's sacking he could not go back on it; but he was quite prepared to discuss the possibility of other changes in his government. Abetz then demanded to see Laval and said he was shocked to hear that he was under arrest. Pétain professed to know nothing of Laval's arrest and ordered his immediate release. There was a further meeting when Laval arrived. Pétain offered to reinstate him either as Minister of Agriculture or Minister of Labour. Laval yet again lost his temper, accused Pétain of 'insincerity and double-dealing with England',[24] became more and more insulting and finally had to be restrained by Abetz himself. At that point it was clear to everybody that Laval had put Pétain in an impossible position. Abetz left for Paris, and Darlan was sent to explain the matter to Hitler, which he did on Christmas Day in a meeting in Hitler's train, emphasising, however, that it was 'the formal wish of the Marshal and his government to pursue the policy of co-operation'.[25]

Laval's sacking went down well in London. On 21 December, Churchill gave a dinner at Chequers for Dupuy. Dupuy told him that 'Pétain, Darlan and . . . Huntziger had spoken to him about the possibility of co-operation in North Africa and Continental France', provided that 'the present atmosphere of tension' between Britain and Vichy could be maintained 'as a smoke screen, behind which contacts could be made and information exchanged'. Churchill replied that 'he was ready to enter into a procedure along the lines suggested above' and that he wished Dupuy 'to inform the French Government of his readiness to send divisions to North Africa in case the French Government should decide to abandon the metropolitan territory or considered it opportune to receive British support in North Africa'.[26]

In spite of leaks to the press, Dupuy went about his mission. Back in Vichy, he sent a report to the Canadian Prime Minister, Mackenzie King, saying that Pétain was fully aware and 'was still hoping for a British victory'.[27] (The awareness was perhaps overstated. Dupuy added later that Pétain had nodded off three times during their conversation and he had had to wake him up by pronouncing the name of General de Gaulle in a loud voice – a procedure which enjoyed immediate success.) Moreover, Dupuy went on to write, on 27 December, to Eden that Pétain, Darlan and Huntziger were at one in suggesting negotiations on commercial matters but 'with the hope that such negotiations might lead to closer collaboration between the two countries'. Dupuy further reported three weeks later. Churchill had drafted a note for Dupuy, stressing the need for urgency, on the grounds that 'the Germans may, by force or favour, come down through Spain, render unusable the anchorage at Gibraltar . . . most important that the Government of Marshal Pétain should realise that we are able and willing to give powerful and growing aid. But this may presently pass beyond our power.'[28]

Dupuy finally reported in mid-January 1941. Neither Weygand nor Pétain had responded to Churchill's note, but he had found Pétain 'much more alert than we had supposed, and anxious for a British victory'.[29] Huntziger, too, was doing 'excellent work behind the scenes, in preparation for the day of liberation' and even Darlan 'was determined not to let his personal animosity against the British Admiralty make him work against a British victory'.[30]

There, for the moment, it rested. As 1940 drew to a close, Pétain, in spite of the blunders, the eccentric diplomacy, the plotting and the sheer bitchiness of Vichy politics, could claim that he had a number of points to his credit. The policy of co-operation with Germany, however wobbly in practice, was still on course. The infrastructure of government was in place. Dialogue with the British had been re-established – in fact, even while Dupuy was playing the go-between an official in the Ministry of Education, Jacques Chevalier, had been in touch with his old friend Lord Halifax. The legitimacy of the Vichy government was not (apart from the interventions of de Gaulle in London) seriously challenged. Above all, he himself had retained the respect, admiration and devotion of his 'children'.

On the debit side, of course, Pétain had had to concede that the sovereignty of France was, to a large measure, dependent on German good will. Moreover, the main plank of his early foreign policy – the imminent collapse of Britain – was starting to look dangerously unstable. Finally, the dream of moving to Versailles or Paris to become the leader of all France had faded as the morning mist. Abetz no longer wanted to see Pétain in or near Paris. Vichy, however small and provincial, whatever the boredom of the place and however bitter the waters – in every sense – was to be his home for the foreseeable future.

21

DARLAN

'Le chef, c'est celui qui sait à la fois se faire obéir et se faire aimer.'

The winter of 1940–1 in Vichy was cold to the marrow. Those who had long family memories said that there had been nothing like it for ninety years. There was ice on the Allier; electric power went on and off without warning; even the old charcoal-burning buses seemed to suffer from sporadic and unpredictable asthmatic attacks. Ministers, wives, diplomats, journalists, let alone the riff-raff of that transient community, spent their time in overcoats and mufflers, trying to warm themselves. There was no remotely recognisable central heating, but by sealing doors and windows with cloth and paper strips and by huddling as near as they could to the old wood-burning stoves, people managed to survive. The politicians and diplomats, of course, were able to survive without much trouble, but others without the privilege of rank or position were suffering – not just from the cold but from a shortage of food and clothing. Moreover, those whose menfolk had surrendered and were in prison camps were starting to complain that there seemed to be no prospect of them coming home. In short, at the beginning of 1941, Pétain's 'children' were cold, undernourished and fractious.

The political climate was as cold as the weather. After Laval's sacking, the German government, at all levels, was instructed that the policy of co-operation outlined at Montoire was now null and void.

Hitler had decided that Pétain was not worth bothering about and that it was better to keep Laval in Paris, with a view to setting up a rival government to Vichy if it seemed worthwhile. Besides, as he told Darlan at their meeting on Christmas Day 1940, it was a matter of indifference to him who was and who was not in the French government. The German attitude was clear. It was called *die kalte Schulter* – 'the cold shoulder'.

The one shoulder which remained relatively warm towards Vichy was that of Abetz. Acting on his own initiative, he tried throughout January 1941 to get Laval reinstated. By way of justifying himself to his superiors in Berlin, he maintained that 'the question of Laval has assumed the character of a test of strength'.[1] Furthermore, he told Baron Jacques Benoist-Méchin, a germanophile intellectual who found himself in the improbable position of representing French prisoners of war in Berlin, that he was – equally improbably – only trying to negotiate Laval's reinstatement out of a deep love of France.

In Vichy, Abetz's insistence could not be ignored. But Pétain was in difficulty. His action in sacking Laval had restored the popularity which he had enjoyed before the unhappy photograph 'at Montoire. Letters of congratulation poured in, praising him for what appeared to be a decisive break in the pro-German policy. His difficulty was that he, along with the other members of his new Directorate, Darlan, Huntziger and Flandin, was determined to continue precisely the same policy. The congratulatory letters, carefully sifted by Ménétrel to select the most unctuous ones, had – much to Pétain's regret since he ever enjoyed the approbation of his 'children' – to be ignored.

The upshot was that early in January 1941 Pétain agreed to see Benoist-Méchin to hear Abetz's case. When he heard that Laval's reinstatement was a necessary condition for Franco-German co-operation, he started, yet again, to waver. It looked as though there would have to be an embarrassing volte-face. Since both Darlan and Huntziger thought that Laval had been shabbily treated, they pressed Pétain to change direction; but they all wanted to know whether Laval really had the support of Berlin. Subject to that pre-condition, they proposed to Benoist-Méchin, for onward delivery, a package for Laval. In return for a letter of apology for his insulting behaviour to Pétain, greater freedom of movement for Pétain in Occupied France (in particular freedom to go to Versailles whenever he liked) and

Vichy censorship of the Paris collaborationist press, which was constantly attacking Pétain, Laval could return as a minister of state and a fourth member of the Directorate.

When told by Benoist-Méchin that he was required to write a letter of apology, Laval exploded. It was he who had been wronged and it was therefore he who should receive a letter of apology from Pétain. It took some hours of patient argument to calm him down. In the end he agreed to write a letter, although it can hardly be said to read like a letter of apology. Nevertheless, it served its purpose, and Pétain agreed to meet Laval on 18 January – at yet another railway station. This time it was La Ferté-Hauterive, on the line from Vichy to Moulins. In order not to attract attention, Pétain and du Moulin de Labarthète left Vichy in a car, pretending they were going for a short country drive. In fact, their drive was only as far as Pétain's train which was waiting in a siding ready to take them to his modest destination.

In the event, Pétain's meeting with Laval came to nothing. Pétain restated his grievances: Laval's unpopularity, his methods, his failure to report properly, his mistrust of colleagues. Laval tried to justify himself, but Pétain still had in the forefront of his mind the intemperate language Laval had used to him the previous December. It was not the sort of thing that Pétain either easily forgot or easily forgave. The two men spent some time circling around Laval's future position, but then Laval spoiled everything by asserting that the Vichy government was not up to the job. Although that may well have been true, it was hardly the remark to endear him to the head of the Vichy government himself. The meeting ended with Pétain grumpily agreeing – for fear of more pressure from Abetz – to be reconciled, while pointing out acidly that Laval's return to a ministerial post might take more than a little time.

By that time, a new character had appeared on the Vichy stage. The United States – in truth, President Franklin Roosevelt – had decided that there was work to be done. In late November 1940, while enjoying a leisurely Sunday morning breakfast in the governor's residence in Puerto Rico, Fleet Admiral William D. Leahy had received a message from Roosevelt summoning him to Washington to become Ambassador to France. The message, to say the least, had come as a surprise. Leahy was, at the age of sixty-four, suitably parked in his retirement from public service. Reasonably enough, he and 'Mrs Leahy', as he always referred to her, thought that they would live out the sunset of their lives in comfort and dignity. The problem, however, was that Leahy was an old friend of Roosevelt. He had known him when Roosevelt was a young assistant secretary of the navy in 1913. Above all, he was one of the few still surviving who had known Roosevelt before he was stricken with polio. When decorating Leahy with the Distinguished Service Cross on his appointment as Governor of Puerto Rico, Roosevelt said in public: 'Bill, if we have a war, you're going to be right back here helping me to run it.'[2] At the time, it did not mean much – it was just Roosevelt's way of trying to be pleasant. But there was a method to this seeming madness. Leahy was an old salt – and far from stupid. Roosevelt needed somebody to go to Vichy, somebody who was an old friend and who could also talk, as one old salt to another, as it were, with Pétain and Darlan.

Leahy and Mrs Leahy duly set off on the cruiser USS *Tuscaloosa* from the port of Norfolk, Virginia, on 23 December 1940 bound for Lisbon. Their journey was quite dreadful. The Atlantic crossing was rough. Meals were served on a tray and Christmas presents were opened while both recipients were prostrate on a long sofa. Things were not much better at Lisbon, where they arrived on 30 December. There was a train to Madrid but they both felt the cold badly. Two days in Madrid, which included 'a tedious interview with British Ambassador, Sir Samuel Hoare',[3] led to a twenty-five-hour rail journey to Barcelona in the company of all sorts of passengers, including, apparently, 'fowls and vegetables'.[4] But that was not the end of it. From Barcelona they were driven by car towards the French frontier, only to find the car nearly submerged when their driver tried to ford a river instead of taking the better option of trusting an unreliable and makeshift bridge. Leahy and Mrs Leahy thought truly that they had met their end – until an obliging farmer came to the rescue and towed their car out of the river with his horse.

They arrived finally at Vichy on 5 January 1941, to do their best to reconcile themselves to the bitter cold and to settle down. On the morning of 8 January Leahy presented his credentials to Pétain. He found Pétain in fine fettle, 'a splendid, soldierly bearing for one of any age, and a pair of remarkably clear blue eyes'.[5] Although Pétain understood some English, he preferred to speak to Leahy in his usual precise and articulate French. They talked about the food situation in Unoccupied France and about what help the United States could give. Leahy tried his best to be encouraging. To that extent, their conversation went well.

The following day, however, Leahy spent another hour – in the late afternoon – with Pétain, this time with Flandin in attendance. 'I was startled', Leahy reported, 'by the contrast in the Marshal's appearance. He showed none of the vitality of the day before. He seemed a tired old man.' Leahy went on to report that 'there were many times when I saw the Marshal in the late part of the day when he appeared thus',[6] and made a mental note to himself to try to see Pétain in the morning rather than in the afternoon.

These conversations were followed with the closest attention in London. Churchill was still trying to persuade Weygand to raise his standard in North Africa. On 7 January he wrote to the British Chiefs-of-Staff that

> we have therefore thought it right to assure Marshal Pétain and General Weygand that we will assist them with up to 6 Divisions, substantial Air forces and the necessary Naval power from the moment they feel able to take the all-important step we so greatly desire. We have also impressed on them the danger of delaying their action until the Germans have made their way through Spain and become masters of the Straits and of Northern Morocco. We can but wait and see what Vichy will do. In the meantime, we enforce the blockade of France fitfully and as naval convenience offers, partly to assert the principle, partly to provide a 'smoke-screen' of Anglo-French friction, and especially not to let the Vichy Government feel that life will be tolerable for them so far as we are concerned if they do nothing.[7]

This message had, in fact, been delivered to Pétain by Leahy on the afternoon of 8 January.

Churchill was most anxious that his message to Pétain had been heard. On 11 January he wrote to Roosevelt that 'it seems, from the report of your Chargé d'Affaires in Vichy, that the Marshal may not have realised that the message was one from myself and that it involved considerably more than a suggestion of assistance in the event of the

French Government deciding to cross to North Africa. The Marshal was no doubt too much embarrassed by the presence of M. Flandin to give as much attention to it as he might otherwise have done.'[8] But Flandin's presence was in truth no embarrassment at all. He was already convinced that a deal between Pétain and Churchill had been struck. The problem was not Flandin's presence but, as Leahy reported, that Pétain was unable to concentrate on what was being said to him. (In fact, whatever the circumstances, Churchill always thought of Flandin as a friend. As a token of continued friendship Churchill wrote a letter to Flandin when he came up for trial in November 1946. It was a friendly letter but, after Churchill's statement to the House of Commons, understandably – and studiously – avoiding Flandin's main point, that a deal had been struck. The letter was delivered by Churchill's son Randolph and read out in open court. The furthest it could go was to say that 'I always regarded you as on our side and against the common foe and his collaborators.')[9]

Leahy's experience was shared by many others. Pétain was alert in the mornings, less so in the afternoons, and usually very tired by the evening. Laval had used this pattern to advantage, presenting laws for Pétain's signature first in the morning, then in the afternoon and finally, for the third time, in the evening when the old man would sign almost anything for a bit of peace. In fact, on a number of occasions Pétain is reported to have signed laws without even reading them through – and then to have been surprised at the result.

It was not just a problem of old age. Ménétrel was up to his old tricks. There was the usual treatment of warm air, oxygen and massages in the morning. But to all that Ménétrel, if other doctors at Vichy are to be believed, apparently added injections of benzedrine, ephedrine or even amphetamine. Weygand, who had no love for Ménétrel, used to say when he met him with his customary sarcasm: 'I don't need I don't know how many injections a day, eh? Nobody has given me an injection at all this morning.'[10] The effect of Ménétrel's attentions, of course, was to brighten the morning – at the expense of a soporific afternoon and evening. Since Ménétrel controlled access to Pétain's suite, he could manage Pétain's visitors as he wished. Indeed, he advised those on his preferred list always to see the old man in the morning.

In giving his first impressions of Pétain to Roosevelt in a report dated 25 January Leahy made only a glancing reference to Pétain's health. He did, however, write at some length about the burden of work which Pétain had assumed and which, in Leahy's view, was 'beyond his physical capacity'.[11] He went on to write that he thought that Pétain favoured 'something like the Fascist government of Italy without its expansionist policy'.[12]

This was not altogether true. There was none of Mussolini's bombast. A more accurate comparison would be the Spanish régime of Primo de Rivera, Pétain's old friend, without a monarch (the monarch, of course, being Pétain himself). For instance, the main vehicle for ensuring support for the government was the Légion Française des Combattants, an amalgam of the various ex-service-mens' organisations that had existed before the war. Pétain was much given to touring the main centres of Unoccupied France and communing with crowds of his 'children'. In fact, it was the part of his job he liked best. These tours were organised by the Légion, whose job it was to distribute favourable literature and ensure that enough people – and the right sort of people – turned out to welcome the Marshal with the utmost enthusiasm. Such was Pétain's drawing power that by mid-1941 the Legion had no fewer than 1.7 million members.

There was also the matter of encouraging doubters to support the government. In this, too, the techniques used owed more to Primo de Rivera than Goebbels. But it was clear where it was all leading. For instance, there was the role of what were called the 'patriots', but who were, in fact, both spreaders of the gospel and informers. The role was described, in a memorandum from the Organe du Comité de Propagande Sociale du Maréchal – intercepted by Canadian intelligence in September 1941- as being in essence 'propaganda by word of mouth'. The objective was, of course, to 'establish a political "climate" and an interpretation of events, even of History, suitable to make more easy and more serene the action of the Government'. To this end, a list of professionals and shopkeepers had been established. Doctors, teachers, clergy, butchers, bakers, grocers and so on were on an extended list. From this list 'the most active and intelligent' formed 'the Marshal's team'. There were secret cells. Each cell had a head, who was responsible only to his superior in the central office in Vichy. Members of the cell were to be known only by their numbers and only the head would know their identity. The main duty of the members was to make reports of anything he or she had heard which could be construed as damaging to the government. In short, they were a form of amateur and secular secret police.[13]

There was also the carefully manoeuvred support of the Catholic hierarchy. Heartened by the revival of religious education and Pétain's obvious belief – whatever his private views – that the Catholic Church was one of the bedrocks on which a properly ordered state rested, the Assembly of Cardinals and Archbishops urged their flock to 'venerate' the Head of State in person and to support his government. There may have been some grumbling among the minor clergy but there was no doubting the enthusiasm of the hierarchy. As Cardinal Gerlier, the Archbishop of Lyon, said, 'Pétain is France and France, today, is Pétain.'[14] Priests were visible even in lay and political posts – for instance, in the departmental committees of the Légion and on local councils. Bishops were frequently to be seen at receptions at the Hôtel du Parc. The Papal Nuncio held ambassadorial rank, and was thus present as of right at all official functions.

Then there were the youth organisations. In spite of pressure from the extreme fascists such as Déat, there was no equivalent to the Hitler Youth, any more than there was a single political party. Pétain himself had refused the idea of a single party; he also refused the idea of a single youth movement. In his view, proper training of young men (young women, of course, were to stay at home and have babies) was essential for the good order of society; but they should not be too militaristic. True, young men of the Chantiers de la Jeunesse, the compulsory youth movement, wore uniforms, were heavily indoctrinated in the themes of the National Revolution and were marched up and down, but their commander was a former Boy Scout whose ideas were little more than an adaptation of the British movement, and the tasks he set his young charges were little more than trivial. But, in competition, there were the Compagnons de France and another six scout groups, all officially authorised by Paul Marion, the minister in charge of propaganda – including, oddly enough, one specifically for Jewish boys. All Marion's efforts to politicise such groups came to nothing, but at least they were supportive of the régime and dedicated personally to Pétain.

Nevertheless, in spite of the Légion, the informers, the cardinals, the bishops and the young Boy Scouts, all was not well in Vichy. True,

Pétain himself commanded wide popular support, and there was general approval – at least until the autumn of 1941 – for the National Revolution and the purge of Masons and Jews. But it was cold and basic foodstuffs were running short. If people are starving they want bread. What they do not want are lectures on how the new France was to arise from the ashes of the old and to be told that the way to this was for them to buckle down and improve themselves as Christians, soldiers and fertile wives. For the first time since the Armistice there was some audible muttering.

January 1941 confronted Pétain, too, with some awkward truths. He had convinced himself that the Armistice would lead to a peace treaty which would allow France to be reborn from under the political rubble of the Third Republic. He had thought that it was his mission, until a peace treaty was duly signed, to lead France to the middle way, staving off the Germans while maintaining relations with the British. But there was more to it than that. He had also thought that his mission would be successful, that he was the man who could come to the rescue of his poor country, as others had done in its history. With the new order, France would regain her true position as the leader of the civilised world.

What, perhaps for the first time, he was now starting to understand was that the enemy with whom he was dealing was much more devious and aggressive than he had ever thought. 'If I go against them', he told Leahy, 'they will come down here, and that would be terrible for my people. They are my people. I am responsible for their welfare.'[15] He was conscious that he had done little, in the face of that threat, for the 1.5 million French prisoners of war – for whom he felt a genuine and constant sense of responsibility. True, he still enjoyed the large crowds at the towns he visited on his travels, but there was no disguising the muttering in the background.

In fact, this muttering, incoherent at first, was leading to small shoots of organised resistance. Groups, centred on Lyon, were starting to organise. Gradually the groups, initially informal, coalesced into more structured organisations with identifiable leadership. Henri Frenay (known as 'Charvet'), Pierre-Henri Teitgen (known as 'Tristan') and Georges Bidault were early leaders. At first, their methods were harmless – small demonstrations, newsletters produced on primitive roneotype, meetings in safe houses. In truth, it was all very small beer. Yet such was the atmosphere created by the network of informers set up by the Ministry for Propaganda that news of these activities soon reached the authorities – and Pétain himself.

Pétain's first reaction was one of disbelief. He had deluded himself – the expression is not too strong – that, as father of the nation, as a Marshal of France and, above all, as the 'Victor of Verdun', his popularity would remain for ever undimmed. His second reaction, once his disbelief had been dispelled, was intense irritation. On 27 January 1941 Constitutional Act no. 7 was announced. It required all secretaries of state, high dignitaries and senior civil servants to swear an oath of personal loyalty to Pétain. The Act gave specific powers to Pétain to order any breach of the oath to be punished either by incarceration or house arrest. Given the network of informers, from then on no senior official could consider himself safe. Moreover, the same officials were obliged, under their oath, to report any sign of anything which could conceivably be regarded as treachery.

Abetz, for one, thought this measure highly satisfactory. But he still was not satisfied with the Directorate. He continued to press for Laval's return – as it happened, against specific instructions from Hitler. Abetz claimed to Ribbentrop (untruthfully) that it was Darlan who suggested he come to Paris to discuss purely administrative matters. On that basis Ribbentrop agreed to the Darlan visit – provided it was understood that Laval was not to return to Vichy. In the belief that Abetz had Ribbentrop's unqualified support, on 3 February Darlan arrived in Paris with a clear proposal for Laval, endorsed, of course, by Pétain. Laval could return to a ministerial post and membership of the Directorate – but no more. Laval immediately rejected the proposal, replying that he would only return as Premier with full powers. Moreover, as Premier, he would sack all existing ministers except Darlan himself and Huntziger. Darlan tried to negotiate, but there was no possible common ground. Darlan went back to Vichy convinced, probably rightly, that Laval had never wanted to return in the first place.

There was one further complication. While Darlan was in Paris, Abetz had, in passing, attacked Flandin with some unusually poisonous venom, on the grounds that he was wholly and irreconcilably opposed to Franco-German co-operation. It was, of course, quite untrue, but Abetz's disapproval was enough. Flandin had, Abetz

Pétain and Darlan in Marseille, January 1941. (*Bettman/Corbis*)

pronounced, to go. Pétain meekly agreed; and on 9 February Flandin, equally meekly, resigned. This entailed yet another governmental reshuffle. Pétain then appointed Darlan Deputy Premier and Minister of Foreign Affairs. (Darlan retained his existing posts of Navy Minister and Commander-in-Chief of the Navy.) The following day Pétain went further: he named Darlan his successor. 'The Marshal has stripped himself of his powers', wailed Serrigny, 'in favour of Darlan . . . Pétain has become Lebrun.'[16] Churchill, too, was horrified. He believed, with justification, that Darlan 'nourishes abnormal and professional resentment against this country' and that 'the matter is very serious in the light of the stories that Pétain at 84 is going to have an operation for prostate gland, which might well carry him off'.[17]

Serrigny gave another example of Pétain's feebleness. It so happened that one of Flandin's ideas before his resignation had been adopted – the appointment of a National Council. It was to be no more than a consultative body, but when the names of the members were announced, it turned out that half of them were former members of the National Assembly and most of those were Flandin's supporters. It did not amount to very much, but Serrigny was appalled. 'In the last few months [the Marshal] has made many mistakes,' he complained. 'The last one, which [Admiral] Fernet told me about just now, was the way the new members of the National Council were designated. Didn't he leave every initiative on this to his ministers? Even so, he didn't even ask to see the final list before signing it.'[18]

The new ministers who assumed office on 9 February 1941 were of an altogether different brand to their predecessors. Out went Alibert, the ideologue of the National Revolution, and Peyrouton, one of the chief conspirators against Laval. In came Pierre Pucheu – from the Banque Worms – at Industrial Production, Jacques Barnaud at Franco-German Economic Relations, and François Lehideux at the Ministry of Equipment. These were not ideologues – any more than Darlan himself. They were technocrats. They believed that the business of running the state was a matter of efficient planning. Moreover, planning required a disciplined approach to corporate governance, in which employers and workers would join together for the greater good. The 'National Revolution' was still a useful tool since it struck a popular chord – but as a pious aspiration not a programme for action. For them, what mattered was efficiency; and efficiency could not be produced by Boy Scouts but by a carefully organised corporatist state. Only in that way would France be able to hold her head up in the new Europe.

Neither Pétain nor Darlan had any particular understanding of these new technocrats, or of corporatism, or central planning or any of the rest of the jargon. Experience shows that generals and admirals are, like diplomats, unaccustomed to the ways of investment bankers. None the less, Pétain dutifully took up their theme in a speech, drafted, like others, by Berl but under instruction from Pucheu, made at St-Etienne on 1 March. The class war, he said, could only be solved by a 'community of work . . . This community is the enterprise . . . its transformation alone can provide the basis of organised professionalism . . .'[19] In fact, as a speech it was far from impressive. As with many of his speeches on economic and industrial affairs, it was ill suited to the painfully slow and tentative delivery of an old man. But then, in mitigation, although he spoke the words, he was doubtless not altogether clear himself what he was meant to be talking about.

Darlan seemed happy with his new team. His political ambition was to see France as an imperial – and naval – power within a German-dominated continental system. France, in the words of a memorandum drafted by Pucheu, Lehideux and Marion and submitted to Abetz, would be Europe's 'Atlantic bridgehead'.[20] For that to happen, France had to be a model of industrial efficiency and inter-class harmony. The new technocrats would make it happen. As an idea, or even as a political ambition, that was all very well. But there was no sign that the Germans were in the least interested in what Darlan was prepared to offer. Apart from Abetz, who considered France to be his personal fiefdom, no senior German figure could be bothered with what was or was not happening at Vichy. Even Abetz was told by Ribbentrop, in a curt telegram, to stop meddling. He should concentrate on keeping the French out of trouble – which meant continuing to threaten a puppet French government in Paris under Laval. Until further notice, the 'cold shoulder' was official policy.

The 'cold shoulder', such as it was, led Pétain to try to curry favour elsewhere. On 27 February he, Darlan, Laure and the French Ambassador to Madrid, François Piétri, assembled in Montpellier to meet Franco and his Foreign Minister, Ramón Serrano Suñer, who were on their way back to Spain from a meeting with Mussolini. There was the customary banquet, after which Pétain and Franco, with the two foreign ministers, sat down for a discussion about North Africa. Pétain spoke of a change in his view of the war from a few months earlier. It would be longer than he had thought. In the end, there would be a compromise peace, as a result of which France would play a full role in a future Europe. To that end, he went on, the differences between France and Spain in North Africa were minor and could easily be settled. Gibraltar, of course, would revert to Spain. All in all, the aim was to rid the Mediterranean of British interests and ensure that it became a sea under the control of France, Spain and Italy.

Franco listened politely, since Pétain was still a respected figure in Spain. But he seemed to pay little attention to the matter in hand. For a start, neither he nor Serrano Suñer trusted the French. Spain had too often suffered from France's changes of mood, and the memory of French vacillation during the Civil War was still too vivid. Moreover,

Pétain and Darlan with Franco at Montpellier, February 1941 (*Keystone*)

Serrano Suñer thought that Pétain secretly favoured a British victory. In any event, by then both Franco and Serrano Suñer knew Hitler well enough to regard French ambitions as the sheerest fantasy. Finally, Franco was far too clever to get embroiled in dealings which would certainly upset the British and, much more important to him, almost certainly upset the Americans. The meeting at Montpellier thus came to nothing. Each of the parties, after expressions of devoted and eternal friendship, went their separate ways.

Almost immediately, there was another surprise, this time on a personal note. On 7 March 1941 Pétain and Nini were married – again. It was, to be sure, a strange affair. Thanks to the efforts of the Papal Nuncio and Brécard, by then Vichy Ambassador to the Holy See, Nini's first marriage had been annulled by an ecclesiastical court in Rome. (The fact that she had borne a child to her lawfully wedded husband had been conveniently ignored – not that Pétain was particularly worried that his stepson Pierre was thereby formally declared illegitimate.) This left Nini free to demand that her civil marriage be regularised by the proper and eternal rites of the Catholic Church. The demand had, as with many of Nini's demands, put Pétain in a quandary. He could hardly refuse. For a head of state of a supposedly Catholic country – and one which had promulgated the 'National Revolution' so enthusiastically – to be living, as it were, in sin, was hardly acceptable if the alternative was available. On the other hand, a religious ceremony in Vichy, however private, would require Pétain to confess his sins in the usual manner. This, so the wags maintained, was altogether too daunting a prospect. Besides, the publicity would no doubt be unpleasant – the bridegroom not being precisely in the first flower of youth.

The solution devised was very neat. He and Nini would be married by proxy. So it was that Nini set off for Paris on the appointed day clutching a sworn affidavit from her husband and, indeed, husband-to-be. Armed with this she appeared in the chapel of the archbishop in the cathedral of Notre-Dame, and knelt solemnly by herself to be joined in holy matrimony to Henri Philippe Pétain, Marshal of France. The deed was duly done; but, reasonably enough, there is no record whether or not there was a reception after the event or, if so, whether there was a toast to the absent bridegroom.

As though by way of relief that the whole thing was over, Pétain spent much of the rest of March and early April visiting the provincial towns. Nîmes, St-Etienne, Le Puy, Grenoble, Vienne, Pau, Lourdes, Tarbes – they were all on his list. Yet again he was received with adulation. But he then made another blunder. Against his – admittedly feeble – opposition, Darlan had succumbed to German demands to set up a Commission Général aux Questions Juives. By early April Xavier Vallat, a former deputy of pronounced anti-semitic views, had become its first head. Its function was to enforce the existing law against Jews, to co-ordinate them with the ordinances issued by the German Military Governor in France – and to devise further laws. Vallat was to prove rigorous in his task, and there was little Pétain could – or wanted to – do to restrain him. Vallat's unpopularity was in time to rub off on Pétain himself. The announcement, and Vallat's appointment, were not just greeted without enthusiasm; in most of Unoccupied France they were greeted with outright hostility.

It was this hostility which encouraged the fledgeling resistance groups to become bolder. There were more people to be seen whispering to one another in the streets; the roneotyped sheets were more strident in their language; and photographs of the Marshal unaccountably disappeared from shop windows. In response, on 7 April Pétain delivered his first attack on the 'dissidents', as he called them. In a radio broadcast he stressed the need for national unity, and went on to criticise 'propaganda, subtle, insidious, inspired by Frenchmen, [which] struggles to break it [unity]. Halted for a moment, the calls to dissidence take up again each day a tone which is ever more arrogant.'[21] To shore up further the government's position, Darlan extended the application of the oath of personal allegiance to Pétain to magistrates and, above all, the Army.

This, however it was presented, was, for Pétain, no small matter. In fact, it can without any exaggeration be described as a personal Rubicon. For the whole of his life, from his childhood stories to Saint Bertin to Arceuil to Saint-Cyr, Pétain had been educated to believe that it was the duty of the Army to obey the instructions of a duly constituted civil authority. If that authority changed complexion the Army would obey the instructions of the new authority. That had been the rule which had proved a binding force in the turbulent French politics ever since the Revolution. That was now to change. From the most senior general to the humblest *poilu*, all were solemnly bound to obey without hesitation or question Pétain's orders, however eccentric they might be and whether or not Pétain was the duly constituted civil authority. Of all the measures which Pétain signed at Vichy it is this measure which brought him – against everything he had learned in his military career – into the ranks of Hitler, Mussolini and Franco. If the Third Republic had been castrated by the National Assembly vote of July 1940, it was just as surely lobotomised by Pétain's signature on the order extending the oath of personal allegiance to judges and, above all, the Army.

On 26 April 1941 Pétain celebrated, if that is the right word, his eighty-fifth birthday. It was noted that he seemed tired and rather depressed. Serrigny had arrived again from Paris two days before, to be told by Laure that Pétain was ageing fast and was now only listening to those who flattered him. Determined that Pétain should know the truth, he barged his way into Pétain's office and told him that his prestige had fallen badly in Occupied France. Obviously put out, Pétain wanted to know why. Serrigny told him that Darlan had recently made a statement to the effect that 'Germany had shown herself more generous than England'[22] – given, naturally enough, wide publicity in the collaborationist Paris press. Soon afterwards Pétain had made a speech in which he said that Darlan had his complete confidence. The two statements were put together by the Parisian press, and the conclusion drawn that Pétain agreed with Darlan's statement. When pressed by Serrigny, Pétain became confused. He replied that he had had no knowledge of Darlan's statement. He claimed that nobody had shown him the newspapers. This was untrue, as Laure subsequently pointed out to Serrigny. Pétain had simply forgotten.

Pétain had, however, let slip to Serrigny that he 'had definitely decided to leave as soon as I believe the moment to have arrived'.[23] On 5 May he went, for the first time since the Armistice, to L'Ermitage. Although he was glad to be back there, not much time could be spent on his possible plans for retirement or, for that matter, on his chickens. Officials, dignitaries, industrialists, bishops, all seemed to want to see him. During the five days he spent there he hardly had time to look at his vines. But, in truth, there was no question of an idle holiday. On 10 May he heard that Darlan was summoned to see Hitler the following day. Return to Vichy could no longer be avoided. He needed to know what Darlan was playing at.

The truth, as Pétain soon found out, was that the 'cold shoulder' was thawing quickly. The Germans found that they had need of French co-operation. This was no longer a matter of mutual agreement for economic or even political co-operation. It was now about the military conduct of the war. Pétain had already received a request from the Germans to authorise their troops to cross Vichy territory on their way to Spain to attack Gibraltar – and from there to occupy Spanish Morocco and thus seal off the western entry point into the Mediterranean. The plan had failed on Franco's reluctance to have anything to do with it. But now there was a new German proposal – one on which Pétain could not hide behind Franco's skirts. The Germans wanted military collaboration – not just civil co-operation – in the French protectorates of the Levant.

Since the outbreak of war the tranquil life of the French forces in the Levantine protectorates, Syria and Lebanon, had hardly been disturbed. They had, of course, welcomed the Armistice, and followed instructions, when they came, from Vichy. Their commander-in-chief was General Henri-Fernand Dentz, an Alsatian whose father had emigrated to France in 1871 to prevent his sons becoming German citizens. Dentz was a faithful supporter of Pétain's government, although he disliked the Germans, on the grounds that they had 'germanised' Alsace in July 1940 and expelled many Alsatian refugees into Unoccupied France. But if there was a post to be enjoyed, Dentz was certainly capable of enjoying it; and Beirut was just such a post. There was not much to do in military terms and social life was particularly agreeable. He was, for instance, on excellent terms with the British Consul-General in Beirut and his charming French wife, and shared with them an affection for good claret.

Dentz had therefore been rather put out in early February 1941 to receive a signal from Darlan instructing him to give all necessary facilities to two German intelligence agents, by the names of von Hintig and Rosen, who duly arrived disguised as commercial travellers. Their activities, of course, were far from commercial. They were there to make contact with German sympathisers – and to survey the possibilities for German use of Syrian airfields.

For the next six months, Dentz's life became a misery. On 2 May the Prime Minister of Iraq, Rashid Ali, after prolonged German wooing, staged an anti-British *coup d'état* in Baghdad and laid siege to the British base at Habbaniya Airport. The overland route to India, as well as the Iraqi oilfields, were in danger of being lost to the British. But Rashid Ali needed German help if he was to fight off the task force of British, Australian and Free French troops which was even then being mobilised in northern Palestine.

Abetz had sent for Darlan while Pétain was at L'Ermitage and had proposed a deal. Procedures at the demarcation line would be made less onerous, the costs of occupation payable by France would be reduced, prisoners of war who had fought in the First World War would be repatriated, and there would be limited permission for rearmament of French naval vessels. In return, the French would provide arms for Rashid Ali and allow German planes to land, refuel and, if necessary, be repaired at French-controlled airfields in Syria.

On 6 May, without consulting the holidaying Pétain, Darlan agreed, and signalled Dentz accordingly. As a result, Darlan was invited to meet Hitler at Berchtesgaden. At the meeting, on 11 May, Darlan expected Hitler to express his gratitude for Darlan's efforts. Hitler, however, was not in that sort of mood. He snapped at Darlan that the sort of co-operation envisaged at Montoire was no longer on the agenda. Since Germany was certainly going to win the war, France had a decision to make: either she collaborated fully or she would suffer the consequences. In other words, she would be treated like Poland, as an appendage to the Greater Reich. That, in his view, was the end of the matter. Darlan was unceremoniously dismissed.

By 14 May Darlan had returned to Vichy. He duly reported to Pétain and his ministerial colleagues. His report was written out in full, and, as though by way of insurance, also sent to the governors of the French colonies. 'If we favour Britain', he wrote, 'France will be smashed, dismembered and will not survive as a nation. If we try to follow a balanced policy between the two adversaries . . . the eventual peace terms will be disastrous. If we collaborate with Germany, without agreeing to make war against England alongside her, we can save the French nation . . . and play an honourable, even important role in the Europe of the future.'[24]

Pétain was yet again in a quandary, which was becoming familiar. He had agreed with the principle of a direct meeting between Darlan and Hitler, and said so in a broadcast the following day. He had also been prepared for German aircraft to use French airfields in Syria. On that basis, therefore, negotiations about an agreement with Germany were allowed to continue, led first by Huntziger and then by Darlan himself. But he had not expected Darlan to go much further. This Darlan did, and Pétain, having given his initial approval, was unable to stop him. By 28 May he had signed three separate agreements. The first was to allow the Germans to use Syrian airfields; the second was to allow Bizerta and Sousse in Tunisia to be used as trans-shipment points for General Erwin Rommel's Afrika Corps in North Africa; and the third was to allow German submarines to use Dakar as a U-boat base from which to attack Allied merchant shipping in the Atlantic.

These agreements, known as the 'Paris Protocols', were brought back by Darlan to Vichy for approval. It was immediately clear that they were a great deal more than the original agreement for the use of Syrian airfields. The second and third Protocols were tantamount to wholesale military collaboration with the Germans, only just stopping short of a declaration of war against Britain. Darlan had wildly exceeded his brief. It was no doubt a bold initiative – but he still had to carry Pétain with him, and Pétain was not to be carried.

It had only been a few days before Darlan signed the Protocols that Pétain had found out what Darlan was up to. Jean Berthelot, an engineer who happened to be under temporary arrest in Paris at the time, had heard all about it from his German guard. Freed from arrest, Berthelot went to Vichy and told Pétain what Darlan was planning. When he heard about it, Pétain was quick to react. As he told Berthelot, there was no question of his approving the second and third Protocols. On the other hand, he could not openly disavow Darlan's signature.

Pétain saw only one way out of the confusion. On 2 June he summoned Weygand from North Africa. As it happened, Weygand had heard about the Protocols and had already decided to fight the battle in Vichy. On his arrival on the evening of 2 June, Weygand marched into Pétain's offices and read him a carefully prepared memorandum, in which he refused, as Governor-General, to put any base in North Africa at the disposal of the Germans or the Italians. French Africa, he went on, would defend itself against whoever attacked it, but France must not, he emphasised finally, deliberately go to war against her former ally.

On the morning of 3 June Pétain called together a small group of ministers, including Weygand. 'I recall the scene,' Berthelot said later. 'Darlan made a cold exposé in an icy silence. He hadn't read the papers. He simply gave an analysis. Weygand was on the Marshal's left; I felt him boiling like a racehorse wanting to jump and Darlan had hardly finished before General Weygand took the offensive – and the word represents precisely what passed. The Protocols were killed on 3 June.'[25]

Weygand went on to say that he would resign. That afternoon Pétain, Huntziger, Laure and others pleaded with him to withdraw. Weygand replied that he would only withdraw if the Germans were asked for concessions in return that they could not possibly grant: French sovereignty over the whole of France; liberation of all prisoners; guarantee of non-intervention in all French colonies; Alsace and Lorraine to be 'ungermanised'; and so on. On 14 June Darlan sent a note to that effect to Abetz. Negotiations on the Protocols were immediately broken off.

There has been much debate on whether Weygand was the decisive voice in forcing Darlan to abandon the military collaboration enshrined in the Paris Protocols, or whether Darlan himself was already having second thoughts; and the matter even now remains in doubt. What is, however, clear is that Darlan drew back from the position he had taken and that, in doing so, he had the support of Pétain. Unless Berthelot's evidence at Pétain's trial is no more than fabrication – unlikely, since it was given under oath – Pétain's view at the time was plain and, unlike his views on previous (and future) occasions, unusually clear. He was not prepared to concede any more than the limited military collaboration already conceded – the use of the Syrian airfields.

As it happened, the Syrian airfields soon passed out of history, and Dentz's misery came to an end. On 8 June the motley Allied army in Palestine crossed into the Lebanon. Dentz's troops formed up to stop them. Although the Free French were led by a band playing the 'Marseillaise' as loudly as possible, the Vichy soldiers were not impressed. One battalion of the Foreign Legion, on the Free French side, refused to fire on their Vichy opponents and had to be withdrawn. It was only when Rashid Ali's rebellion collapsed that the British General Archibald Wavell was able to send reinforcements into Syria. At that point Dentz had had enough, and sued for peace.

There was, however, a strange and revealing twist to the whole episode. On 20 June, while negotiations for an armistice in Syria and Lebanon were about to begin, Pétain decided to renew contact with the British. An emissary was smuggled from Vichy to London by the British secret services. He duly arrived and was ushered in to see Churchill. As a result, on 5 July Churchill instructed Eden, by then Foreign Secretary, to send a message to Oliver Lyttelton, the minister resident in Cairo. 'An agent who we think is sure', Churchill's message went,

> came a fortnight ago to establish a liaison between us and Vichy. Our talks with him were on the dead level. He now sends us the following, dated 5th July: 1. The French Government has given the following general instructions to General Dentz: 'When Syria is occupied by the British the French Civil Servants must remain at their posts and carry on with their duties in collaboration with the Free French Forces. 2. I am requested to beg of you most earnestly to take these instructions into account. Goodwill on your part will make the best impression. 3. Failure to meet this, the first wish expressed by my Government so soon after my return, would have an unfortunate influence on my future actions.[26]

Both Pétain and Churchill were trying to keep lines of communication open, however unorthodox the means. But, as it turned out, there were greater – much greater – events in eastern Europe. On 22 June 1941, at four o'clock in the morning, Hitler's armies invaded the Soviet Union. It was to mark, with all the necessary hindsight, a turning point in a war which had been until then a list of German military successes. Few suspected it at the time, but there was one man who understood very clearly what it meant. When Weygand heard the news, he immediately called Robert Murphy, Roosevelt's personal envoy to North Africa. 'I found him minus his usual composure and in a state of exhilaration,' Murphy later wrote. 'He said without further ado: "When we discussed the war and you expressed your belief that Britain would win in the end, I asked you where the divisions would come from. Now I know where they will come from – Russia. Germany has lost the war!"'[27]

22

THE RETURN OF 'BLACK PETER'

'J'ai des choses graves à vous dire.'

Early in the evening of 12 August 1941 *le tout Vichy*, or at least those who could afford the tickets and the required elegance of dress, arrived at the Opera House for a performance of Mussorgsky's *Boris Godunov*. Since it was the only entertainment available on the day, attendance by the fashionable was almost obligatory, just as it had been for the Grand Prix of the annual race meeting nine days earlier. Ambassador Leahy and Mrs Leahy were, of course, present. Mrs Leahy had managed to overcome her husband's reluctance – he was, as he admitted himself, an unenthusiastic opera-goer. The two therefore sat, she with pleasure and he with a sense of duty, through the prologue and the first three turbulent acts.

In the interval between the third and fourth acts there was an unexpected interruption. Marshal Pétain, it was announced, was to make a radio broadcast which was to be relayed direct to the Opera House. On hearing the news, the whole audience, including the Leahys, rose to its feet. Not only that, but it remained standing throughout the whole of Pétain's statement. The gesture, of course, was made out of respect for the Marshal, but it was a gesture which at least some in the audience probably came to regret, since, in the event, they were to be kept much longer on their feet than they had expected.

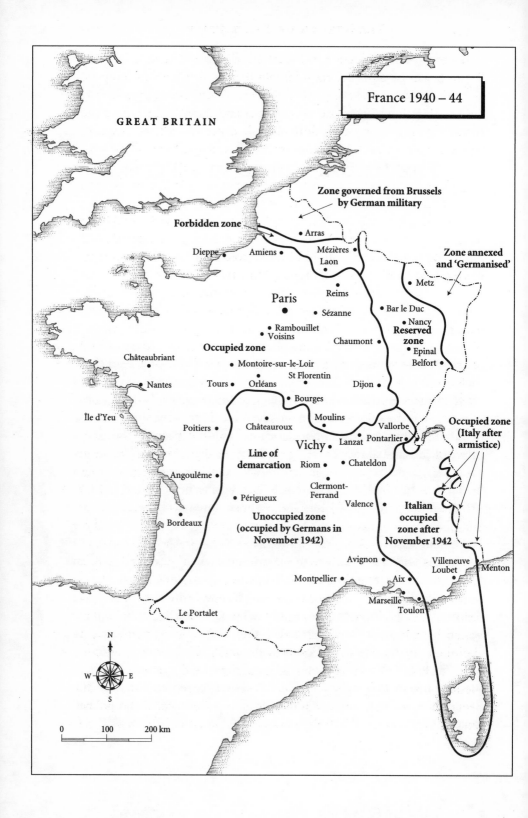

France 1940 – 44

GREAT BRITAIN

Zone governed from Brussels
by German military

Forbidden zone

Zone annexed
and 'Germanised'

Dieppe

Arras

Amiens

Mézières
Laon

Metz

Paris

Reims

Bar le Duc
Nancy

Sézanne

Reserved
zone

Rambouillet
Voisins

Chaumont

Epinal
Belfort

Occupied zone

Montoire-sur-le-Loir

Châteaubriant

St Florentin

Nantes

Tours

Orléans

Dijon

Bourges

Île d'Yeu

Poitiers

Châteauroux

Moulins

Vallorbe

Occupied zone
(Italy after
armistice)

Vichy

Lanzat

Pontarlier

Line of
demarcation

Riom

Chateldon

Angoulême

Clermont-
Ferrand

Valence

Italian
occupied
zone after
November 1942

Périgueux

Unoccupied zone
(occupied by Germans in
November 1942)

Bordeaux

Avignon

Villeneuve
Loubet

Menton

Montpellier

Aix

Marseille
Toulon

N

Le Portalet

W   E

S

0   100   200 km

By way of introduction to what became an extended address, Pétain began by announcing solemnly that he had 'serious things to say'. There was, in what he called 'France' (but presumably referring only to the Unoccupied Zone), disquiet and doubt. The longer the Armistice lasted the more difficult it became to manage relations between the two great countries of France and Germany. Co-opera-tion with Germany was no short-term matter. Patience was of the essence, since Germany was now embarked on the defence of western civilisation against the 'bolshevism' of the east.

As if this was not enough for the audience – still uncomfortably on their feet – Pétain went on to speak about the sins of capitalism. 'I intend that our country should be removed from the most untrust-worthy guardianship: that of money.' How this should be done was far from clear, but it appeared that it had something to do with peasants who had pursued their historic role of providing food for the com-munity. Prisoners of war, of course, 'fortified by life in the camps', would have their role to play in creating 'a free France, powerful and prosperous', as would, so the opera audience was led to believe, all right-thinking people.[1]

By this time the audience – they were still on their feet – must have been feeling some discomfort, but it was out of the question for any-body to sit down while the Marshal was still speaking. Understandably oblivious to these discomforts, Pétain rambled on. France, he said, could only be governed from Paris, but he himself could not take up his position there 'until certain possibilities are offered to me'.[2] Until that was done, France had to stand on her own feet and govern her-self properly.

Thereupon, to the dismay of the opera audience, he proceeded to announce measures which were tantamount to the introduction of a police state. As Leahy listened, he 'had a feeling that Hitler must have written the speech'.[3] 'Authority', Pétain asserted in his by then qua-vering voice, 'no longer comes from below. It is only and entirely that which I grant and that which I delegate.'[4] All political parties were abolished; no political meetings, either in public or in private, were to be held; political literature was no longer to be distributed; parlia-mentary immunity from prosecution was removed as of 30 September; no Freemason could hold any public office; the police budget would be doubled; the powers of regional Préfets were to be increased; all ministers and senior officials were to swear an oath of personal loyalty to himself. 'This first series of measures will reassure Frenchmen who only think of the health of their country.'[5] On that note, he ended – piously – '*Vive la France!*'

There was no more than mild applause in the Opera House when Pétain finished. Most of those present, and certainly all the diplomats, had understood that the Vichy government was entering a new phase. There was then a good deal of whispering before they settled again for the final act of *Godunov* – to witness the downfall of Tsar Boris. By the curious irony of which history is sometimes capable, they sat down to watch the destruction of a previously distinguished and popular military figure who had subsequently claimed for himself authoritarian power. To complete the irony, the language in which they were hearing it was Russian – the language which Pétain believed to be the true language of 'bolshevism'.

Historical and operatic ironies aside, it was the German invasion of Russia which had provided the backdrop for Pétain's hard, authoritarian, almost tsarist, line. Not only had Darlan severed diplomatic relations with Moscow abruptly on 30 June (Leahy had had to intervene on behalf of his friend the Soviet Ambassador Alexander Bogomolov to delay his departure on the grounds that he had a baby too small to travel), but, more important, the Soviets had released French communists from their previous obligation not to attack Germans and indeed encouraged them to use whatever means they chose to do precisely that. The spectre of communism which Pétain – and others – had always feared seemed to be haunting not just Europe but France herself.

It was not only the communists. July 1941 had been an altogether uneasy month in Vichy. Vallat had produced further measures against Jews. They were to be excluded altogether from employment by banks and other financial institutions, and there was to be a ceiling on their numbers in law and in medicine. Darlan had reported to Pétain on 21 July that these measures were unpopular. So they were, but that was, to Pétain, neither here nor there. What was closer to home was Darlan's complaint about Ménétrel, that he was in league with a Colonel Georges Groussard, who, Darlan claimed, was in turn in league with the British and whom he had had arrested. In normal times, all that could be brushed aside as little more than domestic political froth. But these were not normal times, and a quarrel between his immediate deputy and his doctor (and confidant) was a nuisance, and perhaps more than a nuisance, to Pétain himself.

Internationally, too, Darlan had performed badly in July. He had irritated the United States by conceding to Japan the use of French bases in Indo-China, well knowing that the Japanese purpose was to use them to pursue their military ambitions to the south; and he had irritated the Germans by continuing to press for a permanent and comprehensive arrangement to replace the Armistice, claiming that the French military collaboration in Syria merited sympathetic treatment from Berlin. He had thus failed to understand either the strength of American feeling about Japan or the German view that with the collapse of Vichy forces in Syria they no longer had any need of, or wish for, French co-operation.

In short, July had produced for Pétain no successes and a number of failures. The communists had been let out of their cage. It followed to Pétain's military mind that this was not a time to allow internal dissent. Order in 'France' had to be maintained and strengthened. Treason was in the air – Freemasons, as always, apparently to the fore. It was no longer a matter of settling gently the mutinies of 1917, however much he referred to them in his speeches. A hard fist was now needed.

On the day before Pétain's broadcast of 12 August he had appointed Darlan to Weygand's old job of Minister of Defence, giving him overall control of the armed forces, including those in North Africa – much to Weygand's irritation. In his broadcast he also expressed his confidence in Darlan, 'towards whom opinion has not always shown itself to be favourable or fair but who has never ceased to help me with loyalty and courage'.[6] In short, Darlan was the one to apply the hard fist. Moreover, in order to win back favour with Berlin, both he and Darlan would give tacit, and at times open, support to those members of the Legion who volunteered to join with the German Army in the attack on the Soviet Union – even to the point of swearing an oath of personal allegiance to Hitler.

If the 'hard fist' was the new policy, there had to be a parallel effort to repair Pétain's personal image. This was, as many admitted, not easy. His prestige had received something of a battering since the beginning of 1941. It now needed to be restored and, indeed, enhanced. Pétain

himself was quick to give encouragement. In fact, it was his own –
very personal – decision to separate the activity of news management, handled by the Ministry of Information, from the promotion of
his own image. He wanted this under his own close control; and, to
ensure this was so, he put Ménétrel in charge of it.

Ménétrel, wholly unqualified though he was, turned out to be a surprisingly good choice. He did a thorough job. Photographs of Pétain,
statuettes, portraits, porcelain carrying his portrait – all, of course, carefully vetted – were widely distributed. References to Pétain in news
bulletins or newspapers were encouraged and required to emphasise his
wise, patriotic and caring nature. (Nobody, for instance, was allowed to
refer to Pétain in connection with the volunteers from the Legion who
were fighting for the Germans in Russia. Even references to him as the
'Victor of Verdun' were ruled out on the grounds that he would appear
too militaristic.) There were pamphlets, calendars, children's stories and
diaries – all with flattering portraits or potted biographies, or pictures to
colour in. There was a plethora of books, for both children and adults.
Prayers were produced to ask the blessing of the Almighty on the head
of Pétain and were said not only in churches but at the beginning of
each school day. There was even a song composed by two obscure
musicians, one of whom had before the war written for the Moulin
Rouge in Paris. Both the words and the tune were banal almost beyond
belief ('*Maréchal, nous voilà!*' – 'Marshal, there we are!'), but the thing
was played daily on the Vichy radio, sung by two well-known popular
singers, André Dassary and Régine Roche. To cap it all, a special medal
was designed by a jeweller, to be known as *la francisque*, a miniature marshal's baton topped by a double-headed axe, to be awarded to those who
showed particular and personal devotion to the Marshal.

There is no doubt that for the eighty-five-year-old Pétain all this
was a matter of quiet satisfaction. But there was one ceremony he
enjoyed above all. On two Thursdays in each month there was an
opportunity for his 'children' to come to the Hôtel du Parc to greet
him, to bring him presents, a souvenir, a book written about him by
pupils and so on. Groups of Boy Scouts, members of the Legion,
school parties, workers' delegations and any other suitable body
crowded in for the occasion. When all were assembled, Pétain made
a carefully choreographed entry, patted them on the head or shook
their hand as appropriate – and proceeded to give them all presents,

usually portraits of himself in one form or another. These occasions
were dutifully written up by Ménétrel's team and produced in a –
truly dreadful – publication entitled 'The Marshal's Thursdays'.

All that apart, however, life in the autumn of 1941 was far from
easy. The optimism of the first year of government had started to
wane. Pétain was feeling, and looking, tired. A British secret agent
in Vichy reported on 18 September that 'the Marshal has aged
markedly during these last days and Dr Ménétrel, his personal physi-
cian and confidant, has been indispensable to him. Darlan, however,
has been doing his best to keep Ménétrel away from the Marshal.'[7]
This was certainly true. Darlan had shown that he did not like
Ménétrel, and had been quick to tell him so. He thought Ménétrel
to be little more than a shallow and meretricious scoundrel, with an
undue and unwarranted influence over his aged patient. Besides, if
he was to apply the policy of a 'hard fist' he felt it more than ever
necessary to command immediate access to Pétain whenever he

Supporters in the Légion des Anciens Combattants, August 1941.

wished, and Ménétrel seemed to have the key to the Marshal's door.

There was also the problem of Weygand. Abetz had on 25 September relayed a message from Hitler to Pétain describing Weygand's presence in North Africa as being an insurmountable obstacle to any constructive relations between Vichy and Germany. Darlan knew this, and wanted Weygand out of the way so that he could pursue his plan for a final settlement for Franco-German co-operation in the greater Europe.

But Pétain was not yet in a mood to sacrifice Weygand. In fact, he was becoming rather irritated with Darlan himself. Darlan was, after all, only Vice-Premier. He was showing too much independence. He was putting himself about too much. For instance, on his own initiative and without consulting Pétain, he held a number of receptions for the diplomatic corps in September at which he was heard, according to a German agent in Vichy, in a message to Berlin intercepted by the British, to 'speak favourably of German policy and express himself optimistically on the German conduct of the war'.[8] Furthermore, by late September his campaign against Ménétrel was having an effect. His continued attacks wore Ménétrel down to the point where he preferred to leave Vichy and stay with his family on the Côte d'Azur. But Pétain made sure that Darlan's victory was only temporary. Ménétrel was indispensable, and when Pétain took a week off at L'Ermitage in early October Ménétrel joined him there.

Pétain's stay at L'Ermitage was not just designed to rescue Ménétrel from Darlan's assaults. He also wanted to reflect on what had happened since June 1940 and what was likely to happen in the future. Disappointingly, there had been no peace treaty. The whole premise on which the Armistice was based – a quick German victory over Britain followed by a general European settlement in which Germany would be the senior European ally to a France which, thanks to the National Revolution, would have sloughed off the political weaknesses of the past – seemed further away than ever from realisation. But he still believed that co-operation with Germany was the only possible policy. As he had told Serrigny the previous May, 'negotiations [with Germany] will certainly take a long time. But, in spite of everything, they must come to a conclusion. If the war is prolonged, we must be able to live and, above all, to eat. We can only do that with German permission.'[9] In short, the only possible policy was the present one: co-operation with Germany while trying to avoid being drawn to declare war on Germany's enemies.

While at L'Ermitage, Pétain also decided that it was time to bring fully to book, as he put it, those responsible for France's defeat in the previous year. He had already authorised the creation of a Council of Political Justice, the members, of course, to be nominated by himself. On 15 October, by then back in Vichy, he announced that the Council, made up mainly of veterans of the war, had concluded that Daladier, Blum and Gamelin were guilty and should be detained indefinitely, the most severe punishment allowed to the Council. But this was not good enough. Pétain therefore decided to ignore the decision of the Council and to refer the case to the judicial court at Riom. In doing so, he publicly expressed his clear understanding that the court would find them guilty and mete out severer punishment.

Even in Vichy, virtual police state as it had by then become, this procedure was, to say the least, unusual. It was one thing to ask for a trial. It was quite another thing for the Head of State to announce the verdict of the trial in advance. So unusual was it that the presiding judge at Riom, even though he had sworn the oath of personal allegiance to Pétain, announced in open court, on the first day of the hearing, that he would act as though the proceedings in the Council of Political Justice (and, by implication, Pétain's intervention) had never occurred. This allowed the defendants to put up such a spirited defence – Blum's speech was particularly impressive – that the hearing only lasted a few weeks and was abandoned in April 1942, by which time the whole thing had descended into humiliating farce.

October wore on, with all its problems. Pétain tried, albeit half-heartedly, to solve the Weygand problem. On the 16th, Weygand was summoned to Vichy and told he was *persona non grata* with the Germans. Pétain invited him to relinquish North Africa and return to Vichy to another job. Weygand indignantly refused, shouting at Pétain that if he wanted to sack him he had better do so openly. After two days of fruitless talks, Weygand went back to Algiers. On the 22nd, the anniversary of Montoire, Pétain wrote what can only be described as a grovelling letter to Hitler saying that the victory of the Germans over 'bolshevism' offered new hope for a Europe in which the peoples of Germany and France could unite their efforts. Hitler's response was contemptuous. None of that mattered, he replied. What mattered was the assassination of German troops on French territory.

To be fair, Hitler had a point. The communist resistance had become active – and violent. On 21 August their first effort, in Paris, had cost the life of a German soldier. It was only by setting up a special section within the courts with the power to condemn to death anybody found guilty of 'subversion' – another product of the Vichy police state, proposed by Pucheu and approved by Pétain himself – that reprisal executions had been avoided. But just as Pétain's grovelling letter to Hitler was being sent, a German officer was assassinated in Nantes. This time the German authorities were not to be deterred. Fifty hostages, randomly selected in Paris, Nantes and Châteaubriant, were to be shot immediately, and a further fifty in due course unless the culprits were surrendered immediately.

Pétain was having a quiet lunch with friends near Vichy when Ménétrel arrived to tell him the news. By all accounts, Pétain was obviously upset. Innocent Frenchmen were to be murdered by the invader. That was bad enough. But, almost as bad as that, what he believed to be his and Darlan's carefully constructed efforts to join forces with Germany in the new Europe were being undermined by communist criminals. On 23 October he therefore made another broadcast. France, he said, had laid down her arms. She had no right to pick them up again to shoot Germans in the back. 'One guilty man found', he said, 'would save the lives of one hundred Frenchmen.'[10]

The following morning, at seven o'clock, Ménétrel, du Moulin de Labarthète and Laure pushed their way into Pétain's bedroom to announce that the first fifty hostages had indeed been shot, that his broadcast had gone down badly and that public opinion was unanimous in condemning German brutality. Pétain was clearly distraught – almost in tears. He had, he said, spent a sleepless night. This was not at all meant to be the result of co-operation with Germany. Laure and du Moulin then explained their plan. Pétain would announce that he would surrender himself to the German authorities as a hostage in place of the next fifty.

The plan was, quite simply, absurd. Nevertheless, all was prepared. Laure and Ménétrel were to accompany Pétain and stand with him on the Demarcation Line, the line which defined the border between the Occupied and Unoccupied Zones. But there was a snag. The government had to be informed. When they heard about the plan, Darlan and Pucheu said bluntly that it was quite ridiculous. Others chimed in alongside. Faced with this barrage, Pétain conceded. The project was called off. The only result was that the letter which Pétain himself had drafted to von Stülpnagel – for once, in his own hand – was not sent. Instead, it was smuggled out to Switzerland and published verbatim by the *Gazette de Lausanne* and the *Journal de Génève*.

Oddly enough, Serrigny was impressed with what was no more than a futile gesture. Hitler, he opined, 'gave up this time on massive executions'. The news, he went on, got out in Paris, in spite of heavy censorship. 'Unfortunately,' went the next sentence in his diary for 8 November, 'two days later the Marshal sent a bulletin to the French Legion created to fight the Russians in a German uniform. It created the most deplorable effect!'[11] What was meant to be a grand and noble event had descended yet again into farcical confusion. Pétain was reduced to sending a telegram to Hitler deploring the attacks on members of the army of occupation.

As if that was not enough, Pétain was worried about his own position. He believed that Pucheu was aiming to take over his job, that there was a conspiracy centred on the former partners of a certain 'Monsieur Hippolyte Worms, a Judaeo-Christian banker, who had married an English wife'.[12] Pétain even produced to Serrigny a letter written by Pucheu that had been intercepted by the censor, which demonstrated Pucheu's ambition to replace him. But Pétain knew perfectly well that his position was not in doubt as long as he could persuade his 'children' that their future was safe in his hands. In other words, the policy of co-operation – which had almost become total collaboration earlier in the year – had to produce tangible results.

Nevertheless, producing tangible results was not proving easy. In fact, it was becoming more difficult. German pressure, and petty jealousies among ministers, created unpleasant diversions. On 8 November, for instance, Darlan delivered an ultimatum to Pétain: he would resign if Weygand was not sacked. At the funeral of General Huntziger, who had been killed on 11 November when his plane had tried to land at Vichy Airport in bad visibility (and with obsolete radio equipment), Abetz handed Pétain a letter from Hitler stating bluntly that co-operation between the two countries was out of the question while Weygand was still there. Furthermore, Abetz said firmly that no

German negotiator would even bother to sit down with a Frenchman unless Weygand was removed. As though to emphasise his point, he went on to say that he was leaving in Vichy, as Consul-General, one of his closest associates, Roland Krug von Nidda.

Pétain, yet again, caved in. On 16 November Weygand was summoned once more to Vichy. He brought with him a memorandum pointing out the importance of keeping the Germans out of French North Africa. Pétain ignored this, again offered Weygand another job and, when that was refused, on 18 November told him that he was dismissed.

The following day Leahy requested, and was granted, an interview with Pétain – alone. Leahy pointed out

> very clearly that the heretofore friendly and sympathetic attitude of the American Government was based on the assumption that he would not in his relations with the Axis powers go beyond the requirements of the Armistice Agreement and that a removal of General Weygand under German pressure cannot be considered by anybody to be necessitated by the Armistice Agreement. I told him that in my opinion such an unnecessary surrender to Axis demands . . . would have a definitely adverse effect on the traditional amity between our two people . . . I requested that his decision . . . be reconsidered.

Pétain replied that the Germans had exerted increasing pressure, that they had sent him a 'brutal diktat threatening in the event of refusal [to sack Weygand] to occupy all of France, to feed the army of occupation with French food stuffs and to permit the native population to die of hunger'. Faced with such a threat he claimed that he had could do no other than to yield to their demand.[13]

In his comments to Roosevelt on the interview, Leahy was direct. He described Pétain as 'a feeble, frightened old man . . . surrounded by conspirators . . . devoted to the Axis philosophy . . . Darlan . . . Pucheu . . . Benoist-Méchin . . . De Brinon . . . Marion . . . Bouthillier . . . Lehideux.' Pucheu, in particular, not only wanted Pétain's job but 'is busily engaged in building up via the Légion des Anciens Combattants what is intended to become an effective Ku Klux Klan and which is already operating as such to some extent'. Finally, his verdict on Pétain was equally harsh. 'While one may be fully justified in looking at the difficulties of the Marshal's ending years with understanding sympathy, it seems necessary to reluctantly relinquish what was perhaps always a faint hope that it might be possible for me through friendly personal relations and pertinent advice to give some semblance of backbone to a jellyfish.'[14]

Feeble and frightened he might have been, but Pétain thought that he had managed to secure one concession from the Germans. 'The rumour of an interview between [Pétain] and Hitler is true,' the Turkish Ambassador to Vichy signalled Ankara – intercepted by the British. 'It will take place in Occupied France after the capture of Moscow.'[15] It was not to be quite like that – in two respects: first, the Germans failed to capture Moscow and, second, it was not Hitler that Pétain was to meet but Göring.

The meeting took place on 1 December 1941 at St-Florentin in the department of the Yonne. The arrangements were, as before at Montoire, tortuous. Pétain, accompanied by Darlan, Bonhomme and, of course, Ménétrel, left Vichy for Paris on the afternoon of 30 November. From there, in the evening, their train went back on its tracks to La Ferté-d'Hauterive where they all spent the night. At about 6 a.m. the train left again and, some four hours later, arrived at Coulanges-sur-Yonne, where they were met by the German general Hanesse and Fernand de Brinon. The party was then taken by car to St-Florentin, where Göring's train was waiting.

Göring's train was a formidable sight. It was fully armoured, with platforms for anti-aircraft canons and heavy machine guns. Around the station where it was parked a battalion of fully armed infantry patrolled, and a squadron of Messerschmitt 109 fighter aircraft flew up and down overhead. When Pétain and his group arrived, Göring invited Pétain on to his train for a meeting tête-à-tête. Göring wanted from Pétain both military collaboration and the use of North African bases. Pétain in turn wanted German concessions. He recited from a prepared paper, admitting that a head of state cannot govern without the consent of the governed and that he no longer had that support – because the policy of co-operation with Germany had not brought tangible results to his people. There followed a list of French requirements: the liberation of prisoners of war, the removal of the Demarcation Line, the rearming of the French Army and an end to German interference in French administrative matters. He claimed that Germany had broken the promises made at Montoire. Göring listened with impatience – finally saying: 'But, Marshal, I thought that it was you who had been defeated.'[16] Darlan was summoned to the meeting and there was a further nearly three hours of fruitless discussion during which Göring appeared – ostentatiously – bored. At the end, Pétain took his paper out of his pocket and offered it to Göring. It was refused. Finally, Pétain himself lost his temper and pushed the paper into Göring's pocket.

Tempers were calmer over lunch. It was an opulent, and apparently cordial, meal: caviar, roast pork with potato purée, fruit salad, washed down with large draughts of champagne – followed by liqueurs and Turkish cigarettes – and enlivened by military reminiscences. The conversations of the afternoon, to nobody's surprise, were cancelled. Pétain and his group wobbled their way back to their train and arrived back in Vichy that evening. But, Serrigny noted, 'for the first time since the armistice the Marshal had used the language of a leader'.[17]

With Göring in December 1941. (*Keystone*)

The meeting with Göring had, to say the least, not been a success. Pétain had somehow deluded himself that there could be a conversation between former military officers and between the two countries as equals. He had told Göring that Germany could not make peace without France. Göring found this impertinent. Both men emerged from their meeting in anger. But what Pétain failed, yet again, to realise was that Germany had no need of, and no particular affection for, France as such. The only reason the Germans were prepared to talk to the French was because of the French fleet and the North African colonies, which, if they were delivered to the Allies, would make the German military position in Libya untenable.

Matters were made very much more complicated by the German and Italian declaration of war on the United States on 11 December 1941, after the Japanese attack on Pearl Harbor. That, together with the failure of the German armies to break the Soviets in their first onslaught, gave both Pétain and Darlan pause. It was possible – just – that Germany would not, after all, win the war. Given that, they would have to decide where they stood – and they would have to decide quickly, since the Americans would want to know. Sure enough, Leahy was sent to see Pétain and Darlan later that evening to sound them out. Having asked for, and received, an assurance that the French fleet in the West Indies would remain in port, Leahy went on to put the more direct question. It was Darlan who answered, but Pétain clearly agreed. Vichy wished to remain neutral and outside what was now a world war but 'they were powerless to resist German ultimatums'.[18] Pétain intervened to say that the Germans could starve the French civilian population should they so choose. But they reiterated that they wished to remain neutral, and, by way of reassurance, they agreed to set out their position in writing. This was done, and Roosevelt, when he received it, expressed his 'profound satisfaction'.[19]

On 1 January 1942 Pétain broadcast a New Year message. 'For the first time', wrote Serrigny, 'he dared to tell the truth, that is to say that he is not free and traitors are to be found not only in London but also in Paris.'[20] He also repeated the message he had given to Roosevelt, that France wished to stay outside the world war but would watch developments carefully. He went on to say that France's position would be noticed by Germany – and he hoped that it would lead to a softening of the terms of the Armistice. Finally, he warned his compatriots against giving any sympathy to those in the press or on the radio who both preached disunity and attacked the National Revolution (which, he was forced to admit, was not moving ahead with the speed he had hoped).

Du Moulin de Labarthète described the broadcast as signalling a policy of 'wait and see'. For their part, the Germans did not like it at all. It was not published in Occupied France, although it did mysteriously find its way into the *Journal de Rouen*. Roland Krug von Nidda, Abetz's representative in Vichy, remarked that Pétain seemed not to have paid attention to Göring's message – that France had lost the war. But Pétain was unrepentant. In fact, he was rather pleased with himself, particularly since his broadcast had been well received in Unoccupied France. He had also showed Serrigny the end-of-year report of the intelligence service. After a detailed analysis of the military situation it had concluded that of three hypothetical outcomes – a neutral peace, German defeat and a German victory– only the last had now to be totally ruled out.

By the end of January Pétain's policy of remaining neutral in the world conflict was looking very frayed. American intelligence had noted that French ships were transporting heavy-duty lorries and even guns and oil to Rommel in North Africa. Leahy complained to Darlan, who replied that he was under an obligation to honour the agreement he had made with the Italians in December 1941, to make shipments of supplies on a regular basis in order to prevent the seizure of Bizerta. This excuse went down badly in Washington. Leahy was then officially instructed to see Weygand and get him to agree to come out of retirement and return to North Africa under American protection. This Leahy did. But Weygand had resisted Churchill's attempt at seduction and was certainly not going to fall for Roosevelt's. Pétain seems to have been aware of the attempted seduction when Leahy went to see him on 27 January, and was not in the best of moods. He told Leahy irritably that his government would defend France's African colonies against any attacker. 'Does that mean Americans?' Leahy asked. 'It means any attacker, including Americans,' came the reply. Leahy pursued his questioning. 'Would France wish for American military or naval assistance if the Axis powers invaded French colonial possessions?' 'Only if we ask for it.'[21]

If Pétain was being irritable with Leahy it was at least in part because he was under relentless pressure from Abetz and, inside his own government, from Pucheu 'and his friends'.[22] Abetz had hatched a plan, which may even have had Hitler's blessing, for a peace treaty if Vichy would declare public support for the German war effort. In practice, this meant either a declaration of war or a clear and unambiguous statement of support of Germany. The matter was discussed in Vichy in January, and there were those, particularly Pucheu, who were attracted by the idea. Even Darlan wavered. After all, a complete post-war settlement was exactly what he had been working for. Pétain only managed to fend off the plan's supporters by reciting the assurances of French neutrality he had personally given to Roosevelt. On 29 January, a rather morose Darlan was told to make it quite clear to Rudolph Schleier, Abetz's deputy, that Vichy would only declare war if the Allies invaded French territory and that any clear, let alone unambiguous, statement of support for Germany would be so unpopular in Unoccupied France that it would lead to further waves of violence.

Nothing was going well. The weather was, again, cold. Pucheu was a nuisance. When Pétain told him that he was thinking of dismissing a minister, Pucheu replied, 'in that case, we will all resign'.[23] Daladier and Blum made brilliant defence speeches at Riom. The Germans were angry that the Riom trials were about who lost the war rather than who started the war in the first place. Darlan was starting to panic. There was a mad proposal to transfer the French fleet to the Vatican to keep it out of harm's way. Pétain gave his support – until the Papal Nuncio told him that the Vatican was not able to become, overnight, a naval power. All the signs were that Vichy was in political crisis.

On 24 February 1942 Krug von Nidda relayed a message from Abetz to Pétain. The message was blunt. Things were going wrong. Darlan had lost the confidence of the Germans. There was only one way to repair the damaged relations between France and Germany: Pierre Laval should be put back in charge. For Pétain the message was the worst possible news. True, he thought that Darlan's expensive tastes were vulgar and he was irritated at Darlan's obvious scorn for his pet project the National Revolution. But Laval would be even worse. Not only was he just as – if not more – scornful than Darlan about the National Revolution but he was, rightly, perceived as altogether too wedded to the policy of full co-operation with Germany. Pétain realised that his careful assurances to the Americans about French neutrality would go for nothing if Laval were to be put in charge.

Throughout the month of March rumours flew around Vichy. There was, it was said, to be a drastic ministerial reshuffle, the important ministerial posts to be given to German nominees. It was even hinted that the Germans were about to appoint a *Gauleiter*, who would take over from Pétain and run Unoccupied France under instruction from Berlin. This particular rumour was confirmed when Laval's son-in-law – and emissary – René de Chambrun arrived in Vichy on 24 March. He saw Pétain briefly but the main part of his message was delivered to Bonhomme. It was simple. The Germans were disenchanted with Darlan. Either Laval was brought back or the Germans would resort to 'extreme measures (nomination of a *Gauleiter* etc. . . .)'.[24]

There was nothing to be done but to try to pacify Abetz, but it turned out in the end to be yet another exercise in vacillation. Pétain agreed to meet Laval outside Vichy in the forest of Randan on 26 March. It was a favourite place for Pétain's country walks, and he could be seen to go there without raising any suspicion. Once there, Laval told him of the German hostility to Darlan and offered himself as the solution to Pétain's – and Vichy's – problems. But Laval was no more likeable in the spring of 1942 than he had been in the winter of 1940. For the moment, Pétain refused to make any promises.

News of the meeting soon got out. Two days later Leahy was directed by Washington to tell Pétain that the appointment of Laval to any important post in the government would make it impossible for the United States to continue its generally sympathetic attitude towards France. (Privately, the Americans referred to Laval as 'Black Peter'.) The message was delivered on 30 March. The American threat had its effect. On 2 April Laval and Pétain met again, this time openly at the Pavillon Sévigné. Pétain told Laval, as he told Serrigny the following day, that he had given up the idea of recalling him. The Americans would not have it.

Pétain was, to put it crudely, in a mess. He had to find some way of pacifying Abetz without bringing Laval back and offending the Americans. To get himself out of the mess, on 4 April he turned, as he had before, to René Fonck. He explained to Fonck that his way out was to recast his government from top to bottom. Fonck's job was to see his German friends privately and to secure their approval. He drew up a list of possible ministers for Fonck to show to Abetz. The chief figure would be Jacques Barthélemy, a professor of law who was currently holding the Justice portfolio at Vichy, who would become Vice-Premier. The others were from a similar mould – able but colourless. Fonck did indeed show the list to Abetz, who dismissed Pétain's manoeuvre out of hand. But Pétain made the mistake of also showing it to Leahy for his approval. By that time Darlan, Laval and Benoist-Méchin had found out about it (probably from Krug von Nidda) and were duly furious. Pétain was forced to apologise to Darlan for the whole sorry business.

In the mean time, Benoist-Méchin had told Schleier, in charge of the German Embassy in Abetz's absence in Berlin, about what he called the American 'ultimatum'. On 5 April an article appeared in *Le Nouveau Temps*, under the name of Jean Luchaire, stating that not a single day should be lost in putting a stop to American blackmail. It was a question, Luchaire went on, of choosing between Washington and Berlin. The article was broadcast on the Paris radio. There was no doubt about who was behind it all. Abetz was turning up the psychological heat.

On 13 April de Brinon, at Schleier's instigation, flew to Vichy to see Pétain. A quick decision, he said, was essential to avoid a German take-over. Darlan agreed. He would step down as Vice-Premier if Laval became Premier as long as he remained Commander-in-Chief of the armed forces. Pétain finally caved in. Darlan and de Brinon went off to see Laval, who, conveniently, was staying in his house at Chateldon. The deal was done, and was duly sealed in a meeting between Laval and Pétain the following morning. 'The disquiet in the Marshal's entourage', Serrigny noted, 'is very great, because of the feebleness shown by the head of state in this affair as in many others.'[25]

On 18 April 1942 the new government was announced. Laval became Head of Government, Foreign Minister, Minister of the Interior and Minister of Information. Constitutional Act no. 11 was produced to make it all official. It was clear enough. The effective direction of France's internal and external policy was to be assumed by the Head of Government, appointed by the Head of State and answerable only to him. In theory, Pétain was still able to dismiss the Head of Government. In practice, those around him knew that Pétain, if he ever did such a thing, would be inviting a German occupation.

On 26 April Pétain entered his eighty-sixth year. In his old age, he

Petain, Darlan and Laval at Vichy, April 1942. (*Keystone*)

Leahy taking leave of Pétain, April 1942. (*Keystone*)

was pleased, perhaps too pleased, that he was still the object of veneration. But he had been confronted with the truth: he was no longer
in charge of events. The audience at the Opera House which had so
reverentially stood up when he started his broadcast on 12 August
1941 would stand up no longer for a man of power. True, he still had
the dignity of a head of state, but it was little more than a dignity. As
for the audience at the Opera House on that fateful evening, there is
one sad footnote. On the morning of Tuesday 21 April 1942, just as
Leahy was preparing to leave on his recall to Washington, Mrs Leahy
died from a post-operative embolism in La Pergola Clinic in Vichy.
'She was', mourned her husband, 'a grand example of the best type of
American womanhood.'[26] Pétain, to his credit, was courteous to the
end. He sent flowers, and provided a special private car to take her
body on the first stage of its journey back home to her final resting
place in Arlington Cemetery.

Leahy's departure was not just a matter of regret for Pétain.
Churchill, too, was unhappy. He was still trying to persuade Pétain, as
he wrote to Roosevelt, that the successful British military operation
against the Italians in Libya might 'open out . . . Tunis and all French
North Africa to us . . . It is now or never with the Vichy French and
their last chance of redemption'.[27] He was preparing, he wrote further, to make 'an offer, blessing or cursing, to Pétain on the morrow
of a victory in Libya. Trust your link with Pétain will not be broken
meanwhile. We have no other worthwhile connection.'[28] But, whatever Churchill's hopes, there is no doubt that Pétain was the loser. He
had lost, in Leahy and Mrs Leahy, two good and honest friends. In
truth, he had few good and honest friends left.

23

COUNTDOWN TO TORCH

'Je vais lui mettre tellement de responsabilité sur le dos qu'il succombera.'

In mid–April 1942 political Vichy was in a state of the highest excitement. Who was in, it was asked, and who was out? The gossips peddled every latest rumour, one feeding on another's story. Laval had no time to waste if the gossiping was not to get out of hand; and, indeed, he wasted no time at all. On 19 April there was a flurry of announcements. The new government saw most of Pétain's ministers cleaned out, particularly those whom Laval suspected of involvement in the plot against him of December 1940. Pucheu, too, was out – too ambitious and not to be trusted, it was said. Finance went to Pierre Cathala, a known Laval loyalist. Also promoted were Benoist-Méchin and Marion. The ultra-collaborationist de Brinon was brought back from Paris to Vichy as a secretary of state and Abel Bonnard, who had developed a fascination for National Socialism in the 1930s, was given – to much wringing of hands in Pétain's entourage – the Education portfolio. In short, it was, for the most part, all change.

There were, however, some notable absentees. Déat had not been invited, nor the even more overtly collaborationist Jacques Doriot. Both of them had confidently expected to be called from Paris to Vichy. But Laval showed, at least on that occasion, some delicacy. Moreover, he could not ignore the complexities of Vichy politics.

Pétain was, after all, still Head of State, and Darlan was still in command of the armed forces – and Pétain's appointed successor. Furthermore, Laval was not given to political ideologies, be they National Socialism or National Revolution. All he wanted was to construct a government to co-operate with Germany in the new Europe without causing too much offence to the United States. As for Britain, she was just a nuisance. Germany was the future for Europe; Britain only stood in the way. Since Germany would certainly win the war, Britain did not figure in any conceivable equation.

Pétain put up no opposition to Laval's appointments. When asked by Serrigny why he had not protested he replied that 'I had to concede; they had forced me.' But in the same conversation he went on, 'The next months will reveal the game on the military chess board. We will know in October whether the Germans can be victorious. At that moment it will be up to us to decide.'[1] Serrigny hoped that Pétain would stick at that and not be lured yet again into some more German tricks. Others, given their doubts about the old man's resolve, were more decisive. When they heard of Laval's appointments, du Moulin de Labarthète and Laure said that they had finally had enough – and resigned. At that point, it was not only Pétain's remaining friends who were disappearing; his favourite trusties were disappearing as well. The fall-out from Laval's new government was that Pétain not only found his position much diminished but found himself even more dependent for companionship – if only for someone he could talk to – on his personal doctor, Bernard Ménétrel.

It had become a strange relationship. It was as though Ménétrel had assumed the role of a surrogate wife. He not only ran Pétain's personal propaganda machine; he was not only Pétain's doctor; and he was not only the guardian of Pétain's door. He had, by mid-April 1942, become Pétain's only daily confidant. Pétain's true wife, the neglected Nini, might, in terms of the politics of the day, just as well not have existed. Nor was she much welcome even as company. In fact, Pétain, true to form, preferred the company of younger women, of whom there were many in the Vichy of the day to sit at his feet. He even claimed that from time to time he had the occasional 'good month'.

Nevertheless, good months or bad months, Ménétrel saw to it that the rhythm of Pétain's personal life hardly changed. There was the

early and simple breakfast, usually by himself or with Nini, an hour or
so with Ménétrel, submitting to whatever technique the doctor was
employing that day; then another hour reading newspapers – all the
Vichy papers and a digest of the Paris press – and official documents.
At eleven o'clock there was a daily meeting of his staff, and, unavoid-
ably, a short one with Laval. By midday it was time for his walk, a
stroll with Ménétrel in the park, with its exotic trees, which formed
the bank of the Allier. On occasions they were joined by Nini, but
only on occasions, since Nini (by now, of course, known as 'La
Maréchale') disliked Ménétrel – and Ménétrel could not abide Nini.

The walk was a daily ritual. Even in the coldest weather Pétain and
Ménétrel would set out, Pétain with his walking stick, black overcoat
with an astrakhan collar and a black Homburg hat sitting flat on his
head, Ménétrel with a simpler, but equally black, overcoat and a trilby
at a more rakish angle. In the summer, of course, the overcoats were
discarded, the hats were of a lighter colour and Ménétrel's, at least, was
worn at an even more rakish angle. When she joined them – usually
in the summer, since La Maréchale was not one for winter walks – she
also wore a hat, as was proper. Her taste in hats, however, was not of
the greatest elegance. Her preferred hat, such as it was, would be of
simple straw, with a ribbon and, occasionally, as though to lighten the
whole dismal confection, with a long feather sticking out at what can
only be described as a surprising angle.

Nor was Nini altogether successful in her dress sense. Pétain and
Ménétrel wore formal suits (Pétain in a particularly old-fashioned
starched collar and black tie), single-breasted and buttoned carefully in
front. Nini obviously thought it right to wear a suit which matched
the gentlemen. But there was a difficulty. Over the years she had put
on a good deal of weight, and had not had her suits tailored to match.
Buttoning the jacket in front led to unfortunate bulges elsewhere. But
she was at least game. On their walks together she seemed to trail a
metre or two behind the two gentlemen – neither of them, it seemed,
looking back to see where she was; nevertheless, at least on the
summer walks, she held her ground.

It was some two kilometres on the outward journey and another
two kilometres on the way back. Pétain walked at a brisk pace in the
summer, swing his walking stick forward as he went. In the cold of the
winter his walk, as might be expected, became more of a shuffle.

Ménétrel, summer or winter, guarded his patient carefully. He took trouble to deflect the attention of photographers, or just the merely curious, who wanted to take pictures or simply to greet him. Sometimes Pétain would stop and talk, but more often he would just continue his walk. Nevertheless, whatever the weather, the walk went on; and the exercise invariably gave him a keen appetite for lunch.

Pétain's lunch was one of the main events of the day. Apart from all else, Pétain had become, in the French vernacular, *'une bonne fourchette'*. In other words, he was a hearty eater. To be sure, the cuisine at the Hôtel du Parc was not particularly refined, but the helpings were copious, and the food, such as it was, was washed down with Pétain's favourite – ordinary and undistinguished – red wine. On most days there was company – favoured ministers or visitors and, naturally, Ménétrel. Nini was rarely invited; it was, after all, a man's affair. The conversation was, as might be expected, general but respectful of the old man – as always, Pétain was fond of reminding his listeners of his exploits in the First World War – but he was not beyond the occasional waspish sally when the mood took him.

The afternoons also followed a regular pattern. First, it was time for a rest. Then, at about four o'clock, Pétain and Ménétrel went for a drive in the countryside outside Vichy. This provided the opportunity for another walk – not as far or as energetic as in the morning – before a return to the Hôtel du Parc. Then there was evening playtime with the Ménétrel children. Pleasant to the old man as it was, it was often interrupted by a minister on urgent business. In fact, that was Laval's favoured time, since by then Pétain was feeling the strain of the day and apt to sign anything Laval wanted without much argument. There was then another rest before dinner, taken sharp at eight o'clock. Since he was by then not, so it is reported, at his most lively, it was not an occasion for great conviviality. The number of guests was kept to a minimum, and restricted to loyal and understanding friends who happened to be visiting Vichy at the time (and, from time to time, Nini). After half an hour over coffee and a cigarette, Pétain retired – by himself – to his room.

Just as there was a certain military simplicity in domestic life, so was there in the affairs of state. Visitors were often surprised at the severity of Pétain's office and his ante-room. His office, on the third floor of the Hôtel du Parc, was small – some six metres square. There was

The morning walk. (*Keystone*)

Playing with the Ménétrel children (*Keystone*)

a small Second Empire desk with the minimum of clutter: a stand for writing paper, an inkstand and a small clock, and no telephone – only a buzzer with which to summon Ménétrel. Behind the desk was a large and lugubrious wardrobe beside which stood the flag of the Anciens Combattants, and to the side of the desk was a small chest of drawers on which was perched the only table lamp in the room. For a head of state, it could hardly have been more simple.

Laval's accommodation on the second floor was much grander. It was also crowded. He had his personal bodyguard, to protect him from a repetition of the attempt on his life in Paris the previous August. But Laval, whatever may have been his misjudgements, had, when he wanted to turn it on, the politician's requisite – charm. Even Leahy, a fierce critic of his policy, found him engaging. He also had determination. He was not to be deflected from his serious business. In a broadcast on 21 April he therefore announced – bluntly – that France was faced with a choice. It was 'either to be integrated in a new, pacified Europe ... or resign ourselves to seeing the disappearance of our civilisation ... No threat will prevent me from pursuing agreement and reconciliation with Germany.'[2] 'Pierre Laval', as Leahy remarked after their meeting on 27 April, 'is definitely not on our side.'[3]

On 4 May 1942 Laval made another move. He took over the personal direction of the Legion. That done, the Service d'Ordre Légionnaire, originally set up to keep order at the Légion's rallies, was given a wider role – as a shadow police force. Its young recruits would appear in khaki shirts, black berets and ties, wielding thick batons, whenever there was likely to be trouble on the streets of Vichy – or Lyon or Marseille or Toulouse. Joseph Darnand, its commander, was far from shy in the brutal use of force. In fact, Pétain himself approved of Darnand's hard hand, not least because its members were not only required to take the oath of personal loyalty to him (after an all-night vigil reminiscent of the rituals of medieval knighthood) but were dedicated to the fight against communism and for the National Revolution.

As might be imagined, the new authoritarian state was far from popular. Those who opposed the régime were becoming both more numerous and better organised. From the other side, however, came continued political attack – continual sniping from the Paris collaborationists, particularly Déat and Doriot, and from Abetz and Krug von Nidda. There were thus attacks from all sides. But that was not the end of it. In this already heated atmosphere an event occurred which raised the political temperature to even higher levels. On 25 April 1942 there arrived in Vichy a most distinguished escaped prisoner, none other than General Henri-Honoré Giraud.

Giraud was, without a doubt, a figure in the greatest of great French traditions. He had been a hero in both wars. In the first he had been left for dead on the battlefield, had been captured, had escaped and then operated clandestinely behind enemy lines (his description of those adventures had enthralled Churchill when he visited Giraud's positions on the Maginot Line in 1937). In the second war, he had been in the northern sector, commanding first the 7th and then the 9th French Army, with as much distinction as was possible under the circumstances, until he was captured on 19 May 1940. A carefully guarded prisoner of war, on 17 April 1942 he slid down a 150-foot rope to escape from his prison in the fortress of Königstein on the River Elbe, in spite of lameness from an earlier wound which had healed badly. He had then made his way through Switzerland to Unoccupied France – determined to carry on the fight against Germany.

Giraud's arrival in Vichy could hardly pass unnoticed. In that small community, as he walked around the streets, he commanded universal attention. He was very tall – some 6' 5"; and he sported a truly magnificent moustache, curled in the form of a sabre. His walk, too, was most impressive – large strides of elegantly long legs. Above all, he was a five-star general. True, there were those who whispered maliciously that his brain had not grown in the same proportion as his body, but those whispers, at least to the man – and woman – in the Vichy street, did not diminish the grand effect of his physical splendour. Above all, he was a courageous Frenchman who had defied the enemy.

Pétain, of course, welcomed his fellow soldier with the hospitality he deserved, 'with a most generous lunch'.[4] He was perhaps less pleased when Giraud told him roundly that Germany would certainly be defeated and that it was time to strike a deal with the Americans. Laval though, for his part, was very much less pleased. Hitler had been furious at Giraud's escape, and Laval complained that it was a serious blow to his policy of Franco-German co-operation. He was also worried that the French prisoners of war still in Germany would suffer as a result.

Laval then came up with a plan: Giraud should return voluntarily to his German prison. The idea was that he would then be released again formally and without delay. The idea was communicated by Benoist-Méchin to Abetz, who thought it excellent. The problem was that the idea needed Giraud's agreement; and Giraud was certainly not in a mood to agree. He would only return to Germany, he said, if all married prisoners of war were released. The proposition was put to Abetz, who pointed out that that meant some five or six hundred thousand prisoners and that Hitler would never agree to it. Giraud then replied that he would only return to prison if specifically ordered to by Pétain. He knew perfectly well that Pétain would never sign such an order; and when it was suggested to Pétain he did indeed refuse to do so. Giraud then broke off all negotiation on the matter and left for his house in Lyon. Only later did it emerge that when there he immediately started meeting an intermediary sent for the purpose by Roosevelt's envoy in North Africa, Robert Murphy.

In fact, Giraud was not the only one in touch with the Americans. Another, even more prominent, figure was playing the same game. As far back as March Darlan had come to the conclusion that Germany would not win the war. Even then, he had started to plan his escape route. He had asked one of his closest colleagues, Admiral Raymond Fénard, to get in touch with Murphy on his behalf. The conversations had been intermittent; but, with Laval's return, Darlan had even greater reason to jump ship. Not only was he furious at his dismissal but he believed that Pétain had no control over Laval. Pétain's stated view that Laval would 'succumb'[5] under the burdens of office he thought to be quite ridiculous. The old Marshal, in Darlan's view, had lost all control – if, indeed he had ever had much – and that was the end of it. It was time to negotiate seriously with the Americans.

None of this helped Laval in his efforts to secure a solid basis for Franco-German co-operation. In fact, the whole Giraud episode led to what he had feared – the removal of a number of concessions to French prisoners of war. Laval decided to write personally to Ribbentrop. In a letter dated 12 May 1942 he reiterated his determination to pursue co-operation, not least because Germany was waging a historic battle against bolshevism which would determine the future of the whole world. Laval's letter could hardly have been more enthusiastic. Ribbentrop's reply, on the other hand, was 'a frigid document'[6] asking for acts rather than pious hopes.

But there was more to it than a simple exchange of letters. On 21 March Hitler had appointed Fritz Sauckel as Commissar-General for Labour, with a brief to oversee a programme of milking occupied territories of workers to replace – in German factories – those who had left to join the armed forces. Sauckel was, not to put too fine a point on it, a deeply unpleasant Nazi bully. For him, there was no question of negotiation with the French, whether occupied or not. He proposed to transfer to Germany no fewer than 350,000 workers from both zones, half of whom would be skilled workers, mostly from metalworking firms. His deadline for this operation was 15 June.

In spite of Sauckel's deadline Laval did, indeed, negotiate, while assuring Sauckel of his whole-hearted desire to co-operate in his endeavours. The way to get the idea accepted, he argued, was for one prisoner of war to be released for every worker sent to Germany. Sauckel would have none of it. In the end, the deadline of 15 June passed, but on the following day, under pressure from Berlin, Sauckel agreed to reduce the total number to 250,000 and to accept a ratio of one prisoner for every three workers, with the proviso that the prisoners came from farming families. Laval said that both he and Pétain were sincerely grateful for the generous gesture. Whether or not Pétain agreed to the expression of gratitude is not recorded.

On 22 June Laval announced the exchange scheme, know as the *relève* ('relief' in the military sense, of one unit taking over from another). As it turned out, the results were disappointing. By mid-August fewer than forty thousand workers had volunteered. As a result, no more than eleven thousand prisoners of war returned. Needless to say, they were greeted by Pétain himself in his most self-congratulatory mood. He claimed the credit for the policy, and said that it was only the start of what would be a long process to free finally all prisoners of war. What he failed to say was that the Germans were in no mood to make any further concessions, and that the scheme, rather than remaining purely voluntary, would be imposed later on in the year.

While all this was going on an even more sinister policy had been put in place. In January 1942, at a conference on the Wannsee in Berlin, the decision had been taken by a group of senior Nazis, assembled under Heinrich Himmler, to 'cleanse' Europe of all Jews. Furthermore, Unoccupied France was not to be exempt. In mid-June the Germans demanded the deportation of ten thousand Jews from Vichy France. On 2 July Karl Oberg, the SS officer in charge of policing the Occupied Zone, met the Vichy Chief of Police, René Bousquet, to organise the round-up. Bousquet pleaded that it would be something of an embarrassment if the French police were obliged to carry it out. To avoid this embarrassment, Oberg agreed that it would be only foreign Jews who would be arrested. The next day the government ratified the agreement, but only after Laval had insisted that children under sixteen, hitherto excluded, should be put on the list. The sight of screaming children separated from their parents would be politically intolerable. They all had to go together. Moreover, Laval told ministers that the Jews were to be transported to a Jewish state in eastern Europe. He later claimed that he really did believe what he was saying.

The operation went ahead. By the end of August over 6,500 foreign Jews had been taken, many from the concentration camps where they had been interned at the Armistice, to special transit camps before being transferred to the death camps to the east. Although the destination of the deportees was not known, the result in Unoccupied France of the sight of trains rolling out with their desperate cargo was to activate the first serious resistance to Vichy. Solidarité, for instance, set up a Mouvement National Contre le Racisme to publish illegal pamphlets urging the French people to help the Jews and calling on Christian clergymen to open their churches to protect Jews who might be threatened. The Comité de Nîmes, made up of Catholic and Protestant Christian relief organisations, actively worked on behalf of the Jews. The Central Consistory, which represented the Jewish leadership, kept closely in touch with Catholic bishops. Clandestine communist groups sheltered those who were threatened – frequently alerted by broadcasts from London.

On 18 August the Protestant priest Marc Boegner noted in his diary that Cardinal Gerlier had protested vigorously to the Préfet at Lyon about 'the foreign Jews being delivered to Germany and delivered in conditions of inhumanity which were truly scandalous'.

Cardinal Suhard, too, had written to Pétain on the matter. Gerlier was
to follow suit in a further letter to Pétain. 'He believes that given the
facts as established the Churches can no longer keep silent'. But he did
not see any point in writing to Laval. 'His information gave him to
believe that the initiative for the Jewish deportations came from him.'[7]

The clerical protests, the public outrage when news of the deportations leaked out, and the consequent sympathy for the Resistance groups,
had their effect. Pétain, who had received a long and detailed letter
from Boegner himself on the whole subject, told Laval that the policy
was damaging to the government and to the reputation of the Head of
State. On 2 September Laval saw Oberg again and asked not to be
required to arrest more Jews. Yet the deportations continued throughout
the month. On 9 September Pastor Boegner saw Laval himself and
made a detailed complaint about what was happening. Laval claimed that
he did not know about the conditions and that Bousquet was responsible. In any event, he was not going to be deflected from co-operating
with Germany. None the less, by the end of September the deportations
ceased, apart from four in November, until the end of 1942.

Yet Pétain's protests about the Jewish deportations were neither
particularly strong nor particularly principled. His – carefully cultivated – image with his 'children' was being damaged. In this, at least,
he was right. As a senior member of his staff, André Lavagne, told
Boegner, 'Laval is dishonouring the Marshal.'[8] Furthermore, Pétain
himself had already by then gone a long way towards damaging his
own image, fragile as it then was. It was no longer a question of foreign Jews but of the future of Franco-German co-operation. By the
end of May 1942 he had come to the conclusion that sooner or later
there would be Anglo-American attacks on French coasts and on
French North and West Africa. He told Abetz that such attacks were
'inevitable'.[9] He therefore suggested joint Franco-German staff discussions to plan the defence, particularly of North Africa. The
Germans were reluctant, preferring instead to concentrate on getting
their hands on French ships stranded in neutral ports.

Pétain's prediction was well founded. On 19 August British and
Canadian commandos staged a raid on Dieppe. As it happened, the
whole operation was bungled, and the raid was repulsed with heavy
Allied losses. But Pétain was able to use the Dieppe opportunity to
reiterate his request to Hitler that France be allowed to participate in

With Church leaders. (*Keystone*)

the defence of her own territory. No original text of his letter has survived (which led to doubts about its existence at Pétain's trial) but there seems little doubt that it was sent. 'After a meeting I have just had with President Laval', it read, 'and because of the latest British aggression which occurred this month on our territory I propose that you envisage the participation by France in her own defence. I am ready to examine the way to achieve this if you accept the principle. I ask you, Chancellor, to consider this proposal as the sincere expression of my willingness to make a French contribution to safeguarding Europe.'[10]

The intention was perfectly reasonable. If Germany was going to win the war, as Pétain still expected, it was only right that France should join in the defence of her own territory. Yet it handed the Germans another propaganda weapon. On 24 August the German-controlled Radio Paris announced that 'the Marshal had warmly congratulated the Commander-in-Chief of the German forces in the occupied territory on his success in the region of Dieppe . . .'[11] In fact, it is far from clear whether Pétain ever authorised such a message.

Nevertheless, Pétain, by even writing at all in terms which moved from co-operation to military collaboration, had allowed himself to be caught in a dangerous public relations trap.

Pétain was not alone in falling into the trap. Laval had also given voice, and not just to his belief that Germany would win the war. In his broadcast of 22 June about the scheme to exchange French workers for French prisoners of war he had, in the middle, said that he 'wished for a German victory since, without it, bolshevism would tomorrow establish itself everywhere'.[12] In fact, there was nothing particularly new about the sentiment – Laval often said the same thing both before and after mid-1942. But the phrase itself was picked up and used against both Laval and Pétain in 1945. In his pre-trial hearing, Pétain claimed that he had protested violently when the speech was discussed at a later meeting of ministers. Laval countered by claiming that he had discussed the speech with Pétain beforehand and that Pétain had only asked him to omit the words 'believe in' but did not object to the words 'wish for', on the grounds that 'believe in' was an expression of a military opinion which Laval was not in a position to give. When the whole row erupted at Pétain's trial, evidence from Charles Rochat, the head of the Ministry of Foreign Affairs at the time, confirmed Laval's version. Pétain had quite clearly seen Laval's draft. Moreover, at the subsequent meeting of the Council of Ministers on 26 June, the minutes report no sign of Pétain's disapproval. Pétain, to put it politely, was suffering from a serious loss of memory.

At this point, it is important to avoid the benefits of hindsight. Pétain had told Serrigny that October 1942 would be the month of decision. To most observers in the summer and early autumn of 1942, it was quite clear which side was winning the war. The German offensive in Russia had reached as far as the River Volga, and General Erwin Rommel was not very far from the gates of Cairo. The British effort at Dieppe had been swept aside, and the Americans appeared to be more interested in the Pacific war with Japan than in adventures in the European theatre. Stalingrad, Alamein and the invasion of North Africa – code-named Torch – were all in the future. Only Darlan had the foresight to suspect that the tide might be turning, but even he, trimmer as he was, sent a message to Laval congratulating him on his 'moving and courageous speech'.[13]

Where Pétain's judgement failed was in forgetting the lessons of Saint-Cyr and the lessons of 1918. At Saint-Cyr, he had learned that Napoleon's armies had been defeated by the Russian winter and by the strength of Mother Russia, when roused, to defend the homeland. In 1917 and 1918 he had learned that the Great War would be won by the full mobilisation of American strength. Both those lessons had in 1942 been forgotten. The truth was as yet unperceived. What was confronting Germany in the autumn of 1942 was the ferocious resistance of the Red Army and the horrors of the Russian winter, the American decision to concentrate their mighty resources on Europe rather than the Pacific, and the determination of the British in the North African desert.

On 1 November the French commander in North Africa, General Alphonse Juin, received news of heavy British naval concentration at Gibraltar. By the night of 2 November units along the Moroccan coast had been put on high alert. On 7 November, however, Juin signalled Vichy that 'during the [previous] night enemy units had been tracked moving eastwards . . . the alert in Morocco has been stood down'.[14] On the same day Darlan, who was in Algiers, for the purpose – supposedly – of visiting his son in hospital, cabled the Vichy Admiralty. 'I do not think', he wrote, 'that deliberate action against French territories is envisaged by the Anglo-Saxons. The nature and force of the British convoy leads me rather to think that the Anglo-Saxons envisage action against Axis bases in Tripolitania or Cyrenaica to impede reinforcements to the Afrika Corps and attack their rear positions.'[15]

In the early hours of Sunday 8 November Allied troops landed at Algiers, Oran and Casablanca. On the same morning the US Chargé d'Affaires in Vichy, Pinkney Tuck, called on Pétain. Pétain greeted him with the words: 'Monsieur Tuck, I am deeply grieved by what is happening.' Tuck made no reply, but handed Pétain the official message from Roosevelt announcing the landings. Pétain in turn handed Tuck the official French response. It was, he said, simple: 'We are attacked. We defend ourselves.' 'Monsieur Tuck,' he went on, 'a long time ago we took the decision to defend our empire; we must now do what we have said we would do. It is French honour which is at stake.'[16] He then shook Tuck's hand and Tuck left – in tears.

Pétain was not alone in showing defiance. At six o'clock on the same morning in London, de Gaulle was woken by his Chief of Staff, Pierre Billotte, to be told the news. It was not a task that Billotte enjoyed. 'Well,' shouted the General, as he put on his dressing gown, 'I hope the Vichy people are going to throw them into the sea. You can't get into France by breaking and entering.'[17] He then proceeded to give Billotte a foretaste of what he would say to Churchill when he saw him. It lasted two hours.

Thus, the reaction of two Frenchmen, on opposite sides in the war, was the same. The major question, at that point, was what each of them would do next.

24

THE COLLAPSE OF THE
HOUSE OF CARDS

'Le Maréchal reste . . . inerte dans son fauteuil'

Under strict orders from President Roosevelt, General de Gaulle had been kept in ignorance of the plans for Operation Torch. In London, complete security was imposed, and, as it happened, security in London was, unusually, tight and effective. There was no leak – at least not to those who were known by then as Fighting France. Security in Algiers, on the other hand, was, as usual, neither tight nor effective. It was generally known, among those who took the trouble to find out, that Murphy had taken great pains to identify friendly souls who would help to lend assistance to American troops when they landed on the French North African coasts.

There was no guarantee, nor could there be, that rumours about Torch would not leak back from Algiers to Vichy. General Jean Bergeret, who, as he explained in his evidence at Pétain's trial, 'had maintained contacts with the Allies since 1940' in Algiers,[1] was only one of those who had learned about the Allied plan. Unlike others in the know, he promptly went to Vichy to tell Pétain all that he knew about it. Admittedly, Bergeret got the date wrong and had to scurry back to Algiers when he discovered its true date, but he at least had time to tell Pétain what it was all about and why he was hurrying back.

Bergeret's report of rumours in Algiers was, no doubt, only one minor incident in the overall sum of things. Pétain even failed to pass it on to his colleagues. Nevertheless, when he was woken on the morning of 8 November 1942 to be told about the Allied landings and to be presented by Ménétrel with the formal protest – drafted mostly by Laval while he was still asleep – the news came to him as no particular surprise; and, unlike de Gaulle, he had had time to prepare himself.

In his meeting that morning with Pinkney Tuck, Pétain dutifully made his formal gesture of defiance and handed over the formal protest. The French official minute of the meeting, equally dutifully, formally recorded the event. Nevertheless, the French minute differs from Tuck's own report to US Secretary of State Cordell Hull. In Tuck's version, far from being in tears as the French minute describes, he rose to take what he considered to be a dignified leave. When he got up, Pétain grasped him by both hands and looked at him 'steadfastly and smiling'. He then paid Tuck the courtesy of escorting him to the ante-room and 'turned briskly back to his office humming a little tune'.[2]

Tuck took this to mean that Pétain was secretly rather pleased at the turn of events. In this he was, at least partially, right. Memories of the First World War were always in Pétain's mind. Indeed, all his stories about Verdun and the mutinies of 1917 were a constant source of conversation wherever he went. Above all, the memories of the flood of American young men arriving to settle the issue in 1917 and 1918, the way he had helped them with a supply of French tanks and guns when they were held down in the Argonne, the way General Pershing had appealed to him for help and how he had responded – all those memories were rehearsed over and over again. On 8 November 1942 those memories, instead of being the reminiscences of an old general in a past war, suddenly became the stuff of real life. The Yanks, in the words of their marching song in 1917, were coming.

Pétain's dilemma was only too evident. Until November 1942, he had looked to Germany, however unpleasant the Nazi régime, as the only protector of Europe against what he regarded as the ultimate peril of communism; and he had supported Laval, much as he disliked him personally, in his efforts to find some sort of settlement with the Nazis that would be of at least some residual benefit to France and to his 'children'. But on 8 November 1942 a new anti-communist champion had appeared in the lists. Moreover, it was not just a makeweight champion. It was the United States of America. Pétain's memories of 1918 told him that America, if she committed her resources and energy to the priority of winning a European war, would, as in 1918, undoubtedly win it – whatever the British or the Soviets might or might not do; and there is little doubt that, of the two champions in the lists, Germany and America, Pétain's preferred knight in armour was America. Operation Torch told him that America had made the decisive choice. America had decided to win the war in Europe. Japan would wait its turn.

None the less, Pétain's dilemma had, as always, two horns. Much as he might have preferred the Americans, he could not simply dis-avow all that he had hitherto said and done. Apart from all else, he was a head of state; he had made a 'gift of his person' to France; he had what he regarded as a debt of honour to the French prisoners of war still held in Germany; he had embarked on a policy of co-operation with a dominant Germany; his wife had been flattered to the point where she was almost a germanophile; and he had per-sonally endorsed legislation which, on any reading, would not be to the American taste, let alone that of his now perceived rival General de Gaulle, who had been condemned to death in the early days of Vichy for desertion and high treason against the state. The result was that not for the first, and certainly not for the last, time, he was unclear in his mind which way to turn. Added to all that, he was eighty-six years old, tired and often, as Serrigny noted, falling asleep in his armchair after dinner.

Pétain's office on the morning of 8 November can hardly be described as an orderly scene. In short, it was chaotic. Lehideux, who, for no apparent reason, had been summoned from Paris to Vichy, took note. 'There reigned the greatest confusion', he later wrote, '. . . in the course of the morning different men, each claiming to represent some position or some particular competence, marched in succession into Pétain's office to give him, with great authority and in a peremptory manner, wholly conflicting advice'.[3]

At 11 o'clock on that morning there was a meeting of the

Council of Ministers in the Pavillon Sévigné. They were given a full report – full in so far as anybody knew what was going on. Giraud had apparently broken cover and had broadcast an appeal (from Gibraltar, where he was still negotiating his future position with the Americans) to all French forces in North Africa to join with the Allies. There had, it was said, been a Gaullist attempt at a coup in Morocco. The bewildering information duly received, the Council then heard Laval, who reported that he had early that morning asked Krug von Nidda for a German guarantee of French territorial integrity. That request, and the formal protest which Pétain had handed to Tuck, were approved. The German offer of air support, in response to a request from Darlan, was accepted. The business done, Pétain then went for his customary morning walk, this time, however, not with Ménétrel or even Nini, but with Jean Jardel, the secretary to his military group of advisers. On that walk there was, indeed, much to think about.

Laval's request for a German guarantee arrived on Hitler's desk just after noon on the same day. Hitler discussed it briefly on the telephone with Mussolini, who said that he would only join in if France declared war on the United States and Britain. A telegram to that effect was drafted by Abetz, who was unwise enough to add, on his own initiative, that if France declared war Germany would stand by her 'through thick and thin'. This was transmitted personally to Laval by Krug von Nidda at just before three o'clock that afternoon. Laval at first saw it as tantamount to the guarantee which he had sought. With the telegram clutched in his hand he went immediately to see Pétain – who replied firmly that under no circumstances would he agree to declare war on anybody, let alone the United States. That particular horn was not up for negotiation.

The proposal for a declaration of war was finally buried when Weygand, summoned by Pétain himself from his seaside retreat, arrived in Vichy later in the afternoon. He was in time to attend the second Council meeting of the day, which started at just after six o'clock. On their way to the Pavillon Sévigné he and Laval had an angry exchange. Laval was forced to admit that the Abetz telegram did not in reality amount to a guarantee. There was little more he could do. At the Council meeting he did not even mention the German proposal for a declaration of war. He merely said that the Germans requested France to break off diplomatic relations with the United States. He did, however, manage to get the Council to agree to authorise German aircraft to overfly Unoccupied France.

Even as the Council was meeting, the military situation in North Africa was deteriorating. In the late evening Darlan sent a telegram announcing that he had authorised Juin to sign a ceasefire for the city of Algiers and that 'I am to meet the American General [Charles Ryder] who wishes to negotiate, at 10 a.m. local time, a ceasefire for Algeria and Tunisia.'[4] The Americans had suggested that the civil administration remain in place and that it should act under the control of the French government. Darlan had asked whether that meant the Vichy government. Ryder had not replied. The reply would come on the following day, from none other than General Mark Clark, chief of staff to General Dwight Eisenhower, the overall commander of Operation Torch.

On the morning of 9 November Darlan's telegram arrived and was decoded. It was read by ministers just at the moment when Laval was leaving for a meeting with Hitler in Munich to which he had been summoned late the previous evening. The telegram, as it stood, threatened to sabotage the whole purpose of Laval's journey, which was to settle once for all with Hitler the future structure, and defence, of a Europe in which France would hold its position as a great country in its own right. Hitler's purpose, on the other hand, was quite different. It was to instruct France to declare war on the Allies or face the occupation of its Unoccupied Zone. When he heard about Darlan's telegram, Laval immediately set about persuading Pétain to reply to Darlan that, in his absence in Munich, no negotiations with the Americans should take place. Pétain, faced by an angry Laval, agreed.

Thus instructed by a telegram from Pétain, Darlan duly postponed his meeting with Ryder, and contented himself with sending another telegram to Pétain requesting the immediate dismissal of General Mast (who had been acting for Giraud pending his arrival in Algiers) and four other officers for 'having broken their oath of allegiance to the Marshal, having acted dishonourably and having voluntarily facilitated the invasion of [French] territory by a foreign army'.[5] At that point, on 9 November, it seemed clear that Darlan had not yet jumped off the fence on which he had perched himself. His uncomfortable posture was, in fact, made even more painful by the news that Giraud had arrived in Algiers that same day and was claiming that he, and he alone, spoke for the Marshal.

Laval was due to meet Hitler at eleven o'clock on the evening of 9 November. His car was delayed by thick fog as it drove across the Alpine passes, and he did not arrive at Munich until early in the morning of the 10th. But while he was slowly navigating his way, events in Algiers had been moving on. Just before seven o'clock on the evening of the 9th, Ryder and Murphy had presented Darlan with the terms of a ceasefire in Algeria, Tunisia and Morocco. Darlan summarised the terms in a telegram to Pétain. Urgent as it was, by the time it arrived in Vichy Pétain had gone to bed – and, it went without saying, could not be disturbed.

On 10 November, at 11 a.m., without any response from Vichy to his earlier telegram, Darlan was summoned by the Americans. At the meeting, Darlan was confronted not by the gently spoken Ryder but by the irascible General Clark, who had flown in to Algiers the previous evening. Clark kept shouting at Darlan and banging the table, saying, in the crudest language, that he was certainly not going to wait for instructions from Vichy and that if Darlan did not sign straight away he, Clark, would personally put Darlan under immediate arrest (to make sure he was understood Clark leaned forward as though to grab Darlan by the throat) and get Giraud to sign the ceasefire without further ado.

Faced with this unconventional – but effective – diplomacy, Darlan immediately signed the document which Clark had slammed on the table in front of him. He then, as the ceasefire document specified, sent instructions to all military commanders in Morocco, Algeria and Tunisia to lay down their arms. He also pronounced that he was acting on the full authority of 'the Marshal'. So far, as it were, so good. But his instructions were received with some suspicion by its recipients. The Resident General in Morocco, for instance, General Auguste Noguès, received his instruction through his office at 2 p.m. but waited until 4.30 p.m. for a telephone call from Darlan, who, as he wrote two days later to Pétain, 'in your name, ordered the suspension of hostilities for the whole of North Africa'.[6]

Whatever the confusion among the generals in North Africa, it was nothing compared with the confusion among the politicians in

Vichy. When the news of Darlan's signature of a ceasefire agreement reached Vichy, at about lunchtime, the Council of Ministers was deliberating over the reply which they should send to Darlan's earlier message asking for instructions. Weygand was all in favour of a message endorsing Darlan's signature. Others were more doubtful. Rochat, for instance, thought that nothing should be done until Laval returned from Munich. In the middle of the meeting, Laval telephoned from Munich, shouting that he would resign immediately if the Darlan decision was endorsed. That was enough, yet again, to persuade Pétain to concede. A further telegram was sent to Darlan. The order to resist the aggressor, the telegram insisted, still stood.

But that was not the end of the story of 10 November. Radio intercepts were reporting that Darlan was a prisoner of the Americans in Algiers. None the less, the official telegram was sent to him – at 3.14 p.m. Yet at 3.15 p.m., according to Ménétrel, another telegram was sent – from Pétain himself, personally, to Darlan. It was sent by Vice-Admiral Paul Auphan, the Secretary of State at the Admiralty. Ménétrel recorded the event. Pétain wanted to send a coded message to Darlan. Auphan told him that the Admiralty had a secret code which only Darlan knew. 'Immediately', Ménétrel's notes record, 'the Marshal sent a personal and secret message to Admiral Darlan whose exact terms I don't remember but whose sense was: "Pay no attention to my official messages and orders to you, sent under duress. Am fully in agreement with you . . ."'[7]

Ménétrel's notes have, since then, been the subject of dispute. He was, after all, writing after the end of the war, and may have made the whole thing up. Auphan, too, claimed later that the private telegram, such as it was, was no more than a holding operation, only suggesting that there might be a change in official policy once Laval had returned from Munich. Nevertheless, there now seems no doubt that a private telegram from Pétain to Darlan was in fact sent. Whatever its true text, there is equally no doubt that the telegram, such as it was, fits with Pétain's belief that 8 November, marking America's determined entry into the European war, had changed the whole military balance. The dilemma had presented itself. At least for the moment, he had concluded, he should try not to be impaled simultaneously on both its horns.

The official telegram ordering Darlan to rescind the ceasefire agreement arrived at Darlan's office in Algiers at 5.35 p.m. on 10 November. It was, as Weygand had pointed out, absurd. Officers on the ground, he went on, were told to fight from ten o'clock to midday, not to fight from midday until two o'clock and then to continue fighting. To illustrate the confusion, the following morning Juin sent a message back to the Ministry of War that Darlan had authorised him to sign a ceasefire in Algiers on the evening of the 8th, but, in view of Pétain's disapproval, transmitted to him by Darlan on the evening of the 10th, 'to avoid all misunderstanding, it had been agreed with the American commander to wait until this morning [the 11th] before resuming hostilities'.[8] Darlan himself simply gave up. He issued the order, as instructed, to rescind the ceasefire he had signed and declared himself to be a prisoner of the Americans.

It was just at this time, in the evening of 10 November, that Laval was beginning his meeting with Hitler. As might have been predicted, it was not a success. Hitler went straight to the heart of the matter. France had to choose between complete collaboration with the Axis powers or the loss of her whole empire. Laval tried to explain his plans for a greater Europe. Hitler was not in the least interested. In order to try to sweeten the atmosphere Laval suggested that an ultimatum be sent to Vichy demanding a safe passage for German troops landing in Tunisia, and this was done. But it was not enough for Hitler. At 8.30 p.m. he gave the order to his generals to start the occupation of the rest of France on the following morning – Armistice Day.

By the time German troops crossed the Demarcation Line, at 7 a.m. on 11 November 1942, resistance in Morocco had ceased. Noguès sent a telegram that same day to Pétain saying that he had already ordered a complete ceasefire, following Darlan's instruction of 10 November, and that he was to meet Clark on the 12th to discuss the conditions. Casablanca surrendered at the same time. Thus, almost by coincidence, while French North Africa was crumbling to the Americans, Unoccupied France and Corsica were falling to the Germans.

Pétain was still asleep when the Ministry of War sent instructions to area commanders to put up no resistance to the German invasion.

Only General Jean-Marie de Lattre de Tassigny disobeyed the order –
and was promptly relieved of his command and placed under arrest.
By the time Pétain woke up the game was over. At an early meeting
of the Council of Ministers that morning Weygand and Auphan
argued in favour of supporting the North African ceasefire and sending the fleet from Toulon to the African ports. Others argued that
nothing should be done until Laval returned from Munich. Pétain was
only half awake and when everybody turned to him for a decision he
took refuge in the suggested compromise. They should, he pronounced, wait for Laval. In the end, the only point of general
agreement was to approve the appointment of Noguès as the Marshal's
sole representative in North Africa. Almost without being aware of
what he had done, Pétain had burned what remained of his boats. He
had refused to offer any resistance to the German invasion. Never
mind the terms of the Armistice; never mind the humiliations which
France had suffered. In November 1942 Pétain was perceived by the
outside world to have capitulated – in the true sense of the word – to
Germany.

There was then the matter of what sort of protest to make to the
German invaders, in particular to Field Marshal Gerd von Rundstedt,
who was due to see Pétain at 11.30 on the same morning. Negotiated
with Laval on the telephone, it was the feeblest possible effort. It did
no more than state the obvious – that Germany had violated the
terms of the Armistice. Pétain read it out. Von Rundstedt replied
smoothly that everything would be done in the most honourable
way. Pétain then embarked on a longer statement, that he 'was completely won over to this collaboration [with Germany] and a
reconciliation which we will pursue in all good faith'.[9] His speech was
then turned into a communiqué and broadcast. Pétain's dilemma,
already evident in his messages to Darlan, had thus shown its other
horn.

To be fair, Pétain's protest did have some effect. It convinced the
Germans that Pétain was a crucial element in maintaining order in
France. It also gave some heart to those who profoundly resented the
German occupation. Von Rundstedt conceded that Toulon would not
be occupied and that no attempt would be made to seize the French
fleet. Finally, it gave Darlan another opportunity to try to reach an
agreement with Clark without risking being branded as disloyal to the

Marshal. But Darlan was to get yet another shock. Almost at the same time as Pétain's protest was broadcast, a telegram arrived from Vichy announcing Noguès' appointment. To add to the confusion, this was followed immediately by a personal telegram from Pétain to Darlan explaining that the reason why Noguès had been appointed to the post of the 'sole representative of the Marshal in North Africa' was because Darlan was believed to be a prisoner.

Laval arrived back in Vichy at two o'clock in the afternoon. The Council of Ministers was summoned yet again. Auphan argued in favour of a general ceasefire in North Africa. Laval argued against him, on the grounds that a ceasefire would inevitably lead to oppression in France and further maltreatment of the French prisoners of war in Germany. Pétain was, again, persuaded by Laval's argument – and another message was sent instructing Noguès, yet again, to resist the Allies. The result was little short of comic. In one day, French troops had been told to maintain neutrality, to attack the Germans and Italians, then to maintain neutrality – and finally to fight the Allies.

The confusion was made worse by the fact that Noguès was at Fedala in Morocco and was not due back in Algiers until the next day. Darlan, rightly, told Murphy that the Marshal had given his authority to Noguès and that he, Darlan, was unable to take any decisions without his consent. Furthermore, when Murphy explained that Eisenhower himself had promised Giraud the supreme command of French forces in North Africa, Darlan refused to listen. In fact, neither he nor Noguès was on speaking terms with Giraud. Juin, on the other hand, seemed to be taking his own decisions. He refused to order his troops to attack the Americans. All he did was to tell them to suspend attacks on the Germans and Italians. All in all, by the end of 11 November, the situation both in Algiers and in Vichy could hardly have been more chaotic.

When he woke on the morning of 12 November, Clark was in a particularly bad temper. When he heard about what had gone on the previous evening, he summoned 'those yellow-bellied sons of bitches'[10] Darlan and Juin to the Hôtel St-Georges and told them that if they did not do what he said he would arrest them and put them in prison. Darlan tried to explain that he could do nothing without Noguès, Juin lost his temper, and Murphy tried to calm

Clark down – all at the same time. Finally it was agreed, in scenes of bad temper and bad language, that there was nothing for it but to wait for Noguès.

If there was confusion in Algiers on the morning of 12 November, there was equal confusion in Vichy. The urgent question there was what should be done about Weygand. Since Vichy had been occupied – the hotels had been taken over and given over to billeting German soldiers – it was clear that Weygand was in the greatest danger. Pétain asked Ménétrel to make sure that Weygand could evade arrest by providing an official car to take him out of Vichy to what was thought to be a safe place. Weygand's car, however, together with its escort, was followed by the Gestapo. He was stopped, arrested, and taken back to Vichy. Pétain protested, but his protest was brushed aside. Within a few hours, Weygand was whisked off to prison in Germany.

Weygand's arrest had its knock-on effect in Algiers. He was not personally popular as a commanding officer but he was respected by the officers and men of the army in North Africa, above all because he was seen to be resolute in his resistance to Nazi Germany. When Noguès arrived back in Algiers, there was a meeting with Darlan and five senior officers, including Juin. All present gave their opinion. It was unanimous: further resistance to the Allies was fruitless. But they were also unanimous on another point. Under no circumstances would they accept Giraud as their commanding officer. Weygand had cast his formidable shadow on the meeting.

It was at 9.30 on the evening of the 12th that Darlan and Noguès went to the Hôtel St-Georges to meet Clark and Murphy. Clark started off by saying that the Americans wanted nothing to do with Noguès or – for that matter – Pétain himself. Noguès got up to leave, but Darlan managed to grab his sleeve and pull him back. There was a long discussion, at the end of which Clark finally agreed to deal with both of them. At that point, Giraud came in. Noguès refused to shake hands. After some twenty minutes of wrangling, Clark delivered an ultimatum. Unless the three had arrived at an agreement by the next morning he would impose a military government.

It was far from easy to arrive at the agreement which Clark had required. At first, all that was offered to Giraud was to head a group of volunteers. Giraud retired to consider the proposition, but was persuaded by his friends that it would be beneath his dignity. Finally, on the after-noon of 13 November, after Clark had threatened to arrest Darlan and Noguès, a deal was done. Giraud would command the Army, Darlan would be the political leader in North Africa and Noguès would go back to Morocco. Eisenhower arrived to give the deal his blessing. All that was now needed was the nod from Pétain. Noguès sent a long telegram to Pétain explaining the arrangement in detail, and asking him to reappoint Darlan to his former position. His telegram also added that de Gaulle was expected in Algiers at any moment – much to Giraud's irritation.

The Noguès telegram also concluded that 'in reality it is a verita-ble occupation against which we are impotent'.[11] There was, in practice, nothing that Vichy could do but agree. The alternative would have been American military government. Pétain consulted Laval. Both accepted the inevitable, subject to the 'official decision presented to the occupying authorities'.[12] But there was nothing that the German authorities could have done. A North Africa under – conditional – French government was better than a North Africa under total American control. Pétain and Laval duly cabled their approval. That afternoon, Noguès announced that he had ceded his position as the Marshal's representative to Darlan and Darlan announced that he had been reappointed. He went on to say that he was therefore assuming the responsibility for French interests in Africa. Furthermore, he went on, 'I have the agreement of the American authorities with whom I will defend North Africa . . . Long live the Marshal!'[13]

The 'Darlan Deal', as it became known, was greeted with uproar in both Britain and the United States. In Britain, trade unions, Jewish organisations, the press and members of both Houses of Parliament protested angrily and vociferously. The flood of mail to the White House in Washington was almost universally hostile. The very public reaction, of course, only served to convince the Germans that they had been right to agree to it.

Ever since 8 November Pétain had been under pressure from many of his ministerial colleagues to fly to Algiers and declare himself on the side of the Allies. This he refused to do. He gave different reasons at different times to different people. The most frequent one was that he 'had given his person to France' and that he was therefore responsible for all French men and women, be they prisoners of war, workers sent to Germany, or merely those suffering the German occupation. On 13 November Serrigny was briefed by Georges Féat about the Darlan deal. Serrigny asked Féat what Pétain thought of the whole thing. 'He approves,' came the answer.[14]

Serrigny thought that Pétain had finally turned. When he next saw him on 14 November he tried yet again to persuade him to leave France. 'Give straight away all your powers over to Darlan', he urged, 'and go and join him with your fleet, your aircraft, anything you can take with you.' At first, Pétain 'sat inert in his chair . . . Finally he said, "I am told that at my age and in my state of health a journey by air at high altitude would be fatal."'[15] In spite of all his efforts, Serrigny could not shake Pétain out of his 'apathy'.[16] As a last resort, Serrigny pleaded with him to recognise officially Darlan's government. Pétain replied: 'I will try to find a formula.' Immediately afterwards Laval saw Pétain and 'completely turned him round'.[17] He would not recognise officially Darlan's government. Far from it. He signed yet another telegram insisting that resistance to the Allies continue.

Others received other reasons for Pétain's refusal to leave. If he went, he said to one, he would be replaced by Déat who would declare war on the English and Americans, and that he certainly did not want to happen. To another, he claimed that if he went, the whole of North Africa would erupt into war and be burned to ashes. Finally, to a number of others he said he thought he would be shot.

That seems to have been the conclusive reason. Pétain thought he might fall into a trap – as he had thought when Hitler had brought the remains of the Duke of Reichstadt to Paris in 1940. Moreover, he knew that the British support for de Gaulle would bring their protégé finally, and in some sort of triumph, to Algiers – as indeed happened only a few months later. The confrontation between the two would be, to say the least, awkward. But, above all, Pétain feared for his life, either in a plane or by a bullet.

He can hardly be blamed for this. After all, it was only six weeks later that Darlan himself was assassinated. There was a group of hot-headed young Gaullists who had met in a barn just outside Algiers and had drawn lots to determine which of them would take on the latest task that they had devised – the assassination of Admiral Darlan. One of them, Fernand Bonnier – he liked to add 'de la Chapelle' to his name in honour of his mother's ancestry – drew the short straw. While the others melted into the mist, Bonnier was introduced to Gaullist sympathisers who, in turn, introduced him to the British Special Operations Executive. The British then put him through a two-week training course in revolver shooting at their private head-quarters at the Club des Pins. Thus trained, although the revolvers he had been using were changed to avoid detection, Bonnier de la Chapelle, under an assumed name, made his way into Darlan's office on 23 December and shot Darlan – as it happened, painfully in the stomach. Darlan died soon after, and the assassin was beaten up, inter-rogated, given a brief court martial and shot at dawn on 26 December. His coffin had been ordered in advance.

Although Darlan's assassination was in the future, Pétain knew enough about the mesh of Algiers intrigue to know that he would be without any doubt the target of any group – whether of hot-headed Gaullists or hot-headed Axis spies. In terms of preserving his own life, a journey to North Africa was not an option. Serrigny tried to per-suade him that if he died in an aeroplane on the way to North Africa 'you would join Joan of Arc in history. You would reconcile all Frenchmen behind your presumptive heir and de Gaulle, between whom an understanding would inevitably be made. It is sad to say it but France would lose nothing by this accident.'[18] The same might have been true if Pétain had been assassinated in the same way as Darlan. But it was not, to say the least, a very attractive argument – even for an eighty-six-year-old.

If Pétain had decided, as he had done, not to go to North Africa, other alternatives were suggested. He could surrender himself, like the King of the Belgians, as a prisoner; or he could send his ministers to Algiers and stay in France by himself; or he could dissolve his gov-ernment and let civil servants run the country. None of these appealed to Pétain. He would stay where he was.

Nevertheless, even that option was not without its difficulties. Darlan could obviously no longer be Pétain's presumptive successor. In the circumstances, the succession could only be passed to Laval. Furthermore, Laval claimed, with some justification, that he could not, as Head of Government, possibly continue to negotiate with

Hitler and Ribbentrop if every move he made was subject to Pétain's approval.

By that time, Pétain was very tired. At a meeting of the Council of Ministers on the morning of 16 November, he is recorded as saying, apparently in a low and gloomy voice, that he 'asked President Laval, renewing all his confidence in him, to take all decisions which the present circumstances require . . .'[19] There then, immediately after the meeting, came a surprise: Nini had decided to intervene. Pétain had reached the point at which he was resigned to anything which might happen. Nini was worried that he would lose office – and perhaps, like Weygand, be arrested and packed off to Germany – if he detached himself from the Germans and tried to make it up with the Americans. She saw Laval, agreed that he was right to lift at least part of the burden from Pétain's shoulders. (Ménétrel went further, believing that Pétain should retire altogether.)

The rest of 16 November was devoted to the negotiation and drafting of a Constitutional Act appointing Laval as Pétain's successor as Head of State for a period of one month if for any reason he was unable to exercise his functions. At the end of a month it would be for the Council of Ministers to decide on the definitive successor. But by then Pétain's health was giving Ménétrel serious cause for concern. In order to avoid triggering the procedure which would automatically make Laval Head of State, he produced a medical certificate which advised Pétain to take a few days' rest (but only a few – and certainly less than a month). 'The state of the Marshal's health', he wrote, 'temporarily does not allow him to take all the urgent decisions which the situation demands.'[20] Jardel, too, advised a week's rest.

They should have known better. Laval seized on the opportunity to press the case for a transfer of executive powers to him. At the Council meeting on the morning of 17 November, 'the Marshal . . . decided to give to President Laval the powers which are necessary for a head of government to allow him to confront, at any hour and in any place, the difficulties which face France'.[21] Ménétrel and Jardel had thus become the unwitting allies of Laval in securing what amounted to Pétain's virtual abdication. Auphan and two other members of Pétain's staff, seeing the way the wind was blowing, immediately resigned.

There was, however, one more twist to it. Pétain made sure – he required Laval to sign a secret letter – that although he could make laws on his own signature Laval could not sign Constitutional Acts; he could not declare war; he could not appoint ministers without Pétain's approval; he would respect human rights and the French spiritual and philosophical traditions; and, a point Pétain made with special emphasis, he would guarantee the absolute personal and material security of the Alsatians and Lorrainers, the political detainees and all who had found refuge in France.

Pétain from then on did not attend Council meetings. He was not even given sight of the agenda, nor did he know the dates. The only texts he was asked to sign were those which compromised him even further. (For instance, he was required to copy out the verdict on Giraud, convicted of treason, in his own hand so that copies could be distributed by air over Algeria.) He was more and more seen as a prisoner in a country which was wholly occupied. 'From then on', wrote Barthélémy, 'the Marshal was like an organ superfluous to the function of the body of state.'[22]

Events moved on as the month came to its end. On 23 November French West Africa declared for Darlan and the Allies. Darlan tried, and failed, to bring the French fleet over to North Africa. On 27 November the Germans invaded the naval base at Toulon. Admiral de Laborde gave the order to scuttle the fleet. Within a few hours, 250,000 tons of shipping, including three battleships, seven cruisers and one aircraft carrier, were at the bottom of Toulon harbour.

It was the end of any pretence of Vichy independence. In 1940, Unoccupied France had been created as an artificial construct – a short-term arrangement to bridge the gap between the Armistice and a peace treaty. The cards which were the foundation on which the whole ramshackle house had been built were North Africa and the fleet. North Africa was lost and the fleet largely at the bottom of the sea. There was no negotiating hand with which to resist the Germans. The house of cards had finally collapsed.

It is idle to speculate, as have some historians, what would have been the effect of Pétain's arrival in Algiers. 'There was a big wager to win', wrote one. In spite of Montoire, in spite of the Paris Protocols, in spite of the misjudgements of 'collaboration', he would

Scuttling of the fleet at Toulon, November 1942. (*Getty Images*)

have been 'consecrated as the "one who brought freedom to the land" . . . and his name would have been given to more squares, avenues and schools than . . . the late Monsieur Thiers'.[23] That may, or may not, have been so. On the other hand, there were plenty of hot-heads like Bonnier de la Chapelle, who would have happily awarded him the same fate as Darlan. One of those 'hot-heads', as 1943 was to show, was none other than the British Minister in Algiers, Harold Macmillan.

Be that as it may, Pétain's abdication of executive powers is more difficult to understand. True, he was tired and resigned – like a latter-day Wotan ready to accept that his power had passed to the dwarf Alberich. But his reaction to the way the transfer had been announced in the press was to refuse point-blank to make a radio broadcast announcing the event. On 19 November Lavagne noted that 'the Marshal wishes to cling on to his authority in the exercise of his former prerogatives'.[24] In other words, and on Nini's insistence, he wanted everybody to know that he was neither incapacitated nor dead.

Yet the last word on 1942 belongs to Serrigny. In his diary for 19 December he wrote that he had lunched with Pétain at the Hôtel du Parc the previous day. 'The poor man', his diary reads, 'does not appreciate the state of public opinion towards him. The demonstrations the Préfets organise for him with children, nuns and a few idiots give him still the illusion of popularity . . . He believes that Germany will be defeated; he has repeated this to me for the last six months and he throws himself into Hitler's arms!'[25] In other words, the eighty-six-year-old had started to wander into some sort of mental no man's land, with no clear sense of reality.

25

WHICH WAY TO TURN?

'Il est inutile maintenant d'essayer de galvaniser ce pauvre vieillard'

It was no more than, and no less than, an invasion all over again. German soldiers were out on patrol in the streets of Vichy. The Gestapo set up headquarters, as it happened in one of the most pleasant hotels in the town, overlooking the park leading down to the River Allier, and their officers went about their business of arresting, more or less randomly, anybody suspected of harbouring enemy agents or foreign Jews. Deportations of Jews, with the help of the French police, were resumed. The Germans demanded more money from the French to pay for the occupation of their own territory, and Sauckel demanded a further 250,000 French workers to work in the German war machine.

For those living throughout what used to be Unoccupied France, the effects of the occupation were, in the true sense of the word, dreadful. Laval suggested, and the Germans agreed, that a special police force be set up to complement the already overstretched German SS. On 5 January 1943, therefore, the Service d'Ordre Légionnaire adopted the new title of the Milice. Darnand's command was confirmed. That done, he set about recruiting young thugs from the Légion who were to form the core of the Milice, made them swear total loyalty to Pétain, and instructed them in the necessary techniques which were to be used in hunting down Jews, Freemasons and communists. At that point, a miasma of fear seemed to settle on what until then had at least given the appearance of an independent France – a miasma which, in truth, was not to be blown away until the arrival of the fresh wind of the Liberation.

If only by default, Pétain, old as he was and with frequent episodes of attention failure in the afternoons, must bear his share of responsibility. He had, after all, decorated Darnand in the First World War and did not object to – and even encouraged – the Milice oath of personal loyalty. Moreover, he had written to Hitler with the idea of 'a national police force to maintain order in the event of [Allied] occupation'.[1] Seizing on this, Laval had gone much further. On 13 January he sent a letter to von Rundstedt proposing that the Garde Mobile, hitherto a civil police force of some six thousand men, be increased to twenty-five thousand and that a new army, to be called the Phalange Africaine, should be created to form the initial French contribution to the reconquest of North Africa. In fact, neither of Laval's proposals met with German approval and both were watered down to insignificance. Yet out of it all, the Milice grew in strength – and in brutality. Pétain, for his part, simply took far too long to try to put a stop to it.

By then, Pétain himself was under German suspicion. In January 1943 he decided to spend a quiet few days at L'Ermitage. But for this he needed official permission. The Germans, and the Italians who occupied Villeneuve-Loubet, thought that this was a deep plot by Ménétrel to spirit Pétain away to North Africa. Permission was therefore refused. Pétain then tried to get authorisation from General Alexander von Neubronn, the military commander at Vichy. The response was, again, uncompromising. Not only would Pétain be required to stay in Vichy but two Gestapo officers would be assigned to his bodyguard. Pétain was – understandably – furious. But there was nothing he could do about it.

By then, Pétain had reached what seemed to be a conclusion. The news of the surrender of the German 6th Army at Stalingrad and the German defeat at El Alamein did little more than confirm the general belief that Germany would lose the war. On 19 December 1942 Serrigny, puzzled about Pétain's frame of mind and his behaviour, found only one explanation: 'the hope of a compromise peace'.[2] This, in fact, was Pétain's conclusion.

His reasoning was simple. The greatest threat to France – the great and historical France about which he had learned from his earliest peasant childhood – was communism. It followed that the Christian west should unite to defeat that threat. In turn, that meant that France should be in itself united and that Germany should be supported by a united France, Britain and, of course, the United States, in the same enterprise. Even at the time Serrigny was puzzled, Pétain was warning his old friend and colleague, Alfred Conquet, who had worked with him before the war in his old office in the Boulevard des Invalides, to be prepared to make overtures to de Gaulle 'when the Allies have clearly won the match'.[3]

The 'compromise peace' thus became Pétain's new project. The problem, of course, was that he was unable to understand that he was in no position to bring his project to any sort of fruition. He still had not realised that he was now no more than a figurehead in a discredited and occupied state. He still genuinely thought, in discussing the matter with his closest colleagues in the small environment of Vichy, that he could play a role in achieving what was no less than a rebalancing of the world. Old age had brought with it not just a sense of self-importance but a diminishing grasp of reality. To cap it all, he either was unaware – or had not taken in – that the Allies in their conference at Casablanca in January 1943 had declared that they would accept nothing less than unconditional surrender.

There were, of course, several matters which had to be dealt with before Pétain could even start on his project. The first was to ensure that the state of which he was head was properly disciplined – as the Army had to be properly disciplined in 1917 and 1918. But in that there was to be an immediate difficulty. On 16 February 1943 Laval promulgated a new law, the Service du Travail Obligatoire. Voluntary service in Germany had failed to meet Sauckel's targets. Service therefore had to be made compulsory. As a matter of fact, Sauckel's targets were duly met, but there was a corresponding defection by young men who wished to avoid what was then a legal obligation. The result was the formation of bands in the hills – known as the Maquis after the heather on the hills which they adopted as their home. In Pétain's view that was a mutiny against the proper legal authority like the mutinies of 1917, and had, as in 1917, to be suppressed. The result was an upsurge both in violent resistance and equally violent suppression by the Gestapo and the Milice.

The next matter was Laval himself. Apart from personal dislike, Pétain knew that Laval was unacceptable, in any form, either to the Allies or to Giraud – let alone de Gaulle. In fact, Laval shared Pétain's view that the sensible course for France was to work for a 'compromise peace'. He even, like Pétain, believed that he had a role to play in such a negotiation. None the less, Pétain was perfectly aware that, for any possibility of success in negotiations either with Algiers or with the Allies, Laval had to go.

The third matter was how even to start approaching those whom Pétain would have as his allies in his project. Of course, there was no difficulty about the Germans – they were, after all, on his doorstep. But there were difficulties about both the Americans – the friendly Leahy was no longer in Vichy – and his compatriots in London and Algiers, and the British. The problem was how to persuade all possible participants that the Vichy government had legitimacy as a proper evolutionary survivor of the Third Republic. Without that, there could be no hope of French reunification in the post-war resistance to communism. Nor, for that matter, could, without that, a union of all Frenchmen be acceptable to the Americans.

In early January 1943 Pétain was, in so far as age and failing concentration allowed him, giving all this due thought. But little of it filtered down to his colleagues. On 27 January 1943, for instance, Serrigny found Pétain, at dinner, in a mood of 'disconcerting serenity'.[4] When asked by both Ménétrel and Jardel to oppose the law on compulsory service, Pétain is said to have 'kept quiet . . .'. Moreover, 'the disarray increases from day to day. Never has the lie reigned so supreme or inequality so shocking. As for the deportations, the French administration has become German auxiliaries. The appearance of a uniform makes one tremble and only those who have the means to escape are able to hide. As for food, the black market continues to corrupt the French . . .'[5]

Yet Serrigny, or, for that matter, Ménétrel and Jardel had not understood the slow workings of Pétain's mind. Whatever the frailty of old age, Pétain's analytical ability, when fully alert and concentrated on a specific problem, was undiminished. In the early months of 1943 Pétain was slowly digesting the conclusion that Germany would lose the war, and that the right course to follow was his new project of a 'compromise peace'. The end was clear, but the means were far from simple. At the very least, he had to devise a strategy.

At first, his strategy was simply to get rid of Laval while assuring the Germans that he was on their side. On 4 April, he made a speech attacking those who were 'linked to the causes of the disaster and fled its consequences' – in other words, de Gaulle. Yet in the same speech he asserted that 'the National Assembly of July 1940 freely made its decision when it entrusted me with the mandate to fashion a new constitution'.[6] This was a careful preparation for the future battle-ground. That was to be, in the modern vernacular, his Plan B.

So far, so good. But in the Vichy political hothouse it was impossible to keep a secret. Word leaked out to Laval that Pétain wanted to be rid of him. On 23 April Laval told Schleier (Abetz by then being in disgrace for apparently showing too much sympathy for the French) about the plot. Schleier immediately sent a message to Berlin, and, as a consequence, Hitler wrote a stern letter to Pétain – telling him, in the clearest possible terms, to back off – and then, by way of support, summoned Laval to Berchtesgaden. Once there, Laval tried to persuade Hitler to make peace with the Soviets and construct a European Federation which would negotiate honourably with the western Allies. Hitler thought this no more than ridiculous, but he had realised that Laval was a valuable puppet. There were therefore some emollient words, but no more. None the less, Pétain had by then been made fully to understand that his first strategy, simply to be rid of Laval, had foundered on the rock of German opposition.

Towards the end of May 1943, Pétain took a few days off from his official duties – such as they were. He needed time to reconsider. He believed that his project was still in place: to put in place a united France by the settlement of a compromise peace with Germany and then to achieve the overall objective of a united front against communism.

That was all very well. But, his first effort having failed, Pétain devised another. On 23 May 1943 he and Jardel met to discuss it. Jardel told him that the only weapon Pétain had left to defeat Laval was the power vested in him by the National Assembly in July 1940 to promulgate a new constitution. In spite of the – muted – efforts of the Conseil National, which had produced several drafts but led to nothing, the old constitution still stood. Pétain and Jardel therefore started to outline a new constitution designed both to neutralise Laval and to be acceptable to the Americans. This, indeed, was Plan B. The National Assembly, like Lazarus emerging from his tomb, was to be brought back to life.

Three events prompted Pétain to make haste. On 30 May de Gaulle arrived in Algiers to set up, with Giraud, the Committee for National Liberation (CFLN). On 10 July the Allies landed in Sicily; and on 25 July Mussolini was deposed. There was no time to lose. A small committee, chaired by one of Pétain's most faithful confidants, Lucien Romier, was put to work. Their remit was to write, in the shortest time possible, the new constitution.

But Pétain did not stop there. His project of a 'compromise peace' also involved making contact both with the CFLN, jointly chaired at the time by Giraud and de Gaulle, and with the British in Algiers. For these tasks, without mentioning the matter to Ménétrel, Jardel or Romier, he selected a variety of intermediaries. One was Paul Dungler, an Alsatian member of the Resistance, who was summoned by Pétain in July and, by his own account, told to see Giraud and de Gaulle and tell them that Pétain 'proposed that at the Liberation we meet at the Arc de Triomphe when I will transfer to them my powers without reservation'.[7] Dungler duly left for Algiers via Madrid (but when he arrived in Algiers seemed to spend more time in discussing the finances of the Resistance in Alsace than in fulfilling Pétain's commission).

A second intermediary was a Trappist monk, Father Bursby, who had apparently been released from his vow of silence to set up a network of supporters of Giraud in France. One of these was General Henri Lacaille. Lacaille told Bursby that what he was doing was all very well and good, and no doubt Christian, but that he ought to be working for the union of all Frenchmen. To do so, it would be sensible to start with Pétain. Lacaille arranged a meeting, at which Pétain, as expected, was full of enthusiasm for the initiative. But Pétain went on to say that 'I have no specific proposals at the moment but I will welcome and study favourably all proposals which are made to me in that direction.'[8]

That meeting took place on 12 October 1943. But the reason that Pétain had no specific proposals for Bursby was that he had sent another intermediary, this time to make contact with the British. The proposal that his intermediary was to put was, as it happened, very much more ambitious. Whatever the attempts to satisfy the Germans, whatever the inconvenience of leaving his wife and his home in Vichy, whatever the 'gift of his person' to his compatriots, and whatever the personal consequences, Pétain seems – and 'seems' is the only possible word – to have decided that the best way forward for his project of 'compromise peace' was to leave France and place himself in the hands of the Allies. If that were done, he could make peace with de Gaulle, show the Germans that there was a united France – and manufacture the 'compromise peace' in opposition to the Soviets.

On 8 October Lord (Eric) Duncannon, the British staff officer acting as liaison with the CFLN in Algiers, wrote a note, marked MOST SECRET, to Roger Makins, Assistant to the British Resident Minister at Allied Forces Headquarters, Mediterranean, Harold Macmillan. 'Commandant Poniatowski', the note ran, 'asked to see me yesterday on a secret matter which he said was known only to himself and Payolle [sic] in Algiers.'[9] (André Poniatowski was Giraud's ADC and Paillolle (the correct spelling) led an intelligence operation in Algiers.) It appeared that a certain Monsieur Schneider, a 'close associate of Pétain' (those words are in Duncannon's own handwriting) 'and a responsible French industrialist (not of the Schneider Creusot works)',[10] had arrived from France in the previous few days. He was, Duncannon went on, head of a Resistance organisation in Alsace run from funds given him secretly by Pétain, 'who, Poniatowski added, financed a number of such groups in France despite the supervision and control exercised over him by Dr Ménétrel and other Nazi-paid members of his entourage'.[11]

Poniatowski went on to tell Duncannon that Schneider had seen Pétain on 25 August, just before leaving France via Spain for Algiers. 'Pétain told him that he himself was now prepared to leave France and go anywhere except to North Africa.'[12] The question of getting Pétain out would be Paillolle's job in conjunction with the British secret services. Poniatowski wanted the advice of the British on the whole matter.

Neither he nor Payolle [sic] were convinced that it would be a good idea to get Pétain out of France. On the other hand,

Poniatowski emphasised that Pétain was the legal head of state. However much his influence had diminished since November 1942, in the eyes of many Frenchmen he was the legitimate leader and had influence over a large number of army officers. Poniatowski went on to say that Pétain had told Schneider that after leaving France he would release the army from their oath to him. Might it not, therefore, said Poniatowski, be useful to get Pétain out of France a few weeks before the invasion started, if it was considered advisable to bring him out at all?[13]

Duncannon's note duly arrived on Makins' desk. In his scribbled reply Makins wrote:

This is rather a typical piece of political intrigue of Poniatowski. I do not think we can leave it where it is, and I suggest that Lord Duncannon should be authorised to inform Poniatowski that this is a French matter on which we can express no opinion, and that we cannot take any cognizance of it or do anything about it unless asked to do so by the Committee of Liberation. Cdt P might at the same time be reminded of the recent decision of the Committee on the subject of the Marshal. No British source should have anything to do with the affair, and no member of staff should meet M Schneider.[14]

Duncannon then saw Poniatowski again on 11 October. In his record of the ensuing conversation, Duncannon reported that

[Poniatowski] said that he had been thinking over the problem which he put to me last week. The more he thought about it the more he realised that he could do nothing. He was already suspected by Gaullists of being in touch with the enemy. He knew that Giraud, who was already criticised by Gaullists on every possible occasion, would not dare to entertain the proposal. Nor would any other member of the Committee. Even if some of them might personally think that some military advantage might be derived from it they would all be afraid of the consequences, afraid lest Pétain might receive some support outside France at the expense of the Committee of Liberation or afraid lest there might be a Gaullist outcry against the Committee for being a party to his escape. The Committee would never back the proposal. P added that he had no intention of putting the idea to the Americans either . . . It was purely a matter for the British authorities . . . But if the British authorities showed no interest in the matter, it would be dropped.[15]

Makins's answer to this was terse. 'Now reply to Cdt Poniatowski in writing', he scribbled, 'that we can do nothing about this and take no action except on the request of the Committee of Liberation'. With his note on it Duncannon's record was passed on to Macmillan.[16]

It was then Macmillan's turn to show his colours. 'There are no advantages', he noted in manuscript on Duncannon's record, 'in Pétain's escape. The only reason for taking him out of France wd be to execute him as an arch traitor. This is very dangerous stuff indeed. We must act with great circumspection. There are two courses: 1. For Lord D to <u>say</u> that he could not even mention the matter to the Minister; it wd not be worth doing, as he knew that I shd take the line that we cd not touch it with a barge pole; 2. That D <u>write</u> on these lines. I frankly rather fear anything in writing. Please discuss.'[17]

The discussion between Macmillan and Makins duly took place. In spite of Schneider's claim that 'the arrangement of Pétain's escape would not necessarily be a difficult operation' and his conviction that 'if the Marshal escaped and ordered the nation to resist the Germans openly, his action would have a beneficial effect on the 25 to 50% of Frenchmen who still recognised him as their legitimate leader',[18] the result of the discussion was that Duncannon was instructed to inform Poniatowski that he, Duncannon, had mentioned the matter to his immediate superior, who saw no object in putting it up to the minister whose view would most certainly be that he would have nothing whatever to do with it. Duncannon was also instructed to add, as from himself, that the only chance of changing this attitude would be an official request from the Committee of Liberation. This Duncannon did. Poniatowski thereupon abandoned all further efforts.

The story does not end there. A few days later the British Special Operations Executive were asked by Paillolle to train a certain Monsieur Schneider for parachute jumping. They were asked, however, not to allow Schneider actually to make a jump until he was landed in France, adding that if he broke his leg on landing it would not matter as there would be three cars waiting for him. In the event the request was not followed up. It was later learned that Schneider had been dropped into France by the Americans.

It was this which finally sparked off a report to London. On 19 January 1944 Kingsley Rooker of the Office of the British Representative with the CFLN in Algiers wrote to Peter Loxley at the Foreign Office in London. 'Last October,' his letter ran, 'when this strange and fantastic story was brought to our notice Roger Makins decided that it was too far-fetched to merit reporting, more especially as the proposal to send back Schneider had been scotched. His arrival in France through American initiative without any consultation with our people changes the situation and I am therefore giving you the story as we know it up to date.'[19] As though to explain further why there had been no earlier report, Rooker opened his letter by describing Poniatowski as 'an unreliable creature'. It subsequently emerged that it was Giraud who had 'persuaded the [American] O.S.S. to transport him [Schneider]'.[20]

In the cold light of history, leaving aside all the emotions of war, the attitudes of Makins and Macmillan defy rational explanation. An intermediary, apparently authorised by Pétain himself, had indicated that Pétain was prepared to escape from France and release the French armed forces from their oath of loyalty to him. His only stipulation was that under no circumstances would he go to North Africa. Were the proposal genuine, and were Pétain to place himself in the hands of the Allies, there would have been at least some identifiable advantage to the Allies. Pétain would leave France and would openly encourage his compatriots to resist the occupier, with all the prestige he still commanded. The remaining French armed forces would have been able to join openly with Fighting France. It is even possible that the ensuing battle for France would have been much more easily won. At all events, Pétain's suggestion, if genuine, deserved consideration at the highest Allied level.

Even now, Makins's assertion that this was a matter only for the CFLN to decide seems little short of ridiculous. Not only, if genuine, was it a matter of importance to all the Allies – given the impending invasion of the European mainland and the possible saving of Allied lives – but, on a parochial level, the CFLN, packed as it was by then with de Gaulle's supporters, would have never agreed to the idea. As Makins himself pointed out to Duncannon, the CFLN had only recently declared the Vichy government to be treasonable. To brush off the whole thing as a French internal matter was not just ridiculous. It can only be interpreted as a – successful – ploy to kill off the whole idea. The least Makins could have done was to recommend to Macmillan that Schneider's *bona fides* should be properly tested. Moreover, such was the importance of the possible event – however unlikely it may have turned out to be – that Churchill would certainly have wished to have been immediately informed.

There are several possible explanations for Macmillan's reaction – even, perhaps, to the point of dereliction of duty. The first, of course, is that he and Makins thought that Poniatowski was trying to perpetrate some sort of hoax. Makins obviously had no time for Poniatowski and thought that he was engaged in political intrigue. But it is far from clear, if there was political intrigue, what the point of it all was. If the whole thing was a hoax, there were no obvious beneficiaries.

Besides, on the 'hoax' theory, there is a ring of truth in some of what Schneider had reported. True, there is no evidence, other than Schneider's word, that Pétain had financially supported Resistance groups in Alsace or elsewhere. On the other hand, Pétain had used another member of the Resistance, Paul Dungler, to make contact – however unsuccessfully – with Giraud and de Gaulle. The fact that the records of Fighting France keep a trace of Dungler's visit but 'it is no way a matter of Marshal Pétain'[21] is neither here nor there. Such matters are not necessarily – to say the least – put down on paper.

There is a further ring of truth in Schneider's reported assertion to Poniatowski that Pétain was prepared to go anywhere other than to North Africa. Pétain, when he was concentrating, was not stupid. He had seen what had happened to Darlan and knew that he and his government were deemed treasonable by the CFLN. He saw no reason why his life expectancy in Algiers should be any greater than Darlan's.

If the 'hoax' theory does not stand up, a second possible explanation for Macmillan's attitude is that although Schneider might have been asked by Pétain to approach Poniatowski with the suggestion that he would be willing to escape from France, there was no guarantee in the end that the old man would do the deed. He would have to leave his wife, his home, his 'children', renounce 'the gift of his person' and so on. That, of course, given Pétain's record of dithering and indecision when the moment came, was certainly a very strong possibility. But the problem with this explanation is that it was never even addressed either by Macmillan or by Makins. Indeed, it is clear from Macmillan's manuscript comment on Duncannon's note of 11 October that he would tolerate Pétain's escape only if he were immediately to be executed for treason.

The third explanation is by far the most plausible. By August 1943 de Gaulle was in the process of outmanoeuvring Giraud in the CFLN. On 25 September de Gaulle was elected sole President. Giraud was given the consolation prize of leading the force which was to liberate Corsica. In all this, Macmillan was a fervent supporter of de Gaulle. At the Casablanca conference in January 1943 he had done his best to persuade both Churchill and Roosevelt that de Gaulle was the only possible leader of a revived France. By the end of the summer of 1943, as Murphy wrote, 'de Gaulle's Committee had every appurtenance of a full-fledged government, and all of us in Algiers accepted the inevitable'.[22] Macmillan, for his part, 'was overjoyed with the crowning of his efforts, realising that 'de Gaulle now found himself head of what was in effect the Provisional Government of France'.[23] The emergence of Pétain as an alternative leader of France, in whatever form and however it was done, would have spoiled what Macmillan regarded as his own personal triumph.

Added to the political alliance, Macmillan and de Gaulle had developed a bizarre kind of friendship. When, in June 1943, Macmillan decided to visit the Roman ruins at Tipasa de Gaulle had asked if he could accompany him. As they walked through the ruins they 'talked on every conceivable subject – politics, religion, philosophy, the Classics, history (ancient and modern) and so on'. Macmillan then decided to go for a swim, stripped naked and went in, shouting to de Gaulle to join him. De Gaulle refused, and 'sat in a dignified manner on a rock, with his military cap, his uniform and belt . . .' Macmillan went on to describe him as 'this strange, attractive yet impossible – character'.[24]

Pétain could not possibly compete with this. De Gaulle was Macmillan's favourite horse. Nothing, even an obligation to report to Churchill, was to stand in the way of his horse. Pétain had to recognise that any plan to escape from France, or even to make peace with Macmillan and de Gaulle, was bound to fail. That part of his project – the reconciliation of the different French factions in unity with the British – had failed.

Nevertheless, Pétain was not yet ready to give up. Auphan had, on Pétain's instruction, been working on a series of policy initiatives to complement the new constitution which Romier's committee was writing. On 13 September Auphan presented his results. Among other things he suggested that Laval should be replaced, STO scrapped or at least suspended, collaborationist parties outlawed, the anti-Jewish laws relaxed, and contacts made with non-communist Resistance groups. Auphan fully realised that the Germans would oppose practically everything he suggested, and that all those involved would probably be arrested. He considered, however, that this would not matter, and might in fact be a benefit, if Pétain set up a regency council with full authority to exercise his powers if he himself was for any reason prevented from do so.

Pétain, after a few days' reflection, agreed. On 27 September a new draft of Constutional Act no. 4 was prepared. A regency council was to be set up along the lines Auphan had suggested. It was to be composed of seven men (surprisingly including Weygand – still in prison in Germany – and the Gaullist former ambassador Noël, and, unsurprisingly, Auphan himself). In the event of Pétain being permanently unable to or prevented from carrying out his tasks his powers were to pass to the National Assembly, to be exercised by a regency council reporting directly to it.

That done (and kept secret), on 26 October Pétain summoned up the courage to tell Laval that he must resign. Reasonably enough, Laval asked for an explanation. Pétain, rather feebly, told him that he was too unpopular, was too close to the collaborationists Déat and de Brinon, and that the country was on the brink of revolution. What he might have added was that Corsica had been liberated by 5 October and was now in the hands of the Allies, that Allied forces had established a bridgehead at Anzio, that Italy had declared war on Germany, that the Resistance was now active everywhere and that passive opposition in the police and the administration was making the country ungovernable.

Laval immediately told Krug von Nidda of this conversation,

claiming that the right way to solve the problem, if indeed there was a problem, was to purge Pétain's supporters – and in particular Auphan. When this got back to him Pétain responded by preparing yet another draft of Constitutional Act no. 4. This was ready by 12 November. Pétain immediately sent for Laval and told him that he was going to publish the new Act and explain it in a speech the following day. Pétain's new proposal was simple: 'Today', the draft of his speech went, 'I embody French legitimacy. I intend to preserve it as a sacred trust and to return it, upon my death, to the National Assembly from which I received it, if the new constitution is not by then ratified . . . This is the purpose of the Constitutional Act which will be published in the *Journal Officiel*.'[25]

Initially, Laval was quite satisfied with Pétain's proposal. He assumed that he could manipulate the National Assembly just as he had in the past. But he thought that, out of courtesy, Pétain should tell Krug von Nidda about it. This was done. But when the message was passed on to Berlin, Ribbentrop was horrified. At 6.30 p.m. on 13 November, one and a half hours before the by then pre-recorded speech was to be broadcast, de Brinon telephoned Pétain to say that the Germans were not allowing the speech under any circumstances. Moreover, to make doubly sure, German troops occupied the Vichy radio station and the offices of the *Journal Officiel*.

No more than an hour later Pétain made a protest to Krug von Nidda in the most formal terms. He was, he said, no longer able to exercise his constitutional functions. Until the broadcast was allowed, he would simply sit on his hands and do nothing. In other words, he was going on strike. There followed, as might be imagined, a series of rows. Laval had changed his mind and was determined to make Pétain withdraw his proposal in its entirety. Ménétrel and Jardel, and even Romier, were inclined to agree with Laval. But Pétain stood firm. He was determined not to concede to de Gaulle on where the legitimacy of France lay. It lay with him, and not with the rebel general.

Krug von Nidda had originally told Pétain that the embargo on his broadcast was only to last forty-eight hours. In fact, it was three weeks before the Germans finally responded – they needed the time to make their military dispositions in case of serious trouble. But during those weeks, in fact on 23 November, Serrigny arrived unexpectedly in Vichy. Since he was one of the few old friends to whom Pétain could unburden himself, the two had another long conversation. Pétain told Serrigny that he considered himself a prisoner, and that he would act as one. Serrigny pointed out in reply that he certainly was not acting as one at the moment, but that he should. 'You go publicly to Mass every Sunday; you receive delegations; Laval reports to you on the meetings of his Council of Ministers. This is not the way the King of the Belgians behaves – with the result that he has the whole country behind him. Shut your door – to me as well as to the others. The greatest good fortune which could happen to you would be for a German sentry to mount guard in front of the Hôtel du Parc.'[26]

Pétain replied that perhaps Serrigny was right but he could not do all that at the moment as people would think he was ill, and that he could not sack Laval since Berlin had told him that if he did they would send in a *Gauleiter*. 'Marshal, you think too much about Frenchmen and not enough about France!' Serrigny expostulated.[27] He claimed that the German threat was no more than a bluff. 'I believe it is real,' replied Pétain, 'which is why I keep Laval.' Serrigny had done all he could. Pétain kept on saying that perhaps he was right but that time would tell. He then went off to have dinner. 'After the meal, he fell asleep.'[28]

It was Abetz, resuming his role after a year of disgrace, who delivered the final German response to Pétain on 5 December. It was in the form of a long letter from Ribbentrop. The Reich, he wrote, rejected all idea of reviving the National Assembly. It was no longer the expression of the will of the French people, and, furthermore, elections could not be held in time of war. The letter then delivered what amounted to three ultimata: first, all proposed alterations to laws must be submitted to the Reich authorities in good time; second, Laval must reorganise the French Council of Ministers in a way acceptable to the Reich authorities; and, third, the Head of State must remove from the administration all elements hindering reconstruction and ensure their replacement by trustworthy people.

Initially, Pétain was minded to protest. He tried to play for time. But Ribbentrop was not deceived. He insisted on Pétain agreeing to these ultimata in writing. On 15 December Abetz was told to see Laval and to give him the names of those who should be dismissed. Romier and Jardel were among them – Ménétrel was only allowed to stay if he confined himself to medicine. By 19 December Laval had extracted a written pledge from Pétain that all proposed legislative changes would be submitted to the Reich authorities for approval. On 29 December Abetz received Pétain's written agreement not to oppose any of Laval's appointments or any German request for dismissals. Pétain's capitulation was complete. It was sealed by the appointment by the Germans of 'Hitler's special diplomatic representative' to the French Head of State, as Minister Plenipotentiary, Herr Cecil von Renthe-Fink. To be plain, Renthe-Fink was to be – in the modern vernacular – Pétain's 'minder'. Serrigny's prediction had been fulfilled, but in the most humiliating way. The Germans had taken control of Vichy France not by sending in a *Gauleiter* but by ensuring that the existing machine worked entirely to their advantage. Pétain's project of a 'compromise peace' had failed at all stages. He was left, as Auphan found when he saw him in January 1944, sad and alone – and depressed. Serrigny summed it up: 'it is useless now to try to galvanise this poor old man'.[29]

VICHY: THE FINAL ACT

'. . . il n'y a de salut pour la France que dans la reconciliation Pétain–de Gaulle'

The bruising encounters of the last two months of 1943 had left Pétain feeling more than usually depressed. In fact, 1943 had been a bad year for him all round. His 'compromise peace' had proved a chimera, his approaches to the CFLN and the British in Algiers had come to nothing, the Resistance was growing in confidence, and Laval was still head of the government in Vichy. Last, but by no manner of means least, Pétain had to submit to the appointment of a 'minder'.

By the beginning of 1944, therefore, Pétain found himself little more than a tired old warhorse performing ceremonial duties. He made visits to towns damaged by bombing, received what was left of the diplomatic corps, attended the festivities for the Chinese New Year, and so on. Excluded from the process of government, he even had to endure the appointment of Darnand, at the insistence of the SS, as head of the French police, and the presence of two arch-collaborationists, Paul Marion and Philippe Henriot, in Laval's government. True, Laval had managed to deflect Déat by offering him a minor post (which was refused), and Doriot was fighting on the eastern front, but the balance of the government had shifted decisively, as the Germans had insisted, towards overt collaboration. 'I knew',

Pétain wrote in January to his old friend Mrs Pardee, 'that a defeat had disastrous consequences, but I never thought the misfortune which was the result would be so prolonged.'[1]

As 'minders' go, Renthe-Fink was not wholly unpleasant, and, on occasions, he could be reasonably affable. Tall and clean-featured, he took pride in his East Prussian aristocratic ancestry, and considered himself a Prussian of what he would have called the old school. As such, he made sure that his manners – apart from an occasional outburst of bad temper – were studiously correct. His education had been without great distinction, but after his studies in law he had gravitated smoothly, thanks to his aristocratic presence and, perhaps, a few quiet words from his friends, into the Foreign Office in Berlin. Unsurprisingly, his career as a diplomat was not, to put it mildly, on the fast track – a period in the Bern embassy, promotion to a better job in the Copenhagen embassy, and from there to Berlin to supervise the propaganda effort in support of the German campaign in Russia. Nor, for that matter, did he have any position of distinction in the Nazi Party, which he had joined only in 1939.

Renthe-Fink was therefore probably as surprised as anybody to find himself posted from the Berlin office for propaganda on the eastern front to become the '*Kindermädchen*' (nanny), as he himself put it, to the eighty-seven-year-old Marshal Pétain.[2] Nevertheless, although he was apt to shout at Pétain from time to time, Renthe-Fink seems to have got on well with his child. They were both old-fashioned in their manners, and Pétain certainly recognised an aristocrat when he saw one. Renthe-Fink, for his part, called Pétain 'an upright and good man'[3] and regretted being unable to be of help to him after the war.

But there it was. Pétain made up his mind – there was nothing else to do – to live with his nanny. He also had to get used to a new head of his personal staff. Jardel, on German instruction, was replaced by Jean Tracou, a former Préfet of Tours, who had been persuaded by Romier to join him in Vichy – only to find when he arrived on 6 January that Romier had died suddenly of a heart attack. Moreover, on 19 January Bonhomme, Pétain's faithful orderly officer for some twenty years, was killed in a car crash. Pétain had lost two of his most devoted supporters. It is little wonder that he wrote to Mrs Pardee in the depressed mood that he did. Furthermore, there is no doubt that the symptoms of sad old age were becoming more evident. There were more and more moments during the day, even in the mornings, when energy – and sometimes even lucidity – deserted him. It was difficult to remember names, and even the geography of the war, moving daily as it was, seemed from time to time to escape him.

Tracou turned out to be a loyal servant. He in turn brought with him another loyal (and perhaps over-devoted) servant in Louis-Dominique Girard, previously the head of the staff of the Préfecture of Angers. Pétain put them to work on the only role of any consequence which was left to him, the work, left by Romier, on the proposed constitution. The result was not altogether happy. In fact, it was little more than a shambles. A draft was produced at the end of January which Pétain signed without reading it thoroughly (if at all). It was only when it was explained to him that there was to be a return to parliamentary government that he declared himself not at all content with it. As for Laval, when he was shown the document, he said it was ridiculous, rejected it out of hand – and said that he would produce his own proposals.

If the constitutional question was one of confusion, there was also confusion in the maintenance of order in Vichy France. There were constant battles between the resistance in the surrounding hills – the Maquis – and the Milice, particularly in the Haute Savoie, both sides showing such ferocity that it was difficult to tell at times which was the more frightening to ordinary people. The Milice used torture and summary executions, as well as turning over to the Gestapo many of their compatriot prisoners. The Maquis responded by shooting without ceremony anyone from the Milice who fell into their hands. One report to the CFLN in early 1944 described the country as in a state of 'pre-civil war'.[4] The Gestapo, too, joined in the fun, such as it was, with random arrests. Laure, Bouthillier, Bousquet and even Jean Borotra, the Minister for Sport, were all gathered in and packed off to Germany.

By February 1944 Pétain was quite clearly isolated. Since his speeches were minutely examined in draft by Renthe-Fink he was able to be relieved, simply by making a protest, of making them at all. He refused to see more than four or five visitors in any one day. Nini was no longer much in evidence. Of his visitors, and on his morning walks, his preferred companion was Walter Stucki, the Swiss Ambassador, a frequent lunch guest – Pétain himself fretting, as old men tend to do, over the details of the menu. There was talk of the old days, of the First World War and of the beauty of the Swiss countryside. In truth, there was not much else left to talk about. It was up to Laval to stave off the further demands from Sauckel and to try (unsuccessfully) to restrain the excesses of the Milice. Pétain no longer felt able, or willing, to intervene.

But the German pressure on Laval to be more collaborationist was unrelenting. Abetz insisted that Déat be brought into the government. Laval was no longer in a position to resist. On 17 March it was announced that Déat had been made Minister for Labour, with extensive powers to attend to Sauckel's requests for French workers for German factories. Pétain accepted Déat's appointment as yet another which it was futile to oppose. Renthe-Fink had told him that the Reich government attached the greatest importance to Déat's inclusion in the government. Pétain thought about resigning, changed his mind – yet again – and confined himself to a refusal to sign the official decree. He just hoped that Déat would stay in Paris and not come anywhere near Vichy. Stucki reported to his government in Bern that the Déat appointment was the hardest pill for Pétain to swallow, that he had openly told Stucki that his life was intolerable, and that he hoped he would soon be allowed to die.

It was at that point, very late in the day, that the Americans made their approach. A message came from Roosevelt himself – although the method of delivery was tortuous. The context was simple. Roosevelt disliked and distrusted de Gaulle. De Gaulle was, in Roosevelt's own words, 'a nut'.[5] On no account, in Roosevelt's mind, should de Gaulle be allowed to walk into power in France on the back of an Allied landing in which he was not allowed to have any part. Furthermore, Roosevelt had his own plans for the post-war arrangements in France. On 15 March 1944 he had sent a draft directive to Eisenhower, telling him that once he was in France he would be able to deal with any *de facto* French authority, including the CFLN, but not with the Vichy government as such – which, of course, left the door open for dealing with individual members of the Vichy government. This was quite deliberate. Roosevelt had been impressed by his old friend Leahy, who had told him a month earlier that 'when Allied troops enter France, the most reliable person to whom we could look for help in rallying the French was Pétain'.[6]

Roosevelt's proposal to Pétain, delivered on 30 March by Colonel André de Gorostarzu, who had been in Lisbon apparently convalescing from an unspecified illness but who, in fact, had been working secretly on Pétain's behalf, was plain enough. Pétain should resign and play no further part in Vichy. He should follow the example of the King of Denmark, remain in the country but be wholly inactive. When the Americans arrived, they would pick him up out of retirement and he would help them in the post-war reconstruction of his country.

It is not too much to say that Roosevelt's proposal was Pétain's last chance to come out on the right side of history. If he had accepted the proposal, the course of post-war France would certainly have been different. Quite how and in what particular it is fruitless to speculate, but there is no reason to doubt that at least a sizeable part of the population of France thought of Pétain, even then, both as a symbol of the country's successful military past and as the legitimate Head of State.

Yet Pétain, once again, took the wrong turning. He replied that if he did as Roosevelt asked he would be leaving France in the hands of a dangerous group of men without the check which the legitimate head of state symbolised. Moreover, the Germans would certainly not allow him to get away with it. He would be arrested and deported to Germany. Both arguments were, of course, ill-founded. He had no effective control over Laval's government; and, if he had been deported to Germany, it would have been a positive advantage to him. But he went even further, claiming, as always self-importantly, that for him to leave his post would be an act of betrayal. As might be imagined, Roosevelt's proposal was not renewed – indeed, it was not long afterwards that Roosevelt himself announced that the United States was prepared to recognise de Gaulle and the CFLN as the *de facto* authority in France.

As it happened, and purely coincidentally, Pétain's popularity within France made a surprising recovery. The prospect of civil war – the Maquis versus the Milice, as it were – led those in the middle to look again to Pétain as the figurehead which stood above the conflict and which would shield the innocent from brutality – let alone death – from either side. It was, of course, no more than a flight from reality, but when Paris was bombed by the British on 20 April, leaving 651 dead and 461 wounded, General Brécard, by then Grand Chancellor of the

Légion d'honneur, suggested that Pétain should go to Paris to honour the dead. There was, apparently, to be a service of remembrance at the Cathedral of Notre-Dame. Pétain, Brécard said, should be there.

On 24 April Pétain gave a party at the Pavillon Sévigné in Vichy to mark his eighty-eighth birthday. There were some forty guests (including Nini) and much champagne was drunk. Pétain himself made a speech which was too long and rambling. But as the guests tottered out from the occasion and Pétain made his way back to the Hôtel du Parc, Tracou explained the plan to him. The following day they would leave for Paris. The plan would obviously have to be cleared with the Germans but, subject to their approval, Pétain should be ready to move. Nini, it was stressed, was not invited. Pétain thought the plan excellent. Both Renthe-Fink and von Neubronn, when consulted, saw merit in it. Renthe-Fink called Abetz, who agreed. Between them, as well, they agreed that the Germans would keep well into the background, allowing Pétain to present himself to Paris as 'the father of the nation'. But, to be on the safe side, they insisted that both Laval and de Brinon join the party.

On the afternoon of 25 April, Pétain and Ménétrel left Vichy, Laval and de Brinon making their way separately. After a night at the Préfecture of Melun they rose early, and arrived in front of the Hôtel de Ville in Paris at 9.30 a.m. Finding the place deserted, they drove on to Notre-Dame where they were joined by de Brinon (and, although he kept in the background, by Renthe-Fink) and were formally greeted by Cardinal Suhard. The party was then ushered into the cathedral past rows of soldiers of the Republican Guard with arms presented. By the time the solemn Requiem Mass was over, a large crowd had gathered. It was Pétain's first visit to Paris for nearly four years. He was an object of the greatest curiosity – and still, of course, of respect.

The party returned to the Hôtel de Ville, where a large lunch was provided. The champagne was the gift of one of the guests, Pierre Taittinger. During the lunch Tracou was called to the telephone. It was Renthe-Fink, demanding to know why there were loudspeakers on the balcony outside. Pétain should not speak, he said, since no text had been prepared. But Tracou could not get near Pétain. He was talking to councillors of the city of Paris. Pétain then stepped out on to the balcony. The crowd in front of him had grown during lunch as word spread around Paris that Pétain was there and by then filled the square in front of the Hôtel de Ville and the surrounding streets. Moreover, as though to add to the excitement, the Germans had allowed French flags to be displayed – for the first time since the Armistice. Pétain then addressed the crowd. What he said was recorded. He apparently described himself as a 'prisoner', but by the time his words were broadcast the censor had carefully edited them. In the newsreels of the day all that was heard was 'I come to pay you a visit . . . I think often of you . . . But be sure that, as soon as I can do it, it will be an official visit . . . So, I will see you soon, I hope.'[7] There were shouts of '*Vive Pétain*' and the *Marseillaise* was sung. 'The impression was strong and will be long-lasting,' wrote an onlooker; 'the Marshal finally came out of his shell to take sides.'[8]

Pétain and his party then went to the Bichat hospital where he spoke to the wounded, and then drove up the Champs-Elysées, crossed the river and arrived at the Square de Latour-Maubourg, where a number of his friends were waiting, including the former

Paris, April 1944. (*Keystone*)

Spanish Ambassador Quiñones de León. Later, he drove down the Boulevard St-Germain – and left Paris. The visit had been successful – perhaps not quite as successful as the newsreels made out, but the crowds had been noisy and welcoming. The mythology of the Marshal had not yet lost its potency.

The welcome given to Pétain in Orléans and Nancy on his way back was equally enthusiastic. No sooner back in Vichy, however, but he spoiled most of the favourable image he had created – and dented his popularity – by making a speech condemning the Resistance. True, he did it with reluctance, not because he approved the Resistance in all its forms – he thought that much of it was led by foreigners and a large part was overtly communist – but because of the impact the speech would have on his own people. In fact, Renthe-Fink had been pressing Pétain to make such a speech ever since February, but Pétain kept putting him off by claiming that it would lose him all support among his compatriots. Several drafts were prepared by Tracou and Henriot, with Renthe-Fink insisting that somewhere in the speech a sentence should make it clear that Pétain believed that Germany was the only defender of European civilisation against the menace of communism.

Pétain finally agreed, and on 29 April 1944 the speech was made. The Germans, however, were still not satisfied. Many in Berlin thought that Pétain was in some way in league with the Allies and was preparing to go over to them when they landed in France. Renthe-Fink had already told Tracou, and on 5 May he told Pétain, that, for his own safety, he was to move – temporarily – out of Vichy to a château near Paris. In the afternoon of 7 May Pétain, after a feeble protest, left the Hôtel du Parc, accompanied by Nini and Ménétrel. The crowd which turned out to see them leave assumed that they were being taken as prisoners. Many were in tears.

The château in question was at Voisins, not very far from Rambouillet in the Île de France. It was, for those whose taste is for the relatively sober exteriors and lavish interiors of the early twentieth century, a splendid place. The exterior had clean lines, but the interior, characteristically for the period, was full of vast rooms and, the pride of it all, a dining room whose main feature was its walls of marble inlaid with gold. But it had been built, however, in the middle of a dense wood, and the only outlook was on one side to a small

pond fed by a stream which managed to work its way through the
surrounding trees. As Serrigny remarked, 'it seems more suitable to
shelter romantic lovers than an old man of eighty-eight years, who
hates solitude and prefers [proper] gardens to nature'.[9]

Into these gloomy surroundings the Pétain party arrived on the
morning of 8 May, having spent the night at Rambouillet. But there
were problems. One was that the arrival of Pétain's party was so unexpected that they had to wait in the courtyard while the current
German occupants were told to leave. Another was that there were no
sheets for the beds – they had to be borrowed the next day from the
hospital at Versailles. A third was that there was no more than one
bathroom that was truly operational, and, as Nini complained, there
was no running water in the bedrooms – and, above all, no bidet. All
in all, Nini said that she much preferred Vichy.

The following morning, Abetz and de Brinon were the first visitors. Next came Henriot. He was invited, for lack of any other
entertainment, to stay for lunch. It was not a wise move. That very
evening Henriot broadcast – with German encouragement – that 'I
earlier lunched with the Marshal' who was in occupied territory
'. . . to be close to the people for whom he had the greatest care'.[10]
The next day the headlines in the press, in both Paris and Vichy,
repeated Henriot's words. The Germans had not missed a trick.
Pétain, the message conveyed, was not a prisoner but had elected to
go to Voisins of his own free will. When Pétain wanted to talk to
Ménétrel about it, he discovered that Ménétrel had disappeared –
nobody knew where. 'Another extra holiday,' Nini said in a loud
voice.[11] Pétain kept on asking for him.

The charade continued. On 17 May, Déat was invited, at German
request. The next day Laval turned up with his wife, and on the
morning of the 19th Darnand arrived. They were all received with
courtesy. Even von Rundstedt arrived to invite Pétain to inspect the
Atlantic defences. But Pétain was clearly uncertain how to react to his
new position – as a reminder of a glorious past and thus a possible card
to play in the German defence of France. Although he lectured
Darnand on the iniquities of the Milice, he was listened to in scarcely
reverential silence. He was taken to Rouen, by then in ruins, for one
of the interminable anniversaries of Joan of Arc. He was ferried about
to visit neighbouring villages – his almost hysterical reception having

been carefully pre-arranged. He received visits from delegations – mayors, local councillors and so on – all carefully orchestrated.

On 19 May, however, there was a much more welcome event. On the 18th Serrigny, Pétain's old friend and companion in arms, hearing that Pétain was cut off from communication with the outside world, had telephoned and spoken to Pétain's orderly officer at Voisins. When Pétain heard of this, he immediately invited Serrigny to lunch, together with another old friend from the First World War, General Anthoine.

It was not easy for the two old soldiers to reach Voisins. They were stopped repeatedly. There was a roadblock on the route leading from Rambouillet, a German post a few hundred metres further on, French police at the gates of Voisins and a crowd of sinister-looking figures obviously waiting to keep watch on Pétain when he stepped out of the building. When they finally passed all these hazards and got out of their car, they were astonished when Pétain almost ran towards them to 'embrace them with emotion'. 'It is not a familiar gesture for him', Serrigny went on to comment drily.[12] Pétain told them that they were the first real friends he had seen since his arrival at Voisins.

Even more surprising to Serrigny than Pétain's effusive welcome was the account of the visits to villages in the neighbourhood, allegedly damaged by bombing. To be sure, there were crowds of welcomers, and, apparently, most of the villagers thought this 'fine and august old man' had no responsibility for what Laval had done. But he was, as Serrigny noted, yet again deluding himself. He judged his popularity by their welcome, but although 'they were glad that [Pétain] had stayed with them, it is towards de Gaulle and the English that their hearts are turning'.[13] 'Pétain is completely intoxicated,' Serrigny went on, when he heard Pétain sing the praises of, of all people, Henriot. Serrigny's verdict, as he said goodbye to Pétain for what he thought would be the last time, was that he had 'the clear impression that the Head of State no longer at all enjoyed all his clarity of mind'.[14] In other words, Serrigny, his old friend and admirer, thought that Pétain was finally descending into geriatric vacuity.

The stay at Voisins did not last long. On 26 May the party started to move back to Vichy. They passed though Sézanne, Nancy, Epinal and Dijon, with crowds in every case coming out to cheer him on his way. But, although the newsreels of the day represented it as a great return of the Head of State to Vichy, with pictures of Pétain shaking hands with Laval and his ministers (including Henriot), the Germans did not trust him to stay in the Hôtel du Parc. By 7 June, he and Nini had been brusquely moved to yet another château – Lonzat, some seventeen kilometres away fromVichy. He was to be allowed to spend his days at his office in Vichy – but must return to Lonzat every evening.

By the time Pétain and Nini had been parked at Lonzat, the long-awaited Allied landings had taken place. Pétain was persuaded, under some German duress, that he could not remain silent. He therefore broadcast on 6 June. The message was simple. The German and Allied Armies were engaged in battle on French soil. France should remain neutral. In fact, the negotiations about what he would say – in a speech recorded on 17 March, nearly three months before the event itself took place – took six weeks, and the document itself went through ten drafts. Renthe-Fink (one of the drafts was in his own hand) wanted Pétain to announce that, in view of the gravity of the situation, the German occupiers would take over from the civilian authorities the administration of areas where there was likely to be fighting. Pétain refused. France would keep its own administration, but would remain neutral. That was as far as he would go.

Pétain was in Lyon when the news of the Allied landings came through. According to Tracou, he was delighted – he even starting singing, 'It's a long, long way to Tipperary.' His reception in Lyon had been ecstatic. It was the same in St-Etienne on the morning of 7 June, in spite of, or even because of, his broadcast of the previous evening. But when he arrived back in Vichy, it was a different matter. It was reported that five thousand Maquisards were marching towards the Hôtel du Parc. One thousand five hundred German infantry and a squadron of panzers were waiting for them. Renthe-Fink whisked Pétain off to Lonzat.

As it happened, his public appearance before a crowd at St-Etienne was to be the last of its kind. On 11 June, he was told by the Germans not to go to Vichy at all, but to stay where he was until further notice. Those who wanted to see him had to go to Lonzat. In short, he was by then truly a prisoner. On 14 June Darnand was promoted in ministerial rank without Pétain's consent. On 28 June, Henriot was assassinated by the Resistance. Renthe-Fink wanted Pétain to express condemnation. He refused. On 10 July he wrote a letter protesting at the behaviour of German troops, who were killing innocent French civilians as they retreated. It was torn up. On 20 July he refused to write to Hitler congratulating him on escaping assassination by a group of his own officers.

By the beginning of July 1944, Pétain had been allowed back to Vichy. But the visits were no more than day-trips. In the evening he was driven back to Lonzat. On 5 July, for instance, there was a memorial service for Henriot at the church of St-Louis. Pétain was obliged to attend. On 9 July Pétain arrived at the Hôtel du Parc to be confronted by Admiral Charles Platon, who delivered a manifesto signed by the ultra-collaborationists Déat, de Brinon, Doriot, Luchaire, Benoist-Méchin and others in sympathy with them. It demanded the replacement of Laval by a head of government irrevocably committed to supporting the German war effort. Pétain simply told Platon to go away to the country and stop meddling. Laval, when he heard about it, called a meeting of the Council of Ministers for 12 July and accused Platon and the others of trying to foment civil war.

The political air in Vichy became ever more oppressive by the day. Since the Normandy landings the Milice had become even more brutal. Jean Zay, who had been an education minister in the Popular Front government, was shot while being transferred from one prison to another. On 7 July Georges Mandel was also murdered by the Milice in the same circumstances. By way of revenge for Henriot's death Paul Touvier, the head of the Milice in Haute Savoie, rounded up and shot seven Jews. At St-Amand-Montrond, some forty kilometres south of Bourges, the Maquis took hostages. The Germans and the Milice arrived two days later, arrested anybody suspected of links with the Resistance and either shot them on the spot or took them to Vichy to be tortured. The Maquis then hanged thirteen of the hostages, whereupon the leader of the Milice, Joseph Lécussan, a brute who carried in his wallet a Star of David from a Jew's skin, rounded up eighty Jews, had the men pushed into a well and buried them alive under bags of cement. It was far from being an isolated incident. At Oradour-sur-Glane a whole village was massacred in the most horrific way.

There is no doubt that Pétain was outraged by such incidents. He told Renthe-Fink as much: 'You burn villages, you massacre children, you desecrate churches, you cover your country in shame. You are a nation of savages.'[15] On 6 August Pétain wrote a long letter to Laval about the Milice. 'I have talked to you', it started, 'on many occasions and I always hoped that I would hear of improvements in the diverse activities of this political police. The contrary is true . . . Unacceptable and hateful facts are reported to me daily . . .' Pétain then listed some of them. 'By these procedures, the Milice has succeeded in imposing an atmosphere of police terror unknown in this country until now.'[16] It was certainly strong stuff, but it might at least have had some effect if it had come a few months earlier.

Apart from his belated protests about acts of violence, it was by then clear, if it had not been for some time, that Pétain was trying to make his peace with the Allies. Odd as it may seem, Laval was trying to do the same. Laval's plan was to make France, as it were, presentable to the Americans. On 9 August he left for Paris, where he somehow managed to persuade Abetz that it would be a good idea to reconvene the National Assembly. The person to do that, he thought, was Herriot, who was detained in a lunatic asylum near Nancy (although he was perfectly sane). Abetz agreed that Laval himself should go and fetch Herriot, which he did. Herriot was dumbfounded by Laval's unexpected arrival on 12 August. He nevertheless accompanied him back to Paris. But, when there, Herriot said that he was not the President of the National Assembly. Laval should send for Jeanneney, the President of the Senate, who was living somewhere near Grenoble.

Laval did his best to persuade Pétain to come to Paris and endorse the scheme. But Pétain had other ideas. General Brécard, who was in Paris as head of a group known as the 'Friends of the Marshal', was convinced, as he was to tell Pastor Boegner later in the month, that 'there is no salvation for France other than in the reconciliation of Pétain and de Gaulle'.[17] The message was readily accepted by Pétain, who, on 11 August, signed a document giving authority to Auphan to negotiate on his behalf with the Americans and, if possible, to make contact with de Gaulle, with the aim of avoiding a civil war in France and for a transfer of his legitimate authority to de Gaulle. The following day, he signed another document, this time giving authority to Gabriel Jaray, President of the Franco-American Committee, to contact the Americans through Swiss diplomatic channels 'with a view to bringing them up to date with the French political problem and to let

them know my intentions at the moment of the liberation of the territory, with a view to safeguarding the principle of legitimacy which
I incarnate'.[18] But it was all too late – and too naïve. Laval's plan failed
on 16 August, when Herriot was rearrested on direct orders from
Berlin, and Pétain's plan failed because, after the Allied breakout in
Normandy at the end of July and the swift advance thereafter, none of
the Allies were interested in what Pétain had to say.

On 15 August an Allied force, including seven divisions of the 1st
French Army under de Lattre de Tassigny, landed on the southern
coast of France. In a matter of only a few days Toulon had fallen and
Allied troops had started to move up the Rhone valley. The German
19th Army was in full retreat to avoid encirclement. Vichy itself was
threatened. On 17 August Pétain, by then back in the Hôtel du Parc,
was summoned by Renthe-Fink and told to pack his bags. He was to
be moved north-eastward to the frontier town of Belfort in the Jura,
along with Laval and the whole of the Vichy government. Pétain
protested; Ménétrel said that he should escape and join the Maquis, or
even hide in a safe house in Vichy until the Germans moved out. But
it was all to no avail. On the afternoon of 19 August von Neubronn
received his orders. If necessary, he was to arrest Pétain that evening to
move him out of Vichy by force. If there was any resistance, Vichy
would be bombed.

Once again, Pétain conceded. The thought of trying to escape to
the Maquis (Ménétrel had already packed a torch, maps of France,
binoculars, string, knife – as well as a missal and an edition of
Rabelais) was too much for him. He persisted in his view that the
Germans would not take him if he refused to go. He then asked
Stucki to intervene, to tell Renthe-Fink that he was staying put. All
that happened was that Renthe-Fink and von Neubronn read out the
ultimatum once again – this time in Stucki's presence. That was the
end of the matter. Pétain's departure was fixed for the following
morning.

At first light on the 20th Ménétrel was up and about, packing up.
At 6 a.m. a detachment of German soldiers arrived in front of the
Hôtel du Parc. Soon a solitary tank parked opposite the entrance. At
about seven o'clock the soldiers had lost patience. They brushed aside
Pétain's bodyguard – Pétain had ordered them not to shoot – kicked
down the door and found Pétain still getting ready. The German

officer in charge was preparing to arrest him when Ménétrel intervened. Given the long journey which awaited him, and his age, he
thought that at least the Marshal should have some breakfast. The officer gave his assent. Coffee and bread were brought in and eaten in
silence – while Ménétrel was on the telephone to tell the Papal
Nuncio and the Swiss Ambassador about the turn of events.

At eight o'clock Pétain's personal car drew up in front of the
entrance. 'A small group of people', a bodyguard reported to his wife,
'were present, in silence, to see the scene which was to be played out.
The Marshal crossed the doorway, the revolving door having been
demolished, went down the front steps; but his face remained calm; he
raised his hat in greeting, as though to say "adieu", and climbed into
his car.'[19] The curtain had finally fallen on the drama that was Vichy.
Suitably, it was raining.

27

FROM PILLAR TO POST

'Des principes que j'enseignais, de toutes les choses que j'ai librement dit, je ne retire rien.'

The Pétain of the autumn of 1944 and the early spring of 1945 cuts a sorry figure. It was not just a question of age, although he was feeling all of his eighty-eight years. It was worse than that. On the pretext that his personal safety was in danger he had become, as he said himself, a German prisoner. He was no longer able to decide for himself or for his wife where he was to find any sort of a home, or where – or when – he might be directed to go to next. The only constant in this disrupted life was that he would under no circumstances be going back to Vichy.

In fact, he had already said his goodbyes to Vichy. His main goodbye, apart from yet another letter to Hitler protesting at his treatment, had been in the form of a text, written by the old follower of Maurras, Henri Massis, and corrected in Pétain's own hand. The document was not published, but it was reproduced as a poster and put up in various places – although its life was short, since it was soon torn down either by German soldiers or by the Resistance. In it, Pétain recounted his version of events since the defeat of May 1940 and the signature of the Armistice. He claimed that his whole objective had been to 'preserve the body and soul of France'. Not only that, but he asserted roundly that 'if it is true that de Gaulle has boldly raised the sword of France,

I have patiently been the shield [protecting] the French people'.[1] Needless to say, he failed to point out that the shield had not been particularly effective, not just in the current state of near anarchy in the country but – a permanent blot on his record – in the deportation, and in many cases subsequent extermination, of some seventy-five thousand Jews. But it was, after all, his own testament.

None the less, there was in the document a note of defiance. 'Of the principles which I taught, of all the things which I have freely' (the word is worth noting) 'said, I withdraw nothing.'

> It remains true that our country has committed errors against herself which were nearly fatal and which leave its future, for a certain time, compromised. It remains true that, if it persists in the same errors, it will not recover either its rank or its strength. It remains true that France and Germany, condemned by geography to be neighbours to eternity, will have to look, in an effort of mutual understanding, for the conditions of a peace which will last. Germany has known that she is powerless against a coalition; France has known that she could not struggle alone against her neighbour to the east; it is time for the nations of Europe to make up their mind that they do not want to die.[2]

It was a bold statement. (In truth, it could easily have been written by de Gaulle himself. The historical irony, of course, is that it charted a course which de Gaulle followed in the post-war era.) But even apart from this final show of defiance Pétain had started to regain some of the stubbornness of character which had been lost in the feeble compromises of Vichy. On 25 August, he made it clear that he no longer considered himself a head of state, and in consequence would only draw the salary due to him as a Marshal of France. Moreover, he became much more hostile in his resentment towards those whom, at last, he was prepared to recognise as his jailers.

The journey of Pétain and his – by then much diminished – party from Vichy to Belfort was, given the chaotic circumstances of the time, quite dreadful. It took four days, with stops at Saulieu and Dijon, before they were able to settle at the house of the industrialist – and senator – Louis Vieillard at Morvillars, a small village about fourteen kilometres from the centre of Belfort. (By way of an aside, it has

With Nini on the way to Sigmaringen. (*Lebrecht*)

been said that Mme Vieillard was in earlier years the object of Pétain's particular attentions.)

There were, to be sure, some minor compensations. At Belfort itself, a crowd of several thousand had assembled in front of the hôtel de ville in greeting. For them Pétain was the living symbol of French objection to the German oppression under which they all suffered. At Morvillars, too, the Mayor made a respectful speech, although it was rather spoiled by the presence of a sizeable detachment of German troops surrounding the premises. Less happy, perhaps, was Pétain's meeting with Laval, who had arrived at Belfort three days earlier, having told Abetz that he refused to transfer the seat of government from Vichy – thereupon being forcibly abducted and driven, like Pétain, to Belfort. They did agree, however, that neither of them would play any part in government. That would be left, if necessary, to the ultra-collaborationists who had followed in Laval's wake.

Pétain, his wife, Ménétrel and his private secretary, Victor Debeney, spent no more than two weeks at Morvillars. It was not a pleasant stay.

Pétain refused to see anybody other than those permitted by Debeney. He was 'tired, agitated and completely lacking in lucidity'.[3] At times, although physically fit for someone of his age, he seemed to have inexplicable lapses in memory. For instance, on 4 September 1944, he signed a letter to Laval demanding the resignation of his government. Laval, in reply, pointed out, with reason, that since Pétain had abandoned his rôle of head of state he had no powers to ask for anything, even the resignation of the government he had himself approved.

Yet Pétain, much as he might have wished, and occasionally confused as he was, could not escape the circumstance of the time. The Germans wanted to keep him in their pocket. Indeed, on 26 August 1944, the very day of de Gaulle's triumphal march down the Champs-Elysées to a victory ceremony in Notre-Dame, Hitler had sent for Laval. Laval refused the invitation, such as it was. In his stead, Marion, Darnand, Déat, Doriot and de Brinon went off to see, first Ribbentrop, and then, on 1 September, Hitler himself. The message they were given was clear. With his new weapons, Hitler was confident that he would turn the tide of the war. There must therefore be a new government in France. De Brinon – no less – was given the job of seeing Pétain to demand, in the name of the Führer, his endorsement of the new government.

Pétain's response was, for him, unusually robust. He stood firm. First, he refused to see de Brinon. Then he sent Ménétrel, worried, as always, that Pétain would concede, as he had so often in the past, to block de Brinon's way. Debeney was then put to the task of going into Belfort, to receive de Brinon's message and deliver a note in reply. But it was not to be as easy as that. As it happened, de Brinon had struck a sensitive chord. In his message he reminded Pétain of the plight of the French prisoners of war and of those Frenchmen who had been drafted to Germany for forced labour. It was indeed sensitive. It was a matter of those whom Pétain had proclaimed to be under his particular care. Pétain was bound to concede, in his revision of Debeney's note, that de Brinon had a point. The final version of Pétain's reply read that he had 'no objections to M. de Brinon continuing to deal with questions with which he had been previously occupied in respect of civilian interests'.[4]

Whatever that meant, it was Ménétrel who was sent in to Belfort to deliver the message. On 6 September, he read out to de Brinon the text of Pétain's note. It was, of course, heavily qualified – but it was more than enough for de Brinon. The following morning the German press issued a 'call to all Frenchmen', saying that 'Ambassador de Brinon, based on the role of General Delegate [to the Occupied Zone] which the Head of State had entrusted him with, has taken on the task of forming a Governmental Delegation for the defence of national interests'.[5] In this 'delegation', Déat was to be in charge of the maintenance of order, Darnand was to be in charge of defence and Jean Luchaire was to be in charge of information and propaganda.

By that point, the formation of any sort of French government verged on the ridiculous. There was no noticeable France which could be governed by the 'Delegation'. Not only was France itself largely in Allied hands but by then de Gaulle had received the endorsement of the United States. It was General Eisenhower, acting on clear instruction from President Roosevelt, who awarded the accolade. Eisenhower's visit to de Gaulle – on Sunday 27 August 1944 – was clear in its intent. 'I went to call on General de Gaulle promptly', Eisenhower later wrote, 'and I did this very deliberately as a kind of recognition of him as the provisional President of France.'[6] The political die was thus cast beyond any reasonable possibility of doubt. The United States, whatever Roosevelt's dislike of the man, had finally and unequivocally given its support to the unruly General. De Gaulle, in turn, was quick to take his cue. By 5 September he had started to put together a government of 'National Unity', and, on 9 September – after the customary haggling about ministerial posts – had announced his list of ministers.

But there was even more to it than that. When asked by Georges Bidault on 25 August, on the balcony of the Hôtel de Ville in Paris, to 'proclaim the Republic' de Gaulle cut Bidault down. 'The Republic', he said, 'has never ceased to exist . . . Why should I proclaim it?'[7] De Gaulle's view was clear. The vote of the National Assembly on 10 July 1940 was unconstitutional. It followed that the Vichy régime itself was outside the law and was only a 'parenthesis', as he put it, in the long history of the Third Republic. Whether de Gaulle's view was right or wrong – and it has, of course, been disputed down the years – there is no doubt that, in political reality, power in France had passed to de Gaulle and his new government.

In spite of all that was taking place in Paris – and in the real political world – the charade of the remains of what had been the Vichy government continued to play on what was by then a pantomime stage. Yet, pantomime though it might be, Belfort, and Morvillars, were in danger. By early September 1944, General George Patton's tanks were perilously near to Belfort. The result was predictable. Yet again, Pétain and his motley party were told to pack their bags – of course, for their own safety. They were to be transferred to Germany. Pétain wrote a furious letter of protest to Hitler, yet again to no avail, and Ménétrel wrote a farewell letter to his wife. On 7 September Pétain, Nini, Ménétrel and the accompanying party left Morvillars and were conveyed under heavy German escort across the frontier into Germany. They were followed by the group of so-called ministers in the new 'French Governmental Delegation', headed by de Brinon. The journey was, once more, miserable. The next day, they arrived at a small town on the upper Danube.

Sigmaringen was, and still is, with all its beauty, a small and – in political terms – insignificant town. At the time, the population was no more than some five thousand. The war, as almost everything else over the centuries, seemed to have passed it by. The town itself was overlooked by a grand castle. Originally the home of the Princes of Hohenzollern-Sigmaringen – cousins of the ruling family of Prussia – the medieval castle had been destroyed by fire in the 1850s. Rebuilt after the Franco-Prussian War on the same rock overlooking the bend in the River Danube, it was a truly massive example of dubious Prussian nineteenth-century taste. But not only was it ponderous in its architecture; it was also extremely inconvenient. The rooms were linked by long and draughty corridors. There were innumerable staircases and vast drawing rooms. All of them seemed to be no more than extended museums of medieval armour, hunting trophies, antique German furniture and large portraits of forgotten Prussian royalty. There was only one lift into which, it was said, a large motor car could be fitted. Nevertheless, unpleasant as it was, this was to be Pétain's new home. The last Marshal of France had thus become an unlikely resident of a Prussian castle; one, moreover, which had been constructed in the aftermath of the war in which, in Pétain's childhood, France had been decisively defeated.

Pétain and his party were allocated the top floor – the seventh – of the gloomy building. Laval was given the floor below. De Brinon and

Sigmaringen. (*Andrew Cowin-Travel Ink/Corbis*)

his 'delegation' were on the third floor. A newspaper entitled *France*, and a radio station called Ici La France, were run by Luchaire, relating and broadcasting news from the outside world. There were, as might be imagined, numerous squabbles. On 1 October, for instance, the French flag was raised, but both Pétain and Laval, in spite of pleas from Abetz and Renthe-Fink, refused to attend the ceremony. On 4 October de Brinon wrote an irritated letter to Pétain claiming that Ménétrel was undermining his authority. Pétain promptly stripped de Brinon of his *francisque* and wrote to him that he 'should desist from speaking in my name'.[8] He then told Renthe-Fink that he wanted to leave Sigmaringen so as not to continue to suffer the company of de Brinon and of the Milice who were guarding the gates of the castle. His request, needless to say, went unanswered.

It was not just a matter of squabbles and disputes about status. There was fear as well. As the Allies advanced there was much settling of scores in France. What was called the *épuration sauvage* of the summer and autumn of 1944 and the early months of 1945, a series of uncontrolled, random and mostly brutal attacks on those suspected of fraternising with the German occupiers, claimed some nine thousand lives before order was properly restored. There were summary judgements and improvised courts martial. Everybody in Sigmaringen knew what would happen to them if they fell into the hands of their liberated compatriots. The news from Luchaire was thus followed with both hope that Hitler's secret weapons would prevail and dreadful apprehension of the outcome should they fail. By late 1944, show trials were under way. On 10 November 1944 de Gaulle's provisional government set up a High Court of Justice to try all members of the 'governments or pseudo governments which had their seat on metropolitan territory . . . for crimes or offences committed in the exercise of or connected with their functions'.[9] It all sounded very sinister. For Pétain himself, however, there was some comfort in an opinion poll of October 1944. Whatever may be the doubts about the sampling techniques of the time, the message it conveyed was clear: when asked whether Pétain should be punished, 32% of respondents replied 'yes' but 58% replied 'no' (10% did not know).

In the light of all this Pétain, guarded from all visitors – except Abetz and Renthe-Fink, whom he was unable to refuse – by Ménétrel and Debeney, set to work to compile a series of memoranda in justification of all that he had done since the end of the First World War. His preliminary notes, in his own hand, cover his interventions in the Conseil Supérieur de la Guerre in the 1920, his period as a minister, his stay in Spain as Ambassador and, finally, the events of May 1940. Work was interrupted, however, when, on 22 November, Ménétrel was arrested by the SS while returning with Pétain from his daily walk. The arrest, in fact, hardly came as a surprise. Ménétrel had been a constant irritation to de Brinon and his colleagues, and Abetz suspected him of links with the Resistance. Pétain protested yet again – and yet again to no avail. Ménétrel was taken first to the little town of Scheer – and another castle – some ten kilometres south of Sigmaringen, before being transferred in March 1945 to the SS camp at Eisenberg in Bohemia. Pétain was never to see him again.

Pétain had lost – for ever – his doctor and his closest friend. Ménétrel's replacement as Pétain's doctor, the writer and collaborationist Louis-Ferdinand Céline, was not welcomed with any detectable warmth. Not only that, but the war, by the end of 1944 and the spring of 1945, had taken what was to be a decisive turn. On 16 December 1944 the

German Army launched its offensive in the Ardennes. Bold as it was, it was no more than a last throw. By Christmas it had stalled. On 30 January 1945 the Americans launched their own attack on the *Westwall* – the 'Siegfried Line' – and breached it on 4 February. On 22 March they crossed the Rhine at Mainz. On 30 March de Lattre de Tassigny's 1st French Army followed suit and, on 7 April, took Karlsruhe, no more than 120 kilometres to the north of Sigmaringen. They were under orders from de Gaulle to head for Stuttgart and the south. In a week or two, if there was no resistance, they would arrive at the River Danube. In short, they would arrive at Sigmaringen.

Pétain had made up his mind. On 5 April he had learned that all Vichy ministers, including himself, were to be tried by the High Court *in absentia*. This was unacceptable. He was determined to return to France and be tried in person. He therefore would wait for whoever arrived first, French or Americans – it mattered little – at Sigmaringen. He would request whoever came to repatriate him to France. There were moments, too, when he still thought that he could make peace with the Allies and de Gaulle. But the Germans had also made up their minds. They would not let him out of their sight. On the evening of 20 April Otto Reinebeck, a diplomat, and Kurt von Tannstein, an officer at Sigmaringen, who by then had replaced, respectively, Abetz and Renthe-Fink, told Pétain that he was going to be moved. Pétain protested, saying that he wanted to stay where he was and wait for Patton's or de Lattre's arrival. It was, he was told, out of the question. The Gestapo officer present said he would put Pétain in handcuffs if necessary. Pétain's protests were useless. Von Tannstein refused any further argument, and added that they were to move at four o'clock the next morning. In the mean time Pétain, his wife, Debeney and another aide, Admiral Bléhaut, were to be under guard. Yet again, there was nothing to do but fall in with the German demands.

The whole party left Sigmaringen the next morning – very nearly on time. Pétain took rather longer to get ready than the others, and their final departure was not until 4.30 a.m. In the darkness, two Gestapo cars led the gloomy cavalcade. Pétain and Nini followed in the next car, then Debeney in another, Bléhaut and his deputy, Commander Sacy, in a fifth car, a sixth being reserved for their baggage. Reinebeck and two Gestapo cars brought up the rear. Just in case any of the French party should have any unfortunate ideas, all four Gestapo cars bristled with machine guns. Pétain kept muttering that he wanted to go back to France. Nobody seemed to notice, or, indeed, to know where they were going.

At nine o'clock, after taking four and a half hours to cover 120 kilometres, owing to the chaos of a retreating German Army on the road and stoppages to avoid the attentions of Allied aircraft, the party arrived at a place which they were able to identify as the small town of Wangen. They had arrived, as it happened, in a place of beauty. In peacetime, this small town, in the upper valley of the River Argen, which flows south-westward for thirty kilometres or so to debouch into Lake Constance, would have been a pleasant enough place to alight. Pétain and his party, however, were in no mood to admire Wangen's attractions – the surrounding mountain scenery, the Town Hall, particularly its medieval doors, and the Herrenstrasse, with its old merchant houses and its fountains. They only wanted to know where they were to be going next. Their German escort was mute. 'We will see . . .' was the only answer they got.[10]

Needless to say, nobody in Wangen had been warned of their arrival. Since it was bitterly cold, they were all hustled into the Town Hall. The Mayor was summoned and duly appeared, looking flustered at the sudden arrival in his sleepy town of such a distinguished group. He only managed a few stuttering words of welcome. Outside, a crowd was gathering, to stare at the group as though they were 'curious beasts'.[11] The only way the Mayor could disperse them was to sound an air-raid warning. At the sound of the siren the crowd disappeared – as were their instructions in such an event – to their own homes. The Mayor then took Pétain's group to his own home where, apparently, his wife and daughters gave them coffee, bread and Bavarian sausages. For what it was worth, the hospitality was welcome, but, huddled together as they were in the unheated house, the only thought in their minds was where – yet again – they would to be going next.

It was another hour before anybody told them. It was to be to Zeil. There was a fine castle there (belonging, they were told, to the most distinguished gentleman, the Prince von Waldburg) where they were to stay for the rest of the day and one night. Immediately, maps were brought out, and a consultation followed. The conclusion was clear. Far from going south-west to Bregenz and the Swiss frontier, as they had expected, they were going north-east towards Ulm. By now confused as well as distraught, they decided that they were to be taken to the Bavarian redoubt, where Pétain thought Hitler would make his last stand.

On the evening of 21 April, they were all escorted, with the now customary attendance of Gestapo cars and machine guns, to the Prinz von Waldburg's castle at Zeil. In other times, they might have enjoyed the beautiful views from the terraces of the castle. But this was not the moment since, on the morning of 22 April, they learned that the Americans had taken Ulm – and were advancing southwards. It looked as though Pétain's group would be cut off from the Bavarian redoubt and soon overrun by the American forward detachments.

Pétain was quite happy to stay put, take a much needed rest, and wait for them. But at ten o'clock that evening, von Tannstein sent for Debeney and told him to get his party ready to move again. When he heard this, Pétain sent Debeney back to von Tannstein with a message. The message was simple. Pétain refused to move.

At midnight, von Tannstein demanded to see Pétain himself. The others could only listen at the door of Debeney's room, where the meeting was to be held. It started off crisply enough. Von Tannstein explained that the military situation required an immediate departure. Pétain replied that he would not leave. Von Tannstein repeated that an immediate departure was necessary 'to ensure the security of your person'.[12] Pétain was firm. He would not leave. He would wait there for the arrival of French or American troops. He added that his personal security was not in danger. Von Tannstein tried another tactic. He said that he had to obey orders and he pleaded with Pétain to allow him to do so.

At that point, Pétain lost his temper. It was one o'clock in the morning and he was tired. 'It's useless,' he almost shouted. 'You have done nothing but lie to me since Vichy. Where do you want to take me?'[13] When von Tannstein replied that it was to the Swiss frontier, Pétain said he did not believe him, and would not believe him unless he could show that the Swiss authorities had given permission to enter Switzerland. That could be arranged when they got there, was the reply. Pétain said again that he did not believe it, that he had no confidence in von Tannstein at all, that he had always been deceived, that Renthe-Fink had always lied to him. In short, he was staying put.

Von Tannstein became angry in his turn. There followed a heated discussion about German good faith, which lasted the best part of an hour. Bléhaut and Nini were brought into the debate. Nini said that Pétain was tired and needed rest. Bléhaut said that he was sure that they were to be taken to the Bavarian redoubt. Finally, von Tannstein admitted that those were his orders, but that on their own initiative they had decided to deliver Pétain to the Swiss frontier. Nini asked what the German government would think of that. 'There is no government any more,' von Tannstein replied.[14]

At that point, in the middle of the night, their host the Prinz von Waldburg suddenly – and unexpectedly – appeared. He came with the news, which he had heard on the telephone, that French tanks were only twenty kilometres from Zeil. The Prinz's sudden appearance had an immediate effect. Pétain said again that he would wait for the French tanks, and that, moreover, he was now going to bed, and that was the end of the matter.

But he did not have much sleep. At a quarter to six, Reinebeck and von Tannstein burst into Pétain's bedroom. He must leave immediately. He refused. Not only did he refuse; he refused even to get out of bed, saying that he was old and tired – and that he would stay where he was. Only if they could assure him that the Swiss authorities had given their consent would he budge. Reinebeck calmed him down by saying that consent had been requested and would arrive that afternoon. The reply was simple: until and unless the Swiss consent was given in proper form he, Pétain, would stay in bed for a much-needed rest.

Reinebeck was right. The consent from the Swiss Federal Council arrived at around seven in the evening, with the proviso that Pétain sign an assurance that he would stay in the premises allocated to him in Swizerland until the French authorities indicated that they were ready to receive him on French territory. At 10.30 p.m. the whole party gathered itself together, left Zeil, made its way through dense traffic – lorries pulled by tractors, horses, bicycles – and a mass of refugees, and arrived at Bregenz at three the following morning. Rooms were provided, with bad grace by the owner, in a small hotel. At 8 a.m. they were up, not least woken by bombs falling on Bregenz. By 9.30 a.m. the air raid had passed and it was safe to leave. They drove the last ten kilometres to the Swiss frontier, fearful lest they be spotted by Allied aircraft. At 10 a.m. on 24 April 1945, almost on the hour, in four cars, they crossed into Switzerland. That day, Pétain also entered into his ninetieth year.

Pétain's birthday arrival in Switzerland was duly reported to Paris. De Gaulle was immediately informed. For him, given the old relationship, the matter was not easy. In truth, de Gaulle wanted Pétain just to go away and not reappear. But his own government thought itself obliged, such was the ferment of the time, to demand Pétain's extradition to France. De Gaulle then made it known – through the normal unidentifiable channels – that it would be welcome if the Swiss courts could refuse extradition. In that case, Pétain and his wife would pass the remainder of their days in the safety of Switzerland. It was even mooted that if there was a financial problem in maintaining a reasonable Pétain establishment in Switzerland the problem could be resolved without difficulty.

But the problem for the Swiss was that Pétain, far from opposing extradition, was only too anxious for it. The court in Bern took due note of this, and without delay approved an extradition order. Moreover, the order was to be executed immediately. Pétain was to be out of Switzerland as soon as possible. But this was not altogether easy to achieve. The first stop was at a hotel in the little town of Wessen on the Walensee, the brooding lake in almost perpetual shadow from the rock bastions of the Churfisten. The following morning Walter Stucki, by then in charge of the Foreign Affairs Department of the Swiss government, paid Pétain a visit. He was to arrange transit for Pétain and his wife by the most direct route across Switzerland to the French frontier at Vallorbe.

On the morning of 26 April Pétain and his wife said goodbye to the well-wishers of the hotel at Wessen and to his own staff (Debeney was to stay behind to pay the bill – with money provided by Stucki). The route was supposed to be a secret, but their route through Switzerland from east to west was lined by crowds cheering him on, throwing flowers as he passed, and even giving him, just outside Brienne, a cask of wine, as a belated birthday present, for his picnic. They finally arrived, at 4.45 on the evening of 26 April, at the Swiss frontier station of Vallorbe. Nini was asked by a French official whether she wished to accompany her husband as there was no warrant out for her arrest. She replied that under no circumstances would she be separated from him. So it was that at 7.26 precisely, Philippe Pétain and his wife Eugénie, leaving their Swiss escort behind, crossed into France. The Marshal of France, as he had said he would, had returned to defend his honour.

28

LET JUSTICE BE DONE?

'Le vieux Maréchal ne pouvait douter qu'il allait être condamné.'

Pétain's decision to return to France in April 1945 to face his accusers in person was certainly courageous, as de Gaulle was later to write. Some would describe it as foolhardy. He knew perfectly well that as long ago as 3 September 1943 the CFLN in Algiers had, by decree under the signatures of Giraud and de Gaulle, proclaimed him guilty of treason for having sought, and agreed to, the Armistice of 1940. Furthermore, on 9 August 1944 the CFLN had declared null and void 'all Constitutional Acts . . . promulgated on continental territory after 16 June 1940' – the day de Gaulle had left for London.[1] Moreover, even if he had thought that he might surmount the judicial and political obstacles and do some sort of deal with de Gaulle, he had only to look at the fate of one of his ministers, Pierre Pucheu, who had arrived in Algiers under safe conduct signed by Giraud but who had been arrested, tried by a military court, convicted (on dubious evidence) and executed on 20 March 1944. In short, nobody could have possibly said that the omens were anything other than unfavourable.

And yet, at the end of his trial, the three judges proposed Pétain's acquittal on all the charges laid against him. Furthermore, their joint advice and their own votes went against the death penalty, which, in the event, was passed by a majority of only one. Botched prosecution, rambling evidence and some clever and emotional defence almost achieved what at the outset appeared to be beyond the limits of any reasonable possibility. The result in itself was the stuff of drama, but, as it happened, the whole trial turned out to be one of the most extraordinary judicial, political – and theatrical – events in modern French history.

The special train carrying Pétain and his wife from the Swiss frontier towards Paris travelled through the night. There had been an ugly episode at Pontarlier, where the train had stopped. Stones were thrown at his carriage and those who had been able to get close to the train had spat at his windows. Pétain was badly shaken but, fortunately for him, the train sped on without further incident. Early in the morning of 27 April it arrived at the little station of Igny. Pétain and his wife were then driven to the old fort of Montrouge, south of Paris, whose security had been hastily reinforced for the occasion. Pétain was locked in a small cell in which the only furniture was a bed, a cupboard and a bedside table. He was told by the governor, Joseph Simon, that he was to be given no special privileges and was not to be allowed to receive messages or presents. He was permitted to leave his cell for an hour each day for exercise. His food was standard prison fare, but, as a concession, a doctor was on hand if required. To his wife – and she certainly had a case – it seemed to be a deliberate attempt to humiliate a great figure, not least a Marshal of France.

The procedure leading to the trial was by today's standards, to put it mildly, far from satisfactory. The High Court of Justice, itself only appointed by a provisional government without any democratic mandate, had in turn nominated a commission to interrogate the accused. There was no public say on who should be members of the commission and how they should act. Nevertheless, on the afternoon of 30 April its chairman, Pierre Bouchardon, a convinced opponent of Pétain hauled out of retirement for the purpose, arrived at Montrouge to claim authority for the procedure of interrogation which was to follow. Pétain in reply asked Bouchardon for a list of lawyers from which he might select his defence counsel. This was promised. Yet on 8 May (coincidentally the day on which Germany surrendered) Bouchardon returned to Montrouge with a series of questions to which he required immediate replies. He omitted to tell Pétain that he was entitled to refuse to answer questions without the presence of a lawyer. Unaware of his rights, and as yet without legal advice, Pétain signed his consent.

Bouchardon's questioning was overtly hostile. He challenged Pétain immediately. There was, first of all, the vote of 10 July 1940. Bouchardon did not doubt the legitimacy of the vote but attacked the aftermath. Pétain's replies were long and confused. They were a combination of self-justification, in many respects inadvertently – or possibly deliberately – erroneous, and memory lapse – the two, as is frequent in old men, going together.

So far, so bad. But the situation, bad as it then was, had not gone beyond hope of retrieval. Bouchardon had transmitted Pétain's request for legal representation to Jacques Charpentier, the serving President of the Paris Bar. Charpentier visited Montrouge to discuss the matter with Pétain. Their final choice was Fernand Payen, a most distinguished former President of the Bar but who, at the age of seventy-three, was perhaps past his best (apart from all else, he had developed a disconcerting facial tic). In turn, on the recommendation of Pétain's old friend Henry Lémery, Payen chose as his junior the young, thirty-four-year-old, Jacques Isorni, who had caught attention in leading a spirited – but unsuccessful – defence of the collaborationist writer René Brasillach.

On 16 May, Payen and Isorni attended Pétain's second interrogation at Montrouge. Bouchardon was even more aggressive and Pétain even more confused. The more intense the questioning, the less coherent were the prisoner's replies. He even looked appealingly at his lawyers in the hope that they would answer on his behalf. But Payen had decided that both lawyers should stay silent. This was no accident. His strategy for Pétain's defence was to plead senility, and to lay the whole blame for what had happened on Laval – at the time, conveniently, a refugee in Spain. As they left Montrouge, Payen, in the best of humours, was supremely confident in his strategy, pointing out to Isorni that the whole interview had been in itself no more and no less a complete justification of what he had been saying all along. 'Senility' was the only proper defence.

Isorni did not agree. Without even bothering to request authorisation from Payen, he bicycled to Montrouge early the next morning and demanded to see the prisoner. Simon allowed him in – and agreed to keep this sudden visit secret. Pétain was nervous, but when he joined Isorni in the room assigned for the interrogation he was relieved to find Isorni ready and willing to speak up frankly and freely. There was no question of silence. Isorni urged the old man to stand up for himself – to cease to look like 'a gardener accused of stealing vegetables'.[2] When Pétain asked what would be done with him, Isorni simply replied: 'You will be condemned to death.'[3]

Instead of pushing him further into the mood of gloom in which he had been mired ever since the crowd had thrown stones at his train at Pontarlier, Isorni's outspokenness brought Pétain back to life. In short, the old warrior at that point decided to fight. Immediately, the two sat down to plan the defence. Far from being confused, Pétain was now clear in his mind. True, there were lapses of memory, but otherwise he was completely lucid. Together, they went through the whole history of events. Isorni made notes, constantly jogging Pétain's failing memory. In turn, once Isorni had left, Pétain dutifully copied them out in his own hand – so that Payen, when he was presented with them, would think they were all his own work.

Over the next three days, usually in the mornings when Pétain was at his most alert, Isorni came back to Montrouge to spend many hours with the prisoner. Sometimes he made two trips a day. On 21 May, however, while he was closeted with his client patiently going through the history of events – and urging Pétain to try harder to remember precisely what had happened and when – Payen arrived unexpectedly. Furiously, he demanded to know what Isorni was doing there. Isorni had no reply, and was almost prepared to plead guilty. But it was Pétain himself who saved the day. Smiling at Payen, he said that he had not wished to disturb his senior counsel for matters of minor detail and had requested Simon to invite his junior. Whether Payen believed him or not will never be known. Nevertheless, there is no doubt that from that day onwards there was no love lost between the two counsels. In fact, the choice of a third lawyer to complete the required three-man team for the defence was to show the extent of the differences between the senior and the junior.

Inexorably, the interrogation continued. By early June Pétain was very tired. The constant interrogations exhausted him, to the point where the prison doctor intervened to request Bouchardon not to insist on two sessions in one day. But there was more to come. On 1 June the whole Commission turned up, twenty judges, magistrates and members of the Resistance. The meeting was, understandably, chaotic. Everybody seemed to be talking at once. Nothing of consequence was achieved. There was a repeat performance on 8 June, equally chaotic. Each commissioner, on both occasions, wanted to have his say, frequently at inordinate length. Most of the speeches consisted of assertions rather than questions. Payen tried his best, but to no effect, to deflect the attack by demanding in turn that other witnesses be heard, in particular Leahy and Stucki.

By then, the whole procedure was in confusion. Pétain was on the point of collapse, his lawyers were bickering, the commissioners were making speeches rather than putting questions, much of the proceedings were liberally reported in the press and the communist newspapers filled their columns with repeated insistence that the only possible penalty for Pétain – already and quite obviously, of course, guilty of the most horrendous treason – was death by firing squad.

By early June Pétain had the third lawyer in his defence team. Isorni had wanted to recruit Pierre Véron, a well known and well liked former member of the Resistance. When sounded out, Véron agreed to join Pétain's team only on the understanding that he could not defend the race laws or the deportation of Jews. Both Isorni and Pétain accepted his conditions, and on 2 June Pétain wrote to him formally inviting him to act for him – with a copy to Payen. But Payen immediately interposed a veto. It was unacceptable, he said, for a supporter of de Gaulle to be part of Pétain's defence team. The next day he nominated, as replacement, his old friend Jean Lemaire.

Lemaire was, in character, the opposite to both Payen and Isorni. Where Payen was ponderous and heavy-handed, Lemaire could easily dissolve into irreverent giggles. Where Isorni was intense and highly strung, Lemaire could be calm and dispassionate. Calmness and giggles were just what Isorni needed, and he and Lemaire immediately struck up a friendship – much to Payen's irritation. In fact, the two got on so well that Isorni told Lemaire of his confidential meetings with Pétain. Thereafter, the two went together to Montrouge, huddled together in Lemaire's small Simca car, laughing, apparently, most of the way.

The serious business was about to get under way. On 17 June, the anniversary of de Gaulle's flight to London in 1940, the High Court assumed its full legal competence – to try those who had previously been deemed to be traitors. Nevertheless, whatever was or was not its constitutional competence, the court itself was a very odd affair. It consisted of a president, who was at the same time President of the highest Court of Appeal, two fellow judges sitting beside him, respectively the President of the Criminal Division of the Court of Appeal and the President of the Court of Appeal of Paris, and twenty-four lay members.

The lay members – *jurés* in French (translated conveniently but incorrectly into English as 'jurors', since they were allowed to intervene in debates as full members of the court) – were selected by lot from two groups: the first was a group of fifty, chosen by the Constituent Assembly from a list of the eighty parliamentarians who had voted against Pétain and Laval on 10 July 1940; the second was a group of fifty, supposedly freely chosen by the Constituent Assembly but in practice with heavy reliance on a list of members of the Resistance put forward by the commission appointed to oversee the 'cleansing of the state'. Since the (unelected) Assembly consisted of those who, one way or another, had escaped the Vichy régime, it is hardly surprising that the final lists, ratified on 24 February 1945, consisted entirely of Pétain's opponents. As Charpentier himself put it, 'the *jurés* were mostly people of good faith, but what impartiality could the accused expect from somebody who had been deported and who had returned from Buchenwald or from a mother whose son had been shot by the Milice?'.[4]

Matters were made more complicated by an unexpected difficulty in finding a president for the High Court. The sitting President of the Court of Appeal was himself in prison, and nobody else wanted to take on the job. It took seven refusals before somebody was found. The final choice was Paul Mongibeaux; and he was to be flanked by Judge Donat-Gigue and Judge Picard. The difficulty, of course, was that all three of them had taken an oath of allegiance to Pétain personally. Furthermore, Donat-Gigue was a personal friend of Pétain and his wife. Finally, it became evident that the public prosecutor who was to launch the case against Pétain, André Mornet, had not only prosecuted the alleged spy, the glamourous Mata Hari, in 1917 – which much amused the Paris wags – but had applied to be a prosecutor in the Riom trials. (Fortunately for him his request was turned down.)

On 21 July, two days before the trial started, the three defence lawyers attended the procedure of choosing by lot twenty-four jurors, twelve from each group. Lemaire objected to three of those chosen on the grounds that they were communist. One of those rejected shouted, 'that will not prevent the traitor Pétain from getting twelve bullets in the skin!'.[5] There was then a near riot, and Mongibeaux had to intervene to calm things down. What none of the defence lawyers spotted, however, was that one of the parliamentarians was a Communist. His party, supported by their own press, screamed daily for the death penalty. As it happened, the oversight was to prove a costly error.

Much to the indignation of the Parisian public, de Gaulle had decided that the trial should be in a relatively small hall – the First Chamber of the Court of Appeal. The public was expecting a grand event, similar, for instance, to the trials of the Revolution, but de Gaulle refused to allow Pétain to be subject to such popular indignity. In fact, he regarded the whole thing as a 'painful business'.[6] The daily reports to him during the trial from the Minister of Justice, Pierre-Henri Teitgen, were received in the deepest gloom. 'Do your duty,' de Gaulle told him, 'do your duty.'[7]

On 22 July, Pétain and his wife were moved from Montrouge to rooms in the Palais de Justice. The previous day Pétain had summoned his notary to make a new will. He had heard nothing from his relatives in the Pas-de-Calais – as far as they were concerned he seemed to have ceased to exist. His new will was therefore quite simple. His family was to be cut out altogether and his whole estate was to go to Nini and, in the course of time, to his – much disliked – stepson, Pierre de Hérain.

The move from Montrouge was not easy. Pétain and Nini had packed a small suitcase. They were then piled into what was colloquially known as a 'salad basket', the customary vehicle for transferring common criminals – a large but simple black lorry with no windows. There Pétain was put with his two guards, while Nini sat in the front next to the driver. When they arrived at their destination, they found that they were to be put up in the office of the clerk to the Court of Appeal. The window had been barred for the purpose and two iron hospital beds had been installed. There was a washroom next door to the room, but the facilities were little more than primitive. Yet it had to do, since, on the following afternoon, Pétain's trial was to begin.

The morning of 23 July 1945 dawned dry and hot. Paris was in the middle of a heatwave. Even the asphalt in the streets was melting. A storm threatened, but never arrived. By mid-morning the courtroom in the Palais de Justice was an oven. But none of this deterred those who were determined to witness in person what the press called, rightly, a historic trial. By midday the room was full. In the spectators' gallery, people, even distinguished diplomats come to see the fun, were squashed together like very uncomfortable sardines. In the press gallery, journalists were reduced almost to sitting on their neighbours' knees. At 1 p.m. precisely, Pétain entered the courtroom, followed by his three lawyers. On their advice, he appeared in a simple blue uniform, wearing only France's highest military honour, the Médaille Militaire. In his left hand he held his marshal's képi and in his right a roll of paper. It was a dignified entrance. Old as he looked, he held himself upright as he walked to an armchair placed facing the bench on which the judges would sit. The chattering crowd suddenly fell silent, and then, one by one until it became a wave, stood up. Once arrived at his chair, Pétain sat down carefully, placed his képi, gloves and the roll of paper on the table in front of him. 'A sort of abstract sorrow,' *France-Soir* wrote, 'not addressed to mankind . . .'[8] After he had sat down, the onlookers sat down as well – and the chattering started again.

At ten past one the judges entered, robed in the manner required by the court – but sweating heavily in the heat. They were followed by a bustling Mornet, who climbed up to his seat and sat down 'like a vulture settling in his nest'.[9] Immediately, Mongibeaux opened the proceedings. He made what he called a 'declaration'.[10] He wished the trial to take place in serenity and dignity. With this – most optimistic – observation he told Pétain to stand up. This Pétain did and, when asked his name, replied simply: 'Pétain, Philippe, Marshal of France.'[11]

Payen intervened immediately. He made a long speech claiming that the court was not competent to judge the case. He argued that the 1875 Constitution, which was still in place, required that the Senate, sitting as a court, was the only body that could legitimately try the President, the Head of State, for treason. The order of 13 November, setting up the present court, could not possibly alter that. Besides, the judges had taken a personal oath of allegiance to the defendant. On both those grounds, the court should declare itself not competent. Mornet, in reply, pointed out that the oath meant nothing. The judges then retired. At a quarter to three they returned with the decision that they were indeed competent to try the case, since they had been specifically instructed to do so. Right or wrong, Mongibeaux then ordered the indictment to be read.

The final indictment was a curious document, a mixture of fact, opinion and, on occasions, accusations of guilt by association. It was in two parts, the first drawn up in Algiers and the second reflecting Pétain's subsequent interrogation. It started with a recital of events surrounding the Armistice, went on to the vote of 10 July 1940 and then, suddenly, laid the charge that Pétain had been previously plotting against the Republic for many years. As an illustration of the style of the indictment, it quoted a M. Winkler, director of a press agency, who 'related the following conversation reported to him by one of the Marshal's guests – a conversation which he had during a luncheon with the son of Primo de Rivera: "You judge us Frenchmen from the angle of the Popular Front. Wait till next spring; we, too, shall have our national revolution, in the same manner as yours."'[12]

Oddly enough, there was in the indictments no mention at all of the three crimes of which Pétain's régime at Vichy could with justice be accused: the racial laws and subsequent deportation of Jews, the forced labour of Frenchmen sent to Germany to work in appalling conditions, and the terror organised by the Milice. None of those appeared in the main indictment and its supplementary. Since there was no reference to them, Pétain's role in each of them was, at first sight, apparently not to be explored.

It need hardly be said that there were reasons for the omissions. There was, of course, a problem about the Jews. There was no reason to believe that 'liberated France' would be less harsh in its general attitude towards Jews than Vichy. What was objectionable was the inhuman treatment to which they had been subjected. Yet none of the prosecutors in Pétain's trial felt able to bring the matter up. Mongibeaux himself had dispensed justice in Vichy, it was said, 'with a serene conscience'.[13] In other words, the whole subject was a matter of embarrassment, and should be passed over.

The Service de Travail Obligatoire, the system which had obliged

Frenchmen to go to work in Germany, was equally delicate. True, there is in the indictments a short paragraph reproaching 'the Marshal's Government with having contributed to the working of the German war machine, by voluntarily supplying it with products and man-power',[14] but there was no mention of the conditions under which the 'manpower' was forced to work. (In fact, it was the return of the forced labourers, in their bedraggled state, which turned public opinion, if the polls are to be believed, against Pétain.) The trial judges had – when they were at Vichy – made no recorded objection either to the legality of forced labour or to its consequences.

As for the Milice, the indictments are silent. Again, this was a matter of profound embarrassment to the three judges and the Public Prosecutor. They were, after all, there – on the spot. They knew what was going on as well as anybody and had failed to take a stand, even to the point of registering their objections. To bring the whole thing up at this stage would have offered to the defence an open line of attack on the – very sustainable – grounds of hypocrisy.

De Gaulle was not pleased with the indictments and with the conduct of the early stages of the trial. He believed, as he later wrote, that 'the capital fault of Pétain and his government was to have concluded with the enemy, in the name of France, the so-called "armistice" . . . [all the rest] flowed infallibly from this poisoned source'.[15] Yet the trial went on regardless. At the end of the reading of the indictments, the clerk read out the list of those who were to be witnesses and, when they had been told to leave the court, Mongibeaux announced that he was proceeding, as was the custom, to the interrogation of the accused. He asked whether, in view of his great age, Pétain wanted a break. Payen replied that, far from wanting a break, the defendant wished to make a statement. Leave was granted.

Pétain's statement had been prepared – by Isorni – with the utmost care. It went through several drafts, had been revised in discussion, copied out by Pétain in large letters which he would be able to see without his spectacles – and then had been learned by heart. He recited it in a clear voice, starting rather shakily but gathering confidence as he went along. But although Isorni had done his best it was not a happy affair. It was long on his old assertion of his sacrifice to his country and short on explanations of why he had allowed what had been done in his name. He claimed, for instance, that 'the Armistice had saved France and contributed to the victory of the Allies in ensuring a free Mediterranean and the integrity of the [French] Empire', that 'For [the French people] I went as far as to sacrifice my prestige', and that 'While General de Gaulle, outside our frontiers, continued the struggle, I prepared the ways to liberation, in conserving a France sad but alive.'[16] There was no mention of the anti-Jewish laws and deportations, of forced labour or of the Milice (which was perhaps excusable given that they had not been mentioned in the indictment, but perhaps not sensible, in that they were on the minds of much of his audience).

Pétain's speech lasted seven minutes. He had opened by saying that he would make this one speech and then remain silent. He closed by saying that if he was condemned it would be the condemnation of an innocent who would bear the whole burden, 'since a Marshal of France asks pardon from nobody'.[17]

He sat down to silence in the courtroom. Immediately thereafter, first Isorni and then Lemaire attacked, Isorni on the insufficient time given to prepare the trial and the fact that there were still trunkloads of relevant documents which had not even been unpacked, let alone shown to the defence, adding for good measure that Mornet had announced prior to the trial that he would be seeking the death penalty. Lemaire followed up by a personal attack on Mornet, quoting an interview given by Mornet on 28 April to the newspaper L'Aurore. Mornet tried to rebut Lemaire but when there was some shouting in the gallery he made the mistake of saying that 'there are really too many Germans in this room',[18] a remark which was greeted by uproar, some in the crowd applauding and others booing and hissing. There followed an angry exchange between the defence lawyers and Mornet on whether or not Mornet should withdraw his remark. There was a crescendo of noise as the exchange continued, to the point where Mongibeaux ordered the suspension of the sitting and the public galleries to be cleared. In the general confusion a young captain with only one arm leaped over the barrier and ran to shake Pétain's hand. The lawyers withdrew in indignation to listen to the soothing mediation of Charpentier, who had been called in, as the sitting President of the Paris Bar, to settle the matter amicably.

When the court met again, Lemaire picked another row, this time with Mongibeaux himself. He cited an article which had appeared in the *Franc-Tireur* of 21 July, in which Mongibeaux had said to a reporter that 'it is necessary to dispel the equivocation which wishes to make Pétain the man who had tried to save what he could of our unfortunate country but, on the contrary, he who, to satisfy his personal ambition and his political views, advanced himself to the point of treason'.[19] Lemaire wanted a formal denial from Mongibeaux that he had ever said what was reported. Mongibeaux tried to defend himself by saying that he was not in the habit of issuing denials about newspaper articles. But Lemaire, in spite of Payen's tugs at his gown to try to get him to shut up, persisted. Mornet then launched into another defence of the court. After that, the session was again suspended while Mongibeaux and his two colleagues considered the matter.

The upshot of their consideration was that the trial should continue but that Mongibeaux – no doubt to preserve him from further embarrassment – should not proceed along the normal pattern of such trials in setting out in detail the charges against the accused. Consequently, the first witness for the prosecution should be called. By that time, Pétain, who had tried to hear what was going on by cupping his hand over his only viable – left – ear, appeared to have fallen asleep.

The first witness for the prosecution was Paul Reynaud. But it soon became clear that this 'short, elegant figure in a pinstriped suit with a large pocket handkerchief, narrow-eyed, his shiny, wavy hair barely turning grey'[20] was only speaking in self-justification. After the first wearisome hours of his evidence, Mongibeaux decided to call it a day, and the court adjourned. But Reynaud was determined to continue, and did so on the following day. In all, his evidence, admittedly with many interventions from the defence lawyers, lasted over five hours. The one name, however, which he did not mention when the Armistice was discussed was that of Mme de Portes. (Since she was not only Reynaud's mistress but an enthusiastic supporter of the Armistice, the defence missed a trick.) None the less, Reynaud came out, at the end of what, for him, had been a long day, badly damaged – particularly when it was revealed that he had agreed to be Pétain's ambassador to the United States, until Laval's hostility to the idea made him change his mind. It was no surprise that the defence lawyers questioned him closely, and that the lay members of the court – let alone these in the public gallery – had barracked him throughout.

There were to be many such noisy scenes over the three weeks of the trial. There were also revelations of attempts by Pétain's supporters to coerce the jurors into a favourable decision. They were bombarded with hate mail (and worse). Their food had to be checked each day for possible poisoning. At one point the word spread that an unofficial commando group was going to kidnap the jurors, and they were all issued with revolvers and live ammunition. Mongibeaux's call for serenity had quite plainly fallen on deaf ears.

In spite of these diversions, the proceedings continued. Next in line was Daladier who, rightly, asserted that in May 1940 the French Army had not been short of the tools of warfare – tanks, artillery and so on. Their generals had just not known how to use them. Then it was the turn of Lebrun, followed by Jeanneney, Louis Marin, Armand Gazel, the counsellor in Pétain's Madrid embassy, Blum (the most thoughtful and elegant of the prosecution witnesses), Charles-Roux, Michel Clemenceau, General Paul-André Doyen (the first head of the Armistice Commission in Wiesbaden) and a number of figures of lesser importance. Their evidence occupied the remainder of the first week of the trial, but, apart from rambling about, switching from pre-war history to the Armistice, to Vichy and back again to pre-war history, did not add much to what was already known. Each in turn was defending his – or on one occasion her – own role in the melancholy decline of the Third Republic.

By the end of the first week boredom had set in. The press, which had reported extensively the proceedings of the first day – there had been an extra allocation of newsprint for the purpose – started to take less of an interest and to cover other stories more fully. But the thing was none the less vicious. Anonymous letters poured in. The Veterans of Verdun demanded an immediate acquittal. All three defence lawyers received death threats – from both sides. In all this, it was noted that Pétain had not only said nothing ('a Maginot Line of silence', one newspaper commented)[21] but seemed not to hear very much of what was going on and at times was quite clearly asleep.

When the court resumed on the following Monday, 30 July, the last witness for the prosecution appeared. It was Édouard Herriot, yet another veteran of the Third Republic. In spite of a painful attack of gout – he was obliged to keep one of his feet in a slipper – he chose to give his evidence standing up. This was a mistake. In considerable pain,

The trial: Pétain tries to hear what is going on. (*Keystone*)

The trial: Isorni pleads. (*AFP*)

and breathing hard, he was 'alternately vague, bombastic, short-winded, shrill and tearful'.[22] He was no match for Isorni, who reminded him at length that it was he who had woken Pétain in the middle of the night of 17 to 18 June 1940 to demand that his home city of Lyon be declared an open city. Moreover, after the Armistice, Herriot had made a speech in the Council of Ministers on 9 July to any recalcitrant colleagues that they should gather 'around Marshal Pétain, united in the veneration which his name inspires in everybody . . . Take care to avoid disturbing the accord which has been established under his authority.'[23] It was very embarrassing for Herriot. But by that time Pétain had again dozed off. At the end of Herriot's evidence, Mongibeaux asked Pétain if he had anything to say, adding, 'This is the period when he does not hear, but I am obliged to put the question to him.'[24]

That done, it was time for the defence to put their own witnesses forward. There was a long stream of them, nearly fifty in all. But quantity did not make for quality, and, if the defence had come successfully through the first week of the trial, their position was weakened

The trial: Herriot accuses. (*Time Life Pictures/Getty Images*)

by the irrelevance of much of the evidence they put forward. There was, however, a good start. The first witness, Loustanau-Lacau, said immediately that he owed Pétain nothing. Indeed, he had been sacked in early 1940 from Pétain's office, had been arrested by Weygand in May 1941, had escaped and taken to the hills, had been rearrested and handed over to the SS, had spent six months working in the caves of the notorious Commandant Geissler, had undergone fifty-eight interrogations, had been condemned to death and transferred to the camp at Mauthausen. He was freed just in time, but not before his body had been broken and his face laced with scars. He was unable to walk without the aid of sticks. It was all the more impressive, then, when he asserted roundly that Pétain had never been involved with the Cagoule, that he had known nothing of the 1937 plot to overthrow the government of the day. He finished by saying that 'as for Marshal Pétain, I wish to say that, although he dropped me in a disgusting manner, I ask here that everybody reflect that, for France's misfortune, the blood of Marie-Antoinette and Marshal Ney is enough'.[25]

It was then time for Weygand, who took the stand in the afternoon of 31 July, saluting Pétain as he walked past him leaning on his stick. (Pétain returned the salute.) Weygand was, as usual – and in spite of his age and the fact that he had just come from the prison hospital – robust and direct. But he was also very long-winded, explaining in full the history of events leading up to the Armistice and defending his actions and those of Pétain. His first statement lasted three hours. He did, however, manage to make perfectly clear the difference between 'armistice' and 'capitulation'. Since the surrender of Marshal Bazaine at Metz in the Franco-Prussian War 'capitulation' was the gravest offence a commander in the field could commit, punishable by death. In fact, he went on, if France had 'capitulated' the whole country would have been occupied and the fleet seized. Not only that, but the way would have been open for the German Army to march through Spain – occupying Gibraltar and handing it to Spain as the reward – and to land in Morocco. The whole of North Africa would have been lost. The same would have happened if the French Army had fought on and, as would certainly have happened, been mopped up with heavy casualties. At the end of his evidence, for the first time Pétain spoke up, to say that he had not heard much of what was going on, but that he considered Weygand somebody on whom the greatest reliance could be placed.

At that point Reynaud intervened. He had been listening to Weygand with mounting anger. His anger spilled over when Isorni asked Weygand whether it followed from his evidence that the first people to mention the Armistice in the War Committee were not himself and Pétain but Lebrun and Reynaud. Weygand agreed that that was so. This was the start of a bad-tempered row between Reynaud and Weygand, which nobody seemed able to stop. Each was trying to lay the blame for the defeat on the other. So heated did it become that Mongibeaux declared an end to it – until the following day.

The session of 1 August started with the second act of the row between Reynaud and Weygand. By that time the court – and the press – was getting bored with it, and was only brought to life by the arrival of a letter from Leahy, which was hastily produced by Payen. In spite of Payen's enthusiasm, it did not add much to the debate. Leahy reiterated the views he himself had expressed when in Vichy as American Ambassador. He was certain, he wrote, that Pétain had resisted many of the demands of the Axis. 'I was then, and I am now, convinced that your main aim was the well-being and protection of the French people who had been abandoned. On the other hand, I must in all honesty repeat my opinion expressed to you at the time, that a complete refusal to make the slightest concession to Axis demands, which might have led to greater punishment for your people, would not in the long term have been disadvantageous . . .'[26] In truth, Leahy's letter did little more than give ammunition to both sides.

That done, and the Weygand–Reynaud row concluded, there followed more evidence from Generals Hering and Georges, from Ambassador Noël (long and pompous), Serrigny (effusive in praise of Pétain), and the President of the Paris Municipal Council during the Occupation, Charles Trochu. Once they had been heard – with varying degrees of press and public disinterest – a rumour spread quickly around the court: Pierre Laval was back in Paris, and was to be called the next day.

The rumour turned out to be true. Laval was indeed back in Paris. He had been sent back by Franco, after the three months' asylum which he had been granted, on the same German plane that had brought him to Spain and back to Austria to the same base, Linz. On arrival there, he was immediately arrested by American military police, taken to Innsbruck and delivered to the French authorities – to be shipped straight back to Paris. When they heard the news, the defence lawyers were horrified. Laval, if he was allowed to give evidence, might lead the court they knew not where. It was essential, and Payen argued the case to Mongibeaux, that there should be a preliminary interrogation. Mongibeaux refused the argument and the request. Laval, he announced, would appear the following day.

By midday on 3 August the public galleries in the First Chamber were full. The oppressive heat had returned – one or two of the spectators fainted in the indoor temperature. Conditions were made much worse by the court police who, fearing an assassination attempt, exercised what they thought was appropriate discipline, which mostly involved pushing the crowd in the public gallery back on themselves. Journalists arrived in their dozens – and were only let in through the dark corridors behind the chamber itself.

At 1.30 p.m. Mongibeaux led his two colleagues to their places, all of them sweating profusely under their heavy gowns. Once seated, he lost no time in calling the first witness of the day: Pierre Laval. Laval then appeared, escorted by his guards. Gone was the confident street politician of the pre-war years. Instead, there entered a shabby, almost dirty, figure in a crumpled grey suit, grubby white tie, his hair plastered flat, his moustache yellow from nicotine. 'We were expecting a combination of vice and crime,' wrote one journalist. 'What we had before us was a village idiot from the Auvergne, speaking to local magistrates for the first time.'[27]

Mongibeaux started proceedings by saying that he wished to ask no questions that would prejudice the subsequent interrogation of an accused person. He then went on to do precisely that. As Laval answered – the first question was directed at the origins of his political relationship with Pétain – he constantly looked around him at the audience in court, reading, as best he could, the temperature and the mood. As he spoke about the days of the 1930s and of French relations with Italy, his voice grew in confidence. He made more of his Auvergnat accent – the rs fully rolled (oddly enough, Hitler, the Austrian, had the same trick) until they became almost mesmeric. He spoke on, about his period as Minister of Foreign Affairs in 1934, about the Duke of Windsor, the defence of the franc, his hatred of war.

All that took up twenty-five minutes. By then, Laval was into his stride. He swatted aside an intervention from a juror, and even sneered at Mongibeaux, who had started to muddle his dates and had to be corrected not just by defence lawyers but by the witness himself. The more he went on the more confident he became. Even the hostile journalists started to put down their pencils to admire what was a most impressive performance. When he saw this, Laval turned to a nearby journalist and asked if he could have some water. One or two of the foreign correspondents asked Mongibeaux – out loud. Of course, was the answer, and an usher was called. He went out and came back – with a bottle of Vichy water. Even the most hardened and hostile journalist could not resist a wry chuckle.

By the time the session was adjourned after two hours, two things had become clear: first, that the court was dealing with a professional, who was confident in public speaking and quite prepared to go on the offensive when it suited him; second, much to the relief of the defence lawyers, Laval was not going to attack Pétain. In fact he went out of his way to align himself with the positions Pétain had taken. True, he was concerned to protect his back – he pointed out, much to the general surprise, that the Constitutional Acts Pétain had signed were null and void since they lacked the essential words 'After consultation with the Council of Ministers'[28] – but he went on to claim that that was no more than an example of Pétain's lack of political experience. He was also firm in his view that the National Assembly had constitutionally and in due form approved the Armistice.

At the start of the next session, Laval had a nasty moment. The former Secretary to the Senate, a M. de la Pommeraye, claimed that Laval had said, on signing the Constitutional Acts himself, 'and that's how you throw over the Republic'.[29] Laval said he could not possibly remember, and replied that he and M. de la Pommeraye disliked one another from the start. But he was thrown off balance and took a little time to regain it. He drew more fire when he talked of Montoire, claiming – amidst general clamour – 'Do you think that in 1940 any man of good sense could imagine anything other than a German victory?'[30] He also had to fend off accusations about his 'wishing' for a German victory. In fact, his defence was ingenious. Having been required by Pétain to cut out the words 'I believe', he still felt that a gesture was necessary to placate the Germans. Indeed, if Pétain had asked him to cut out the words 'I wish' he would have argued strenuously for their retention. With that, and with a sentimental flourish about his love of France, his village of Chateldon and the Auvergne, he was ushered out.

Pétain immediately made one of his rare interventions. 'I reacted very strongly', he said angrily,

> when I heard, in the speech, this phrase of M. Laval . . . he said earlier that he had come to find me with M. Rochat of the Ministry of Foreign Affairs, to show me that phrase. Well, M. Rochat would never have accepted keeping that phrase in, and I agreed with him. And then when I heard it on the radio . . . I thought it was done, that he had arranged the matter . . . and when I heard that the phrase had been repeated on the radio, I jumped up. I hadn't realised. I believed that it had been left out. I am very sad that it was left in.[31]

In fact, it was yet another example of Pétain's selective memory. Laval's version was correct.

The second day of Laval's evidence, Saturday 4 August, was much less theatrical than the first. The press was still hostile in spirit (*France-Soir* published a cartoon, under the caption 'Call Pierre Laval', showing judges, police and journalists holding their noses as he entered the chamber) but the journalists who were there were still admiring his performance. There was a session of an hour and a half which was devoted entirely to questions to Laval on all the matters which had been covered previously, to which Laval in turn gave clever but oblique answers. When the court reconvened at four o'clock it was clear that Laval had little more to say. There were some desultory questions about the murders of Georges Mandel and Jean Zay and the arrests of Reynaud, Daladier, Blum and Gamelin, but none of the points made scored serious hits. But by the time he had finished Laval had shown himself to have sided with Pétain but, more important, he had shown Pétain to have sided with him. 'Like a patient, cunning spider', wrote one onlooker, 'he had trussed up the Marshal in his statements and insinuations which could never be untied.'[32]

Laval by then off the stage, the press again lost interest. During the afternoon of 6 August the news suddenly spread that the Americans had dropped an atom bomb on Hiroshima. This, for the press, was a much more interesting story than the succession of generals and Vichy ministers who were wheeled out by the defence. In fact, by producing so many witnesses who had so little to say, the defence seemed to lose momentum. The following day, *Le Monde* devoted the whole of its front page to the Hiroshima bomb and one column on an inside page to the Pétain trial.

The public, such as it was, did not miss much. In truth, among the many defence witnesses who were heard, only three points of interest were raised. The first was in the evidence, on 7 August, of the former Vichy Minister for National Education, Jacques Chevalier. He reported Pétain telling him on 1 February 1941 that

> I am caught between two policies: one, that of co-operation with the English, which I greatly prefer; the second the law of the victor which I am bound to submit to because the victor is there and he is imposing it on the people that I must defend from him . . . I do not follow a policy of 'double game' . . . I only have one word to give; I am faithful; I am loyal to the one as to the other. With the one, I have signed the Armistice, I respect the Armistice . . . With the other I am loyal and friendly with the English since as far as I am free to do so — which is not very far — I do all in my power to facilitate their task.[33]

A less charitable view, however, was put on 8 August by General Jacques Campet, the head of Pétain's military *cabinet* during 1941, 1942 and 1943. In the middle of an incoherent ramble he suddenly produced a sentence which startled the court. His job had been to brief Pétain on the military situation from day to day. 'Questions of sentiment', he announced, 'did not arise for the Marshal; only questions of practicality were important. It was not a question of knowing whether the Marshal desired the victory of the Allies or the Germans but of knowing who would win the war, in order to be able to stick close to the victor and to profit from his victory.'[34]

The second point of interest was in the evidence of Captain Édouard Archambaud on the following day. He confirmed that he had been instrumental in putting into code the three telegrams sent to Darlan: on 10 November 1942, that he should understand that the order to defend North Africa 'was necessary for current negotiations'; on 11 November, that he was not appointed the Marshal's representative in North Africa 'only because you were thought to be a prisoner'; and on 13 November, in response to the proposals for a binding agreement with the Americans sent earlier by Darlan to Vichy, a telegram drafted by Auphan himself saying, 'Close agreement between Marshal and Laval but before answering you the occupying forces are to be consulted'.[35] Archambaud went on to say that at that point Laval was on the telephone to Abetz. In other words, his message was that Pétain approved the American plan but Laval scuppered it.

The third point of interest was the written evidence of General Juin who, in November 1942, was one of the generals commanding in North Africa. The defence lawyers had asked the court to get in touch with Juin, who had been mysteriously sent by de Gaulle on a mission abroad – a mission, apparently, due to last the same length of time as Pétain's trial. Contact was duly made, and Juin's reply was read out to the court on the morning of 10 August. Juin was categorical. 'On the 13th or the 14th [of November 1942], I cannot remember which, Admiral Darlan, who had taken charge, told me of another telegram from Admiral Auphan speaking of a "close agreement of the Marshal" . . . I can state that these two telegrams from Admiral Auphan were of great help to us. They allowed us to calm down a number of consciences tormented by the oath [they had made to Pétain] and still hesitant.'[36] Juin's written evidence, coming from a former Vichy general who had switched sides to de Gaulle, showed beyond doubt, at least in the view of the judges and the remaining impartial observers, that Pétain had been ready and willing to support Darlan in the deal he had done with the Americans.

It was time for the final speeches. On the afternoon of Saturday 11 August, Mornet started his summing up. Fortunately, the weather had broken and there were showers about. The court settled down in reasonable comfort to hear what was obviously going to be a long speech. Indeed it was. It was also tiring to the listeners. It was hard to believe the argument, supported by numerous quotations of doubtful force, that Pétain had hatched a plot while he was Ambassador in Madrid and then refused to join Daladier's Council of Ministers. It was even harder to believe that Pétain and Weygand together had planned the Armistice with the deliberate purpose of overthrowing the government. After two and a quarter hours, during which the court listened with a mixture of boredom and incredulity, Mongibeaux gave the court a merciful fifty-minute break.

During the break the defence lawyers tested the general opinion. They were quite satisfied. Mornet had thus far failed to make much of an impact. His voice was strained and at times difficult to hear. But after the break he found a second wind. He threw all the most powerful accusations at Pétain: acceptance of defeat amounting to capitulation; humiliation of France; devious war against the Allies; the provision to Germany of men to work and to fight for the Germans; in short, treason under the definition of Article 75 of the Penal Code. With a final flourish he concluded 'not without profound emotion but in the knowledge that a stern duty is accomplished' that 'it is the penalty of death which I demand this High Court of Justice to pronounce against he who was Marshal Pétain'.[37]

It was then Payen's turn. He had decided that he would plead three times, first himself, then after Lemaire and finally after Isorni. On the afternoon of Monday 13 August, Payen therefore stood up. After a long recital of Pétain's life history, he attacked the indictment, on the grounds that most of it was speculation. He took the witnesses for the prosecution to task for defending themselves and, in doing so, trying to throw blame on to Pétain. But his delivery was not good, and, like Mornet, in many parts of the chamber he could not be heard. Some jurors started to fall asleep. Pétain himself had already dozed off. They only woke up because Payen had finished and had abruptly sat down.

Lemaire then stood up, and immediately started to pick a quarrel with Mornet. Payen tried to stop him, but Lemaire was determined. Mornet jumped up to reply, but by that time Mongibeaux had succeeded in defusing what threatened to become an unpleasant personal dispute. Lemaire went on to attack the indictment, but the most effective part of his speech was his destruction of the evidence for a plot. He was able to show that the much touted memorandum reporting a conversation with Alibert was no more than tittle-tattle. In fact, the author of the memorandum had confessed that the subject matter was simply no more than rumours which were running around the Resistance at the time.

Payen spoke again. Although he was still difficult to hear, this time his speech had a better flow to it. First of all he summarised the views of Laval and his colleagues. Britain in 1940 was doomed. Germany was going to dominate Europe. Pétain, on the other hand, believed in an ultimate British victory. For the time being there was no question of resisting the occupying power. The only sensible policy was to give as little as possible to the Germans. He had therefore refused to give them the fleet, the bases they asked for in North Africa, refused to go to Berlin, refused to approve the Paris Protocols and refused to declare war on Britain. And then, Payen went on, age had taken its toll. He started to explain in the quietest possible tones that Pétain was senile. As though by way of agreement, Pétain had fallen asleep, but then so had a number of jurors.

The stage was now set for Isorni. He made full use of it. At the start he was nervous – his mouth parched, his voice uncertain. But as he calmed down, his delivery became stronger and he started to use the gesture of his arms, supplicating as though in prayer, familiar to the journalists who had seen him in action before. Tall and thin, with a high forehead, he loomed over Pétain, as the most hostile journalist of all, Madeleine Jacob of the *Franc-Tireur*, wrote, 'like an archangel'.[38]

Isorni did his best with Riom, the racial laws and deportation of the Jews, the Milice, and forced labour – the matters which had been in everybody's mind but had hardly been mentioned in the previous evidence. It was skilful enough, although he begged too many questions for it to be entirely convincing. It was when he started his long peroration that his speech caught fire. He moved into the middle of the court and addressed himself directly to the 'Gentlemen of the Resistance'. 'For half an hour everyone believed that Pétain was in truth the saint and martyr described by the lawyer, the leader of the French Resistance admired by men of integrity . . .'[39] As an orator, Isorni was in those moments almost irresistible. 'Judges of the High Court, listen to me, hear my plea. You are only judges. You are only judging a man. But you hold in your hands the destiny of France.'[40]

It was Madeleine Jacob who wrote, 'it seems to me that when, in years to come, people talk about the Pétain trial, it is the name of Maître Isorni that will dominate the whole story'.[41] Even Mornet rushed across to congratulate him. In his room Pétain embraced him. 'I had never seen him so moved before,' Madame Pétain said of her husband. 'He thinks of you as a son.'[42] But when the court reconvened after a short break, Payen rose to speak yet again. He spoke for three hours. After Isorni's fireworks Payen seemed dull and flat. Although his speech was worthy enough, it was unnecessary – and an anti-climax. When Payen had finished, Mongibeaux asked Pétain whether he had anything to say. Pétain made a short and dignified speech. 'Deal with me according to your consciences,' he said. 'Mine brings me no reproach, since during a life that has already been long, and having arrived at the threshold of death, I affirm that I have had no other ambition than to serve France.'[43] With that, the court adjourned to arrive at a verdict. It was five past nine in the evening.

First things, of course, came first. The members of the court had to be fed. A buffet had been laid out in the President's chambers, cold fish with mayonnaise, cheese and fruit, with plentiful supplies of wine and Vichy water. They were all invited by Mongibeaux to help themselves. In fact, some of them had difficulty in recognising their president. He had laid aside his robes and his hood, and 'looked like an old provincial poet, with his little goatee and his bow tie'.[44] None the less, his invitation was accepted and they all helped themselves liberally. Glasses were filled repeatedly – and emptied just as quickly. It was not until the fruit had finally vanished that Mongibeaux opened the door of the room in which they were to deliberate and invited them in.

The jurors sat down in front of two narrow tables covered in green cloth. Once they were comfortable, Mongibeaux addressed them. 'Gentlemen,' he said, 'my colleagues and I wish to ask you whether you would agree to a sentence of five years' exile.'[45] In other words, he was suggesting what was tantamount to an acquittal. Picard followed him. He did not believe either in the plot against the Republic or in Pétain's guilt, and gave the jurors a long discourse on the meaning of the word 'treason'. Donat-Guigue also gave his view that treason had not been proved.

All this was too much for the lay jurors to stomach. The leader of the parliamentarian jurors, Gabriel Delattre, himself a trial lawyer, spoke of the importance of the verdict in the public perception. There was then a question about the sentences provided for under Article 80 and Articles 75 and 87 of the Penal Code. The answer was that Article 80 entailed a sentence of hard labour for life – but this could not apply to anybody over seventy; Articles 75 and 87 entailed the death sentence.

There followed a long debate, at the end of which there was a vote. Jurors were asked to record, in secret ballot, whether they opted for Article 75 or for Article 80. When the result was declared, eighteen had voted for Article 75 against eight for Article 80. Mongibeaux, who had not voted, announced the result but pointed out that it was only provisional. There would have to be a further vote on whether or not to apply the death penalty. If that vote turned out to be against the death penalty, that would be the end of the matter, and a lesser sentence could be passed.

The argument dragged on into the night. At about one o'clock some of the jurors called for the second vote to be taken. In silence the ballot box was passed around the table. Nobody spoke while Mongibeaux counted the votes. All waited tensely for the result. When it came, it was as close as could be: fourteen for death, thirteen against. It soon appeared that the three judges had voted against the death penalty, that nine of the Resistance jurors had voted in favour, along with five parliamentarians. The vote that tipped the balance was cast by Louis Prot, the communist deputy for the Somme. That done, the penalty of 'national indignity' was proposed and carried. Pétain was to lose his rank, his decorations and his property. It was only then that a recommendation was passed that, in view of Pétain's great age, the death sentence should not be carried out.

Mongibeaux put away the text he had drafted when he expected an acquittal and drafted the text of condemnation. It was after four o'clock in the morning when the court reassembled. Pétain, who had spent the hours in his room making his confession and hearing Mass, was summoned. He listened in silence while the judgement was read out. It was humiliating. A Marshal of France, the 'Victor of Verdun', had been found guilty of treason. But nobody was in any doubt about the seismic shock of the event. It was a shock which would resonate, with all its aftershocks, down the years.

29

PRISON FOR THE REST OF HIS LIFE

'Je n'ai jamais accepté ma condemnation.'

No time was wasted. After the sentence was pronounced, Pétain was taken down and immediately told to put on civilian clothes. Most important, his hat, a dark grey Homburg, was brought to him to stand in for the marshal's képi which his sentence had taken from him. Then, under the guard of Simon, five soldiers, a doctor and several policemen, he was driven to the military airport of Villacoublay, where de Gaulle's own personal aircraft – a DC3 Dakota painted with the Cross of Lorraine on its fuselage – was waiting. Nini, much to her disgust, was left behind. At six o'clock on the morning of 15 August 1945 the plane took off.

The whole thing had been swift. De Gaulle, reasonably enough, wanted to avoid any possibility of disturbances – even riots – after the sentence was announced. Swift it may have been, but the continuing challenge to an unsatisfactory verdict and a continued fear of ambush from Pétain's supporters dragged out what might have been temporary confinement to prison for the rest of his life.

De Gaulle's aircraft, carrying Pétain and his guards, landed at the airport of Pau, in the deep south of France, at about eight o'clock on the same morning. It was met by the local Préfet with suitable support, even at that early hour, from a handful of local dignitaries. The prisoner, as Pétain now was, was then invited to get into a car, to be driven – under heavy motor-cycle escort – to the fort of Le Portalet, high in the mountains of the Pyrenees and only a few kilo-metres from the Col du Somport and the Spanish frontier. As the cavalcade passed through the towns and villages on its route, people who were out on the streets to celebrate the annual feast of the Assumption of the Blessed Virgin Mary stopped and stared, and even waved to the well-known figure – who responded, as always, by raising his hat to them.

Pétain, old as he was, had not yet come down from the excitement of his trial. In fact, he was rather enjoying the attention. His only complaint was that the aircraft had flown above the clouds and he was unable to see the ground at all. In short, the flight had been rather boring. The cheerfulness vanished, however, when he saw the cell in which he was to be lodged. It was the same cell in which Georges Mandel had been confined by the Vichy government, with Blum, Reynaud, Daladier and Gamelin as neighbours.

In his first letter to Nini from Le Portalet, Pétain described his accommodation as 'lamentable. If I had known it as I know it now I would never have sent my worst enemy . . . There can be no question of you making the journey . . . we will receive soon the visit of an inspector . . . I hope that we can convince him [to order] an immedi-ate change of location, which everybody wishes.'[1] The description was apt. His cell was on the level of the third basement – the fort itself almost clinging to a cliff; it was damp; there was only one electric fire, which had to be kept going night and day; and there was nowhere to walk but a small terrace which could only be reached by a steep and dangerous staircase of thirty-two steps.

The inspector came and went. Pétain's hopes for an early change of prison came to nothing. True, de Gaulle had signed on 17 August an order commuting the death sentence to one of life imprisonment, and had in mind, as he later wrote, that Pétain, 'after having been detained for two years in a fortified place he would go to his home near Antibes to finish his life'.[2] But de Gaulle, to say the least, had much to think about during the second half of 1945 and the conditions of Pétain's imprisonment were nowhere near the top of his list. Besides, there were many who thought that Pétain should have a taste of the medi-cine which he had given others. The fact, as it turned out, that the previous occupants of the fort had a much easier time of it – Reynaud spent his days with a twenty-three-year-old secretary ('very pretty, too', Simon was told);[3] Mandel had regular visits from his mistress, Mme Béatrice Bretty of the Comédie Française, and was looked after by his black valet Baba; Daladier's sons frequently came to see him, and all of them had their food sent up from the Hôtel des Voyageurs in the valley town of Urdos – was neither here nor there to those who were looking for revenge.

By the end of August Pétain's morale, resilient as it had been up till then, was starting to break. On the 30th he told Simon that he was living on the edge of the grave and that he had nothing more to expect from life. But perhaps more revealing was his remark that 'I made the gift of my person, it is said, but in truth it is in words, since one holds on to life . . .'[4] At last, he was admitting that the 'gift of his person', proclaimed with great ceremony while he was in power, was little more than a rhetorical gesture. Holding on to life was more – much more – important than rhetorical gestures. But if he had finally come round to admitting that 'the gift of his person' was no more than a gesture, there had been no sign as yet that his morale had sunk into anything near to suicidal desperation.

The sign came two months later, after his lawyers had come and gone – promising repeal of the trial verdict on a rehearing – and Nini had paid her first visit, spending much of her time bickering with her husband and shouting at his jailer, provoking Simon to write in his diary that he would like to 'kick her up the backside'.[5] On 20 October Simon noted that Pétain was badly depressed. The prospect of long years in prison and disappointment with his wife led him to burst out: 'If there were no bars on the window, I would have thrown myself into the Gave [the river below].'[6]

By that time Simon, who at Montrouge had been openly hostile to his charge, had become sympathetic, indeed almost affectionate. The two had daily conversations about the world in general, Pétain with his customary courtesy and Simon with his Breton bluffness. Simon noted, too, how the doctors who looked after Pétain had become devoted to him, how the local *curé* who came to say Mass every Sunday enjoyed his visits, and how even the guards were happy to exchange a joke or two with the prisoner on his walks on the terrace. He also noted Pétain's surprisingly good physical health. True, there were times when Pétain's morale was so low that he refused to eat or to shave himself, and Simon had to encourage one of the guards to play cards with him. In fact, the only thing that cheered him up at all was a series of letters from Isorni promising favourable – but unspecified – developments in the review of his case on appeal. After reading these he was apt, in his most cheerful mood, to tell Simon about what he knew was to happen – a transfer to the Mediterranean island of Ste-Marguerite, perhaps, or another equally suitable island.

Another island it was to be, although not any of the ones he had imagined. By the end of October 1945 the magistrate in the Ministry of Justice charged with following the case, Alain Jégou, had come to the conclusion that Pétain should not stay at Le Portalet for the winter. The climate was too harsh and, although the fort itself was secure from possible raids by Pétain's followers to get him out, the Spanish frontier was too close for comfort. There were rumours that groups of Spaniards were preparing to make a marauding raid to whisk him off to Spain and to demand political asylum for him from Franco. Real or imaginary, the threat itself was enough for Paris. The last thing the de Gaulle government wanted was Pétain, as it were, on the loose.

At the beginning of November Simon received instructions from Jégou. The prisoner, he was told, was to be moved from Le Portalet to the island off the western coast of France known as the Île d'Yeu. The move was to be accomplished in the greatest secrecy, yet again to give no opportunity to Pétain's friends to take advantage of the move to mount an ambush. The fear was, perhaps, exaggerated. Simon at least thought so. Nevertheless, at half past eleven on the night of 14 November a new cavalcade left Le Portalet. There were, in all, five cars. In the third car Pétain sat, uncomfortably perched between Simon and Jégou. Simon and the rest of the guard were equipped with sub-machine guns to fend off an ambush – much to Simon's disgust. As an old soldier he knew how to handle them but the raw police guard were, he thought, bound to be trigger-happy; so much so that he asked for two army sergeants to come along to keep control of them.

The cavalcade bypassed Pau to take the road to Bordeaux, and drove through the night. As it happened, it was held up by one of the cars breaking down twice on the way – dirty petrol, it was said. A garage in Bordeaux fixed the problem, but not before a group of

Bordelais had come out to gawp at the former marshal, whose face they knew well. It was therefore not until eleven o'clock in the morning of the 15th that the party reached the Atlantic coast. The everpresent fear of ambush – however ridiculous – led them to avoid the usual ports of access to the Île d'Yeu, Fromentine and Saint Gilles, and to make for the nearby little fishing harbour of La Pallice. There a corvette was waiting to take them on what should normally be no more than an hour or two's passage to Port-Joinville, the main port – and capital – of the island.

The corvette left La Pallice at about noon on the 16th. What should have been a short and comfortable journey started out well. Pétain himself was particularly pleased. The officers on board the corvette addressed him again as 'Marshal'; he was given the two rooms normally occupied by the captain and was served at the luncheon table by the captain's butler. The food, too, was to his liking. He proceeded to hold court, recounting to his amiable and willing companions the story of his previous visit to the Île d'Yeu in August 1921 and the enthusiastic welcome given to him by the fishermen of the island and their families. So content was he in finding such an agreeable environment that he seemed to think himself back to the days of 1921. He even tried, when he went for his afternoon rest, to prevent his guards entering the apartment which the captain had put at his disposal.

The journey ended badly. The sea became rough, to the point where the corvette was unable to dock at Port-Joinville. The party was forced to transfer to a small fishing boat to be towed into port by a coastguard launch. It was not the most dignified landing, but they managed to scramble on to the jetty without falling into the water. There were, of course, onlookers. A small – and 'impassive'[7] – crowd had assembled to watch the performance. As he walked towards the cars which were waiting for him Pétain, yet again, raised his hat to them.

The Île d'Yeu is even now, whatever the tourist literature claims, not a particularly attractive place. An island 9.5 kilometres long and 4 kilometres wide, it lies some eighteen kilometres off the western coast of the French mainland. It is an appendage, if that is the right word, of the department of the Vendée, and its administration, as well as the subsidies needed to maintain it, derive from the city of Nantes. It is an old island, geologically going back 360 million years or so and historically the victim of many invasions from both English and French marauders in the Middle Ages until, after many changes of ownership, it was finally bought by Louis XVI in 1785 to prevent smuggling of salt and tobacco. Climatically, it suffers from the Atlantic weather. It is buffeted on its eastern side by the strong currents flowing down from the Brittany peninsula and on its western side by fearsome oceanic waves. Port-Joinville, its capital, has a pretty enough centre, but the narrow streets and small houses tell of the poverty of a population of little over two thousand souls. Nowadays, of course, there are groups of second homes, owned by businessmen from Nantes – or even Paris – both on the edge of the little town and also scattered among the havens where there are sheltered patches of green grass, but these are for summer visitors only. The winters are always bleak and unfriendly.

About a kilometre to the west of the capital is La Citadelle, whose main feature is the fort of Pierre-Levée. It is, even for today's visitor, a gloomy place. There is a central building of two storeys, in the middle of which is an archway which is the only entrance to the fort. At either end of the building two wings of barracks form an enclosure on three sides of a large courtyard. The entrance is protected by a drawbridge. As such, it is secure, suitably so, since it was a military prison during the Napoleonic Wars. Of course, its security is enhanced by the daunting prospects for any escapee even attempting to get off the island.

In this depressing establishment Pétain was allocated two rooms above the entrance to the fort, looking inwards, in so far as a small barred window allowed him to look, on to the square. In one room there was a metal bed, a small chest of drawers, two upright wooden chairs and little wood stove; in the second there was a largeish table, an armchair and another little stove. There was a small bathroom and lavatory next door. Drinking water had to be fetched by the guards from an outside tap some 250 metres away, and the electricity only functioned in the evenings until eleven o'clock. But such as they were, which is not much, these quarters were to be Pétain's home for the next five and a half years.

Apart from Simon and three attendant guards, the most important figures in Pétain's new life at Pierre-Levée were the doctor, the priest

In the courtyard of Fort Pierre-Levee. (*L'Illustration/Sygma*)

Supper in late 1950. (*Le Bot Alain/Gamma*)

and his wife – possibly in that order. The doctor at Port-Joinville, who was instructed to look after him, Dr Emmanuel Imbert, was a cheerful enough character. But he led what can only be described as a colourful life. In short, he was apt to drink too much. In one of his more lively moments he had led a group of sailors to smash up the main hotel in Port-Joinville on the grounds that the owner had made a fortune during the Occupation by denouncing his fellow citizens to the Gestapo – an escapade for which he was fined two thousand francs and shipped off to the mainland to cool down. Alcohol, however, was not his only difficulty. He was also rather too fond of young sailors. As a result, there was some doubt in the minds of the authorities whether he was a suitable person to be looking after Pétain's health. In the end the doubts were swallowed and Imbert got the job. In fact, he turned out to be a pleasurable companion for his patient, even though it was recognised that it was unwise to try to call him out after seven o'clock in the evening and that he was apt to disappear from time to time on a fishing boat crewed by, among others, a particularly attractive young sailor.

Abbé Germain Ponthoreau was altogether different. Like many of the clergy of the Vendée he was a Pétain sympathiser, and was very happy to engage every Thursday in long conversations with the prisoner. A gentle man, he was considered by his flock to be 'a priest of exceptional qualities, both spiritual and human'.[8] He kept detailed notes of his talks with Pétain but thought it better, possibly on the advice of his superior, to destroy his manuscript in case it revealed too much sympathy and admiration for his distinguished interlocutor.

Pétain's wife, of course, was another matter. Their relationship had had, to put it mildly, its ups and downs. But in his isolation Pétain became, almost like a child, dependent on her. When she was there, she could do no right; when she was not there, she was instantly missed. His letters to her from the rest island, summoning her back, become more and more alluring as time passes. 'I embrace you with every tenderness' of February 1946 becomes 'I embrace you with all my heart which grows every day closer to yours' in June.[9] It goes without saying that when Nini did come to visit him there were the usual arguments, even in front of the guard who was required to be present. None of this is particularly surprising. Pétain was lonely. He spent most of the day alone – at one point he tried to keep himself entertained by improving his poor English. He ate his meals alone – the same food as the guards, including a quarter-bottle of wine. He made his own – iron – bed alone. The only personal task he did not perform alone was to cut his toenails. (He explained that at Vichy he had had a pedicure for the task and now did not know how to do so.) Any company – even his wife's – was better than none.

Old age, loneliness and boredom were starting to take their toll. He was still in good physical health, but periods of depression became more frequent. Furthermore, the world outside the Île d'Yeu was changing, and not to his advantage. In January 1946 de Gaulle suddenly resigned and walked off home to Colombey-les-Deux-Églises. With him went the last serious possibility of Pétain's early release. True, the lawyers were doing their best, but Payen had died and neither Isorni nor Lemaire had the political weight needed to overcome what turned out to be the nervous dilatoriness of the various ministers who, in frequent succession, succeeded de Gaulle. Certainly, Pétain was cheered to learn from his wife, on a visit at the end of June 1946, that President Harry Truman had asked the French Government to release him, sending the message that if release was politically embarrassing the United States was ready to grant Pétain asylum. There were committees for his release forming as well, not only in Paris but in Switzerland, Italy, the United States, Brazil – and in Britain. Queen Mary, the Queen Mother, for instance, and the Duke of Windsor were particularly active on his behalf.

But it all came to nothing. Life in prison went on as before. Nini asked for another armchair for the prisoner. Simon refused. 'Everything this woman does is calculated,' Simon complained in his diary. 'For me, she has no affection for her husband but she holds on to him because of the prestige which, in spite of everything, rebounds on to the wife of the ex-Marshal.'[10] Pétain was caught in the crossfire between his wife and his surly jailer. 'She knows', he explained to Simon, 'that without me she is nothing. If she is "la Maréchale" she owes it to me. But at the moment she is perfect, I would never have believed she could be so nice . . . it's a revelation to me.'[11] Simon himself was getting fed up with looking after the old man and made it clear to his superiors.

The second winter of Pétain's imprisonment on the Île d'Yeu began on that sour note. None the less, 1947 itself began promisingly. Isorni and Lemaire were given permission again to visit the prisoner. The Constitution of the Fourth Republic was in place. Elections had been held and a government, under Pétain's old colleague and opponent Ramadier, had been formed. On 16 January Vincent Auriol was elected President of the new republic. It was customary, the lawyers told Pétain, for an amnesty to follow the election of a new head of state. They were quick to follow up. On 10 February Isorni and Lemaire went to see Auriol full of high hopes – to be immediately brushed aside. Neither Auriol nor Ramadier had any intention of altering the present state of affairs in any way whatsoever. On the same day, Pétain asked for authorisation for Nini to stay near him in La Citadelle when she came to visit. Authorisation, again, was refused.

In the early weeks of 1947, Pétain's health was poor. His legs were swollen (Nini proclaimed loudly that he had been poisoned) and one hip was painful. Mentally, too, he was starting to slip further. The 'eclipses' became longer and more frequent, and he would occasionally fall asleep in the middle of a sentence. There was little Dr Imbert could do. Nini, too, was of little help. She was still furious at not being allowed to stay with him in the fort. 'She was unable to restrain herself from calling those responsible s . . . and f . . ., descriptions usually regarded as impolite by lorry drivers.'[12] Moreover, she treated the inhabitants of Port-Joinville with contempt, and shouted at Pétain's guards – all of whom asked for a transfer in the event of her being allowed to stay in La Citadelle. Islanders and guards alike said that she was only 'wanting to show Grandfather's supporters the calvary she had to climb to be near her husband'.[13] ('Grandfather' was the name given to Pétain by the islanders.)

Pétain's health recovered in time for a further visit from Isorni and Lemaire on 24 April 1947 – his ninety-first birthday. Their visits always cheered him up, and they found him on his best form. They reported that the Académie Française was recruited to the cause, working for his release. At the same time, he was also cheered to receive a telegram from his great-niece, Yvonne de Morcourt. It was the first time he had heard from any of his family since his arrival in the Île d'Yeu. She wrote that she wanted to come to visit him. The news was more than welcome, and Pétain replied as much, saying that he was sure that she would be allowed to do so if she came with Nini.

Yet when they had all gone, and the reply to Yvonne de Moncourt had been sent, Pétain fell again into despair. He told Simon that his lawyers kept on telling the same story and he kept on trying to believe them. He also asked continually for his wife. In fact, he had forgotten that she was close by, since by then Nini was spending most of her time at the Hôtel des Voyageurs in Port-Joinville, in a small apartment set up for the purpose in an annexe. But he seemed not to care about where or how she lived. In fact, life, even for her, was not easy. She had no companions other than a small radio, and she trekked up the hill each day to La Citadelle on the long walk to see her husband. Besides, she could not fend for herself, and a maid from the hotel was detailed to look after her. ('Why not?' she said to Simon. 'I don't know how to do anything and if I were alone I would die of hunger.')[14]

Moreover, Pétain's attitude to her remained, as always, ambivalent. When she went back to Paris for a week or two, he wrote affectionate letters to her saying how much he missed her. On 16 February 1947, for instance, he noted that he was writing at two o'clock in the afternoon, the time for her visit when she was on the island: 'It is the hour, impatiently waited for each day, during which I am allowed to go and embrace you . . . soon, I hope, my darling, I will embrace you with my whole heart.'[15] And yet on 2 March he told Simon that 'she only wanted to be near me to be able to say later that she had shared all my misfortunes'.[16] At times he seemed happier playing on his daily walks in the courtyard, as a child plays, with a little dog which Simon had found and brought into the fort to catch the rats which infested the place – known as Miquette, or 'Mickey' as Pétain called her – than he was seeing his wife. Simon summed up the mood in September 1947 after one of Nini's departures: 'What calm for everybody when she is not there. If she could never come back, how happy we would be, the prisoner and the personnel.'[17]

On 7 June 1947 Isorni wrote to Nini at the Hôtel des Voyageurs that there was to be a visit to the Île d'Yeu by the parliamentary commission set up to inquire into the events in France during the period 1933–45. Nini tried to block the visit, on the grounds that her husband was not up to it, but, yet again, she protested in vain. On 10 July the commission, thirteen of them (and three secretaries), including Blum, Daladier and Gamelin, arrived on a warship at Port-Joinville, and immediately went up to La Citadelle to see Pétain. Nini, however, was not to be denied. She went up to Pierre-Levée a couple of hours before the commission arrived there. Her purpose was plain: 'to insist with the prisoner that he say "no" to every question asked'.[18]

It was advice that Pétain would have done well to heed. Instead, he told the commissioners that he would answer questions, although he tried to make it clear that his memory was not what it was. But it turned out to be worse than that. When questions were put to him he kept on referring back to the First World War. He claimed never to have heard of books to which he had contributed a preface. He could not remember having sent Reynaud, Gamelin, Daladier, Blum and Mandel to prison – above all Blum, for whom he claimed to have the highest regard. In fact, when the commission left him after nearly two hours they were none the wiser. But they were suspicious of his memory lapses – perhaps, they thought, Pétain was up to his old tricks. And yet they were impressed by his bearing, and their initial hostility – some wanted just to call him without ceremony 'Pétain' – turned to grudging respect. 'Whatever one can think about Vichy,' said one deputy on leaving, 'he is all the same somebody [of consequence].'[19]

On 9 September Isorni paid Pétain another visit. He found that he had 'let his moustache grow again. He has found again his physiognomy of 1918.'[20] He also found Pétain quite ready to admit to the lapses of memory which had raised such suspicion among the members of the commission, but still mentally alert. Isorni reminded him of a conversation they had had about Reynaud and Albert Lebrun and what he thought about them. 'Nothing' had been the reply. 'That "nothing" made him laugh a lot,' Isorni recalled. '"That's exactly right!" he added . . .'[21]

1947 dragged on. On 17 September Pétain noted the marriage of his (much disliked) stepson Pierre. He wrote to Nini, after having some difficulty with his pen, which he had not used for some time, that 'I am overjoyed that you have met a daughter-in-law to your taste. I am ready, by way of advance, to give her my admiration and my confidence.'[22] It was not very welcoming, even for his new step-daughter-in-law, Odette. In fact, Pierre had visited his mother several times on the island and Odette had come too; but she (he had not even tried) had been unable to secure authorisation to visit La Citadelle.

On 8 October Simon's wife died. Pétain, Nini and Isorni all wrote letters of condolence. But when Simon returned to duty, quite clearly in grief after his wife's funeral, he found he had a much more difficult prisoner to deal with. On 7 or 8 November – the exact date is uncertain – Pétain refused his daily walk. He did not even recognise Simon. 'Who are you?', he asked.[23] When Nini arrived for her daily visit he did not recognise her either. She tried her best to revive his memory, explaining that they had been living together, one way or another, for twenty-eight years and that they had been married. Her promptings went without noticeable response. He was surprised when she told him that she had been at his side in Vichy and had followed him to Sigmaringen. Later in the day he recovered his memory, but Dr Imbert, after prolonged examination, was obliged on the 9th to report that, although physically he was well, 'these breakdowns, at the moment not very serious because of their short duration and their rare occurrence, point to an unavoidable state of ageing . . .'[24] When Pétain was brought his morning coffee on the next day, he was in tears and, for the first time, refused to make his bed.

What was then bad became even worse. On 2 December, Pétain denied ever having been married to Nini and demanded a marriage certificate to prove the contrary. On 11 December, he soiled his trousers in front of his guards and a weeping Nini. Again and again he was heard by Simon letting out cries of despair. By the end of 1947 it had become clear that the 'eclipses' were becoming more frequent and ever longer in duration. True, in the intervening periods of clarity he was mentally alert, but, as Simon noted, they faded ever more quickly. As 1947 passed into 1948, in the cold and loneliness of his prison, the old Marshal of France seemed gradually to be slipping into what Isorni was later to describe as an eternal night.

There it rested, over the long and dark months of winter of 1947. In the late spring of 1948, however, when the small group of flowers bordering the courtyard of Pierre-Levée were blooming, there was an incident on the island which seemed to bring Pétain back to something near to his old life. On 10 May Dr Imbert suddenly, and unexpectedly, committed suicide. He had, according to Simon's report of the incident, an incurable illness and had wished to die without pain. Pétain was told on the following day when he was having one of his brighter periods. 'Poor doctor, how sorry I am for him. He was very charming and competent.'[25] But Pétain's brighter mood was yet again no more than temporary. On the day Imbert's replacement arrived from the mainland Pétain was moaning to Simon, helplessly and in tears, that he had had enough, that nobody cared about him, and that they all wanted him to die.

Imbert's replacement, the young doctor Jean Jouhier, who had only recently finished his training at the hospital of La-Roche-sur-Yon, knew nothing of the island or its most famous resident. His first examination, to which the patient submitted meekly, showed excellent physical health. 'I was surprised', he reported, 'by the vitality and musculature of this body of ninety-three years.'[26] The patient's mental health was another matter. Isorni and Lemaire came on another visit on 4 June, to talk about the committee which had been set up to promote the cause. On the first day of their talks Pétain was lively and interested. The next day he had forgotten all that had happened the previous day, rambled, and kept asking the same questions over and over again. 'One had the feeling', runs Isorni's report, 'that he can no longer bear imprisonment, that his forces are starting to abandon him.'[27]

The summer of 1948 went by without incident. But even Nini was starting to feel depressed. She had every day to walk up the hill to La Citadelle, cross the drawbridge into the fort, spend an hour and a half with Pétain, repeating the reasons for continued hope without any great conviction. Her life improved, however, in August, when she was presented with a little car by one of Pétain's sympathisers and she found a local driver who could take her to the fort and back. She had developed a painful sciatica in her leg – and she was, of course, badly overweight. The car was a great blessing. For his part, Pétain, in so far as his attention had not wandered, was glad of her visits. From time to time he spoke to her, but what he said was full of gloom. He no longer, he told her, even made a pretence of believing in his lawyers.

On 4 September 1948 Isorni and Lemaire arrived yet again on the island. 'The Marshal', Isorni noted, 'is slowly losing his lucidity or, more precisely, the lucid intervals are becoming rarer . . . one whole part of his brain has ceased to function.'[28] They tried to explain to him that the government was likely to fall and that they were hoping that Henri Queuille, a doctor by background, would be asked to form the next government. It turned out that they were right, and on 26 September they went to see Queuille, by then the new Head of

Government. There were, indeed, words of sympathy. Queuille fully understood the problem and thought a transfer to the military hospital of Val-de-Grâce in Paris would be eminently sensible. Unfortunately, given the political circumstances of the day, Queuille was sorry to say that he could not possibly accede to their request.

Early in November 1948, for no immediately apparent reason, the government decided to make a film of Pétain, his wife and those who regularly visited him, including his new doctor, Dr Jean Potéreau. A naval lieutenant, Ernest Laspougeas, was to be in charge of what turned out to be a very old-fashioned camera. In turn, he was to be assisted by a Monsieur Cocu, a naval rating, to be in charge of the lighting. Its purpose was not ever explained to the prison staff, but Simon assumed that it was partly to show that Pétain, contrary to the case put forward by his wife and his lawyers, was kept in reasonably good conditions and partly to demonstrate to the veterans of the Resistance, contrary to their insistent opinion that Pétain was receiving preferential treatment, that the rules governing prisoners were being scrupulously applied.

The event, whatever its purpose, certainly had its comic side. Laspougeas was told to explain to Pétain that he was a workman come to work on changes to the fort. Unfortunately he found Pétain on one of his good days. 'The only change required here', the old man replied crisply, 'is for me to change residence.'[29] When things got going, there was another incident. M. Cocu, on the evening before the shooting, decided to investigate the entertainment available in Port-Joinville. Finding the possibilities no more than extremely limited, he decided to return to the fort, only to find the drawbridge closed against him and that he had to spend the night in the cold November air. Yet there was also an element of pathos. When Pétain was filmed shaving, his dentures, provided by the – much distrusted – local dentist, fell out into the little basin in front of him. He took several minutes, fumbling about in the hot water, to locate them. (To give him his due, Laspougeas was duly abashed.) When the film party left, Pétain was not at all sure who they were. In fact, he asked them to come back often – life, he said, was much more interesting when they were there.

As it happened, the film was never shown – at least not until 1975. Nevertheless, it was enough to show Isorni that the government was taking an interest. He tried to explain this to Pétain during his New Year visit to the Île d'Yeu on 3 and 4 January 1949. At first he was quite successful. Pétain seemed to be having one of his better days. But the next day it was all lost. He talked about 'Napoleon, Verdun, Vichy – mixing them up . . . He repeated over and over again, "You cannot imagine the complexity of large battles."'[30] It was enough to move Isorni to ask Nini herself (at his dictation) to write to Queuille explaining her husband's real state and challenging the conclusions of the most recent medical examination.

Nini's letter achieved its intended effect. Queuille made sure that three distinguished doctors were sent from Paris to the island to make a thorough examination of the prisoner. The three duly arrived at Port-Joinville on 25 February, to be met by Simon in his car and driven to La Citadelle. They then saw Pétain in his cell late that evening and again the following morning, making meticulous notes on his general state of health, his heart and his mental capacities. Their opinion, signed by all three, was emphatic. Pétain, they reported, was not fit to remain where he was and should be moved forthwith to Paris and the Val-de-Grâce.

So much was clear. But, as it turned out, it was not be as easy as that. The Council of Ministers met on 3 March 1949 to discuss the experts' recommendation. There was, by all reports, a violent argument. The former (mostly self-proclaimed) heroes of the Resistance insisted that Pétain stay in prison. Others took a more humane view. The upshot was that no consensus was reached and, therefore, no decision was taken, except one on which they could all agree – to improve the medical facilities available to the prisoner. As a result, yet another young military doctor, Alphonse Zeude, was posted, much against his will, to the Fort Pierre-Levée. His duty was to see Pétain each morning and evening, and twice a week to make a full examination of the prisoner to be reported to Paris. Two nurses were also to be sent in support.

Zeude reported faithfully, as was his duty. But by mid-May he was also requesting more nursing help. The two nurses had arrived, but were refusing to do the menial work which they regarded as being more suitable for a personal maid and were sitting in their rooms doing no more than twiddling their useless thumbs. Besides, his patient was starting to hallucinate. He had become convinced that he was in the middle of battles, that naked women were dancing around in his room. It was no good appealing to his wife. She had gone back to Paris for treatment on her bad leg, where Pétain had written her a letter, referring to his prison – much to her consternation – as 'home'.[31] The matter was becoming urgent. Zeude needed help. So desperate was his call that it was immediately answered. At the end of May four male nurses arrived, one from a naval hospital and the others from the military hospital at Rennes. It was by then plain that, whatever might be its official designation, the prison was gradually being turned into a hospital.

In fact, that whole process was completed by the middle of 1949. Simon received his long-awaited posting; the guards were replaced by nurses (Nini was furious that one of the guards had claimed ownership of Miquette, 'the little dog who was the only entertainment for the Marshal and who never left him', and had taken her away);[32] Pétain was allowed a battery-powered radio; and a new director, Charles Boulay, previously in charge of the hospital prison at Liancourt, arrived on 1 July.

With the change from prison to hospital the rhythm of Pétain's life also changed. Doctors and nurses came and went, their stay on the island never lasting more than six months. Sometimes, in default of nurses, nuns from the island's convent were called in. Pétain was bemused by the comings and goings, as was Nini, but at least there was some relaxing of the strict régime imposed by Simon. Indeed, Nini was heartily glad to see the back of him, particularly since Boulay allowed her to eat her meals with her husband.

By then, it seemed that everybody was simply waiting for Pétain to die. In August 1949 instructions were issued to all concerned on how to act when death finally occurred. Elaborate telephone codes were set out for every eventuality; the precedure for laying out the body by nuns fully specified (the corpse to be dressed in civilian clothes); only the family and the authorities were to be present at the funeral, with the possible exception of a few journalists with special authorisation; religious service in the fort's chapel, and so on. That was all very well but, as it turned out, they all had to wait another two years.

In fact, the expectation of Pétain's early death was justified by the marked deterioration in his health towards the end of 1949. Physically, he had developed cardiac arrhythmia, had become incontinent at nights and had low blood pressure; mentally, 'Senile dementia [is] practically complete,' as the doctors reported on 24 November.[33] There were only fleeting moments of lucidity. The doctors also recorded that Pétain had lost a sense of modesty and was given to exposing himself to the nurses. When he was moved to the ground floor of the fort to allow him to go out into the courtyard for a walk (although he was unable to put one foot in front of another without support from his nurse) and put in better accommodation, he 'started urinating and spitting almost everywhere'.[34]

It would be otiose (and tasteless) to dwell on Pétain's condition during the last two years of his life. Although physically he seemed to improve during the early months of 1950, mentally he remained where he was. Without him being more than even half conscious of the attempt, in May 1950 his lawyers submitted a request for the 1945 verdict to be overturned. The Ministry of Justice said it would study the matter – and did nothing. Nor was he aware that on 25 February Franco gave an interview to the newspaper *Arriba* on the 35th anniversary of Verdun. In it he had praised Pétain as 'a great soldier and a gentleman'. He had gone on to say that he had advised Pétain to stay in Spain in 1939. '"You are the victor of Verdun. Do not join your name to what others have lost." "I know," Pétain had replied, "but my country calls me and I owe myself to her."' When asked by the editor of *Arriba* whether there was anything that Spain could do for Pétain, Franco replied: 'Very little, since it is involving the intimate affairs of another country. We can only mourn his distress and, if the occasion arises, offer him the hospitality of our country, where he can pass his remaining years in respect and affection.'[35]

On Saturday 7 April 1951 Pétain started struggling for breath. It was the start of the congestive heart failure which was to be the final cause of his death. He was confined to his bed, and his doctors ordered twenty-four-hour nursing. The prognosis was anything but good. Yet, once again, Pétain surprised his doctors by making at least some sort of recovery. By 24 April he was able to be propped up in bed for his ninety-fifth birthday. As it turned out, the event was not as depressing as those summoned to the feast expected. Nini had supervised the baking of a large cake, and on to its top were crowded ninety-five candles of red, white and blue. His two lawyers were at the party, as were

Birthday: Nini, the cake and ninety-five candles. (*Paris Match*)

Yvonne de Moncourt and her children. Franco sent a basket of fruit
from Spain, and flowers came from all over France. Moreover, to add
to the jollity, Pétain was having one of his best days for a long time.
Not only was he able to be propped up in his bed but he seemed fully
to realise what was going on. 'How pretty it is!' he said of the cake,
and with his finger he pointed to one candle that was unlit.[36]

But it was only a temporary remission. On 12 May President
Auriol was alerted to the daily medical reports. After much hesitation,
he finally agreed that Pétain ought to be moved, and on 8 June signed
a decree commuting Pétain's sentence from prison to a 'hospital establishment'[37] – provided he was fit enough to survive the transfer. The
decree was kept secret, for obvious electoral reasons, until after the
general election for the National Assembly, due to take place on 17
June. That done, on 25 June the fort of Pierre-Levée was formally
designated as a military hospital. At that point, however, Pétain could
no longer leave his bed. He slept a great deal, had to be fed by his

nurses and, when at all awake, was either silent or babbled without cease.

Nevertheless, to everyone's astonishment, Pétain suddenly had a period of near total lucidity. He recognised his lawyers, his wife and his doctors. It seemed that he was perfectly capable of being transferred to the house in Port-Joinville – no. 27 rue Guist'hau, owned by the lawyer Paul Luco – which, for the purpose, had been named as an annexe to the military hospital at Nantes. In spite of last-minute official nervousness, at seven o'clock on the morning of 29 June the rue Guist'hau was sealed off by police. 'Operation Luco', as it was called, which had been rehearsed no fewer than four times, was under way.

Pétain was gently manoeuvred on to a large stretcher and carried to a small military lorry which was parked in the courtyard of the fort. His doctor rode with him to monitor his pulse throughout the journey. Then, escorted by a battered old police car, the lorry moved off at 7.04 a.m. The journey to the Luco house, at a strict six kilometres an hour, lasted eleven minutes. The transfer had been achieved without a hitch. Medicin-Général Tabet, who had been in charge of the operation, was particularly pleased. Over aperitifs in the Hôtel des Voyageurs later in the morning he was expansive. 'As Dante wrote in *The Divine Comedy*', he told the breathless journalists, '"in everything there has to be a leader."'[38]

For a time, Pétain's condition remained as it had been at the time of his transfer – sleeping most of the time but with bursts of lucidity in an otherwise semi-conscious day. By 18 July, however, it was clear that he was moving towards his death. On 20 July Queuille summoned Isorni to tell him that there was no time to waste. There were arrangements to be made. There was no question of the body being buried at Douaumont alongside the dead of Verdun, as Pétain had wished. The whole thing was politically far too sensitive. It would have to stay on the Île d'Yeu. His wife could make what dispositions she liked there as long as it was a private event and did not cause too much trouble.

Isorni and Lemaire hurried back to the island, to meet those who were gathering at Pétain's bedside – Yvonne de Moncourt and her children as well as Nini and her son Pierre. The lawyers were nearly too late. During the day of the 21st Pétain had slipped into a coma. Nini had moved into the Villa Luco. In the end, he stayed in a coma throughout the 22nd and, at 9.22 on the morning of 23 July 1951, he died. A nurse held his hand as he went and, when he had gone, gently laid it on his dead body. Nini leaned over and kissed his fore-head. A nun knelt in the corner saying her rosary. She was praying, as was appropriate, for the repose of the old man's troubled soul.

The prayers said, the nurses and the nuns then busied themselves with laying out the body. Contrary to the official instruction, at Nini's request he was clothed in simple military uniform, the Médaille Militaire pinned to his breast. His bed, which had been brought from Pierre-Levée, was surrounded by flowers – the pots shrouded in black crape – and six large candlesticks. Outside, in the street, a small crowd gathered, but the police made sure that there was no disturbance. The telephone lines between the island and the mainland were blocked for an hour while the government was informed. The Council of Ministers met and decided to take all necessary precautions. Police were deployed in the streets of Paris. Everybody seemed suddenly to be very nervous.

In fact, so nervous were ministers about the political impact of Pétain's final passing from the scene that they immediately decided that the funeral should be completed with the greatest possible speed.

The funeral procession. (*Keystone*)

The decision turned out to be amply justified. Pétain's death was not only a major public event but, politically, a highly charged one. There were demonstrations in most French cities. The Veterans of Verdun made sure of that. A number of them wanted to go to the island to pay their last respects. They went; but permission to enter the Villa Luco was refused. Nevertheless, they did obtain one concession: they were allowed to be the main pall-bearers in the funeral procession.

At 10 a.m. on 25 July an aircraft bearing French military markings flew low over the island and circled over Port-Joinville. As it passed over the cemetery where Pétain was to lie, bystanders saw a wreath gently floating to earth. Nobody knew who the pilot was or where the aircraft came from – and nobody was minded to find out. At 10.30 the ferry docked, bringing Weygand, Héring and Fernet, as well as the Bishops of Luçon and Angers. Telegrams were still flooding in from those who could not attend: Franco, Stucki, Cardinals Gerlier and Liénart, Poniatowski, Primo de Rivera's grandson, and a number from members of the Académie Française. Even General Juin sent a telegram – much to Auriol's fury – expressing his 'profound grief at the loss of the great soldier of Verdun'.[39]

At eleven the passing bell started to sound. Led by a choirboy carrying the processional cross and by the assembled clergy, the coffin was brought into the church of Notre-Dame de Bon-Port and placed on the catafalque. It was draped in the French flag. On top was placed Pétain's marshal's képi. The service then followed the customary pattern, the only bizarre note being struck by the owner of the Hôtel des Voyageurs singing, after the Gospel, a curious little ditty with accompaniment from the choir. Solemnity returned with the sermon, which reminded the congregation, and those outside who could not get into the church, of Pétain's military achievements. 'We will pray', the Bishop of Luçon intoned, 'that God will forgive the sins and crown the merits of this long and tragic life, and we will pray even with the Marshal himself, since I am sure that he wishes it, for the desire and the dream of his life: the union of all Frenchmen and the greatness of France.'[40]

At 12.30 the procession set off from the church to the cemetery. On its way, in the brilliant sunshine, it passed crowds of islanders and tourists (many of them in their bathing suits). It wound its way up the gentle hill leading out of the town. When they arrived in front of the newly dug grave, the bishops and attendant clergy formed a circle round it. The Bishop of Angers blessed the coffin, which was then lowered slowly to its resting place. By one o'clock the last rite had been duly performed. Pétain's long life had finally come to its close.

ACKNOWLEDGEMENTS

It is difficult to know where to start. In the course of this endeavour I have benefited from the wise advice and detailed knowledge of so many that it is difficult to know how even to begin to acknowledge them properly. But a start must be made, however inadequate the result. My main guides as the book has progressed have been Philip Bell and Nicholas Atkin, both with the greatest patience for my various solecisms as well as an acute perception of instances where I was wandering into dangerous historical territory. Martin Alexander has been kind enough to read my final draft and make life-saving corrections. Christopher Arnander and Jane Nissen have read through the proofs with the greatest diligence. I owe them all more than I can say – debts that I am afraid I will never be able to repay – while accepting, as is appropriate, that any errors which have slipped through the fine mesh of their scholarly net are my responsibility and mine alone.

Others have helped on specific topics. Audrey Bonnery, Agnes Ooms and Jaime Alvarez have been indefatigable in research on my behalf, respectively in France, Germany and Spain. Mia Stewart-Wilson has been a brilliant researcher of pictures; Renata Propper has been kind enough to write a penetrating analysis of Pétain's handwriting; Matthew Buck has been wholly persuasive on the subject of the Pétain–de Grandmaison alleged disagreements in their lectures at the École de Guerre; Hugh Thomas has been full of information about Spain, and unsparing in the attention he has given to my questions; Martin Gilbert has given me the benefit of his great knowledge of Winston Churchill; Julian Jackson has been most helpful on the events of May 1940 and the Vichy period; Gerd Krumeich and Holger Afflerbach have contributed to my understanding of Germany in the First World War; Maurice Vaïsse has been most informative on French military history; Père Montagnes of the Couvent des

Dominicains in Toulouse and Père Duval of the Couvent Saint Jacques have been most helpful on Pétain's education; and Richard Griffiths has followed up his earlier book with some generous suggestions to me. My thanks to all of them.

Others have helped me with vital pieces of information or by pointing to sources: Robert Boyce, Jean Crouzat, Philippe Denis, Piers Dixon, Alexei Filitov, Jonathan Haslam, Ken Morgan, Jacques Le Groignec, Denis Lesage, Gilles Nolleau, Felipe Propper, Hew Strachan. I must also record the unstinting and friendly help I have always received from the House of Lords library, in particular from David Jones, Shorayne Fairweather and Caroline Auty. Sarah Tyack and William Spencer at the National Archives in Kew have gone beyond the call of duty in assisting me to unearth hitherto ignored primary material, as have the staff of the Archives Nationales in Paris and the staff of the Service Historique des Armées de Terre at Vincennes. Finally, I thank Richard Beswick and Stephen Guise of Time Warner Books, Andrew Wylie and Tracy Bohan of the Wylie Agency for their enthusiasm and efficiency in bringing the ship safely into port.

The book is dedicated to my stepfamily, Justin and Caroline and their children Tim, Katharine, Peter, Eleanor and Hannah, in the hope that their love of France will not be diminished by my efforts in French history. It goes without saying that none of this could have happened without the full-hearted and loving support of their mother and grandmother – in other words, my wife.

NOTES

INTRODUCTION

Epigraph: 'Whatever one may think about Vichy, he is all the same somebody [of consequence].' A parliamentary commissioner after a visit to Pétain in prison in 1947, quoted in J Isorni: *Souffrance et Mort du Maréchal*; Paris, Flammarion, 1951, p. 198.

CHAPTER 1: 'THE SON OF MY SORROW'

Epigraph: 'So it is with our past. It is labour in vain if we to look to recapture it, all the efforts of our intellect are useless.' M. Proust: *Du Côté de chez Swann*; Paris, Gallimard, 1954, p. 44.

1. *Journal de Genève*, 27.iv.45.
2. *Le Monde*, 28.iv.45
3. Quoted in L.-D. Girard: *Mazinghem, ou la vie secrète de Philippe Pétain 1856–1951*; private publication, 1971, p. 59.
4. Quoted in L.-D. Girard: *op. cit.*, p. 60.
5. Quoted in G. Wright: *Rural Revolution in France*; Stanford, CA, Stanford University Press, 1964, p. 11.
6. P. Berrier: *Cauchy-à-la-Tour, des origines à 1945*; L'Association historique et archéologique auchelloise, Auchel, 1992, p. 111.
7. E. Weber: *Peasants into Frenchmen*; London, Chatto & Windus, 1977, p. 140.
8. E. Weber: *op. cit.*, p. 167.
9. Letter to L.-D. Girard from M. Occre of Cauchy-à-la-Tour, quoted in L.-D. Girard: *op. cit.*, p. 63.

CHAPTER 2: FROM THE CRUCIFIX TO THE SABRE

Epigraph: 'Don't doubt the sombre atmosphere in which we grew up in a France humiliated and murdered . . . brought up for a revenge which would be bloody, fatal and perhaps useless.' Romain Rolland, quoted in C. Digeon: *La Crise allemande de la pensée française (1870–1914)*, Paris, Presses Universitaires de France, 1959, pp. 519–20.

1. I. Robertson: *Blue Guide*; London, A. & C. Black, 1997, p. 67.
2. E. Poteau: *Ces Messieurs de Saint-Bertin . . .*; Lille, Université Charles de Gaulle, 1994, p. 1.
3. J. W. Padberg SJ: *Colleges in Controversy*; Cambridge, Mass., Harvard University Press, 1969, p. 279.
4. M. Perrot and A. Martin-Fugier in M. Perrot (ed.): *A History of Private Life*, Vol. IV; Cambridge, Mass., Harvard University Press, 1990, p. 216.
5. P. Gerbod: *La Vie quotidienne dans les lycées et collèges au XIXè siècle*; Paris, Hachette, 1968, p. 101.
6. *L'Indépendant du Pas-de-Calais*, 7.xiii.1873.

7. T. Zeldin: *France 1848–1945*, Vol. II; Oxford University Press, 1977, p. 148.
8. Ibid.
9. Ibid., p. 151.
10. A. Lehembre: *Le Bertinien*, St-Omer, April 1931.
11. R. Tombs: *France 1814–1914*; London, Longman, 1996, p. 44.
12. Quoted in M. E. Howard: *The Franco-Prussian War: The German Invasion of France, 1870–1871*; London, Hart-Davis, 1961, p. 208.
13. Archives Nationales, Paris (AN), W 111 277.
14. M. E. Howard: *op. cit.*, p. 397.
15. M. Ducrocq: *Le Collège Saint-Bertin de 1561 à nos jours*; Collège Saint-Bertin, 1998, p. 124, n. 204.
16. L. Lecuyer: *La Revanche par l'éducation*; Paris, 1871, p. 24.

CHAPTER 3: THE LONG APPRENTICESHIP (1)

Epigraph: 'Cold. Improves on acquaintance, is perhaps not yet entirely made, will make a good officer.' Pétain's report from the École Supérieure de Guerre (École de Guerre), 1890.

1. A. Teller: *Souvenirs de Saint-Cyr*, Paris, 1886, quoted in T. Zeldin: *France 1848–1945*, Vol II.
2. D. R. Porch: *The March to the Marne: The French Army 1871–1914*; Cambridge University Press, 1981, p. 40.
3. Commandant A. Thieblemont: *Saint-Cyr, École Spéciale Militaire, tradition 1823–1979 – Création et mutation d'un symbole: la 'Galette'*; *Revue historique des armées*, No. 1, 1980, p. 86.
4. Extract from the official register of the *mairie* of Béthune.
5. E. Titoux: *Saint-Cyr et l'École Spéciale Militaire en France*; Paris, Firmin Didot, 1898, p. 408.
6. AN, W 111 277.
7. R. Tombs: *France 1814–1914*, p. 41.
8. Quoted in L.-D. Girard, *Mazinghem*, p. 93.
9. AN, W 111 277.
10. Quoted in D. R. Porch, *op. cit.*, p. 43.
11. M. Perrot (ed.): *A History of Private Life*, Vol. IV, pp. 586–7.
12. P. A. Bourget: *Témoignages inédits sur le Maréchal Pétain*; Paris, Fayard, 1960, p. 26.
13. AN, W 111 277.
14. Ibid.
15. Letter from Mme Jean Deffieux, Célina Brassart's great-niece, quoted in L.-D. Girard, *op. cit.*, p. 111.
16. Letter from Mlle Henriette Laurent, quoted in L.-D. Girard, *op. cit.*, p. 114.
17. AN, W 111 277.
18. Individual report of the École Supérieure de Guerre, 1890.
19. AN, W 111 277.

CHAPTER 4: THE LONG APPRENTICESHIP (2)

Epigraph: 'And I refused to surrender so as not to owe anything to one of the most open activists in the Dreyfus affair.' Pétain in 1945: AN, W 111 277.

1. Quoted in H. Amouroux: *Pétain avant Vichy*; Paris, Fayard,1967, p. 23.
2. Quoted in H. Lottman: *Pétain*; Paris, Seuil, 1992, p. 39.
3. M. Harry: *Mon Amie, Lucie Delarue-Mardrus*; Paris, Ariane, 1946, p. 38.
4. AN, W 111 277.
5. R. Pichot-Duclos: *Réflexions sur ma vie militaire*; Paris, Arthaud, 1947, p. 41.

6. Mme Pétain, as reported in P. A. Bourget: *Témoignages inédits*, p. 29.
7. D. Bredin: *The Affair: The Case of Alfred Dreyfus*, quoted in R. Tombs: *France 1814-1914*, p. 466
8. R. Tombs: ibid.
9. AN, W 111 277.
10. Capitaine Targe, quoted in D. R. Porch: *The March to the Marne*, p. 92.
11. D. R. Porch: *op. cit.*, p. 93.
12. One of Pétain's pupils, quoted in J.-R. Tournoux: *Pétain et de Gaulle*; Paris, Plon, 1964.
13. Pétain, letter to his nephew, quoted in L.-D. Girard: *Mazinghem*, p. 134.
14. Ibid.

CHAPTER 5: THE ROAD TO RETIREMENT

Epigraph: 'Truly, the little schoolboy of Saint-Bertin did not expect to have such a fine career.' Pétain during interrogation in 1945, AN, W 111 277.

1. J.-R. Tournoux: *Pétain et de Gaulle*, p. 49.
2. P. Pelissier: *Philippe Pétain*; Paris, Hachette, 1980, p. 44.
3. Ibid.
4. Quoted in G. Pedroncini: *Pétain, le soldat et la gloire 1856–1918*; Paris, Perrin, 1989, p. 28.
5. Ibid. p. 29.
6. M. Buck: *French Army Notes*; unpublished, 2004, p. 2.
7. L. de Grandmaison: *Deux Conférences faites aux officiers de l'état majeur de l'armée*; Paris, Berger Levrault, 1911.
8. Author correspondence with M. Buck.
9. Quoted in D. B. Ralston: *The Army of the Republic*; Cambridge, Mass., MIT Press, 1967, p. 329.
10. Quoted in J.-R. Tournoux: *op. cit.*, p. 49.
11. Quoted in J. Pouget: *Un Certain Capitaine de Gaulle*; Paris, Fayard, 1973, p. 51.
12. Quoted in J.-R. Tournoux: *op. cit.*, p. 54.
13. Pétain to Eugénie Hardon, 12.iv.14, AN, 523 Mi.
14. Pétain to Eugénie Hardon, 14.v.14, AN, 523 Mi.
15. Ibid.
16. *Le Memorial artésien*, St-Omer, 16–17.vii. 1914.

CHAPTER 6: THE DOGS OF WAR

Epigraph: 'It was . . . really the first "cruel" day of the war'; Pétain, quoted in E Laure: *Pétain*; Paris, Berger-Levrault, 1941, p. 28.

1. E. L. Spears: *Liaison 1914*; London, Eyre & Spottiswoode, 1930, p. 20.
2. M. Egremont: *Under Two Flags*; London, Weidenfeld & Nicolson, 1997, p. 23.
3. E. L. Spears: *op. cit.*, p. 384.
4. E. Laure: *op. cit.*, p. 25.
5. E. L. Spears: *op. cit.*, p. 14.
6. C. de Gaulle: *Lettres, notes et carnets*, Vol. I; Paris, Plon, 1980–6, p. 88.
7. Quoted in L.-D. Girard: *Mazinghem*, p. 206.
8. Quoted in G. Pedroncini: *Pétain, le soldat et la gloire*, p. 51.
9. E. Laure: *op. cit.*, p. 46.
10. E. L. Spears: *op. cit.*, p. 272.
11. E. L. Spears: *Two Men Who Saved France*; London, Eyre & Spottiswoode, 1966, p. 12.
12. E. Laure: *op. cit.*, p. 29.

13. H. Strachan: *The First World War*, Vol. I; Oxford University Press, 2001, p. 250.
14. E. Laure: *op. cit.*, p. 31.
15. Ibid., p. 33.

CHAPTER 7: KILL OR BE KILLED

Epigraph: 'Goodbye 1914 and long live 1915 which will be the year of victory.' E. Fayolle: *Cahiers secrets de la Grande Guerre*; Paris, Plon, 1964, p. 71.

1. E. L. Spears: *Two Men Who Saved France*; pp. 12–13.
2. M. Egremont: *Under Two Flags: The Life of Major-General Sir Edward Spears*; London, Weidenfeld & Nicolson, 1997, p. 5.
3. Ibid. Spears diary entries of 16 and 27.xi.14.
4. Ibid., p. 46.
5. B. Serrigny: *Trente Ans avec Pétain*; Paris, Plon, 1959, p. 22.
6. Ibid., p. 8.
7. Order of 14.xii.14; Service Historique des Armées de Terre, Vincennes (SHAT), 22 N 1792.
8. E. L. Spears: *Liaison 1914*, p. 9.
9. Ibid.
10. Joffre, note of 15.i.15; SHAT, 22 N 1793.
11. Pétain to d'Urbal, 6.v.15; SHAT, 22 N 1794.
12. D'Urbal to Pétain, 10.v.15; SHAT, 22 N 1801.
13. D'Urbal to Pétain, 25.v.15; SHAT, 22 N 1832.
14. E. Laure: *Pétain*, p. 49.
15. Lt-Col. S. Clive, report, 9.vi.15: Kitchener Papers; National Archives, Kew, Public Record Office (NA (PRO)), 30/57/54.
16. Ministère de la Guerre: *Les Armées françaises dans la grande guerre* (AFGG), Vol. III (1931), p. 539.
17. Pétain's report of 1.xi.15; SHAT, 19 N 427.

CHAPTER 8: THE VICTOR OF VERDUN?

Epigraph: Gen. J. J. Pershing to Pétain in 1929, P. Pétain (tr. MacVeagh): *Verdun*; London, E. Matthews & Elliot, 1930, p. 16.

1. A. Horne: *The Price of Glory: Verdun 1916*; London, Macmillan, 1962, p. 36.
2. Ibid., p. 39.
3. Quoted in I. Oulsby: *The Road to Verdun*; London, Jonathan Cape, 2002, p. 43.
4. H. Afflerbach: *Falkenhayn: Politisches Denken und Handeln im Kaiserreich*; Munich, R. Oldenbourg Verlag, 1994, p. 363.
5. Pétain to Eugénie Hardon, 11.i.16; AN, 523 Mi.
6. Pétain to Eugénie Hardon, 22.ii.16, ibid.
7. I. Oulsby: *op. cit.*, p. 66.
8. P. Pétain: *op. cit.*, p. 76.
9. B. Serrigny: *Trente Ans avec Pétain*, p. 44.
10. Ibid., p. 45.
11. Ibid., p. 46.
12. Pétain to Eugénie Hardon, 3.iii.16; AN, 523 Mi.
13. B. Serrigny: *op. cit.*, p. 46.
14. Ibid., p. 48.
15. Ibid., p. 50.
16. Pétain to Eugénie Hardon, 3.iii.16; AN, 523 Mi.
17. B. Serrigny: *op. cit.*, p. 64.

18. A. Horne: *op. cit.*, p. 162.
19. B. Serrigny: *op. cit.*, p. 83.
20. Ibid., p. 82.
21. G. Loustanou-Lacau: *Mémoires d'un Français rebelle*; Paris, Fayard, 1948, p. 36.
22. C. Mangin: *Lettres de guerre 1914–1918*; Paris, Fayard, 1950, p. 100.
23. Quoted in A. Horne: *op. cit.*, p. 233.
24. B. Serrigny: *op. cit.*, p. 95.
25. P. Pétain: *op. cit.*, pp. 134–9.
26. Quoted in H. Lottman: *Pétain*, p. 57.

CHAPTER 9: 'THEY REFUSE TO ADVANCE TO BE BUTCHERED'

Title: Bertie of Thame to Foreign Office, 29.iv.17; NA (PRO), FO 800/169.
Epigraph: 'I am only called in catastrophes.' Pétain to Henry Bordeaux in H. Bordeaux: *Images du Maréchal Pétain*, Paris, Sequana, 1941, p. 23.
1. E. Fayolle: *Cahiers secrets*, p. 197.
2. Pétain to Eugénie Hardon, 25.i.17; AN, 523 Mi.
3. Ibid.
4. *Le Matin*, 17.ii.17.
5. E. Fayolle: *op. cit.*, p. 196.
6. J. de Pierrefeu (tr. Street): *French Headquarters 1915–1918*; London, Bles, n.d., p. 141.
7. E. L. Spears: *Prelude to Victory*; London, Jonathan Cape, 1939, p. 337.
8. Ibid., p. 364.
9. Ibid., p. 365.
10. Ibid., p. 507.
11. G. Pedroncini: *Les Mutineries de 1917*; Paris, Presses Universitaires de France, 1967, p. 58.
12. R. M. Watt: *Dare Call It Treason*; London, Chatto & Windus, 1964, p. 163.
13. Pétain to Eugénie Hardon, 28.iv.17, AN, 523 Mi.
14. Bertie to Balfour, 30.iv.17; NA (PRO), FO 371/2937.
15. LeRoy-Lewis to Chief of Imperial General Staff, 29.iv.17; NA (PRO), WO 33/913.
16. B. Serrigny: *Trente Ans avec Pétain*, p. 131.
17. Haig diary entry, 4.v.17, in R. Blake (ed.): *The Private Papers of Douglas Haig 1914–1919*; London, Eyre & Spottiswoode, 1952, p. 227.
18. *Le Figaro*, 13.v.17.
19. Bertie to Balfour, 16.v.17; NA (PRO), FO 371/2937.
20. Pétain to Eugénie Hardon, 21.v.17; AN, 523 Mi.
21. J. de Pierrefeu: *op. cit.*, p. 163.
22. B. Serrigny: *op. cit.*, p. 144.
23. Haig diary entry 18.v.17, in R. Blake, *op. cit.*, p. 232.
24. B. Serrigny: *op. cit.*, p. 145.
25. NA (PRO), WO 158/48/92623.
26. L. Freedman, P. Hayes and R. O'Neill (eds.): *War, Strategy and International Politics: Essays in Honour of Sir Michael Howard*; Oxford, Clarendon Press, 1992 (D. French: 'Who Knew What and When? The French Army Mutinies and the British Decision to Launch the Third Battle of Ypres'), p. 143.
27. Ibid., p. 142.
28. R. M. Watt: *op. cit.*, p. 160.
29. Directive 1, GQG, 19.v.17; SHAT, 22N 1832.
30. Pétain to Eugénie Hardon, 23.v.17, AN, 523 Mi.
31. R. M. Watt: *op. cit.*, p. 170.

32. L. Freedman et al.: *op. cit.*, p. 146.
33. AFGG, Tome V, Vol. II, p. 198.
34. Pétain to Eugénie Hardon, 15.vi.17, AN, 523 Mi.
35. J. J. Pershing: *My Experiences in the World War*, London, Hodder & Stoughton, 1931, p. 55.
36. Ibid., p. 68.
37. E. L. Spears, *Liaison 1914*, p. 596.
38. H. Desagneaux (tr. Adams): *A French Soldier's War Diary*, London, Elmfield Press, 1975, pp.48–49.
39. L. Freedman et al.: *op. cit.*, p. 150.
40. Haig memo of 19.x.17; NA (PRO) WO 158/48/92623.
41. Haig diary entry, 16.xii.17, in R. Blake, *op. cit.*, p. 274.

CHAPTER 10: WILL IT EVER END?

Epigraph: 'The French Army is what it should be, what I wished that it should be.' Pétain, quoted in H. Bordeaux: *Images du Maréchal Pétain*; p. 62.

1. Pétain, quoted in J. de Pierrefeu: *French Headquarters 1915–1918*, p. 64.
2. *Journal Officiel*, 20.xi.17, p. 2963.
3. Haig diary entry, 7.i.18, in R. Blake (ed.): *The Private Papers of Douglas Haig*, p. 278.
4. Pétain to Clemenceau, 18.i.18, quoted in G. Pedroncini: *Pétain, le soldat et la gloire*, p. 252.
5. F. Foch (tr. B. Molt): *The Memoirs of Marshal Foch*, London, Heineman, 1931, p. 27.
6. Haig diary entry, 27.i.18, in R. Blake: *op. cit.*, p. 280.
7. Haig to Lady Haig, 31.i.18, in R. Blake: *op. cit.*, p. 281.
8. NA (PRO), WO 158/48/92623.
9. Haig diary entry, 1.ii.18, in R. Blake: *op. cit.*, p. 281.
10. NA (PRO), WO 158/48/92623.
11. Haig diary entry, 19.iii.18, in R. Blake: *op. cit.*, p. 293.
12. A. J. P. Taylor (ed.): *Lloyd George: A Diary by Frances Stevenson*; London, Hutchinson, 1971, p. 138.
13. Ibid., p. 286.
14. Haig to Lady Haig, 20.iii.18, in R. Blake: *op. cit.*, p. 294.
15. Haig diary entry, 21.iii.18, ibid., p. 296.
16. Haig diary entry, 25.iii.18, ibid., p. 297.
17. E. Fayolle: *Carnets secrets*, pp. 262–3.
18. Haig diary entry, 26.iii.18, in R. Blake: *op. cit.*, p. 298.
19. F. Foch: *op.cit.*, p. 300.
20. E. Fayolle: *op. cit.*, p. 267.
21. Churchill, quoted in M. Gilbert: *Winston S. Churchill*, Vol. IV, *1916–1922*; London, Heinemann, 1975, p. 98.
22. Ibid.

CHAPTER 11: THE STRIFE IS O'ER, THE BATTLE DONE . . .

Epigraph: 'Is it possible that they will refuse me that?'; Pétain quoted in P. A. Bourget: *Témoignages inédits*, p. 44.

1. Haig diary note, 14.iv.18, in R. Blake (ed.): *The Private Papers of Douglas Haig*, p. 303.
2. Haig diary note, 19.iv.18, ibid., p. 304.
3. Haig diary note, 2.v.18, ibid., p. 308.
4. G. Pedroncini: *Pétain, le soldat et la gtoire*, p. 362.
5. E. Fayolle: *Cahiers secrets*, p. 277.

6. Derby to Balfour, 5.vi.18, NA (PRO), FO371/3214.
7. J. de Pierrefeu: *French Headquarters 1915–1918*, p. 272.
8. Ibid.
9. E. Fayolle: *op. cit.*, p. 283.
10. Haig diary note, 4.vi.18, in R. Blake, pp. 313–14.
11. Ibid.
12. Pétain to Eugénie Hardon, 28.vi.18, AN, 523 Mi.
13. E. Fayolle: *op. cit.*, p. 285.
14. AFGG, Tome VI, Vol. 2, p. 468.
15. G. Pedroncini: *op. cit.*, p. 395.
16. E. Fayolle: *op. cit.*, p. 296.
17. J. J. Pershing: *My Experiences . . .*, p. 571.
18. Ibid., p. 593.
19. Ibid., p. 622.
20. Ibid., p. 634.
21. J. Keegan: *The First World War*, p. 442.
22. Haig diary note, 5.x.18, in R. Blake: *op. cit.*, p. 330.
23. Haig diary note, 19.x.18, ibid., p. 333.
24. Ibid.
25. Haig diary note, 25.x.18, ibid., p. 336.
26. J. J. Pershing: *op. cit.*, p. 670.
27. Haig diary note, 19.x.18, in R. Blake: p. 334.
28. Haig diary note, 24.x.18, ibid., p. 336.
29. Haig diary note, 25.x.18, ibid., p. 337.
30. Pétain to Eugénie Hardon, 11.xi.18; AN, 523 Mi.
31. C. de Gaulle: *Mémoires d'espoir*, Vol. I; Paris, Plan, 1970, p. 173.
32. E. Fayolle: *op. cit.*, p. 299.
33. Pétain, quoted in P. A. Bourget: *op. cit.*, p. 44.

CHAPTER 12: NINI

Epigraph: '. . . I note that I love you deeply . . .' Pétain to Eugénie Hardon, 19.ii.19; AN, 523 Mi.

1. B. Serrigny: *Trente Ans avec Pétain*, p. 142.
2. Pétain to Eugénie Hardon, 2.ii.19; AN, 523 Mi.
3. Pétain to Eugénie Hardon, 6.ii.19; ibid.
4. Pétain to Eugénie Hardon, 19.ii.19; ibid.
5. Pétain to Eugénie Hardon, 25.ii.19; ibid.
6. Ibid.
7. Pétain to Eugénie Hardon, 21.iii.19; ibid.
8. J. Doise and M. Vaïsse: *Diplomatie et outil militaire 1871–1969*; Paris, Imprimerie Nationale, 1987, p. 268.
9. Quoted in G. Pedroncini: *Pétain, la victoire perdue*; Paris, Perrin, 1995, p. 75.
10. Pétain to Eugénie Hardon, 2.viii.19; AN, 523 Mi.
11. Pétain to Eugénie Hardon, 10.ix.19; ibid.
12. Quoted in L.-D. Girard: *Mazinghem*, p. 245.
13. Pétain to Eugénie Hardon, 27.vii.20; AN, 523 Mi.
14. G. Pedroncini: *op. cit.*, p. 101.
15. Quoted in R. A. Doughty: *The Seeds of Disaster*; The Shoe String Press, Hamden, Conn., 1985, p. 9.
16. Quoted in G. Pedroncini: *op. cit.*, p. 111.

CHAPTER 13: THE SPANISH CONNECTION (1)

Epigraph: 'The Marshal is a great man who . . . died in 1925.' De Gaulle, quoted in J.-R. Tournoux: *Pétain et de Gaulle*, p. 356.

1. Quoted in R. Griffiths: *Marshal Pétain*; London, Constable, 1970, p. 108.
2. Pétain to Eugénie Pétain, 13.i.25; AN, 523 Mi.
3. Pétain to Eugénie Pétain, 11.vi.25; AN, 523 Mi.
4. Pétain to Eugénie Pétain, 22.vii.25; AN, 523 Mi.
5. Pétain to the Minister of War, 22.vii.25; SHAT, 3 H 609.
6. Pétain to Painlevé, 20.x.25; SHAT, 3 H 609.
7. ABC Madrid, 29.vii.25.
8. Ibid.
9. Courson: 2nd Report to Ministry of War, 16.ix.25; SHAT, 3 H 100.
10. ABC Madrid, 31.vii.25.
11. Pétain to Painlevé, 20.x.25; SHAT, 3 H 609.
12. Ibid.
13. French liaison officers' report, 30.x.25; SHAT, 3 H 607.
14. Quoted in D. S. Woolman: *Rebels in the Rif*, Stanford, CA, Stanford University Press, 1969, p. 195.
15. Quoted in R. Griffiths: *op. cit.*, p. 122.
16. ABC Madrid, 4.ii.26.
17. ABC Madrid, 5.ii.26.
18. ABC Madrid, 6.ii.26.
19. Ibid.
20. ABC Madrid, 7.ii.26.
21. Ibid.
22. ABC Madrid, 15.vii.26.
23. S. Ben-Ami: *Fascism From Above*; Oxford, Clarendon Press, 1983, pp. 165–6.
24. *New York Times*, 10.ix.25.

CHAPTER 14: 'THE MEMORY IS WEAKENING'

Epigraph: 'I have never been subjected to such an avalanche of questions in three days . . .' Pétain to Eugénie Pétain, 4.ix.27; AN, 523 Mi.

1. Minute of meeting of 22.1.34; *Cahiers du redressement français*, 2e Série, No. 11.
2. *Revue des Deux Mondes*, March 1935, p. 1.
3. J.-R. Tournoux: *Pétain et de Gaulle*, p. 55.
4. Ibid., p. 58.
5. C. de Gaulle (tr. G. Hopkins): *The Edge of the Sword*; London, Faber & Faber, 1960, dedicatory note.
6. Pétain to Eugénie Pétain, 16.x.25; AN, 523 Mi.
7. Quoted in J. Pouget: *Un Certain Capitaine de Gaulle*; Paris, Fayard, 1973, p. 187.
8. Pétain to Eugénie Pétain, 1.viii.28; AN, 523 Mi.
9. J.-R. Tournoux: *op. cit.*, p. 133.
10. Quoted in P. C. F. Bankwitz: *Maxime Weygand and Civil–Military Relations in Modern France*; Cambridge Mass., Harvard University Press, 1967.
11. Harold Macmillan, quoted in A. Horne: *To Lose a Battle*; London, Macmillan, 1969, p. 543.
12. Clemenceau, quoted in P. C. F. Bankwitz: *op. cit.*, p. 29.
13. *Le Populaire*, 25.i.31.
14. ABC Madrid, 18.iii.30.
15. *New York Times*, 6.xi.31.

16. J.-R. Tournoux: *op. cit.*, p. 160.
17. Ibid., p. 161.
18. Ibid., p. 162.
19. A. J. Toynbee: *Survey of International Affairs 1931*; London, Royal Institute of International Affairs, 1932, p. 22.

CHAPTER 15: THE HOLLOW YEARS

Epigraph: '. . . I have never practised politics and I do not wish to do so.' Pétain, quoted in E. Laure: *Pétain*, p. 362.
1. Quoted in L.-D. Girard: *Mazinghem*, p. 333.
2. Pétain to Eugénie Pétain, 8.ix.34; AN, 523 Mi.
3. E. Laure: *op. cit.*, p. 361.
4. Ibid., p. 362.
5. M.-G. Gamelin: *Servir*, Vol. II; Paris, Plon, 1947, p. 128.
6. M. S. Alexander, 'In Defence of the Maginot Line', in R. Boyce (ed.): *French Foreign and Defence Policy 1918–1940*; London, Routledge, 1998, p. 172.
7. A. Conquet: *Auprès du Maréchal Pétain*; Paris, Editions France-Empire, 1970, p. 57.
8. E. Laure: *op. cit.*, p. 366.
9. A. Conquet: *op. cit.*, p. 19.
10. Ibid., p. 75.
11. Ibid., p. 77.
12. Ibid., p. 78.
13. Ibid., p. 80.
14. Göring, speech in Essen, 4.xii.34, in *Göring, Reden und Aufsätze* (ed. E. Gritzvach); Munich, Zentralverlag der NSDAP, 1942.
15. Quoted in R. Griffiths: *Marshal Pétain*, p. 193.
16. Sir J. Burnett-Stuart, quoted in M. S. Alexander: *The Republic in Danger: General Maurice Gamelin and the Politics of French Defence*; Cambridge University Press, 1992, p. 246
17. *La Victoire*, 6.ii.35.
18. *La Victoire*, 18.ii.35.
19. *Le Jour*, 22.v.35.
20. Pétain to Eugénie Pétain, 19.v.35; AN, 523 Mi.
21. Pétain to Eugénie Pétain, 4.viii.35; ibid.
22. *Vu*, 30.xi.35.
23. François-Poncet, quoted in G. A. Craig: *Germany 1866–1945*; Oxford, Clarendon Press, 1978, pp. 688–9.
24. *Le Journal*, 30.iv.36.

CHAPTER 16: THE UNPOPULAR FRONT

Epigraph: 'If the barometer announces rain, is it the barometer which is wrong?' Quoted in A. Conquet: *Auprès du Maréchal Pétain*, p. 284.
1. Quoted in 'Pertinax' (*nom de plume* of A. Géraud): *The Gravediggers of France: Gamelin, Daladier, Reynaud and Laval*; New York, Editions de la Maison Française, 1944, p. 342.
2. Quoted in A. Conquet: *op. cit.*, p. 284.
3. Ibid., p. 283.
4. Quoted in G. Warner: *Pierre Laval and the Eclipse of France*; London, Eyre & Spottiswoode, 1968, p. 164.
5. *Procès du Maréchal Pétain. Compte rendu officiel in extenso des audiences de la Haute Cour de Justice (Procès Pétain)*; Paris, Editions Louis Pariente, 1976, p. 234.
6. Ibid.

7. G. Loustanau-Lacau: *Mémoires d'un Français rebelle*, p. 112.
8. SHAT, 1 K 224.
9. Quoted in A. Conquet: *op. cit.*, p. 152.
10. Ibid., p. 199.
11. Ibid., p. 151.
12. *Revue Militaire Générale*, 1/37, p. 22.
13. Pétain to Eugénie Pétain, 5.ii.37; AN, 523 Mi.
14. Pétain to Eugénie Pétain, 28.iv.37; ibid.
15. H.-J. Hansen (ed.): *Auf den Spuren des Westwalls*; Aachen, Helios Verlags-und Buchvertriebs-Gesellschaft, 1998, p. 59.
16. Pétain to M.-A. Pardee, 10.iii.38, in M.-A. Pardee: *Le Maréchal que j'ai connu*; Paris, Editions André Bonne, 1952, p. 14.
17. Pétain to Eugénie Pétain, 11.ix.38; AN, 523 Mi.
18. Pétain, quoted in M. Cornick: 'Fighting Myth With Reality: The Fall of France, Anglophobia and the BBC', in V. Holman and D. Kelly (eds): *France at War in the Twentieth Century: Propaganda, Myth and Metaphor*, Oxford and New York, Berghahn Books, 2000, p. 13.
19. 'Conversazione R. Ambasciatore-Maresciallo Pétain': *Affari Politici Francia 20*; Foreign Ministry Archives, Rome, quoted in M. Cornick, *op. cit.*, pp. 2–3.
20. O. Bullitt: 'For the President: Personal and Secret Correspondence Between Franklin D. Roosevelt and William C. Bullitt', 1973; 6.ii.39, quoted in J. Jackson: *The Fall of France: The Nazi Invasion of 1940*; Oxford University Press, 2003, p. 70.
21. Pétain to Eugénie Pétain, 9.ix.38; AN, 523 Mi.
22. Pétain to Eugénie Pétain, 10.ix.38; ibid.
23. Quoted in G. A. Craig: *Germany, 1866–1945*, p. 704.
24. Pétain to Eugénie Pétain, 14.ix.38; AN, 523 Mi.
25. Quoted in H. Amouroux: *Pétain avant Vichy*, p. 204.
26. Quoted in A. Conquet: *op. cit.*, p. 284.

CHAPTER 17: THE SPANISH CONNECTION (2)

Epigraph: M Peterson: *Both Sides of the Curtain*, London, Constable, 1950 p. 179.
1. Pétain to Eugénie Pétain, 1.iii.39; AN, 523 Mi.
2. *Le Populaire*, 3.iii.39.
3. *Candide*, 8.iii.39.
4. Pétain to Eugénie Pétain, 17.iii.39; AN, 523 Mi.
5. Pétain to Eugénie Pétain, 2.iv.39; ibid.
6. A. Gazel in *Procès Pétain*, p. 96.
7. Quoted in *New York Herald Tribune* (Paris edition), 25.iii.39.
8. M. Peterson: *op. cit.*, p. 175.
9. Pétain to Eugénie Pétain, 19.iv.39; AN, 523 Mi.
10. *Madrid*, 19.iv.39.
11. M. Peterson: *op. cit.*, p. 175.
12. *Madrid*, 7.v.39.
13. Pétain to Eugénie Pétain, 13.v.39; AN, 523 Mi.
14. Quoted in H. Amouroux: *Pétain avant Vichy*, p. 213.
15. *Arriba*, 3.viii.39.
16. Pétain to Eugénie Pétain, 7.vii.39; AN, 523 Mi.
17. Pétain to Eugénie Pétain, 15.vii.39; ibid.
18. Quoted in E. Laure: *Pétain*, p. 427.
19. Pétain to Daladier, 11.ix.39; AN, AG 2 11.
20. Quoted in *Le Monde*, 24.i.53.

21. Pétain to Eugénie Pétain, 16.xi.39; AN, 523 Mi.
22. M. Peterson: *op. cit.*, p. 178.
23. Pétain to Eugénie Pétain, 25.xii.39; AN, 523 Mi.
24. Pétain to Eugénie Pétain, 3.i.40; ibid.
25. M. Peterson: *op. cit.*, p. 179.
26. Quoted in A. Horne: *To Lose a Battle*, London, Macmillan, 1969, p. 212.
27. Quoted ibid., p. 213.
28. Pétain to Eugénie Pétain, 27.iii.40; AN, 523 Mi.
29. Pétain to Eugénie Pétain, 31.iii.40; ibid.
30. Quoted in J. Szaluta: *French Historical Studies*, Vol. VIII, Part 4 (1974), p. 529.

CHAPTER 18: DEFEAT

Epigraph: '. . . I make the gift of my person to France to lessen her distress . . .' Quoted in E. Laure: *Pétain*, p. 435.
 1. Pétain to Eugénie Pétain, 22.v.40; AN, 523 Mi.
 2. Lebrun in *Procès Pétain*, p. 64.
 3. Quoted in B. Vergez-Chaignon: *Le Docteur Ménétrel, Éminence grise et confidant du Maréchal Pétain*; Paris, Perrin, 2001, p. 83.
 4. E. Spears: *Assignment to Catastrophe*, Vol. I; London, Heinemann, 1954, p. 183.
 5. Ibid., pp. 231–2.
 6. Quoted in B. Vergez-Chaignon: *op. cit.*, p. 35.
 7. Ibid.
 8. Pétain to Eugénie Pétain, 22.v.40; AN, 523 Mi.
 9. Ibid.
10. Campbell to Halifax, NA, FO 800/312.
11. W. S. Churchill: *The Second World War*, London, Cassell, 1949, p. 100.
12. E. Spears: *op. cit.*, p. 319.
13. E. Spears: *Assignment to Catastrophe*, Vol. II; London, William Heinemann, 1954, p. 19.
14. Pétain to Eugénie Pétain, 4.vi.40; AN, 523 Mi.
15. Ibid.
16. Campbell to Halifax, 5.vi.40, Cabinet Papers 65/13, in M. Gilbert: *Churchill War Papers*, Vol. II, *May 1940–December 1940*; London, Heinemann, 1994, p. 253.
17. E. Spears: *op. cit.*, p. 84.
18. Ibid.
19. E. Spears: *op. cit.*, p. 138.
20. The Earl of Avon: *The Eden Memoirs: The Reckoning*; London, Cassell, 1965, p. 115.
21. E. Spears: *op. cit.*, p. 175.
22. J. Colville, diary entry, 12.vi.40: *The Fringes of Power: Downing Street Diaries 1939–1955*, London, Hodder and Stoughton, 1985, p. 154.
23. Quoted in E. Laure: *op. cit.*, p. 433.
24. G. Warner: *Pierre Laval and the Eclipse of France*, p. 174.
25. Quoted in E. Spears: *op. cit.*, p. 286.
26. Ibid., p. 292.
27. Quoted in J. Jackson: *The Fall of France*, p. 138.

CHAPTER 19: THE ROAD TO VICHY

Epigraph: 'It happens that a peasant at home sees his field laid waste by hail. He does not despair of the next harvest.' Pétain, speech of 23.vi.40, in P. Pétain: *Quatre Années au pouvoir*, Paris, La Couronne Littéraire, 1949, p. 50.
 1. Minute of meeting, Huntziger/von Stülpnagel, 8.viii.40; AN, 3 W 283.

2. Laval in *Procès Pétain*, p. 235.
3. Pétain, radio broadcast, 17.vi.40.
4. Pétain, broadcast of 17.vi.40, in P. Petain: *op. cit.*, p. 47.
5. Herriot, in *Procès Pétain*, p. 144.
6. P. Baudouin: *Neuf Mois au gouvernement*; Paris, La Table Ronde, 1948, p. 227.
7. English text of Armistice in *Documents on German Foreign Policy 1918–1945*, HMSO, 1957.
8. Quoted in G. Warner: *Pierre Laval and the Eclipse of France*, p. 199.
9. Flandin, in *Le Procès Flandin devant la Haute Cour de Justice, 23–26 juillet 1946*; Paris, Librairie de Médicis, 1947.
10. *Journal Officiel Débats*, 10.vii.40.
11. B. Serrigny: *Trente ans avec Pétain*, p. 180.
12. Ibid., p. 181.
13. Quoted in H. du Moulin de Labarthète: *Le Temps des illusions: souvenirs (juillet 1940–avril 1942)*; Geneva, Les Editions du Cheval Ailé, p. 106.

CHAPTER 20: NOUS, PHILIPPE PÉTAIN . . .

Epigraph: 'This policy is mine . . . It is me alone that history will judge.' Pétain, in P. Pétain: *Quatre Années au pouvoir*, p. 71.

1. B. Serrigny: *Trente ans avec Pétain*, p. 179.
2. René Gillouin, quoted in R. Griffiths: *Marshal Pétain*, p. 263.
3. British Foreign Office circular, 'Intelligence Summary on French African Colonies', June 1940; NA (PRO), FO371/2846.
4. Quoted in W. Tute: *The Reluctant Enemies*; London, Collins, 1990, p. 107.
5. *Daily Mirror*, 28.ix.40.
6. Quoted in J. Jackson: *The Dark Years*; Oxford University Press, 2001, p. 171.
7. H. du Moulin de Labarthète: *Le Temps des illusions*, p. 35.
8. B. Serrigny: *op. cit.*, p. 186.
9. Pétain in *Quatre Années au pouvoir*, p. 62.
10. P. Baudouin: *Neuf Mois au gouvernement*, p. 379.
11. Documents on German Foreign Policy, London, HMSO, 1959–61, Series D, Vol. XI, no. 227.
12. Laval in *Procès Pétain*, p. 246.
13. NA (PRO), FO 370/2769.
14. NA (PRO), PREM 7/7.
15. Memorandum of E. M. Young, 15.vi.64; NA (PRO), FO 370/2769.
16. Letter from J.-P. de Dadelsen to M. Yourcenar, 27.x.40, quoted in B. Vergez-Chaignon: *Le Docteur Ménétrel*, p. 130.
17. Pétain in *Quatre Années au pouvoir*, p. 69.
18. Ibid., p. 70.
19. J. Colville: *The Fringes of Power*, p. 339.
20. Quoted in M. Gilbert: *Winston S. Churchill: Finest Hour*; London, Heinemann, 1983, p. 960.
21. Matthews to Hull, 16.xi.40, in *Foreign Relations of the United States*, Vol. 2, p. 411.
22. M. Peyrouton: *Du Service public à la prison commune*; Paris, Plon, 1950, p. 179.
23. Laval in *Procès Pétain*, p. 250.
24. H. du Moulin de Latarthète, *op. cit.*, p. 80.
25. L. Noguères: *Le Véritable Procès du Maréchal Pétain*; Paris, Fayard, 1955, p. 652.
26. Quoted in M. Gilbert: *op. cit.*, p. 957.
27. Ibid., p. 958.
28. Ibid., p. 959.

29. Ibid., p. 960.
30. Ibid.

CHAPTER 21: DARLAN

Epigraph: 'The leader is he who knows at the same time how to make himself obeyed and how to make himself loved.' Pétain: *Quatre Années au pouvoir*, p. 81.

1. Abetz to Foreign Ministry, 26.xii.1940, *Documents on German Foreign Policy*, Series D, Vol. XI, no. 569.
2. W. D. Leahy: *I Was There*; London, Victor Gollancz, 1950, p. 12.
3. Ibid., p. 20.
4. Ibid.
5. Ibid., p. 21.
6. Ibid., p. 22.
7. Churchill to Chiefs of Staff, 7.i.41, in M. Gilbert: *Churchill War Papers*, Vol. III, *The Ever-Widening War*, London, Heinemann, 2000, p. 42.
8. Churchill to Roosevelt, 11.i.41, ibid., p. 64.
9. Churchill to Flandin, 14.xi.45, Churchill papers 2/146, M. Gilbert: *Winston S. Churchill*, Vol. VII, *Never Despair*, London, Heinemann, 1988, p. 169.
10. AN, 3 AG 2 318.
11. W. D. Leahy: *op. cit.*, p. 26.
12. Ibid., p. 27.
13. NA (PRO), FO 371/8104.
14. Quoted in J. Jackson: *The Dark Years*, p. 268.
15. W. D. Leahy: *op. cit.*, p. 28.
16. B. Serrigny: *Trente Ans avec Pétain*, p. 192.
17. Churchill to Foreign Office and Chiefs of Staff Committee, 15.ii.41, in M. Gilbert: *op. cit.*, p. 220.
18. B. Serrigny: *op. cit.*, p. 192.
19. P. Pétain: *op. cit.*, p. 79.
20. Quoted in R. O. Paxton: *Vichy France: Old Guard and New Order 1940–1944*; New York, Columbia University Press, 1982, p. 113.
21. Pétain: *op. cit.*, p. 89.
22. B. Serrigny: *op. cit.*, p. 193.
23. Ibid., p. 194.
24. AN, 2 AG 656.
25. J. Berthelot in *Procès Pétain*, p. 341.
26. Churchill to Eden, 9.vii.41, Churchill papers 20/40, M. Gilbert: *Churchill War Papers*, Vol. II, p. 919.
27. R. Murphy: *Diplomat Among Warriors*; London, Collins, 1964, p. 113.

CHAPTER 22: THE RETURN OF 'BLACK PETER'

Epigraph: 'I have serious things to say to you.' Pétain: *Quatre Années au pouvoir*, p. 105.

1. P. Pétain: *op. cit.*, p. 110.
2. Ibid.
3. W. D. Leahy: *I Was There*, p. 59.
4. Pétain: *op. cit.*, p. 110.
5. Ibid.
6. Ibid., p. 112.
7. NA (PRO), HW 1/74.

8. NA (PRO), HW 1/84.
9. B. Serrigny: *Trente Ans avec Pétain*, p. 195.
10. P. Pétain: *Actes et Ecrits*, (ed. J. Isorhi); Paris, Flammarion, 1974, p. 41.
11. B. Serrigny: *op. cit.*, p. 198.
12. Ibid., pp. 198–9.
13. Leahy to Roosevelt, 22.xi.41; Franklin Delano Roosevelt Library, New York.
14. Ibid.
15. Turkish Ambassador at Vichy to Ankara, 29.xi.41; NA (PRO), HW 1/277.
16. B. Serrigny: *op. cit.*, p. 200.
17. Ibid.
18. W. D. Leahy: *op. cit.*, p. 84.
19. Ibid., p. 85.
20. B. Serrigny: *op. cit.*, p. 203.
21. W. D. Leahy: *op. cit.*, p. 96.
22. B. Serrigny: *op. cit.*, p. 203.
23. Ibid.
24. Ibid., p. 207.
25. Ibid., pp. 209–10.
26. W. D. Leahy: *op.cit.*, p. 123.
27. Churchill to Roosevelt, 20.xi.41; Cabinet papers 65/24, in M. Gilbert: *Churchill War Papers*, Vol. III, p. 1481.
28. Churchill to Roosevelt, Churchill papers 20/46, ibid., p. 1611.

CHAPTER 23: COUNTDOWN TO TORCH

Epigraph: 'I am going to put so much responsibility on his back that he will collapse.'
Pétain to Serrigny in Serrigny:, *Trente Ans avec Pétain*, p. 212.
1. Ibid.
2. *Le Temps*, 22.iv.42.
3. W. D. Leahy: *I Was There*, p. 114.
4. H.-H. Giraud: *Mes Evasions*; Paris, Juillard, 1946, p. 131.
5. B. Serrigny: *op. cit.*, p. 212.
6. G. Warner: *Pierre Laval and the Eclipse of France*, p. 299n.
7. P. Boegner: *Carnets du Pasteur Boegner 1940–1945*; Paris, Fayard, 1992, p. 192.
8. Ibid., p. 200.
9. Abetz to Auswärtiges Amt 1.vi.42, quoted in G. Warner: *op.cit.*, p. 312.
10. Reproduced in L. Noguères: *Le Véritable Procès du Maréchal Pétain*, unnumbered page at end.
11. P. Boegner: *op. cit.*, p. 195.
12. *Le Temps*, 24.vi.42.
13. Quoted in L. Noguères: *op. cit.*, p. 399.
14. Juin to Ministry of War, 7.xi.42; SHAT, 1 P 17.
15. Darlan to Admiralty, 7.xi.42; SHAT, 1 P 17.
16. Minute of meeting Pétain/Tuck, 8.xi.42; SHAT, 1 P 17.
17. P. Billotte: *Le Temps des armes*; Paris, Plon, 1972, p. 239.

CHAPTER 24: THE COLLAPSE OF THE HOUSE OF CARDS

Epigraph: 'The Marshal rests . . . inert in his chair'. B. Serrigny: *Trente ans avec Pétain*, p. 225.
1. Bergeret in *Procès Pétain*, p. 333.
2. Tuck to Hull, 8.xi.42; Foreign Relation of the United States, 1942, Vol. II, quoted in G. Warner: *Pierre Laval and the Eclipse of France*, p. 323.

3. F. Lehideux: *De Renault à Pétain – Mémoires*; Paris, Pygmalion, 2001, pp. 392–3.
4. Darlan to Admiralty, 8.xi.42; SHAT, 1 P 17.
5. Darlan to Pétain, 9.xi.42; SHAT, 1 P 17.
6. Noguès to Pétain, 12.xi.42; SHAT, 1 P 17.
7. Quoted in L. Noguères: *Le Véritable Procès du Maréchal Pétain*, p. 449.
8. Juin to Ministry of War, 11.xi.42; SHAT, 1 P 17.
9. Quoted in B. Vergez-Chaignon: *Le docteur Ménétrel*, p. 207.
10. Quoted in H. Coutau-Bégarie & C. Huan: *Darlan*; Paris, Fayard, 1989, p. 611.
11. Noguès to Pétain, quoted ibid., p. 617.
12. Telegram reproduced in facsimile, ibid., p. 619.
13. Quoted ibid., p. 620.
14. B. Serrigny: *op. cit.*, p. 224.
15. Ibid., pp. 224–5.
16. Ibid.
17. Ibid.
18. Ibid., p. 226.
19. Ménétrel's notes, in L. Noguères: *op. cit.*, p. 508.
20. AN, 2 AG 617, quoted in B. Vergez-Chaignon: *op. cit.*, p. 211.
21. Minute of Council of Ministers on 17.xi.42, in L. Noguères: *op. cit.*, p. 511.
22. J. Barthélémy, *Le Ministre de la Justice. Memoires de Vichy 1941–1943*; Paris, Pygmalion, 1989, p. 133.
23. J.-P. Azéma: *De Munich à la libération*; Paris, Seuil, 1979, p. 204.
24. A. Lavagne, diary entry for 19.xi.42, quoted in J.-R. Tournoux: *Pétain et la France*, p. 435.
25. B. Serrigny: *op. cit.*, pp. 227–8.

CHAPTER 25: WHICH WAY TO TURN?

Epigraph: 'It is useless now to try to galvanise this poor old man'. B. Serrigny: *Trente Ans avec Pétain*, p. 230.
1. Ibid., p. 225.
2. Ibid., p. 228.
3. A. Conquet: *Auprès du Maréchal Pétain*, p. 385.
4. B. Serrigny: *op. cit.*, p. 230.
5. Choppin to Féat, 8.iii.43; AN, 2 AG 610, quoted in B. Vergez-Chaignon: *Le Docteur Ménétrel*, p. 219.
6. P. Pétain: *Quatre Années au pouvoir*, pp. 137–8.
7. Paul Dungler, quoted in B. Vergez-Chaignon: *op. cit.*, p. 229.
8. *Procès Pétain*, p. 287.
9. Duncannon, note of 8.viii.43; NA (PRO), FO660/149.
10. Ibid.
11. Ibid.
12. Ibid.
13. Ibid.
14. Ibid.
15. Duncannon, note of 11.x.43; NA (PRO), FO660/149.
16. Ibid.
17. Ibid.
18. Ibid.
19. Rooker to Loxley, 19.i.44; NA (PRO), FO660/149.
20. Draft telegram (unsigned) to Foreign Office, 9.ii.44; NA (PRO), FO660/149.
21. B. Vergez-Chaignon: *op. cit.*, p. 229.
22. R. Murphy: *Diplomat Among Warriors*, p. 231.

23. Macmillan, quoted in A. Horne: *Macmillan 1891–1956*; London, Macmillan, 1988, p. 190.
24. Macmillan diaries, quoted ibid, p. 189.
25. L. Noguères: *Le Véritable Procès du Maréchal Pétain*, p. 568.
26. B. Serrigny: *op. cit.*, p. 234.
27. Ibid., p. 235.
28. Ibid., p. 236.
29. Ibid., p. 230.

CHAPTER 26: VICHY: THE FINAL ACT

Epigraph: '. . . there is no salvation for France other than in the reconciliation of Pétain and de Gaulle', Brécard, reported in P. Boegner: *Carnets du Pasteur Boegner*, p. 287.
1. Pétain to M.-A. Pardee, 11.i.44, in M.-A. Pardee: *Le Maréchal que j'ai connu*, p. 79.
2. Agnes Ooms telephone conversation with Frau Cornelia Lutze (Renthe-Fink's daughter), 1.xii.03.
3. Agnes Ooms telephone conversation with Frau Gabriele von Heiden (Renthe-Fink's granddaughter), 1.xii.03.
4. A. Kaspi: *La Libération de la France*, quoted in J. Jackson: *The Dark Years*, p. 534.
5. W. D. Hassett: *Off the Record With FDR, 1942–1945*; London, Allen & Unwin, 1949, p. 257.
6. Halifax to Foreign Secretary, 3.ii.44; NA (PRO), FO 954/9.
7. *France Actualités*, quoted in B. Vergez-Chaignon: *Le Docteur Ménétrel*, p. 275.
8. Lavagne to Ménétrel, 1.v.44; AN, 2 AG 76, quoted in B. Vergez-Chaignon: *Le Docteur Ménétrel*, p. 275.
9. B. Serrigny: *Trente Ans avec Pétain*, p. 237.
10. French radio, quoted in B. Vergez-Chaignon: *op. cit.*, p. 277.
11. Quoted ibid., p. 278.
12. B. Serrigny: *op. cit.*, p. 237.
13. Ibid.
14. Ibid., p. 238.
15. Quoted in J. Tracou: *Le Maréchal aux lions*; Paris, André Bonne, 1948, p. 309.
16. L. Noguères: *Le Véritable Procès du Maréchal Pétain*, pp. 653–5.
17. P. Boegner: *op. cit.*, p. 287.
18. AN, 3 W 300, in B Vergez-Chaignon: *op. cit.*, p. 290.
19. Letter from a bodyguard to his wife, 20.vii.44, quoted ibid., p. 297.

CHAPTER 27: FROM PILLAR TO POST

Epigraph: 'Of the principles which I taught, of all the things which I have freely said, I withdraw nothing.' Message of 20.viii.44, in J.-C. Barbas (ed.): *Philippe Pétain: Discours aux Français, 17 juin–20 août 1944*; Paris, Albin Michel, 1989, p. 340.
1. Ibid.
2. Ibid.
3. Captain Renault (at Sigmaringen), quoted in L. Noguères: *La Dernière Etape: Sigmaringen*; Paris, Fayard, 1956, p. 60.
4. Ibid., p. 64.
5. Ibid., pp. 98–9.
6. Quoted in D. Cook: *Charles de Gaulle*; London, Secker & Warburg, 1984, p. 251.
7. Quoted in J. Lacouture: *De Gaulle: Le rebelle*; Paris, Seuil, 1984, p. 834.
8. Pétain to de Brinon, 9.x.44; NA (PRO), GFM 33/123.
9. Quoted in C. de Gaulle: *Mémoires de guerre*, Vol. III; Paris, Plon, 1954, pp. 222–3.

10. Eugénie Pétain account; AN, W 111 288.
11. Ibid.
12. Ibid.
13. Ibid.
14. Ibid.

CHAPTER 28: LET JUSTICE BE DONE?

Epigraph: 'The old Marshal could have had no doubt that he was going to be convicted.'
C. de Gaulle: *Mémoires de guerre*, Vol. III, p. 112.

1. *Journal Officiel de la République française* (Algiers), 10.viii.44.
2. J. Isorni: *Mémoires*, Vol. I; Paris, Robert Laffont, 1984, p. 409.
3. Ibid.
4. Quoted in J.-M. Varaut: *Le Procès Pétain, 1945–1995*; Paris, Perrin, 1995, pp. 80–1.
5. Quoted in J.-M. Varaut: *op.cit.*, p. 105.
6. C. de Gaulle: *op.cit.*, p. 248.
7. Teitgen interview in *De Gaulle vu d'ailleurs* (video of contemporary newsreels: LMK Images).
8. Quoted in J. Roy: *Le Grand Naufrage*; Paris, Julliard, 1966, p. 24.
9. Ibid., p 26.
10. *Procès Pétain*, p. 7.
11. Ibid.
12. Ibid., p. 15.
13. J. Roy: *op. cit.*, p. 26.
14. *Procès Pétain*, p. 13.
15. C. de Gaulle: *op. cit.*, pp. 248–9.
16. *Procès Pétain*, pp. 15–16.
17. Ibid., p. 16.
18. Ibid., p. 18.
19. Ibid., p. 19.
20. J. Roy: *op. cit.*, p. 38.
21. Quoted ibid., p. 104.
22. Ibid., p. 107.
23. *Procès Pétain*, p. 149.
24. Ibid., p. 151.
25. Ibid., p. 158.
26. Ibid., p. 198.
27. Quoted in J. Roy: *op. cit.*, p. 144.
28. *Procès Pétain*, p. 240.
29. Ibid., p. 243.
30. Ibid., p. 247.
31. Ibid., pp. 255–6.
32. Quoted in J. Roy: *op. cit.*, p. 178.
33. *Procès Pétain*, p. 325.
34. Ibid., pp. 344–5.
35. Ibid., pp. 356–7.
36. Ibid., p. 384.
37. Ibid., p. 429.
38. Quoted in J. Roy: *op. cit.*, p. 286.
39. Ibid.
40. *Procès Pétain*, p. 472.
41. Quoted in J. Roy: *op. cit.*, pp. 287–8.

42. Ibid.
43. *Procès Pétain*, p. 490.
44. Quoted in J. Roy: *op. cit.*, pp. 293–4.
45. Ibid., p. 295.

CHAPTER 29: PRISON FOR THE REST OF HIS LIFE

Epigraph: 'I have never accepted my conviction.' Pétain's instruction to his lawyers on 7.ix.46, quoted in J. Varaut: *Le Procès Pétain*, p. 395.
1. Pétain to Eugénie Pétain, 16.viii.45; AN, 415 AP 2 Mi.
2. C. de Gaulle: *Mémoires de guerre*, Vol. III, p. 250.
3. J. Simon (ed. P Bourget): *Pétain, mon prisonnier*, Paris, Plon, 1978 (Simon diary entry, 18.viii.45), p. 55.
4. Ibid., (diary entry, 30.viii.45), p. 59.
5. Ibid., (diary entry, 6.x.45), p. 73.
6. Ibid., (diary entry, 20.x.45), p. 79.
7. Ibid., (diary for 14–16.xi.45).
8. Letter from Mme Nolleau to P. Bourget: quoted ibid., p. 353.
9. Pétain to Eugénie Pétain, 20.ii.46 and 9.vi.46; AN, 415 AP 2 Mi.
10. J. Simon: *op. cit.*, (diary entry, 9.vii.46), p. 109.
11. Ibid., (diary entry, 10.vii.46), p. 111.
12. Simon to Jégu, 4.iii.47; ibid., p. 155.
13. Ibid., footnote to p. 156.
14. Ibid., (diary entry, 11.ix.47), p. 189.
15. Pétain to Eugénie Pétain, 16.ii.47; AN, 415 AP 2 Mi.
16. Ibid., (diary entry, 2.iii.47), p. 154.
17. Ibid., (diary entry, 22.ix.47), p. 190.
18. Ibid., (diary entry, 9.vii.47), p. 181.
19. Quoted in J. Isorni: *Souffrance et mort du Maréchal*; Paris, Flammarion, 1951, p. 198.
20. Ibid., p. 197.
21. Ibid., p. 199.
22. Pétain to Eugénie Pétain, 17.ix.47; AN, 415 AP 2 Mi.
23. J. Simon: *op. cit.*, (diary entry, 7.xi.47), p. 194.
24. Ibid., (diary entry, 9.xi.47), p. 196.
25. Ibid., (diary entry, 2.v.48), p. 230.
26. Report of Dr Jouhier, ibid., p. 233.
27. J. Isorni: *op. cit.*, p. 213.
28. Ibid., p. 216.
29. J. Simon: *op. cit.*, (note to diary entry, 4.xi.48), p. 239.
30. J. Isorni: *Le Condamné de la Citadelle*; Paris, Flammarion, 1982, p. 257.
31. Pétain to Eugénie Pétain, 16.v.49; AN, 415 AP 2 Mi.
32. Eugénie Pétain to J. Isorni, quoted in Simon: *op. cit.*, p. 287.
33. J. Simon: *op. cit.*, (diary entry, 24.xi.48), p. 301.
34. Simon report of 21.vii.50; quoted ibid., p. 307.
35. British Ambassador to Madrid, report to Foreign Secretary, 25.ii.51; NA (PRO), FO 371/9617.
36. J. Isorni: *op. cit.*, p. 347.
37. Decree of 9.vi.51, ibid., p. 424.
38. *Paris Match*, 14.vii.51.
39. J. Isorni: *op. cit.*, p. 380.
40. Quoted ibid., pp. 378–9.

BIBLIOGRAPHY

BIBLIOGRAPHICAL NOTE

There are many thousands of books and articles relevant to Pétain's life and times. There is no point in compiling an arbitrary list. I have therefore confined myself to those which I have found particularly useful. An excellent bibliographical essay on Pétain can be found in Professor Atkin's book (listed below), and further bibliographical information can be found in those books I have labelled 'General'. The bibliography which follows below is therefore selective and, I imagine, regrettably incomplete. Where direct quotations have been used, they are acknowledged in the Notes, as are references to some other specialist works, as well as magazines and newspapers not listed here. Archives which I and those who helped me have consulted are not listed either, but are referred to in the Notes. On the first occasion it appears the full name of the archival source is given, together with the abbreviation or acronym subsequently used.

Translations are always a problem, as are names. In general, I have translated French quotations myself, but where a translation has been made by an authoritative source I have used it. As far as names are concerned, I have used what I believe to be common sense, even at the expense of consistency. Thus, where there is a French or German spelling of a place where the English have a variant (Reims or Rheims, for instance) I have tended to use the French or German version unless the context seems to require otherwise. There is a further complication. Spears only anglicised his name from Spiers in September 1918. Throughout the First World War he was known, rightly, as Spiers. I have taken the feeble way out to avoid being accused of pedantry. Even more difficult is the matter of Eugénie Hardon. Known as Nini in her youth and beauty, she has seemed to me to have a suitable nickname to be preserved in her less than attractive old age. Pétain in his later, and less passionate, letters addressed her as 'Annie'. I have stuck with 'Nini', if only for the sake of avoiding confusion.

GENERAL

Abetz, O.: *Das öffene Problem: Ein Rückblick auf zwei Jahrzehnte deutscher Frankreichpolitik*; Cologne, Greven Verlag, 1951

Adler, J.: *The Jews and Vichy: Reflections on French Historiography*; Cambridge University Press, 2001

Alexander, M. S.: *The Republic in Danger: General Maurice Gamelin and the Politics of French Defence*; Cambridge University Press, 1992

Argenson, Marquis de: *Pétain et le pétinisme*; Paris, Editions Créator, 1953

Aron, R.: *Histoire de Vichy*; Paris, Fayard, 1954

Atkin, N. and Tallett, F.: *The Right in France 1789–1997*; London and New York, Tauris, 1997

Auphan, G.: *Histoire élémentaire de Vichy*; Paris, Editions France-Empire, 1971

Azéma, J.-P.: *From Munich to the Liberation 1938–1944*; Cambridge University Press, 1979

Azéma, J.-P. and Bédarida, F. (eds.): *La France des années noires*; Paris, Seuil, 2000

Barbas, J.-C.: *Philippe Pétain. Discours aux français, 17 juin 1940–20 août 1940*; Paris, Albin Michel, 1989

Barreau, J.-M.: *Vichy contre l'École de la République*; Paris, Flammarion, 2001

Barthélemy, J.: *Le Ministre de la justice. Mémoires, Vichy 1941–1943*; Paris, Pygmalion, 1989

Bell, P. M. H.: *A Certain Eventuality*; London, Saxon House, 1974

Ben-Ami, S.: *Fascism From Above*; Oxford, Clarendon Press, 1983

Bessborough, E.: *Return to the Forest*; London, Weidenfeld & Nicolson, 1962

Boyce, R. (ed.): *French Foreign and Defence Policy 1918–1940*; London, Routledge, 1998

Brinon, F. de: *Mémoires. De Vichy à la Haute Cour*; Paris, La Page Internationale, 1959

Brissaud, A.: *Pétain à Sigmaringen*; Paris, Perrin, 1966

Buck, M.: *French Army Notes*; unpublished paper, 2004

Burrin, P.: *La France a l'heure allemande, 1940–1944*; Paris, Seuil, 1995

Burton, R. D. E.: *Blood in the City: Violence and Revolution in Paris, 1789–1945*; Ithaca, NY, Cornell University Press, 2003

Carcopino, J.: *Souvenirs de sept ans, 1937–1944*; Paris, Flammarion, 1953

Carré, H.: *Les Grandes Heures du Général Pétain; 1917 et la crise du moral*; Paris, Editions du Conquistador, 1952

Churchill, W. S.: *The World Crisis*; London, Cassell, 1931

Clayton, A.: *Paths of Glory; The French Army 1914–18*; London, Cassell, 2003

Cointet, J.-P.: *Pierre Laval*; Paris, Fayard, 1993

Cointet, M.: *Pétain et les Français 1940–1951*; Paris, Perrin, 2002

Cointet-Labrousse, M.: *Vichy Capitale*; Paris, Perrin, 1993

Coutau-Bégarie, H. and Huan, C.: *Darlan*; Paris, Fayard, 1989

Craig, G. A.: *Germany 1866–1945*; Oxford, Clarendon Press, 1978

Dallas, G.: *At the Heart of a Tiger: Clemenceau and His World 1841–1929;* London, Macmillan, 1993

Darlan, A.: *L'Amiral Darlan parle*; Paris, Amiot-Dumont, 1952

De Wailly, H.: *L'Effondrement*; Paris, Perrin, 2000

Digeon, C.: *La Crise allemande de la pensée française 1870–1914*; Paris, Presses Universitaires de France, 1959

Discours de M. le Maréchal Pétain à l'Académie Française et réponse de M. Paul Valéry; Paris, Plon, 1931

Doise, J. and Vaïsse, M.: *Diplomatie et outil militaire 1871–1969*; Paris, Imprimerie National, 1987

Ducrocq, M.: *Le Collège Saint-Bertin de 1561 à nos jours*; Arras, Société des Antiquaires de la Morinie, 1998

Duroselle, J.-B.: *Clemenceau*; Paris, Fayard, 1988

Duroselle, J.-B.: *La France et les Français*; Paris, Editions Richelieu, 1972

Duroselle, J.-B.: *L'Abîme. Politique étrangère de la France, 1939–1944*; Paris, Imprimérie Nationale, 1982

Egremont, M.: *Under Two Flags: The Life of Major-General Sir Edward Spears*; London, Weidenfeld & Nicolson, 1997

Fayolle, M.-E.: *Cahiers secrets de la Grande Guerre, ed. H. Contamine*; Paris, Plon, 1964

Fernet, J.: *Aux Côtés du Maréchal Pétain*; Paris, Plon, 1953

Fischer, D.: *Le Mythe Pétain*; Paris, Flammarion, 2002

Foch, F. (tr. Bentley Mott): *The Memoirs of Marshal Foch*; London, Heinemann, 1931

Frankenstein, R.: *Le Prix du réarmament français 1935–1939*; Paris, Publications de la Sorbonne, 1982

Gaulle, C. de: *Vers l'Armée de métier*; Paris, Berger-Levrault, 1934

Gerbod, P.: *La Vie quotidienne dans les lycées et collèges au XIX siècle*; Paris, Hachette, 1968

Gervereau, L. and Peschanski, D. (eds): *La Propagande de Vichy, 1940–1944*; Paris, Collections des Publications de la BDIC, 1990

Gillouin, R.: *J'Étais l'Ami du maréchal Pétain*; Paris, Plon,1996

Girard, L.-D.: *Montoire; Victoire diplomatique*; Paris, André Bonne, 1948

Girardet, R.: *Mythes et mythologies politiques*; Paris, Seuil, 1986

Gorce, P.-M. de la: *The French Army: A Military-Political History*; London, Weidenfeld and Nicolson, 1963

Griffiths, R.: *The Intelligent Person's Guide to Fascism*; London, Duckworth, 2000

Guiral, P. and Thuillier, G.: *La Vie quotidienne des professeurs de 1870 à 1940*; Paris, Hachette, 1982

Horne, A.: *The Price of Glory: Verdun 1916*; London, Macmillan, 1962

Hubscher, R. H.: *L'Agriculture et la société rurale dans le Pas-de-Calais du milieu du XIXe siècle à 1914* (2 vols.); Arras, Mémoires de la Commission Départmentale des Monuments Historiques du Pas-de-Calais, 1979

Hughes, J. M.: *To the Maginot Line: The Politics of French Military Preparation in the 1920s*; Cambridge, Mass., Harvard University Press, 1971

Isorni, J.: *C'est un Péché de la France*; Paris, Flammarion, 1962

Isorni, J.: *La Correspondance de l'Île d'Yeu*; Paris, Flammarion, 1966

Isorni, J.: *Le Condamné de la Citadelle*; Paris, Flammarion, 1982

Isorni, J.: *Mémoires*; 3 vols.; Paris, Robert Laffont, 1984–8

Isorni, J.: *Philippe Pétain*; 2 vols.; Paris, La Table Ronde, 1972

Isorni, J.: *Souffrance et Mort du Maréchal*; Paris, Flammarion, 1961

Jäckel, E.: *Frankreich in Hitlers Europa*; Stuttgart, Deutsche Verlags-Anstalt, 1966

Jackson, J.: *France: The Dark Years*; Oxford University Press, 2001

Jackson, J.: *The Fall of France: The Nazi Invasion of 1940*; Oxford University Press, 2003

Jaray, G. L. (ed.): *Le Maréchal Pétain; Paroles aux Français; Messages et ecrits 1934–1941*; Lyon, H. Lardanchet, 1941

Jeantet, G.: *Pétain contre Hitler*; Paris, La Table Ronde, 1966

Joll, J.: *The Origins of the First World War*; London, Longman, 1984

Kaspi, A.: *Le Temps des Américains; Le Concours Américain à la France en 1917–1918*; Paris, Publications de la Sorbonne, 1976

Kedward, H. R.: *In Search of the Maquis: Rural Resistance in Southern France, 1942–1944*; Oxford University Press, 1993

Kedward, H. R.: *Occupied France: Collaboration and Resistance*; Oxford, Basil Blackwell, 1985

Keegan, J.: *The First World War*; London, Hutchinson, 1998

Keiger, J. F. V.: *France and the World Since 1870*; London, Arnold, 2001

Kessel, J.: *Jugement dernier*; Courtry, Editions Christian de Bartillat, 1995

Freedman, L., Hayes, P. and O'Neill, R. (eds.): *War, Strategy, and International Politics: Essays in Honour of Sir Michael Howard*; Oxford, Clarendon Press, 1992

Leahy, W. D.: *I was There;* London, Victor Gollancz, 1950

Lehideux, F.: *De Renault à Pétain – Mémoires*; Paris, Pygmalion, 2001

Turpin, M. and Maloire, A.: *Le 24è Bataillon de chasseurs*; Paris, Editions Berger-Levrault, 1959

MacMillan, M.: *Peacemakers: The Paris Conference of 1919 and Its Attempt to End War*; London, John Murray, 2001

Mangin, C.: *Lettres de guerre 1914–1918*; Paris, Fayard, 1950

Marrus, M. R. and Paxton, R. O.: *Vichy France and the Jews*; New York, Basic Books, 1981

Maurois, A., tr. H. Miles: *Marshal Lyautey*; London, Bodley Head, 1931

May, E. R.: *Strange Victory: Hitler's Conquest of France*; London, I. B. Tauris, 2000

Michel, H.: *Le Procès de Riom*; Paris, Albin Michel, 1979

Miller, G.: *Le Pousse-au-jouir du Maréchal Pétain*; Paris, Seuil, 1975

Ministère de la Guerre: *Les Armées françaises dans la grande guerre*; Paris, 1931

Mosse, G.: *Fallen Soldiers: Reshaping the Memory of World Wars*; Oxford University Press, 1990

Moulin, A.: *Les Paysans dans la société française de la Révolution à nos jours;* Paris, Seuil, 1992

Moulin de Labarthète, H. du: *Le Temps des illusions*; Geneva, A l'Enseigne du Cheval Ailé, 1946

Murphy, R.: *Diplomat Among Warriors*; London, Collins, 1964

Newhall, D. S.: *Clemenceau: A Life at War*, Lewiston, NY, The Edwin Mellen Press, 1991

Noguères, L.: *La Dernière Etape: Sigmaringen*; Paris, Fayard, 1956

Noguères, L.: *Le Véritable procès du Maréchal Pétain*; Paris, Fayard, 1955

Oulsby, I.: *The Road to Verdun*; London, Jonathan Cape, 2002

Painlevé, P.: *Comment j'ai Nommé Foch et Pétain*; Paris, Librairie Félix Alcan, 1932

Pardee, M. A.: *Le Maréchal que j'ai connu*; Paris, Editions André Bonne, 1952

Paxton, R. O.: *The Anatomy of Fascism*; London, Allen Lane, 2004

Paxton, R. O.: *Vichy France: Old Guard and New Order, 1940–1944*; New York, Columbia University Press, 1982

Perrier, G.: *Rémy, l'agent Secret no. 1 de la France libre*; Paris, Perrin, 2001

Perrot, M. (ed.): *A History of Private Life*, Vol. IV, *From the Fires of Revolution to the Great War*, Cambridge, Mass., Harvard University Press, 1990

Pershing, J. J.: *My Experiences in the World War*; London, Hodder & Stoughton, 1931

Philpott, W. J.: *Anglo-French Relations and Strategy on the Western Front, 1914–1918*; London, Macmillan, 1996

Pierrefeu, J., tr. C. J. C. Street: *French Headquarters 1915–1918*; London, G. Bles, n.d.

Porch, D.: *The March to the Marne: The French Army 1871–1914*; Cambridge University Press, 1981

Price, R.: *A Social History of Nineteenth-Century France*; London, Hutchinson,1987

Procès du Maréchal Pétain: Compte rendu officiel in extenso des audiences de la Haute Cour de Justice; Paris, Editions Louis Pariente, 1976

Prost, A.: *Histoire de l'enseignment en France 1800–1967*; Paris, Librairie Armand Colin, 1968

Pryce-Jones, D.: *Paris in the Third Reich: A History of the German Occupation*; London, HarperCollins, 1983

Ralston, D. B.: *The Army of the Republic: The Place of the Military in the Political Evolution of France, 1871–1914*; Cambridge Mass., MIT Press, 1967

Robbins, K.: *The First World War*; Oxford University Press, 1985

Rossignol, D.: *Vichy et les Franc-maçons: La Liquidation des sociétés secrètes 1940–1944*; Paris, J. C. Lattès, 1981

Rothschild, M. de: *Si j'ai Bonne mémoire*; Paris, Editions Monelle Hayot, 2001

Rougier, L.: *Mission secrète à Londres; les accords Pétain–Churchill*; Paris, La Diffusion du Livre, 1946

Rousso, H.: *Le Syndrome de Vichy, 1944–198.*; Paris, Seuil, 1987

Rousso, H.: *Un Château en Allemagne, Sigmaringen*; Paris, Ramsay, 1980

Rousso, H.: *Vichy: Un Passé qui ne passe pas*; Paris, Fayard, 1994

Roy, J.: *Le Grand Naufrage*; Paris, Perrin, 1966

Roy, J.: *The Trial of Marshal Pétain*; London, Faber & Faber, 1968

Simon, J.: *Pétain, mon prisonnier; presentation, notes et commentaires de Pierre Bourget*; Paris, Plon, 1978

Smith, G.: *Until the Last Trumpet Sounds: The Life of General of the Armies John J. Pershing*; New York, John Wiley, 1998

Spears, E. L.: *Liaison 1914: A Narrative of the Great Retreat*; London, Eyre & Spottiswoode, 1930

Spears, E. L.: *Prelude to Victory*; London, Jonathan Cape, 1939

Spears, E. L.: *Assignment to Catastrophe*; 2 vols.; London, William Heinemann, 1954

Stevenson, D.: *French War Aims against Germany, 1914–1919*; Oxford, Clarendon Press, 1982

Strachan, H.: *The First World War*, Vol. I, '*To Arms*'; Oxford University Press, 2001

Stucki, W.: *La Fin du régime de Vichy*; Neuchatel, Editions de la Baconniere, 1947

Stucki, W.: *Von Pétain zur Vierten Republik*; Bern, Verlag Herbert Lang, 1947

Tombs, R.: *France 1814–1914*: London, Longman, 1996

Tracou, J.: *Le Maréchal aux liens*; Paris, André Bonne, 1948

Usborne, C. V.: *The Conquest of Morocco*; London, Stanley Paul & Co, 1936

Varaut, J.-M.: *Le Procès Pétain*; Paris, Perrin, 1995

Vergez-Chaignon, B.: *Le Docteur Ménétrel, eminence grise et confidant du Maréchal Pétain*; Paris, Perrin, 2001

Watt, R. M.: *Dare Call It Treason*; London, Chatto & Windus, 1964

Weber, E.: *My France: Politics, Culture, Myth*; Cambridge, Mass., Harvard University Press, 1991

Weber, E.: *Peasants into Frenchmen*; London, Chatto & Windus, 1977

Weber, E.: *Action Française*; Stanford, CA, Stanford University Press, 1962

Weber, E.: *Varieties of Fascism*; New York, Van Nostrand, 1964

Webster, P.: *Pétain's Crime*; London, Papermac, 1991

Werth, L. (ed. C. Kantcheff): *Impressions d'audience – Le Procès Pétain*; Mayenne, Editions Viviane Hamy, 1995

Wilhelm, Crown Prince of Germany: *My War Experiences*; London, Hurst & Blackett, 1922

Wilhelm, Crown Prince of Germany: *The Memoirs of the Crown Prince of Germany*; London, T. Butterworth, 1922

Woolman, D. S.: *Rebels in the Rif: Abd El Krim and the Rif Rebellion*; Oxford University Press, 1969

Wright, G.: *Rural Revolution in France*; Stanford, CA, Stanford University Press, 1964

Zeldin, T.: *France 1848–1945*; Oxford University Press, 1977

BIOGRAPHIES AND PART BIOGRAPHIES

Alméras, P.: *Un Français nommé Pétain*; Paris, Laffont, 1995

Amouroux, H.: *Pétain avant Vichy; La Guerre et l'Amour*; Paris, Fayard, 1967

Atkin, N.: *Pétain*; London, Longman, 1998

Ferro, M: *Pétain*; Paris, Fayard, 1987

Girard, L.-D.: *Mazinghem, ou la vie secrète de Philippe Pétain*; Paris, private publication, 1971

Griffiths, R.: *Marshal Pétain*; London, Constable, 1970 and 1995

Laure, E.: *Pétain*; Paris, Berger-Levrault, 1942

Lottman, H. R.: *Pétain, Hero or Traitor?*; New York, Viking, 1984

Lottman, H. R., tr. B. Vierne: *Pétain*; Paris, Seuil, 1984

Pedroncini, G.: *Pétain, le soldat et la gloire, 1856–1918*; Paris, Perrin, 1989

Pedroncini, G.: *Pétain: La Victoire perdue, 1918–1940*; Paris, Perrin, 1995

Pedroncini, G: *Pétain: Général en chef*; Paris, Presses Universitaires de la France, 1974

Planells, A. J.: *Pétain, Mariscal de Francia*; Madrid, Viena, 2000

Ryan, S.: *Pétain the Soldier*; New York, A. S. Barnes & Co., 1969

INDEX